GARRY KASPAROV ON GARRY KASPAROV

PART II: 1985-1993

Gloucester Publishers plc   www.everymanchess.com

EVERYMAN CHESS

First published in 2013 by Gloucester Publishers Limited, Northburgh House,
10 Northburgh Street, London EC1V 0AT

First published 2013 by Gloucester Publishers Limited

British Library Cataloguing-in-Publication Data
A catalogue record for this book is available from the British Library.

ISBN: 978 1 78194 024 2

Distributed in North America by The Globe Pequot Press, P.O Box 480,
246 Goose Lane, Guilford, CT 06437-0480.

All other sales enquiries should be directed to Everyman Chess, Northburgh House,
10 Northburgh Street, London EC1V 0AT
tel: 020 7253 7887 fax: 020 7490 3708
email: info@everymanchess.com
website: www.everymanchess.com

EVERYMAN CHESS SERIES
Chief advisor: Byron Jacobs
Commissioning editor: John Emms
Assistant editor: Richard Palliser

Translation by Ken Neat.
Typesetting and editing by First Rank Publishing, Brighton.
Cover design by Horatio Monteverde.
Printed and bound in Estonia.

Contents

Foreword

This second volume of the autobiographical trilogy *Garry Kasparov on Garry Kasparov* contains one hundred of the most memorable games and endings played during the eight years when I was FIDE champion (1985-1993). This period was the peak of my playing career, as is confirmed by both my competitive results, and the quality of the games.

The era described was an extremely tense and most unusual one for me. In the first four years, from the moment when I won the title of world champion (November 1985) until the conquering of the 2805 rating (November 1989), a cosmic figure for those times, I consolidated my domination in the world chess arena. I twice defended my champion's title in dramatic matches with Anatoly Karpov (1986 and 1987), took or at least shared first place in all the tournaments in which I participated, and convincingly won the tournament championship of the planet – the World Cup (1988-1989).

However, the year 1990 began with tragic, extraordinary events. Returning to Baku after lengthy wanderings abroad, I found myself in the very thick of an ethnic conflict – the Armenian pogroms. My mother and I as well as our relatives had to take flight. Thus in the year of the next match for the world championship I was suddenly deprived of both my native home, and my long-standing training base in Zagulba. This was a severe psychological blow, the collapse of my entire customary way of life.

Not surprisingly, at precisely that time my battle with FIDE for the rights of chess players and with the USSR State Sports Committee for professional sport grew into a battle for changes in the country. After settling in Moscow I became an active political figure, inspired by the ideas of Andrey Dmitrievich Sakharov (our acquaintance, unfortunately, was very short-lived).

There were also substantial changes to the composition of my training team, with which I prepared for my fifth match with Karpov. Nikitin departed and, with the exception of Shakarov, no one remained from those who were with me on my way to the chess crown. In this sense too, the 1990 match also became an historic landmark. Despite all the upheavals, I managed to win it, but the history of the legendary team of the 1980s had come to an end: from then on completely new people appeared in it.

From the early 1990s talented young players began assuming the leading roles in chess (Anand, Ivanchuk, Gelfand, Short, Kamsky, Shirov, Topalov), and Karpov and I were no longer able to dominate as we had done before. Paradoxically, in 1991 in none of the super-tournaments in Linares, Amsterdam and Reggio Emilia did either of us take first place! But by effort of will I was able to break the negative trend. With the help of Sergey Makarychev I renovated my opening repertoire – and I won not only Tilburg 1991, but also Linares two years in succession (1992 and 1993).

On this occasion my domination in the chess arena lasted less than two years, but on the other hand this time was perhaps the most fruitful in the creative respect. In clashes with young, inventive and tenacious opponents, some brilliant and unforgettable games were created.

In February 1993 Nigel Short, the winner of the next qualifying cycle, unexpectedly suggested to me that we should play our match for the world championship outside of the FIDE framework. Thinking that this would be a convenient opportunity to at last put chess on a professional basis, I agreed. Because of the rapid rehabilitation after the crisis of 1991, my sense of danger had evidently been dulled. The moment chosen for the declaration of war on FIDE was unfortunate, and the decision taken proved to be a mistake with far-reaching consequences.

In response FIDE President Campomanes took an unprecedented step: stripping me and Short of our rights of champion and challenger, he arranged a match 'for the world championship' between the two reserve candidates who had lost to Short in the qualifying cycle – Timman and Karpov. A new spiral in chess history began...

I should like to express my gratitude to my former trainers Alexander Nikitin and Alexander Shakarov, and also the chess compilers Vladislav Novikov and Yakov Zusmanovich, for their help in preparing the manuscript for publication.

Chapter One

Match after Match

Matches with Hübner and Andersson

Six-game training matches: **Kasparov**-Hübner (Hamburg, 27 May – 4 June 1985): 4½-1½; **Kasparov**-Andersson (Belgrade, 12–20 June 1985): 4-2.

Preparations for the second match with Karpov began almost at once after Campomanes's memorable February press conference, which forcibly terminated the protracted first match 'without a final result'.

Realising that time was short, we drew up a precise schedule for the next six months, including both relaxation and independent work, two training matches (essential practice!), and three twenty-day sessions with the whole training team. Initially we needed to rest on our own after the months of close contact, and to cool down after the sharp and intense disputes. And we separated for a time, each with his own home assignment. But early in May the team assembled in Zagulba for the first session. We worked intensively, mainly on the reconstruction of my opening repertoire and the improving of my positional technique. We also did not forget about physical preparation, the conditions for which were simply ideal.

As far as I remember, the idea of short training matches belonged to Botvinnik, who regarded them as a highly effective method of practical preparation (especially since no appropriate tournaments were anticipated). And I decided to play two successive matches abroad, the opponents and venues being carefully chosen with the future main match in mind. I was to play the West German grandmaster Robert Hübner in Hamburg and the Swedish grandmaster Ulf Andersson in Belgrade. I judged that West Germany and Yugoslavia were ideal places as regards public interest, since, after my criticisms, the roles played by the German Alfred Kinzel (co-chairman of the appeals committee) and the Yugoslav Svetozar Gligoric (the chief arbiter) in the halting of the unlimited match had become topics of heated debate in their own countries.

At the end of May I arrived in Hamburg, in order to contest a match of six games with the best German player, conduct two unusual simultaneous displays (against chess computers and blindfold) and to give an extensive interview to the well-known news magazine *Der Spiegel* – the organiser of this entire enterprise. It was noteworthy that it was not a trainer who the USSR Sports Committee sent me with, but my long-standing KGB guardian Viktor Litvinov, furnished with instructions regarding the forthcoming interview (whereas Hübner was assisted by a chess expert – none other than Spassky!). At that time such 'individual' foreign visits were still unusual, and when we landed in Frankfurt we were anxious about whether anyone would meet us. But our hosts received us very well, and the following day I was invited to the editorial office of *Der Spiegel* for the interview.

I remember that Litvinov was terribly nervous, afraid that I would say something out of place. This was the first appearance by a Soviet sportsman on the pages of a serious Western publication, and I endeavoured to tell all: about the role of Campomanes and Karpov in the scandalous ending of the first match, about the intrigues that then followed, and about the campaign that had been launched against me on the threshold of the new match. The issue of the magazine with my revelations came out while I was still in Hamburg – on 3rd June, on the day of the 5th game of the match with Hübner. Although by present-day standards the interview looks absolutely harmless, at the time it came like a bombshell and was reprinted in dozens of publications around the world. As it transpired a couple of months later, it was not without reason that Litvinov had been nervous...

Hübner was a player of solid positional style, with considerable match experience – in 1980 he even got as far as the final Candidates match. And in the spring of 1985 he

had won (together with Ljubojevic) the super-tournament in Linares. I think that for the encounter with me he prepared quite seriously. I did not need any special preparation: very many ideas had been stored up for the matches with Karpov. By the summer I had already fully recovered from the strain of the many recent months of combat. I was just 22 years old – I had energy in abundance! Of course, this form of training put at risk my status as the no.1 contender to the title (this aspect was discussed with Botvinnik), but I believed in myself.

The tone of the entire match was set by the first game: it stunned my opponent, who was playing White. Although it lasted 28 moves, in reality the outcome was decided earlier, so that in principle it can be regarded as a miniature. And this in the solid English Opening!

Game 1
R.Hübner-G.Kasparov
Training Match
1st Game, Hamburg 28.05.1985
English Opening A21

---

1 c4 e5 2 ♘c3 d6

I did not make any special preparations for the game, and since I wasn't very keen on playing ...♘b8-c6 here, I employed a variation which I had studied with Timoshchenko before my match with Korchnoi (1983).

3 d4

Hübner had already played this against Balashov (Rio de Janeiro Interzonal 1979). After 3 ♘f3 there would have followed 3...f5 4 d4 e4, seizing space – this complicated, fighting position appealed to me, even though it is strategically dangerous for Black, who concedes the f4-square to the opponent. And if 3 g3, then 3...f5 4 ♗g2 ♘f6

5 d4 ♗e7 or 5 d3(e3) g6, followed by ...♗g7, ...0-0 and ...c7-c6, also with interesting play (as in *Game No.82*).

3...exd4 4 ♕xd4

4...♘f6!?

More cunning than the usual 4...♘c6, which leads after 5 ♕d1 ♘f6 6 e4 ♗e6 (preventing ♘ge2) 7 ♘f3 g6 8 ♗e2 ♗g7 9 0-0 0-0 to a well-known *tabiya*, favourable for Black (Kotov-Konstantinopolsky, Moscow 1940; Alatortsev-Boleslavsky, Moscow 1942).

5 ♕d2 ♘f6 6 b3 is more ambitious, although in the afore-mentioned Hübner-Balashov game, after 6...♗e6 (to the immediate 6...a5!? 7 ♗b2 a4 there is the strong reply 8 ♘d5!, L.Popov-Vaganian, Skara 1980) 7 e4 a5 8 ♘ge2 a4 9 ♖b1 axb3 10 axb3 g6 11 g3 ♗g7 12 ♗g2 0-0 13 0-0 ♘d7 14 ♘d5 ♘c5 15 b4 ♘a4 16 ♕c2 ♘e5 17 ♘ef4 ♗d7 18 ♖e1 c6 19 ♘e3 Black could have maintained the balance by 19...b5! (Hübner).

5 g3

On encountering a slight surprise, White chooses the most natural move. In the event of 5 b3 there is no need to transpose into the variation from the previous note (5...♘c6 6 ♕d2 etc.) 5...♗e7 is possible, with a solid position, but the main point is 5...g6!? (this is probably what I would have played) 6 ♗b2 ♗g7, when nothing is given by 7 ♘d5 ♘bd7

8 ♕e3+ ♔f8 (Ornstein-Ree, Budapest 1977), since the black king calmly castles artificially, while after 7 g3 0-0 8 ♗g2 ♖e8 9 ♕d2 ♘bd7 10 ♘f3 ♘c5 11 0-0 both 11...♘fe4 (Smejkal-Mokry, Trnava 1989) and the more aggressive 11...a5 (Miles-Smejkal, Bad Wörishofen 1985) are good.

5...♘c6 6 ♕d2 ♗e6

Of course. Now, when g2-g3 has been played instead of b2-b3, the picture is altogether different.

7 ♘d5

Black is better after 7 e4 a5 8 b3? a4 (8...♘xe4!? 9 ♘xe4 d5) 9 ♖b1 axb3 10 axb3 ♘xe4! 11 ♘xe4 d5 12 cxd5 ♗b4 13 ♘c3 ♗xd5 14 f3 (Palatnik-Lputian, Irkutsk 1983) 14...♕f6! and wins (1985 analysis), or 7...♗e7 8 b3? ♘xe4! 9 ♘xe4 d5 10 cxd5? (10 ♗g2 is more resilient) 10...♗b4 11 ♘c3 ♗xd5 12 f3 ♕f6! 13 ♗b2 0-0-0 and wins (Benko-Psakhis, Aruba 1992).

7...♘e5 8 b3 ♘e4! (the main move in this line) **9 ♕e3**

If 9 ♕d4 there is the tempting 9...♘c5 10 f4 ♘c6 (10...c6!?) 11 ♕e3 ♗e7 (Taimanov-Smyslov, 34th USSR Championship, Tbilisi 1966) or 9...f5 10 ♗g2 g6, when White loses ignominiously after 11 ♗b2? c5! 12 ♕d1 ♗xd5 13 ♕xd5 ♕a5+ 14 ♔d1 ♘d3!! (J.Kristiansen-Reinert, Denmark 1985).

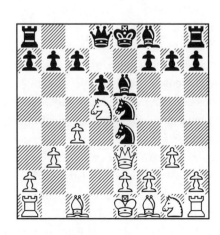

9...♘c5!?

An idea devised at the board (I have to admit that I thought it was a novelty). The variation 9...c6 10 ♕xe4 cxd5 11 cxd5 ♕a5+ 12 ♗d2 is perfectly safe for Black in view of 12...♕xd5 (the same 1985 analysis), or 12...♗xd5 13 ♗xa5 (13 ♕f4 ♕d8!) 13...♗xe4 14 f3 ♗c6 (Ftacnik-Timman, Wijk aan Zee 1985), but I was not interested in going into such a prosaic endgame: Hübner would surely have steered his ship into a drawing haven. Therefore I decided to complicate the play – move my knight from e4, only then play ...c7-c6 and, after driving the white knight from d5, obtain certain tactical counter-chances.

10 ♗b2?!

Annotating this game in *Informator*, I rightly recommended 10 ♗g2 – it is important to free the f1-square for the king as soon as possible. If 10...c6, both 11 ♘c3 ♕a5!? (the *Informator* suggestion 11...a5 is unclear because of 12 ♗a3!) 12 ♗b2 g6 (to Stohl's move 12...♗e7 there is the good reply 13 ♘f3 ♘xf3+ 14 exf3!) 13 ♘f3 (13 ♖d1?! ♗g7!) 13...♗g7 14 0-0 0-0 15 ♖ad1, and 11 ♘f4 g6!? (my earlier move 11...♕f6 is parried by 12 ♗b2 ♘ed3+ 13 exd3 ♕xb2 14 ♖d1) 12 ♘f3 ♘xf3+ 13 ♗xf3 ♗g7 14 ♖b1 0-0 15 ♘xe6 ♘xe6 16 0-0 are acceptable for White. Both lines lead to complicated, roughly equal 'King's Indian' play, where each side has his trumps.

The seemingly natural 10 ♗b2 dangerously increases the dynamic possibilities in the position (the white king is after all stuck on e1) – Hübner did not sense this in time.

10...c6 11 ♘f4?

Again a natural move: if 11 ♘c3, then 11...♕b6! is strong – the threat of ...♘xc4 (the bishop has moved prematurely to b2) forces the awkward retreat 12 ♘d1, and after 12...♗e7 13 ♘f3 ♘g4 Black has a slight

initiative: 14 ♕f4 ♗f6 15 ♗xf6 ♘xf6 or 14 ♕c1 0-0 15 ♗g2 a5 16 h3 ♘f6 17 ♘d4 a4. But now White encounters real problems.

11...♘g4!

This is, indeed, a novelty! White's idea is fully justified after the passive 11...♗e7? 12 ♘xe6 ♘xe6 13 ♗h3 (Smejkal-Rogoff, Amsterdam 1980).

12 ♕d4

After 12 ♕f3 ♘e4! 13 a3 d5 14 ♘xe6 ♕a5+! 15 ♗c3 ♘xc3 16 ♘xf8 ♘a2+! 17 b4 ♘xb4 18 ♗h3 ♘c2+ 19 ♔f1 ♖xa1 or 12 ♘xe6 ♘xe3 13 ♘xd8 ♘c2+ 14 ♔d1 ♘xa1 15 ♘xb7 (weaker is 15 ♘xf7?! ♔xf7 16 ♗xa1 ♗e7) 15...♖axb3! 16 axb3 ♘xb7 17 ♗g2 ♔d7 Black would have gained a material advantage (although in this last variation the two bishops promise White some compensation for the exchange).

At this point Hübner looked calm and confident: 13 ♘xe6 is threatened, and against the queen check on a5 there is the defence ♗c3. But after my reply the opponent's face changed and he even flinched.

12...♘e4!! (under attack by the queen!) **13 ♗h3!**

The best chance of retaining a not altogether clear situation. 13 ♕xe4?? ♕a5+ or 13 ♘g(f)h3? ♕a5+ 14 ♔d1 d5! is fatal. We will analyse three other continuations:

1) 13 ♘xe6 fxe6 14 ♗h3 (14 a3 ♘exf2) 14...♘gxf2 15 ♗xe6 ♗e7! 16 ♕xg7 ♖f8 (Stohl) 17 ♘f3 ♘xh1 18 ♔f1 ♗f6 19 ♗xf6 ♖xf6 20 ♕g8+ ♔e7 21 ♕xh7+ ♔xe6 22 ♕xe4+ ♔d7, and it is doubtful whether White can save the game;

2) 13 ♘d3, after which Black has two good options:

a) 13...d5 14 cxd5 ♗xd5 15 ♘f3, and here instead of the unclear 15...c5 16 ♕a4+ ♗c6 17 ♕c4 b5 (At.Schneider-Z.Lehmann, Budapest 1995) 18 ♕c1!, there is the strong 15...♘gxf2! 16 ♘xf2 ♕a5+ 17 ♘d2 ♘xf2 18 ♕e5+ ♔d8! 19 ♗c3 ♗b4 and wins, or 15 f3 c5 16 ♕a4+ ♗c6 17 ♕c4 b5 18 ♕c1 c4 with a powerful attack – 19 fxe4?! ♗xe4, and if 19 ♗h3, then 19...♕a5+ or 19...h5!?;

b) 13...f5, and if 14 c5? (N.Maiorov-Votava, Pardubice 2001) or my *Informator* suggestion 14 ♗c1(?), then 14...♗e7! is decisive, but also after 14 f3 c5 15 ♘xc5 ♕a5+! 16 ♗c3 dxc5 17 ♗xa5 cxd4 (Stohl) 18 fxe4 fxe4 19 ♗g2 ♗f5 20 ♗d2 e3 21 ♗a5 ♘f2 22 ♗xb7 ♖c8! White is in trouble;

3) 13 b4!? – an interesting move, suggested by an unknown chess fan at one of my subsequent lectures. However, after 13...♘gxf2 White loses a pawn: 14 ♗g2 ♕b6! or 14 ♘gh3 d5! 15 cxd5 ♕b6!! (at the board it is not easy to 'unearth' this!) 16 a3 ♗xh3 17 ♗xh3 ♕xd4 18 ♗xd4 ♘xh1 19 dxc6 bxc6 20 ♗g2 0-0-0 21 ♗xa7 ♘hxg3 22 hxg3 f5, and Black has every chance of converting his exchange advantage.

Instead, Hübner made the most obvious move, at last freeing the f1-square for his king, and he appeared to calm down.

13...♕a5+

13...♘gxf2 was also possible, since 14 ♗xe6? (for 14 ♘xe6 fxe6 15 ♗xe6 ♗e7! see above, but 14 ♘f3!? ♘xh3 15 ♘xe6 ♕a5+ 16 ♔f1 is more resilient – see the next note) 14...fxe6 15 ♘xe6 ♕a5+! (and not 15...♗e7?!

16 ♘h3!) 16 ♔f1 would have led to a position from the game. In my notes for *Informator* I condemned this move order because of 16 ♗c3(?), overlooking the murderous 16...♕f5! 17 ♘c7+ ♔d7 18 ♘xa8 c5! and ...♘xh1 – the black knight will escape from h1, but White's will not escape from a8.

14 ♔f1 ♘gxf2

15 ♗xe6?

The decisive mistake, although 15 ♘xe6 was also insufficient: 15...fxe6 16 ♗xe6 ♕e5! (my previous recommendation 16...♗e7(?) 17 ♕xg7 ♖f8 is worse because of 18 ♘f3! ♘xh1 19 ♔g2) 17 ♕xe5 dxe5 18 ♗f5 ♗c5 19 ♗xe4 ♘xe4 20 ♘f3 (20 ♘h3?! 0-0+ 21 ♔g2 g5 22 ♖hf1 g4 23 ♘g1 ♘d2 and wins) 20...♘f2 21 ♗a3 ♗e3 22 ♖g1 ♘g4 (22...e4!?) with an obvious advantage, or 17 ♕xf2 ♕xe6 18 ♕e3 d5 19 ♔g2 ♗c5 20 ♗d4 ♗xd4 21 ♕xd4 dxc4 22 ♕xc4 ♕xc4 23 bxc4 0-0-0 24 ♘f3 ♘c3, winning one of the weak pawns.

Two other continuations are better:

1) 15 ♘f3!? ♘xh3 16 ♘xe6 ♘hf2 17 ♘xf8 ♕f5! 18 ♖g1 ♖xf8 19 ♖g2, and here 19...♘g4 20 h3 ♘gf6 21 g4 ♕e6 is satisfactory, or 19...♘h3 20 ♕xg7 h5 21 g4 ♘d2+ 22 ♔e1 ♘xf3+ 23 exf3 ♕xf3 24 ♖e2+ ♔d7 25 ♕f6 ♕xf6 26 ♗xf6 ♖fe8 27 gxh5 ♘f4 28 ♖xe8 ♖xe8+ 29 ♔f2 ♘xh5 etc;

2) 15 ♗g2!? – after which Black would have replied either 15...♘f5 16 ♘gh3 ♘xh3, or 15...d5 16 ♗xe4 ♘xe4 17 cxd5 cxd5 18 ♘f3 0-0-0.

Although in all the variations given White would have remained a pawn down, he could still have resisted.

15...fxe6 16 ♘xe6

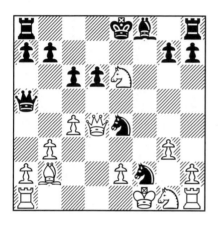

16...♔d7!

A spectacular move, leading to a win, but the no less strong 16...♕f5! 17 ♘c7+ ♔d7 18 ♘xa8 c5! was simpler, forcing 19 ♕d5 ♕xd5 20 cxd5 ♘xh1 21 ♘h3 ♗e7 22 ♔g2 ♘hxg3 23 hxg3 ♗f6 and ...♖xa8 with a technically won endgame: it is not just that White is a pawn down, but he also has chronic weaknesses.

17 ♘h3

This makes things easier for Black. However, he is also close to success after 17 ♘xf8+ (17 ♔g2 ♖e8!) 17...♖axf8 18 ♘f3 (18 ♕xg7+ ♔c8!) 18...♕h5! (Stohl gives only the less effective 18...♖e8 19 ♖g1) 19 ♔g2 (now if 19 ♖g1 there is the thunderous 19...♖xf3! 20 exf3 ♖f8!) 19...c5! 20 ♕d5 ♕xd5 21 cxd5 ♘xh1 22 ♖xh1 ♕f7 or 18 ♔g2 ♕h5! 19 ♖f1 (19 ♕xa7 ♔c7) 19...c5 20 ♕e3 ♕g6 and wins.

17...♘xh3! 18 ♕xe4

For an instant it may seem that White has

fortunately extricated himself, but he is short of literally one tempo.

18...♖e8 19 ♘c5+ (it turns out that 19 ♕g4 ♖xe6 20 ♕xh3 is not possible because of 20...♕d2) **19...♕xc5 20 ♕g4+ ♔c7 21 ♕xh3**

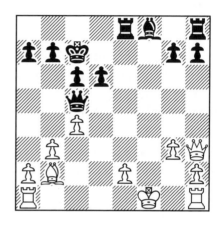

21...♗e7! (simply completing Black's development and threatening ...♖hf8+) **22 ♗xg7**

Clearly realising that all the same he was losing, Hübner decided to check whether there was a mate here. And indeed, both 22 ♖g1 ♕e3! and 22 ♔g2 ♗f6! (Stohl) were hopeless, as was 22 ♕g4 ♖hf8+ 23 ♔g2 ♖f2+ 24 ♔h3 ♕e3! 25 ♗c1 (25 ♗xg7 h5!) 25...♕e5 26 ♗f4 ♕e4.

22...♖hf8+! 23 ♗xf8 ♖xf8+ 24 ♔e1 ♕f2+ 25 ♔d1 ♕d4+ 26 ♔c2

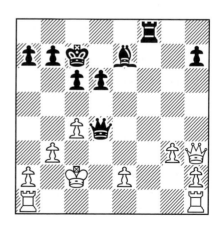

26...♕e4+! (now mate is inevitable) **27 ♔d2**

27 ♔b2 ♛xe2+ or 27 ♔c3 ♛e3+ 28 ♔b4 d5+ was no better.

27...♗g5+ 28 ♔c3 ♛e5+ 0-1

After 29 ♔b4 the quickest way to mate is by 29...♔b6!: for example, 30 a4 ♗f6 31 a5+ ♔a6 or 30 ♔a3 ♛a5+ 31 ♔b2 ♛d2+ and ...♗f6.

The psychological effect of this win was great. When in the 2nd game, in a quiet and roughly equal Queen's Gambit position, I unexpectedly opened the centre, within a dozen moves it again all concluded with a direct mating attack: 2-0! And after a draw in the very complicated 3rd game, I also won the 4th, in which I did not achieve anything from the opening, but I gradually outplayed my opponent in an instructive knight endgame. Apparently Hübner thought that he would gain a draw without difficulty, but I was able to exploit my spatial advantage. The confident handling of endings had become a new feature of my play, acquired in the battles with Karpov.

Thus I gained the desired 3½ points ahead of schedule, and fighting draws in the 5th and 6th games determined the final score in the match: 4½-1½. A convincing victory over one of the most successful western grandmasters increased my optimism. I felt that I was playing well.

Immediately after the match with Hübner, on 5th June, I gave a simultaneous display in Hamburg against chess computers, in which 32 machines participated – eight from each of the four leading production firms. I easily won game after game, but in one I ended up in a bad position, precisely against a computer from the firm Saitek, with which I had an advertising contract. Fearing that in the event of a loss or even a draw I would be accused of promoting my 'own' product, I strained every sinew and in the end I also won this game. Five hours' play produced a 32-0 result, which was not surprising for that stage in the development of chess computer technology.

And on 7th June, also in Hamburg, I gave a blindfold simultaneous display on ten boards – for the only time in my career (I considered the excessive strain experienced when playing blindfold to be damaging to one's health). One of my opponents again turned out to be a computer, and against it I announced a forced mate with sacrifices in 10 moves. The overall score was +8=2.

Then Litvinov and I set off for Belgrade, where on 12th June my match with Ulf Andersson was to begin, organised on the occasion of the 40th anniversary of the well-known 'Partisan' sports society. On the day before, the participants gave a press conference, conducted by an active supporter of mine, grandmaster Milunka Lazarevic. As also in Hamburg, the journalists peppered me with questions about the intrigues surrounding my past and future matches with Anatoly Karpov, and when I was asked to assess my present opponent, I replied: 'Ulf has a distinctive chess style, a very subtle positional feeling, and I think that a match with a player of such a level and such a style may prove very beneficial to me before the meeting with Karpov.'

Although Andersson was not such an esteemed grandmaster as Hübner, he had the reputation of being an opponent who was very hard to beat. It was not without reason that in the USSR v. Rest of the World Match (1984) he was put on board 1 against Karpov. In 1985 he had won tournaments in Rome and Rio de Janeiro, and the match with me was part of his preparations for the forthcoming Biel Interzonal Tournament in July. Breaching Andersson's defences was a psychologically difficult task: in our preceding seven meetings I had managed to do this only once (Game No.61 in *Garry Kasparov on Garry Kasparov Part I*).

On this occasion I had White in the 1st game and I employed a novelty in the Catalan Opening, but Ulf managed to neutralise my initiative – draw. In the 2nd game after a quiet opening, unpretentiously played by my opponent, a very serious battle flared up with chances for both sides, but in the end it again all concluded in a draw.

At this point an old acquaintance arrived to help me – the Hungarian grandmaster Andras Adorjan. We did not carry out any large-scale chess analysis, but he helped me with valuable advice and created an optimistic mood. Adorjan gave me a taste for Schweppes tonic water, and earlier, in Hamburg, I took to eating a steak before every game. Of course, this was not the most diet-orientated food, but it seemed to give me energy, and things continued this way for nearly ten years.

In the 3rd game I decided to improve on White's play compared with the 1st game.

Game 2
G.Kasparov-U.Andersson
Training Match
3rd Game, Belgrade 15.06.1985
Catalan Opening E04

---

1 d4 ♘f6 2 c4 e6 3 g3 d5 4 ♗g2 dxc4 5 ♘f3 c5 6 0-0 ♘c6 (my opponent always employed this system) **7 ♘e5**

In my game with Andersson in Niksic (1983) the variation with a queen sacrifice occurred – 7 ♕a4 cxd4 8 ♘xd4 ♕xd4 9 ♗xc6+ ♗d7 10 ♖d1 ♕xd1+ 11 ♕xd1 ♗xc6 and here, instead of 12 ♕c2, which was usual at that time, I made the fresh move 12 ♘d2!?. After some thought Ulf chose the

solid 12...b5 13 a4 ♗e7, and after 14 axb5 ♗xb5 15 ♘xc4 0-0 16 b3 ♖fd8 in the end Black was able to set up a fortress.

7...♗d7 8 ♘a3!?

A novelty from the 1st game, which was prepared back in the summer of 1983, but in Niksic I decided to keep it for the forthcoming match with Korchnoi. For a long time before that they played 8 ♘xc6 ♗xc6 9 ♗xc6+ bxc6 10 ♕a4 cxd4 11 ♕xc6+ ♘d7 12 ♕xc4 ♗c5 13 ♘d2 0-0 with an equal game (an example: Petrosian-Andersson, Moscow 1981) or, more rarely, the gambit 8 ♘xc4 cxd4 9 ♗f4. Neither of these inspired me, and I devised 8 ♘a3, which for a long time became the main move, although Black gradually found a way of neutralising it.

8...cxd4 9 ♘axc4

For the sacrificed pawn White has dangerous pressure in the centre.

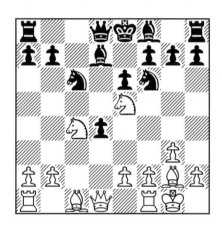

9...♘d5?

The 1st game went 9...♖c8 10 ♕b3 ♘xe5 11 ♘xe5 ♗c6 12 ♘xc6 bxc6 13 ♖d1 c5 14 e3 ♗d6 15 exd4 c4 16 ♕b5+ ♕d7 17 a4! with some advantage for White, and I came to the conclusion that subsequently I could have played more strongly. Andersson decided not to tempt fate and he deviated first, having decided to simplify the position immediately at the cost of his extra pawn.

But, as often happens in little-studied situations, he went from the frying pan into the fire.

Six months later the main continuation became 9...♗c5 (now 9...♗e7 has also come into fashion) 10 ♕b3 0-0 (Nogueiras-A.Sokolov, Montpellier Candidates 1985), returning the pawn for the sake of rapid development. After 11 ♕xb7 ♘xe5 12 ♘xe5 ♖b8 13 ♕f3 Serper's move 13...♗d6 (Kasparov-Deep Blue, 2nd match game, Philadelphia 1996) allows White slightly the better chances – 14 ♘xd7 ♕xd7 15 ♕d3 e5 16 b3 (Beliavsky-Pavasovic, Hungary 2008), but 13...♘d5 is perfectly safe, since the showy 14 ♗g5 f6 15 ♕g4!? is parried by 15...h5! 16 ♕h3 fxg5 17 ♗xd5 g4 18 ♕g2 ♖xb2 (Sulava-Dizdarevic, Cattolica 1993) or 18...♗c8!?.

10 ♘xc6 ♗xc6 11 ♕xd4 ♘b4 12 ♗xc6+ ♘xc6

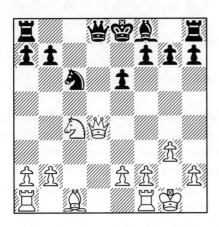

13 ♕c3!

The attack on the g7-pawn hinders the development of the opponent's kingside (much weaker is 13 ♕e4? ♕d5!, Cherniaev-Janssen, Wijk aan Zee 2003). Now White has no need to devise anything: he has the initiative for free with the material equal.

13...f6

This move would be good if Black were

able to complete his development, but alas... However, it is already unclear what he should do: if 13...♖c8 there follows 14 ♗e3(f4), if 13...♘d4 – 14 ♕d3 (with the threat of ♖d1) 14...♘c6 15 ♕b3!, while if 13...♕d4 (or 13...♕f6 14 ♕b3) 14 ♕b3 ♕d5, then 15 ♕xb7 (more forceful than 15 ♗e3, which has been played) 15...♘d4 16 ♕xd5 exd5 17 ♘e5 with the better endgame.

Perhaps Black should have tried to confuse matters by 13...b5 14 ♘e5 ♘d4, although here too after 15 ♕d3 he has an unpleasant position: 15...♗c5 16 ♖d1 f6 17 e3! or 15...♕d5 16 ♗f4 (16 ♗e3!?) 16...♖d8 17 ♖ac1 etc.

14 ♗e3 ♗e7 15 ♖fd1 ♕c7

After 15...♕c8 16 ♖ac1 0-0 17 ♘a5! ♘xa5 18 ♕xa5 ♕e8 19 ♕c7 b6 20 ♕c4 White has such powerful pressure on the open files that Black is obliged to try and relieve it by giving up his e6-pawn.

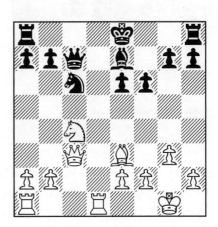

16 ♕b3! (gradually aiming at the e6- and b7-pawns) **16...g5**

Comparatively the best chance – already some sharp advance has to be made. 16...♔f7? is weak because of 17 ♗f4 ♕c8 18 ♗d6 and wins, while if 16...0-0?! the simplest is 17 ♘d6.

17 ♖ac1

A natural developing move, but 17 f4!? at

once is also strong, aiming to open the position as soon as possible and create an attack on the weakened black king.

17...♖d8?

More saving chances were offered by 17...♔f7 18 f4 ♖hd8 19 fxg5 fxg5, although even here after 20 ♘d2 ♖d5 21 ♘e4 or 20 ♖f1+ ♔g8 21 ♘a5 White has an obvious advantage.

18 ♖xd8+ ♗xd8 19 ♕xb7!

It is hard for a human to refrain from such a pretty stroke, but the computer rates highly the less aesthetic 19 ♘a3!? ♕d7 20 ♖d1 ♕e7(c8) 21 ♘b5, also winning a pawn, but keeping the queens on the board.

19...♕xb7 20 ♘d6+ ♔d7 21 ♘xb7 ♗b6 22 ♘c5+ ♗xc5 23 ♗xc5

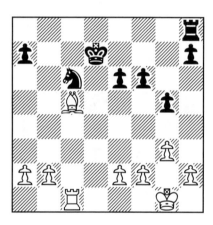

An endgame has been reached with a mobile bishop against a knight and a sound extra pawn for White. It was for this that I had aimed, wishing to demonstrate that I had improved in technical endings.

23...f5

23...a5 24 ♖d1+ ♔c7 was somewhat more resilient, but this position is also hopeless for Black, since he is not helped by the exchange of rooks.

24 ♖d1+ ♔c7 25 ♖d6 ♖e8

Passive defence makes things easier for me. 25...♖b8 26 ♖xe6 (26 b4!?) 26...♖xb2

was sharper, but nevertheless Black's downfall is bound to be caused by the vulnerability of his kingside pawns.

26 b4 a6 27 f3 h5 28 h4 (fixing the weakness on h5) **28...gxh4 29 gxh4 ♖g8+ 30 ♔f2 ♖g6**

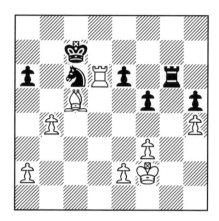

Now, when the black rook has moved away to g6, White creates a passed pawn on the queenside.

31 a4 f4 32 b5 axb5 33 axb5 ♘e7 34 ♖a6 ♘f5 35 ♖a7+ ♔c8 36 b6 ♖g7 37 ♖a4 ♔b7 38 ♖xf4 ♔c6 39 ♖c4+ ♔b5 40 ♖b4+

After almost holding out until the time control, Black resigned (**1-0**).

This unpretentious game decided the outcome of this short match: after it Andersson somehow drooped and did not demonstrate even a hint of aggression. In the 4th game against the English Opening I chose the double fianchetto 'à la Adorjan' and easily gained a draw: 1 ♘f3 ♘f6 2 c4 b6 3 g3 c5 4 ♗g2 ♗b7 5 0-0 g6 6 b3 ♗g7 7 ♗b2 0-0 8 ♘c3 ♘a6 (later Andras reproached me for rejecting 'large-scale play' – 8...d6 and ...♘bd7) 9 d4 d5 etc.

The 5th game proved to be the longest and most difficult in the match. I methodically built up the pressure and adjourned the game with a big advantage. It was resumed the day after the drawn 6th game, and it brought me a second win, and with it overall success: 4-2.

My contests with Hübner and Andersson raised the public interest in my autumn match with Karpov. At the same time, a considerable stir had been caused by my interview in *Der Spiegel* and an open letter to the Belgrade newspaper *Politika*, where I revealed my dispute with Gligoric regarding the events in February. In addition, I stated my point of view in several letters to FIDE, without clearing these in advance with the USSR Chess Federation.

As was anticipated, Karpov's supporters tried to have me disqualified for my statements, which were unpardonably audacious by Party standards. On 9th August, three weeks before the start of the title match, they set a date for the reprisal – a special meeting of the USSR Chess Federation Praesidium, at which my 'anti-State' behaviour was to be considered. There was every likelihood that my punishment would be disqualification, but here an intervention was made by one of Gorbachev's men, the new director of the Communist Party Propaganda Department Alexander Yakovlev. When the problem was explained to him, he said, briefly and clearly: 'The match must take place.'

I have to admit that I had to endure some unpleasant minutes: it was not until just before the meeting that I learned that it had all been decided differently. Not even all the initiators of the 'reprisal' knew about the new Party directive, and so this 'historic' meeting of the USSR Chess Federation Praesidium of 9th August 1985 resembled an absurd and at times comical play. And it concluded with a recommendation that Soviet grandmasters should not give interviews to the western media. That was all!

The summer months flew by very quickly.

And by September, despite all the off-the-board intrigues, I felt far more confident than a year earlier. I had become stronger and had more stamina, and my style of play was more balanced and universal. My store of opening ideas had been thoroughly replenished. In short, I was prepared for the new battle with my mighty opponent.

Second Match with Karpov
World Championship Match Karpov – **Kasparov** (Moscow, 1 September – 10 November 1985): 11-13.

As though in confirmation of Karpov's words that 'opening preparation is the strongest aspect of Kasparov's play', in the very first game I took my opponent aback with my choice of opening.

Game 3
G.Kasparov-A.Karpov
World Championship Match
1st Game, Moscow 03.09.1985
Nimzo-Indian Defence E20

---

1 d4 ♘f6 2 c4 e6 3 ♘c3

In my matches with Korchnoi (1983), Karpov (1984/85), Hübner and Andersson (1985) I avoided the Nimzo-Indian Defence by 3 ♘f3 or 3 g3.

3...♗b4 4 ♘f3

A surprise! Earlier I normally played 4 e3 (*Game No.26*), for which Karpov would undoubtedly have prepared before the first match. The immediate 4 g3 was rejected because of 4...d5.

4...c5

The most popular reply. After 4...0-0 the pin 5 ♗g5 is unpleasant (7th and 11th games). If 4...♘e4, then 5 ♕c2 (*Game No.6*). The Queen's Indian 'hybrid' 4...b6 5 ♗g5 leads to complicated play (*Game Nos.9, 10, 11, 18, 20*).

5 g3

Here Karpov thought for nearly half an hour. Strangely enough, the then fashionable Romanishin Variation had never occurred in any of his or my games, although it was in the opening repertoire of several of the champion's helpers, and most probably he would never have devoted much attention to it, reckoning that I was unlikely to employ it in the match. Add to this the particular importance of the first game, and it is not hard to understand why the initial five moves took Karpov 50 minutes (an unprecedented occurrence in his games!).

Although the great Rubinstein played it a couple of times, the strategic defects of the variation are obvious and it is by no means suitable for everyone. I reckoned that the resulting positions would not appeal to Karpov and that they would be difficult for him to play. Here the rules that operate are poorly perceived by 'classical' players, since one constantly has to operate with different values, exchanging material and positional weaknesses for the initiative. And my reckoning was fully justified! In terms of points, the effect of 4 ♘f3 proved stunning: +3=2.

5...♘e4

Subsequently my opponent played only 5...♘c6 (13th and 17th games) or 5...cxd4 6 ♘xd4 0-0 7 ♗g2 d5 (*Game No.13*).

6 ♕d3 ♕a5 (avoiding both the *tabiya* of those years 6...cxd4 7 ♘xd4 ♕a5, and also the present-day *tabiya* 7...♗xc3!? 8 bxc3 ♘c5) **7 ♕xe4 ♗xc3+ 8 ♗d2 ♗xd2+ 9 ♘xd2**

9...♕b6

A rare move of the Hungarian grandmaster Vadasz (usually 9...♘c6 10 dxc5 or 10 d5 is played – cf. *Revolution in the 70s*, pp.277-278). On encountering a surprise, Karpov endeavoured to find the path which he assumed had been least studied by the opponent in his preparation, and after lengthy thought he chose a variation leading to simplification and a seemingly tenable endgame. As our first match showed, the champion judged an exchange of queens to be *a priori* in his favour, and this continuation stemmed from his general logic of taking decisions in non-standard situations.

10 dxc5

Nothing is promised by 10 0-0-0 cxd4 11 ♘b3, if only because of 11...♕c6 (11...♘c6!?, Pinter-Vadasz, Budapest 1979) 12 ♖xd4 b6 13 ♗g2 ♗b7 14 ♔b1 ♕xe4+ 15 ♗xe4 ♗xe4+ 16 ♖xe4 ♘c6 with equality (Ubilava-Vyzhmanavin, Tashkent 1984).

10...♕xb2 11 ♖b1 ♕c3

11...♕xa2 is dangerous, and not only because of 12 ♕d4 0-0 13 ♕c3 ♕a4 14 ♗g2 ♘c6 15 0-0 ♕a5 16 ♕xa5 ♘xa5 17 ♖a1 ♘c6 18 ♘e4 with the better ending, but also in view of 12 ♗g2 with a highly promising lead in development.

If 11...♕a3 (Ubilava-Lerner, Tallinn 1983), then 12 ♕d4! is strong: 12...0-0 13 ♗g2 ♘c6 14 ♕d6 ♕xa2 15 0-0 ♕a5 16 ♖a1 ♕d8 17 ♖fb1 with serious pressure (Itkis-A.Ivanov, Borzhomi 1984). The undeveloped state of Black's queenside also tells after 13...♘a6 14 ♘e4 (14 ♘b3!?) 14...♕a5+ (14...f5 15 ♘d6 ♖b8! is better) 15 ♕d2 ♕c7 16 ♖b5 (Ubilava-Rozentalis, Kharkov 1985; Bluvshtein-Riazantsev, Khanty-Mansiysk 2011).

12 ♕d3! (White is forced to offer the exchange of queens) **12...♕xd3**

12...♕a5?! could have ended in disaster: 13 ♖b5 ♕a4 14 ♕c3 0-0 15 ♗g2 ♘c6 16 ♗xc6! a6 17 ♖b6! dxc6 18 ♖b3 and wins.

13 exd3

It was on this ending that Karpov was pinning his hopes: he has retained material equality, his king is in the centre, and without the queens, the problem of developing his queenside is hardly a fatal one. This was also played occasionally after the match, Black apparently being guided by the same considerations.

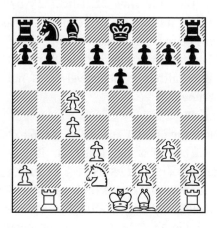

White's separated pawns have been transformed into a dynamic pawn mass. He has pressure on the b-file and the h1-a8 diagonal, while Black has a weak d6-point, for where the white knight will aim, and a weak b7-pawn. And all because of the white c5-pawn! Therefore it must be exchanged, but first Black has to develop his knight.

13...♘a6

With an attack on the c5-pawn. After the natural 13...♘c6 14 ♗g2 b6 I was planning 15 ♘e4! (15 d4!? bxc5 16 dxc5 is also interesting) 15...♔e7 16 ♔d2 f5 17 cxb6 axb6 18 ♘c3, or immediately 16 cxb6 axb6 17 ♘c3 (not exchanging the a2- and b6-pawns) 17...♖a6 18 ♔d2 with pressure on the weak b6-pawn – ♖b2, ♖hb1 and so on.

14 d4! (but not 14 ♘e4 in view of 14...♔e7 15 d4 b6! 16 cxb6 ♗b7! with counterplay)

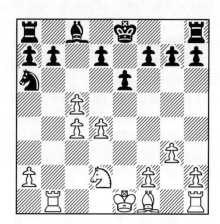

14...♖b8

Karpov again plays on the basis of general logic. He hopes to free himself without resorting to extreme measures and without hurrying to create new weaknesses in his position. But it soon transpires that the planned ...b7-b6 is insufficient for equality.

This is precisely the kind of situation which demands a combination of general strategy and concrete, dynamic play. The opponent's pawn mass could have been broken up in a different way – 14...e5!?. Although after 15 ♗g2! ♖b8 (15...exd4 is weaker in view of 16 ♖xb7! ♖b8 17 ♖xb8 ♘xb8 18 ♘e4) 16 dxe5 ♘xc5 17 0-0 b6 18 ♗d5 (18 ♘b3!?) 18...♗b7 19 f4 and ♘f3-d4 White gains some clear targets to attack, there is less material left on the board, which eases Black's defence.

15 ♗g2 ♔e7?!

Missing the last chance to undermine the centre – 15...e5 16 dxe5 ♘xc5, transposing into the previous variation. 15...b6 is premature, since after 16 cxb6 axb6 (16...♖xb6 17 ♔e2!?) 17 ♔e2 ♗b7 18 ♗xb7 ♖xb7 19 c5 and ♘c4 Black's b-pawn is too weak.

16 ♔e2(?!)

'According to general endgame rules the king should be in the centre, but here specific tactical features associated with the position of the king at e2 prove more important, and by exploiting them Black could have gained good drawing chances. 16 0-0! was correct,' I wrote in the book *Dva matcha*. Well, let's have a look. After 16...d6 17 cxd6+ ♔xd6 18 c5+ and ♘c4 things are depressing for Black, irrespective of the white king's position. And if after 16 0-0 Black replies 16...♖d8 17 ♘e4 b6, as in the game, then again 18 ♘d6!.

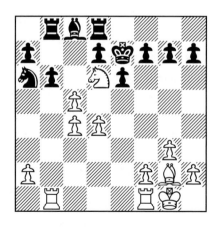

Analysis diagram

In the event of 18...bxc5 19 ♖xb8 ♘xb8 20 dxc5 the piece sacrifice 20...♘a6 (cf. the note to Black's 18th move) is no longer so effective because of 21 ♘xc8+ ♖xc8 22 ♗b7 ♖xc5 23 ♗xa6 ♖a5 24 ♗c8 ♖xa2 25 ♖d1 d6 26 ♖b1 or 24...♖c5 25 ♗b7 ♖xc4 26 ♖e1 ♖a4 27 ♗d5 with real winning chances.

And the 'Karpov line' – this is undoubtedly what he would have played – 18...♘c7 19 ♖b4 ♘e8 20 ♘xe8 ♔xe8 (without the king on e2 there is no point in playing 20...♖xe8 21 ♖fb1 ♗a6? in view of 22 c6! dxc6 23 ♖a4) 21 ♖fb1 ♗a6 (21...♗b7 22 d5) now runs into 22 f4 (if immediately 22 a4, then 22...♖bc8!) 22...♖dc8 23 a4 with a clear advantage to White: 23...d6 (23...♗b7 24 a5) 24 c6 ♔d8 25 f5! (25 a5!?) 25...♔c7 26 fxe6 fxe6 27 d5, creating a protected passed pawn.

However, with the removal of the white king from the centre Black has acquired the possibility of 16...b6!, which promises him better saving chances: 17 cxb6 axb6 18 ♖b3 ♗b7 19 ♖fb1 (the bishop on g2 is defended!) 19...♗xg2 20 ♔xg2 ♘c7, while after 21 ♖xb6 ♖xb6 22 ♖xb6 ♖a8 23 ♖b2 ♖a4! and ...♘a6-b4 Black is saved by his active rook. The breakthrough 21 c5! is much stronger, with the idea of 21...b5 22 a4 b4 23 ♖xb4, but the clever manoeuvre 21...♘d5! makes things difficult for White – after 22 cxb6 ♖b7! (the only way: 22...♖hc8? 23 b7!) 23 ♘c4 ♖a8, despite his two connected passed pawns he may be unable to win.

Therefore it is rather difficult to criticise 16 ♔e2, although objectively it is not the best move.

16...♖d8

Now the gambit 16...b6?! 17 cxb6 axb6 18 ♖b3 ♗b7 19 ♗xb7 ♖xb7 20 ♖hb1 ♘c7 (after 20...♖hb8 21 c5 b5 22 ♘c4 ♘c7 23 a4 all the same Black loses his b-pawn) 21 ♖xb6 ♖xb6 22 ♖xb6 ♖a8 23 ♖b2 ♖a4 is parried by the simple 24 ♔d3. And if 16...e5 Averbakh suggested the excellent centralisation 17 ♔d3 exd4 18 ♔xd4 ♘c7 19 ♖he1+ ♘e6+ 20 ♔c3 f5 21 ♖e5 ♔f6 22 f4, restricting the opponent's actions.

17 ♘e4 b6 (this undermining move cannot be delayed, as otherwise ♖b2 and ♖fb1 could lead to complete paralysis) **18 ♘d6**

The critical position.

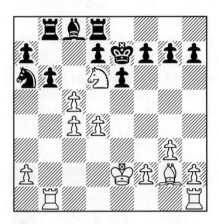

18...♘c7

In aiming to exchange the powerful knight on d6, Karpov misses an excellent tactical resource – 18...bxc5!?. In the event of 19 ♘xc8+ ♖dxc8 20 ♗b7 Black sacrifices the exchange – 20...♖xb7 21 ♖xb7 cxd4 22 ♖xa7 ♘c5, obtaining good counterplay (23 ♖b1 e5 24 a4 e4).

At first sight 19 ♖xb8 ♘xb8 20 dxc5 is stronger, almost stalemating Black, but an unexpected piece sacrifice – 20...♘a6! 21 ♘xc8+ ♖xc8 22 ♗b7 ♖xc5 23 ♗xa6 ♖a5 leads to an unclear ending, since in contrast to the variation with 16 0-0 the a2-pawn is captured with check: 24 ♗b7 ♖xa2+ 25 ♔e3 ♖c2 with good drawing chances (26 ♖a1 ♖xc4 27 ♖xa7 ♖c7), or 24 ♗c8! ♖xa2+ 25 ♔e3 ♔d8 (more resilient than 25...♖c2 26 ♖d1 d5 27 ♗a6!? ♖a2 28 ♗b7 dxc4 29 ♖d2! or 28...♖b2 29 ♗c6 dxc4 30 ♖d7+ and ♖xa7) 26 ♗b7 ♖c2 27 ♖a1 ♖xc4 28 ♖xa7 ♖c7 29 ♖a8+ ♔e7 30 ♗e4 h6, and it is very difficult,

if at all possible, for White to win.

19 ♖b4 (intensifying the pressure) **19...♘e8**

Logical. The variation 19...♗a6 20 ♖hb1 ♘d5 21 ♖4b3 bxc5 22 ♖xb8 ♘c3+ 23 ♔d3 ♘xb1 24 ♖xd8 ♔xd8 25 dxc5 ends with the trapping of the knight.

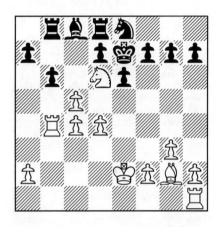

20 ♘xe8!

The correct move: after 20 ♘xc8+ ♖dxc8! 21 ♖hb1 ♖c7 22 ♔d3 (22 cxb6 ♖xb6 is equal) 22...♖bc8! 23 cxb6 axb6 24 a4 ♘f6 25 ♖1b2 d6 26 f4 ♘d7 Black could at last have breathed freely: he clearly has more chances of drawing than White of winning.

20...♔xe8?

A critical moment. Black misses another opportunity to exploit the king's position on e2 – 20...♖xe8! 21 ♖hb1 ♗b7 22 d5 exd5 23 cxd5 ♖ec8! (not my previous suggestion 23...♔f8+?! 24 ♔d2 ♖a8 25 ♖1b2!) 24 cxb6 ♗a6+ 25 ♔d2 ♖xb6 26 ♖xb6 axb6 27 ♖xb6 ♗c4 28 a4 ♖c5 with quite good saving chances (here d5-d6 is not threatened, in contrast to the variation in the following note).

21 ♖hb1 ♗a6

The bishop is finally developed, but... too late! It is now bad to play 21...♗b7 22 d5 (White has no reason to exchange the bishops, unless he gains some clear plus – say, a pair of connected passed pawns) 22...exd5

23 cxd5 ♖dc8 24 cxb6 ♗a6+ 25 ♔d2 ♖xb6 26 ♖xb6 axb6 27 ♖xb6 (27 d6!?) 27...♗c4 28 a4 ♖c5 29 d6 or first 29 ♔c3!.

22 ♔e3?!

The natural move, but 22 ♔d2! was more accurate, with the idea of 22...♖dc8 23 a4!, when 23...e5? loses to 24 cxb6 ♖xb6 25 ♖xb6 axb6 26 c5! bxc6 27 ♖b6 etc.

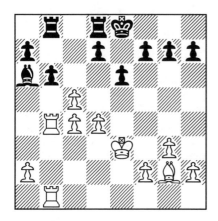

22...d5?

Cracking under the pressure. 22...♖dc8 was necessary, after which I recommended 23 ♗f1 ♖a8 24 ♖a4 winning a pawn, although after 24...♗b7! 25 cxb6 axb6 26 ♖xa8 ♖xa8 27 ♖xb6 ♗c6 28 ♖b2 ♖a3+ 29 ♗d3 f5 30 ♔d2 ♗e4 there are serious problems with its conversion. And 23 a4 runs into 23...e5! with the threat of ...exd4+. Therefore 23 c6! is stronger: 23...♖c7 (23...dxc6? 24 ♖a4) 24 d5!? ♔e7 (24...dxc6? 25 d6) 25 ♖a4 ♗c8 26 ♖d1 d6 27 f4 – Black has a difficult but for the moment defensible position, and there is still a lot of play.

23 cxd6!

After 23 cxd5 exd5 24 cxb6 axb6 25 ♖xb6 ♖xb6 26 ♖xb6 ♗c4 27 a4 ♖a8 28 ♖b4 ♖a6 Black would have acquired hopes of a defence.

23...♖bc8 (Black would have lost immediately after 23...♖xd6 24 c5 ♖dd8 25 c6! ♖bc8 26 ♖a4) **24 ♔d3**

The imminent prospect of taking the lead in the match paralysed me, and I was no longer calculating variations, but aiming to play as solidly as possible. The game would have been quickly and spectacularly concluded by 24 ♖a4! ♗xc4 25 ♗b7 b5 26 d7+! ♔xd7 27 ♗xc8+ ♔xc8 28 ♖xa7.

24...♖xd6 25 ♖a4 b5 26 cxb5 ♖b8 27 ♖ab4

Averbakh and Taimanov recommended 27 ♔e3. In any event, White has no reason to hurry: he can simply advance his queenside pawns.

27...♗b7 28 ♗xb7 ♖xb7 29 a4 ♔e7 30 h4 h6 31 f3 ♖d5 32 ♖c1 ♖bd7 (nothing would have been changed by 32...♔d6 33 ♖bc4 or 33 ♖c6+ and ♖c5) **33 a5**

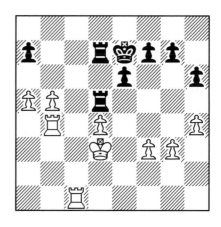

The presence of all four rooks on the board does not help Black: he is not only a pawn down, but also without counterplay. In time-trouble Karpov initiates activity on the kingside, which leads merely to the exchange of a few pawns.

33...g5 34 hxg5 ♖xg5 35 g4 h5 36 b6 axb6 37 axb6 ♖b7 38 ♖c5 f5 39 gxh5 ♖xh5 40 ♔c4! (this, the last move before the time control, settles matters) **40...♖h8 41 ♔b5 ♖a8 42 ♖bc4**

The sealed move. The following day Black resigned without resuming (**1-0**). Times: 2.32–2.28.

Many were surprised by the outcome of the first game – after all, the previous match had instilled the thought that decisive results in our games should not often be expected. Besides, before this Karpov had never lost three games in a row (if one includes his two losses at the finish of the previous match), just as he had never lost the first game in a world championship match.

Whereas I was somewhat perplexed and did not yet know how I would cope with the burden of leading, which had been acquired so quickly, Karpov too found himself in the unaccustomed role of pursuer. Therefore the second game had an obvious psychological implication: how would the two contestants perform with these new roles and in an unfamiliar situation?

Game 4
A.Karpov-G.Kasparov
World Championship Match
2nd Game, Moscow 5/6.09.1985

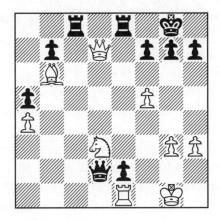

34...♛h6?

In time-trouble – Karpov and I each had about 3-4 minutes left – I was tempted by a double attack and I missed an opportunity

to bring the game to a rapid and highly spectacular conclusion: 34...♖f8! 35 ♔f2 (after 35 ♗c7 ♖xc7 White is two pawns down, while after 35 f6 ♖c1! he loses a piece) 35...♖c3 36 ♘e5 ♖f3+!! (another combination on the theme of overloading and diversion) 37 ♔xf3 ♛xe1 38 ♗f2 ♛d1. However, 34...♛h6 does not throw away the win.
35 ♗f2 ♛c6! (into the endgame!) **36 ♛xc6** (36 ♘c5 ♛xd7 37 ♘xd7 ♖c2 38 ♘b6 h5 is also hopeless for White) **36...♖xc6**

It turns out that the a4-pawn cannot be defended.
37 ♖b1 (by now White had just one minute left) **37...♖c4 38 ♖xb7 ♖xa4 39 ♗e1 ♖a3 40 ♖d7 a4 41 ♔f2**

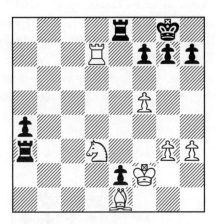

Here the game was adjourned. White has securely blockaded the e2-pawn, but it is obvious that he is unlikely to be able to cope with the passed a-pawn without losing material, and Black can expect to win.
41...♖b3 (5)

My sealed move does not yet spoil anything, although before the resumption it seemed to me to be second-rate. When he saw it on the board the following day, Karpov breathed a sigh of relief. White's position remains difficult, but if Black had played 41...♖a8! or simply given his king an escape square with 41...h5! and only after 42

♘f4 gone 42...♖b3! 43 ♖a7 (43 ♘xh5? ♖a8) 43...h4 44 gxh4 a3, he would have won the game far more easily.

42 ♘c1 (weak is 42 ♘f4? ♖a8 or 42 ♘c5? ♖b5! 43 ♘xa4 ♖xf5+ 44 ♔g2 ♖f1) **42...♖b1!**

The correct move, but I had not fully evaluated all its consequences. Initially my trainers and I analysed 42...♖b5 and in the variations with 43 g4 ♖a8! we found a clear win: 44 ♖d2 a3 45 ♖xe2 ♖b2 46 ♗c3 (46 ♘a2 ♖e8) 46...♖xe2+ 47 ♔xe2 a2 48 ♗a1 ♖b8 (48...♖a3!?) 49 ♗c3 a1♕ 50 ♗xa1 ♖b1. But literally two hours before the start of the resumption, we suddenly discovered a strong reply for White – 43 ♖a7!, immediately beginning a battle with the dangerous a4-pawn. After 43...♖xf5+ 44 ♔g2 ♖f1 (44...♖d5 45 ♘a2!) 45 ♘d3 ♖d8 46 ♖xa4 g5 47 ♖a3 ♖xd3 (47...f5 48 ♗f2) 48 ♖xd3 ♖xe1 49 ♖e3 and 50 h4 at best Black would have obtained a drawn ending with f- and h-pawns. A feverish search for other ideas began...

43 ♘a2

But not 43 ♘xe2? ♖b2 and ...a4-a3.

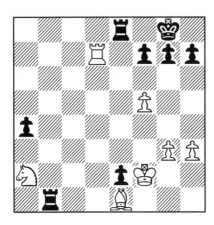

43...♖a8? (5)

This would appear to throw away the win, although White still has considerable difficulties. One of the two continuations studied at home should have been chosen:

1) 43...h5 44 ♘c3 a3 45 ♖a7 ♖b3 46 g4 h4, fixing the h3-pawn. Lack of time prevented us from evaluating this position exactly, and only later did we establish that this would have promised Black a win, since it extends the defensive front and White is unable to protect all his weaknesses;

2) 43...♖a1 (this tempting possibility was found 15 minutes before we set off for the resumption) 44 ♘c3 h5 45 ♖a7 a3 or 44 ♘b4 h5 45 ♖a7 ♖e4 etc.

Black also had a third way to win – 43...♖b5!: for example, 44 g4 ♖b3 45 ♘c3 a3 46 ♖a7 h5! 47 gxh5 ♖e5! 48 f6 ♖xh5. But, alas, after a sleepless night spent analysing, I was in a disorganised state and at the board I was unable to work out the situation correctly.

44 ♖e7! (15) **44...♖b2 45 ♖xe2 ♖xe2+** (45...♖ab8! was stronger) **46 ♔xe2 ♖e8+ 47 ♔f2**, and by accurate defence White gained a draw on the 65th move. Times: 3.50–3.59.

For the win (and a score of 2-0!) I lacked just a little something... Failures such as this are always vexing, but in a match for the world championship everything is perceived with particular intensity, and Karpov seized the psychological initiative. After a quiet draw in the 3rd game he scored two successive wins and took the lead: 3-2.

I needed, firstly, to regain my composure as quickly as possible; secondly, to play forcefully and with the utmost self-discipline, so as not to allow Karpov a chance to build on his success; and, thirdly, to go in for a complicated struggle, in order to regain the match initiative and if possible wear out my opponent. This objective was achieved in the period between the 6th and 10th games. All these five draws were tense encounters and they took a great deal of effort. The character of the play began to change. I employed drastic measures – in all these games I sacrificed a pawn: with Black in order not to concede the initiative, and with White in order to seize it.

In the 10th game I saved myself, in the words of the commentators, 'with a series of stunning sacrifices', as a result of which Karpov must have been left with a feeling a deep disappointment. Of course, his oversight on the 22nd move in the next game, the 11th, was something quite out of the ordinary, but it should not be forgotten that it came after ten very tough battles, the last two of which (the 9th and 10th games) had demanded of him an enormous expenditure of nervous energy. Besides, in the 11th game itself he was initially in difficulties, and when the worst was over, it would seem that he prematurely relaxed. The price of a moment's weakening proved very high.

The match score became level, and it remained so up to the 16th game, which for many years I regarded as my best creative achievement.

Game 5
A.Karpov-G.Kasparov
World Championship Match
16th Game, Moscow 15.10.1985
Sicilian Defence B44

1 e4 c5 2 ♘f3 e6 3 d4 cxd4 4 ♘xd4 ♘c6 (a move order tested in the 12th game, and before that in the 3rd game of the previous match) **5 ♘b5**

So, not 5 ♘c3 d6 6 g4!? (14th game). Instead, Karpov felt prepared for a theoretical duel.

5...d6 6 c4 ♘f6 7 ♘1c3 a6 8 ♘a3 d5?!

This departure from the standard 8...♗e7 9 ♗e2 0-0 10 0-0 b6 (Game No.7 in *Kasparov vs. Karpov 1975-1985*), which first occurred

in the 12th game, looked like a bolt from the blue. Many journalists christened this pawn sacrifice the 'Kasparov Gambit' and 'novelty of the year', although it first occurred in the old and well-forgotten game Honfi-Dely (Hungarian Championship 1965). I did not know it and I found the idea 8...d5 in the spring of 1985, moving the pieces on a pocket set during a flight between Baku and Moscow. I wanted to exploit the unpretentious position of the white knight on a3.

9 cxd5 exd5 10 exd5 ♘b4 11 ♗e2

This move, which I considered to be harmless, was made instantly by the champion, rejecting the line tested in the 12th game: 11 ♗c4 (Honfi played 11 ♕a4+?! ♗d7 12 ♕b3 against Dely, but this was a loss of time) 11...♗g4! 12 ♗e2 (after 12 ♕b3 ♗d6, 12 f3 ♗f5 13 0-0 ♗c5+, or 12 ♕d2 ♕e7+ 13 ♔f1 b5 Black has a comfortable game, while after 12 ♕d4!? I was planning the sharp 12...b5) 12...♗xe2 13 ♕xe2+ ♕e7 14 ♗e3 ♘bxd5 with a quick draw.

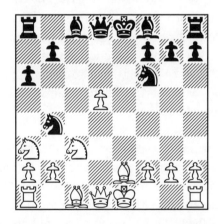

For the sake of the rapid development of his pieces White returns the pawn. In the variations with 11...♘bxd5 he retains an advantage: 12 ♘xd5 ♕xd5 13 0-0 ♕xd1 14 ♖xd1 ♗g4 (14...♗c5 15 ♗f3!) 15 ♗xg4 ♘xg4 16 ♖e1+ ♔d7 17 h3 ♗xa3 18 bxa3 ♘f6 19 ♗b2 etc.

At our training sessions we also analysed 11...♘fxd5!?. Now in the event of 12 0-0 (or 12 ♘xd5 ♕xd5 13 0-0 ♗e6) 12...♗e6 (12...♗e7!?) 13 ♘xd5 ♕xd5 the active knight on b4 helps Black to equalise (Ernst-Brodsky, Helsinki 1992). 13 ♕a4+!? is more dangerous for him: 13...b5 (13...♗d7?! 14 ♕b3; 13...♕d7 14 ♕xd7+ is also unattractive) 14 ♘axb5 axb5 15 ♗xb5+ ♔e7 16 ♘xd5+ ♘xd5 17 ♕e4 f5 18 ♕f3 ♔f7 19 ♖d1 with two pawns for the piece and an attack (the source game: Almasi-J.Horvath, Hungarian Championship 1993), although it is by no means decisive: 19...♗e7! 20 ♗c6 (20 ♗c4 ♖a5 21 ♗e3 ♕a8!) 20...♖a5 21 ♗e3 (21 g4?! is weaker: 21...♖f8! 22 gxf5 ♔g8 23 ♕e4 ♗f7) 21...♕d6 22 b4 ♕xc6 23 bxa5 ♕b5 etc.

However, already before the match itself I had conceived an unexpected, genuine gambit idea, involving the invasion of the knight from b4 to d3.

11...♗c5?!

This move, which we thought was very good, was also made quickly and firmly, after which Karpov became anxious, on realising that he had again not guessed the direction of our thorough home analysis, and that he would have to carry out the main work at the board against a well-prepared opponent.

12 0-0?! (5)

Natural development. 12 ♗e3! ♗xe3 13 ♕a4+! and ♕xb4 was far stronger. This was overlooked by me and my trainers! Soon afterwards the Kiev master A.Kostyuchenko published a brief analysis devoted to this improvement. 13...♘d7?! 14 ♕xb4 ♗c5 15 ♕e4+ ♔f8 16 0-0 leaves White with a clear advantage (Karpov-van der Wiel, Brussels 1986), while after 13...♗d7 14 ♕xb4 ♕b6 15 ♕xb6 ♗xb6 16 ♘c4 ♗c5 17 ♗f3 (Karpov) or 17 0-0 the endgame would appear to be tenable, although Black is condemned to an

unpleasant struggle for a draw. Thus the 11...♗c5 gambit turned out to be not altogether correct.

Fortunately for me, I brought out my bishop without thinking and did not notice the reply 12 ♗e3. And yet if my opponent had played this or if I had avoided 11...♗c5, the match could have turned out differently. Fate decreed otherwise...

12...0-0

White is at a crossroads.

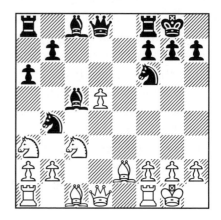

13 ♗f3 (13)

Karpov later claimed that he could have gained an advantage by 13 ♗g5. However, in my view, in the ending after 13...♘bxd5 14 ♘xd5 ♕xd5 15 ♗xf6 ♕xd1 16 ♖xd1 gxf6 and ...♗e6 Black should be able to draw without particular difficulty: the two bishops compensate for his pawn weaknesses.

But why should White voluntarily part with his material advantage, at a time when Black does not appear to have any threats, nor even any serious counterplay? And although he undoubtedly sensed that I had made a through study of the resulting positions, Karpov nevertheless felt obliged to play for a win. However, at that point he could hardly have imagined just how deep his opponent's analysis had been.

13...♗f5

Black's first achievement: it is now not easy for the knight on a3 to come into play, and in addition the d3-square is weakened. In the event of 13...h6? 14 ♗e3! the knight would have escaped from a3.

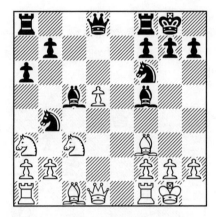

14 ♗g5

The attempt to activate the knight – 14 ♘c4 is parried by 14...♗c2 15 ♕d2 ♗d3. Another tempting continuation – 14 ♗e3 ♗xe3 15 fxe3 could have been answered by 15...♗d3 16 ♖e1 ♕b6, when the e-pawn becomes a target, or even 15...♕b6 16 ♘c4 (16 ♕d2 ♗d3!) 16...♕c5 17 ♕d4 ♕xd4 18 exd4 ♗d3 19 ♘b6 ♗xf1 20 ♘xa8 ♗xg2! with an unclear ending. Therefore Karpov simply develops his pieces, hoping that subsequently his extra pawn will tell.

Indeed, how can Black expect to create counterplay? He does not have any lead in development, and, apart from the knight on a3, all the opponent's pieces are quite reasonably placed. But Black's position contains colossal dynamic resources, which are not easy to foresee. The main point is the immediate prospect of the black pieces seizing all the dominating 'heights' in the position, and White, strangely enough, has to act very energetically.

On the other hand, it is not easy to force yourself to hurry, when you have an extra

pawn and, at first sight, a solid position. It is possible that, for the entire first half of the game, Karpov was quite unable to escape from this psychological impasse.

14...♖e8 (17)

It is essential to take control of the e4-square. It only needed some haste on Black's part –14...b5?, and after 15 ♗e4 or 15 d6 all his chances would have vanished. And the immediate 14...h6 would have allowed White a loop-hole for the simplifying 15 ♗xf6 ♕xf6 16 ♗e4.

15 ♕d2 (10)

There was no point in White sharply changing the character of the play and returning the extra pawn by 15 ♘c4 ♗d3 16 a3 ♗xc4 (16...♗xf1? 17 ♔xf1) 17 axb4 ♗xb4, since in the complicated positions after 18 ♕d4 ♗xf1 19 ♕xb4 ♗b5! or 18 ♖e1 ♖xe1+ 19 ♕xe1 h6 the chances are rather with Black.

15...b5! (depriving the knight on a3 of the c4-square) **16 ♖ad1** (15)

Again the most obvious continuation. White would not have achieved anything with 16 d6 ♖a7 17 ♖ad1 ♖d7 or 16 ♕f4 ♗g6 17 ♗xf6 ♕xf6! 18 ♕xf6 gxf6.

16...♘d3! (9)

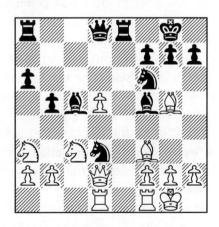

A cherished leap, which I first carried out earlier on my pocket set. The knight could not have dreamed of a better career! It is destined to play a brilliant role in the ultimate victory. With their excellent advanced outpost at d3, the black pieces are ready for a decisive invasion of the enemy position.

White must now recognise the threatened danger of complete suffocation and urgently undertake something, decide on some form of action...

17 ♘ab1? (08)

Another natural move (defending against the fork ...b5-b4: 17 ♗e2? ♘xf2! 18 ♖xf2 b4), which proves to be a serious mistake. Indeed, 17 d6! was essential.

Now White has the advantage after 17...b4 18 ♗xa8 ♕xa8 19 ♗xf6 gxf6 20 d7! ♖d8 21 ♘a4 bxa3 (21...♗a7 22 ♘c4) 22 ♘xc5 ♘xc5 23 ♕a5! axb2 24 ♕xc5 b1♕ 25 ♖xb1 ♗xb1 26 ♖xb1 ♖xd7 27 ♕c4, or 17...♖a7 18 ♗e2! ♘xf2 (18...♘e5 19 ♘d5) 19 ♖xf2 b4 20 ♕f4 ♗g6 21 ♘a4 ♗xf2+ 22 ♕xf2 with an attack on the rook (22...♖d7 23 ♗xf6 ♕xf6 24 ♘c4, and if 24...♗c2, then 25 ♕xf6 gxf6 26 ♖d2 ♗xa4 27 ♘b6 a5 28 ♗g4). He can also be satisfied with 17...♖b8 18 ♘d5! (18 ♗e2? ♘xf2) 18...♗xd6 19 ♗xf6 gxf6 20 ♘c2 or 18...♕xd6 19 ♗xf6 gxf6 20 ♕c3 ♘e5 21 b4.

However, after 17 d6 I was planning a promising exchange sacrifice – 17...♕xd6! 18 ♗xa8 ♖xa8 with highly tactical play in which Black has the initiative: 19 ♗xf6 (19 h3 comes into consideration too, but not 19 ♘e2?! ♘g4 20 ♘g3 ♕e5) 19...♕xf6 20 ♘c2 (20 b4 ♘xb4) 20...♘xb2 21 ♕d5 (21 ♘d5 ♕d6) 21...♖c8 22 ♖d2 ♘c4 23 ♖e2 ♗e6 – Black has excellent compensation for his minimal material deficit and after 24 ♕f3 there is still all to play for.

That which happened in the game was far worse for White. By retreating his knight, Karpov was probably hoping soon to evict the knight from d3 by ♗f3-e2, but he is not

in fact able to do this.

17...h6 (4)

At a convenient moment Black succeeds in making an important move: it is useful to drive back the bishop, so that it can never return to e3.

18 ♗h4

Both 18 ♗xf6 ♕xf6 and 18 ♗e3 ♗xe3 (or even 18...♖xe3!?) 19 fxe3 ♕b6 are bad for White.

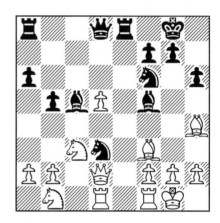

18...b4! (5)

Continuing his restriction strategy, Black not only dislodges the knight on c3 from its good position, but also deprives the knight at b1 of any future.

19 ♘a4?! (11)

'The second knight also has to move to the edge of the board' (*Dva matcha*). Even so, 19 ♘e2 was somewhat better – although 19...g5 (19...♘e5 20 ♘d4! is unclear, but 19...♕b6!? is of interest) 20 ♗xg5 ♘xf2 21 ♖xf2 (21 ♗xf6? ♘e4+!) 21...hxg5! 22 ♕xg5+ ♗g6 23 ♘d2 ♘xd5 (23...♕b6 24 ♕g3 ♖ac8 will also do) 24 ♕xd8 ♖axd8 cannot satisfy White, after 20 ♗g3 g4 21 ♘c1 ♘xb2 22 ♕xb2 gxf3 he has better chances of defending.

19...♗d6 (6)

A position for which I had aimed in my home analysis! 19...♗a7 was also good.

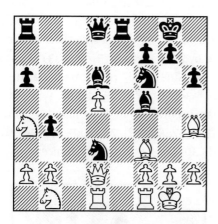

Now Black's achievements are patently obvious. White's minor pieces are scattered about, stuck on both flanks, and are quite unable to coordinate, the placing of his knights being particularly depressing. But Black's main achievement is the wonderful ♗f5 and ♘d3 duo, which completely paralyses all three of White's major pieces (not without reason did Keene call the knight on d3 an 'octopus'). A very rare occurrence in a practical game.

Even so, despite the paralysis of the enemy pieces, Black's ultimate success is by no means obvious, since for the moment White has no glaring weaknesses, and if he should succeed in driving the knight on d3 from its dominating post, the worst for him will be over. Black, naturally, will want at any price to maintain his bridgehead in the enemy camp. It is around this that the struggle revolves over the next few moves, with Black proving his case with the help of various tactical means.

20 ♗g3 (5)

The only sensible move. Both ...♗f4 and 20...♗xh2+ 21 ♔xh2 ♘g4+ were threatened, and if 20 ♕c2?, then 20...♖c8 21 ♕b3 ♘f4, with the threats of ...♗c2 and ...g7-g5-g4. But now White is planning b2-b3 and ♘b2.

20...♖c8 (26)

After a long think I found an interesting way of forestalling White's plan. 20...♘e4 seemed very strong to me, but then I noticed that after 21 ♗xe4 ♗xe4 22 ♕e3! White, by activating his queen, solves all his problems. On the other hand, I would have retained the advantage after 20...♗xg3 21 hxg3 (21 fxg3?! ♕d7! 22 b3 ♕a7+ 23 ♔h1 ♕d4 is worse for White) 21...♕d6!? (21...♕a5 22 b3 ♖ad8 23 ♘a3!? ♘xd5 24 ♘c4 ♕b5 25 ♘cb2 is not so clear) 22 ♗e2 ♘e5, but I already had more ambitious plans.

21 b3 (5)

At first sight it seems that Black cannot prevent the freeing manoeuvre ♘a4-b2, but now fresh forces join the battle.

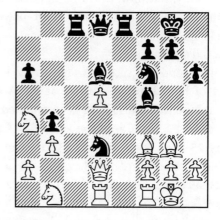

21...g5! (14)

The advance of this modest pawn looks more energetic than 21...♗e5!? 22 a3 a5, and it finally tips the scales in Black's favour. In a normal situation such a pawn thrust, weakening the king's position, would be anti-positional, but here, on the contrary, it contains a profound positional point: 22 ♘b2? is not possible because of the loss of a piece – 22...♘xb2 23 ♕xb2 g4 (24 ♗e2 ♖c2). The result is that for the moment White is unable to get rid of the knight on d3 (22 ♗e2? ♘e4!).

22 ♗xd6 (16)

The sharp 22 h4 would have run into 22...♘e4! (22...♘f4!? is also interesting) 23 ♗xe4 ♗xe4 with a very strong attack: 24 ♕e3 (24 f3 ♗h7!) 24...♗f4! 25 ♕d4 gxh4 26 ♖xd3 hxg3, 24 ♗xd6 ♕xd6 25 ♘b2 (25 hxg5 ♘f4!) 25...♘f4 26 ♘c4 ♕g6 and wins, or 24 hxg5 ♗xg3 25 fxg3 ♕xd5 26 ♔h2 (not 26 ♕e3 ♗g6 or 26 gxh6 ♖e6!) 26...♕b7 with the idea of ...♘e5, and White cannot hold out.

22...♕xd6 23 g3

In solving the problem of the defence of his f4-point, White creates new weaknesses in his position. Again it was not possible to drive the knight from d3 – after 23 ♗e2? ♘f4 Black's attack would have developed too swiftly. But now, at last, it appears that nothing can prevent White from playing ♘a4-b2...

23...♘d7!? (11)

Black sends his second knight to the support of his advanced outpost at d3. A big advantage would also have been retained by the quiet 23...♗g6, with the idea of 24 ♘b2 ♘e5 25 ♗g2 ♘e4 and ...♘c3, or even by relieving the guard – 23...♘e5!? 24 ♗g2 ♗d3 25 ♖fe1 (25 ♘b2? ♘e4!) 25...♖c2 26 ♖xe5 ♖xd2 27 ♖xe8+ ♘xe8 28 ♘xd2 ♕c7, and White only has practical chances of a draw.

24 ♗g2?! (4)

Missing the last opportunity to combat the outpost by 24 ♘b2. Because of the mass of tempting possibilities, it is not so easy for Black to choose the correct course. 24...♘7e5 is not bad, but the best is 24...♕f6!, for example:

1) 25 ♘xd3 ♗xd3 26 ♗g2 (fatal is 26 ♗g4? ♘e5! or 26 ♕xd3? ♘e5!, and the white queen is trapped in the middle of the board!) 26...♗xf1 27 ♖xf1 a5 with the exchange for a pawn and a dominating position;

2) 25 ♘c4 ♖xc4! 26 bxc4 ♘7e5, and my previous recommendation 27 ♗e2 ♘xc4 28 ♕c2 ♘f4 29 ♗d3 (if 29 ♕c4 there is a pretty mate by 29...♘xe2+ 30 ♔g2 ♗h3+! 31 ♔xh3 ♕f3 32 ♖de1 h5!) is incorrect because of 29...♘h3+! 30 ♔g2 ♗g4 and wins, but a queen sacrifice is more resilient – 27 ♕e2 ♘xf3+ (27...♘b2!?) 28 ♕xf3 g4 29 ♕xd3 ♗xd3 30 ♖xd3 with saving chances.

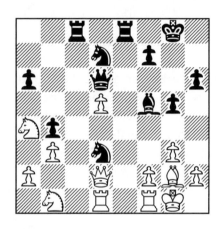

24...♕f6! (4)

The b2-point is now conclusively under Black's control. In contrast to the examined variation with 24 ♘b2 ♕f6 25 ♘c4, the knight at a4 does not in fact come into play. The fate of the game is essentially decided – the white pieces are completely pinned down within their own territory.

25 a3 a5 26 axb4 axb4 27 ♕a2 (27 h3 ♘7e5!) **27...♗g6!** (4)

Suppressing the slightest attempt by White to free himself. 27...♘e1 or even 27...♖e5 was also very strong.

28 d6 (12)

At last Karpov decides to give up his extra pawn, but now with a very modest aim – to at least develop his pieces somehow: 28...♕xd6? 29 ♘d2. Bad alternatives were 28 ♘d2? ♖e2! and 28 ♗h3? ♘f4! or 28...♘3e5, while if 28 h3 Black could have made the pretty and, apparently, winning move

28...♘e1!?, or simply played 28...h5 29 ♕d2 h4, developing a decisive attack: 30 ♔h2 (30 gxh4 ♘f4!) 30...♘7e5! 31 ♕e2 g4 32 hxg4 hxg3+ 33 fxg3 ♕g5.

28...g4! (11)

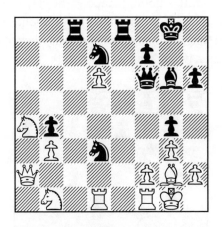

This position could be used as a striking example on the theme of 'domination' – with the board full of pieces, White is practically stalemated! It is not surprising that on his next six moves Karpov used up nearly all of his remaining time before the control.

29 ♕d2 (8) ♔g7 30 f3 (4)

In search of at least some air. 30 f4 was no better because of 30...♕d4+ 31 ♔h1 ♗f5!.

30...♕xd6 31 fxg4

Nothing would have been changed by 31 ♘b2 gxf3 32 ♗xf3 ♘7e5 33 ♘xd3 ♕b6+ 34 ♕f2 (34 ♔h1 ♗xd3) 34...♘xf3+ 35 ♔g2 ♖e3 – complete domination!

31...♕d4+ 32 ♔h1 ♘f6! (4)

The start of a direct attack on the king.

33 ♖f4 (5)

If 33 h3, then again 33...♘e4 is decisive, but I was planning 33...♖e3 – the powerful concentration of black pieces in the centre demolishes White's position (34 ♖f4 ♕e5).

33...♘e4 34 ♕xd3 (3)

The knight, which has caused White so much trouble, nevertheless perishes. But it is perhaps highly symbolic that for it White

has to give up his queen.

34...♘f2+ 35 ♖xf2 ♗xd3 36 ♖fd2 ♕e3! (the most effective) **37 ♖xd3 ♖c1!**

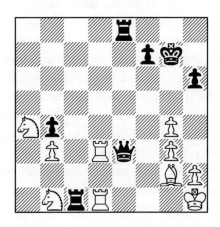

White has lots of pieces, but there is still no coordination.

38 ♘b2 ♕f2! (swift and pretty) **39 ♘d2 ♖xd1+** (39...♖e2!?) **40 ♘xd1 ♖e1+ 0-1**

Times: 2.29–2.20.

Such victories are remembered for a long time. This game was judged to be the best in the 40th volume of *Informator*. None of my earlier creations on the chess board can compare with it as regards the grandiosity of the overall conception.

I again took the lead: 8½-7½. The changed situation demanded a psychological adjustment: I had to become accustomed to the role of leader. Indeed, after two tense draws, I was able to win the 19th game in good style.

> *Game 6*
> **G.Kasparov-A.Karpov**
> World Championship Match
> 19th Game, Moscow 24.10.1985
> *Nimzo-Indian Defence E21*

1 d4 ♘f6 2 c4 e6 3 ♘c3 ♗b4 4 ♘f3 ♘e4

A very rare move. On this occasion Karpov avoids both 4...c5 (*Game Nos.3, 13*), and 4...0-0 (7th and 11th games), already on the 4th move directing the game along almost unknown lines. Black's idea is the same as in the variations with 4...c5: to double the opponent's pawns on the c-file and then to attack them, especially the c4-pawn (light-square strategy). However, in the aforementioned variation the d6-point was weakened, and one of the white pieces was constantly aiming for there, whereas here, for the moment, Black does not create any unnecessary weaknesses in his position.

5 ♕c2 f5

A move which has been known since the late 1920s. The 19th game of the Euwe-Alekhine return match (1937) went 5...d5 6 e3 c5 7 ♗d3, and Black brought his knight back – 7...♘f6, thus admitting the failure of his idea. In his notes to this game Botvinnik wrote: 'In the spirit of the position, of course, was 5...f5 followed by ...b7-b6 and ...♗b7.'

6 g3

There is no reason for White to avoid the fianchetto of his king's bishop. 6 e3 b6 7 ♗d3 ♗b7 would lead to a favourable variation for Black of the Nimzo-Indian Defence: 4 e3 b6 5 ♗d3 ♗b7 6 ♘f3 ♘e4 7 ♕c2 (the gambit 7 0-0!? is more energetic) 7...f5 8 0-0 ♗xc3 9 bxc3 0-0 with a complicated struggle – possibly this is what Karpov expected of me (later I had to uphold Black's position against Graf, Geneva (rapid) 1996). Knowing my disposition, he could also have expected the extravagant 6 g4, although such thrusts are suitable for less important events. 6 g3 is a sounder and more logical move, but after it Karpov sank into thought...

6...♘c6

A novelty. 6...b6 7 ♗g2 ♗b7 occurred back in the first half of the 20th century, but then went out of fashion. The game Balogh-Keres

(correspondence 1936-7) continued 8 ♘d2! (driving the knight from e4) 8...♗xc3 9 bxc3 ♘d6, and here White should have avoided the exchange of the light-square bishops – 10 d5!, with some advantage.

From this point, independent play began. Both players began thinking for a long time and on the next seven moves they each spent a whole hour.

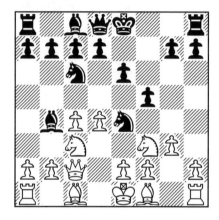

7 ♗g2

The timid 7 ♗d2, with the aim of avoiding the spoiling of White's queenside pawn structure, would have made things easier for Black: 7...♘xd2 8 ♕xd2 0-0 9 ♗g2 ♕f6 10 a3 ♗xc3 11 ♕xc3 d6 intending ...e6-e5.

7...0-0 8 0-0 ♗xc3 9 bxc3 ♘a5

Karpov carries out a plan which is an unusual hybrid of the ideas in the 13th and 17th games. It appears that Black should easily achieve an excellent game: the c4-pawn cannot be successfully defended, but after its advance there follows ...b7-b6 or ...d7-d6, and after the exchange cxb6 or cxd6 – pressure on the open c-file.

10 c5! d6

After 10...b6, 11 c4! is also strong, when White is better after both 11...♗a6 12 ♘d2 ♘xd2 13 ♗xd2 ♘xc4 14 ♗b4! (14 ♗xa8?! ♕xa8 gives Black excellent play for the exchange) 14...c6 15 cxb6 d6 16 bxa7 ♖xa7

17 ♖fc1, and 11...♗b7 12 ♖d1 bxc5 (12...♕e8 13 ♗f4) 13 ♗a3!?.

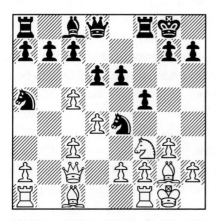

11 c4!

Intuition suggested to me that this pawn sacrifice, opening up the game, was perfectly correct, since after its acceptance the scattered nature of Black's forces and the absence of his dark-square bishop are felt. The routine 11 cxd6? would have justified the opponent's opening plan: 11...cxd6 12 c4 ♗d7 and 13...♖c8, with good counterplay.

11...b6!

A strong and forceful reply (as we will see, I wrongly condemned it in the book *Dva matcha*). Karpov, also most probably intuitively, does not capture the pawn and aims for clarity. His idea is to play ...♗a6 and nevertheless force the exchange of pawns on the c-file, in order to use it for active play. 11...dxc5 would have led to a very complicated position, full of tactical nuances:

1) 12 dxc5 ♘c6 (12...♘xc5? 13 ♗a3 and wins – Averbakh) 13 ♖d1 ♕e7 14 ♗a3, and now not 14...♘xc5? 15 ♘e1!, but 14...a5 or 14...e5 with double-edged play;

2) 12 ♗a3 (this is probably what I would have played) 12...♘c6 13 ♖ad1, and the unexpected 13...e5?!, with the idea of 14 ♘xe5 ♘xd4 15 ♕b2 ♕f6 16 ♗xe4 fxe4 17 ♗xc5 ♕xe5 18 ♗xd4 ♕e7 with equality

(Moiseenko-Shulskis, Kharkov 2003), is parried by 14 dxe5!, while if 13...♕e8 White retains the initiative by 14 ♕b2.

12 ♗d2!?

'It is possible that Karpov underestimated the strength of this subtle move.' (Averbakh, Taimanov). I even attached an exclamation mark to it, but in the light of what follows I am not now sure that it is the best move. However, little is also promised by 12 ♘d2 d5 13 ♘xe4 (13 cxd5 exd5 14 ♘b3?! is weak: 14...♘c4 15 f3 ♘g5!) 13...fxe4 14 ♗f4 ♘xc4 15 ♗xe4 dxe4 16 ♕xc4 ♖f7 17 ♖fc1 ♕d5 18 cxb6 ♕xc4 19 ♖xc4 cxb6 with a drawn ending, or 14 cxd5 exd5 15 f3 exf3 16 ♖xf3 ♖xf3 17 ♗xf3 ♗e6 18 ♗f4 c6 19 ♖f1 ♕d7 followed by ...♖f8 and ...♘c4, and it is not possible to breach Black's defences.

Perhaps the only virtue of 12 ♗d2 is that it led to the winning of the game!

12...♘xd2

Black could hardly be satisfied with his broken pawns after 12...dxc5?! 13 ♗xa5 bxa5 14 ♘d2! (more active than 14 ♖fd1) 14...♗b7 15 ♘xe4 ♗xe4 16 ♗xe4 fxe4 17 ♕xe4 cxd4 18 ♖ad1 c5 19 e3 ♕f6 20 exd4 ♖ad8 21 d5 exd5 22 ♖xd5, or 14...♘xd2 15 ♕xd2 ♖b8 16 d5 ♗a6 (16...♖b4 17 a3! ♖xc4 18 ♖ac1) 17 ♕xa5 ♗xc4 18 dxe6 ♗xe6 19 ♕xc5.

13 ♘xd2

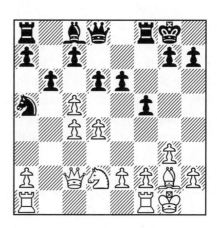

The most important moment of the battle.

13...d5?

A move which was unconditionally condemned by the commentators. 'In the variation 13...♗b7 14 ♗xb7 ♘xb7 15 c6 ♘a5 16 d5 ♕e7 17 ♕d3 Black would have had more chances of obtaining counterplay.' (Averbakh, Taimanov). After 17...e5 or 17...♖ae8 (for the moment not lifting the pressure on the d5-pawn) he has a solid enough position. The out-of-play knight at a5 partly ties down White's pieces by the need to defend the c4-pawn (if he rushes into an attack on the kingside, Black will play ...a7-a6 with the idea of ...b6-b5, and after a2-a4 the knight will obtain the b3-square). 16...♕f6 is also playable, or even the immediate 16...e5.

13...d5? leads to far more serious consequences, and it can be regarded as an irreparable positional mistake. But its psychological implication is also interesting. Karpov did not like playing with bad pieces such as the knight on a5, which altogether has no moves. After 13...♗b7 14 ♗xb7 ♘xb7 15 c6 ♘a5 16 d5 he may even have considered the idea of ♘b3 to be unpleasant for Black, and if ...♘xb3 – axb3 with pressure on the a-file. He thought in different concepts: this position did not suit him, and in principle it seemed 'incorrect' to him. It was this approach that induced Karpov to choose 13...d5, which, though bad, was a more understandable continuation. Here roles were also played by his dislike of inferior, non-standard positions, his anxious match situation ('minus one' – he must not lose!), and the opponent's unpleasant initiative.

14 cxd5 exd5 15 e3

The main defect of Black's position is his hopelessly weakened e5-point. However, it is not possible to exploit this factor immediately – the knight on d2 must guard the c4-

square. Generally speaking, it is not so easy to find a clear plan for converting White's positional advantage – for the moment Black is able to cover his weaknesses.

On occasions I have failed to win far more favourable positions. But in the given instance I understood exactly how to do this. I needed, as Botvinnik taught, to play 'like Capablanca' – don't hurry, suppress active attempts by Black, gradually increase the pressure, prepare an attack on the f5-pawn, and above all – seek a favourable moment to transfer my knight to e5.

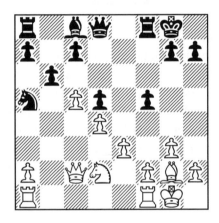

15...♗e6

Black cannot establish his knight on c4: 15...b5 16 ♕c3 ♘c4 17 a4, or 15...♗a6 16 ♖fc1 ♘c4 17 ♗f1, and after 17...♘xd2 18 ♗xa6 ♘e4 19 cxb6 cxb6 20 ♗b7! ♖b8 21 ♕c6 White is in charge on the queenside: 21...♘f6 22 ♕e6+ ♔h8 23 ♗a6 b5 24 ♖c6 ♘e4 25 ♖ac1 etc.

16 ♕c3 (necessary prophylaxis against ...b6-b5) **16...♖f7 17 ♖fc1**

Not only a demonstration of strength on the queenside, but also a preparation for the transfer of the knight to e5.

17...♖b8

It is not altogether clear why this was played, but in any case Black is condemned to waiting.

18 ☖ab1 ☖e7

If 18...c6 there would have followed 19 a4 ☖fb7 (after 19...b5?! 20 axb5 the passed c5-pawn is too strong) 20 ☗f1!, when ...b6-b5 is no longer possible, and 20...bxc5 21 ♕xc5 is clearly advantageous to White. But the regrouping in the game also makes things easier for him. Black should have kept his rook on f7 and played ...g7-g6, in order only after h2-h4 to reply ...h7-h6.

19 a4 ☗f7

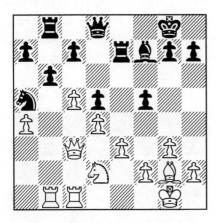

20 ☗f1! (it is essential to keep control of the c4-point) **20...h6?!**

Karpov further weakens his position – note that 21 ♘f3 ♘c4 22 ♘g5 was threatened. 20...☗h5!? 21 ☗d3 ♕f8 was possible – this would at least have forced White to devise something. Thus if 22 ♔g2 g5 23 h4 Black has the unclear 23...f4!, and it would somehow be a pity to exchange the long-suffering knight at a5 with the unexpected move 22 ♘b3!?, although this leads to the disintegration of the enemy queenside: 22...♘xb3 23 ☖xb3 ☗f3 24 a5 etc.

21 ☗d3

21 ♘f3 ♘c4 22 ☗xc4 dxc4 23 ♘e5 ☗d5 24 cxb6! axb6 25 ♕c2 was also sensible, or first 21 ♕c2!? with the intention of ♘f3-e5.

21...♕d7 22 ♕c2

In the press centre grandmaster Po-

lugayevsky analysed an 'interesting queen sacrifice' – 22 ♕xa5?! bxa5 23 ☖xb8+ ☗e8 24 c6 ♕d6 25 ☖b3, but in the computer age such things are not suggested (especially since Black has 25...f4!? 26 gxf4 ☗g6).

22...☗e6

White has achieved his aim – he has not allowed the activation of the bishop. 22...g6 23 ♘f3 also held little joy for Black.

23 ☗b5 (23 ♘f3 ♘c4 24 ☗xc4 dxc4 25 ♘e5 was already possible, but I was not in a hurry) **23...♕d8** (after 23...c6 24 ☗d3 Black would merely have acquired new weaknesses) **24 ☖d1!**

Intensifying the threat of 25 ♘f3, since if 24...♘c4 there follows 25 ☗xc4 dxc4 and the breakthrough 26 d5!.

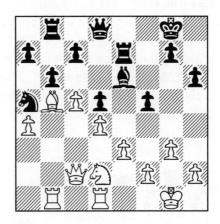

24...g5?!

Karpov is tired of waiting passively, and he launches a desperate counterattack, realising that the strategic battle has been lost, but hoping in the approaching time scramble to obtain some tactical chances. However, White is far better prepared for such a turn of events, and in the end Black's activity on the kingside rebounds against him.

Therefore he should have stood still and 'done nothing' – 24...♕c8! (also defending the f5-pawn), when after 25 ♘f3 (25 ☖dc1!?)

25...c6 26 ♗d3 ♘c4 27 ♖b3 b5 Black's position is not easy, of course, but his knight has been switched to c4 and all is not yet totally clear. But after this new weakening, created under serious pressure, it can be said that the fate of the game is finally decided.

25 ♘f3! (now the ♘d2-f3-e5 manoeuvre is carried out under favourable circumstances)

25...♖g7

After 25...♘c4 26 ♗xc4 dxc4 27 d5! Black's position collapses: 27...♗xd5 28 ♕xf5 c6 29 e4! ♕f8! (29...♖xe4 30 ♕g6+ ♔f8 31 ♕xh6+ is completely bad) 30 ♕xf8+ ♖xf8 31 exd5 ♖xf3 32 cxb6 axb6 33 dxc6 ♖d3 34 ♖dc1 ♖b3 35 a5!, a precise deciding rejoinder. If 35...bxa5, then 36 ♖xb3 cxb3 37 c7, while if 35...b5 the simplest is 36 a6 ♖a7 37 ♖a1.

26 ♘e5 (the knight has safely arrived at its appointed place, while the black bishop is still shut in) **26...f4**

Activating the bishop in the hope of 27 exf4 gxf4 followed by ...♕d8-f6 and ...h6-h5-h4 with counter-chances, but, of course, White has no need at this point to open the g-file.

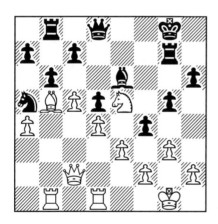

27 ♗f1

Having done its job on the a6-f1 diagonal, the bishop returns to its lawful place (g2), where it will cover the king and prepare a decisive breakthrough in the centre. Previ-

ously I attached an exclamation mark to this move, but 27 ♗d3!? with the idea of e3-e4 or exf4 was also strong, although the best was 27 gxf4! ♕f6 (27...gxf4+? loses to 28 ♔h1 and ♖g1!) 28 ♔h1! etc. But this demands accurate machine calculation, whereas a human can win almost without calculating variations – therefore the solid move 27 ♗f1, made in a nervy atmosphere and when short of time, also deserves an exclamation mark.

27...♕f6 28 ♗g2 ♖d8 29 e4! dxe4 30 ♗xe4

Now the knight at a5 is unable to come into play, whereas the finely-placed knight at e5 will play one of the leading roles in the imminent attack.

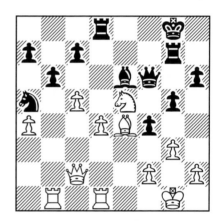

30...♖e7 31 ♕c3

The all-seeing computer discovers 31 gxf4! gxf4 32 ♔h1 ♖g7 33 cxb6 cxb6 34 ♖g1 and wins, or 31...♕xf4 32 ♘g6 ♕g4+ 33 ♔h1 ♖g7 (if 33...♖ee8(f7), then 34 f3 and ♘e5) 34 d5 ♗d7 (34...♗c8 35 d6!) 35 f3 ♕h3 36 ♘e5, and Black is lost.

31...♗d5?!

A positional move – which loses the game: Karpov underestimated the threat of ♘g4. True, 31...♗f5 32 ♖e1 was also insufficient, while after the most resilient 31...♗a2! (creating a certain lack of harmony in the opponent's ranks) 32 ♖a1 ♗f7 33 ♗g2 (33 f3!?; 33 ♖e1!?) 33...♘b3 34 ♘xf7 ♕xf7 (34...♘xd4? 35 ♘xh6+) 35 ♖ab1 f3!? (35...♘a5 36 d5!) 36 ♗h1 ♘a5 37 ♕xf3 White should convert his advantage, but not without some difficulties: the knight escapes from a5.

32 ♖e1?!

There was an immediate win by 32 ♘g4! ♕g7 33 ♗xd5+ ♖xd5 34 ♖e1 ♖dd7 35 gxf4! gxf4 36 ♔h1, or 32...♕c6 33 ♗xd5+ ♖xd5 34 ♖e1 ♖e6 35 h3!, defending the knight with the simple idea of 36 ♖xe6 ♕xe6 37 ♖e1.

32...♔g7?!

Resistance would have been prolonged by 32...♗xe4 33 ♖xe4 ♖de8 34 gxf4 (better than 34 f3) 34...♕f5 35 ♖be1 gxf4 36 ♔h1 ♖f8 (36...♔h7 37 ♕f3) 37 f3 ♖g7 38 ♘g4 etc.

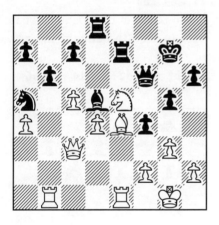

33 ♘g4!

The consequences of the move ...g7-g5 begin to be distinctly felt – White creates an irresistible attack against the denuded black king.

33...♕f7 34 ♗xd5 ♖xd5 35 ♖xe7 ♕xe7 36 ♖e1 ♕d8 37 ♘e5

Black has seized control of the d5-point, but the open position of his king causes his downfall. Both 37 ♖e6!? and 37 gxf4! gxf4 38 ♘e5 would also have won.

37...♕f6

If 37...fxg3 the simplest is the 'anti-positional' 38 fxg3 with the decisive opening of the f-file. But after 37...♕f6 I found another couple of 'anti-positional' exchanges.

38 cxb6!

Opening another invasion line. The black queen is forced to move away from its king.

38...♕xb6 (38...cxb6 39 ♕c7+ ♔g8 40 ♘g4 etc.) **39 gxf4!**

Another timely capture, opening up the play on the kingside.

39...♖xd4?!

A blunder in severe time-trouble, but also after 39...gxf4 40 ♕f3 or 39...c5 40 ♕f3 ♖xd4 41 fxg5 Black's agony would not have lasted long.

40 ♘f3 ♘b3 41 ♖b1 ♕f6

Here the game was adjourned, and the arbiter invited me to seal my move. But in such a position it can also be made on the board...

42 ♕xc7+

This provoked a storm of applause in the auditorium: it was a unique occurrence in matches for the world championship (and also a rarity in grandmaster play) for a sealed move to be made openly. But what do you do, if the opponent does not find in himself the strength to resign in a hopeless position? Karpov did this only the following morning, by phoning one of the two chief arbiters (**1-0**). Times: 2.32–2.29.

The win in this game took the score to 10½-8½ and gave me very real chances of overall victory in the match. However, at this difficult moment Karpov was able to display his will-power and enormous match experience. As for me, I was even more oppressed by the 'champion phenomenon': every now and then my chess calculations were affected by the thought that for the moment I was still just the challenger.

The draw in the 20th game was the result

of an exhausting nine-hour struggle. In the 21st game I had an obvious advantage, but, stupefied by the proximity of victory in the match, I missed some good winning chances. And in the 22nd game I got into time-trouble, blundered and lost. It was as though I had set myself the aim of doing everything to ensure that the competitive intrigue was retained to the very last second of the match! But Karpov should be given his due: at a critical moment of the match he showed he had nerves of steel, and he was rewarded for his patience and resourcefulness. The gap was reduced to one point, and after a draw in the 23rd game I led 12-11.

And so, everything was to be decided in the final game. On the result of it depended the fate of the entire marathon of 72 games, unparalleled in the history of chess. Today, after thorough computer analysis, I realise particularly clearly that Karpov and I played this unforgettable game each in his own style, each his kind of chess. This is a vivid example of a clash of different playing conceptions! The game turned out to be not only uncommonly dramatic, but also valuable in the theoretical sense, for a long time pointing the way in one of the main lines of the Scheveningen. As for Karpov, after it he gave up playing 1 e4 and switched completely to closed games.

Game 7
A.Karpov-G.Kasparov
World Championship Match
24th Game, Moscow 09.11.1985
Sicilian Defence B85

---

1 e4

At the decisive moment Karpov remains true to his favourite (until that day!) first move. When with exaggerated confidence he advanced his king's pawn, I felt glad: now the battle would take place on my territory – my opponent was aiming not for protracted manoeuvring, but for a hand-to-hand fight, which would give me a definite competitive advantage (and in the end it was this that told).

1...c5

Black also sticks to his principles: he does not avoid the Sicilian Defence, which nearly always leads to complicated, double-edged play. The well-known 'Capablanca rule' states: always employ those openings which bring good results, irrespective of the positions arising.

2 ♘f3 d6 3 d4 cxd4 4 ♘xd4 ♘f6 5 ♘c3 a6 6 ♗e2 e6 7 0-0 ♗e7 8 f4 0-0 9 ♔h1 ♕c7 10 a4 ♘c6 11 ♗e3 ♖e8

A continuation of the opening debate begun back in the 5th game of the previous match.

12 ♗f3 ♖b8 13 ♕d2 ♗d7 14 ♘b3 b6

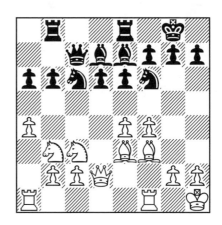

15 g4

Instead of the quiet 15 ♗f2 (18th game), this move signals the start of an assault. The energetic 15 g4 occurred in the game A.Sokolov-Ribli (Montpellier Candidates 1985), played a couple of weeks earlier, and, of course, both players were aware of it. Karpov evidently decided that this attacking plan was most in accordance with the spirit of this last, deciding game.

15...♗c8 16 g5 (½-½ Dely-Sax, Hungarian Championship 1974) **16...♘d7 17 ♕f2!?**

And this was the move that we expected, considering it to be a 'significant improvement'. Sokolov played 17 ♗g2 ♘a5 18 ♕f2 and after 18...♗f8?! 19 ♖ad1 ♘c4 20 ♗c1 b5 21 axb5 axb5 22 ♖d3 g6 23 ♖h3 ♗g7 24 f5! he won with a direct attack on the king.

18...♘xb3 19 cxb3 ♘c5 is also hardly good in view of 20 ♕c2, but with the immediate 18...♘c4 Ribli could have hindered the switching of the queen's rook to the kingside – both I and my trainers judged that this manoeuvre would favour Black. However, experience showed that after 19 ♗c1 ♗b7 (19...b5?! is weaker: 20 axb5 axb5 21 ♖a7) 20 ♘d4! ♗f8 (20...♖bc8 21 f5) 21 b3 ♘a5 22 ♗b2 the initiative remains with White (Timoshenko-Lesiege, Koszalin 1999). In addition, instead of 18 ♕f2 there is the interesting 18 ♘xa5!? bxa5 19 b3.

A cunning point of 17 ♗g2 is also revealed in the spectacular variation 17...♗f8?! 18 ♖f3! g6 19 ♖h3 ♗b7 20 ♕f2 ♗g7 (Hübner-Hjartarson, Munich 1988) 21 ♕h4! ♘f8 22 f5! ♗xc3 23 f6!! with a powerful attack. 17...♗b7! is correct – after 18 ♖f3 there is now the good reply 18...♘a5, and if 19 ♕f2 ♘c4 20 ♗c1 d5! with sharp play.

Extolling 17 ♕f2, I wrote: 'But now in the event of the slow 17...♘a5 the white rook succeeds in crossing to d1 – 18 ♖ad1 ♘c4 19 ♗c1.' But it turned out that here after 19...b5! 20 axb5 axb5 21 ♗g2 (White does not have 21 ♖a7 – the rook has moved off the a-file!) 21...b4 22 ♘e2 ♘c5 Black has sufficient counterplay: 23 f5 ♗f8 24 g6 ♘xb3 25 cxb3 ♘e5 26 gxf7+ ♕xf7 27 ♘d4 exf5 28 exf5 ♗b7 29 ♘e6 ♖bc8 with equality (Topalov-Anand, Las Palmas 1996). Therefore it is better to play 18 ♘d4!? or 18 ♗g2!?,

transposing into a favourable position for White from the Sokolov-Ribli game.

Well, in pre-computer times, chess theory was sometimes truly 'short-sighted'. Today the moves 17 ♗g2 and 17 ♕f2 are considered equally good, since they are links in the same plan: the bishop makes way for the rook to go to h3 and strengthens the threat of f4-f5, while the queen aims for h4. But in the first case Black must reply only 17...♗b7! (although 17...♘a5 suggested itself), while in the second case both 17...♗b7 and 17...♗f8 are possible – it was this defensive set-up that we had prepared.

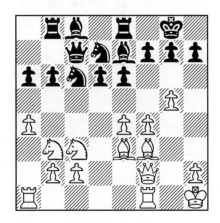

17...♗f8 (18)

This solid move is the start of a universal plan with ...♗b7, ...g7-g6 and ...♘b4, pressing on the c2-pawn and controlling the d5-point, in order to answer f4-f5 with ...exf5, opening up the position without having to fear ♘d5. Black simply completes his development, relying on the flexibility and solidity of his position, and also planning in the future to meet White's attack with the counter-stroke ...f7-f5.

18 ♗g2

The direct 18 h4 ♗b7 19 h5 is also interesting (Beliavsky-Kasparov, Barcelona 1989) – soon Black committed some inaccuracies and ran into difficulties, although in the end he managed to win with a counterattack on the kingside. In those years, under the influence of my wins over Karpov, I sincerely believed that the g2-g4 thrust was ineffective, since Black could comfortably arrange his pieces and then advantageously exploit the weakening of the white king's defences. However, practice demonstrated that White's active resources cannot be underestimated.

18...♗b7 19 ♖ad1 (8)

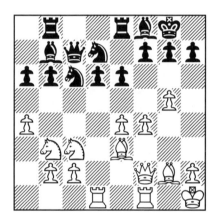

White completes his development and takes aim at the d6-pawn. This arrangement of the white and black pieces, which later became typical, first occurred in the game Velickovic-Jansa (Zrenjanin 1980), which went 11...♗d7 12 ♘b3 b6 13 ♗f3 ♖ab8 14 g4 ♗c8 15 g5 ♘d7 16 ♗g2 ♖e8 17 ♕e2 ♗f8 18 ♖ad1 ♗b7 19 ♖f3 (19 ♕f2!? would have led to a position from our game) 19...♘b4 20 ♖h3 g6 21 ♖d4 ♘c6 22 ♖d2 ♘a5 with double-edged play.

19...g6 (4)

A position that was little-known at that time has arisen: it had been reached by transposition in only two previous games.

Looking for ways to develop his initiative, Karpov thought here for 44 minutes. For the greater part of this time I circled around the stage or sat in the rest room. In the corridor

leading to it I chanced upon a placard which had been made in advance with the inscription: 'Anatoly Evgenevich, congratulations on your victory!' But this creation had the opposite effect – not at all that for which it was hoping.

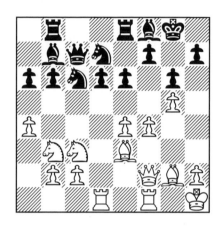

20 ♗c1!?

A new and promising idea. The bishop retreat clears the third rank for the rook on d1 to switch to the kingside, significantly strengthening White's attacking potential. 20 f5?! is clearly premature because of 20...♘ce5, but 20 h4!? comes into consideration (Radjabov-Babula, Saint Vincent 2005).

20...♖bc8?! (19)

A pointless waiting move. Although the rook stands better on the c-file, a loss of time in such a tense situation often has unpleasant consequences. Thus after 20...♗a8 21 ♖d3 the optimistic 21...b5?! 22 axb5 axb5 23 ♖h3 b4 24 ♘d1 f5 (Berndt-Wahls, Bundesliga 2004) gives White a dangerous attack: 25 gxf6! ♘xf6 26 f5 followed by ♗g5 and ♕h4. It is better to play 21...♘b4!? 22 ♖h3 (22 ♖d4 ♘c6) 22...♗g7 23 ♗e3 f5! 24 ♕h4 ♘f8 25 ♗d4 e5 with chances for both sides.

I was not afraid of the ♖d3-h3 manoeuvre, but following the principle 'better safe than sorry' it made sense to prevent this – 20...♘c5! (the most precise; the unclear

20...♞b4 21 ♖d4 d5 does not appeal to me). Here it is far more difficult for White to build up his attack: 21 ♞xc5 bxc5! (21...dxc5 22 f5!?) 22 ♖d3 ♞d4 23 ♖h3 ♛e7!? (intending 24 ♛h4 h5 – a typical defensive idea), and Black has a solid position with decent counterplay.

21 ♖d3 (4)

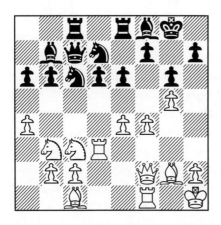

21...♞b4

Again underestimating the danger, although this is excusable: both players are making their way through virgin territory, and each step they take has a psychological implication. The 'sideways' knight move is not so bad, but it gives White the chance of launching a swift, although not deadly attack.

Perhaps 21...♝g7!? should have been preferred. For example: 22 ♖h3 f5 (22...♞e7!? with the idea of ...d6-d5 is also interesting) 23 gxf6 ♞xf6 24 f5 exf5 25 exf5 ♞e7 26 fxg6 ♞xg6, and the queen's knight comes to the aid of the king, or 22 ♖fd1 d5!? (an unexpected break!) 23 f5! (23 exd5 ♞b4! or 23 e5 ♞e7 is weaker) 23...♞ce5 24 ♖h3 dxe4 25 f6 ♝f8 26 ♝f4 ♖ed8 27 ♛h4 h5 28 gxh6 ♚h7 with double-edged play.

22 ♖h3 ♝g7

There is no longer anything better. 22...♞e7? will not do: 23 ♛h4 (23 f5!?) 23...h5

24 gxh6 with the threat of f4-f5, while 22...f5?! is risky in view of 23 gxf6 ♞xf6 24 f5! exf5 25 exf5 ♝g7 26 ♝g5! ♞h5 27 f6 ♖f8 28 ♖xh5! gxh5 29 ♞d4 or 26...♞g4 27 ♛h4! with a dangerous attack.

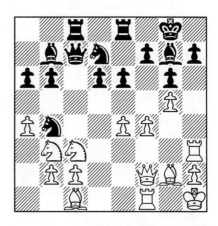

The critical moment of the game and of the entire match – it was not surprising that this highly interesting position generated a great deal of debate. White has concentrated a great amount of force on the kingside and he must find a way of decisively strengthening his attack. The most obvious way is to make use of the resource f4-f5.

23 ♝e3?!

Here Karpov thought for just three minutes (!) and remained true to himself: he does not hurry to force events, but prefers consistently to strengthen his position – he takes aim at the weak b6-pawn and creates the unpleasant threat of ♝d4. In passing he sets a transparent trap – 23...♝xc3? 24 bxc3 ♛xc3 25 ♝d4 ♛xc2 26 ♖xh7! with mate. In addition, White prevents ...f7-f5: if 23...f5, then 24 gxf6 ♝xf6 (after 24...♞xf6 25 ♝xb6 ♞g4 26 ♛g1 Black has insufficient compensation for the pawn) 25 ♝d4 or 25 f5!? exf5 26 ♝d4 with the initiative.

Meanwhile, the immediate 23 f5! was stronger. After the forced 23...exf5 24 exf5

White simultaneously has two threats: 25 ♕h4, with a double attack, and 25 fxg6.

However, soon after the match I found and then published the main variation of a successful defence: 24...♗xg2+ 25 ♔xg2 ♕b7+ 26 ♔g1 ♖c4! 27 fxg6 ♖g4+ 28 ♖g3 ♖xg3+ 29 hxg3! (but not 29 ♕xg3 hxg6 30 ♕f4 ♘e5 31 ♕xb4? ♘f3+) 29...♘e5! 30 gxh7+ (30 ♘e4 ♕xe4 or 30 gxf7+ ♕xf7 31 ♕xb6? ♘f3+ is worse) 30...♔h8, and for the sacrificed pawns Black has active counterplay.

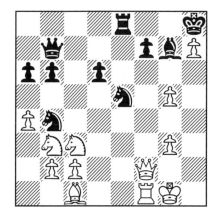

Analysis diagram

Under the watchful eye of the computer let us analyse the three tempting possibilities for White, mentioned in the book *Dva matcha* – 31 ♗f4, 31 ♘d4 and 31 ♕f5:

1) 31 ♗f4 (not 31 ♗d2 ♘xc2!) 31...♔xh7!, eliminating the insidious pawn and coolly parrying the threats: 32 ♗xe5 (32 ♕e2 ♔g8!) 32...♖xe5 33 ♕d4 ♘d5 34 ♘xd5 (34 ♕d3+ ♔h8!) 34...♕xd5 35 ♕xd5 ♖xd5 36 ♖xf7 ♖xg5 with a probable draw, or 32 ♘d4 ♘bd3! 33 ♕h2+ (33 cxd3 ♘g4) 33...♔g8 34 ♗xe5 ♘xe5 35 ♕h5 b5! 36 axb5 (36 ♘f5 bxa4) 36...♕a7 37 ♘ce2 axb5 with counterplay;

2) 31 ♘d4 ♘ed3! 32 cxd3 ♘xd3 33 ♕d2 ♗xd4+ 34 ♔h2 ♗xc3 35 ♕xd3! (35 ♕xc3+

♘e5) 35...♗g7 36 b3 b5, and Black is close to the drawing haven;

3) 31 ♕f5 ♘xc2! 32 ♕xc2 ♘f3+ 33 ♖xf3 ♕xf3 34 ♕f2 ♕d3 35 ♗d2 ♕c4! 36 ♕xb6 ♔xh7 with equality, or 32 ♗d2 b5! 33 axb5 axb5 34 ♕xc2 (34 ♖f2 b4 35 ♘e4 ♕d5!) 34...♘f3+ 35 ♔f2 ♘h2, gaining a draw.

As we see, in many variations Black is saved by the typical Sicilian break ...b6-b5, opening the a7-g1 diagonal for his queen.

But to judge by the speed with which my opponent played 23 ♗e3, he did not even delve into the details of the complications arising after 23 f5: here a mass of unclear variations would have had to be calculated. Tal would certainly have gone 23 f5 (but against Tal I would have played differently!), whereas Karpov evaluated the situation on the basis of *his* concepts. Even at critical moments he was unable to change his character, and he always aimed to play 'Karpov-style' – strengthen the position, but do not seek a denouement. It is probable that in the depths of his heart he was not convinced about the correctness of the attack on the kingside and therefore he was unable to conduct it boldly and firmly. Suppose that 23 f5 led only to premature simplification and a draw?

Considering that only a win would do for Karpov, his pressurising, strictly positional move with the bishop looks very logical and strong: it is not immediately apparent how Black is to defend against the threat of ♗d4 with the exchange of bishops, since ...e6-e5 is bad because of fxe5, when the f7-pawn is under attack (or, after ...♘xe5, the b6-pawn). But after a long think I was able to find an unusual and, it would seem, the only defence. I am sure that if I had not found it and I had lost this game, everyone would have attached two exclamation marks to 23 ♗e3 as being a 'brilliant, typically Karpov move'!

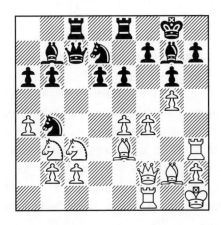

23...♖e7! (28)

An original manoeuvre, which for the moment has a very modest aim – to defend the f7-point in advance. In essence, this is the most difficult move in the game, after which White's attack begins to peter out. Who could then have thought that in time the ...♖e8-e7 manoeuvre would become a typical idea in such positions...

24 ♔g1 (29)

Now if 24 ♗d4 there is the simple 24...e5 25 fxe5 (25 f5? exd4 26 f6 dxc3 27 fxe7 ♘e5) 25...♗xe5 26 ♗xe5 dxe5 and ...♘f8. Little is also promised by 24 f5 exf5 25 exf5 ♗xg2+ 26 ♕xg2 (26 ♔xg2? ♗xc3! 27 bxc3 ♕xc3) 26...gxf5 or 26...♖ce8, as well as 24 ♘d4 e5 25 ♘de2 exf4 (but not the reckless 25...♘xc2?! 26 f5!) 26 ♘xf4 ♖ce8! 27 ♕h4 ♘f8 and Black's chances are not worse.

After a long think, having convinced himself that nothing concrete could be achieved immediately, Karpov continued playing in the same unhurried, positional manner – he made a prophylactic move of the category 'just in case', as though inviting Black to declare his intentions. But this is not at all easy – at first sight White has successfully restricted his opponent's active possibilities.

24...♖ce8?! (14)

The doubling of the black rooks on the closed (!) e-file looks absurd, but to me it seemed well-founded: firstly, the f4-f5 advance, which like a sword of Damocles has been hanging over Black's position, now finally loses its strength, and, secondly, Black himself prepares for active play on the kingside.

However, the waiting move with the rook (an unfortunate one, in contrast to that of its workmate) allows White to intensify the pressure in the centre, whereas the immediate 24...f5! would have relieved Black of all difficulties. After 25 gxf6 (25 exf5 exf5!) 25...♗xf6 he does not have to fear either 26 f5 exf5 27 exf5 ♗xg2 28 ♕xg2 ♕c6 or even 26...gxf5!? 27 exf5 ♖g7, or 26 ♕d2 ♖f8 (26...♘c5?! 27 ♘d4!) 27 ♘d4 e5! 28 fxe5?! ♘xe5 or 27 ♖d1 ♗g7, and the weaknesses in White's position balance his pressure on the d6-pawn.

25 ♖d1!

White promptly probes a vulnerable point in the opponent's position (the d6-pawn), again forcing him to solve some difficult defensive problems.

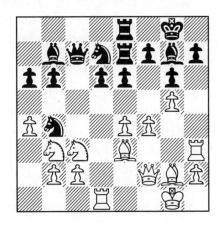

25...f5 (8)

This activity is practically forced, and from this moment the latent spring of Black's position gradually begins to uncoil.

26 gxf6! (4)

After 26 ♕d2 (26 exf5?! exf5!) apart from 26...e5 (my previous recommendation) 27 exf5 ♗xg2 28 ♕xg2 gxf5, Black could also play 26...fxe4! 27 ♕xd6 (27 ♘xe4 ♘d5!) 27...♕xd6 28 ♖xd6 e5!, when it is now White who has to concern himself with how to equalise.

26...♘xf6

I don't know what evaluation sign to attach to this surprising move. According to higher chess mathematics, it would seem that 26...♗xf6 should be played, but with the unexpected pawn sacrifice 26...♘xf6 I won the match!

The faint-hearted 26...♗xf6 would after 27 ♕d2! have left White with the initiative: 27...e5 28 f5 gxf5 29 exf5! ♖g7 30 ♖g3 ♖xg3 31 hxg3 ♗xg2 32 ♕xg2, or 27...d5 28 e5 ♗g7 29 ♘d4 ♘c6 30 ♘ce2 with quite persistent pressure. In view of the match situation, such a development of events would have suited Karpov.

The consequences of 26...♘xf6 are far less clear. In addition, I made this move very confidently and quickly – who knows, perhaps it was this confidence that disturbed my opponent. An important moment arose, and an extremely interesting one from the standpoint of chess psychology.

27 ♖g3?!

As if in unison, Karpov also replied quickly. He hardly calculated the variations with 27 ♗xb6, fearing 27...♘g4 (here there will be exchanges, and he needs to win), and he made a move dictated by the logic of match play. Karpov took me 'at my word', reckoning that the b6-pawn would not run away.

However, only the immediate 27 ♗xb6! could have given him real chances of success. There seems to be an acceptable reply in 27...♕b8 28 a5! (recommended by Igor Zaitsev) 28...e5 (otherwise Black has insuffi-

cient compensation for the pawn), and if 29 f5 gxf5 30 exf5 (30 ♕xf5? ♗c8), then 30...♗xg2 31 ♕xg2 ♔h8 with counterplay. But White has a subtle tactical stroke – 29 fxe5! ♖xe5 30 ♕d4, forcing 30...♘xe4! (if 30...♘xc2? 31 ♕d3!, trapping the knight and securing the desired win) 31 ♕xb4 ♖g5 32 ♕c4+ ♔h8 33 ♘d5 ♕a8 34 ♘e3 ♘f2! 35 ♔xf2 ♗xg2 36 ♖g3 ♖xg3 37 hxg3 ♕f3+ 38 ♔g1 ♗h3 39 ♕f4 ♖xe3 40 ♕xf3 ♖xf3 41 ♔h2 ♗g4 42 ♖xd6 ♗xb2 43 ♗d4+ ♗xd4 44 ♘xd4 ♖a3 45 ♖xa6 ♔g7 with saving chances.

And even the knight leap 27...♘g4!, the move which concerned White, would also have led to an endgame a pawn down: 28 ♗xc7 ♘xf2 29 ♗xd6! ♘xd1 30 ♗xe7.

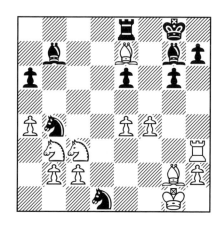

Analysis diagram

In the event of 30...♖xe7 31 ♘xd1 ♘xc2 32 e5! ♗xg2 33 ♔xg2 g5! 34 ♖c3! ♘b4 35 fxg5 ♖d7 (or 35...♗xe5 36 ♖c4) 36 ♘f2 ♗xe5 37 ♖c4 Black's position is dangerous. On the other hand, excellent drawing chances are given by the unexpected 30...♘xc3! 31 bxc3 ♘xc2 – Black's activity compensates for the pawn deficit, and the poor position of the white rook at h3 is also felt. For example:

1) 32 ♗d6 e5! 33 f5 gxf5 34 exf5 (34 ♘c5

♗c8) 34...♗xg2 35 ♔xg2 e4 or 33...♗c8!? 34 ♘c5 (34 ♖g3 ♗h6! 35 fxg6 ♗e3+ 36 ♔h1 ♖d8) 34...♖d8! 35 ♗e7 ♖d1+ 36 ♔f2 ♖d2+;

2) 32 ♗g5 presents Black, apart from 32...e5, with the additional idea 32...♗f8!? (planning ...♗c6) 33 e5 ♖b8, 33 ♘d4 ♗c5 or 33 ♘a5 ♗a8 34 ♔f2 e5 35 f5 gxf5 36 exf5 ♗c5+ 37 ♔g3 ♗xg2 38 ♔xg2 e4 39 ♖g3 ♔f7 40 ♘b7 ♖e5 41 f6 ♗f8 with equality.

Thus Karpov was perhaps right to intuitively avoid the simplification, being afraid of losing all his chances. Nevertheless, the position after 27 ♗xb6 would have been far better for White than that which he obtained in the game.

27...♖f7! (4)

Karpov underestimated the strength of this move: Black succeeds in successfully regrouping his rooks. The similar manoeuvres in the 18th game (18...♖bd8 and 19...♖f8) come to mind. The preceding moves were not found easily by the two players and had taken much time. The final, fifth hour of play in this match was beginning...

28 ♗xb6 ♕b8 29 ♗e3

In contrast to the variation 27 ♗xb6 ♕b8 28 a5, White's weakened kingside has become a source of constant concern for him: now if 29 a5 there is the good reply 29...♘h5 30 ♖f3 ♖ef8. It turns out that Black has very powerful compensation for the pawn, and to avoid the worst White must now make a draw.

29...♘h5 30 ♖g4 (if 30 ♖f3 Black can repeat moves – 30...♘f6, but it is far stronger to play 30...♗xc3! 31 bxc3 ♘a2 32 ♗a7 ♕a8 33 ♘d2 ♘xf4) **30...♘f6**

Here the competitive factor came to the fore: a draw was equivalent to a loss for Karpov, and he avoided 31 ♖g3 ♘h5 with a repetition of moves.

31 ♖h4

After some hesitation. 31 ♖g5? is too dangerous in view of 31...♗h6 32 ♖g3 ♘h5 33 ♖f3 ♖ef8 34 ♗h3 ♗c8!. In a normal game Karpov would never have played 31 ♖h4, but what was he to do?

An amusing detail: the two sides' rooks have moved between what look like unusual magic squares. Black's via f8-f7-e7-f7, and White's via h3-g3-g4-h4. When they concluded their mysterious manoeuvres, the evaluation of the position was decided.

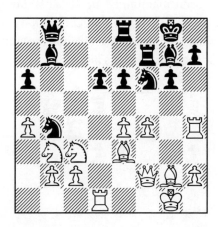

31...g5! (4)

Black's initiative becomes threatening, although the resulting irrational positions involve great risk for both sides.

32 fxg5 ♘g4!

Black pins his hopes on the strength of his two bishops and the poor placing of the white knights. It is more important to eliminate the opponent's dark-square bishop than his central pawn by 32...♘xe4. Here 33 ♕xf7+(?) ♔xf7 34 ♘xe4 seemed to me to be 'absolutely unclear', but after 34...♘xc2 35 ♘xd6+ ♔g6(g8) White's activity comes to nothing and Black retains the advantage. On the other hand, 33 ♕e2! ♘xc3 34 bxc3 ♘d5 35 ♗xd5 ♗xd5 36 ♕xa6 ♗xc3 37 ♕d3 leads to extremely double-edged play.

33 ♕d2 (12)

After this Karpov had only four minutes

left on his clock – very, very little for such a dangerous situation. The intensity of the battle was approaching its peak...

33...♘xe3 34 ♕xe3 ♘xc2 35 ♕b6!

Not conceding the a7-g1 diagonal and the b-file: 35 ♕h3? would have lost to 35...♗c6!.

35...♗a8! (3)

I was proud of this rapid reply, assuming that with the exchange of queens, the lack of harmony in the placing of the white pieces should tell. After 35...♗e5 the balance would have been maintained by 36 ♖c1!, but the unexpected bishop retreat caused Karpov to go wrong: in severe time-trouble he quickly made the most obvious move.

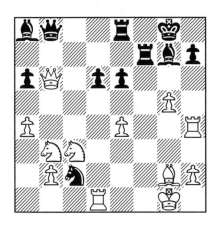

36 ♖xd6?

A blunder, which loses the game. It was essential to play 36 ♕xb8 ♖xb8 37 ♗h3! (37 ♖d2? ♘e3!) with wild complications, such as one does not often see even with the queens on. Had Karpov found this resource, it is not clear how the time scramble would have ended. However, he would certainly have been able to hold out to the adjournment:

1) 37...♖xb3 38 ♗xe6 ♗d4+! (now Black is one move closer to the time control, and the white king is one move further away from the centre) 39 ♔h1 ♖xb2 40 ♖f1 ♗xc3 41 ♖xf7 ♘d4 42 ♖a7 (42 ♗c4? d5!) 42...♘xe6 43 ♖xa8 (Averbakh, Taimanov) 43...♔g7 44

♖a7+ ♔g8 with a draw;

2) 37...♖e7 (a quieter course) 38 ♖xd6 ♖xb3 39 ♖d8+ (39 ♗xe6+ ♖xe6 40 ♖xe6 ♘d4!) 39...♔f7 40 ♖xa8 ♖xb2 with sufficient compensation for the pawn.

Thus after 36 ♕xb8 ♖xb8 37 ♗h3! Black would still have had good play, and a draw would have been the logical conclusion of the game.

36...♖b7!

Up until now this rook has moved only in small steps, uncharacteristic of such a powerful piece (...♖f8-e8-e7-f7), but its first 'long' active move proves decisive.

37 ♕xa6 ♖xb3?!

In his joy Black gets carried away. There was an immediate win by 37...♘b4!, whereas now the battle could have been prolonged.

38 ♖xe6

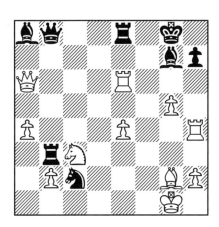

38...♖xb2?

And this throws away the win, although it does not throw away the desired draw! In the press centre this error was not noticed: there they were no longer calculating variations – they were preparing for a change of world champion.

38...♘e3! 39 ♖xe8+ ♕xe8 would have been decisive. White has three pawns for the piece, but in positions of this type (where both kings are exposed) the piece is far more valuable, and in addition Black is better prepared for an attack: 40 ♕e2 ♗d4 41 ♔h1 ♕f7 or 40 ♗h3 ♖xb2 41 ♕e6+ (a forced exchange) 41...♕xe6 42 ♗xe6+ ♔h8 43 ♘d5 ♖g2+ 44 ♔h1 ♗xd5 45 exd5 ♖f2 46 ♗h3 ♖d2 47 ♔g1 ♗d4 and Black wins.

39 ♕c4 ♔h8 (3)

'For a draw (and victory in the match!) 39...♕a7+ 40 ♔h1 ♖xe6 41 ♕xe6+ ♕f7 42 ♕c8 ♕f8 was sufficient. But Kasparov is aiming for a win.' (Averbakh, Taimanov)

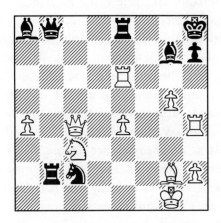

40 e5?

This instantly-made move, the last before the time control, loses almost as instantly: when there are only seconds left on the clock, all sorts of mistakes are possible. For a long time I thought that 40 ♖xe8+ ♕xe8 41 ♘d1 ♘a3 42 ♕d3 was also bad in view of 42...♖a2! (after 42...♖b1 43 e5! h6 44 ♖d4! it is now Black who is forced to maintain the balance by 44...♖b8!) 43 ♘e3 ♕f8! etc. But in 2007 I discovered the following elegant computer geometry: 43 g6! h6 44 ♖xh6! ♗xh6 45 ♕c3+ ♗g7 46 ♕h3+ ♔g8 47 ♕b3+ with perpetual check.

In addition, I examined 40 g6 h6 41 ♖xe8+ ♕xe8 42 ♘d1 ♘a3, thinking that in the endgame after 43 ♕f7 ♕xf7 44 gxf7 ♖b1 45 ♗f3 ♘c4 Black would gradually be able to

convert his advantage. But here too White is saved by 43 ♖xh6+! ♗xh6 44 ♕c3+ ♗g7 45 ♕h3+ followed by 45...♔g8 46 ♘xb2, and the black king cannot hide from the checks.

40...♕a7+ 41 ♔h1 ♗xg2+ 42 ♔xg2 ♘d4+ 0-1

Preferring to win a whole rook, rather than queen for rook after 42...♘e3+ 43 ♔h3 ♘xc4 44 ♖xe8+ ♗f8.

What different fates the black rooks have experienced! One, the queen's rook, made a couple of awkward movements, and to the end of the game stood in its place, but the other, the king's rook, conducted itself heroically and decided the outcome by giving the last check.

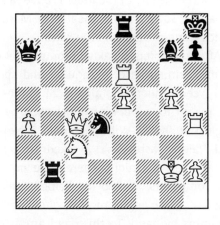

Karpov appeared to freeze. A few more agonising minutes passed, and finally he held out his hand and congratulated me on my victory and on winning the title of world champion. And the thunderous roar which broke out in the hall at that moment finally convinced me – yes, yes, it was true! I had done it! I triumphantly raised my arms over my head... Times: 2.33–2.25.

The following day, 10th November, the closing ceremony of the match took place. I remember the faces of Campomanes, Sevastyanov and Krogius. It was a piquant situation: I was crowned with a laurel wreath by the very people who had done everything within their powers to try and ensure that this did not happen.

Matches with Timman and Miles

Six-game training matches: **Kasparov** – Timman (Hilversum, 14-22 December 1985): 4-2; **Kasparov** – Miles (Basel, 14-21 May 1986): 5½-½.

World champion! Initially the weight of this title had a paralysing effect, which kept me in a state of euphoria (I should remind you that I was just 22 years old). We wildly celebrated the victory over Karpov, and five days after the end of the match I gave talk at a packed Sovremennik Theatre in Moscow which went on deep into the night.

After returning to Baku, I promptly set off to my training base in Zagulba and spent two weeks annotating all the 24 games of the match for a book commissioned by an English publisher. With Alexander Shakarov and Valery Tasturyan I worked furiously, literally day and night. There were not yet any computers, and so my helpers used a typewriter, while my mother glued in the diagrams by hand. To this day I am astonished by how quickly the book was produced. But at that time all manuscripts were sent abroad via the All-Union Copyright Agency, and it kept my book for four months – because, by Soviet standards, the introduction was over-seditious.

After all this strain I was faced in December 1985 with playing a short match against the top Dutch grandmaster Jan Timman, who was rated No.3 in the world. That year he had won tournaments in Wijk aan Zee, Zagreb and the Interzonal in Taxco (with 12 out of 15!), then in the autumn he shared 4th place with Tal in the Candidates Tour-

nament in Montpellier, and after an additional match (3-3) he broke through to the Candidates semi-finals.

For a champion who had won the title only a month earlier, it was an unusual action to contest a match with such a strong opponent: I was risking my reputation and simply could not afford to lose. But an agreement regarding this unofficial encounter had been reached early in the summer in Hamburg. Every year the Dutch TV company KRO arranged such matches for Timman in Hilversum, and before me he had already played Korchnoi, Spassky (both 3-3) and Portisch (3½-2½). The organisers, naturally, wanted the 'descendent of Euwe' also to play me. The prize fund was quite modest, but money wasn't the aim of my trip to Holland; rather a desire to show the world how the new champion played.

At a press-conference before the start Timman admitted that he had made a careful study of my play and had found a number of improvements in positions that had occurred in my games. For my part, I said: 'Let's see what sort of champion I am.' On this occasion, instead of Litvinov, I was accompanied by Yuri Mamedov, the leader of my delegation at the first and third matches with Karpov. And Andras Adorjan arrived from Budapest – to play Timman not only without any preparation, but also without the help of a second, would have been altogether flippant. That said, in the openings I was relying mainly on the ideas accumulated in my preparations for the world championship battles.

The match was opened by Anatoly Blatov, the Soviet ambassador in Holland. We played in a television studio of the KRO company, which accommodated four hundred spectators, and a further one and a half thousand followed the games in a neighbouring room, with demonstration boards and commentators. Apart from the local media, the event was covered by journalists from seven countries, including Soviet, French and Yugoslav TV.

Timman and I endeavoured not to disappoint the public. In the first game I drew the black pieces.

Game 8
J.Timman-G.Kasparov
Training Match
1st Game, Hilversum 15.12.1985
Ruy Lopez C93

1 e4 e5

Against my Sicilian with 1...c5 2 ♘f3 e6 3 d4 cxd4 4 ♘xd4 ♘c6 5 ♘c3 d6 my opponent used to employ the variation 6 f4 ♘f6 7 ♗e3 ♗e7 8 ♕f3, which on closer inspection did not appeal to me. And an hour before the game started, I decided that a world champion should play solid openings, and besides the Spanish had already occurred in my game with Timman from the 3rd round of the USSR v. Rest of the World match (1984).

2 ♘f3 ♘c6 3 ♗b5 a6 4 ♗a4 ♘f6 5 0-0 ♗e7 6 ♖e1 b5 7 ♗b3 d6 8 c3 0-0 9 h3 ♗b7 10 d4 ♖e8 11 ♘bd2 ♗f8

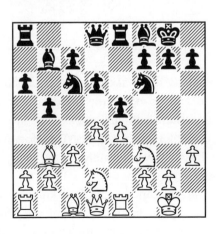

12 a3

This could have been expected: it was what Timman played against Karpov (Tilburg 1979). Instead, in his aforementioned game with me, after including the moves 11 ♘g5 ♖f8 12 ♘f3 ♖e8 13 ♘bd2 ♗f8, he chose 14 ♗c2 ♘b8 15 b4 ♘bd7 16 a4 ♘b6 17 axb5 axb5 18 ♖xa8 ♕xa8 19 ♗d3, but after 19...exd4 20 ♘xd4 ♘xe4 Black obtained comfortable play. I myself preferred 12 a4 with White (*Game Nos.16, 17, 69, 74*).

12...h6 13 ♗c2 ♘b8 14 b4 ♘bd7 15 ♗b2 g6

I had also looked at 15...c5 16 bxc5 exd4 17 cxd4 dxc5 with a complicated game (Karpov-Smejkal, Moscow 1981), although after 18 d5 I preferred White's position.

16 c4

The immediate opening of the position allows Black to maintain the balance. After this match White more often began playing 16 ♕b1 (the source game: Romanishin-Timoshchenko, 49th USSR Championship, Frunze 1981), reinforcing the e4-pawn and planning ♘b3-a5, while if 16...♘b6, then 17 ♗b3 and at a convenient moment c3-c4.

16...exd4 17 cxb5 axb5 18 ♘xd4 c6

Not altogether aesthetic (the b7-bishop is blocked), but all Black's pieces are well developed, he has acquired the ...d6-d5 resource, and the main thing is that for the present White has no real threats.

19 a4

An attempt to probe the weaknesses in the opponent's position. No particular benefits are promised by either 19 ♖c1 ♕b6 20 ♗d3 ♗g7, or 19 ♘2b3 ♖c8 (Chiburdanidze-Akhmylovskaya, Moscow 1983), while 19 ♘4b3 (Hübner-Kavalek, Tilburg 1979) allows 19...c5.

19...bxa4 (as the computer age has shown, 19...d5! is stronger, with a very sharp, roughly equal game, Svidler-Bacrot, Poikovsky 2005) **20 ♗xa4**

Timoshchenko and I had studied this position in 1984.

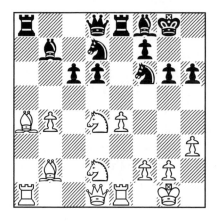

20...♕b6

Karpov defended more passively against Timman – 20...♖c8?! 21 ♖c1 c5 22 bxc5 dxc5 23 ♘4f3 ♗c6 and after 24 ♗xc6 ♖xc6 25 ♘c4?! (25 e5! ♘h5 26 ♘e4 would still have retained an advantage) 25...♘b6 26 ♕xd8 ♖xd8 he gained a draw, but by 24 ♗b3! ♘h5 (24...♘xe4? 25 ♕c2 and wins) 25 ♕c2 ♗g7 26 ♗xg7 and ♘c4 White could have placed his opponent in a difficult position.

21 b5

The unsuccessful result of a long think. 21 ♕b3 d5! is also unconvincing (Maryasin-Dydyshko, Minsk 1983), but in the 3rd game Timman played 21 ♘c2! ♕c7 22 ♗b3 and after the superficial 22...♗a6?! (Game No.95 in *Revolution in the 70s*), with 23 ♘e3! he could have fought for an advantage.

22...♖xa1 23 ♗xa1 (23 ♕xa1 ♘h5!?) 23...♗g7 24 ♘e3 c5 is more solid, intending 25 bxc5 ♘xc5 with equality (Timman-Karpov, Bugojno 1986), but here 25 b5! ♘xe4 26 ♘d5 ♗xd5 27 ♗xd5 ♘ef6 28 ♖xe8+ ♘xe8 29 ♗c6 is more energetic, with promising play for the sacrificed pawn.

21...cxb5 22 ♗xb5 d5 23 ♖xa8 ♗xa8 24 ♕a4

It would appear that at this point Timman

wavered: he couldn't decide whether to curtail the game (say, by 24 exd5 ♖xe1+ 25 ♕xe1 ♗xd5 26 ♕a1 with a quick draw), or nevertheless try to exploit the white pieces in the first game with the new world champion. The queen thrust and the next few moves reflect this wavering, which in the end leads to disaster.

24...♘c5 25 ♕c2 (25 ♕a2 ♖d8!? 26 e5 ♘fe4 27 ♘2f3 ♗b7 is somewhat better for Black)

25...♖b8

Setting up an X-ray on the b-file.

26 exd5

It would probably have been simpler for my opponent to play the roughly equal position with a blockade of the isolani on d5 – 26 e5!? ♘fe4 27 ♘2f3 ♘e6 28 ♖b1 etc.

26...♘xd5

Now, when both sides are left with just three pawns on one wing, White's pieces are somewhat hanging.

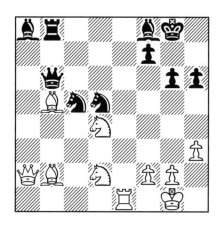

Whereas the black bishops are distantly placed and do not come under attack, the white bishops are vulnerable, leaving Black with latent tactical threats. Therefore Timman has to play accurately.

27 ♘c4

'A rare instance – the four knights have come together in the centre of the board' (Razuvaev). One can understand White wanting to attack the queen, but 27 ♗a1 ♗g7 (27...♘b4 28 ♕c3) 28 ♗c4 ♘f4 29 ♘e2! was more appropriate – this far from obvious move equalises, as it turns out that 29...♘xg2? is weak on account of 30 ♖b1 ♕a7 31 ♖xb8+ ♕xb8 32 ♕xg6.

27...♕c7 28 ♘e5

The exchange of the active black rook would have simplified the defence – 28 ♖e8!? ♖xe8 29 ♗xe8 ♘f4 (29...♕e7 30 ♕e2) 30 ♘e3, when it would appear that Black has little serious prospect of an advantage:

1) 30...♗xg2 31 ♘xg2 ♘xh3+ 32 ♔h1 ♕e5 33 ♘c6 ♕xe8 34 ♕c3 ♘xf2+ 35 ♔g1 f6 36 ♕xf6 ♘g4 37 ♘e7+! ♕xe7 38 ♕xg6+ ♗g7 39 ♕xg4 with equality;

2) 30...♘fd3 31 ♗a1 ♗g7 (31...♕a7 32 ♗c3) 32 ♗b5 ♕a7 33 ♕d1 intending ♘dc2 with equality;

3) 30...♖e4! 31 ♕c4 ♕e7 32 ♗c6 (32 ♗a3 is also suitable) 32...♘cd3 33 ♗a1, and nothing is given by any of 33...♕a3 34 ♕a4!, 33...♘e5 34 ♕a4 ♘xc6 35 ♘xc6, 33...♗g7 34 ♗xe4 ♕xe4 35 ♘b3 ♘e2+ 36 ♔f1 ♘g3+ 37 ♔g1, or the combinative 33...♘xf2 34 ♔xf2 ♕h4+ 35 g3 ♘xh3+ 36 ♔e2 ♕xg3 37 ♗xe4 ♕f2+ 38 ♔d1 ♕xe3 39 ♗d5 with an adequate counterattack.

28...♗g7

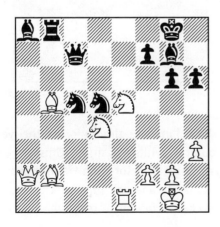

After this it transpires that loss of mate-rial for White is now inevitable – he has to give up two pieces for a rook (true, for the moment without ruinous consequences).

29 ♘ec6?

A serious oversight in an anxious position. It was also bad to play 29 ♗c6? ♗xe5 30 ♕xc5 ♖xb2 31 ♕xd5 ♗xd4 32 ♕xd4 (32 ♖e8+ ♔h7!) 32...♕xc6 or 30 ♗xa8 ♗h2+ 31 ♔h1 ♘b4 32 ♕e2 ♘bd3 33 ♘b5 ♕d7 34 ♔xh2 ♕xb5, winning a piece. And to Razuvaev's recommendation 29 ♘ef3 there is the strong reply 29...♘f4!.

However, after the consolidating move 29 ♗f1! White could still have firmly counted on a draw:

1) 29...♖xb2 30 ♕xb2 ♗xe5 31 ♕a3! (the only move!) 31...♘b6 32 ♘b5 ♕e7 33 ♕e3 (White regains the material, exploiting the pin on the e5-bishop; 33 ♖c1 ♘ba4 34 ♖xc5 is also not bad) 33...♖e4 34 f3 ♘d5 35 ♕a3 ♕h4 36 ♖c1 ♗f4 37 ♖xc5 ♗e3+ 38 ♔h2! ♕f4+ 39 ♔h1 ♗xc5 40 ♕xc5 ♘e3 41 ♗e2 with a draw;

2) 29...♗xe5 30 ♘b5 ♗h2+ 31 ♔h1 ♕c6 32 ♔xh2 ♖xb5 33 ♗xb5 ♕xb5 34 ♔g1 ♕c6 35 ♕e2, and the power of the b2-bishop compensates White for his material deficit: 35...♘f6 36 f3 ♘cd7 37 ♖d1, or 35...♘e6 36 ♕e5 ♘c3 37 ♕g3! ♘e4 38 ♕b8+ ♘f8 39 ♖c1 ♘c5 40 f3 etc.

29...♗xc6 (perhaps Timman had been counting on 29...♖xb5? 30 ♖e8+ ♔h7 31 ♖xa8 or 30 ♘xb5 ♕xc6 31 ♘a7! ♕b7 32 ♖e8+ ♔h7 33 ♗xg7 ♘b4 34 ♖h8+! ♔xg7 35 ♕c3+ f6 36 ♖xa8 with a draw) **30 ♗xc6 ♘f4!**

All three of White's minor pieces are under attack. 'Kasparov loves this sort of play' (Razuvaev).

31 ♗b5

After 31 ♕xc5 ♖xb2 32 ♘b5 ♘e2+! 33 ♔h1 ♕a5! Black has a decisive attack (was it this that my opponent had overlooked?), for example: 34 ♖d1 ♘c3 35 ♗e8! – a clever reply, hoping for the pretty variation 35...♖xb5 36 ♗xf7+ ♔h7 37 ♕c6 ♖g5 38 ♕e8 h5 39 ♖d6 ♕f5 40 h4 ♖g4 41 ♗g8+ ♔h6 42 ♖xg6+! ♖xg6 43 ♕e3+ ♖g5 44 ♕xg5+ ♕xg5 45 hxg5+ ♔xg5 46 g3 with a not altogether clear endgame, but the rigorous 35...♔h7! 36 ♗xf7 ♕xb5 refutes this idea.

And in the event of 31 ♖e8+ ♖xe8 32 ♗xe8 Black wins prettily by either 32...♘ce6 33 ♘c6 (33 ♕xc7 ♘xc7 with the threats of ...♘xe8 and ...♗xd4) 33...♗xb2 34 ♕xb2 ♘g7!, trapping the bishop, or 32...♕d8!? 33 ♕xc5 ♕xe8, when White unexpectedly loses a piece.

31...♖xb5?

In my joy I quickly grabbed the bishop, missing a certain win: 31...♘ce6! (31...♕b7!? 32 f3 ♘cd3 33 ♗xd3 ♕xb2 34 ♘c6 ♕xc2 35 ♗xc2 ♖b2 was also good enough) 32 ♕xc7 ♘xc7 33 ♗c1 ♘fd5, winning a piece. It was not so difficult to calculate these variations.

32 ♘xb5 ♕c6 33 f3 ♕xb5 34 ♗xg7 ♔xg7 35 ♕c3+ ♔g8!

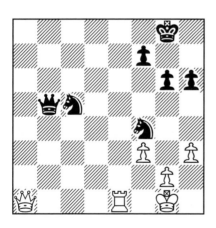

A position with two knights against a rook has been reached by force. From afar I thought that, with the queens on the board, the win for Black would be merely a question of time, but here I began to realise that the path to the goal was a very difficult one. Black is not able to make a double attack with his knights on the g2-pawn, whereas White can combine play against the enemy king with the threat of exchanging queens, leading most probably to a drawn endgame. True, in practice it is not easy for White to defend: he has to manoeuvre with great accuracy and caution.

36 ♕e5 ♘fe6 37 ♖a1 ♕b7 38 ♕d6 h5! 39 ♔h1 (39 ♔h2!?) 39...♔h7 40 ♖c1 ♕a7

The first time control was reached, but the game was not adjourned: in my matches with Timman and Miles the time control was 40 moves in 2 hours, then 20 moves in 1 hour, followed by an adjournment.

41 ♖b1

This allows a favourable regrouping of the knights. White should have tried to keep the black knight on c5 by 41 ♕d5, after which I was planning the invasion 41...♕a3 and ...♕e3.

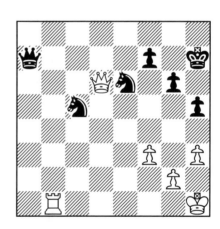

41...♘g7!

'The knights are aiming for g3, the weakest point in White's position' (Gipslis). Here I began to scent victory: the knight heads for f5, the other one will replace it at e6, and after ...h5-h4 mating threats will be in the air.

42 ♖b8 ♘ce6 43 ♕e5?

An error in a difficult position. 43 ♕b4(b6) ♕a1+ 44 ♕b1 was more resilient, although here too after 44...♕d4 Black has an escalating attack.

43...♘d4! (this is the whole point: now both knights are rampant) **44 ♖b1 h4?!**

An obvious but over-hasty move. Black gets slightly out of step – the immediate 44...♘gf5! would have won more forcefully, for example:

1) 45 ♕d5 ♘e2 46 ♕e5 h4 (it was for this position that I was aiming: the knights are ideally placed, and the rook can no longer be activated) 47 ♔h2 (47 ♖a1 ♕b6) 47...♕f2 48 ♕f6 ♔h6, and White has no defence;

2) 45 ♕b8 ♘xf3! (a spectacular stroke, which immediately resolves matters) 46 gxf3 (if 46 ♕xa7 ♘g3 mate) 46...♕f2 47 ♖g1 ♕xf3+ 48 ♔h2 ♘e3 and ...♘f1+, regaining the exchange and remaining two pawns up.
45 ♕b8 ♕e7 46 ♕b4 ♕f6

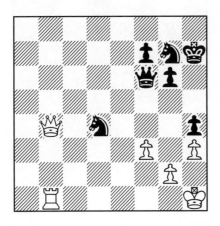

47 ♕f8?!

An empty blow, but 47 ♕b6 ♘ge6 followed by ...♘f5 would have led to a similar finish.

47...♘e2 (launching a mating attack) **48 ♖d1 ♘f5 49 ♕b8 ♘e3 50 ♕d8 ♕f4 51 ♖e1 ♘f1 0-1**

Or 51...♘f5!. But as it was White resigned (52 ♖xf1 ♘g3+ 53 ♔g1 ♕e3+).

Success with Black in this exciting first game improved my mood. Whereas Timman, in the opinion of Yuri Razuvaev, the Moscow commentator on the match, *'after his unexpected loss in this game was certainly in a state of confusion, which was increased in the 2nd game.'*

> ### Game 9
> ### G.Kasparov-J.Timman
> Training Match
> 2nd Game, Hilversum 16.12.1985
> *Queen's Indian Defence E13*

1 d4 ♘f6 2 c4 e6 3 ♘f3

I think that after 3 ♘c3 ♗b4 4 ♘f3 (*Game Nos.3, 7, 13*) all the same there would have followed 4...b6.
3...b6 4 ♘c3 (4 a3 – *Game No.32*) **4...♗b4**

Playing Timman at that time it was easy to guess the opening after 1 d4: either the Nimzo-Indian, or the Queen's Indian, or a hybrid of these two defences. In the event of 4...♗b7 I would have chosen the 5 a3 system, with which I was familiar.

5 ♗g5 ♗b7

Nowadays, to avoid the reply 6 ♘d2, many have reverted to 5...h6!? 6 ♗h4 g5 7 ♗g3 ♘e4 (the source game: Gligoric-Taimanov, Zurich Candidates 1953; recent examples: Bacrot-Topalov, Nanjing 2010, Nakamura-Anand, Wijk aan Zee 2011).

6 e3

Later they also began playing 6 ♘d2!?, excluding the set-up with 6...h6 7 ♗h4 g5 and ...♘e4, and after 6...♗xc3 and ...d7-d6 immediately setting up a 'big centre' by f2-f3 and e2-e4. I also employed the knight move – against Psakhis (2nd match game, La Manga 1990) and Onischuk (Tilburg 1997). True, with Psakhis after 6...♗xc3 (nowadays even 6...h6 7 ♗h4 ♘c6!? is being tried) 7 bxc3 h6 8 ♗h4 g5 9 ♗g3 d6 10 e3 the normal position was reached (as in *Game No.18*), but 10 f3!? was possible with the idea of e2-e4.

6...h6 7 ♗h4 g5 (7...♗xc3+ 8 bxc3 d6 is more restrained – *Game No.18*) **8 ♗g3 ♘e4**

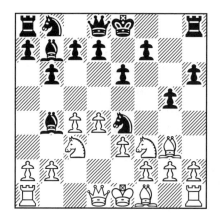

One of the *tabiyas* of the 'hybrid', in which for many years the automatic continuation was 9 ♕c2 (*Game Nos.10, 11*). But I was able to surprise Timman with a gambit move.

9 ♘d2!?

This pawn sacrifice, known since the time of the game Stein-Langeweg (Amsterdam 1969), was one that I looked at with Timoshchenko before my match with Korchnoi (1983). It was thought that here Black had good play, but a promising idea had occurred to me (at that time I was literally bursting with similar ideas).

'Kasparov aims to "drag" his opponent out of his armour of knowledge and experience, and into an open battle. He has an excellently developed feeling for positions with disrupted material balance (which is practically impossible to cultivate – it rarely occurs and it has to be inherently instilled in a player). For the moment only a pawn is sacrificed...' (Razuvaev)

9...♘xc3 (9...♘xg3 is not so critical – *Game No.20*) **10 bxc3 ♗xc3 11 ♖c1 ♗b4**

In our preparations for the 4th game Adorjan and I did not like 11...♗a5 12 h4 ♖g8 (Crouch-Harikrishna, London 2001), and I reverted to the classical lines (9 ♕c2). However, after 13 ♕h5 White has sufficient compensation for the pawn. Therefore even now, more than a quarter of a century later, this gambit seems to me to be fully correct and safe for White.

12 h4 gxh4?! (12...♖g8 is more solid, not exposing the weak h6-pawn) **13 ♖xh4!**

Here is the fresh idea! Stein played 13 ♗xh4 ♗e7 14 ♗g3, which was a loss of time (14...d6 with equality). The bishop at g3 is on its optimal square, and the rook must be brought into the battle.

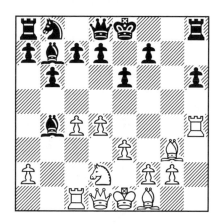

13...♗d6

A controversial decision – in the words of Razuvaev, the exchange of bishops 'looks uncouth'. However, after 13...♗e7 14 ♖h5 (14 ♕h5!?) 14...d6, in contrast to the Stein game, White's rook is already on h5, and he has 15 c5! dxc5 16 dxc5 ♗xc5 17 ♖hxc5 bxc5 18 ♖xc5 with excellent compensation for the exchange and a pawn (our preparation of 1983). In Gelfand-Vallejo (Moscow 2004), after some thought Black replied 14...♗d6, but after 15 ♕g4 (15 ♗xd6!?) 15...♕f6 16 c5 ♗xg3 17 ♕xg3 ♘a6 White could have retained some advantage by 18 c6! dxc6 19

♗xa6 ♗xa6 20 ♖xc6.

And in 1985 there was also the *Informator* recommendation 13...♘c6 by Agzamov and Nadyrkhanov. After this I considered 14 d5 ♘e7 15 ♗d3 to be promising, but there is also the interesting 15 dxe6 ♘f5! (not 15...dxe6? 16 ♕a4+ ♘c6 17 ♖d4 ♕g5 18 c5! Bartel-Berkes, Istanbul 2005) 16 exf7+ ♔f8 17 ♖g4(h3) ♘xg3 18 ♖xg3 ♕f6 19 c5! with a dangerous initiative.

14 ♕g4

The queen breaks out into the open, at the same time defending the rook. From this point I was very happy with my position.

14...♗xg3

In the event of 14...♕e7!? 15 ♗xd6! (weaker is 15 c5 ♗xg3 16 ♕xg3 ♘c6 and ...0-0-0, Plaskett-Short, Brighton 1984) 15...cxd6 (15...♕xd6 16 c5!) 16 ♕g3 f5 17 c5 (Agdestein-Hellers, Gausdal 1987) or 16 ♕f4!? White would also retain the initiative.

15 ♕xg3

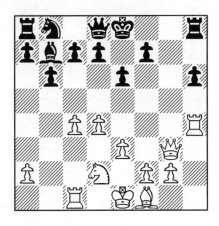

15...♘c6?!

After a long think Timman makes the most natural move, avoiding the known continuation 15...♘a6 16 c5!. After 16...♕e7?! (Eingorn-Nadyrkhanov, Volgograd 1985) there is the strong reply 17 ♖h5(h3). The correct defence is 16...♘b4 17 a3 ♘d5 18 e4 ♘e7, but after 19 ♖h5 or 19 ♕g7 this is also favourable for White.

16 d5! (White has to hurry with his attack, as otherwise Black will succeed in castling queenside) **16...♘e7 17 ♗d3!**

Timman obviously did not like this developing move: it turns out that he has a difficult choice. 'The light squares on the b1-h7 diagonal are taken under control, and how is Black now going to complete his development?' (Razuvaev).

17...d6

If 17...♖g8 there would have followed 18 ♕h2 exd5 19 ♖xh6.

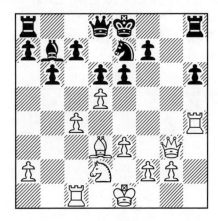

18 ♕g7

Preventing the black king's flight to the queenside. True, after 18 dxe6 fxe6 19 ♗e4! White also has sustained pressure: 19...♗xe4 20 ♘xe4 ♔d7 21 ♘f6+ ♔c8 22 ♖e4 e5 23 c5!, or 19...♘f5 20 ♕g6+ ♔d7 21 ♗xf5 exf5 22 ♕xf5+ ♔e7 23 ♘e4 ♕f8 24 ♕b5 a6 25 ♕b4.

18...♖g8 19 ♕h7!

The simple-minded capture of the pawn – 19 ♕xh6?! would have allowed Black to solve all his problems: 19...♘g6! 20 ♗xg6 (20 ♖g4 ♕f6) 20...♖xg6 21 ♕f4 ♕g5!. However, the unexpected queen manoeuvre, of which I was very proud, confused my opponent.

19...♖f8?

Timman decided to play 'safely', but he

went wrong. 19...♕d7? 20 ♘e4 ♖g6 21 ♕h8+ ♘g8 22 ♘xd6+! and ♗xg6 was even worse, while 19...exd5? 20 cxd5 ♗xd5 was weak on account of 21 ♘e4 ♖g6 (21...♗xe4? 22 ♖xe4 and wins) 22 ♘c3! etc.

However, 19...♖xg2 was more resilient, after which White had two tempting continuations: the quiet 20 ♖f4 ♘f5 21 ♗xf5 exf5 22 ♕xf5 ♖g7 23 ♘f3! ♗c8 24 ♕h5 ♕e7 25 ♕xh6, regaining the pawn with unpleasant pressure, or the flamboyant 20 ♗e4!! ♖g1+ 21 ♔e2 ♖xc1 22 dxe6 fxe6 23 ♗xb7 ♔d7 24 ♘e4 ♕h8 25 ♗xa8 ♖c2+ 26 ♔d1 ♕xh7 27 ♘f6+ ♔d8 28 ♘xh7 ♖xf2 29 ♖xh6 ♖xa2 30 ♗f3 ♘f5 (30...e5? 31 ♘f6 and wins) 31 ♖xe6 with a piece for two pawns and winning chances.

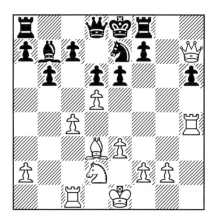

20 ♘e4?

Returning the favour. Tempted by the threat of a pretty mate in one move (♘f6), I overlooked the simple 20 ♖xh6 with a decisive advantage after 20...exd5 21 cxd5 ♗xd5 22 ♘e4 ♗xe4 23 ♕xe4 a6 24 ♖xc7! or 20...♕d7 21 dxe6 fxe6 22 ♘e4 ♗xe4 23 ♕xe4 and ♖xe6.

20...♘f5?

Timman also gains his 'revenge', missing the saving move 20...♘g8! (it is psychologically difficult to return the knight to its initial square – I did not even consider it),

when 21 c5!? ♗xd5! 22 cxd6 cxd5 23 ♖f4 e5 is unclear, while after 21 ♖f4 e5 (this way, rather than 21...♕e7? 22 c5!) 22 ♖f3 ♕e7 and the unavoidable ...0-0-0 Black would have solved all his problems.

21 ♖h3

21 ♖h5!? ♕e7 22 g4 ♘h4 23 ♖xh6 was no less convincing, when my *Informator* suggestion 23...♘g6 is bad because of 24 ♕g7! with the threat of ♘f6+ (if 24...0-0-0, then 25 ♖xg6), while after 23...♘f3+ there is a win by 24 ♔e2 ♘g5 25 ♘xg5 ♕xg5 26 dxe6 ♕xg4+ 27 ♔d2 ♕g5 (27...♕f3 28 ♖f1) 28 f4 or 24...♘e5 25 ♘f6+ ♔d8 26 g5, when Black is helpless.

21...♕e7 22 g4 ♘h4

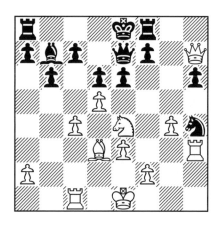

23 ♕g7!

A pretty move, which stunned Timman: he was counting on 23 ♕xh6? ♘g6, when Black could at last breathe freely. But now the knight at h4 is in danger – the interference move ♘f6+ is threatened.

23...0-0-0

Allowing the decisive invasion of the knight on f6. However, going into an ending would hardly have helped – 23...f5 24 ♕xe7+ ♔xe7, after which I was planning 25 ♘c3! ♘g6 (25...♘g2+ 26 ♔e2! fxg4 27 ♖h2, and the knight is trapped) 26 ♖xh6 ♘e5 (26...♖f6? 27 g5) 27 ♖xe6+ ♔d8 28 ♗xf5 followed by the victorious march of the kingside pawns (28...♗c8 29 f4! etc.).

24 ♘f6

A picturesque situation: Black's army is completely paralysed, and with the board full of pieces he loses his knight!

24...exd5 25 cxd5 ♔b8 26 ♖xh4 ♗xd5 27 g5

Here I relaxed slightly, whereas I should have done a little calculation and played 27 ♘xd5! ♕xh4 28 ♘xc7 with crushing threats: 28...♕e7 29 ♘a6+ or 28...♕h1+ 29 ♔d2 ♕b7(f3) 30 ♘a6+ etc.

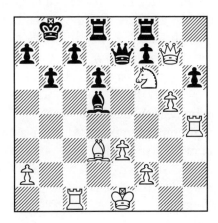

27...♗xa2

27...hxg5 28 ♘xd5 ♕e5 would have sharpened the play somewhat, after which White has a choice between 29 ♕xe5 dxe5 30 ♘b4 ♖xd3 31 ♘xd3 gxh4 32 ♘xe5 with a won endgame, and the more energetic 29 ♘f6! gxh4 30 ♘d7+! ♖xd7 31 ♕xf8+ ♔b7 32 ♗a6+! or 29...♕a5+ 30 ♔e2 gxh4 31 ♘d7+ ♔b7 32 ♘xf8, and the curtain comes down.

28 gxh6 (there now follows a brief agony) **28...d5 29 h7 ♕a3 30 ♖d1 ♖h8 31 ♘g8 ♗b3 32 ♖a1** (or 32 ♕xh8 ♗xd1 33 ♔d2!) **32...♕c5 33 ♕xh8 d4 34 ♖xd4** (34 ♕f6!) **34...♕c3+ 35 ♔e2 1-0**

The score became 2-0, and after such a resounding win I was already beginning to think about a maximum, 'Fischer' result.

Alas, the 3rd game brought me down to earth. The main events in it took place in a time scramble. On the 31st move Timman went wrong, but instead of a winning queen move, I made a dreadful move with my rook. My opponent could have gained an obvious advantage, but he preferred to launch into an unclear attack with a knight sacrifice, and after my blunder on the 35th move he also won in crushing style. 2-1! From the press: *'The Dutch fans were unable to restrain their joy. Timman picked up his six-year-old daughter and carried her on to the stage'.*

The second half of the match was no less intense than the first. Both players played for a win in every game, irrespective of the colours. And the best was the drawn 4th game, which was uncommonly gripping and mind-boggling. Razuvaev: *'It is extremely hard to analyse, and in general it is hard to believe that it was played now, and not in the time of La Bourdonnais.'*

Game 10
G.Kasparov-J.Timman
Training Match
4th Game, Hilversum 19.12.1985
Queen's Indian Defence E13

1 d4 ♘f6 2 c4 e6 3 ♘f3 b6 4 ♘c3 ♗b4 5 ♗g5 ♗b7 6 e3 h6 7 ♗h4 g5 8 ♗g3 ♘e4 9 ♕c2

For this game Adorjan and I did a little bit of preparatory work and as we were temporarily disillusioned with 9 ♘d2 (*Game No.9*), we reverted to a traditional set-up, which had occurred several times in my opponent's games.

9...♗xc3+ 10 bxc3 d6 (10...♘xg3 11 fxg3!?, Vaganian-Timman, London 1984) **11 ♗d3 f5**

After 11...♘xg3 here too 12 fxg3!? is good

(the source game: Spassky-Polugayevsky, 29th USSR Championship, Baku 1961).

12 d5

A position which has been known since Alekhine's times.

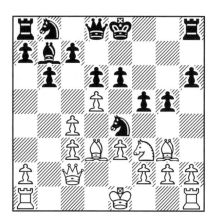

12...♘c5

Timman's invention – on his advice this was first played by Ribli against Vaganian in the USSR v. Rest of the World match (London 1984). 12...exd5?! is weaker: 13 cxd5 ♗xd5 14 ♘d4 ♘d7 15 f3 ♘xg3 16 hxg3 ♕f6 17 ♗xf5 0-0-0 18 ♕a4 a5 19 ♔f2 with advantage in view of the weaknesses in Black's position (Keres-Taimanov, 22nd USSR Championship, Moscow 1955).

However, things are unclear after 12...♘d7 (intending ...♘dc5) 13 ♗xe4 fxe4 14 ♕xe4 ♕f6 15 0-0 0-0-0 16 ♕xe6 ♕xe6 17 dxe6 ♘c5 18 ♘d4 ♖de8 19 f3 ♗a6 (Ree-Taimanov, Hamburg 1965), or the fashionable 12...♘a6!? 13 ♗xe4 (13 ♘d4 ♘ac5 14 0-0 ♕e7! Bacrot-Topalov, Nanjing 2010) 13...fxe4 14 ♕xe4 ♕f6 15 0-0 0-0-0 16 ♕xe6+ ♕xe6 17 dxe6, and apart from 17...♘c5 (transposing into the 12...♘d7 variation), there is 17...♗xf3! 18 gxf3 ♘c5 with equality (Wang Yue-Adams, Baku 2008).

Later, to avoid 12...♘c5 13 h4!, Timman twice played 12...♕f6, in order after 13 ♘d4

♘c5 to transpose into a position from the note to White's 13th move, but Salov (3rd match game, Saint John 1988) and Adianto (Amsterdam 1996) retained the initiative by 13 ♗xe4 fxe4 14 ♕xe4 ♕xc3+ 15 ♔e2 ♕b2+ 16 ♘d2 ♕f6 17 h4 g4 18 h5! ♘d7 19 ♗h4 ♕f5 20 ♕xe6+ ♕xe6 21 dxe6 ♘c5 22 e7.

13 h4!?

Here is the novelty that we had analysed, hoping that Timman would play 12...♘c5: he was always noted for his principled approach to the opening. In the Vaganian-Ribli game, after 13 ♘d4 ♕f6 14 f4 gxf4 15 exf4 ♘ba6 16 ♘xe6 ♘xe6 17 dxe6 0-0 18 0-0 ♘c5 19 ♖ae1 (19 e7 ♖f7) 19...♖ae8 Black obtained excellent play, but there is an unpleasant piece sacrifice – 17 ♗xf5!? ♘g7 18 ♗g6+ ♔d7 (Ribli) 19 0-0! ♖af8 20 f5. Therefore 15(14)...♘bd7!? is more solid.

An attempt to improve White's play with 14 h4 did not succeed in view of 14...♘ba6 15 ♘xe6 ♘xe6 16 dxe6 ♔e7 17 ♗xf5 ♘b4! with equality (Kir.Georgiev-Kudrin, Amsterdam 1985).

13...g4?!

A rather quick reply. Later too many blocked the flank, apparently fearing the opening of the h-file. Meanwhile, 13...♕f6!? 14 hxg5 (14 ♘d4 ♘ba6 – cf. above) 14...hxg5 15 ♖xh8+ ♕xh8, which occurred at the turn of the century, leads to complicated play: 16 0-0-0 ♕f6 17 ♘d4 f4 18 ♗h2 e5, or 16 ♘xg5 and now White is better after 16...exd5 17 0-0-0! ♗c6 18 ♕d2 ♕g8 (18...♕f6 19 ♗h4) 19 cxd5 ♕xd5 20 ♗b1!, but the sharp 16...♘xd3!? 17 ♕xd3 ♕h1+ 18 ♔d2! ♕xa1 19 ♘xe6 (with the threats of ♕xf5 and ♘xc7+) 19...♕xa2+ 20 ♔e1 ♕a1+ 21 ♔e2 (dreaming of hiding on f3) 21...♕a4! 22 ♘xc7+ ♔d8 23 ♗xd6 ♘a6 24 ♘xa8 ♗xa8 promises a draw.

14 ♘d4 ♕f6 15 0-0 (after 15 ♘xe6?! ♘xe6 16 dxe6 ♗xg2 17 ♖g1 ♗f3! 18 ♗xf5

♘a6(c6) Black has a comfortable game) **15...♘ba6**

The problems are not solved by 15...♘xd3?! (*Game No.11*).

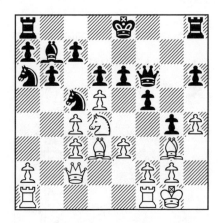

16 ♘xe6! (breaking up Black's pawn chain and exposing his king) **16...♘xe6 17 ♗xf5!**

Of course, not 17 dxe6? 0-0 18 e7 ♖f7. My idea was to sacrifice a piece for two pawns followed by f2-f3.

17...♘g7 18 ♗g6+ ♔d7 19 f3!

At this Adorjan and I concluded our analysis. I believed in the power of the two bishops and I assumed that I would cope after this on my own, by combining the attack with an advance of the pawns. Although it all proved not to be so simple, my intuitive assessment of the position was correct.

19...♖af8 20 fxg4 (for the piece White now has three pawns) **20...♕e7 21 e4**

The e4-e5 breakthrough is in the air. In this rather wild position White is threatening not so much a direct attack on the king, but rather to transpose into an endgame, the outcome of which will be decided by the passed pawns on the kingside.

21...♔c8

Aiming to remove the king from the centre. 21...♖f6? would have lost ignominiously after 22 ♖xf6 ♕xf6 23 e5! ♕e7 24 exd6 or 23...dxe5 24 ♖f1.

In *Informator* I gave 21...♘c5 22 ♕e2 ♖f6(?) 23 h5 as being better for White. He also has the advantage after 22...♔c8 23 e5 ♗a6?! 24 e6 (Ivanchuk-Anand, Monte Carlo (rapid) 1993), but 23(22)...♘e8! retains an unclear situation. But it is far stronger to postpone the planned exchange of rooks for the sake of an immediate breakthrough – 22 ♖fe1! (Yrjola) 22...♔c8 23 e5 ♕d7 (23...dxe5 24 ♗xe5! assists the bishops) 24 e6 ♕e7 25 ♖f1! ♗a6 (25...♘cxe6?! 26 ♕e2) 26 ♖f7! ♖xf7 27 exf7 ♗xc4 28 ♕f2 ♘d7 29 ♖e1 or 28...♕f8 29 ♕d4, and Black is in a bad way.

22 ♕d2

White intends to treat himself to the weak h6-pawn. Apparently the sharp 22 e5!? (activating the g3-bishop) was even better: 22...dxe5 23 ♕e4 ♘e8 24 ♕xe5 ♕c5+ 25 ♔h2 or 24...♕xe5 25 ♗xe5 with an overwhelming position. But I decided to manage without therapeutic measures.

22...♔b8

Soon afterwards in the game Miles-Timman (Tilburg 1986) Black tried 22...♘c5, but after 23 ♖xf8+ ♖xf8 24 ♕xh6 (24 ♖e1!?) 24...♕f6?! (24...♗a6 is more resilient) 25 ♗f5+ (25 e5!? dxe5 26 ♖e1) 25...♘xf5 26 ♕xf6 ♖xf6 27 exf5 he was unable to restrain the pawn avalanche.

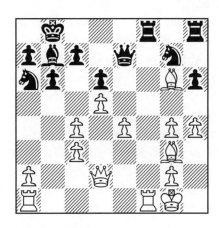

23 ♖xf8+?

'White needs to play e4-e5, and this aim was best served by 23 ♕d4.' (Razuvaev). Indeed, after 23...♘e8 (23...♘c5 24 e5!) 24 ♖f7! (the crux of the idea: in *Informator* I considered only 24 ♖xf8 ♖xf8 25 ♖f1, while in *New in Chess* Timman gave the equally unclear 24 e5 dxe5 25 ♕xe5) 24...♖xf7 25 ♕xh8 ♖f8 (25...♕f8 26 ♕d4!) 26 ♕xh6 ♘c5 27 h5 ♘d7 28 ♗f5 White has a winning position (Salov-Timman, 5th match game, Saint John 1988).

23...♖xf8 24 ♕xh6

I thought that four pawns for the piece would be sufficient for a win, but now Black gains counterplay.

24...♗c8! (24...♕f6? 25 e5!)

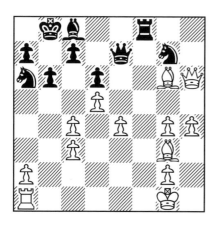

25 ♖e1?!

I suddenly got carried away by the unrealisable idea of a 'textbook-style' rout. The g4-pawn should not have been given away so lightly. True, my *Informator* suggestion 25 g5 ♘c5 26 ♖f1 ♖xf1+ 27 ♔xf1 ♗a6 was altogether harmless. It was far more interesting to transpose into an endgame by 25 ♗f2!? ♗xg4 26 ♗d4 ♘e8 27 ♖f1! ♖xf1+ 28 ♔xf1 ♘c5 29 ♕g5! ♕xg5 30 hxg5, although after 30...♗d7! and ...♔c8-d8 Black would have retained drawing chances.

25 ♗f5! was a more suitable way of fighting for an advantage: 25...♘c5 26 ♖e1

(Timman gave only 26 ♕g5?!) 26...♘d7 27 ♗xd7! ♕xd7 28 g5 or 26...♘d3 27 ♖e3 ♘e5 28 ♗xe5! dxe5 29 ♔h2, and the pawns are stronger than the piece.

25...♗xg4

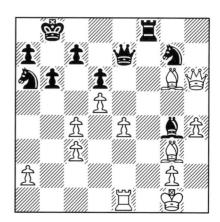

26 c5?!

This 'brilliant' move strongly suggests itself, but, alas, I overlooked Timman's genuinely brilliant reply. The thematic 26 e5! was correct, and if 26...dxe5 – either 27 ♗xe5 ♘f5 28 ♗xf5 (28 ♗xc7+? ♘xc7!) 28...♖xf5 29 ♖e4! ♖h5 (29...♗d1 30 d6) 30 ♕f6, or 27 ♖xe5 ♕c5+ (27...♕f6 is rather worse: 28 ♕g5! ♗f5 29 ♕xf6 ♖xf6 30 ♗xf5 ♘xf5 31 ♗f2 ♔c8 32 g4 ♘d6 33 h5) 28 ♔h2 ♖f1 29 ♕e3 ♘f5 30 ♕xc5 ♘xc5 31 ♗xf5 ♗xf5 32 h5, and everywhere it is most probably a draw, although Black is the one in more danger of losing.

26...♕f6!

It unexpectedly transpires that there are no crushing continuations for White, and he loses material. I had reckoned on 26...♘xc5 (26...bxc5? 27 e5!) 27 e5 dxe5? (27...♘d7? 28 exd6 ♕f6 29 dxc7+ ♔b7 30 ♕g5 is even worse) 28 ♗xe5 ♘f5 29 ♗xc7+! ♔a8 30 ♖xe7 ♘xh6 31 ♗e8 (31 h5!?) 31...♗c8 32 h5 with good winning chances. However, after the cool-headed 27...♔b7 28 exd6 ♕f6 Black would have defended: 29 ♖e7 ♘h5(f5) 30

♖xc7+ ♔b8! and ...♘xg3, or 29 ♕h7 ♗f5 30 ♖e7 ♗xg6 31 ♖xc7+ ♔a6!, intending ...♕f1+ and ...♗e4.

27 cxd6 ♗h5!

Of course! This turn of events put me in a state of shock. Fortunately for me, a saving pawn storm was brewing...

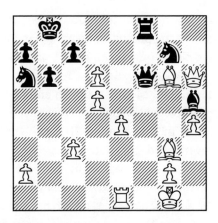

28 e5!

After 28 dxc7+? ♔b7 the passed pawns lose their strength: 29 d6 ♕xg6 30 ♕xg6 ♗xg6 31 e5 ♘e6 etc. However, 28 d7 ♕xg6 (28...♗xg6? 29 ♖e3!) 29 ♕xg6 ♗xg6 30 e5! ♘c5 31 e6 would have led to a position from the game.

28...♕xg6 29 ♕xg6 ♗xg6

'White is playing an endgame two pieces down! But how to assess such an unusual position?' (Razuvaev).

30 e6! ♘c5 31 d7

The immortal McDonnell-La Bourdonnais game comes to mind, although the creation of a third connected passed pawn – 31 dxc7+? is bad due to 31...♔c8! and ...♖g8.

31...♘xd7!

The correct decision: such pawns cannot be endured. In the event of 31...♖d8? 32 ♗e5 (Stohl) the scales would again have tipped in White's favour.

32 exd7 ♖d8 33 ♖e6?

A flamboyant thrust, but White should

have maintained the balance by 33 ♗e5! ♖xd7 34 g4 or 33...♘f5 34 g4 ♘xh4 35 ♔f2 ♗f7 (35...♖xd7 36 ♔g3) 36 ♗f6 ♖xd7 37 ♗xh4 ♗xd5 38 a3.

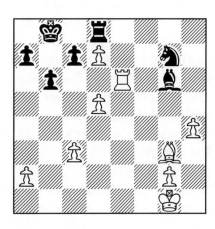

33...♗h5?

After 33...♘xe6? 34 dxe6 it is Black who would have had to attain a draw: 34...♗e8 35 h5 ♗xd7 36 ♗h4 ♗xe6 37 ♗xd8 ♗xa2 etc. But 33...♗f5! leads to an advantage:

1) 34 ♖e7 ♖xd7 35 ♖xd7 ♗xd7 36 ♗e5 ♘f5 37 h5 (Razuvaev) 37...♗e8! 38 g4 ♘e3 39 h6 ♗g6, or 36 ♔f2 (36 ♔h2 ♗g4!) 36...♘f5 37 ♔f3 ♘xg3 38 ♔xg3 ♔c8 39 ♔f4 ♔d8 40 g4 ♔e7 with winning prospects;

2) 34 ♖h6 ♖xd7(!) 35 ♗e5 (my *Informator* recommendation) 35...♘e8 36 ♖h8 ♖e7 37 ♗f4 ♔b7 38 ♖f8 ♗b1 39 a3 ♗a2 40 g4 ♗xd5 41 ♔f2 ♗f7 42 h5 ♘f6 43 ♔g3 ♘xh5+ 44 gxh5 ♗xh5, and Black converted his extra pawn (Lerch-Helmreich, correspondence 1986-87);

3) 34 ♖f6 ♖xd7(!) 35 ♗e5 (Timman) 35...♔b7! 36 g4 (36 c4 ♖e7! and ...♗d3) 36...♖xd5 37 ♗d4 ♗d7, or 35 d6 cxd6 36 ♗xd6+ ♔b7 37 ♗e5 ♗b1 38 a3 ♖e7 39 ♗d6 ♖e4 40 ♖f7+ ♔c6 41 ♗b8 ♘e6, and again things are not easy for White.

34 ♗e5 ♖xd7 35 ♖h6 ♗f7

Not the best move, which also applies to 35...♗e2 (Keene) 36 ♖h7 ♖e7?! (36...♗c4 is correct) 37 d6! (37 ♗xg7 ♔b7! and ...♗d3) 37...♖xe5 38 d7 ♖d5 (38...♘e6? 39 ♖e7! Timman) 39 ♖h8+ ♔b7 40 d8♕ ♖xd8 41 ♖xd8, when the rook and pawns are stronger than the two minor pieces.

35...♗d1! was more accurate. In time-trouble Timman was afraid of 36 ♖h7(?), overlooking the reply 36...♖e7! with the unexpected idea of 37 ♗xg7 ♔b7! and ...♗c2 or 37 ♗f4 ♔c8!. However, the energetic 36 g4! would have sufficed to give me a draw (Stohl's move 36...♖e7 is parried by 37 d6! ♖xe5 38 d7).

36 ♗xg7 ♗xd5

'The pieces are now equal, but the resulting endgame with opposite-colour bishops and passed pawns on opposite wings is exceptionally interesting.' (Razuvaev)

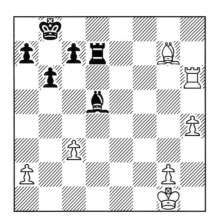

37 ♗e5

Black would have been caused more problems by 37 ♗f8! (to restrain the newly-created passed a-pawn) 37...♗xa2 38 g4, but after 38...c5 39 h5 ♔c7 he would nevertheless have gained a draw (40 ♖f6 ♖f7).

37...♗xa2 38 h5

The assessment of this double-edged position as equal would not have been changed by 38 g4 ♔b7 39 g5 a5. As they used to say in the old days, one passed pawn advances more quickly than two...

38...♔b7 39 g4 (more ambitious than 39 ♖g6 a5 40 h6 a4 41 ♖g7 ♖xg7 42 ♗xg7 ♗b1 43 c4 ♔c6 44 ♗d4 with a draw) **39...♗c4**

In *New in Chess* Timman gave a different move order – 39...a5 40 g5? (40 ♖f6! is equal) 40...♗c4, which, however, does not play any particular role.

40 g5?

The last move in time-trouble before the control. In my pursuit of an ephemeral win I missed clear equality: 40 ♖f6 a5 41 h6 a4 42 ♖f4 b5 43 ♖d4! ♖xd4 (43...♖e7 44 ♗g7) 44 ♗xd4 ♗d3 45 c4 with a drawn ending with opposite-colour bishops.

40...a5 41 g6 (threatening ♖h7) **41...♖d5!**

I overlooked this move, expecting only 41...a4? 42 ♖h7, when in the event of 42...♔c6? 43 ♖xd7 ♔xd7 44 ♗f4 a3 45 ♗c1 a2 46 ♗b2 ♗d3 (46...♔e7 47 h6) 47 ♔f2 ♔e6 48 ♔e3 White has a won bishop endgame, while after 42...♖xh7 43 gxh7 a3 44 h8♕ a2 45 ♕g7 a1♕+ 46 ♔h2 Black is a pawn down, but with drawing chances.

42 ♗f4 (42 ♗g7? ♖f5! and ...a5-a4 would be fatal) **42...♖f5!**

After 42...a4? 43 ♖h7 ♖c5 44 ♗c1! White would have stopped the pawn, whereas now ...a5-a4 is threatened.

43 ♗g3! a4 44 ♖h7 ♖c5 45 h6 (but not 45 ♗d6? a3!) **45...a3**

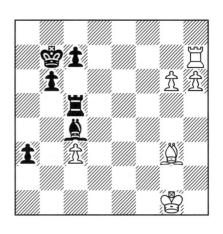

'A fascinating pawn race!' (Razuvaev)

46 ♖e7!

White finds the only moves to save himself, by succeeding in returning his rook to a1 via the defended e1-square. If 46 ♖d7?, then 46...a2 47 ♖d1 ♖b5! 48 h7 ♖b1 and wins.

46...a2 47 ♖e1 ♖h5 48 h7 ♗d3 49 ♖a1 (49 ♗e5? ♖xe5!) **49...♗xg6 50 ♖xa2 ♖xh7**

The situation has cleared and an objectively drawn endgame has been reached. Even so, it is not very pleasant to be a pawn down, and I was already thinking that Timman would drag out the game until the adjournment, and then there would be a lengthy resumption. However, all the problems were resolved surprisingly easily.

51 ♔f2 ♖d7 52 ♔e2 ♖d5 53 ♖a4! (53 ♖d2 ♖c5! – Timman) **53...c5 54 ♖f4 ♗e8** (54...♖d3 55 ♖f3) **55 ♔e3 ♖d1 56 ♖e4 ♗b5**

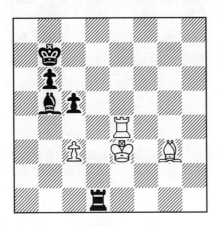

57 c4! (an important defensive resource: it is difficult for Black to exploit the weakness of this pawn) **57...♗d7?!**

After 57...♗a4! 58 ♔e2 ♖d7, intending ...♗b3 and ...♔a6-a5-b4, it was still possible for Timman, if not to win, then at least to torment White.

58 ♔e2 (the king breaks across to the queenside) **58...♖g1 59 ♖e7! ♖xg3**

Apparently my opponent imagined that there might be chances of success in the rook endgame. True, little was also promised by 59...♔c6 60 ♖g7 or 59...♔c8!? 60 ♗f4! (but not 60 ♖g7?! ♗e6!).

60 ♖xd7+ ♔a6 61 ♔d2 ♔a5 62 ♖d6 ½-½

Draw: there is no way for Black to improve his position.

Raymond Keene, who had arrived from London, declared: *'What a game! Sacrifices and counter-sacrifices. The spectators were staggered'*. Both players were left unhappy with the outcome: each, not without justification, thought that he had missed good winning chances.

In the 5th game, after choosing the Exchange Variation of the Spanish, Timman obtained somewhat the better endgame and he methodically built up his initiative. To maintain the balance, I gave up the exchange for a pawn and with difficulty gained a draw on the 35th move.

The score became 3-2, and to win the match it was sufficient for me to draw the 6th, concluding game. Ideally I should have played solidly, but everyone was expecting a grand battle – not without reason were there 3,000 spectators at the match that day! And the game turned out to be very sharp and entertaining, abounding in mutual blows.

Game 11
G.Kasparov-J.Timman
Training Match
6th Game, Hilversum 22.12.1985
Queen's Indian Defence E13

---

1 d4 ♘f6 2 c4 e6 3 ♘f3 b6 4 ♘c3 ♗b4 5 ♗g5 ♗b7 6 e3 h6 7 ♗h4 g5 8 ♗g3 ♘e4 9 ♕c2 (9 ♘d2 – *Game No.9*) **9...♗xc3+ 10 bxc3 d6 11 ♗d3 f5 12 d5 ♘c5 13 h4 g4?! 14**

♘d4 ♕f6 15 0-0 ♘xd3?!

A novelty (instead of 15...♘ba6 – *Game No.10*), but Adorjan and I had prepared for it. **16 ♕xd3 e5 17 ♘xf5** (of course, not 17 ♘b5? ♘a6) **17...♗c8**

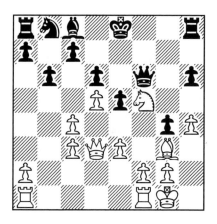

At this point Timman looked very content. After sacrificing a pawn, Black eliminates the errant knight and would appear to obtain a comfortable game: for example, 18 e4?! ♗xf5 19 f4 (19 exf5 ♘d7! Miles-Timman, Cologne 1986) 19...gxf3! 20 ♖xf3 ♘d7 21 ♖xf5 ♕g7 and ...0-0-0. But all is not so simple...

18 ♘d4?!

'A piece sacrifice with the aim of improving the pawn structure!' (Razuvaev). Alas, this pretty idea contained a flaw. It is a pity that a 'simple' transposition of moves did not occur to me – 18 f4!! ♕xf5 (18...♗xf5 19 e4 or 18...gxf3 19 ♖xf3 is no better) 19 e4 and fxe5 with crushing threats: Black is a piece up, but he does not manage to get developed (Miles-Beliavsky, Tilburg 1986).

18...exd4 19 cxd4

I thought that White had excellent compensation for the piece in the form of his mobile pawn mass, but in fact the position is completely unclear.

19...♕f5?

Confusion: the queen voluntarily moves

to where it can be attacked, and White's idea proves fully justified. 19...♘d7?! was also not altogether accurate on account of 20 f4! followed by e3-e4.

The correct reply was 19...0-0!, since now if 20 f4(?!) there is the undermining move 20...c6!. And also after 20 f3 ♕g7 Black has no reason for complaint: 21 ♔h2?! ♘d7 22 e4 ♘f6 23 f4 (Gligoric-Popovic, Budva 1986) 23...♘h5!, or 21 fxg4 and now not 21...♖xf1+ 22 ♖xf1 ♗xg4 (Gligoric) because of 23 c5!, but simply 21...♘d7!. 20 e4 is preferable, but then after 20...♕g6 Black has an extra tempo compared with the game.

20 e4 ♕g6

'For the moment the advance of the dangerous pawn mass is halted, but for how long?' (Razuvaev).

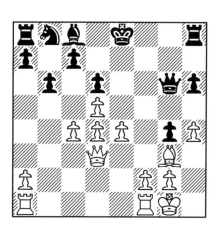

21 ♕c3 (21 ♕a3 was also not bad, but on c3 the queen is more solidly placed) **21...0-0 22 ♖fe1**

A useful preparatory move. 22 e5 at once would have allowed the freeing 22...dxe5 23 dxe5 ♗f5! 24 e6 ♘a6 and ...♘c5.

22...♘d7

In the event of 22...♘a6 23 e5 dxe5 (with the idea of 24 dxe5 ♗f5!) there is the good reply 24 ♖xe5! ♗f5 25 ♖ae1 ♖ae8 26 c5, exploiting the remote position of the knight on a6.

23 e5

A critical position, in which I rated my chances very optimistically, in view of my powerful centre and the weak defences of the black king.

23...♗b7?! (an unfortunate idea – 23...♗a6 was better) **24 ♖e3?!**

With the obvious intention of ♖ae1, but after 24 exd6! cxd6 25 ♖e7 Black would immediately have encountered problems.

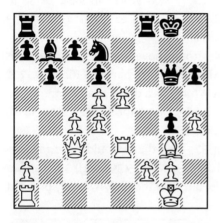

24...b5?

In my view, Timman underestimated White's threats. The undermining of the pawn centre, planned with 23...♗b7, creates fatal weaknesses in Black's own position. Razuvaev preferred 24...♖f5(?!) 25 ♖ae1 ♘f8, but after 26 exd6 cxd6 27 ♕a3 White has very unpleasant pressure. Apparently the best move was the patient 24...♖ae8(c8).

25 ♕a5! (the attack changes direction!) **25...♘b6** (25...dxe5? 26 ♕xc7) **26 ♕xb5 ♕c2**

Black was relying on this thrust, but it leads to disaster. However, what should he play instead? There is the impending breakthrough c4-c5. If 26...♖ad8(e8), then for the moment 27 ♖ae1!. If 26...♗c8, then 27 e6! is strong, or if 26...dxe5 – 27 ♖xe5!. And even the cleverest defence – 26...♖ac8!? (with the idea of 27 ♖ae1?! c6!) would have left Black with few saving chances after 27 exd6 cxd6

28 ♖e7! ♖f7 29 ♖ae1 ♕f5 30 ♖1e4 ♖xe7 31 ♖xe7 ♗a8 32 ♖xa7 ♘xc4 33 ♖xa8 ♖xa8 34 ♕xc4.

27 exd6 cxd6

It turns out that the alternatives are bad: 27...♕xc4? 28 ♕b1! (an unexpected retreat: Black perishes on 'his own' light squares!) 28...♖f7 29 ♕g6+ (not my *Informator* suggestion 29 ♖e7(?) because of 29...♕xd4!) 29...♖g7 30 ♖e8+ ♖xe8 31 ♕xe8+ ♔h7 32 ♕e4+ ♔g8 33 ♕e6+ ♔h7 34 ♕f5+ ♔g8 35 ♖e1 with a mating attack, or 27...♘xc4 28 ♕xb7 ♘xe3 29 dxc7! ♘f5 (Razuvaev) 30 ♔h2! ♕e4 31 ♖b1 or 30...♘xg3 31 fxg3, and the passed pawns are irresistible.

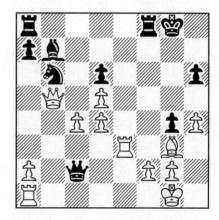

28 ♖e7

28 ♖ae1!? also came into consideration (after 28...♘xc4 29 ♖3e2 the bishop on b7 is lost), as did 28 c5!? and now 28...♕c4 29 ♕b1! ♕xd5 30 ♕g6+ ♔h8 31 ♕xh6+ ♔g8 32 ♕g6+ ♔h8 33 ♗e5+! (in my old analysis I did not see this move, and I thought that White had only perpetual check) 33...dxe5 34 ♕h5+ ♔g8 35 ♕xg4+ ♔h7 36 ♕h5+ ♔g7 37 ♖g3+ ♔f6 38 dxe5+ ♔e7 39 cxb6 with a mass of pawns for the piece plus an attack, or 28...dxc5 29 dxc5 ♘c4 (29...♘xd5 30 ♖e2!) 30 c6 ♗xc6 31 dxc6 ♘xe3 32 fxe3, and Black cannot hold out. However, the move in the game is also good.

28...♖f7

The attempt 28...♗c8 29 ♕c6 ♗f5 (29...♕g6 30 c5!) did not work on account of 30 ♕xd6! ♘c8 31 ♕xh6 ♘xe7 32 ♗e5 ♔f7 33 d6 and wins.

29 ♖xf7 (29 ♖ae1!? was an alternative, with the idea of 29...♕xc4? 30 ♕b1! or 29...♖af8 30 ♖xf7 ♖xf7 31 ♖e6) **29...♔xf7 30 c5**

30 ♖e1!? ♕d3 31 ♗xd6 ♗xd5 32 a4 (32...♕xc4 33 ♕b1!) would also have been decisive, but in the fifth hour of play the idea of 30 c5 attracted me by its comparative simplicity.

30...♕c4

After 30...♗xd5, apart from the normal human continuation 31 cxb6 ♕e4 32 ♕f1 axb6 33 ♖e1! ♕xd4 34 ♕b5 or 32...♗c6 33 d5! ♕xd5 34 ♖d1 ♕e4 35 f3! gxf3 36 gxf3 ♕e3+ 37 ♔h2 with a winning attack, there is the murderous computer move 31 ♖e1!.

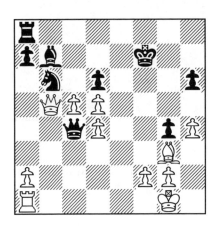

31 ♕b1!

The decisive stroke. 'White's entire play is based on this tempo!' (Razuvaev).

31...♕xd5

At last Black has created a threat – mate by ...♕xg2, but with checks White picks up the g4-pawn and defends against the mate. If 31...♔g7 there is a win by both 32 h5 ♕xd5 33 ♕g6+ ♔h8 34 ♕xh6+ ♔g8 35 ♕g6+ ♔h8 36 ♕f6+ ♔g8 37 f3, and 32 c6

♗a6 33 h5 ♕d3 34 ♕b4 ♖d8 35 c7 ♖d7 36 ♗xd6 etc.

32 ♕h7+ ♔f6 33 ♕xh6+ ♔f7

Here I got the feeling that Timman was hoping for a draw by perpetual check, which would give me victory in the match. For an instant the position still seemed not altogether clear, but... only for an instant.

34 ♕f4+ ♔g8 (34...♔e8 35 ♖e1+) **35 ♕xg4+ ♔h7**

35...♔f7 was worse in view of 36 ♗xd6 ♖g8 (36...♘c4 37 ♖e1) 37 ♕f4+ and f2-f3.

36 ♗f4!

A strong move, which gave me pleasure. All the threats are parried (36...♖g8 37 ♗g5), and White has a decisive advantage.

36...♗c8 37 ♕g3 (or 37 ♕e2 ♗b7 38 ♕d3+) **37...dxc5**

If 37...♘c4 there would have followed 38 h5! ♗f5 (38...♕xh5 39 ♖e1!) 39 ♕g5 ♖e8 40 cxd6, but now the rook is simply brought up.

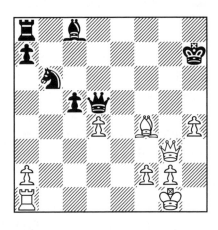

38 ♖e1! ♕f7 39 ♕g5 ♘d5 (defending against ♖e7, but the attack again changes direction) **40 ♕h6+ ♔g8 41 ♖e5 1-0**

My favourite construction has been achieved: all my pieces are in the attack, while nearly all the opponent's army is stuck on the opposite wing and is unable to help its king. 'A brilliant finale to a brilliant match!' (Razuvaev).

This spectacular win in the last game gave me victory by the convincing score 4-2. A worthy debut by the young world champion! That same evening the closing ceremony took place, and at night I urgently annotated the 1st game for the *New in Chess* magazine.

The next morning, 23rd December, at a two-hour press conference in Amsterdam, I spoke out openly against the staging of the return match which was being imposed on me, and was being planned by FIDE – an unprecedented occurrence! – for between 10th February and 21st April 1986. The arguments regarding this raged for a whole month. I was supported by the recently founded European Chess Union and by grandmasters Timman, Larsen, Najdorf, Ljubojevic, Seirawan and Short (who declared that 'the world championship cycle stinks'). But my opponents firmly stood their ground, again threatening me with disqualification, and on 22nd January Karpov and I reached a compromise to play this match no earlier than the end of the summer.

Immediately after the Amsterdam press conference I flew to Hamburg and the same day I gave an eight-board simultaneous display with clocks – against a professional team of the West German Bundesliga! The score was 3½-4½ (more details of this and other unusual displays will be given in the next volume). The next day I celebrated the Catholic Christmas as a guest of a new friend, the Hamburg journalist and computer expert Frederic Friedel (we met during my match with Hübner), and then I also gave a simul' in Munich...

In the spring of 1986 active preparations for the return match began. Nikitin: *'Beginning in March, for three months and with only small breaks, the training base in Zagulba became the home for our team.'* At the same time, despite all the anxiety and being so busy, with the help of Trades Union officials I resurrected the Botvinnik school, in which at one time I had begun my way into top-class chess. Now it became known as the 'Botvinnik-Kasparov school', and in April 1986, in Petsov on the outskirts of Moscow, Mikhail Moiseevich and I held its first session, in which 13 young talents from the far corners of the country took part.

Prior to a battle for the world title I was not eager to play in tournaments, and I followed my usual mode of preparation: why change a successful habit? In the middle of May I flew to Basel in Switzerland, where I played another six-game training match, already the fourth that year, with one of the top western grandmasters – this time the 31-year-old Englishman Tony Miles.

Razuvaev: *'The choice was not accidental and it did not surprise the chess world: Miles was the leader of a powerful new wave, which had made England a chess power after an interval of nearly a century. Like many young people of the 1960s and 70s, he was sympathetic to the 'hippy' movement. Eccentricity became his style both in life, and in chess* (thus at the 1980 European Team Championship he inflicted a sensational defeat on Karpov, after replying to 1 e4 with the audacious 1...a6?! – G.K.). *Tony plays sharply, powerfully, forcefully and without prejudice, with something of a disregard for analytical principles and chess convention. Everything is absolutely concrete – this is his creative credo. Journalists have given him the nickname 'street-fighter', and Miles greatly values his status, missing no opportunity to support the fame of chess nihilism. In September 1985, on the advice of a doctor, he exchanged his chair at the chess table for a special couch, and from a prone position he won the super-tournament in Tilburg'.* More precisely, in 1985 Miles shared 1st-3rd places with Korchnoi and Hübner, but in 1984 in Tilburg he had taken 1st place on his own.

Again I played a training match almost 'at sight', relying merely on the solid preparation for my battles with Karpov. I was again helped by Andras Adorjan. In the 1st game Miles drew the black pieces, and he endeavoured to avoid a theoretical duel.

Game 12
G.Kasparov-A.Miles
Training Match
1st Game, Basel 15.05.1986
Czech Benoni A56

1 d4 ♘f6 2 c4 c5

A surprise, although Miles often employed 'quirky' openings. Here I thought: now it will be a Benko Gambit...

3 d5 e5

No, a set-up known as the Czech Benoni. This suited me: I loved to seize space, and back in my youth I played a mass of training games on this theme with Nikitin. If the opponent wanted to neutralise my preparation and create a position that was unfamiliar to me, this was not the best decision.

4 ♘c3 d6 5 e4 ♗e7 6 ♘f3 0-0 7 h3! ♘bd7 8 g4

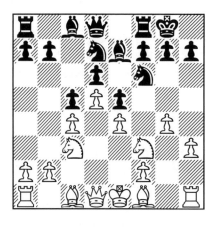

Setting up a typical bind. Razuvaev: 'With the centre closed, White begins a flank attack. This method of play became popular after Spassky's games with Ghitescu (Beverwijk 1967) and Petrosian (9th match game, Moscow 1969).'

8...♘e8

White is also slightly better in the event of 8...a6 9 a4 ♖b8 10 ♗d3 ♖e8 11 ♖g1 ♘f8 12 g5 ♘6d7 (12...♘h5 13 ♘xe5!) 13 h4 ♘g6 14 ♘e2 ♗f8 15 ♕c2 (Christiansen-Miles, New York 1987).

9 ♗d3 a6

With the knight on e8, 9...g6 is logical, although after 10 ♗h6 ♘g7 11 ♕d2 or 10 ♗e3 ♘g7 11 ♖g1 ♘f6 12 ♕e2 (Ivanchuk-Seirawan, Reykjavik 1990) all the same White has more space.

10 a4

Continuing to play for a bind. 10 ♕e2 is also played, not weakening the queenside in anticipation of 0-0-0.

10...♖b8

Here too the traditional 10...g6 is more appropriate, but Miles has altogether decided to avoid playing ...g7-g6 and ...♘g7, and instead is intending to transfer his e8-knight to support ...b7-b5.

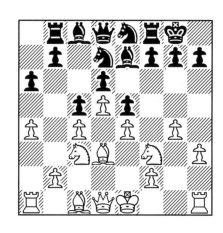

11 ♖g1! ♘c7 12 b3

12 a5!? came into consideration, with the

idea of 12...b5 13 axb6 ♖xb6 14 b3 and ♗c2, killing Black's counterplay on the b-file and retaining good prospects of an attack on the kingside. However, I had a more double-edged plan.

12...♖e8 13 h4!? b5!

Black avoids blundering a piece (13...♗xh4? 14 g5) and he does not wish to conduct a tedious defence after 13...♘f8 14 h5 and g4-g5, or 13...h6 14 h5! ♘f6 (14...f6 15 a5 and ♘h4) 15 g5 ♘xh5 (15...hxg5 16 ♘xg5) 16 gxh6 g6 17 ♘xe5 ♗f6 18 ♕xh5 ♗xe5 19 ♗d2 b5 20 ♖b1 etc.

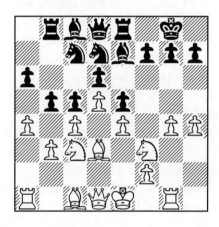

14 g5!?

Not responding to Black's actions! Miles was counting on 14 cxb5 axb5 15 axb5 (15 ♘xb5 allows the freeing 15...♘xd5! 16 exd5 e4 17 ♗xe4 ♗f6 18 ♘xd6 ♗xa1 19 ♔f1 ♘f6! 20 ♘xe8 ♘xe4 21 ♗f4 ♖b4 or 21...♘c3) 15...♘f8 16 h5 ♗d7 17 ♕e2 ♕c8 18 ♘d2 ♕b7 19 g5 ♘xb5 with counterplay against the b3-pawn. But my unexpected reply confused him.

14...♘f8?!

A passive reply in anticipation of cxb5, but White avoids this. 14...bxc4! was correct: 15 ♗xc4 f5 16 ♗d3 (16 exf5 e4! 17 ♘xe4 ♘b6 or 16 gxf6 ♘xf6 17 ♘g5 ♗f8 is no better) 16...fxe4 17 ♗xe4 ♖b4, or 15 bxc4 a5 16 h5 ♘a6 17 ♘b5 ♘b4 with complicated play.

15 h5 ♗d7 (15...bxc4!? 16 ♗xc4 ♘d7) **16 ♘h2** (16 ♘h4!?) **16...bxc4**

Alas, with a delay. However, 16...b4 17 ♘e2 or 16...bxa4 17 ♘xa4 a5 18 ♗c2 also gave no joy.

17 ♗xc4!

This is the whole point: now, when the black knight has gone to f8 and the ...♘d7-b6 manoeuvre has become more difficult, the capture with the bishop promises more than 17 bxc4 ♖b4.

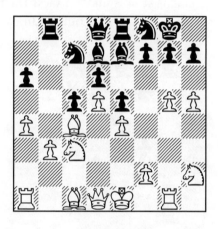

17...f5 (a risky undertaking, but what else was there to do?) **18 exf5 ♗xf5 19 ♘f1?!**

'The white knight heads for an excellent post in the centre' (Razuvaev), although 19 ♘g4 or 19 ♕f3 and ♘g4 was more energetic.

19...♕d7?! (the bishop should have been preserved from exchange – 19...♗c8) **20 ♘e3** (now ♕f3 is threatened) **20...e4 21 ♗b2** (even better than 21 ♘xf5 ♕xf5 22 ♕g4, transposing into a favourable ending) **21...♗d8 22 ♘e2?!**

22 ♕c2! ♕f7 23 0-0-0 ♘d7 24 f4!, depriving Black of his last hopes of counterplay, would have led to a strategically won position. But I decided 'simply' to bring up my knight to the main battlefield.

22...♕f7 23 ♘f4

What tells, apparently, is the anxiety typical of the first game. An advantage would still have been retained by 23 ♘g3 ♗d7 24 ♕d2, although after 24...♕f3! (preventing queenside castling) 25 ♗e2 ♕f4! with the threat of ...♗xg5 (25...♕f7?! 26 ♖a3! is less good) nothing terrible for Black is apparent – thus after 26 ♗xg7?! ♔xg7 27 ♘ef5+ ♕xf5 28 ♘xf5+ ♗xf5 29 ♕c3+ ♖e5 the white queen and pawn are hardly any stronger than the three minor pieces.

23...♗c8

The knight at f4 is under attack! The rest took place in an escalating time scramble.

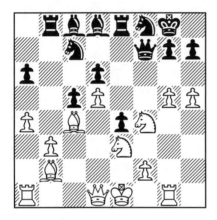

24 ♖g4!?

This spectacular move stunned Miles. 'In recent times Kasparov has begun often employing Petrosian's favourite weapon – the positional exchange sacrifice.' (Razuvaev). Double-edged play would have resulted from 24 g6 ♕xf4 25 gxh7+ ♔h8! 26 h6 ♕xh6 27 ♗xg7+ ♕xg7 28 ♖xg7 ♔xg7 or 26 ♖xg7 ♗f6 (to my *Informator* suggestion 26...♖e5 27 ♗xe5 dxe5 there is the good reply 28 ♖g3) 27 ♖f7 ♘xh7 28 ♗xf6+ ♘xf6 29 ♖xc7 ♕(♖)e5.

24...♕e7?

In the event of 24...♗xg4? 25 ♕xg4 none of the following lines will do: 25...♘d7 26 g6, 25...g6 26 hxg6 hxg6 (26...♘xg6? 27 ♘f5) 27 0-0-0, or 25...♕e7 26 ♘e6 ♘fxe6 27 dxe6 d5

(27...♘xe6 28 g6) 28 ♘xd5 ♘xd5 29 ♗xd5 c4 30 ♗f6! or 26 ♘h3!? ♕d7 27 ♘f5 ♖e7 28 g6 and wins.

Only the computer move 24...g6! (for a human it is hard to decide on such a weakening of the long diagonal) offered a defence: 25 hxg6 ♘xg6! 26 ♘h5 ♘e5 27 ♗xe5 ♖xe5 28 ♖f4 ♕g6 29 ♘f6+ ♔g7, and White has only perpetual check (30 ♘h5+ etc.), or 25 ♕d2!? gxh5 26 ♘e6 ♘cxe6 27 dxe6 ♗xe6 28 ♕c3 ♗a5! 29 ♕xa5 ♗xc4 30 ♕c3 ♘g6 31 ♖f4! ♖xb3! 32 ♖xf7 ♖xc3 33 ♖g7+ ♔xg7 34 ♗xc3+ ♔g8 35 ♘xc4 d5 with sufficient compensation for the piece.

25 ♖g3! ♕f7 26 ♘fg2! ♘a8

Again it is hard to offer Black any good advice. Thus 26...g6 is fatal in view of 27 hxg6 hxg6 28 ♕d2 or 27...♘xg6 28 ♕h5 and 0-0-0.

27 a5?

An impulsive time-trouble move. After 27 ♗e2!, with the threat of g5-g6, White would have retained a big advantage.

27...♘c7 (the knight has acquired the loophole b5-d4) **28 ♘h4 ♘b5**

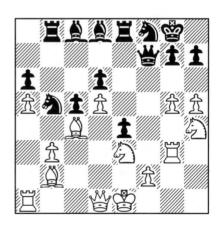

29 g6

The activated knight should have been exchanged – 29 ♗xb5! ♖xb5 30 ♘c4 (30 ♔f1 c4!), after which 30...e3! is acceptable: 31 fxe3 ♕f4 32 ♕f3 ♕xf3 33 ♘xf3 ♗c7 with a complicated endgame, or even 32...♕xh4 33 ♘xd6 ♖e7.

29...hxg6 30 ♘xg6?

Allowing the knight to go to d4. 30 hxg6?! ♕f4 was also unfavourable for White (31 ♘eg2 ♕h6 32 ♗c1 ♕h8!), but 30 ♗xb5! would still have maintained equality: 30...♖xb5 31 ♘xg6 ♗f6 32 ♕c2 or 30...♗xh4 31 hxg6 ♘xg6 32 ♗xe8 ♕xe8 33 ♖g2 ♗h3 (33...♘e5 34 ♖a4) 34 ♖h2 ♘f4 35 ♖xh3! etc.

30...♗f6?

An answering error in time-trouble. After 30...♘d4! the picture would have changed. 31 ♔f1(?), given by me in *Informator*, is bad because of 31...♘xg6 32 hxg6 ♕f4 33 ♕h5 ♕h4 and wins. And after 31 ♗xd4 cxd4 32 ♕xd4 ♗f6 33 ♕d1 ♗c3+ 34 ♔e2 Black could have won the exchange for a pawn or retained his powerful dark-square bishop and an unpleasant initiative.

31 ♗xb5! (finally it dawned on me) **31...♖xb5** (31...♗xb2? 32 ♗xe8) **32 ♕c2 ♗xb2?** (after 32...c4! 33 ♘xc4 ♖xd5 Black would have been okay) **33 ♕xb2 ♘xg6**

The assessment of the position has again swung in White's favour. 33...c4 was too late in view of 34 ♘xc4 e3 (34...♖xd5 35 ♘f4!) 35 fxe3 ♘xg6 36 hxg6 ♕xd5 37 ♕h2 ♕h5 38 ♕xh5 ♖xh5 39 0-0-0!.

34 ♖xg6 ♖e5

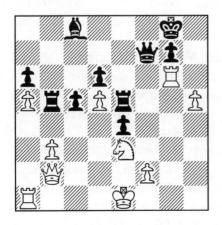

35 0-0-0!

'It is not often that you see castling on the 35th move!' (Razuvaev). In an instant White evacuates his king from the centre and includes his queen's rook in the attack. I think that in the fourth hour of play Miles simply forgot that this move was possible.

35...♖xh5 (35...♔h7 36 ♖dg1 was no better) **36 ♖dg1 ♖h7**

36...♖b7 37 ♖xg7+! (37 ♖xd6!?) 37...♕xg7 38 ♖xg7+ ♔xg7 39 ♕f6 ♖h2 40 ♔b2 ♗d7 41 ♔a3 followed by ♕xd6 was also hopeless for Black.

37 ♘c4 (37 ♖xd6!? ♕f8 38 ♖f6 ♕d8 39 d6 would have won more simply) **37...♕f4+ 38 ♔b1 ♖b7 39 ♘xd6?!** (this move suggests itself, but 39 ♖xd6 ♗f7 40 ♔a1! was correct) **39...♗f5!**

A brilliant defensive resource – a desperate and pretty attempt in time-trouble.

40 ♖f6

Also after 40 ♘xb7 ♗xg6 41 ♖xg6 e3 42 ♖g1 ♕e4+ 43 ♔a2 ♕xd5 44 fxe3 ♕xb7 45 ♕e5 ♕f7 46 ♖g5 ♖h1 Black could have fought for a draw.

40...♕h2?

With his last move before the time control Miles misses the only saving continuation 40...e3+! 41 ♘xf5 exf2 when 42 ♖xg7+! ♖hxg7 43 ♘e7+ ♖bxe7 44 ♖xf4 ♖e1+! 45

♔a2 f1♕ 46 ♖xf1 ♖xf1 would have led to an endgame with queen against two rooks, with an extra passed pawn for White. My *Informator* moves 47 ♕c2(e5) are inaccurate in view of 47...♖gg1!, but also 47 d6 ♔f8 with the same idea of ...♖gg1 would have left Black with real saving chances.

41 ♖g3 (now it is all over) **41...♕h1+ 42 ♔a2 1-0**

A grand battle, despite the numerous mistakes. However, it was not this game that was Miles's undoing, but the 2nd. In it he gained an advantage from the opening (a mixture of the Grünfeld and the Slav), and for a long time he persistently played for a win, but after the first time control, by then in an equal position, he overstepped the mark and again lost.

Whereas in the first two games there was a roughly equal battle, in the 3rd, after employing a highly unusual defence (1 d4 ♘f6 2 ♘f3 c5 3 d5 b5 4 ♗g5 ♘e4) and obtaining an acceptable position, Miles lost very quickly. In the 4th game with White, to avoid the worst, he made a quick draw. But in the 5th, where at the board I devised a novelty in the Botvinnik Variation, Miles resigned as early as the 28th move, and in the 6th he was unable to refute my defective novelty in the Meran (15...♔f6?!), making a serious mistake on the 18th move and resigning on the 30th.

After the last game Miles thanked me for the lesson, and in an interview he lamented: *'I thought I would be playing the world champion, not a monster with a hundred eyes!'* Yes, the win of the match by 5½-½ (of course, not without some good fortune) created a furore, and resembled the times of Fischer.

In Basel another noteworthy event occurred. The young founders of ChessBase, Frederic Friedel (the driving force behind the project) and Matthias Wüllenweber (an expert programmer), demonstrated the very first version of a chess database, created for the Atari ST computer. This program greatly appealed to me, and from 1987 I began using it, foreseeing that soon it would conquer the entire chess world.

Then in Frankfurt I gave a clock simul' against the West German junior team (6½-1½), in Barcelona I received my third chess 'Oscar' (for 1985), and then I dropped in at London to see how things were going with regard to the organisation of the first half of my return match with Karpov.

On returning to Baku, I immediately shut myself away in Zagulba and concentrated entirely on preparing for the main match. I was diverted only by the defence of my long-prepared diploma work (earlier, because of the unlimited match, I had been given academic leave of absence), and on 30th June 1986 I received the diploma after completing my course at the Azerbaijan Institute of Foreign Languages.

There was little time left, but my team of trainers worked most productively. Remembering the sad fate of Smyslov and Tal, and with Botvinnik's steely training behind me, I carried out an enormous amount of preparatory work and I sensed that I had reached a new level of chess understanding.

Third Match with Karpov

Return match for the world championship **Kasparov** – Karpov (London – Leningrad, 26 July – 9 October 1986): 12½-11½.

My third match with Karpov began with three draws. In the 4th game I gained my first win, of which I had every right to feel proud – unusual decisions in the middle-game and the confident conversion of an advantage in the endgame enabled a complete game to be produced.

Game 13
G.Kasparov-A.Karpov
World Championship Match
4th Game, London 04.08.1986
Nimzo-Indian Defence E20

1 d4 ♘f6 2 c4 e6 3 ♘c3 ♗b4 4 ♘f3

Once again, for the eighth time in our games, the Nimzo-Indian Defence occurred, and each time in reply to 4 ♘f3 Karpov chose a new variation. Such a persistent avoidance of a theoretical duel was something of a record in matches for the world championship. In this game my opponent finally employed a continuation which was soon to kill my desire to play 4 ♘f3 (and I would switch to 4 e3 or 4 ♕c2). However, during the course of the match the solidity of Black's defences was not yet obvious either to me or to Karpov.

4...c5 (4...♘e4 – *Game No.6*) **5 g3 cxd4**

For the first time Black chooses the main line of the variation, instead of 5...♘e4 (*Game No.3*), 5...♘c6 6 ♗g2 ♘e4 (*Game Nos.65, 69* in *Kasparov vs. Karpov 1975-1985*), or 6...d5!? (*Game No.2*). To judge by Karpov's determined appearance, there could be no doubt that here he had done some serious preparation.

6 ♘xd4 0-0 7 ♗g2 d5

As we will see, in the third match Karpov played completely differently compared with the second match, discarding the largely mythical idea of winning the white c-pawns (which possessed him during the entire second half of our previous match), in favour of free development.

8 ♕b3

At that time this continuation was full of fresh ideas. Two other moves – 8 0-0 dxc4 9 ♕a4 and 8 cxd5 ♘xd5 9 ♗d2 or 9 ♕b3 – were hardly analysed at all in our preparations.

8...♗xc3+ 9 bxc3

The critical move: White spoils his own pawn structure in the hope of exploiting dynamic factors, the pair of powerful bishops, and the threat of ♘b5. I took notice of 9 ♕xc3 e5 10 ♘b3 only in the late 1990s.

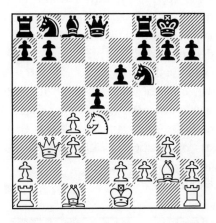

I will explain the story of how Black's next move came into being. Initially 9...e5 10 ♘b5 dxc4 was successfully played here, but then Georgian players introduced 11 ♕a3!, and after the game Georgadze-Polugayevsky (Moscow 1983), which went 11...♘c6 12 ♗e3! ♗e6 13 ♖d1 ♕b8 14 0-0 ♖d8 15 ♕c5 ♖xd1?! 16 ♖xd1 a6 17 ♘d6 ♘d7 18 ♕a3 ♕c7 19 ♕a4!, the evaluation of the variation changed in favour of White.

Black had to seek a new way – 9...dxc4, but here too 10 ♕a3! is possible. It was around this gambit idea that the main discussion developed. For the pawn White has sufficient compensation, and games played in 1983-86 confirmed this assessment. The character of the play appealed to me and could hardly satisfy Black.

Therefore in our preparations for the match we looked for other ways of defending.

Black's main problem is the development of his queenside pieces, and an attempt to solve it suggested to us the idea of exploiting the development of the queen at b3 by 9...♘c6! 10 cxd5 ♘a5!. But my opponent too was not idle, especially since one of his trainers, Ubilava, was the 'godfather' of the 8 ♕b3 variation.

9...♘c6!

Karpov made this move with lighting speed – apparently, with the aim of stunning me. Obviously, the searches for the strongest continuation for Black had proceeded in parallel...

10 cxd5 ♘a5!

The crux of Black's idea. 10...exd5 is weaker on account of 11 0-0! ♖e8 12 ♗g5 (and if 12...♘xd4 13 cxd4 ♖xe2, then 14 ♖fe1), or 11...h6 12 ♗f4 (Jobava-Sturua, Tbilisi 2001) with pressure.

11 ♕c2 ♘xd5

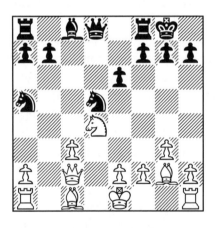

'With the c-file open and his pieces able to develop normally, the weak c3-pawn alone should be sufficient for Black to gain good counterplay', I wrote in *Revolution in the 70s*. Of course, we realised that this position looked very promising for Black, and yet we had found a possibility of fighting for the initiative.

12 ♕d3!?

After 12 0-0 Black has two good replies: 12...♗d7, and 12...♕c7!? 13 e4 ♘b6 (Barlov-Stone, New York 1988), when if 14 f4 there is 14...e5 15 fxe5 ♘ac4, or 13 ♖e1 ♗d7! 14 e4 ♘b6 15 e5 ♗a4 16 ♕d3 ♕c4 17 ♕f3 ♘c6 18 ♖e4 ♘xd4 19 ♖xd4 ♗c6 with equality (Nakamura-Kramnik, Dortmund 2011). It was this that gave rise to the unusual move 12 ♕d3, but a mistake had crept into our home analysis.

12...♗d7?

It is paradoxical, but true: this seemingly natural move, which in our preparations we considered to be best, turned out to be second-rate, and the genuinely best reply 12...♕c7!, which was subsequently recommended by the commentators, was not seriously examined by us! After briefly assessing 13 ♘b5 ♕c4? 14 ♕xc4 ♘xc4 15 ♗xd5 exd5 16 ♘c7, we did not return again to this line, but later it transpired that 13...♕c6! is far stronger, and if 14 ♗a3, then 14...♖d8 15 e4 a6 or 15...♘c4 with equality (Izeta-Smagin, Novi Sad 1986). Nothing is also given by 14 a4 a6! (Shchukin-Aseev, St. Petersburg 1998) or 14 0-0 ♗d7 15 a4 a6! 16 e4 axb5 17 exd5 ♕c4.

Soon in a game with Suba (Dubai Olympiad 1986) I again chose this variation, hoping that my opponent would not know the latest recommendations, but in fact he replied 12...♕c7!. I decided to avoid 13 ♘b5 ♕c6! and take a risk (how else could I play for a win?): 13 0-0 ♗d7 14 e4?! (14 ♗xd5 exd5 15 ♗f4 was more solid) 14...♘b6 15 f4, but after 15...e5 16 fxe5 ♘ac4 17 g4?! ♘xe5 18 ♕g3 ♘bc4 19 ♗f4 ♕c5 I ended up in an inferior position and gained a draw literally by a miracle.

This was a very important moment in the match. 12...♕c7, solving all Black's problems, was overlooked not only by me, but also by Karpov! We both considered the best move to be 12...♗d7, after which White retains the initiative. I was unaware of the improvement right up to the time when we moved to Leningrad, when an exchange of information occurred and one of the trainers said to me: 'In that line there is 12...♕c7 13 ♘b5 ♕c6!'. To all appearances, Karpov also did not immediately learn about this: right to the end of the London half of the match – in the 8th, 10th and 12th games – he avoided the Nimzo-Indian Defence, answering 1 d4 only with 1...d5.

Thus we proceeded along parallel analytical courses. Our 'dispute by correspondence' in this game concluded two moves later...

13 c4 (13 ♗a3?! is weaker in view of 13...♖e8) **13...♘e7**

Also after 13...♘b6!? 14 c5 ♘bc4 15 0-0! ♖c8 16 ♘b3 ♗c6 17 ♗xc6 ♖xc6 18 ♖d1 White would have had somewhat the better chances: for example, 18...♕xd3 19 exd3 ♖a6 20 ♖b1 ♘xb3 21 ♖xb3 ♘a5 22 ♖a3 ♘c6 23 ♖xa6 bxa6 24 ♗e3 etc.

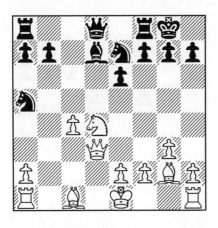

In our home analysis we had planned 14 ♗a3 here, in order after 14...♖c8 to play 15 ♖c1 'with advantage', but at the board I saw that 14...♖e8 15 0-0 ♘ec6! was far stronger – Black provokes favourable simplification (16 ♘f3 e5 17 ♕c3 ♗e6). Karpov was clearly aiming for this position! What was I to do?

After some thought, I devised a stronger move.

14 0-0!

For the present it is too early to bring out the bishop to the vulnerable a3-square – it may also be developed at g5 or e3, and it may also remain at c1.

From this moment on both players began acting spontaneously. And Karpov also sank into thought: Black has certain problems to solve.

14...♖c8?!

This first move of his 'own' is seemingly the most consistent (it attacks the c4-pawn), but it is not the best. If 14...♘ec6 both 15 ♘f3 e5 16 ♘g5 and 15 ♘b3 are unpleasant, since after 15...♘e5 16 ♕c3 ♘exc4 17 ♘xa5 ♖xa5 18 ♗b2 f6 19 ♖fd1 White has strong pressure for the pawn.

The best chance was 14...♗c6!? (Gufeld). It is psychologically not easy to present the opponent with two bishops against two knights – 15 ♘xc6 ♘exc6, but here the knights coordinate well, whereas it is hard for the white bishops to expand their influence (say, 16 ♗f4 ♕xd3 17 exd3 ♖fd8 18 ♖fd1 ♖d7 and ...♖ad8). Therefore in my preparations for the 8th game I was intending 15 ♗a3! ♗xg2 16 ♔xg2, retaining the initiative (16...♖c8 17 ♘b5!).

'Everywhere White is a little better' – this was the conclusion we arrived at in London, not yet being aware of 12...♕c7!, and we tirelessly analysed the position after 14 0-0. However, it was never to occur again...

15 ♘b3!

A very strong move, forcing the opponent to agree to the exchange of the weak c4-pawn for the pawn on b7. At the same time White not only rids himself of a chronic weakness, but also evicts the black knight from c4 with an unusual bishop manoeuvre.

15...♘xc4 16 ♗xb7 ♖c7

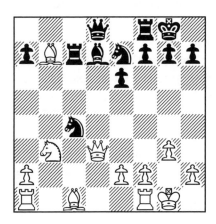

17 ♗a6!

The light-square bishop has fulfilled its mission on the long diagonal (17 ♗e4?! ♘g6 does not give anything real), and it changes direction. The knight at c4 is an outpost for Black, with which his hopes of counterplay are associated. From this point on, with every move White confronts his opponent with direct threats.

17...♘e5

The little tactical trick 17...♘g6 (with the idea of 18 ♗xc4 ♘e5) runs into a strong rejoinder – 18 f4!.

18 ♕e3

18 ♕d6 also came into consideration, although it is unclear whether White achieves anything after 18...♘7g6: for example, 19 ♗e3 ♗c8 20 ♕xd8 ♖xd8 21 ♗b5 ♘e7 with a slightly inferior, but perfectly tenable ending for Black.

18...♘c4?

A tempting, but in fact faulty move. The correct continuation was 18...f6! 19 ♗a3 ♗c8!, when White's advantage would have remained minimal: 20 ♖fd1 ♘d5 21 ♗xf8 ♕xf8 22 ♖xd5 exd5 23 ♗xc8 ♕xc8 24 ♕d2 ♖d7 etc.

19 ♕e4!

Not 19 ♗xc4 ♖xc4 20 ♕xa7 ♘d5 with adequate counterplay. Now, though, White

achieves his aims: he either drives the knight from c4, or forces the exchange of queens under very favourable circumstances.

19...♘d6

It is hard to say whether 19...♕a8 was any better: 20 ♕xa8 ♖xa8 21 ♗f4!? e5 22 ♗g5 f6 23 ♖fc1 fxg5 (23...♗e6? 24 ♗e3 leads to the loss of material) 24 ♖xc4 ♖xc4 25 ♗xc4+ ♔f8 26 ♘c5, also with a great advantage.

20 ♕d3!

The three-move dance has concluded to White's clear advantage: the queen has returned with honour to its chosen square, whereas the black knight is not destined to do the same. Apparently Karpov was hoping to solve his problems thanks to the symmetry of the pawn structure, but he is let down by his 'hanging' knights.

20...♖c6 (20...♗c8 21 ♗a3 ♗xa6 22 ♕xa6 was no better for Black) **21 ♗a3 ♗c8**

The attempt to exploit the 'errant' bishop on a6 does not succeed: 21...♕b6? 22 ♘d4! ♕xa6 23 ♘xc6 and wins.

22 ♗xc8 ♘dxc8

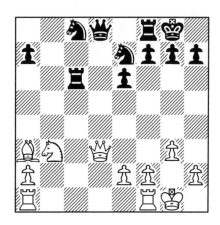

23 ♖fd1!?

A psychologically unpleasant move for Black – after the forced exchange of queens the rhythm of the play changes. 23 ♕f3 suggested itself, but after 23...♕b6 24 ♖fd1 ♖d8! for the moment no direct gain is evident. In the given specific instance it is with the queens off the board that the main drawback of Black's position becomes apparent – the insecure, poorly coordinated placing of his pieces. It is very important that White is able to gain complete control of the d-file.

23...♕xd3 24 ♖xd3 ♖e8

After 24...♖a6 25 ♘c5 ♖c6 26 ♖b1 ♖e8 27 ♖b7 or 24...♖c2 25 ♖d7 ♖e8 26 ♘d4 ♖c4 27 ♖c1 ♖xc1+ 28 ♗xc1 ♘d5 29 ♗d2, despite the pawn symmetry and the limited material, White has considerable winning chances.

25 ♖ad1

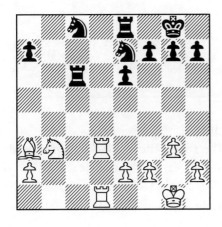

25...f6?

Again seemingly the most natural move (creating an escape square for the king), but it does not take into account the concrete nuances of the position. For ...e6-e5 Black lacks just one tempo, and he loses.

25...h6?! 26 ♖d8! was also bad for Black, but 25...g6 would have enabled him to avoid loss of material – 26 e4 ♖c2 27 ♖d8 ♖xd8 28 ♖xd8+ ♔g7 29 ♖e8 with the hope of exploiting the weakness of the dark squares: 29...♖c7 30 e5! ♖d7 31 ♘c5 ♖c7 32 ♘e4, or 29...f5!? 30 ♘d4 (30 ♗xe7 ♔f7! is unclear) 30...♖c4 31 ♘f3 fxe4 32 ♘g5, and although Black is far from lost, his position is very

dangerous. That is also the case after 25...♘d5!? 26 e4 ♘f6 (26...♘c3? 27 ♖d8) 27 ♘d4 (27 ♖d8!?) 27...♖c4 28 f3 ♘b6 29 ♘b5 ♖c2 30 ♖d8 h6 31 ♖xe8+ ♘xe8 32 ♖d8 ♖c8 33 ♖xc8 ♘xc8 34 e5 etc.

But here it would still have been possible to defend, whereas now the issue is decided unexpectedly quickly.

26 ♘d4! ♖b6

Or 26...♖a6 27 ♘b5. The sacrifice of the e-pawn by 26...♖c4 27 ♘xe6 ♘c6 28 ♘f4 was no worse than the game continuation, where the a-pawn was lost, but for the moment it is not clear why Black should give up material.

27 ♗c5

Suddenly it transpires that the rook has nowhere to go.

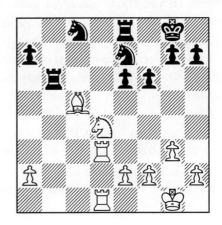

27...♖a6

It was hardly any better to play 27...♖b2 28 ♘xe6 ♘c6 (but not 28...♖xa2? 29 ♘c7 ♖f8 30 ♖e3 or 28...♖xe2 29 ♘c7 ♖f8 30 ♖d7 etc.) 29 ♘d8 ♘xd8 (29...♘e5 30 ♖3d2) 30 ♖xd8 ♖bxe2 31 a4 a5 32 ♖1d7, when the a5-pawn is doomed.

28 ♘b5! ♖c6

28...♖xa2? was bad in view of 29 ♘c7, but 28...♘d5 29 e4 ♖c6 30 ♗xa7 ♘db6 was somewhat more resilient.

29 ♗xe7!

Another non-routine decision, based on concrete calculation. Now Black loses a pawn in an unfavourable situation.

29...♘xe7 (29...♖xe7? 30 ♖d8+ ♔f7 31 ♖xc8) **30 ♖d7**

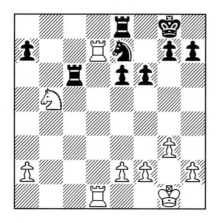

White creates the threat of 31 ♘d6 and occupies the 7th rank, retaining a positional advantage and winning material. The fate of the game is decided; with desperate resistance Black merely succeeds in postponing his defeat.

30...♘g6

If 30...♘c8, then 31 ♖c7 ♖b6 32 ♘xa7 is strong (32...♘d6 33 a4), as is the immediate 31 ♘xa7 ♖c2 32 ♖b1 ♖xa2 33 ♘xc8 ♖xc8 34 ♖bb7 with a won double-rook ending: 34...♔h8 35 ♖xg7 ♖xe2 36 ♖xh7+ ♔g8 37 h4 etc.

31 ♖xa7 ♘f8 32 a4 ♖b8 (temporarily preventing a4-a5) **33 e3 h5 34 ♔g2 e5** (or 34...♖c2 35 ♖d3!) **35 ♖d3!**

With the idea of ♖c3 (35 ♖d6 ♖c2 is less convincing). The exchange of a pair of rooks deprives Black of his last saving hopes.

35...♔h7

After 35...♘e6 there would have followed 36 ♖d6 ♖xd6 37 ♘xd6 – Black is unable both to defend his weakened kingside, and to prevent the advance of the a-pawn: 37...♖b2 38 a5 ♖a2 39 a6 ♔h7 40 ♖e7 ♘d8

41 ♖d7 ♘c6 42 ♘e8 ♖xa6 43 ♖xg7+ ♔h6 44 ♖f7.

36 ♖c3 ♖bc8 (forced) **37 ♖xc6 ♖xc6 38 ♘c7** (38 a5 ♘e6 39 h4 was also good) **38...♘e6 39 ♘d5**

White activates his pieces, at the same time creating tactical threats.

39...♔h6 40 a5 e4

Here the game was adjourned.

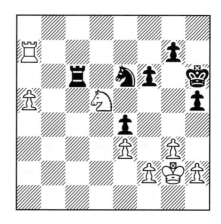

41 a6!

The sealed move. Black resigned without resuming **(1-0)**: 41...♖d6 (41...♘c5 42 ♖c7) 42 ♘e7 ♖d1 43 ♖a8 ♔h7 44 a7 ♖a1 45 ♘c6 ♘g5 46 ♖e8 and wins. Times: 2.39–2.29.

I consider that this game, conducted consistently and energetically by White from beginning to end, was one of the best that I played in my long-running duel with Karpov.

Alas, the scores were immediately levelled: in the 5th game, with a series of strong moves, my opponent refuted the audacious plan prepared by me, which was based on an analytical mistake. This opening disaster strengthened an unpleasant feeling, which first arose during the 4th game: that my opponent was following a parallel analytical course, as if he knew beforehand what variation I was intending to employ. I became nervous and was tormented by my doubts, since I trusted my trainers completely...

The psychological initiative in the match passed to Karpov, but after two fighting draws in the 6th and 7th games it again began to swing my way. The intensity of the struggle in these encounters was high, but even so it was nothing compared with what happened in the following game. One grandmaster said: *'The excitement of the time scramble gave me stomach cramp. It was a ferocious game, but in the complications Kasparov's nerves proved stronger.'*

Game 14
G.Kasparov-A.Karpov
World Championship Match
8th Game, London 15.08.1986
Queen's Gambit Declined D35

---

1 d4 d5

I wanted again to test the solidity of the Nimzo-Indian Defence, but from that day Karpov switched to his reserve opening (the improvement on the 4th game, 12...♕c7!, had not yet come within our field of view).

2 c4 e6 3 ♘c3 ♗e7

When it was necessary to hold out, the Queen's Gambit also served me faithfully, but by the irony of fate, the overall result was in favour of my opponent. By contrast, Karpov, who experienced greater problems with Black, had until this game successfully avoided defeat.

4 cxd5 exd5 5 ♗f4

A position from the previous game has been reached – the opening duel is continued with a change of colours! This occurred several times in our matches, but in the given instance the two players quickly avoided 'repeating the past' and events developed far more dynamically than before.

5...♘f6

'My' move from the previous match, instead of the approved 5...c6 6 e3 (*Game No.73* in *Kasparov vs. Karpov 1975-1985*) or 6 ♕c2 (7th game).

6 e3 0-0

In the words of Pushkin 'We all learned little by little...' In the 22nd game of the 1985 match Karpov had the white pieces here, but now he is ready to defend the same position with Black.

Ubilava's gambit line – 6...♗f5 (with the idea of 7 ♕b3 ♘c6 8 ♕xb7 ♘b4 9 ♗b5+ ♔f8) had not yet acquired its 'seal of approval'. Karpov was to employ it only in the 12th game of our next match, and after a quick draw it began to come into fashion. Although Timoshchenko and I were already looking at 6...♗f5 in 1986, our team focussed on 6...0-0. This move also attracted my opponent.

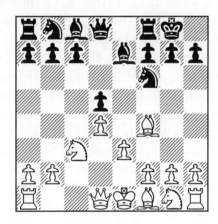

7 ♗d3

It is logical not to allow the development of the black bishop to f5. In the event of 7 ♘f3 c5?! 8 dxc5 ♗xc5 9 ♗e2 ♘c6 10 0-0 Black is left with an 'eternal' weakness at d5 (10...d4? 11 ♘a4), but after 7...♗f5! his position is quite acceptable, and it is unlikely that Karpov was concerned about the plan with 8 h3 and g2-g4, which he himself chose in the 22nd game of the previous match. In the 20th game he had prevented ....♗f5 by 6 ♕c2 0-0 7 e3, weakening his control over d4, which allowed the typical 7...c5! 8 dxc5 ♗xc5 9 ♘f3 ♘c6 10 ♗e2 d4 etc.

With 7 ♗d3 White has also weakened his control over d4, which the opponent immediately exploits by initiating play in the centre.

7...c5 (this was planned by me back in the 1985 match) **8 ♘f3**

It is advantageous for White to maintain the tension in the centre. After 8 dxc5 ♗xc5 he is unable to prevent the simplifying ...d5-d4, for example: 9 ♘f3 ♘c6 10 0-0 d4 11 ♘a4 ♗d6! 12 ♗xd6 ♕xd6 13 ♘xd4 (13 exd4 ♗g4) 13...♘xd4 14 exd4 ♗g4! or 13 ♘c3 ♗g4 14 ♘b5 ♕d7 15 ♘bxd4 ♘xd4 16 exd4 ♖ad8, regaining the pawn with full equality.

In our preparations we initially studied 8 ♘ge2!? ♘c6 9 0-0. Now after 9...cxd4 10 ♘xd4 ♘xd4 11 exd4 White has a small but enduring plus. Therefore we preferred 9...♗g4 (even after 8 ♘ge2) 10 dxc5 ♗xc5 11 h3 ♗xe2 12 ♘xe2 (12 ♕xe2 d4!) 12...♗d6, when after 13 ♕b3 (Wojtaszek-Fressinet, Wijk aan Zee 2011) Black has a slightly inferior but acceptable position, since it is difficult for White to prevent ...d5-d4.

We also analysed 8 ♘f3 ♘c6 9 0-0 c4 with the evaluation 'unclear', and 9...♗g4 10 dxc5 ♗xc5 11 h3 ♗xf3 12 ♕xf3 d4 13 ♘e4 ♘xe4 14 ♗xe4 dxe3, 'and Black is alright, since 15 ♕h5 after 15...exf2+ 16 ♔h1 f5 17 ♗xf5 g6 18 ♗xg6 hxg6 19 ♕xg6+ gives only perpetual check.' Our team analysis ended with this conclusion, and later Timoshchenko and I looked at these positions separately. In the last variation Gennady found a serious improvement for White, about which no one knew, apart from the two of us.

8...♘c6 (8...b6 is more passive: 9 ♘e5! ♗b7 10 ♕f3, Tal-Abramovic, Moscow 1982) **9 0-0**

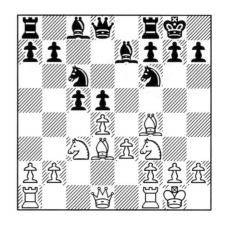

As has already been said, the exchanges 9...cxd4 10 ♘xd4 ♘xd4 (10...♗g4?! is weaker: 11 ♕a4 ♘xd4?! 12 ♕xd4! ♕d7 13 h3 ♗e6 14 ♖fd1 ♖fc8 15 ♗e5, Kasparov-Tal, Skelleftea 1989) 11 exd4 favour White: for example, 11...♗g4 12 ♕b3 or 11...♕b6 12 ♖e1 ♗e6 13 ♘a4 ♕a5 14 a3 and b2-b4 with unpleasant pressure.

9...♗g4?!

This move surprised me: in contrast to my opponent, I knew that it did not promise Black an easy life. 9...c4 is better, stabilising the situation in the centre and transferring the battle to the wings: 10 ♗c2 ♗g4! 11 h3 ♗h5 12 g4 ♗g6 13 ♘e5 ♗b4! with the idea of ...♗xc3, relieving the pressure on the d5-point (Vyzhmanavin-Timoshchenko, Irkutsk 1986), or 10 ♗b1 ♗g4 11 h3 ♗h5 12 g4 ♗g6 13 a3 ♗xb1 14 ♖xb1 ♕d7, also with unclear play.

10 dxc5 (a forced exchange; it is impossible to maintain the d4-point) **10...♗xc5**

Nothing is changed by 10...d4 11 ♘e4! ♘xe4 12 ♗xe4 ♗xc5 13 h3!, and since after 13...♗h5 14 ♖c1 ♗b6 15 g4 ♗g6 16 ♗xc6 bxc6 17 ♘xd4 White has an obvious advantage, there only remains 13...♗xf3 14 ♕xf3, transposing to the game.

11 h3! ♗xf3

Maintaining the pin by 11....♗h5 was not

possible: 12 g4! ♗g6 13 ♗xg6 hxg6 14 g5 with the win of a pawn – 14...♘h5(e4) 15 ♕xd5. The retreat 11...♗e6 would have led to a standard position with an isolani, where White has gained a tempo with h2-h3 (12 ♖c1! Janowski-Schlechter, Ostend 1905), but the move in the game gives White the advantage of the two bishops.

12 ♕xf3 d4

For the moment all in accordance with our analysis. After making this thematic advance, Black can normally regard the future with equanimity. It would appear that this is also the case here, especially since it is not apparent how White can gain any perceptible benefit from his two bishops. After 13 exd4?! ♘xd4 14 ♕xb7? ♘e6! the bishops come under attack, and one of them is lost. However, by exploiting tactical nuances associated with the presence of his light-squared bishop, White avoids simplification and retains the initiative.

13 ♘e4!

After this move Karpov sank into thought for the first time. I was very pleased to have gained such a promising position, and I was hoping to employ our home preparation.

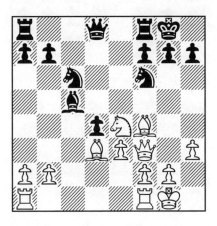

13...♗e7 (23)

The ex-world champion's sense of danger did not betray him – at the last moment he avoided the 'drawing possibility' 13...♘xe4 14 ♗xe4 (threatening ♗xh7+) 14...dxe3? (if 14...♕b6 15 ♖ac1, but the gambit line 14...♗b6!? 15 ♗xc6 bxc6 16 ♕xc6 ♖c8 is more resilient) 15 ♕h5 (later 15 fxe3!? was also successfully employed) 15...exf2+ 16 ♔h1 f5 17 ♗xf5 g6 (17...♖xf5 18 ♕xf5 is insufficient, since the f2-pawn inevitably falls) 18 ♗xg6! hxg6 19 ♕xg6+ ♔h8, for which he was unanimously – and unjustly! – criticised by the commentators.

In fact White does not give perpetual check, but includes his rook in the attack – 20 ♖ad1 (it was this that Timoshchenko discovered) 20...♕f6 21 ♕h5+ ♔g8 22 ♖d5 ♖f7 23 ♗g5 ♕h8 24 ♕xh8+ ♔xh8 25 ♖xc5 ♖e8 26 ♗d2 and g2-g4 with good winning chances, or, even stronger, 20 ♕h5+ ♔g8 21 ♕g4+! ♔h8 22 ♖ad1 ♕e7 (22...♕f6 23 ♖d5) 23 ♖d5! (but not 23 ♖d7? ♕xd7 24 ♕xd7 ♖xf4 25 ♕xb7 ♖e8 26 ♕xc6 ♖e1 with a draw) 23...♖f7 24 ♗g5 ♕f8 25 ♕h4+ ♔g8 26 ♗h6 ♗e7 27 ♕g3+ ♖g7 28 ♗xg7 ♕xg7 29 ♕b3 or 21...♔h7 22 ♖ad1 ♗d4 23 ♗e3 ♕f6 24 ♗xd4 ♘xd4 25 ♖xd4 ♖f7 26 ♕h5+ ♔g8 27 ♖g4+ ♖g7 28 ♕d5+, winning the f2-pawn and the game.

But now it was my turn to think: how should White continue, to avoid his initiative petering out? In the event of 14 exd4 ♕xd4 15 ♖ad1 ♖ad8 there is nothing real. White is slightly better after 14 ♘xf6+ ♗xf6 15 e4 ♘e5 16 ♗xe5 ♗xe5 17 ♕g4 (17 ♕e2 ♕g5!) 17...♕c8!? (17...♕e7 18 f4! Yakovich-Timoshchenko, Barnaul 1988) 18 f4 ♕xg4 19 hxg4, but this simplifies the game too much.

I wanted more: to concentrate my forces in the centre, quickly complete my development and switch to an attack on the kingside. With this aim a rook move to d1 suggests itself. And again there is the eternal dilemma – which rook to place on this square, the queen's or the king's? Reckoning that after 14 ♖ad1 White would create a powerful piece grouping, I decided to retain for my rook on f1 the prospect of coming into play on the kingside.

14 ♖ad1 (22)

If 14 ♖fd1, then 14...♕a5 would lose its point (the a2-pawn is not hanging), but 14...♕b6 would gain in strength, since now after 15 ♗d6(g5) Black equalises by 15...♘xe4! 16 ♗xe7 (16 ♕xe4 g6 17 ♗xe7 ♖fe8) 16...♘xf2!, while 15 ♘g3 g6 is unclear (but not 15...♖fe8?! 16 ♘f5! Milov-Toth, Liechtenstein 1996).

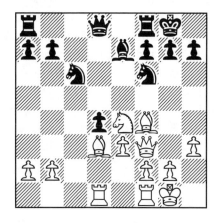

14...♕a5 (30)

The queen takes control of the fifth rank and, in addition, an attack on the queenside pawns forms the basis of Black's counterplay. Therefore 14...♕b6 also came into consideration, although after 15 ♗d6! ♘d5 (15...♘xe4?! 16 ♗xe7!) 16 ♘g5! ♘f6 (16...♗xg5? 17 ♗xf8 ♘xe3 loses to 18 ♗xg7! etc.) 17 ♗xe7 ♘xe7 18 ♘e4 Black remains under positional pressure.

15 ♘g3! (17)

An unusual and, at first sight, strange idea – White removes a piece from the centre. But he prepares an attack on the kingside, in which the rook at f1 will come in useful.

The 'obvious' 15 ♗g5 is parried by the

accurate 15...♘xe4! 16 ♕xe4 (16 ♗xe7?! ♘d2!) 16...g6 17 ♗xe7 ♖fe8 18 b4!? (18 ♕h4 ♖xe7 19 exd4 ♕b4! 20 ♗e4 ♖ae8 21 ♗xc6 bxc6 is equal) 18...♕c7! 19 b5 ♖xe7 20 ♕h4 dxe3!, with the idea of 21 bxc6 e2 (here the rook at f1 'comes in useful' to the opponent). However, White would have retained some advantage with 15 ♗c4!? ♘xe4 16 ♕xe4 ♗f6 17 exd4 ♖fe8 18 ♕f3 or 15...♖ad8 16 exd4 ♘xd4 17 ♘xf6+ ♗xf6 18 ♕xb7, and Black still has to think about how to regain the pawn.

Thus the variation from my old analysis employed by Karpov – 9...♗g4?! 10 dxc5 ♗xc5 11 h3 ♗xf3 turned out to be dangerous for Black (perhaps even more dubious than 11...♗e6). To avoid being 'burned alive', he had to display miracles of resourcefulness.

15...dxe3?!

15...♕xa2 16 ♘f5 ♕d5! is safer – after 17 ♕g3 (17 e4 ♕e6) 17...♘h5 18 ♕g4 g6 19 ♗h6 ♖fe8 20 ♗e4 ♕e6 21 ♗xc6 ♕xc6 22 ♘xe7+ ♖xe7 23 ♕xd4 White's pressure is still tolerable.

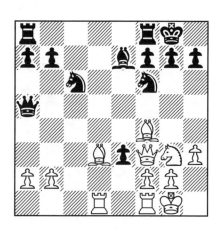

16 fxe3!

This cool-headed capture is more accurate than 16 ♘f5, although even here after 16...exf2+ 17 ♔h1! Black's defence is difficult: 17...♕xa2 18 ♗h6! or 17...♗c5 18

♘xg7!, while if 17...♖fe8 (Gutov-Rustemov, Moscow 1999), then simply 18 ♕xf2 with dangerous threats – 18...♘e5 19 ♗xe5 ♕xe5 20 ♖de1 ♕c7 21 ♖c1! etc. White is also better after 17...♖ad8! 18 ♗h6! ♘e8 (18...♖d5? 19 ♘xg7!) 19 ♕e4 ♖xd3 (19...♘f6 20 ♕h4!) 20 ♖xd3 ♗f6 21 ♗e3 or 18...♕e5!? 19 ♗xg7 ♘d4 20 ♘xd4 ♗d6 21 g3 ♔xg7 22 ♘f5+ ♔h8 23 ♖xf2.

16...♕xa2!

A highly practical decision and one typical of Karpov. It is not only a matter of the a2-pawn, but the choice by Black of the shortest path to e6, where the queen will cement the defence and control the strategically important e5-point. Neither 16...♔h8?! 17 ♘f5 nor 16...g6?! 17 ♗h6 ♖fe8? 18 ♘e4 was any good.

17 ♘f5 ♕e6 (5)

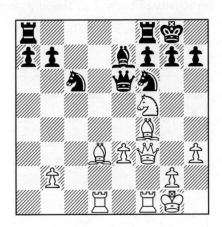

18 ♗h6! (17)

It was hard to refrain from such a spectacular move, beginning a direct attack on the king. Besides, it would be a pity for White to exchange his fine knight, which later might play one of the leading roles – 18 ♘xe7+?! ♘xe7 (18...♕xe7? 19 ♗d6!) 19 ♕xb7, especially since after 19...♘g6 his advantage evaporates.

18...♘e8

For the moment Black is not able to launch a counterattack: 18...♘e5? 19 ♕xb7 ♘xd3 20 ♘xe7+ ♔h8 21 ♗xg7+ ♔xg7 22 ♘f5+ ♔h8 23 ♖xd3 or 19...gxh6 20 ♕xe7, and White must win.

19 ♕h5! (6)

The danger approaches ever closer to the black king. 19 ♗e4 was much weaker on account of 19...gxh6 20 ♗xc6 bxc6 21 ♕xc6 ♘d6!.

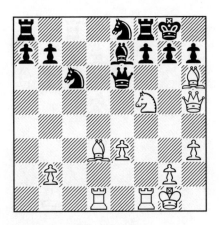

19...g6! (5)

The only sensible decision – Black sacrifices the exchange, but retains a defensible position. He would have lost ignominiously after 19...♘f6? 20 ♕h4! ♘d5 21 ♘xe7+ ♘dxe7 22 ♗xg7!.

20 ♕g4 (5) **20...♘e5!** (7)

'An excellent post for the knight! The position begins to stabilise: Black loses the exchange (the rook on f8 cannot leave its post), but the pawn plus two nimble knights will give him definite counterplay.' (Gufeld)

The knight move is necessary, since otherwise the white bishop switches to the a2-g8 diagonal with decisive effect: 20...♗f6? 21 ♗c4 ♘e5 22 ♗xe6! ♘xg4 23 ♘e7+! ♗xe7 24 ♗xf8, and 24...♘xe3 is not possible on account of 25 ♖xf7! with inevitable mate, or 20...♘d6?! 21 ♘xe7+ ♕xe7 22 ♕f4!, and if 22...♖fe8?! or 22...♘e5?! there is the murderous 23 ♗b1! and ♗a2, and therefore

Black has to give up the exchange – 22...♖fd8 23 ♗g5 etc.

Thus, in a desperate situation, when to many it appeared that Black's defences on the kingside would be quickly swept aside, Karpov displayed admirable tenacity in defence and with a series of brilliant moves succeeded in parrying the first wave of the attack.

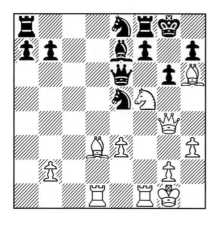

21 ♕g3?! (11)

White's striving at all costs to decide the game by a direct attack on the king diverts him from the correct path – 21 ♘xe7+ ♕xe7 22 ♗xf8 ♔xf8 23 ♕f4, winning the exchange and taking the game into a technical phase (say, 23...♔g7 24 ♗e4 ♘d6 25 ♗d5 ♖d8 26 ♕d4), although the conversion of the advantage is not easy. However, here it would have been easier for Black to take decisions...

21...♗f6! (17)

This cool-headed reply came at a high price to Karpov: he now had just 12 minutes left on his clock.

22 ♗b5?! (10)

After 22 ♗xf8 ♔xf8 23 ♘d4 ♕e7 24 ♗e4 ♘d6 25 ♗d5 Black has obvious compensation for the exchange – control over a complex of dark squares, centralised pieces, and weak pawns to target on e3 and b2. At the board I came to the conclusion that I had incorrectly assessed my possibilities on the previous move, when I assumed that the opposite-colour bishops would help the attack: the black bishop is too strong! Even so, White would still have had some advantage – even with the opposite-colour bishops he would have chances of converting the exchange after e3-e4, b2-b3 and ♘f3, with the exchange of one of the black knights (against Andersson in Moscow 1981 I tried for a long time to win a far less promising position).

After 22 ♗b5 the chances become objectively equal, but an already tense situation is sharply inflamed. It was important that by this point both players (especially Karpov) were seriously short of time. I realised that such tactics were risky, but I intuitively relied on the activity of my pieces. The initiative at any cost – this is the keynote of White's subsequent play!

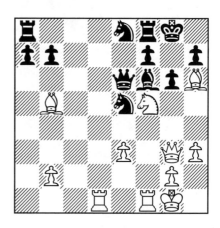

22...♘g7! (5) **23 ♗xg7** (23 ♘d4 ♕e7 would have signified the collapse of White's hopes) **23...♗xg7 24 ♖d6 ♕b3** (24...gxf5? 25 ♖xe6 fxe6 26 e4 was bad for Black) **25 ♘xg7 ♕xb5 26 ♘f5**

26 ♘h5 is parried by 26...♘f3+! 27 ♕xf3 ♕xh5 with an easy draw.

26...♖ad8

On this move Karpov used nearly all of his already little remaining time, leaving himself with just one minute for 14 (!) moves. It would seem that he was looking for winning chances – and could not find any. A draw would have resulted from 26...f6 27 ♘h6+ (27 ♘d4? ♕xb2) 27...♔g7 28 ♘f5+ ♔g8! (after 28...♔h8?! 29 ♘d4 White has a dangerous initiative).

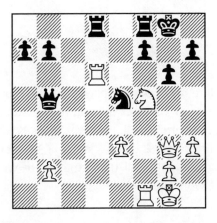

27 ♖f6 (8)

At this moment I was convinced that the conflict was not yet exhausted. The rook move, increasing the tension, was unpleasant for my opponent, who was in desperate time-trouble.

27...♖d2

Intuitively Karpov makes a speculative move, which in itself does not spoil anything – Black trains his fire on the second rank, hoping to create counterplay against the white king. But, in readjusting to playing for a win, Black wastes his last seconds of precious time. 27...♕xb2, 27...♖d7 28 h4! ♕xb2 and 27...♔h8!? (the safest) were all perfectly possible too.

28 ♕g5?!

The only moment in the game when White overstepped the mark. The surest way of maintaining the balance was 28 b4!, removing the pawn from attack and hindering the activation of the black queen.

28...♕xb2?!

Black chooses the wrong time to treat himself to a second pawn. Apparently the absence of real threats dulled Karpov's vigilance. By 28...♔h8! 29 ♕h6 ♖g8 he could have gained an advantage, for example:

1) 30 ♘e7 ♕xb2 (30...♖g7!?) 31 ♕g5 ♖g7! 32 ♖e6!. A spectacular reply, but after 32...♘c6! 33 ♖xf7 (alas, 33 ♘xc6? fxe6! 34 ♘d4 is bad because of 34...h6! 35 ♕xh6+ ♔g8 36 ♕g5 ♖xd4 37 exd4 ♕xd4+ 38 ♔h1 ♕d5 39 ♕g4 ♕e5) 33...♖xg2+ 34 ♕xg2 ♕xg2+ 35 ♔xg2 ♖xf7 36 ♘xc6 bxc6 37 ♖xc6 ♔g7 38 e4 White has only one hope – to save himself in a rook endgame where he is a pawn down;

2) 30 ♘d6 ♕d5! (30...♕xb2 is weaker: 31 ♕g5 ♖f8 32 ♘xf7+) 31 ♕g5 ♖f8! (now ...♘f3+ is threatened) 32 h4 ♖d1 33 ♘xf7+ ♘xf7 34 ♕xd5 ♖xd5 35 ♖xf7 ♖xf7 36 ♖xf7 ♖b5 37 ♖f2 ♔g7, and again White has an inferior rook endgame.

However, in time-trouble such as Karpov was experiencing, an objective assessment of the position was out of the question: at any moment White might surprise his opponent with an unexpected move.

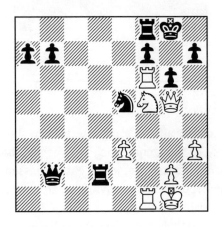

29 ♔h1!

This is essential prophylaxis and a strong

psychological resource: White 'stands still' – perhaps Black can do the same?

29...♔h8?

An instantaneous reply and the decisive mistake. The prolonged and unpleasant pressure finally disconcerted Karpov, and with his flag about to fall he was unable to adjust to the rapidly changing situation, although he could still have fought for a draw:

1) 29...♖d7 30 ♘h6+ ♔g7 31 ♖6f5! f6 32 ♖xf6 ♘f7 33 ♕f4! ♕b3 34 ♔h2 b5 35 e4 ♕c4 36 g4! b4 37 g5 (threatening 38 ♖xf7+ and ♕e5+) 37...♕c7 38 e5 b3 39 e6, and White nevertheless wins;

2) 29...a5 30 ♘e7+ ♔g7 (30...♔h8? 31 h4!) 31 ♖6f4! h5! 32 ♕f6+ ♔h7 33 ♖d4! ♖xg2 (33...♖xd4 loses after 34 exd4 ♕xd4 35 ♘xg6! fxg6 36 ♕xf8 ♕d7 37 ♖b1!) 34 ♕xe5 f6 35 ♕f4 ♕e2 36 ♖dd1 ♖f7 37 ♘d5 ♖g5 38 ♕f2 or 38 ♖g1 with winning chances.

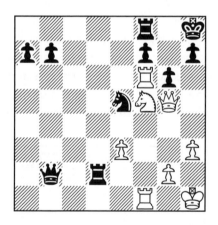

30 ♘d4!

Cutting off the black queen from the defence of the knight. Such unexpected 'backwards moves' are most easily missed in time-trouble. Now White's threats are irresistible.

30...♖xd4 (alas, 30...♖e8 would have led to a catastrophe on the f7-point – 31 ♖xf7 ♘xf7 32 ♕f6+, and mate in three) **31 ♕xe5!**

The final touch.

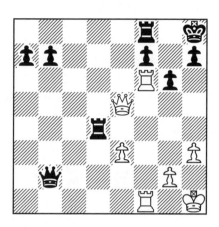

Here my opponent played 31...♖d2, but – the flag on his clock fell and he overstepped the time limit **(1–0)**. However, after 32 ♕e7! ♖dd8 33 ♖xf7 ♖xf7 34 ♖xf7 ♔g8 35 e4 or 35 ♔h2 and e3-e4 all the same White would have won. Times: 2.26–2.30.

I again took the lead: 4½-3½. Overstepping the time limit 10 moves before the control in a lost position was a shocking occurrence, a unique one both in matches for the world championship and in Karpov's career (in Linares 1993 he broke his anti-record – cf. *Game No.98*). It is hard to overestimate the psychological significance of the 8th game for the entire subsequent struggle. It was a defining moment: in contrast to earlier times, Karpov was unable to punish me for my audacious, provocatively sharp play.

In the 9th game I succeeded in quickly equalising, and Karpov immediately forced a draw by repetition. In the 10th game the ex-champion had to conduct a gruelling defence right from the opening until deep into the endgame, but in the end, not wishing to adjourn the game immediately after the time control on move 40, with a hasty pawn advance I missed some winning chances.

Naturally, everyone expected that in the 11th game there would be a large-scale battle: playing White, Karpov was obliged to make use of his last real chance to level the scores in the London half of the match. By that time the queues for tickets had turned into crowds, and in Green Park an enormous demonstration board was set up for those who were unable to gain admission.

Game 15
A.Karpov-G.Kasparov
World Championship Match
11th Game, London 25.08.1986
Grünfeld Defence D93

1 d4 ♞f6 2 c4 g6 3 ♞c3 d5 4 ♗f4 ♗g7 5 e3 c5 6 dxc5 ♕a5 7 ♖c1 dxc4 8 ♗xc4 0-0 9 ♞f3 ♕xc5 10 ♗b3 ♞c6 11 0-0 ♕a5 12 h3 ♗f5 13 ♕e2

On this occasion, instead of 13 ♞d4 ♗d7! (9th game), Karpov chooses the main, more critical continuation.

13...♞e4 (otherwise White plays e3-e4 and becomes active in the centre) **14 ♞d5** (nowadays 14 g4 is fashionable, and 14 ♞xe4 is also played) **14...e5**

Practically forced, since 15 ♗c7 was threatened.

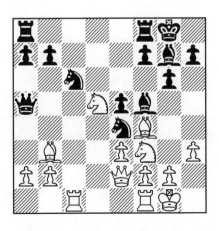

A position known since the early 1970s, and a key one for the evaluation of the entire variation. Before this 15 ♗h2 was played here, and after 15...♗e6! 16 ♖fd1 ♖fd8! 17 ♕c4 ♞f6 a double-edged struggle developed. In our preparations we studied the continuation 18 e4 ♖ac8 19 ♞g5 ♞d4 20 ♞e7+ ♔f8 21 ♞xe6+ ♔xe7 22 ♞xd8 ♖xc4 23 ♗xc4 from the game Smejkal-Saidy (Tallinn 1971), which went 23...♔xd8? 24 b4! ♕c7 25 ♖xd4+ with advantage to White. And before the 7th game we essentially killed the variation, by discovering 23...♞xe4 24 ♞xf7 ♕b6! 25 ♞xe5 ♗xe5 26 ♗xe5 ♞f3+! 27 gxf3 ♕xf2+ with perpetual check (Timman-Ivanchuk, 5th match game, Hilversum 1991). 23...♗h6 is also not bad (Huzman-Dorfman, Lvov 1988) or 23...♞e8 24 ♞xf7 b5! (Kramnik-Kamsky, Moscow 2008).

After the 14th move I was hoping that at last I would be able to surprise Karpov with something in the opening. But, alas, in this match only he was able to spring any surprises...

15 ♖xc6!

A shock! The main virtue of Karpov's novelty was that it was dramatic and unexpected (for which it deserves an exclamation mark). It enables White to sharply change the character of the play, disrupting both the material and the positional balance, while for the moment not straying beyond the risk zone. But the main thing is that it proved profitable in the psychological sense: I involuntarily took my opponent 'at his word' – just imagine, Karpov himself sacrifices the exchange!

15...exf4?! (5)

Instinctively I did not like the fact that after 15...bxc6! 16 ♞e7+ ♔h8 17 ♞xc6 (it is amusing that the line 17 ♞xe5?! ♗xe5 18 ♞xc6 ♕d2!, which was condemned by me, nevertheless occurred later in the game I.Sokolov-Shirov, Wijk aan Zee 1999) 17...♕b6 18 ♘cxe5 with pretty knight leaps White picks up two pawns. However, as the future showed, 18...♗e6! gives Black good play – we arrived at this conclusion before the 13th game. Everywhere White has sufficient compensation for the exchange, but also Black, whose pieces are active, has no reason for complaint – his rooks may be able to display their strength. And it was not without reason that Karpov never played 15 ♖xc6 again, nor indeed the variation with 4 ♗f4 ♗g7 5 e3.

After 15...exf4 Black also has a defensible position, and yet White now has clear play with various threats, which at the board are not so easy to parry.

16 ♖c7! ♗e6 (37)

Beginning an operation to drive out the rook from c7. If 16...fxe3? 17 ♕xe3 ♗e6 18 ♕e1! White has an obvious advantage: 18...♘c3 19 ♘e7+ ♔h8 20 ♖xc3 or 18...♕xe1 19 ♖xe1 ♗xd5 20 ♗xd5 ♘d6 21 ♗xb7.

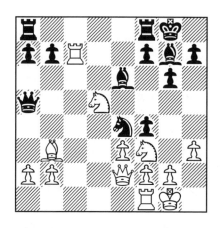

17 ♕e1!

To judge by the speed with which Karpov made this move, this was all prepared in his home laboratory and the unexpected queen manoeuvre was the point of White's plan. In the event of 17 ♘e7+ (but not 17 ♖xb7?

♘d6!) 17...♔h8 18 ♖fc1 ♗xb3 19 axb3 fxe3 20 ♕xe3 ♘d6 21 ♕f4 ♖ad8 the chances are equal.

17...♕b5 (5)

The only move: the endgame after 17...♕xe1? 18 ♖xe1 is obviously advantageous for White. Here, for the first time, Karpov thought for a long time, which is quite understandable: the variation with the exchange sacrifice only arose in the course of the match and there simply wasn't time to analyse in detail all the subsequent complications.

18 ♘e7+! (27) **18...♔h8 19 ♗xe6 fxe6** (7)

After 19...♕b6? 20 ♘d5 ♕xe6 21 ♘xf4 White's deeply entangled knight escapes, and he retains a clear advantage: 21...♕xa2 22 ♕b4 or 21...♕b6 22 ♕c1.

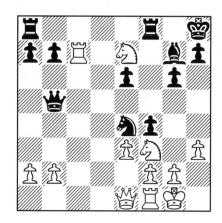

20 ♕b1 (5)

An ambitious plan of attack – the queen stands in ambush, aiming from afar at the g6-point and supporting the rook on c7 and knight on e7. But 20 ♕c1! ♕xb2 21 ♕xb2 ♗xb2 22 ♖xb7 was objectively stronger, with a somewhat better endgame.

20...♘g5! (12)

This is the safest, since it forces drawing simplification.

21 ♘h4! (28)

To judge by the time spent by Karpov, my

20th move came as an unpleasant surprise to him, but he nevertheless found the best practical chance, guaranteeing White at least a draw by perpetual check. After 21 ♘xg5 ♕xg5 22 exf4 (22 ♕e4 fxe3 is equal) 22...♖xf4! 23 ♖xb7 ♖af8 or 23...♗d4 (but not Dlugy's move 23...♖e8?! because of 24 ♕c1!) Black has excellent compensation for the pawn.

21...♘xh3+ (12)

I could not resist the temptation to make this showy move, although by 21...fxe3! I could have forced a draw: since Black is better after 22 fxe3? ♘xh3+! 23 gxh3 ♕g5+ 24 ♘g2 ♗e5! 25 ♘xg6+ (25 ♖d7?! ♕g3) 25...hxg6 26 ♖cf7 ♖xf7 27 ♖xf7 ♔g8!, all that remains for White is to give perpetual check with the sequence 22 ♘hxg6+ hxg6 23 ♘xg6+ ♔g8 24 ♘e7+ (24 ♘xf8? e2 25 ♖e1 ♖xf8) etc.

22 ♔h2!

The knight is taboo: 22 gxh3? ♕g5+ 23 ♘g2 f3 and wins. But now Black has some problems.

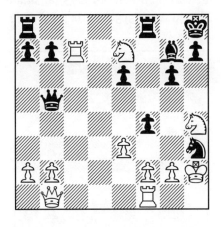

22...♕h5?

A small mistake gives rise to a bigger one. Here, to maintain equality, Black by now had to display some resourcefulness:

1) 22...♖xf2!? (a provocative sacrifice) 23 ♖xf2! (23 ♘exg6+ hxg6 24 ♘xg6+ ♔g8 25 ♘e7+ with perpetual check, but not 24 ♕xg6? ♕e5!) 23...fxe3 24 ♖xf8+ ♖xf8 25 ♔h3 (again avoiding the draw after 25 ♘hxg6+) 25...e2 (25...♕h5 26 ♘exg6+ hxg6 27 ♕xg6 ♕h6 28 ♖e7 ♔g8 29 ♖xe6 ♕xg6 30 ♘xg6 ♖f2 is also sufficient, or 25...♖f1 26 ♖c8+ ♗f8 27 ♖xf8+ ♖xf8 28 ♘hxg6+ ♔g7! 29 ♘xf8 ♕h5+), nevertheless forcing White to sue for peace – 26 ♘exg6+ (26 ♕e4? ♕h5 with the threat of ...g6-g5) 26...hxg6 27 ♘xg6+ ♔g8 28 ♘e7+;

2) 22...fxe3! (an invitation for White to play 23 ♘hxg6+) 23 ♔xh3! hoping for 23...e2? 24 ♖h1! (24 ♕e4?, with the mating idea 24...exf1♕!? 25 ♘hxg6+, loses to the very pretty stroke 24...♖f3+!! – a unique diversion sacrifice!) 24...♕h5 25 ♘exg6+ hxg6 26 ♕xg6 ♕e5 27 ♖xb7 ♖xf2 28 ♖xg7 ♕xg7 29 ♔g3 with winning chances. But the accurate 23...♖xf2! again forces 24 ♘hxg6+ hxg6 25 ♘xg6+ ♔g8 26 ♘e7+ ♔h8! 27 ♘g6+ with a draw.

23 ♘exg6+ (4)

It would have been naïve to expect 23 ♔xh3? g5!. Which knight White captures with on g6 is of no particular importance (slightly later he can reach the same position), but even so 23 ♘hxg6+ hxg6 24 ♕xg6 was more precise, maintaining the attacking construction with the knight on e7.

Now 24...♕a5? 25 ♘d5 is bad for Black, as are 24...♕e5? 25 ♕g4 (or the brilliant 25 ♔xh3 ♖f6 26 ♔g4!!), and 24...♕h7 (Polugayevsky) 25 gxh3! ♖f6 26 ♕g4 fxe3 27 fxe3!. The only defence is 24...♖f5!, although after 25 ♕xh5+ ♖xh5 26 gxh3 fxe3 27 ♘g6+ ♔g8 28 fxe3 ♖g5 (28...♗xb2?! 29 ♖g1!) 29 ♖g1 ♖xg1 30 ♔xg1 ♗xb2 31 ♖xb7 ♗f6 followed by ...a7-a5 and ...♖c8 Black faces a difficult fight for a draw in an ending a pawn down.

23...hxg6

Another critical moment.

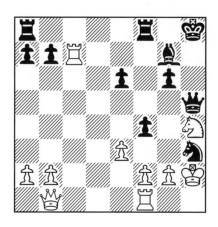

24 ♕xg6? (3)

An obvious oversight, overlooking my reply. 24 ♘xg6+ ♔g8 25 ♘e7+ ♔h8 (25...♔f7? is bad because of 26 ♘f5+ ♔f6 27 ♘xg7 ♕e5 28 ♕h7! or 27...♕h4 28 g3! ♕h6 29 g4! and ♘h5+) 26 ♕g6! was correct, transposing into the advantageous position which could also have arisen from 23 ♘hxg6+.

24...♕e5! (3)

The only reply, but an adequate one. Black eliminates all the danger, and it is now White who has to play accurately.

25 ♖f7?! (41)

This move came as a complete surprise to me. My calculations involved White's numerous other possibilities:

1) 25 ♖fc1 (not 25 ♖xg7? fxe3+ and ...♕xg7) 25...fxe3+ 26 ♔xh3 exf2 27 ♕g4! ♔g8 28 ♘f3 (28 ♘g6? loses to 28...♕e3+ 29 g3 f1♕+! 30 ♖xf1 ♖xf1) 28...♕f6 29 ♔g3 ♖ad8 with equality, or 27...♕e3+!? 28 g3 ♕h6 with the idea of a counterattack by ...♖f6 and ...♖g8;

2) 25 ♕c2 fxe3+ 26 ♔xh3 ♔g8 27 f4 (27 ♖xb7 ♖ad8) 27...e2 28 ♖e1 ♖xf4 29 ♖xe2 ♕h5 30 g3 ♖xh4+ 31 gxh4 ♕f3+ 32 ♔h2 ♕f4+ with perpetual check;

3) 25 ♖xb7 ♘xf2! 26 ♘f3 ♕f6 27 ♕h5+ ♔g8 28 ♖xf2 fxe3 29 ♖e2 ♖ab8 with equality.

Now, however, the initiative passes to Black, and he is the one who is thinking of winning. Why did Karpov spend so much time and still commit an oversight? Perhaps he was reproaching himself for his mistake on the previous move...

25...♖xf7! (13) **26 ♕xf7 ♘g5!** (forcibly transposing into a favourable endgame) **27 ♘g6+** (27 ♕xb7? fxe3+) **27...♔h7 28 ♘xe5 ♘xf7 29 ♘xf7 ♔g6!**

It is probable that this important move was also overlooked by Karpov (not surprising in such a tense battle), and that he was expecting only 29...fxe3 30 ♘g5+ ♔g6 31 ♘xe6 with equality.

30 ♘d6 fxe3 (the bishop, which for a long time has been asleep, finally wakes up) **31 ♘c4!**

Already the only move: White must get rid of the insidious pawn on e3. After 31 f4? ♖d8 or 31 ♘xb7? ♖f8 32 ♘c5 (32 ♔g3 ♗e5+) 32...♗xb2 33 ♘e4 ♗d4 it would have become a powerful passed pawn.

31...exf2 (6) **32 ♖xf2 b5 33 ♘e3 a5** (33...♖d8 34 ♖e2 was no better) **34 ♔g3** (8) **34...a4 35 ♖c2 ♖f8 36 ♔g4** (5) **36...♗d4** (7) **37 ♖e2**

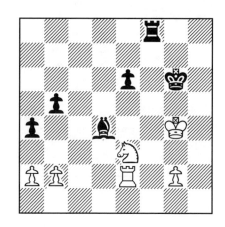

37...♗xe3?! (9)

With this exchange, which effectively signifies an agreement to a draw, I hurried to secure victory in the London half of the match (after all, in the 12th game I had the white pieces). I should have displayed greater persistence, although with accurate play White would still have gained a draw:

1) 37...e5 38 g3 ♖f7 39 ♘d5 ♖f1 40 b3! (40 ♘c7?! is weaker: 40...b4 41 ♘b5 ♔f6 42 ♖d2 ♗c5) 40...♖c1 41 ♖h2 or 40...a3 41 ♖c2 ♔f7 42 ♘c7 b4 43 ♘d5;

2) 37...♖c8!? 38 ♔f4 ♗g7 39 ♔e4 (39 ♖d2!?) 39...♖d8 40 g3 ♖d4+ 41 ♔f3 ♔g5 42 ♖c2 ♖b4 43 ♘d1! (but not 43 ♖c5+? ♔g6 44 ♖c6 ♖xb2 45 ♖xe6+ ♔f7 46 ♖b6 ♗d4! 47 ♖b7+ ♔e6 48 g4 ♗xe3! 49 ♔xe3 ♔d6 and wins) 43...♗d4 44 ♘c3 ♔f6 (44...♔f5 45 g4+) 45 ♘d1 e5 46 ♖e2 ♔e6 47 ♖c2 or 44...♗xc3 45 bxc3 ♖c4 46 ♔e3 ♔g4 47 ♔d3 ♔xg3 48 ♖e2.

38 ♖xe3 ♖f2 39 b3 (39 ♖xe6+ ♔f7 40 ♖b6! ♖xb2 41 a3 would also have done) **39...♖xg2+ 40 ♔f3 ♖xa2 41 bxa4 ½-½**

The resources are exhausted. 6-5! Times: 2.27–2.26.

The organisers of the London half of the match put up a special prize from the firm Save and Prosper (£10,000 in gold sovereigns) for the best of the 12 games. The jury was made up of members of the English team, headed by Tony Miles. By awarding this prize to both players for the 11th game, the English displayed their customary tact and political correctness, once again confirming their neutrality. And as a result Karpov and I each received 64 gold sovereigns from the time of Queen Victoria!

After a quiet draw in the 12th game the match moved on to Leningrad, where a week later the 13th game took place. Although it also ended in a draw, it was a fighting, tense game, and it set the tone for the second half of the match.

The next few games showed that Karpov was aiming at any cost to seize the match

initiative. Behind on points and with his unprecedented opening preparation, he was induced into extremely risky and vigorous action. This was most certainly apparent in 14th game.

Game 16
G.Kasparov-A.Karpov
World Championship Match
14th Game, Leningrad 08.09.1986
Ruy Lopez C92

1 e4 e5 2 ♘f3 ♘c6

I was intending once again to test Black's defences in the Petroff Defence – against 2...♘f6 (6th game) a new conception with 3 d4 had now been prepared. But Karpov pleasantly surprised me...

3 ♗b5 a6 4 ♗a4 ♘f6 5 0-0 ♗e7 6 ♖e1 b5 7 ♗b3 d6 8 c3 0-0 9 h3

The classical Spanish, that inexhaustible mine of original strategic plans, subtle positional manoeuvring, swift attacks and counterattacks, was Karpov's favourite opening. Since his youth he felt confident in it, irrespective of what colour he was playing. The range of openings played in our games was quite diverse, but up until then in the Spanish I had not managed to win: in three games I achieved highly promising positions, but they all ended in draws, and one game I even lost. Therefore this next dispute was of a crucial nature, and we had prepared very seriously for it.

9...♗b7 10 d4 ♖e8 11 ♘bd2 ♗f8 12 a4 (the main line; 12 a3 – *Game No.8*) **12...h6 13 ♗c2**

One of the *tabiyas* simultaneously of two variations – the Smyslov and the Zaitsev.

13...exd4

In the 9th game of the 1985 match Karpov chose the solid but passive 13...♘b8 14 ♗d3 c6, but now he goes in for the most topical and sharp continuation: Black concedes the centre, obtaining in return the b4-square for his knight, and the possibility of beginning active play on the queenside and then attacking the opponent's pawn centre.

14 cxd4 ♘b4 15 ♗b1 c5

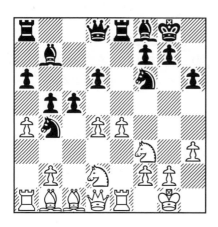

The main reply, although we also already had experience of playing the variation with 15...bxa4 (*Game No.69*).

16 d5 (to fight for an advantage, the centre has to be closed) **16...♘d7**

Hoping to exploit the position of the knight on b4 to undermine the centre by ...f7-f5, or, after ...c5-c4, to occupy the d3-point. After 16...g6 17 ♘f1 (Sax-Greenfeld, Lucerne Olympiad 1982) or 16...bxa4?! 17 ♖xa4 (Grünfeld-Frey, Lucerne Olympiad 1982) it is more difficult to create counterplay.

17 ♖a3!

Preparing for ...f7-f5 and the switching of the rook to the kingside. The routine 17 ♘f1?! prevents the plan with ...c5-c4 and ...♘c5, but encourages 17...f5! 18 exf5 ♘f6 (Gavrikov-Razuvaev, 52nd USSR Championship, Riga 1985, De Firmian-Beliavsky, Tunis Interzonal 1985).

17...c4

17...g6 is weaker: 18 ♘f1 ♗g7 19 a5! (Gufeld-Timoshchenko, Kislovodsk 1982). In

our 1990 match Karpov was to try against me the alternative 17...f5 (*Game No.74*).

Of course, the move ...c5-c4 has a drawback – White obtains the d4-square for his knight, but also Black gains the opportunity of invading at d3.

18 axb5 (15)

A new idea, found in preparation for the match: the knight will go to d4 with gain of tempo, by threatening the b5-pawn. At that time the experience with this variation was limited to the game A.Sokolov-Psakhis (Volgograd 1985), where after 18 ♘d4 ♘e5 (18...♕f6! – *Game No.17*) 19 axb5 ♕b6 20 ♘2f3 ♘bd3 21 ♗e3 ♘xe1 22 ♘xe1 ♕c7 a complicated battle developed.

18...axb5 19 ♘d4

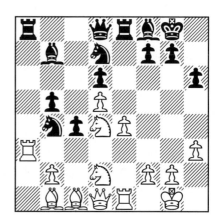

19...♖xa3!?

An unexpected reply, which – and this was also psychologically important – was made instantly. We had looked at a different pawn sacrifice – 19...♘e5 20 ♖xa8 ♕xa8 21 ♘xb5 (Anand-Kamsky, 7th match game, Las Palmas 1995), but we considered it insufficient and concluded that Black should go in for 19...♕b6!? 20 ♘f5.

Now 20...♘e5?! is dangerous for him: 21 ♖g3 g6 22 ♘f3 ♘ed3 23 ♗e3! (if 23 ♕d2, then 23...♘xe1, but not 23...♗xd5? 24 ♘xh6+! Anand-Adams, San Luis 2005)

23...♛d8 24 ♝xh6 ♛f6 (24...♞xe1 25 ♞3h4!) 25 ♞3h4! ♝xd5 (Kotronias-Berend, Heraklion 2007) 26 ♝d2! or 25...♞xe1 26 ♝g5! ♛xb2 (26...♛h8 27 ♝d2!) 27 ♞xg6 fxg6 28 ♝h4! with crushing threats.

However, after 20...g6 21 ♞f1! ♜xa3! (only not 21...gxf5? 22 ♜g3+ ♚h8 23 ♝xh6! or 22...♚h7 23 ♛h5 ♞e5 24 exf5) 22 bxa3 ♞xd5 23 exd5 ♜xe1 24 ♛xe1 gxf5 no advantage is apparent: 25 ♝e3 ♛d8 (De Firmian-A.Ivanov, Las Vegas 1996), 25 ♝xf5 ♞e5 (Volokitin-Azarov, Moscow 2007), or 25 ♞e3 ♛d4 26 ♞xf5 ♛xd5 27 f3 – it seemed to us that here Black's defence was difficult, but after 27...♛e5 he holds on.

Nevertheless, in his 'parallel' analysis Karpov rejected this line and prepared a far from obvious pawn sacrifice, which I had overlooked. It was clearly aimed at unsettling me, but here he was unlucky: on encountering a new position and forced to work out its subtleties directly at the board, I did not become flustered and, despite a couple of slips, I played one of my most subtle positional games.

20 bxa3 ♞d3 21 ♝xd3 cxd3

Here I thought for a long time, searching for a way to retain the initiative.

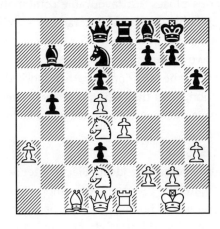

22 ♝b2 (17)

White sets his sights on the opponent's kingside. He has two other possibilities: 22 ♞xb5 ♛a5! – although I took my opponent 'at his word', Black does, indeed, have good compensation for the pawn (an example: Shirov-Karjakin, Bilbao 2009), or 22 ♜e3 (before the 1987 match we thought this was the main way to fight for an advantage) 22...♞c5 (22....♞e5 23 ♞4f3!) 23 ♝b2 ♛a5 (23...♝c8?! 24 ♞c6, Anand-Beliavsky, Madrid 1998) 24 ♞f5! g6 25 ♞g3 b4! 26 ♞h5 bxa3 27 ♞f6+ ♚h8 28 ♝a1 ♜c8 29 ♞h5+ ♚g8 30 ♞f6+ with a draw (Volokitin-Kasimdzhanov, Wijk aan Zee 2009).

Thus White's three continuations are roughly equivalent. However, 22 ♝b2 proved to have one undoubted virtue: Karpov thought for a long time over his reply, and it became clear that he had not considered this move at home (years later Igor Zaitsev confirmed that the ex-champion had focused all his attention on the variations with 22 ♜e3 and especially 22 ♞xb5).

22...♛a5 (45)

22...♞c5 (a move that suggests itself) could have led to a position from the previous note after 23 ♜e3.

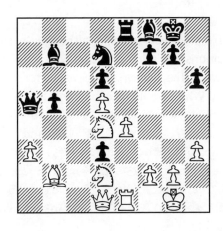

23 ♞f5! (30)

Forward! A 'squabble' over the winning of the far-advanced black pawn would be inappropriate.

23...♞e5 (20)

On his last two moves White had spent nearly an hour, and Black even more: in a critical position the choice of a move is always difficult. Karpov intuitively chose a solid move – he blocked the dangerous diagonal with his knight. Also good and 'in accordance with the spirit of fighting for the initiative' was 23...g6, which I recommended in the book *Dva matcha*: after 24 ♞e3! ♞e5! 25 ♞b3 ♛a4 26 ♝xe5 ♜xe5 27 ♞g4 ♜e7 28 ♞f6+! ♚h8! 29 ♛xd3 ♝g7 30 ♛f3 (30 ♛c3 ♛a8!) 30...♛xa3 Black is okay (Grischuk-Karjakin, Bilbao 2009).

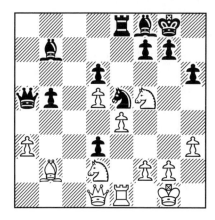

24 ♝xe5!

I replied very quickly, although in such positions one's hand naturally reaches out towards the f-pawn. However, after 24 f4 ♞c4! White would have had only a draw: 25 ♞xc4 (25 ♝xg7? ♛xd2) 25...bxc4 26 ♞xh6+ (26 ♝xg7? ♝c8! 27 ♝xf8 ♚xf8 and wins) 26...gxh6 27 ♛g4+ ♚h7 28 ♛f5+ with perpetual check, or 25 ♞b3 ♞xb2 26 ♞xh6+! ♚h7! 27 ♞xa5 ♞xd1 28 ♜xd1 gxh6 29 ♞xb7 ♜xe4 30 ♜xd3 ♜xf4 31 ♜b3 ♜a4 with equality.

24...dxe5 (14)

After 24...♜xe5 25 ♞f3 ♜xf5 26 exf5 ♝xd5 27 ♜e3 ♝c4 28 ♛e1! Black does not have sufficient compensation for the ex-

change (if 28...♛xa3 the invasion 29 ♜e8 is decisive).

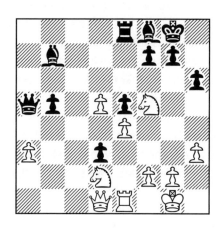

25 ♞b3

The paradoxical exchange of bishop for knight had a solid positional basis: White has obtained a protected passed pawn in the centre (which, incidentally, will decide the game), the d5-e4 pawn wedge restricts the bishop on b7, and both his knights are well placed. The knight on b3 deprives Black of active counterplay on the queenside (where the b5-pawn may be vulnerable), while the knight on f5 is potentially dangerous on the kingside (where Black may possibly have to weaken himself with ...g7-g6). For such obvious pluses – a favourable combination of dynamic and strategic factors – White does not begrudge allowing his opponent the two bishops, especially since for the moment the position is rather blocked. In addition, I had the feeling that such a development of events would not be to Karpov's liking.

25...♛b6 (24)

An aggressive idea: Black intends to eliminate the a3-pawn with another piece. Karpov is still hoping to seize the initiative, thinking that White's activity is only temporary, and relying on his two bishops.

Meanwhile, 25...♛xa3, a move unjustly

condemned by the commentators, was quite acceptable: for example, 26 ♕xd3 g6 (if 26...♕b4, then 27 ♖b1 is strong) 27 ♕xb5 (27 ♘e3 ♕a6, and if 28 ♕d2, then 28...h5 with equality) 27...♕b4!, forcing a draw – 28 ♘xh6+ ♔g7 29 ♕xe8 ♕xe1+ 30 ♔h2 ♕xf2 31 ♕xe5+ ♔xh6! (31...f6? 32 ♘g4) 32 ♕h8+ ♔g5 33 ♕xf8 ♕f4+. The balance would also have been maintained by 25...♕c3!? 26 ♖e3 ♕c2 27 ♖xd3 ♕xd1+ 28 ♖xd1 ♗c8! 29 ♘a5 ♗xf5 30 exf5 ♖a8 31 ♘c6 ♗d6.

This analysis shows that White has lost his opening advantage (possibly already with 18 axb5).

26 ♕xd3 ♖a8?!

26...♗c8! was correct, and if necessary ...♗xf5 or ...♗d7, defending the b5-pawn and blocking the enemy passed pawn. This multi-purpose move would have enabled Black to regroup successfully and organise a defence: 27 ♘a1 ♗xf5 28 exf5 ♗c5 29 ♖e2 e4 with equality, or 27 ♘d2 ♗d7 with counterplay against the a3-pawn, compensating for the slight material deficit. After missing this chance, Karpov could have ended up in a difficult position.

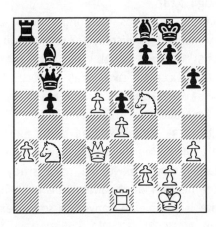

27 ♖c1?! (30)

I was very proud of this move (later I was told that the manoeuvres of the white rook in this game created an enormous impres-

sion on Karpov), and in the book *Dva matcha* I attached an exclamation mark to it, with the following commentary: 'One of the most difficult prophylactic moves in the game. Now the bishop dare not leave the c6-square undefended. 27 d6 was premature in view of 27...♖d8.'

However, in the computer era it is not difficult to establish that the energetic 27 d6! was the only way to retain the advantage:

1) 27...g6 28 ♘e7+ ♔g7 29 ♖c1 ♖d8 30 ♕g3 ♔h7 31 ♘c5 ♖xd6 32 ♘xb7 ♕xb7 33 ♘d5 ♖c6 34 ♖b1! and with queens and rooks on the board, the 'eternal' knight on d5 makes it hard for Black to defend;

2) 27...♖d8 28 ♕g3 g6 29 ♖e3! ♖e8 (29...♗xd6?! 30 ♘xh6+ ♔g7 31 ♖f3!) 30 h4! ♔h7 (30...♖e6 31 h5) 31 ♕f3! with the initiative.

And today, taking into account the objective evaluation, I am reluctantly forced to assess the move 27 ♖c1 as dubious.

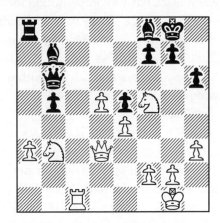

27...g6

The normal reply. 27...♖xa3? (weakening the back rank) would have lost after 28 d6 ♖a8 29 ♘c5 ♖c8 30 ♔h2! or 28...g6 29 ♘e7+ ♔g7 (29...♔h8 30 ♖c7!, while if 29...♔h7, then 30 ♕f3 f5 31 ♘xf5! is also good) 30 ♕g3 ♔f6 31 ♖d1.

But 27...♗xa3 was not as bad as I thought, for example: 28 ♕g3 ♕f6 29 ♖a1 ♗xd5 or 28 ♖a1 ♗f8 29 ♖xa8 ♗xa8 30 ♕c3 ♕b8, and Black's fortress is difficult to approach.

28 ♘e3

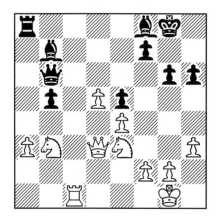

28...♗xa3!

The best move. 28...h5 was recommended, but after 29 ♘c2 it is now bad to play 29...♗xa3? because of 30 ♘xa3 ♖xa3 31 d6!, and otherwise there follows ♖b1 and ♘d2-f3, when Black has no compensation for the pawn. However, 28...♖xa3 was acceptable: 29 ♕c2 (29 ♘g4 f6! 30 ♕c2 h5 is equal) 29...♖a8 30 ♘g4 ♕d6 31 ♕d2 f5 32 ♘xh6+ ♗xh6 33 ♕xh6 fxe4 and ...♗xd5 with good drawing chances.

29 ♖a1 ♖a4

29...♗d6? is weak: 30 ♖xa8+ ♗xa8 31 ♘g4 h5? 32 ♘f6+ ♔h8 (32...♔g7 33 ♘e8+, ♘xd6 and ♕xb5) 33 ♕d2 with a decisive attack. White would have been left with some advantage after 29...♗f8 30 ♖xa8 ♗xa8 31 ♕c3 ♕b8 32 ♘g4 ♗g7 33 ♕e3! (33 ♘c5 h5 34 ♘e3 ♕c8 is less good) 33...h5 34 ♘h6+! ♗xh6 35 ♕xh6 or 33...♔h7 34 ♕f3 ♕a7 35 ♘f6+ ♔h8 36 ♘e8.

Therefore the most accurate continuation would have been to restrict the knight by 29...h5! 30 ♕c3 f6. Now in the event of 31 d6 ♕c6! it is unclear how White can strengthen

his position, while after 31 g4!? (breaking up the opponent's defences on the kingside) 31...hxg4 32 ♘xg4 ♖a4! (but not the passive 32...♗e7?! 33 ♖xa8+ ♗xa8 34 ♕c8+ ♕d8 35 ♕a6) Black has an equal game: 33 ♖d1 ♕d6 or 33 ♕g3 ♗f8 34 ♖e1 ♗c8, while if 33 ♖xa3 there can follow 33...♖xa3 34 ♕b4 ♖xb3 35 ♕xb3 ♗c8 or even 33...b4 34 ♕f3 ♖xa3 35 ♘xf6+ ♔g7 36 ♘e8+ ♔g8, forcing a draw.

After 29...♖a4 the position remains roughly equal, but Black has some problems to solve.

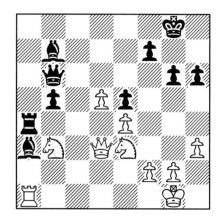

30 ♘g4 ♗f8?

Simple solutions no longer work and Black needed to display some ingenuity – 30...h5! 31 ♘xe5 ♗b2!, when 32 ♖xa4 (32 ♘d7?! ♖xa1+ 33 ♘xa1 ♕a5 34 ♘c2? ♕c7 35 ♕b3 ♗g7 36 ♕xb5 ♗c8 or 34 ♘b3 ♕e1+ 35 ♔h2 ♗c8! is unfavourable for White) 32...bxa4 33 ♘c4 ♕xb3 34 ♕xb3 axb3 35 ♘xb2 h4! (fixing the enemy pawns on light squares) would have led to a study-like endgame with knight against bishop, where White is unable to convert a sound extra pawn: 36 f3 ♔f8 37 ♔f2 ♗a6 38 ♔e1 ♔e7 39 ♘d1 ♔d6 40 ♔d2 f5! 41 ♔c3 ♗e2 42 ♘e3 f4 43 ♘g4 ♗f1 44 ♔xb3 ♗xg2 45 ♘f2 ♗xf3 with a draw.

However, Karpov did not yet see the need

to find a way to save the game – with 30...♗f8 he was undoubtedly pinning his hopes on 31 ♘xe5? ♗g7 32 ♘d7 ♖xa1+ 33 ♘xa1 ♕c7, but...

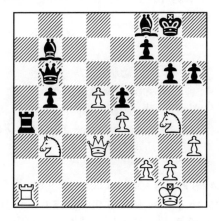

31 ♖c1!

Here this move is indeed strong. With subtle manoeuvres White has imperceptibly achieved complete domination – the rook 'pendulum' has disrupted the harmony in the opponent's ranks. Black's defensive problems were also aggravated by severe time-trouble.

31...♕d6? (8)

Worn out by the complicated struggle, Karpov makes a decisive mistake. However, it was not easy to find the correct move. The comparatively best chance was 31...f6!, although even here after 32 d6! (if 32 ♕f3 there is the saving reply 32...♖a6!) 32...♕xd6 33 ♕xb5 ♖a7 (33...♖b4?! 34 ♕e8 ♗xe4 35 ♘c5 is dangerous for Black) 34 ♕e8 ♗xe4 35 ♘c5 ♕e7 36 ♕xe7 ♗xe7 37 ♘xe4 f5 38 ♘xh6+ (38 ♖c6!?) 38...♔g7 39 ♘g4 White obtains an ending with an extra pawn and winning chances.

32 ♘c5! (11)

Forcibly transposing into a won endgame. Karpov was probably hoping for 32 ♕xb5?! ♖b4 with counterplay: if 33 ♕e8?! ♖xb3 34 ♘xh6+ ♔g7 35 ♘xf7 ♕e7 36 ♕xe7 ♗xe7 37

♘xe5 ♗d6 38 ♘g4 ♔f7 39 e5 ♗e7 the bishops should be able to cope with the white infantry, while after 33 ♕d3 h5 34 ♘e3 ♗a6 Black has some compensation for the pawn.

32...♖c4 (there is nothing else) **33 ♖xc4 bxc4 34 ♘xb7 cxd3** (if 34...♕b4 the simplest is 35 ♕d1 ♕xb7 35 d6 or 35...♕b3 36 ♘e3) **35 ♘xd6 ♗xd6 36 ♔f1!**

Heading for the d3-pawn. The h6-pawn does not tempt White: 36 ♘xh6+?! ♔g7 37 ♘g4 f5, and the win becomes problematic.

36...♔g7

Here it was possible to set an interesting trap: 36...h5 37 ♘e3 ♗c5 in the hope of 38 ♔e1? ♗xe3 39 fxe3 f5 40 exf5 gxf5 41 e4! (the only move) 41...h4! (instead of 41...fxe4? 42 g4 Black fixes the white pawns, devaluing the opponent's material advantage) 42 exf5 e4, unexpectedly saving the pawn ending. However, the accurate 38 ♘d1! would have deprived Black of his last hopes: 38...f5 39 f3 ♗d4 40 ♔e1 with the inevitable fall of the d3-pawn.

37 f3 f5 38 ♘f2 d2 39 ♔e2 ♗b4 40 ♘d3 ♗c3 (here the game was adjourned) **41 ♘c5**

The sealed move.

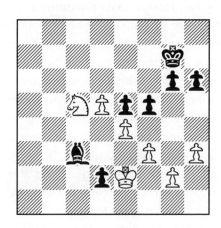

Now ♘b3xd2 is inevitable, with the threat of playing the king to b5 and the knight to e6 – Black cannot simultaneously combat the d6-pawn and defend his king-side pawns. And after the active 41...♚f6 42 ♘b3 ♚g5 43 ♘xd2 ♚f4 the simplest is 44 d6! ♗a5 45 ♘c4 ♗d8 46 g3+ ♚xg3 47 ♘xe5 or 44...♗b4 45 d7 ♗e7 46 ♚d3 ♚g3 (46...♚g5 47 ♚c4) 47 ♘c4 etc. Black resigned without resuming the game **(1–0)**. Times: 2.32–2.28.

Even today I rate this win among my best creative achievements, especially since it was gained on Spanish territory. Yes, Karpov made a few errors, and on the 27th move I also played inaccurately, but in general to obtain decisive positional gains original play was demanded of White.

Thus I was able to increase my lead to two points (8-6), although my opponent again easily found his bearings in an opening position that was new to him and skilfully avoided my home preparation. Therefore the joy of victory was tinged with a feeling of alarm...

I think that Karpov was very disappointed with the draw in the 15th game: even after employing a high-quality novelty against the Grünfeld, he was unable to set Black any real problems. The forecasts regarding the 16th game were unanimous: a fierce battle was to be expected. However, it was not hard to predict this, bearing in mind how uncompromising the Leningrad encounters had been, and – the number of the forthcoming game! After all, it was in the 16th game of the previous match that the conclusive turning-point had occurred. There is no doubt that such crushing defeats are remembered for a long time not only by the winner, but also by the loser...

And for this game, despite the disappointments of the two previous ones, Karpov arrived aiming for full-scale revenge. He decided to fight in an untraditional way for him, by not avoiding the most forceful and risky continuations. As for myself, it is not in my nature to avoid an open battle. Besides, I believed in the lucky star of the 16th game, and I was dreaming of creating another masterpiece.

Game 17
G.Kasparov-A.Karpov
World Championship Match
16th Game, Leningrad 15.09.1986
Ruy Lopez C92

1 e4 e5 2 ♘f3 ♘c6 (of course, not 2...♘f6) **3 ♗b5 a6 4 ♗a4 ♘f6 5 0-0 ♗e7 6 ♖e1 b5 7 ♗b3 d6 8 c3 0-0 9 h3 ♗b7 10 d4 ♖e8 11 ♘bd2 ♗f8 12 a4 h6**

Black demonstrates his readiness to continue the analytical debate begun in the 14th game.

13 ♗c2 exd4 14 cxd4 ♘b4 15 ♗b1 c5 16 d5 ♘d7 17 ♖a3!

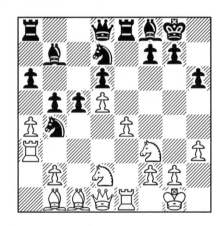

17...c4

And this is a familiar motif, evoking memories of the previous year's 16th game: the black knight intends to establish itself at d3, causing confusion in the white ranks. We made these opening moves quickly, virtually at blitz speed.

18 ♘d4

Abandoning 18 axb5 (*Game No.16*) for the moment, I followed the aforementioned A.Sokolov-Psakhis game, where I was intending to demonstrate an improvement that had just been found for White.

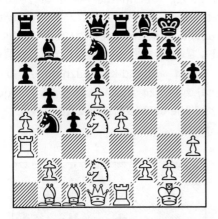

After 18...♘e5 19 axb5 ♕b6 instead of the modest 20 ♘2f3 ♘bd3 I had devised an unexpected knight sacrifice – 20 ♘xc4!! ♘xc4 21 ♖g3, cutting the Gordian knot. This idea came to me during the night after the 15th game, and our entire team began looking at it the day before the 16th. And our collective analysis showed that White's attack is very dangerous – his well-coordinated pieces literally demolish the black king's position. After 21...axb5? 22 ♘f5 g6 23 ♕h5! Black is in a sorry state. And after the best reply 21...♗c8 we initially looked at 22 ♗xh6 axb5 23 b3 with sufficient compensation for the piece, but in the end we deemed the strongest to be 22 b3! ♘e5 23 ♗e3, when Black's defence is difficult (A.Sokolov-Portisch, Brussels 1988).

After checking our old analyses, I have again ascertained that this sacrifice is very favourable for White, since it gives him several important pluses. His rook instantly swings across to g3, while the black knights are deprived of their strong point at d3, and

the knight on b4 begins to 'hang', coming under attack with gain of tempo (♕d2). For the moment the extra piece does not play any particular role – White continues to build up the pressure on the kingside, and in some cases he can even switch to a purely positional course.

I remember my joyful anticipation: would I succeed at last in employing in this match a genuinely destructive novelty? Before the game I warned my mother: 'Today I'm going to sacrifice a knight, so don't faint.' But my opponent proved ready for this and he was the first to employ a novelty...

18...♕f6! (6)

This apparently pointless attack on the knight at d4, dislodging White from his home analysis, left me slightly shocked – again Karpov avoided a 'mine'! True, he made the queen move without enthusiasm, and soon the impression was gained that he had prepared the entire variation in a hurry.

19 ♘2f3 (33)

White does not want to remove his knight from the centre and lift the attack on the b5-pawn, and therefore he is forced to block the rook's access to g3. Now, having safeguarded his king, Black can make use of his trumps, associated in particular with his outpost at d3.

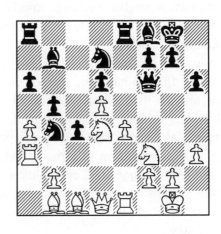

19...♘c5

For the second time in succession in a similar position, Karpov goes in for a pawn sacrifice, hoping in return for indefinite positional compensation. Such an occurrence, frankly speaking, was very rare for him: 'pawn sacrifice for the initiative' was never one of Karpov's favourite chess procedures. And over the long history of our encounters he showed himself to be a staunch supporter of a material advantage and at any convenient moment he would accept pawns sacrificed by me. Now the eternal creative debate – 'material or the initiative?' – is given a new impulse, but unexpectedly with reversed colours. It is apparent that Karpov was eager at any price to provoke a crisis in the match...

The move 19...♘c5 was made without hesitation, which looks intriguing, since here Karpov disregarded another, no less interesting possibility, which was more in accordance with his style: 19...♘d3!? 20 ♗xd3 b4!. At the board this variation concerned me, after the game I discussed it with my trainers, and later, before the 1987 match, I devised a pretty exchange sacrifice: 21 ♖b3! (21 ♗xc4 bxa3 with equality, Anand-Kamsky, 5th match game, Las Palmas 1995) 21...cxb3 22 ♘xb3 – White has enduring compensation for the exchange and comfortable play, but objectively the position is bordering on equality.

To judge by Karpov's speed of play, the plan with 18...♕f6 had been worked out at home, and it is hard to imagine that both he and his helpers had failed to see 19...♘d3. Although, as I know from my own experience, in the commotion of a match (when dangers seem exaggerated) oversights occur both in analysis and in the assessment of a position, especially when work has to be done hastily...

20 axb5

If White is to suffer, then at least he'll have a pawn. After 20 ♖ae3?! ♘bd3 (20...bxa4!?) 21 ♗xd3 ♘xd3 22 ♖xd3 cxd3 he merely has compensation for the exchange (Timofeev-Yakovenko, Oropesa del Mar 2001). And in the event of 20 ♖ee3 ♘bd3 (20...bxa4?! 21 ♖ac3! A.Sokolov-Karpov, Rotterdam 1989) 21 axb5 axb5 22 ♘xb5 ♖xa3 23 ♘xa3 ♗a6!? (not 23...♖xe4 24 ♘xc4 Anand-Kasimdzhanov, Bastia (rapid) 2006) 24 ♗xd3 cxd3 Black has good play (cf. the note to Black's 23rd move).

20...axb5

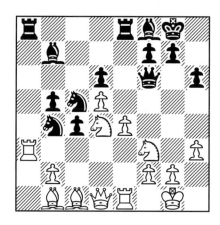

21 ♘xb5 (15)

Now the white knight will have to take up a poor post at a3. This could have been avoided by 21 ♖xa8!? ♖xa8 22 ♘xb5. Here 22...♘bd3 is good, but I did not like the invasion of the rook – 22...♖a1, when 23 ♗e3 ♘bd3 24 ♗d4 ♕g6 promises no more than a repetition of moves (25 ♘h4 ♕g5 26 ♘f3 ♕g6), while 23 ♘c3 ♘bd3 24 ♖f1 seems passive, although in fact after 24...♘b3 25 ♗e3! ♘xb2 26 ♕c2 ♘d3 27 ♖d1 White seizes the initiative, but after 24...♖xb1!? 25 ♘xb1 ♘xe4 26 b3 the position is roughly equal.

21...♖xa3 22 ♘xa3

After the alternative 22 bxa3?! ♘bd3

Black quickly regains the pawn and he has the resource ...♕a1.

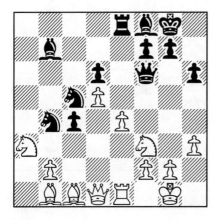

22...♗a6

Before the invasion on d3 Black strengthens his position to the maximum, although 22...♘bd3 23 ♗xd3 cxd3 would also have given him good compensation for the pawn. However, here 23...♘xd3?! would allow White to consolidate successfully – 24 ♖e3! ♗a6! (after 24...♘xb2 25 ♗xb2 ♕xb2 26 ♘xc4 or 24...♘c5 25 ♕c2 Black is simply a pawn down) 25 ♕a4! ♖a8 26 ♕c6 with a dangerous initiative.

23 ♖e3!

Essential prophylaxis. White prepares in advance for the appearance of a black knight at d3.

23...♖b8

The final preparation for the invasion. Karpov played this move (which was not possible after 20 ♖ee3) without particular thought, and later it became the standard one.

Meanwhile, Black had several other tempting moves, in particular 23...♘bd3. This was wrongly criticised by the commentators, including myself in *Informator* No.42, since after 24 ♗xd3 cxd3 (24...♘xd3?! 25 ♕a4!, as in the note to Black's 22nd move) 25 b4 (25 ♕e1 ♘b3 or 25 ♘d2 ♕d4 is less

good for White) 25...♘xe4 26 b5 (26 ♕a4? ♖c8) 26...♗b7 27 ♕xd3 (27 ♖xd3 ♖c8!, and White's extra pawn is not felt) 27...♕a1 28 ♕b1 (28 ♖e1?! ♘xf2!) 28...♕xb1 29 ♘xb1 ♖c8 an equal ending is reached.

But this assessment is of purely theoretical interest, since Karpov was aiming for more, as he was well ahead on the clock and he thought that he had caused me definite discomfort. Even so, Black's pressure is not so strong as to force White to passively await the development of events. 'There is no need to panic', I said to myself. 'I must boldly press forward: in the resulting complications everything will be decided by enterprise and ingenuity.'

24 e5! (19)

Black would have been quite satisfied with 24 ♖c3 ♘bd3 25 ♗xd3 cxd3 26 ♗e3 (26 ♘d2 ♕d4!) 26...♘xe4 27 ♖c6 ♖a8 (Anand-Timoshchenko, Frunze 1987), when if 25 ♘xc4?? he has 25...♕xc3!. On observing this simple trap, for a moment I felt sad: the black knight on d3 reminded me too strongly of the events in the 16th game of the previous match. Besides, the time showing on my opponent's clock clearly demonstrated that this was not the first time he had seen this position.

White is not promised anything by 24

♘e1 ♘bd3 25 ♘xd3 cxd3, 24 ♘d2 ♘bd3 25
♗xd3 cxd3, or 24 ♘d4 ♘bd3 25 ♗xd3
♘xd3 (Shirov-Anand, Moscow (blitz) 2007),
but 24 ♘h2!? deserved some consideration:
24...♘cd3 25 ♘g4 ♕d4 26 ♘c2 ♘xc2 27
♗xc2 h5 28 ♘h2 g6 29 ♘f3 (Milos-Mecking,
Buenos Aires 2001) 29...♕c5 with a double-
edged game.

In my view, 24 e5 was the most correct
move, from both the chess (opening lines for
attack) and the psychological point of view –
it came as a surprise to Karpov.

24...dxe5 25 ♘xe5

By exploiting the removal of the black
rook from the e-file, White has radically
changed the character of the play. True, he
has had to part with his strong pawn centre
(which has lost its original value, since Black
has managed to get round it from the flank),
and for the moment the d5-pawn is more of
a weakness than a strength. In return White
has sharply activated his pieces and, given
the opportunity, he is ready to create threats
against the black king. I felt that I would
always have sufficient counterplay against
the opponent's actions in the centre and on
the queenside: nearly all my pieces are
eyeing the kingside, whereas most of the
opponent's are on the other side. The position is one of dynamic balance.

Here, to my surprise, Karpov thought for
more than an hour! This is another point in
the game which is hard to explain. Given
thorough home preparation it is hardly
possible to overlook the e4-e5 break (it is a
very obvious idea), but if it is assumed that
the entire analysis of the plan with 18...♕f6
was made in great haste, the picture begins
to become clear. At any event, the fruit of
this long think (which, incidentally, equalised the reading on our clocks) was a move
which immediately placed Black in a critical
position...

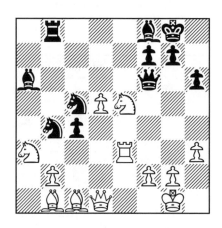

25...♘bd3? (63)

The start of a comedy of errors, which
pursued the two players for three moves in
succession. Of course, at first sight 25...♘bd3
looks more logical – all other things being
equal, simultaneously Black also includes his
rook in the play. However, here 25...♘cd3!
was necessary, retaining control of c2. White
does not have a great choice, and the simplest is to force an immediate draw by 26
♗xd3 ♘xd3 27 ♖xd3 cxd3 28 ♘d7 ♕d6 29
♘xb8 ♕xb8 30 ♘b1 (30 ♕a4 is also possible) 30...♕e5 31 ♘c3 ♗b4 32 ♗d2 ♗xc3 33
♗xc3 ♕xd5.

But I was intending the fighting 26 ♘g4.
Now where should the queen move?
26...♕h4 is not bad – 27 ♖g3 ♔h8 28 ♗d2
(Nunn-Psakhis, Hastings 1987/88) 28...♗c5!,
prettily forcing a draw: 29 ♕f3 f5! 30 ♘e3 f4
31 ♘f5 ♕xg3 32 ♘xg3 fxg3 33 ♕e4 ♖f8 34
♗xb4 ♗xf2+ 35 ♔f1 ♗c5+ 36 ♔e2 ♖f2+ 37
♔d1 ♖f1+.

However, 26...♕d4! is stronger – in the
centre the queen occupies a far more aggressive position and controls the key a1-h8
diagonal. White has two main continuations:

1) 27 ♖g3 ♔h8! (the sharp variations with
27...♗d6 also lead to a draw, whereas
27...♘xc1? loses: 28 ♘xh6+ ♔h8 29 ♘xf7+

♔g8 30 ♕h5) 28 ♗e3 ♕xb2 29 ♘xh6 gxh6 30 ♕h5 ♕f6 31 ♖f3! ♕g6 32 ♗d4+ ♗g7 33 ♗xg7+ ♕xg7 34 ♖xf7 ♕g5 35 ♕f3 ♔g8 36 ♖f5 ♕g7 37 ♕e3, and White's attack is nevertheless sufficient for a draw;

2) 27 ♘c2! (a more positional method – a bad piece is exchanged, and in addition the annoying knight at d3 is deprived of support) 27...♘xc2 (27...♕xd5? 28 ♘f6+!) 28 ♗xc2, when 28...♗c5? is bad because of 29 ♕f3! ♖d8 (29...♘xc1 30 ♘xh6+! Dvoirys-Timoshchenko, Barnaul 1988) 30 ♗e4 ♕xd5 31 ♘xh6+! gxh6 32 ♖g4+ ♔h7 33 ♕f6 ♗f8 34 ♕xa6 and wins. But Black has a reasonable choice: 28...♗d6!? 29 b3 ♕a1 30 bxc4 ♗xc4 31 ♗xd3 ♗xd3 32 ♖e1 ♗g6 with a rapid draw (Dvoiris-Timoshchenko, Naberezhnye Chelny 1988), or 28...h5! 29 ♘h6+! (29 ♘e5 ♕xd5, which has occurred in the 21st century, is less good) 29...gxh6 30 ♖g3+ ♗g7 31 ♗xd3 h4! 32 ♖xg7+ ♔xg7 33 ♕h5 or 30...♔h7 31 ♕f3! ♗g7! 32 ♕xf7, in each case with a draw.

Thus 25...♘cd3! would have fully justified Black's opening idea and given him a good game, whereas after 25...♘bd3? the scales could have tipped in White's favour.

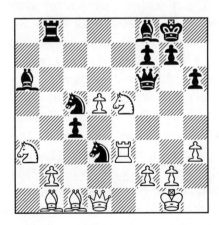

26 ♘g4? (14)

This places White on the verge of defeat! The problem was that for me Black's 25th move came as something of a surprise. Awaiting Karpov's reply, I sat in my rest room, mentally calculating the unclear variations with 25...♘cd3 26 ♘g4. Therefore, when I encountered a surprise, I did not instantly readjust, but decided to continue as planned. Of course, the opened b-file and the agile knight on c5 are serious arguments for Black in the coming battle, changing the situation to his advantage, but nevertheless I was hoping that the imminent attack on the king would safeguard White, even if his queenside were to be completely destroyed.

However, with an hour for thought, I should have found both the drawbacks to the planned move, and the best decision – 26 ♕c2!. After other moves Black is alright, whereas with this brilliant reply White could have gained a clear advantage, although on the way to his goal he would have had to display considerable resourcefulness: 26...♖b4 (the only move; 26...♘b3? 27 ♘d7!) 27 ♘c6! (27 ♖e2? ♘b3) 27...♖b6! 28 ♖e8! ♖xc6 (this exchange sacrifice is forced: after 28...♘d7? both 29 ♘e7+ and 29 ♘a5 are strong) 29 dxc6 ♕xc6 30 ♖d8!. White's idea is to return the exchange at a convenient moment and obtain an extra passed pawn. And he achieves this: for example, 30...♕e4 (30...♗b7 31 f3 or 30...♕b6 31 ♖a8 is no better) 31 ♗d2 ♗b7 32 f3 ♕h4 33 ♗a5! ♘e6 34 ♘xc4!? ♘xd8 35 ♕xd3 ♗c5+ 36 ♔h2 ♘e6 37 ♗d2.

The other question is how great are White's chances of converting his material advantage. Black may be able to save himself (although at the board, with the clock ticking away, this is highly problematic), but in any case he would have faced a difficult struggle for a draw.

It is probable that, when he played 25...♘bd3?, Karpov simply overlooked the move 26 ♕c2! and he found it only after the conclusion of the game – just as I did, and also all the commentators. Perhaps he was expecting 26 ♗xd3 cxd3 (avoiding 26...♘xd3 27 ♖xd3 cxd3 28 ♘d7 with the same forced draw as after 25...♘cd3), but after 27 ♘b1 (intending ♘c3) 27...♗d6 28 ♘c6 ♖a8 29 b4 ♘d7 30 ♕b3 ♕h4 or 30...♗b5 he would merely have achieved a dynamic balance. At any event, his risk almost proved justified: now the scales could have tipped in favour of Black.

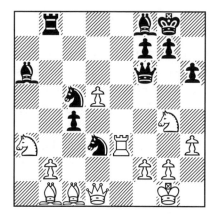

26...♕b6?

After this quick and obvious reply everything fell into place: Karpov began preparing to win material, while I set about assembling a striking force for storming the king's fortress; i.e. each was engaged in his favourite business!

Meanwhile, 26...♕f5! was stronger, not moving the queen away from the kingside. In previous analyses I considered only variations that are obviously favourable for Black after 27 ♖f3(?) ♕xd5 and 27 ♖g3(?!) ♔h8 28 ♖f3 ♕xd5 29 ♘e3 ♕d7! etc. But things are far harder for him after 27 ♗xd3!? cxd3 28 ♘b1! ♘e4 29 ♘c3 ♘xc3 30 bxc3 ♗d6 31 ♕a4 ♕c8 32 ♗d2 ♗c4 33 ♖e1 ♖a8 34 ♕c6 ♕xc6 35 dxc6 or 27...♘xd3 28 ♖f3 ♕d7 (28...♕xd5? 29 ♘f6+) 29 ♖g3 ♔h8 30 ♗xh6 ♕xd5 (30...f5 31 ♘e3) 31 ♘e3 ♕e6 32

♘axc4 ♗xc4 33 ♘xc4 ♕xc4 34 ♗xg7+ ♔xg7 35 ♖xd3 ♗xb2 36 ♕h5+ ♔g8 37 ♖g3+ ♔f8 38 ♕h6+ ♔e7 39 ♖e3+ ♔d7 40 ♕g5, and White has good drawing chances.

Karpov could, nevertheless, have set me serious problems, whereas now...

27 ♖g3 (14)

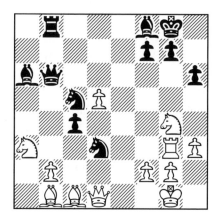

An unequivocal hint at a direct attack. It is interesting that at this very important moment Karpov replied largely intuitively, almost without thinking.

27...g6 (4)

All the same Black could not avoid a weakening of his king's pawn screen: 27...♔h8 28 ♘xh6! ♘e4! (forcing White to think also about defence) 29 ♘xf7+ ♔g8 30 ♖e3 ♘exf2! 31 ♕h5 ♗c5! with equality, or 30 ♗e3 ♕xb2 31 ♕h5 ♘xg3 32 fxg3 ♗xa3! (as in the following variation). 27...♘e4 is also possible: 28 ♘xh6+! ♔h7 29 ♗e3! ♕xb2 30 ♘xf7 ♘xg3 31 fxg3 with an attack, good enough to save the game: 31...♔g8 32 ♕h5 ♗xa3! or, alternatively, 31...♗xa3! 32 ♕h5+ ♔g8 33 ♗xd3+ cxd3 34 ♘g5 d2, immediately forcing perpetual check.

Black eliminated the threat of the sacrifice on h6 in the most radical way – he removed the pawn from g7, rightly assuming that it would not be easy for White to redirect the fire of his attack against the g6-point. With his cool-headed decision Karpov clearly let it be known that he considered White's attack to be short-lived, and he was ready (guided by Capablanca's well-known principle – the minimum number of pieces in defence) to assail the opponent's defenceless queenside.

28 ♗xh6! (14)

Here the knight is a far more valuable attacking piece than the dark-squared bishop. After 28 ♘xh6+? ♗xh6 29 ♗xh6 ♕xb2 30 ♗xd3 cxd3 nothing comes of the attack. 28 ♘xc4?! ♗xc4 29 ♗xd3 ♘xd3 30 ♖xd3 ♗xd3 31 ♕xd3 h5! is also unfavourable for White.

28...♕xb2 (7)

It would seem that Black has clearly been more successful: he has already broken through on the queenside and is ready to win the knight on a3, whereas White has not yet created any real threats against the king.

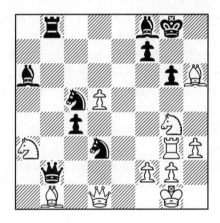

29 ♕f3!

The inclusion of White's strongest piece sharply changes the situation on the kingside. The black king begins to feel uncomfortable – the defensive lines around it look unconvincing compared with the opponent's powerful piece grouping.

29...♘d7 (7)

By covering the f6-square, Karpov follows his conception (defence with minimal means), but underestimates the opponent's attacking potential. Strangely enough, this natural move, which in itself is not bad, hinders Black's subsequent play: his control of the d3-point is weakened, and now at an appropriate moment White can get rid of the knight on d3.

After 29...♕xa3 30 ♘f6+ ♔h8 the attack and the material advantage would have balanced each other: perpetual check results from both 31 ♗xf8 ♖xf8 (not 31...♖xb1+? 32 ♔h2 ♕c1 because of 33 ♕h5+!!) 32 ♔h2 ♖g4! ♕c1+ 33 ♔h2 ♔g7! 34 ♘h5+ ♔g8 35 ♘f6+, and the spectacular 31 ♕h5!? ♖xb1+ 32 ♗c1+ ♔g7 33 ♘e8+ ♔g8 34 ♘f6+.

It is not possible to gain an advantage by 29...♖b6 on account of 30 ♔h2! ♗d6 31 ♗e3!? (with the threat of ♘h6+; 31 ♗xd3 with equality is more modest) 31...♔g7 and here, apart from the prosaic 32 ♘xc4 ♗xc4 33 ♗xd3 ♗xd3 34 ♗xc5 ♗xc5 35 ♕xd3 with equality, there is the incredible resource 32 ♗a2!! with a spectacular knockout in the event of 32...♗xg3+ 33 fxg3 ♕xa2? 34 ♘h6+! ♔g8 35 ♕e3! ♖e6 36 ♕d4! ♕b2 37 dxe6!! ♕xd4 38 e7 – Black is now a queen up, but he is absolutely helpless: 38...♕d7(e4) 39 ♘f6+, while the defence 38...♗b5 is killed by the 'dead' knight on a3! Therefore 32...f5!? is correct: 33 ♘xc4 ♗xc4 34 ♗xc4 ♘e1! 35 ♕d1 ♘c2 36 ♗xc5 ♗xc5 37 ♗d3 ♗d6! 38 ♗xc2 fxg4 with equality.

If immediately 29...♗d6(?), attacking the dangerous rook, then 30 ♗e3! is even more successful: 30...♗xg3 31 ♘h6+! (instead of my previous 31 ♘f6+ ♔g7 32 ♕xg3, which only promises a draw) 31...♔h7 32 ♕xg3, and Black has great problems: 32...♘e4 33 ♕h4 or 32...♕e5 33 ♕h4 ♕h5 34 ♕f6(e7) ♕e5 35 ♕xf7+ ♕g7 36 ♕f3! with an unceasing attack.

But Karpov still did not believe in the seriousness of White's attack, and he was dreaming of calmly picking up the lone knight on a3 and then converting his material advantage.

30 ♗xf8 ♔xf8

In the event of 30...♖xf8 31 ♘h6+ ♔g7 (31....♔h7? 32 ♘xf7) 32 ♘f5+ Black would have been fighting only for a draw. But what can White do now?

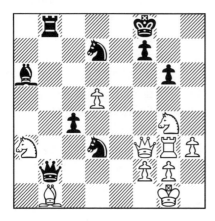

31 ♔h2!

This important prophylactic move is one which has occurred in many branches of this game: before the assault the king must move off the weakened back rank. It transpires that Black has definite problems which are beginning to unnerve him. However, he has an energetic manoeuvre.

31...♖b3!

31...♕d4!? was also not bad. After making his move, Karpov calmly stood up and began leisurely strolling up and down the stage, transferring his triumphant glance from the board to the auditorium and back again. Indeed, the rook comes into play with great effect, creating an unpleasant 'X-ray' along the third rank, the aim of which is to reach the rook standing in ambush at g3 (with its exchange, the potential of White's attack will be exhausted). And after safeguarding himself against the combined threats, Black will at last be able to pick up the stray knight on a3.

The the grandmasters watching the game were sure that I was losing. White has no choice, but his only sensible reply radically changes the situation.

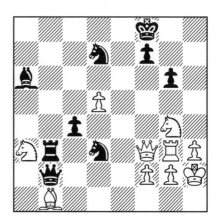

32 ♗xd3!

By this point I had less than 10 minutes left on my clock, whereas Karpov had slightly more than half an hour, but after 32 ♗xd3 I became absolutely calm, since I felt intuitively that White had nothing to fear. Of course, Black can win a piece, but on the other hand the white queen can steal right up on the enemy king.

To all appearances, this turn of events came as a surprise to Karpov. His expression changed and he spent nearly all his remaining time, trying to choose the best of the four possible captures (a unique instance: two pieces are *en prise* – and both can be captured in two ways!), but after any one of them White's threats were by now very obvious. Stupefied by the mass of highly complicated variations, which were hardly possible to calculate, Karpov lost control over the position and in pursuing the mirage of victory he overstepped the fatal mark...

32...cxd3?! (27)

And Karpov now had just three minutes left... The move made by him aggravates Black's problems, but 32...♖xa3 33 ♕f4 ♖xd3

(33...cxd3? 34 ♖f3!) 34 ♕d6+ etc. looked dangerous, while the obvious 32...♖xd3 would have led by force to an endgame a pawn down – 33 ♕f4 ♕xa3 34 ♘h6 ♕e7 35 ♖xg6 ♕e5 36 ♕xe5 ♘xe5 37 ♖xa6 ♖xd5, although White's winning chances would be very limited: 38 ♖a8+ (38 ♘f5?! ♘f3+!) 38...♔e7 39 ♘f5+ ♔e6 40 ♘e3 ♖c5 41 ♖a2 f5 42 f4 ♘d3 43 ♖c2 c3 44 ♘d1 ♘xf4 etc. But such a metamorphosis obviously could not satisfy Karpov: effectively a piece up, to go into a colourless ending? And he chose the sharp capture with the pawn, hoping to queen it in the time scramble.

33 ♕f4

Of course!

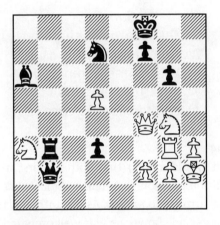

33...♕xa3?

In the end, now in desperate time-trouble, Karpov loses his nerve and grabs the knight which has plagued him for so many moves. However, this loss of tempo allows White to whip up a decisive attack with lightning speed. Immediately after the game some of the commentators recommended 33...♖xa3(?), but after 34 ♖f3! Black's position collapses.

The only correct continuation was 33...d2! 34 ♘h6 ♘f6!, when Black holds on literally by a thread:

1) 35 ♖xb3 ♕xb3 36 ♕xf6 ♕xd5 37 ♘xf7

(after 37 ♕h8+ ♔e7 38 ♘g8+ ♔d6 39 ♕f6+ ♔c5 the king escapes) 37...d1♕ (37...♔e8? 38 ♘b1! d1♕ 39 ♘c3! – a fork of both queens!) 38 ♘d6+ ♔g8 39 ♕xg6+ ♔f8 40 ♕f6+ ♔g8 41 ♘f5! ♕xf5! 42 ♕xf5 ♕d6+ 43 f4 ♕xa3, and the three pawns for the piece give White no more than a moral advantage;

2) 35 ♕d6+ ♔e8 (35...♔g7? 36 ♘f5+ ♔h7 37 ♕f8 etc.) 36 ♕xa6 d1♕ 37 ♕c8+ ♔e7 38 ♕c5+ (against two queens one cannot take liberties: 38 ♘c4 ♕xf2! 39 d6+? ♕xd6) 38...♔d7! 39 ♕c6+ ♔e7 40 d6+ ♔f8 (40...♔e6 41 ♕c8+ ♘d7 42 ♕e8+ ♔d5 43 ♕xf7+ ♔c6! 44 ♘c4 ♕f6 is also possible) 41 ♕c8+ ♔g7 42 ♘f5+ ♔h7 43 ♕f8 ♘g4+ 44 ♖xg4 ♖xh3+!! (grandiose!) 45 ♔xh3 ♕h1+ 46 ♔g3 ♕e5+ 47 ♖f4 g5! 48 ♕xf7+ ♔h8 49 ♕f8+ ♔h7, and the desperate attempt to play for a win – 50 ♕e7+ ♕xe7 51 dxe7 gxf4+ 52 ♔xf4! (after all, it is not easy for the black queen to battle on its own: 52...♕c1+? 53 ♔g4 ♕c8 54 ♘b5 ♕c4+ 55 ♘bd4) is most simply parried by exploiting a study-like motif: 52...♕xg2! 53 e8♕ ♕g4+ 54 ♔e5 ♕e4+ 55 ♔xe4 – stalemate!

34 ♘h6 ♕e7 35 ♖xg6 ♕e5

For an instant Black has everything in order – White's strongest piece is crippled.

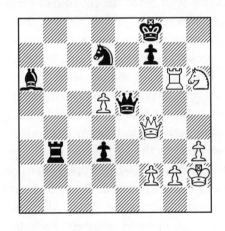

36 ♖g8+ ♔e7 37 d6+!

When I landed this deadly blow with an

undefended pawn, a storm of applause broke out in the auditorium. The chief arbiter Lothar Schmid vigorously waved his arms, calling on the spectators to be quiet, and for a time he succeeded.

37...♔e6 (time-trouble agony) **38 ♖e8+ ♔d5 39 ♖xe5+ ♘xe5 40 d7 ♖b8 41 ♘xf7**

After making this move, I went off to the rest room for a short time, and when I returned to the board to sign the scoresheets the spectators again rewarded me with an ovation. From force of habit Karpov could have adjourned the game, but in such a position he decided not to and he left the stage without the traditional handshake **(1-0)**. Times: 2.25–2.29.

In my view, for all the mistakes by both sides, this game is unique as regards the intensity and scale of the problems which the players faced in a new, very complicated position, which later became one of the fashionable *tabiyas* of the Ruy Lopez (incidentally, Karpov's desire to get even in this opening was to cost him our 1990 match, where he suffered two crushing defeats in the Zaitsev Variation – *Games 69, 74*).

The outcome of this grandiose battle essentially symbolised the collapse of Karpov's hopes of revenge. The knock-out in the 16th game practically decided the match – my enormous lead (9½-6½) and my obvious playing advantage did not leave this in any doubt, but, alas, after the great emotional stress a distinct slump occurred in my play.

After declining to take my last time-out, I went along to the 17th game in a disorientated state and failed to cope with another novelty by the opponent. This failure did not yet greatly distress me: 'Well, what can be done – an opening disaster!' Such things happened – it was something that had to be expected. The match situation remained

favourable, one win by me could effectively settle the outcome, and in the next 'White' game I was in the mood to engage my opponent in a decisive battle, assuming that Karpov would not avoid one.

And a battle took place! In the 18th game, in the words of the observers, I played 'brilliant and original chess'. Two of my moves especially staggered the commentators. One of them wrote: 'Typical Kasparov! The entire board was in flames.' This unforgettable game, which Taimanov called 'the prefinishing culmination of a fascinating duel', nearly became my best creative achievement in our matches. Alas, only nearly...

> *Game 18*
> **G.Kasparov-A.Karpov**
> World Championship Match
> 18th Game, Leningrad
> 19/20.09.1986
> *Queen's Indian Defence E13*

1 d4

It would appear that both my first move and the position soon reached did not come as a surprise to Karpov. As the 14th and 16th games had shown, he was well prepared for the Ruy Lopez. The other reason why I played 1 d4 was that I had something in store for my opponent in the set-ups he usually employed: I had prepared an improvement in the Queen's Gambit and I was now ready for the Queen's Indian Defence. In addition, a change of approach usually produces a certain psychological effect. But not in this case!

1...♘f6 2 c4 e6 3 ♘f3 (avoiding 3 ♘c3 – I should remind you that in the variation from the 4th game we both now knew about the move 12...♕c7!) **3...b6**

And here is confirmation of Black's striving for a large-scale battle – the Queen's Gambit is given a rest.

4 ♘c3 (after 4 g3 ♗a6 at that time I did not see any particular prospects for White)

4...♗b4

Earlier, in the 10th and 32nd games of the first match, Karpov preferred 4...♗b7 5 a3 d5 6 cxd5 ♘xd5 – here we both had great experience. But now he chose one of the most complicated variations – the 'hybrid', which I had successfully tested with White in my match with Timman (1985). Again with unusual boldness he challenged me on my own territory!

5 ♗g5 ♗b7 (5...h6!?) **6 e3** (6 ♘d2!?) **6...h6 7 ♗h4**

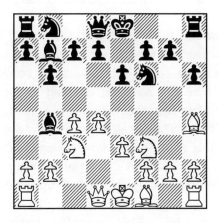

7...♗xc3+

But not immediately 7...d6? because of 8 ♕a4+ ♘c6 9 d5. Here Timman and Miles acted more 'sweepingly' – 7...g5 8 ♗g3 ♘e4 (*Game Nos.9-11, 20*).

8 bxc3 d6

Black has quite a flexible position, and it has to be ascertained what in fact are more important – the defects in White's pawn chain or the strength of his centre, and whether the white bishops are 'dangerous' or 'lack scope'.

9 ♘d2

A logical plan, known since the game Bot-

vinnik-Keres (12th USSR Championship, Moscow 1940): 9...e5 10 f3 ♕e7 11 e4 ♘bd7 12 ♗d3 g5 13 ♗f2 etc.

9...g5

At that time this half-forgotten move had only just once again appeared on the scene. The bishop is driven away from h4 before White prepares a retreat for it at f2, and now carrying out the 'Botvinnik plan' will involve the loss of a tempo. But White can change his plan: the early ...g7-g5 allows him to seize the h-file by h2-h4.

Therefore it is better not to hurry with either 9...e5 or 9...g5 – later games showed that 9...♘bd7 10 f3 ♕e7 is more flexible, and then 11 ♕a4 e5 12 e4 0-0 or 11 e4 g5 12 ♗f2 ♘h5 (13 g3 f5) with roughly equal play.

10 ♗g3

The first critical moment.

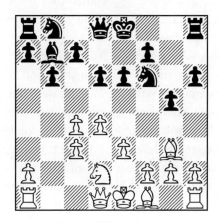

After the usual 10...♘bd7 I was planning to play 11 h4! ♖g8 12 hxg5 hxg5, and now (instead of 13 ♕c2 or 13 f3 which had previously occurred) to prevent queenside castling by 13 ♕b3!? (with the idea of 13...♕e7 14 c5) or 13 ♕a4!? (Bareev-Gavrikov, 54th USSR Championship, Minsk 1987), judging the position to be in favour of White. Similar motifs are in evidence after 10...♘c6 11 h4! ♖g8 12 hxg5 hxg5 13 ♖h6 ♕e7 14 ♕f3! ♖g6 (14...♘d7 15 c5!) 15 ♖xg6 fxg6 (Bacrot-

Adams, Sarajevo 2000) 16 ♘e4 (16 c5!?) 16...♘xe4 17 ♕xe4 ♕f6 18 c5!.

10...♕e7!?

Also a rapid reply, but an unexpected one for me – and yet another novelty by Karpov in this match! By retaining the option of ...♘b8-c6, he diverts me from my intended new plan of attack. It can be imagined how shocked I was: 'Again the opponent anticipated an improvement on my part! From where does he get such insight?'

Light on the origin of this phenomenon was shed by an article entitled 'Autumn on Kamenny Island' by a member of Karpov's team, the psychologist and journalist Igor Akimov, published soon after the match in the magazine *Studenchesky Meridian*. Here there is some amazing evidence – it turns out that on the eve of the game Karpov spent a sleepless night analysing the position after 10...♕e7, since he was completely sure that it would occur!

But why after two crushing wins in the Ruy Lopez should I change tack, and begin the game not with the king's pawn, but the queen's pawn? Let us suppose that Karpov made a brilliant guess. But, even knowing the opening, how could he picture in such detail the structure of the opponent's preparations? How could he possibly foresee exactly what would be 'on the board tomorrow', if I was intending to employ a continuation that I had never played before?! And at the same time to be sure that I had 'honed this position at home', and that 'it was familiar to me' (indeed, we had several pages of analysis), and that Black's 10th move would come as a surprise to me! It has to be agreed that there is only one sensible explanation...

On the day of the game the incredible happened: from Karpov's chess table at home the position migrated on to the stage of the concert hall of the Leningrad Hotel. Instead of the natural 10...♘bd7, Black preferred the clever 10...♕e7 – what Karpov was avoiding, no one realised, apart from he and I.

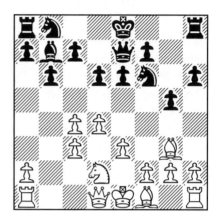

11 a4

A useful move, directed against Black's queenside castling, but with an accurate reply he can solve his opening problems. Therefore later the main line became 11 h4 ♖g8 12 hxg5 hxg5. Here 13 a4 is now weaker in view of 13...♘c6! (with the idea of ...0-0-0 and ...♖h8) 14 ♘b3 ♘e4 – the g3-bishop has been prematurely deprived of support. If 13 ♗e2 again there is the sound reply 13...♘c6! (13...♗xg2?! 14 ♖h6! Bareev-Dolmatov, 54th USSR Championship, Minsk 1987) 14 ♕c2 0-0-0 15 0-0-0 ♖h8 with equality (Kasparov-Psakhis, 2nd match game, La Manga 1990). 13 ♖h6 ♘bd7 14 ♕a4 is more topical, but here too White has not achieved any tangible results.

The unclear gambit 13 c5!? dxc5 14 ♗b5+ has also occurred (V.Mikhalevski-Ligterink, Leeuwarden 1995) or immediately 11 c5!? dxc5 12 ♗b5+ (Zviagintsev-Solozhenkin, Elista 1995). Generally speaking, pawn sacrifices and other 'drastic' measures are typical of White's play in this set-up. And this is understandable: the static elements of the position (such as the integrity of the pawn structure) 'vote' for Black, and White has to play energetically.

11...a5

'This contradicts the idea of 10...♕e7. Karpov played 11...a5 very quickly, having probably decided that the inclusion of 11 a4 a5 does not greatly change the situation on the board. However, this is not so. 11...♘c6! was more logical.' (Makarychev). Apparently Karpov was concerned about 12 ♘b3 with the threat of a4-a5, but after 12...h5! 13 f3 (13 h4 ♘e4 with equality) 13...h4 14 ♗f2 a5 and ...0-0-0 Black has a good game (Dokhoian-Lerner, Lvov 1990).

It would appear that during his urgent night-time analysis my opponent simply did not have time to delve into certain nuances of an unfamiliar position.

12 h4

'Play over the entire front, emphasising the insecure position of the black king. White's desire to open the position is associated with the presence of his two bishops.' (M.Gurevich)

12...♖g8

As yet no one has tried 12...g4 (avoiding the opening of the h-file) 13 h5 ♘bd7 (if 14 ♗h4 Gurevich recommended 14...♕f8).

13 hxg5 hxg5

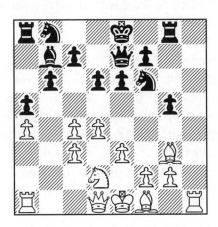

14 ♕b3!

A very important moment – White tries to prevent the opponent from completing his development. 'The main attacking resource is the c4-c5 breakthrough, and operations on the h-file are kept in reserve.' (Taimanov). The modest 14 ♖h2 ♘bd7 15 ♗e2 (Kozlov-Tukmakov, Novosibirsk 1986) would have allowed 15...0-0-0 and ...♖h8.

14...♘a6

'A courageous decision, signifying an almost complete rejection of active counterplay for the sake of erecting a powerful defensive wall.' (Makarychev). 14...♘bd7? is weak: 15 c5! dxc5 16 ♗xc7, and 14...♘e4?! is also insufficient on account of 15 ♘xe4 ♗xe4 16 c5! dxc5 17 ♖d1. After 14...♘c6 15 c5! (otherwise 15...0-0-0) 15...dxc5 16 dxc5 ♕xc5 17 ♗xc7 ♘d5 18 ♘e4 (Makarychev) 18...♘d4! (18...♕e7? 19 ♗d6) 19 cxd4 ♕xc7 20 ♔d2 and ♖ac1 the initiative is again with White.

However, 14...♗c6!? would have retained the possibility of the normal development of the knight at d7. After this the immediate 15 c5 is not very dangerous for Black in view of 15...bxc5 (15...dxc5?! 16 ♗b5!) 16 dxc5 d5 (Makarychev), but 15 ♖b1 ♘bd7 16 c5 bxc5 17 ♗b5! is more interesting, with sharp play (Rashkovsky-Dolmatov, 54th USSR Championship, Minsk 1987).

Of course, at a6 the knight is not very well placed. However, Karpov is hoping to castle and then seize the h-file.

15 ♖b1!

'This rook will exert considerable (although indirect) pressure on the black king, bishop and knight at a6, and will make the c4-c5! breakthrough possible. Kasparov's play in a very complicated position just after the opening creates a strong harmonious impression – a combination of a deep strategic plan with controlled concrete decisions.

However, the world champion soon began to run seriously short of time.' (Makarychev)

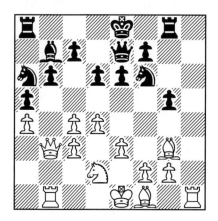

15...♔f8!

15...0-0-0? is too dangerous: 16 c5! dxc5 17 ♘c4 with the threats of ♘xa5 and ♕xb6!. It is also unfavourable for Black to play 15...♘e4?! 16 ♘xe4 ♗xe4 17 ♖d1 (or even 17 c5 immediately), since after exchanging the passive white knight on d2 he remains with the same unresolved problems: where to hide his king, and how to coordinate his forces? And if 15...♗c6 the thematic 16 c5! is good.

White's achievements are evident: Black has a bad knight at a6 and his king is still insecurely placed on the kingside. However, if Black should succeed in playing ...♔g7 and ...♖h8, the bishop on g3 will begin to come under threat by ...♘h5. Therefore White must act!

16 ♕d1!

Clearly demonstrating to the opponent the gravity of the problems facing him. If 16...♔g7 there follows 17 ♖b5!, but that is not all: White has taken control of the g4-square and outlined a plan of mobilising his forces on the kingside (♖h2!, ♗d3, then e3-e4-e5, etc.).

'One of the strongest moves of the entire return match, disclosing the colossal re-

sources concealed in the position. Sometimes it is unexpected moves such as this that sharply change the picture of the battle! If 16 ♕c2 there could have followed Yudasin's suggestion 16...♖e8 with the idea of 17 e4(?) e5 18 f3(?) exd4 19 cxd4 ♘b4, and the black pieces come alive.' (Gurevich). Or, as in the game, 16...♗c6.

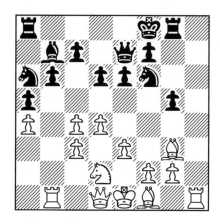

16...♗c6!

Preventing ♖b5 (in order to play ...♔g7) and at the same time aiming at the a4-pawn. If 16...e5?! (in order after 17...exd4 18 cxd4 to regroup the knight by 18...♘b4) White has the strong reply 17 c5! exd4 18 cxd6 cxd6 19 ♘c4! dxe3 20 fxe3 (not 20 ♗xd6? exf2+ and 21...♘e4+) 20...♘e4 (20...♔g7 21 ♖xb6) 21 ♗xd6 ♘xd6 22 ♕xd6 ♘c5 23 ♖xb6 with an extra pawn and winning chances.

17 ♖h2

'Having delayed the plan of ...♔g7 and ...♖h8, White prepares the development of his f1-bishop (the g2-pawn is defended) followed by e3-e4-e5. It is clear that Black cannot wait.' (Makarychev)

17...♔g7?!

Now it only remains for the rook to be played to h8. 'In the event of 17...♘b8?! 18 ♗d3 ♘bd7 19 e4 Black's strategic problems would merely have been aggravated:

19...♔g7? is still dangerous on account of 20 e5 dxe5 21 dxe5, while if 19...e5, then 20 f3! followed by ♘f1-e3-f5.' (Makarychev)

But 17...♕d7! with the idea of ...e6-e5 was more accurate: for example, 18 ♖b5!? (Gurevich) 18...e5! 19 dxe5 dxe5, and the e5-pawn is taboo on account of 20...♘g4!, or 18 ♗d3 e5! 19 ♔f1 (19 c5 exd4!) 19...♔g7 20 c5!? ♖h8! and ...♖xh2 with good counterchances. And if 18 c5 bxc5 19 ♗b5 there is time for 19...cxd4!, when after 20 exd4 ♘b8 Black has a solid pawn chain.

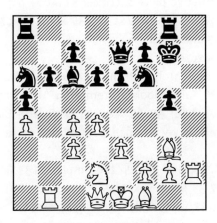

18 c5!

'Once again we see Kasparov's favourite idea – a pawn sacrifice for the initiative.' (Gurevich). This sacrifice is very timely: Black, who was all ready to neutralise the consequences of his dangerously-played opening, now faces new problems.

18...bxc5

It is easier for White to attack in the event of 18...dxc5?! 19 ♗e5! (threatening ♕h5) 19...♔f8 (19...♖h8? 20 ♕g4) 20 ♗b5: for example, 20...♘b8? 21 dxc5 bxc5 (21...♗xb5 22 ♖xb5!) 22 ♖h6 ♘e8 (22...♘d5? 23 c4! ♗xb5 24 cxd5) 23 ♕h5 f6 24 ♖h7! ♘g7 (24...♖g7 25 ♕h6) 25 ♕h3! and wins, or the more resilient 20...♗b7 21 ♖h6 ♖g6 22 ♖xg6 fxg6 23 ♘f3! ♘g4(e4) 24 ♕d3 etc.

19 ♗b5 (the Ruy Lopez!) **19...♘b8?**

Now White's initiative becomes threatening. However, he also has the better chances after 19...♕d7 20 f4! (exploiting the king's position on g7), or 19...♗xb5 20 axb5 ♘b8 21 b6, and after retreats by the bishop – 19...♗d5 20 ♕e2 cxd4 (20...♘b8?! 21 e4!) 21 exd4 ♘b8 22 f4!, or 19...♗b7 20 ♕e2! (not my earlier move 20 ♗d3 because of 20...cxd4! 21 exd4 ♗c6) 20...♖h8 21 ♗d3, creating problems for the opponent with the bishop on b7.

20 dxc5 d5?!

It is now hard to offer Black any good advice. After 20...♗xb5 21 ♖xb5! dxc5 22 ♕f3 ♘bd7 23 ♗xc7 the bishop also breaks free with destructive effect. 20...dxc5 also does not help in view of 21 ♗e5! ♔f8 22 ♖h6 with crushing threats (as in the note to Black's 18th move). And after the restricting 20...e5 there is the strong reply 21 ♘c4! ♖d8 22 cxd6 cxd6 23 f3! ♗xb5 24 ♖xb5 ♕c7 25 ♕d3 ♖a6 26 e4 and ♘e3.

The move made by Karpov does not spoil his pawn chain, but it so weakens the dark squares (around his king!) that it induces White to search for decisive continuations. Was this a lure on the part of my opponent? If so, it hit the target: here I spent much time seeking a clear way to win, but failed to find one – in the position it turned out that there were too many complicated tactical nuances, too many tempting possibilities...

21 ♗e5 ♔f8 22 ♖h6 ♘e8 23 ♕h5!

The strongest move (also involving a trap – 23...♗xb5? 24 ♖h7! and ♕h6+), although the variations after it are mind-boggling, and I already had little time left.

23...f6 24 ♖h7 ♘g7

There is also no defence after 24...♖g7 25 ♕h6 fxe5 (25...♗xb5? 26 ♖h8+! ♔f7 27 ♕h5+ ♖g6 28 ♖h6 ♗d3 29 e4) 26 ♖h8+ ♔f7 27 ♘f3 ♕f6 28 ♕h5+ ♖g6 29 ♖h6 e4 30 ♖xg6 ♕xc3+ 31 ♘d2 ♘g7 32 ♖xg7+ or

29...♔g7 30 ♖h7+ ♔f8 31 ♘xe5! etc.

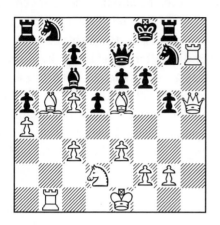

25 ♕f3!

Alas, here I grew nervous and I spent 9 out of my remaining 15 minutes to the time control (how I missed them later!) calculating a bishop sacrifice – 25 ♕h6? fxe5 26 ♘f3, leading after 26...♗xb5 merely to complications and a draw: 27 axb5 (27 ♘xe5? ♗e8 and wins) 27...♘d7 28 c6 g4!, or 27 ♖xb5 ♘c6 28 c4! (winning the e4-square for the knight; 28 ♘xg5 ♔e8!) 28...dxc4 29 ♘xg5 ♔e8 30 ♘e4 ♔f7(f8).

25...♔f7 26 ♕h5+ ♔f8 27 ♕f3! ♔f7 28 ♖h6?!

After repeating moves to save time, I took a decision which was far from best. I could have won by the unexpected 28 ♗e2 (and then on to h5), the sharp 28 e4, the cool-headed 28 ♔e2, or the lethal 28 c4! – now 28...♘d7 29 ♗xc6 ♘xe5 30 ♕h5+ ♔f8 31 ♗xa8 ♘xh5 32 ♖b8+, 28...♗xb5 29 axb5 and 28...g4 29 ♕f4 ♗xb5 30 axb5 are all hopeless for Black.

28...♘e8 (not 28...♘d7? because of 29 ♗xf6! ♘xf6 30 ♗xc6 or 29 ♗xc7! ♕xc5 30 ♗e5!)
29 e4?

A pawn joins the attack (30 ♗xf6 ♘xf6 31 e5 is threatened), but – the wrong one! 29 c4!? was far stronger. After 29...g4 30 ♕f4 ♗xb5 31 ♖xb5 ♘d7 32 ♗b2! e5 33 ♖h7+

♖g7 34 ♕h6 Black is helpless, while if 29...♗xb5 there is the decisive 30 cxd5! ♗d3 31 d6! (Makarychev) or 30...exd5 31 ♕xd5+ ♔g7 32 ♖xb5 ♔xh6 33 ♕xa8 ♕xe5 34 ♖xb8 ♕a1+ 35 ♔e2 ♕xa4 36 ♕d5.

29...g4 30 ♕f4 ♗xb5 31 ♖xb5

After the hasty 31 ♗xf6? ♘xf6 32 e5 Black had prepared 32...♗d3! (covering the h7-square) 33 ♖xf6+ ♔e8.

31...♘d7

Karpov has almost defended himself. Instead, 31...♘c6? would have allowed a destructive piece sacrifice: 32 ♖h7+ ♖g7 33 ♖xg7+ ♘xg7 34 ♗xc7 e5 35 ♕xg4 ♕xc7 36 exd5 and wins.

32 ♗xc7!?

Desperately fighting for the initiative. 32 ♗xf6 also looked tempting, but after 32...♘dxf6! 33 e5 ♖g6 34 ♖h8 ♖g8 Black would have retained possibilities of resisting.

32...♘xc5 (if 32...e5? the simplest is 33 ♖h7+ ♖g7 34 ♕h6! ♘xc5 35 ♕h5+ ♔f8 36 ♖h8+ ♖g8 37 ♗xa5 ♘d3+ 38 ♔f1) **33 ♕e3!**

Both forced and strong. In principle White's chances are better, but the position is now close to dynamic equilibrium: Black has managed to develop his pieces.

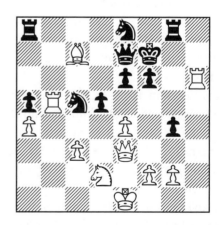

33...♘xe4?

A losing move! 33...♘xc7?! 34 ♖xc5 ♖g7

35 g3 was also insufficient, but the fearless 33...♘xa4! 34 ♗xa5 ♕d7 would have retained real hopes of saving the game, although after both 35 ♕d3 ♘b2 36 ♖xb2 ♖xa5 37 ♘c4! or 35...♖c8 36 c4! ♘c5 37 ♕d4 dxc4 38 ♕xd7+ ♘xd7 39 ♖b7 ♔e7 40 e5 fxe5 41 ♗b4+ ♔d8 42 ♖xe6, and 35 exd5 exd5 (35...♕xb5? 36 ♕xe6+ ♔g7 37 ♖h4! ♔f8 38 ♖h7! ♘g7 39 ♕xf6+ ♔e8 is bad because of 40 ♕g6+! ♔f8 41 ♘e4! ♕b1+ 42 ♔d2) 36 ♕d3 ♘b2 37 ♖xb2 ♖xa5 38 ♘b3 Black would have had to defend accurately.

34 ♘xe4 dxe4 35 ♗xa5 f5 (Black does not want to lose his e4-pawn, but this catastrophically weakens the dark squares) **36 ♗b4**

The immediate 36 ♕d4! was even better. In any event, White has an irresistible attack. However: 'The group of pawns in the centre and the opponent's severe time-trouble give Black definite counter-chances.' (Gurevich).

36...♕d7 37 ♕d4! (centralisation – and a trap: 37...♕xd4? 38 ♖b7+!) **37...♖a7**

The only defence against a rapid rout: 37...♖d8 38 ♖b7! ♕xb7 39 ♕xd8 g3 40 ♕h4! gxf2+ 41 ♔xf2 ♕a7+ (41...♖g6 42 ♖h8) 42 ♔f1 ♘g7 43 ♖f6+! ♔e8 44 ♕h7.

38 ♖h7+?

Even now, more than a quarter of a century later, I cannot look at this and my next move without a shudder – a 'combination' of the two weakest moves in my career! They disrupt the entire harmony of White's position, and no time-trouble can excuse them.

And yet there were just three moves to make before the time control – any three normal moves, and that would have been the end both of the game, and of any struggle in the match! The most practical was 38 ♗c5 ♕xd4 39 ♗xd4 ♖d7 (39...♖c7 40 a5) 40 ♖b8 (precisely three moves) or 38...♖b7 39 ♖h7+ ♖g7 40 ♖xg7+ ♘xg7 41 ♕xd7+ ♖xd7 42 a5 with an elementary win. The most

surprising – 38 ♗d6!? ♖g6 39 ♖h8 ♖g8 40 ♖b8!, and the most 'attacking' – 38 ♕e5!? ♖g6 (38...♖xa4? 39 ♖b7!) 39 ♖h7+ ♖g7 40 ♖xg7+ ♘xg7 41 ♖b8! ♘e8 42 ♕h8! and wins.

I cannot find any explanation for what happened. For 37 moves in this game Black has not once 'raised his head', and suddenly he receives an enormous gift!

38...♘g7

I overlooked this defence.

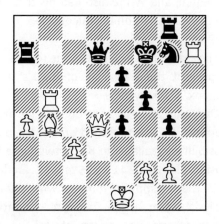

39 a5??

During the last few seconds before the fall of my flag I completely lost my head. 39 ♗c5! (Gurevich) would still have won after 39...♕xd4 (there is nothing better) 40 ♗xd4 ♖d7 41 ♖h6 and a4-a5 or 40...♔g6 41 ♗xa7 ♔xh7 42 ♖b7(b8). Instead of this White even manages to lose!

39...♔g6?!

Karpov had about two minutes left and in the time scramble he hurried to exchange the queens, although he could have gained a decisive attack by 39...♕xb5! 40 ♕xa7+ ♔g6 41 ♖h4 ♖d8! (Makarychev; 41...♕d3?! 42 ♕d4!) 42 ♕e3 ♘h5 etc. After 39...♔g6 the win for Black is by no means so obvious.

40 ♕xd7 ♖xd7

Here the game was adjourned. For some ten minutes I stared at the board, trying to understand what had happened in the time scramble and what had become of White's advantage.

Initially I wrote on my scoresheet the panicky 41 ♖xg7+?, in order to rid myself of the ill-starred rook which was now out of play (the conversion of the exchange advantage would not have presented a difficult problem for Black). But then I managed to take myself in hand and I realised that I could still fight for a draw: in the end, material was still equal, and White also had his trumps – the passed pawns on the queenside.

41 ♖h4

The sealed move. 'From h4 the rook is able to prevent the activation of Black's pawn phalanx.' (Makarychev)

Our team analysis went on until six in the morning. It was established that, of the main possibilities available to Black, two were the most unpleasant – 41...♘h5 and 41...♖gd8.

On the resumption, miracles with 'parallel analysis' again began to occur – identical key ideas and even oversights by the two players.

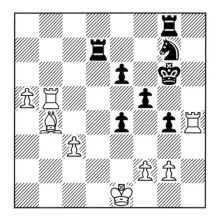

41...♖gd8!

The first coincidence: we also came to the conclusion that 41...♘h5 was weaker. However, in the variation 42 g3 (forced) 42...e3 43 ♖b6! exf2+ 44 ♔xf2 ♔g5 we only considered

45 ♗d6?! (45 ♖xe6? ♘xg3) 45...♖gd8 46 ♖xh5+ or the immediate 45 ♖xh5+?!, whereas after 45 ♖h1! ♘f6 46 ♖e1 ♘e4+ 47 ♖xe4 fxe4 48 ♗b5+ ♔f6 49 ♔e3 and ♔xe4 White does, indeed, have better drawing chances than in the game.

42 c4

Preventing the invasion of both black rooks. After 42 ♗c5? both 42...♖d1+ 43 ♔e2 ♖8d2+ 44 ♔e3 g3! 45 fxg3 ♖g2 and the preparatory 42...♔g5 would have been decisive.

42...♖d1+ 43 ♔e2

The key position of this variation: which of the white pawns should Black first take under control – 'a' or 'c'?

43...♖c1?

Our analysis of this second-rate continuation turned out to be deplorable – and Karpov once again struck at the most vulnerable point... The a-pawn is more dangerous (it is closer to the queening square), and therefore our main attention had been focused on 43...♖a1!. Now White loses after both 44 g3? ♖a2+ 45 ♔e1 e3 46 fxe3 ♖d3 47 ♗c5 ♘h5, and 44 ♗c5? g3! followed by ...♘h5. We were counting on 44 ♗c3 ♖c1! 45 ♗e5 (45 ♗xg7 ♖c2+ 46 ♔e3(e1) ♔xg7 is insufficient) 45...♖c2+ 46 ♔e1 ♖dd2(?) 47 ♖h6+! ♔g5 48 ♖h7 with a draw, but many years later it transpired that here too after 46...♘h5! (with the threat of ...♖dd2) 47 ♖b2 ♖xc4 things are bad for White.

Thus, after 43...♖a1! only a miracle could have saved White. But in our analysis of the drawing move 43...♖c1? a 'hole' had crept in on the very first move! Karpov was about 10 minutes late for the start of the adjournment session. According to his second, Sergey Makarychev, in analysis a win for Black had not been found and which of the two continuations (43...♖a1 or 43...♖c1) to choose was decided by the ex-world champion only five minutes before the start of play. And the move he chose was obviously the weaker one!

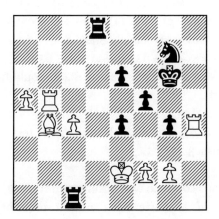

44 a6?

A blunder – it was on this terrible 'hole' that our conclusions were based. And yet White's problem was not in fact so difficult: he needed to activate his unfortunate rook on h4. This idea is realised by the obvious 44 ♗c5! (to e3 as quickly as possible – it would have been impossible to set up this ideal construction after 43...♖a1!), and things head for a draw: 44...♘h5 45 g3 (but not immediately 45 ♗e3? because of 45...♖c2+ 46 ♔e1 g3! 47 a6 ♖d3! 48 a7 ♖a3 and wins) 45...♖c2+ 46 ♔e1 ♖xc4 47 ♗e3! (a fortress!) 47...♖a4 48 ♖b6 ♖a1+ 49 ♔e2 ♖d3 50 ♖xh5 ♔xh5 51 ♖xe6 ♖a2+ 52 ♔f1! or even 50 ♖xe6+!? ♔f7 51 ♖a6 ♘xg3+ 52 fxg3 ♖a2+ 53 ♗d2 ♖axd2+ 54 ♔e1 ♖d1+ 55 ♔e2 ♖3d2+ 56 ♔e3 ♖d6 57 ♖b6 ♔f6 58 ♖h6+ ♔e5 59 ♖hxd6 ♖xd6 60 ♖b3 ♖d1 61 ♖a3 ♖f1 62 ♖a4 with a draw.

Unfortunately, I bashed out 44 a6 at blitz speed, whereas I should have stopped to think at the board...

44...♖c2+!

In our analysis we overlooked this intermediate check. 44...♖a1 was also good, since 45 ♖b6 ♖a2+ 46 ♔e1 would have led to a

position from the game, while after my planned 45 ♗d2 Black could have increased his advantage by 45...♘h5 46 ♖b2 ♖a8.

45 ♔e1 (if 45 ♔e3 Black decides matters with 45...♖d3+! 46 ♔f4 ♖xc4, when ...e4-e3 cannot be prevented) **45...♖a2 46 ♖b6**

After 46 ♗c5? ♖xa6 47 ♗e3 ♖a1+! 48 ♔e2 ♖a2+ 49 ♔e1 ♘h5 (shutting in the rook) 50 g3 ♖d3! with the threats of ...♘xg3 and ...♖xe3 White's fortress would have quickly collapsed. And if 46 ♗a5, then 46...♖a8!. Therefore White is forced to waste time on the defence of his a6-pawn, and Black activates his second rook.

46...♖d3

Preparing a decisive attack. The mistakes on moves 38-39 and in the analysis of the adjourned position had demoralised me, and during the resumption I played with a feeling of doom. I was especially vexed by the fate of my once formidable king's rook.

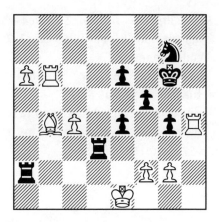

47 c5?

Too submissive! 47 ♗c5! g3! 48 fxg3 ♖xg3 49 ♔f1 was more resilient, although after 49...♖gxg2! 50 a7 ♖gc2 51 ♖b1 ♖xc4 52 ♗e3 ♘h5 53 ♖h2! ♖a3! 54 ♖g2+ ♔f6 55 ♗b6 ♘f4 56 ♖g8 ♖ca4 it is doubtful whether White can save the game.

47...♖a1+ 48 ♔e2 ♖a2+

'With the aim of keeping a large reserve of

time for the last moves before the time control, which had extended beyond our home analysis.' (Makarychev). One senses that Karpov too had not analysed 43...♖c1 very thoroughly.

49 ♔e1 g3

49...♔g5! would have won much more simply, including all the forces in the attack: 50 c6 (50 ♖h7 ♘h5) 50...♔xh4 51 c7 ♖a1+ 52 ♔e2 f4 with unavoidable mate, or 50 g3 ♖a1+ 51 ♔e2 f4.

50 fxg3 ♖xg3 51 ♔f1

'An interesting idea, which almost proved successful. If 51 ♖h2, then 51...f4 would have been decisive.' (Makarychev)

51...♖gxg2 52 ♗e1 ♖gc2 (combining an attack with prophylaxis) **53 c6 ♖a1 54 ♖h3 f4** (54....♘e8!?) **55 ♖b4**

Also after 55 ♖hb3 ♘f5 (55...♖cc1? 56 ♖b1!) 56 ♖b1 ♖aa2 there is no way of saving the game.

55...♔f5

55...♘h5(f5) was simpler: 56 ♖xe4 ♘g3+ 57 ♖xg3 fxg3 58 ♖g4+ ♔f5 59 ♖xg3 ♖xc6, and White can resign.

56 ♖b5+ e5 (not 56...♔g4? 57 ♖h4+ with perpetual check) **57 ♖a5 ♖d1**

The next time control had been reached, and Black could have played more accurately: 57...♖ac1! 58 c7(a7) e3!.

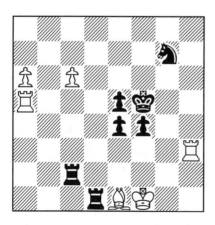

58 a7

58 c7! was better with the idea of 58...♖xc7 59 a7, but after the subtle 58...e3! 59 ♖h2! ♖cc1! 60 c8♕+ ♖xc8 61 a7 f3! (with the threat of ...♖xe1+) or 60 ♖e2 ♘e6! 61 a7 ♘xc7 62 a8♕ ♘xa8 63 ♖xa8 ♔e4 64 ♖a4+ ♖d4 65 ♖a3 ♖d3 66 ♖a4+ ♔f5 67 ♖h2 ♖d2 68 ♖e2 ♖cc2 all the same Black would have won.

58...e3! 0-1

Mate is unavoidable, and White resigned. Times: 3.39–3.42.

All I could do was bitterly regret that I had ruined a masterpiece. And it brought to mind the tragic 6th game of the first match, where I also unexpectedly returned my queen to d1, then failed to find the murderous 25 ♕h5! and also contrived to lose (Game No.94 in *Kasparov vs. Karpov 1975-1985*). The situation in the match again changed – my lead was reduced to the minimum and the psychological initiative had obviously passed to my opponent.

Playing after two successive defeats is very difficult; in fact it's pretty terrible: you imagine cracks appearing in the most reliable set-ups. In the 19th game I again went down in flames in the Grünfeld Defence – and earned my third successive nought! My recent enormous advantage had evaporated like the morning mist. The score was now equal: 9½-9½. In this desperate situation my trainers and I decided to aim for a short draw in the 20th game, in the 21st to parry the opponent's onslaught, and to make the 22nd the 'retribution game'. And that is what happened.

On the day of the 22nd game it rained incessantly, but as we set off for the start it suddenly stopped. And when I got out of the car, over the Leningrad Hotel was the most brilliant rainbow I had ever seen in my life. It was wonderful! For my romantic and rather superstitious nature, this was like a sign from on high. And indeed, this game granted me some unforgettable moments...

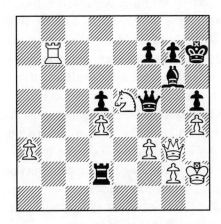

Game 19
G.Kasparov-A.Karpov
World Championship Match
22nd Game, Leningrad
3/4.10.1986

The time scramble had just come to an end and here the game was adjourned. Having just played ...♖c2-d2, Karpov looked very content: in a difficult battle for equality he appeared to have achieved much. I sank into thought... The most natural move for White is 41 ♖b4, but after 41...f6! 42 ♘xg6 ♛xg6 43 ♕xg6+ ♚xg6 Black has excellent chances of saving the rook ending. At the adjournment it was this development of events that was predicted by all the commentators.

However, I did not consider any move other than 41 ♘d7 (which had been conceived 'in rough' on the 37th move). Delving into the position, fairly soon I also discovered the third move of the combination (43 ♖b4). Staggered by its beauty, for 17 minutes I

checked and re-checked the variations, not believing my own eyes and gaining enormous aesthetic pleasure. Then I wrote down 41 ♘d7, but within a short time I again picked up my pen. Many thought that I had changed my initial decision. Nothing of the sort! It was simply that 'for safety's sake' I decided once again to overwrite the sealed move (a photocopy of the scoresheet was published soon afterwards in *Literaturnaya gazeta*), and only then did I seal my scoresheet in the envelope.

'Either I am going mad, or else I have a forced and very pretty win' I informed my trainers, who, incidentally, were looking rather despondent (they too had been analysing only 41 ♖b4). I remember their first reaction: 'No, that sort of thing doesn't happen.' But it turned out that it does happen! We analysed the position for a long time: we had to check over and over again that our eyes were not deceiving us.

My opponent arrived for the adjournment session with a heavy heart. It stands to reason that he had found the combination, and one can imagine with what feelings he awaited the revealing of the sealed move, and with what difficulty he appeared to remain completely calm. When the arbiter was opening the envelope, Karpov stared into the audience, but even so he was unable to restrain himself and he cast a glance at Schmid's hand, when the latter was taking the scoresheet out of the envelope. Even before the move was reproduced on the board, Karpov saw it and understood everything...

41 ♘d7!!

'The grandmasters unanimously called this move a study-like solution.' (Keene)

41...♖xd4

It is not a matter of the pawn, but of the exchange of queens, which Black wishes to

offer (from f4). How to defend against this?
42 ♘f8+ ♚h6 43 ♖b4!!

The crux of the combination! White's small army operates so harmoniously that Black is unable to break up the mating net without great loss of material.

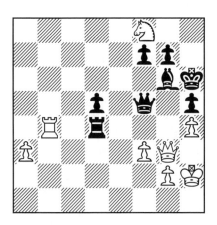

43...♗c4

Here Karpov thought for no more than a minute. The following variation is especially pretty: 43...♖xb4 44 axb4 d4 45 b5 d3 46 b6 d2 47 b7 d1♕ 48 b8♕ (threatening check and mate from f4) 48...♕c1 49 ♘xg6 ♕xg6 50 ♕h8+ ♕h7 51 ♕gxg7 mate.

He would also have lost after 43...♖d3 (43...♖d1 44 a4!) 44 a4 (the simplest, but 44 ♖b8 is also good) 44...♖e3 (not 44...d4? 45 ♖b5 or 44...♖a3 45 ♖d4! ♕f6 46 ♖xd5) 45 ♖b8 ♗h7 (45...♕e5 46 ♕xe5 ♖xe5 47 ♘d7 with the mating threat ♖h8+ and ♘f8) 46 ♕g5+ (46 a5!?) 46...♕xg5 47 hxg5 ♚xg5 48 ♘xh7+ etc.

Botvinnik: 'After 43...♖d3 in his adjournment analysis Kasparov was not satisfied with the simple win of a piece, but sought a problem-like continuation of the attack with 44 ♕e1. Capablanca thought that it was unaesthetic to play for brilliancy, if there was a simple win. And in the given instance he was proved right: candidate master M.Chudakov (and after him grandmaster

J.Nunn) showed that 44...♕c8! 45 ♕e7 ♕f5 46 f4 (*46 ♕c7! – G.K.*) 46...♕f6 would have repelled the attack. Yes, a striving for brilliancy sometimes prevents Kasparov from reaching the truth... Here with experience everything should come right.'

Instead of 45 ♕e7, White has the crushing stroke 45 ♕e5!, since the knight cannot be taken – 45...♕xf8? because of 46 ♖b8 ♕xb8 47 ♕xb8 ♖xa3 (47...♚h7 48 ♕b2 and a3-a4) 48 ♕h8+ ♚h7 49 ♕c8! (pretty geometry: the threat is ♕c1+ and ♕xa3 or ♕g5 mate) 49...♖a1 50 ♕c3 and wins, while if 45...♕f5 there follows the unexpected 46 ♕g3! ♖xa3 47 ♖d4!! (a study-like move: the threat is ♖xd5!) 47...♖a5 48 ♕c7 with the threat of ♕c1+ and an irresistible attack. It is not often that one encounters such a 'box' as the one in which the black king found itself. It is greatly hindered by its own pawns on g7 and h5 as well as the ill-starred bishop, and the role of the key to this construction is played by the white knight.

44 ♖xc4 dxc4 45 ♕d6! c3 (the only defence against 46 ♕d2+) **46 ♕d4 1-0**

Now 47 ♕e3+ is threatened, and if 46...♗h7 (46...♕d3? 47 ♕f4 mate), then 47 ♕xc3 g5 48 ♕d4 or 47...♗g8 48 ♕e3+ g5 49 ♕xg5+ with a straightforward win. Times: 2.42–2.32.

Thanks to its study-like finish, this game, which was of colossal competitive importance and which essentially decided matters, was simultaneously the best in the match, and also in the 42nd issue of *Informator*.

In the remaining two games I needed half a point to retain the title of champion, but I made two draws. As the sports commentator Kote Makharadze remarked, 'the victory of one Soviet grandmaster over another was reported on television in such a voice that you'd think the commentator had just lost a close friend.' The closing ceremony also resembled a funeral, with many of the 'select' audience wearing mournful expressions. There were few people on the stage, and the senior officials of the Sports Committee, and even Sevastyanov, the chairman of the Chess Federation, were absent. The lavish celebrations that had been planned for a different outcome were put off for another occasion.

By winning a second match against Karpov, for the first time I took the lead in the overall number of wins in our matches (13-12). Psychologically this was an important turning-point: I was no longer in any doubt that I was a better player than my opponent. Everything suggested that I was beginning to feel comfortable as champion. I experienced joy and relief, little suspecting that a year later a *genuine* return match awaited me.

For the First Time on Board 1

27th World Chess Olympiad (Dubai, 14 November – 2 December 1986): 1. USSR – 40 out of 56; 2. England – 39½; 3. USA – 38½; 4. Hungary – 34½; 5–7. Iceland, Bulgaria and China – 34; 8–12. Czechoslovakia, Cuba, France, Argentina and Peru – 33, etc. (altogether 108 teams). The winning team comprised **Kasparov** (8½ out of 11), Karpov (6 out of 9), A.Sokolov (6 out of 9), Yusupov (10 out of 12), reserves Vaganian (7 out of 10) and Tseshkovsky (2½ out of 5).

Immediately after the return match I annotated all the games from it, and whereas my book about the 1985 match appeared only in England (1986), the collection *Dva matcha* was published in Moscow (1987). In October 1986 I also began working on the book *Child of Change* (co-authored by Donald Trelford, a prominent English politi-

cal commentator, and editor-in-chief of the Sunday *Observer*).

Then in November Karpov and I headed the Soviet team at the next Olympiad. We had missed the previous one, which took place during the unlimited match of 1984/85, but even without us the USSR team had taken first place, ahead of England, USA, Hungary and so on. These same teams were also our main rivals on this occasion, in the sultry heat of Dubai, to where the flight from the cold of Moscow took more than seven hours.

This Olympiad was a difficult test for me: for the first time I appeared on board 1 and at the same time I took part in the work of the FIDE Congress, lobbying delegates late into the night to get them to vote against Campomanes in the forthcoming presidential election. Inspired by the recent removal of Vitaly Sevastyanov from the post of Chairman of the Soviet Federation, I was hoping also to overcome my opponent in FIDE. However, I completely overlooked the strength of the alliance between the Sports Committee and Campomanes, forged by the participation of both sides in the events of February 1985. The official announcement of the USSR's position predetermined the results of the votes. All the pro-Soviet countries voted for Campomanes, which also influenced the delegates who had been wavering. Also solidly behind the Filipino were the Arab states and the delegates of those Third World countries who had travelled to the Olympiad at the organisers' expense. In the end Campomanes was triumphantly elected for a second term, and I promptly set about creating an independent organisation – the Grandmasters Association (GMA).

This late-night campaigning did little to help my chess, and in the middle of the

Olympiad I suffered a serious slump. But I started well, as did the team as a whole: we defeated Lebanon 4-0, dropped just half a point in each of the matches with Peru and Czechoslovakia (I won against Granda and Smejkal) and overcame Hungary by the minimum margin (I let Portisch off the hook, but Karpov beat Ribli).

However, the next five days turned out to be the most agonising period of our stay in Dubai: of the four matches, we drew three and did not win a single one! In the 5th round there was a difficult drawn match with Yugoslavia (I was rested, and Karpov lost to Ljubojevic). In the 6th round we met the unprecedentedly strong English team and within two hours (!) we had already lost the two 'Black' games: Sokolov to Nunn and Vaganian to Chandler. Fortunately, Yusupov methodically outplayed Short, while 'by tradition' I overcame Miles.

> ## Game 20
> ### G.Kasparov-A.Miles
> World Chess Olympiad
> 6th Round, Dubai 21.11.1986
> *Queen's Indian Defence E13*

1 d4 ♘f6 2 c4 e6

On this occasion, instead of 2...c5 (*Game No.12*), Miles decided to play as Timman did in his match with me.

3 ♘f3 b6 4 ♘c3 ♗b4 5 ♗g5 ♗b7 6 e3 h6 7 ♗h4 g5 (7...♗xc3+ 8 bxc3 d6 – *Game No.18*) **8 ♗g3 ♘e4 9 ♘d2!?**

Although the opponent's choice came as a surprise to me, I again preferred the pawn sacrifice (9 ♕c2 – *Game Nos.10, 11*).

9...♘xg3 (rejecting 9...♘xc3 10 bxc3 ♗xc3 – *Game No.9*) **10 hxg3 ♗f8!?**

An original novelty. Avoiding the usual 10...♗xc3+ 11 bxc3 d6, Black asserts that

with two bishops he can afford to play recklessly. A similar plan – 10...♘c6 11 ♕c2 ♗f8 had already been employed by Miles against Schussler (Reykjavik 1986), and after 12 a3 ♗g7 13 ♗e2 ♕e7 14 g4 0-0-0 15 0-0-0 ♔b8 he achieved a good game. Even so, this is not the most appropriate idea.

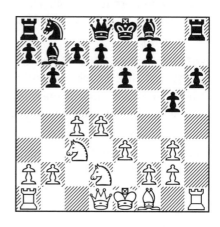

11 f4?!

A completely unnecessary move: I did not immediately grasp what I should do, and I was afraid of taking my king to the queen-side, because of the illusory counterplay with ...♗g7 and ...c7-c5. 11 ♕a4!? followed by 0-0-0, ♔b1 and ♖c1 was correct, planning after ...0-0-0 an attack with c4-c5 and ♗a6.

11...♗g7 12 ♕a4

I was even thinking about 12 ♔f2, but after 12...♘c6 13 ♗e2 ♕e7 14 d5 ♘a5 (intending ...0-0-0) the king on f2 is not best placed.

12...♘c6

Yefim Geller, the chief trainer of our team, criticised this move for its rejection of the idea of ...c7-c5, and he recommended 12...c5 or the preparatory 12...♕e7. However, if 12...c5 there would have followed 13 d5!, when 13...♗xc3 14 bxc3 exd5?! 15 cxd5 ♗xd5 16 0-0-0 is advantageous for White, while if 12...♕e7 13 0-0-0 c5, then again 14 d5! ♗xc3 15 bxc3 exd5?! 16 cxd5 ♗xd5

(16...♕xe3? 17 ♕e4+) 17 e4 ♗c6 18 ♕c2(b3) with excellent play for the pawn: it is not easy for Black to safeguard his king.

13 0-0-0

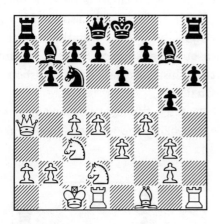

13...♕e7?!

The drawback to f2-f4 would have been emphasised by 13...♘e7! (in order by ...♘f5 to attack the weakened pawns on e3 and g3) 14 ♗d3!? (essentially a forced pawn sacrifice) 14...♗xg2 15 ♖h2 ♗b7 16 ♕c2 with unclear play. But Miles sticks to the plan with ...0-0-0.

14 ♗e2 0-0-0 15 ♔b1 ♔b8

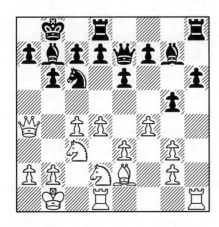

16 ♖c1

This move suggests itself. 'Black has a solid, but passive position' (Geller), and White tries to develop his initiative, by concentrating his forces on the queenside with the idea of c4-c5 and ♗a6.

16...♕b4

Miles drives the white queen away from his king. The defensive try 16...f5 17 a3 g4 18 ♘b3 a6 19 c5 b5 would have been refuted by 20 ♗xb5! axb5 21 ♘xb5 with the decisive threat of ♘a5 (and if 21...d6, then first 22 ♖c3!).

17 ♕d1 ♕f8 (intending ...♘e7-f5) **18 ♗f3**

18 ♘b3 (but not 18 d5?! ♘e7) 18...f5 (18...♘e7 19 ♗f3!) 19 c5 was also possible, but I did not want to block the queen's path to a4.

18...f5 (now 18...♘e7?! is dangerous on account of 19 ♗xb7 ♔xb7 20 c5!) **19 ♕a4**

The reply 19...♕b4 is ruled out, and again c4-c5 is threatened.

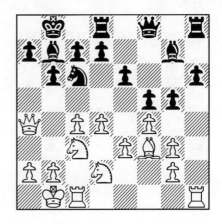

19...g4

19...a6 20 ♗xc6! dxc6 21 c5 e5 22 fxe5 ♗xe5 23 ♖hf1 is also unclear, but the weakening ...a7-a6 is not to everyone's taste. Miles blocked the kingside, probably in the expectation of 20 ♗e2?! h5! with good counterplay, but I had prepared a surprise for him.

20 ♗xc6! dxc6

20...♗xc6 is no better in view of 21 ♘b5 ♗xb5 (forced: 21...a5? 22 c5!) 22 cxb5 (22 ♕xb5 also gives a small plus) 22...♕d6 (my

Informator recommendation with the idea of ...♕d5 'with equality') 23 ♖c3! ♕d5 24 ♖hc1 ♖c8 25 ♕c2 ♕b7 26 a4 ♗f8 (otherwise a4-a5) 27 ♘c4, and White retains the initiative (here the knight is somewhat more active than the bishop).

21 c5! (restricting still further the actions of the black bishops) **21...e5!**

A counter-breakthrough in the centre. 21...bxc5?! is too risky in view of 22 ♘b3! cxd4 23 exd4 with an attack.

22 fxe5 ♗xe5 23 ♘e2!

A highly unusual semi-open position has arisen. Miles was relying on his two bishops, but the white knights have more prospects: for the moment one of them goes to f4, while the other, after ♖c3 and ♖hc1, may be able to worry the black king. Nevertheless, all the play still lies ahead.

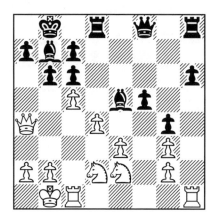

23...♗f6 24 ♘f4 ♕e8 25 ♖c3 b5

All the same Black cannot avoid this – say, 25...♖h7 26 ♖a3 a6 27 ♕b3 (27 ♕c2 ♖e7!) 27...b5 28 ♕d3 ♗c8 etc.

26 ♕c2 ♗c8 27 a4 ♖h7

A loss of time. If 27...a6 in *Informator* I recommended 28 ♘b3 – and indeed, after 28...♗g5 29 ♘d3! ♗e6 30 ♘b4 White has a dangerous attack. However, the immediate 27...♗g5! with the idea of ...♗xf4 (now 28 ♘d3? is not possible because of 28...♗xe3)

would have retained approximate equality.

28 axb5 cxb5 29 c6 (29 ♖d3 ♗e7 30 ♕b3 ♗g5 31 d5 a6 is unclear) **29...a6 30 ♖c1 ♖d6?**

And this is already the decisive mistake (30...♖e7?! 31 ♕b3! was also weak). Again 30...♗g5! and ...♗xf4 was the correct defence, but Miles stubbornly does not want to part with his active dark-squared bishop.

31 ♕b3!

If 31 ♕d3, then 31...♖e7 was now suitable, provoking the far more modest move 32 ♘f1.

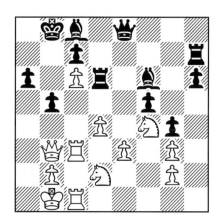

31...♖e7?

A time-trouble error, which hastens the end. In avoiding the fatal 31...♔a7(a8)? 32 ♖c5! ♖e7 33 ♖1c3, Miles allows a combination which in fact exploits the position of the rook on e7. The only chance of complicating matters was 31...h5 32 ♖c5! h4 33 gxh4 ♗xh4, in the hope of the unclear 34 ♖1c3?! ♔a7 35 ♕a3 ♗e1! 36 ♖e5 ♕f8, although after 34 ♘d5! (with the terrible threat of 35 ♖xb5+! axb5 36 ♕xb5+ ♔a7 37 ♘b4) Black has a barely defensible position.

32 ♘c4! (a mating attack has suddenly arisen) **32...♖xc6**

If 32...♖d8, then 33 ♘b6 is possible, but 33 ♘a3! ♕f7 34 ♕b4 with the threat of ♘xb5 wins outright.

33 ♘a5 ♖xc3

If 33...♖d6, then 34 ♘d5! ♖ed7 35 ♘xc7 ♕e4+ 36 ♔a1 ♗b7 37 ♘xb7 ♔xb7 38 ♘xb5! or 37...♕xb7 38 ♘e8! ♖b6 39 ♖c7 and wins.

34 ♕xc3 ♗b7 35 ♘xb7 ♔xb7 36 ♘d5 (after 31...h5 this would not have worked because of the reply 36...♕e4+) **36...♖f7**

If 36...♗g5 it is possible to take the exchange – 37 ♘xe7, but 37 ♘xc7! ♕d7 38 ♕a3 is more forceful.

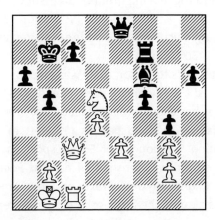

37 ♘xf6

There was a win by direct attack after 37 ♘xc7! ♕e4+ 38 ♔a1 with the threats of ♕a5 and ♘xb5, but in time-trouble I played more simply, taking the game into a technical phase.

37...♖xf6 38 ♕xc7+ ♔a8 39 ♖c5! (this invasion leads to the gain of material; ♖e5 is threatened) **39...♕b8?**

This loses immediately, but 39...♖f7 40 ♕b6 ♕e4+ 41 ♔a2! ♕b7 42 ♕xh6 ♔a7 43 ♕g6 was also insufficient.

40 ♕d7 ♖f8 (40...♖d6 41 ♕xf5) **41 ♖c6 1-0**

If 41...♕b7 42 ♕d6(d5).

My win enabled us to save the match with the English. The paradoxical feature of this important game was that Miles usually preferred knights, while I preferred bishops,

but here it all turned out the other way round: I successfully, 'in Chigorin style', manoeuvred with my knights, while Miles suffered with his bishops.

In the 7th round the Soviet team was unable to beat Iceland: I won against Helgi Olafsson, but Karpov failed to finish off Hjartarson, and Tseshkovsky lost to Petursson. And half way through the tournament we lost the lead: England and USA – 20 out of 28, USSR – 19½.

It was hard to overestimate the importance of our match with the Americans in the 8th round. In the fourth hour Yusupov and Vaganian drew, Sokolov lost an obvious advantage in his game with Christiansen, while I was continuing to seek a way to win against the desperately resisting Seirawan. But on the neighbouring boards the English crushed Iceland 4-0, threatening to burst ahead, and at the end of the fifth hour my nerve failed me: I made an untimely exchange of bishop for knight, blundered in a sharp rook ending, and suffered a painful defeat. As a result we lost the match (1½-2½), which had a considerable psychological effect: the US President Reagan even sent his compatriots a congratulatory telegram!

The Soviet team unexpectedly dropped to 6th place, now 2½ points behind England. The situation was desperate, but not hopeless. In the 9th round we crushed France (3½-½), although I again slipped up: playing White against Spassky, in the opening I incorrectly sacrificed a pawn, ran into an improvement, and to avoid the worst I accepted the draw offered by my opponent. The gap between us and the leaders was reduced by just half a point.

In the 10th round came an uncommonly dramatic match with Romania. After playing what was then my main variation against the Nimzo-Indian Defence, I encountered a novelty 12...♛c7! (cf. *Game No.13*, note to Black's 12th move), immediately ended up in a difficult position, for a long time fought for equality and only by a miracle gained a draw. Fortunately, Yusupov defeated Ghinda in a subtle endgame with opposite-colour bishops, and we won the match (2½-1½). That day the English suffered a sensational defeat against the young Spanish team (3½-½!), and we at last caught up with them. However, four rounds before the finish we were still a point behind our 'offenders' – the Americans.

On the day of the 11th round match with Bulgaria I entrusted board 1 to Karpov and spoke at a meeting of the FIDE Central Committee, where its attitude to the creation of the Grandmasters Association was considered: we invited the FIDE leadership to hold a joint meeting in Brussels early in 1987. One of the officials asked indignantly: *'What's all this about – today the grandmasters set up an association, tomorrow it'll be international masters, and then something else for arbiters?'* I replied: 'These are people who represent chess. But what you represent, I don't know. It's of no importance whether or not you exist, but it's on them that the development of chess in the world depends!' (Not so long ago, at the 2010 Congress in Khanty-Mansiysk, I again encountered such officials who effectively control world chess, and this depressed me). Campomanes seemed to be interested in our project – at any event he agreed to hold a special meeting of the FIDE Executive Council in Brussels, to discuss the founding of the GMA and meet its leaders.

Meanwhile, the match with Bulgaria took a difficult course: again Tseshkovsky could not cope with his nerves, Karpov failed to win with White against the young Kiril Georgiev, and yet wins by Yusupov and Vaganian tipped the scales in our favour: 2½-1½. But the gap between us and the leading Americans rose to one and a half points.

We needed to increase the tempo, and we managed to pull ourselves together. In the next two rounds we defeated the tiring Spanish (3½-½) and the Italians (3-1), matches in which I won against Fernandez and, not without difficulty, Tatai. Before the finish there was an extremely tense situation in the leading group: USA – 36½ out of 52, USSR – 36, England 35½. Some were already calculating the tie-break scores, as in the 1980 Olympiad.

It stands to reason that I was anxious: had we lost the Olympiad, there would no doubt have been recriminations against me for engaging in chess politics rather than upholding the honour of Soviet sport. In the last round we were paired against Poland, the English against Brazil, and the Americans against the more solid Bulgarian team. In view of the fact that England might win 4-0, we decided to play for a win in all the games: 'And the last fight let us face!'[1]

But to play for a win with White is one thing (thus, Karpov and Vaganian successfully employed important novelties), whereas with Black it is quite another, especially when you feel terribly tired. And my opponent Wlodzimierz Schmidt was quite a solid grandmaster. On looking at his games, I discovered that in the Benko Gambit he did not capture the pawn on b5. This is something Black can only dream of! After consulting with Nikitin, who was helping me for the first time at the 'Tournament of Nations', I therefore decided to play the Benko.

---

[1] Words from *The Internationale* – Translator's note.

1 d4 ♘f6 2 c4 c5 3 d5 b5 4 a4

Schmidt was surprised by my choice, but he did not take the pawn. I employed the Benko Gambit very rarely, precisely because of 4 cxb5!. Now Black has far fewer problems.

4...b4!

Blocking the queenside. After 4...bxc4 5 ♘c3 and e2-e4 White has too easy a game.

5 ♘d2 g6

Strangely enough, a novelty. I considered this to be more dynamic than 5...e5 6 e4 d6 followed by ...g7-g6 and ...♗g7 (which, however, is also not bad).

6 e4 d6 7 ♘gf3

Later various moves occurred here, and the best of them, in my view, is 7 b3!? followed by ♗b2, immediately opposing the powerful bishop on g7.

7...♗g7 8 g3?! (8 ♗d3 0-0 9 0-0 is obviously better, after which there is a choice between ...e7-e5 and ...e7-e6) **8...e6!**

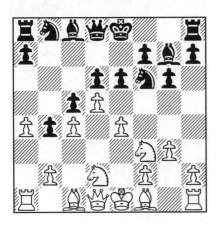

Very timely: after the opening of the cen-

tre White already has to think about how to complete his development.

9 ♗h3?!

The exchange of the light-squared bishops favours Black. But after the natural 9 ♗g2 (not 9 dxe6?! ♗xe6 and ...♘c6) 9...exd5 10 0-0! 0-0! (10...dxe4?! 11 ♘xe4! ♘xe4 12 ♕d5) 11 cxd5 ♗a6 12 ♖e1 ♘bd7 he has a comfortable variation of the Modern Benoni (which I used to play in my youth), and also in the event of 11 exd5 ♖e8 12 ♖e1 ♘bd7 White can only think in terms of maintaining equality (by 13 ♖a2 with the same idea b2-b3).

9...exd5 10 ♗xc8 ♕xc8 11 cxd5?!

In the event of 11 exd5 ♕h3 or 11...0-0 12 0-0 ♕f5 and ...♘bd7 Black would have had an excellent position, and yet this was the lesser evil.

11...0-0?!

The intense pressure of the last round tells. A clear advantage in the endgame would have resulted from 11...♕a6! 12 ♕e2 (there is nothing else) 12...0-0 (more accurate than my *Informator* suggestion 12...♕xe2+) 13 ♕xa6 ♘xa6, and White's e4-pawn is extremely weak.

12 0-0 c4

Showy, but not very effective. The developing 12...♘bd7 and ...♖e8 was more solid.

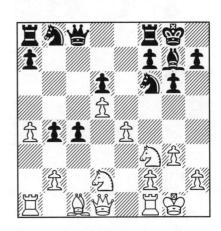

13 ♕c2?

Now my idea proves justified. White should have attacked the c4-pawn by 13 ♕e2! – then after 13...c3 14 bxc3 bxc3 (14...♖e8 15 cxb4 ♘xd5 16 ♘c4! is no better) he would have the forceful reply 15 ♘c4 ♕a6 16 ♘d4! with chances for both sides: 16...♘xd5 17 ♘b5! or 16...♖e8 17 f3 ♘xe4 18 ♘b5! ♘f6 19 ♕a2 ♘bd7 20 ♘c7 ♕b7 21 ♘xa8 ♖xa8 22 ♗a3, and although Black has obvious compensation for the exchange, it is hard to speak of any advantage for him.

13...c3 14 bxc3 bxc3! (this capture was underestimated by Schmidt, who was hoping to defend the inferior position after 14...♕xc3 15 ♖a2!) **15 ♘b3 ♕g4!**

'An early mopping-up begins.' (Nikitin)

16 ♘fd4 ♕xe4 17 ♕xc3 ♘xd5!

After 17...♕xd5 18 ♗b2 White has more chance of compensating for the loss of the pawn.

18 ♕d2 ♘b6! (making way for the queen and aiming for the c4-point) **19 ♖e1 ♕d5 20 ♕d1 ♘8d7 21 ♖a2?!**

21 ♗f4(e3) ♖fb8! etc. was somewhat more resilient.

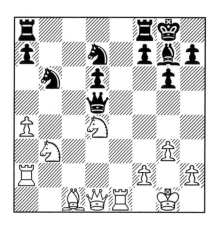

21...♗xd4?!

After easily achieving an overwhelming advantage, I decided that Black could win as he pleased, and I relaxed. Such a bishop

should not have been exchanged – after 21...♘c5! a second pawn could simply have been won. I think that in this case I would have been the first of the Soviet grandmasters to finish, not the last.

22 ♖d2 ♘e5

Again missing an opportunity to win a second pawn: 22...♗xf2+!? 23 ♔xf2 ♕f5+ 24 ♔g1 ♘e5 25 ♖f1 ♕h3(d7) with winning prospects.

23 ♘xd4 ♘bc4?! (23...♖fe8! was more accurate) **24 ♖c2** (if 24 ♖de2?, then 24...♕xd4 25 ♕xd4 ♘f3+ 26 ♔g2 ♘xd4 27 ♖e4 ♘c2 and wins) **24...♖ac8 25 ♖c3!**

The only chance of holding on. I was counting on 25 ♗e3? ♘xe3 26 fxe3 ♘f3+!.

25...♘b6?!

A more appreciable advantage would have been retained by 25...♕a5!? or 25...♖fe8! 26 ♖f1 ♕a5. However, here I grew nervous and I immediately began chasing the a4-pawn.

26 ♗b2 ♖xc3 (26...a5!?) **27 ♗xc3 ♖c8** (27...♕c4 28 ♘b5 a6 29 ♗xe5! dxe5 30 ♘d6 is also not altogether clear) **28 ♗a1**

Compared with a few moves ago, White has achieved a great deal: after the inevitable f2-f4 he will gain counterplay.

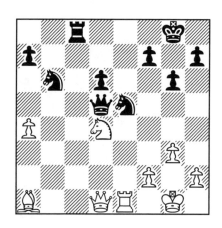

28...♖c4

This looks like a decisive invasion, but

more chances of converting the extra pawn were promised by 28...a6!? (preventing ♘b5) 29 f4 ♘ed7.

29 ♘b5

29 f4!? was more resilient – after this I could have fought for victory by 29...♘ed7 30 ♘b5 ♖xa4 31 ♕xd5 ♘xd5 32 ♘xd6 f6 or 29...♕c5!? 30 a5 ♘bd7 31 ♔g2 ♘c6 (31...♕d5+ 32 ♔h3!) 32 ♖e8+ ♘f8 33 ♘b3 ♖c2+ 34 ♖e2 ♖xe2+ 35 ♕xe2 ♕d5+ 36 ♕f3 ♕xf3+ 37 ♔xf3 f5.

29...♖xa4?

Only here did I see that 29...♘f3+? would be refuted by 30 ♕xf3! (the weakness of the a1-h8 diagonal and the back rank!), and in my 'grief' I simply captured the pawn, throwing away the greater part of my advantage. 29...♖e4! was correct, and only after 30 ♖f1!, 30...♖xa4 31 ♕xd5 ♘xd5 32 ♘xd6 ♘d3, reaching an endgame far more favourable for Black than in the game.

30 ♕xd5 ♘xd5 31 ♗xe5?

An error in reply in time-trouble – exchanging this powerful bishop. Real saving chances were offered by 31 ♔g2! f6 32 ♘xd6 ♘d3 33 ♖b1.

31...dxe5 32 ♖xe5 ♘f6 33 ♖e7 a5 34 ♘d6 (after 34 ♖a7 ♘e4! things are also not easy for White) **34...♖d4! 35 ♘xf7 ♔f8 36 ♖a7 ♖d7 37 ♖xd7 ♘xd7 38 ♘d6**

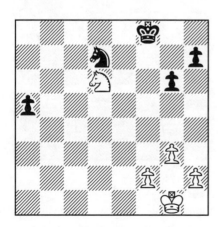

'The resulting knight endgame is won for Black. Matters are decided by the outside passed pawn and the active king, but in view of the small number of pawns a certain accuracy is required. Despite some annoying errors, Kasparov did not display signs of confusion. After the game he thanked Karpov for the winning method, which he demonstrated in a similar situation against Gheorghiu (Lucerne 1982).' (Nikitin)

From this point my game was the only remaining unfinished one in the leading group, and was the focus of attention for several thousand spectators, who were assembled in the enormous hall of the exhibition pavilion. The Americans had already bowed out of the battle for 1st place, after drawing 2-2 with the Bulgarians. But the English quickly crushed the Brazilians 4-0 and were anxiously following the decisive USSR-Poland match. To our opening triumphs by Karpov and Vaganian had been added another with Black by Yusupov, who played brilliantly in Dubai. The score became 3-0, and now we were half a point behind the English, but with this ending in reserve.

As it transpired, a draw would have been enough for us: in the event of a share of 1st-2nd places with the English, the USSR team would have the better tie-break score. But I was continuing to fight for a win, and was not even contemplating a draw. True, this endgame, despite the generally-accepted precept 'knight endings are like pawn endings', proved to be far more complicated than I imagined at the time.

38...♔e7 39 ♘c4 a4 40 ♔f1 ♔e6 41 ♔e2 ♔d5 42 ♘e3+ (42 ♘a3?! ♔d4) **42...♔d4 43 ♔d2**

Weaker is 43 ♘c2+ ♔c3 44 ♘a3 (44 ♔d1 ♔b2) 44...♘f6 45 f4 ♘e4 or 45 f3 ♘d5 46 ♔d1 ♔b3 etc.

43...♘e5! 44 ♔c2

For the moment everything is more or less forced: if 44 ♘c2+, then 44...♚e4 45 ♚e2 ♘f3 with the threats of ...♘xh2 and ...♘d4+ is decisive. White's only chance is to meet the a-pawn with his king and try to eliminate both black pawns on the kingside by means of exchanges and the sacrifice of his knight. For his part, Black must prevent this.

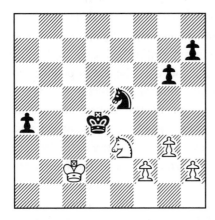

44...♘d3

Forcing the opponent to retreat his knight to d1, but is this so important? 44...♚e4! (with the threat of ...♚f3) 45 f4 ♘f3 was more accurate, when there is no way of saving the game:

1) 46 ♘f1 (in *Informator* I wrongly attached an 'unclear' assessment to this move; White also loses after 46 ♘c4 ♘xh2) 46...h5 47 ♚c3 (47 ♚b2 ♚d3 is no better) 47...a3 48 h3 ♘g1 49 g4 ♚xf4 50 gxh5 gxh5 51 ♚b3 ♘xh3 52 ♚xa3 ♚f3 and wins;

2) 46 ♘g4 h5 47 ♘f2+ ♚f5! (not my *Informator* suggestion 47...♚e3(?) 48 ♘d3 ♘xh2 because of 49 f5! gxf5 50 ♘f4 ♘f1 51 ♘xh5 ♚d4 52 ♚b2 ♚c4 53 ♚a3 ♚b5 54 ♚b2 ♚b4 55 ♚a2 with a draw) 48 h3 ♘d4+ 49 ♚b2 ♘e2 50 g4+ ♚xf4 51 gxh5 gxh5 and wins.

45 ♘d1 ♘e1+ 46 ♚b2 ♘f3?!

Here too Black would have won by 46...♚e4! (with the same idea of ...♚f3;

46...♚d3!?) 47 f4 ♘f3 48 ♘c3+ ♚f5!, for example:

1) 49 h3 ♘g1 50 ♘xa4 (50 h4 h5! 51 ♚a3 ♚g4 or 51 ♘d5 ♘e2!) 50...♘xh3 51 ♘c3 ♘f2! 52 ♘d5 ♘g4 53 ♚c3 ♚e4 54 ♘e7 ♘e3 55 ♘g8 ♘d5+ 56 ♚c4 h5 with the deadly threat of ...♘xf4 and ...h5-h4;

2) 49 h4 h5 50 ♚a3 ♚g4! (50...♘d4 will also do) 51 ♘e2 ♘xh4! (not satisfying himself with the simple 51...♘d2 and ...♘e4 or 51...♘h2 and ...♘f1) 52 gxh4 ♚xh4, and again the h-pawn cannot be stopped.

47 h4 ♘e5

In the event of 47...♚d3?! 48 ♘e3 ♚e2 both 49 h5 gxh5 50 ♘d5 ♚xf2 51 ♘f6 (given by me in *Informator*) 51...♘d2 52 ♚a3 ♚f3 53 ♘xh5 ♘e4 54 ♚xa4 ♘xg3 55 ♘f6 h6 56 ♚b4, and 49 ♘g4 h5 50 ♘f6 ♘e5 51 f4 ♘c4+ 52 ♚c3 ♘e3 53 f5 ♘xf5 54 g4 hxg4 55 ♘xg4 ♘xh4 56 ♘f6 ♘f5 57 ♘h7 or 50...♚xf2 51 g4 hxg4 52 ♘xg4+ ♚g3 53 ♘f6 ♚xh4 54 ♚a3 would have led to a draw.

The last critical position has been reached. 'The whole question is whether with his knight alone White can manage to eliminate the black pawn pair. The white pawns are doomed.' (Nikitin).

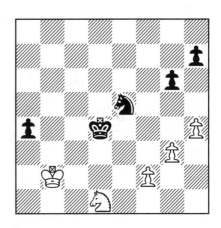

48 ♚a3?!

Moving the king away loses quickly, whereas 48 ♘c3! (neither of us saw this brilliant resource) could have complicated my task – 48...♘c4+! 49 ♔c2 a3, for example:

1) 50 ♔b3 ♘d2+ 51 ♔c2 ♘e4 52 ♘b5+ ♔e5 53 ♘xa3 ♘xf2 54 ♘c4+ ♔f5 55 ♘b6 ♘e4 56 ♔d3 ♘xg3 57 ♘d7 h6! 58 ♘f8 ♘h5 59 ♔e3 ♘f4 60 ♔f3 ♘d3 61 ♔g2 ♘c5! with the decisive threat of trapping the white knight;

2) 50 g4 ♘e5 51 ♘b5+ (51 g5 ♔c4!) 51...♔e4 52 ♘c3+ ♔f3! 53 g5 ♔f4 54 ♘d5+ ♔f5 55 ♔b3 (55 ♘e3+ ♔e4 56 ♔b3 ♘f3 57 ♘g4 ♔f5! is no better for White) 55...♘f3 56 ♔xa3 (in the event of 56 ♘e3+ ♔f4 57 ♘d5+ ♔e5! 58 ♘b6 ♔f5 59 ♘d7 there is the decisive 59...♘xg5!) 56...♘xh4 57 ♔b3 ♔xg5 58 ♔c2 ♘g2 59 ♔d2 h5 60 ♘e7 ♘f4 61 ♔e3 ♔g4, and nevertheless Black should be able to convert his extra pawn.

48...♔e4 (at last!) **49 h5** (desperation: 49 ♔xa4 ♔f3 50 ♔b3 ♘g4 and ...♘xf2) **49...gxh5 50 ♘e3 ♔f3 51 ♘d5** (or 51 ♘f5 ♘g4! 52 ♘g7 ♘f6 and ...♔xf2) **51...♘g4! 52 ♘e7**

52 ♘f4 is also pointless in view of 52...h4 or 52...♘f6.

52...♘xf2 53 ♘f5 ♘e4 54 ♔xa4 ♘xg3 55 ♘h4+ ♔e4 56 ♔b4 ♘f5 0-1

When Schmidt raised his hands in a sign of capitulation, a storm of applause broke out in the hall. I was mobbed by a crowd of excited spectators, and my colleagues with difficulty brought me out of the 'encirclement'.

This memorable game was not without its faults, but it was of great competitive importance. By winning 4-0, the USSR team nevertheless took sole first place, which had been hard to imagine a few days earlier. And by winning my last three games, I achieved a score of +7−1=3 and simultaneously won three gold medals (true, the metal out of which they were made did not even look

precious): for the team victory, for the best score on board 1, and for the absolute best score at the Olympiad!

Tournament Debut as Champion

Double-round super-tournament in Brussels (9-21 December 1986): 1. **Kasparov** – 7½ out of 10; 2. Korchnoi – 5½; 3-4. Nunn and Hübner – 5; 5. Short – 4; 6. Portisch – 3.

In my first individual tournament as world champion, played after a three-year break from tournament appearances, I began with a cold and tiredness, which was the result of the nervous strain in Dubai, lengthy flights and the abrupt change in climate. For almost a week in Moscow I fought a bad cold with all possible means, and initially in Brussels I wanted more than anything to sleep. Meanwhile, I faced a double-round battle with five top-class grandmasters – for the first time the organisers had succeeded in assembling a category 16 tournament, at that time the highest category.

We played to the newly-fashionable six-hour time control: 40 moves in 2 hours, plus 20 moves in an hour, followed by adjournment. Nikitin: *'It was suggested that play should begin at 13.00 hours, and that adjourned games be resumed the following day from 9.00 to 11.00. All the remaining time before the start of the first round was spent seeking an acceptable compromise, and the meeting of the six super-grandmasters would have produced no result had not the champion stood up and announced that he would not sit down at the chess board earlier than 15.00. The rounds began at 15.00. The start time to which all were accustomed was restored.'*

In the 1st round I won surprisingly easily with Black against Nunn in the Poisoned

Pawn variation of the Sicilian Najdorf. Nunn chose a dubious plan of attack – he sacrificed a second pawn, to prevent my king from castling, but I was able to walk the king into the corner and soon it was all over.

In the 2nd round I gained a very difficult draw against Korchnoi. In the original variation 1 d4 ♘f6 2 c4 e6 3 ♘f3 ♗b4+ 4 ♗d2 c5 5 g3?! he employed a novelty – 5...♕b6!, which unsettled me. After sacrificing a pawn, I played unconvincingly and ended up in a hopeless position, but in a wild time scramble Korchnoi missed a certain win.

Inspired by this miraculous save, I played with great determination in the 3rd round against Hübner.

Game 22
R.Hübner-G.Kasparov
Brussels, 3rd Round, 12.12.1986
Grünfeld Defence D90

1 d4 ♘f6 2 c4 g6 3 ♘c3 d5 (at that time this was my main fighting opening) **4 ♘f3 ♗g7 5 ♕a4+**

My opponent decided to surprise me with a rare variation, but I had studied it before my match with Korchnoi (1983), when we were looking for a 'refutation' of the Grünfeld Defence.

5...♗d7 6 ♕b3 dxc4 7 ♕xc4 0-0 8 e4

Nowadays 8 ♗f4 ♘a6 9 e4 c5 10 e5 is sometimes employed, exploiting the fact that the bishop on d7 deprives the f6-knight of its ideal retreat square.

At this moment Hübner looked content, assuming that he had restricted Black's possibilities to just 8...♗g4 (with a transposition into the variation 5 ♕b3 dxc4 6 ♕xc4 0-0 7 e4 ♗g4 from the 15th and 17th games of my recent match with Karpov). But now came a little surprise.

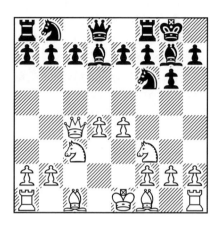

8...b5!

Played without particular hesitation, although I had not looked at this position in detail. There is no time for 8...a6?! because of 9 e5, and so Black sacrifices a pawn to create counterplay, exploiting the position of the bishop on d7 and his lead in development, aiming to attack the white king!

9 ♕b3

The first sign of confusion. 9 ♘xb5 is more critical, although after 9...♘xe4 Black has the advantage after 10 ♘xc7?! ♘c6! 11 ♘xa8 ♕a5+ 12 ♗d2 ♘xd2 13 ♘xd2 ♘xd4 (Bönsch-Jasnikowski, Harkany 1985), 10 ♕d5?! c6 11 ♕xe4 ♗f5, or 10 ♗d3?! ♘d6! 11 ♘xd6 cxd6, while after the best move 10 ♕xc7 ♘c6 11 ♗d3 ♘b4 12 ♗xe4 ♗xb5 13 ♕xd8 ♖axd8 14 ♗d2 f5 (14...♘d3+!? 15 ♗xd3 ♗xd3, Giorgadze-Stohl, Senek 1998) 15 ♗xf5 ♖xf5 16 ♗xb4 (Giorgadze-Khalifman, Bundesliga 1997/98) 16...e5 or 16...♗c6 and ...♗xf3! he has full compensation for the pawn. But the position is simplified, and White is not in any danger.

9...c5! (already seizing the initiative) **10 e5?!**

A dubious novelty. 10 ♗xb5?! is weak: 10...♗xb5 11 ♘xb5 ♘xe4 12 0-0 cxd4 13 ♕c4 ♘d6 14 ♕d5 ♘d7! 15 ♘bxd4 ♘b6 16 ♕b3 ♘bc4 (Anikaev-Malisauskas, Klaipeda 1983), but 10 dxc5 ♘a6 11 e5 ♘g4 (Ubilava-

Kengis, Kiev 1984) 12 ♗xb5! ♘xc5 13 ♕c4 ♖c8 14 0-0 is more solid, although here too Black has a comfortable game.

10...♘g4 11 ♗xb5?!

Another small step towards the precipice. 11 ♕d5?! cxd4! was also bad for White: 12 ♕xa8 dxc3 or 12 ♘xd4 ♕b6! 13 ♗xb5 ♗xe5 14 ♗xd7 ♘xd7 15 ♕xd7 ♘xf2! and wins. 11 dxc5 was necessary, even though, apart from 11...♘a6 (cf. the note to 10 e5), Black has acquired the resource 11...a6!, when he inevitably regains the pawn while retaining the initiative.

11...cxd4 12 ♘xd4 ♗xb5

12...♗xe5 also deserved consideration: for example, 13 ♘f3 (13 ♕d5?! ♕b6!, as in the note to 11 ♗xb5) 13...♗xc3+! 14 bxc3 ♕b6 15 ♘d4 (Stohl) 15...e5! 16 ♗xd7 ♘xd7 17 ♕xb6 ♘xb6 with a favourable endgame. However, I wanted more.

13 ♘dxb5 a6 14 ♘a3

With 14 ♕a4 White would have avoided the sufferings with his bad knight on a3, but after 14...♘c6 15 ♕xg4 ♘xe5 or 15 0-0 ♘xh2! 16 ♔xh2 axb5 17 ♕xb5 ♘xe5 he would not have escaped from the pressure.

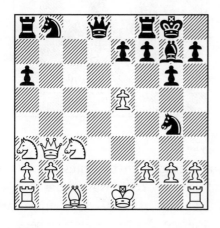

14...♕d4!

Preventing castling: in the variation 15 0-0?! ♕xe5 16 g3 ♕h5 17 h4 ♘c6 Black builds up a fearfully strong attack.

15 ♕c2 ♘c6 (now ...♘b4 is also threatened)
16 ♕e2 (again 16 0-0?! ♕xe5 17 f4 ♕c5+ 18 ♔h1 ♖fd8 is unsatisfactory for White)
16...♕xe5

There is no longer any point in Black avoiding the exchange of queens: his aim is to establish his knight on d3. 16...♘gxe5 17 0-0 ♕d3 (Stohl) was a worthy alternative.

17 ♕xe5?!

17 ♘c4?! was weak: 17...♕xe2+ 18 ♘xe2 ♘b4 19 0-0 ♖ac8. But 17 ♘c2 would have caused more problems – after, say, 17...♘xh2 18 ♕xe5 ♗xe5 19 f3 (Stohl) 19...♗g3+ 20 ♔e2 f5 it is not to easy to convert the extra pawn, and therefore 17...a5!? is interesting, with the idea of 18 h3 ♘b4!.

17...♘gxe5 18 0-0 ♘d3

Evoking pleasant associations with a memorable game (*Game No.5*). However, Hübner was hoping to hold out – in the last resort, with three pawns against four on the same wing.

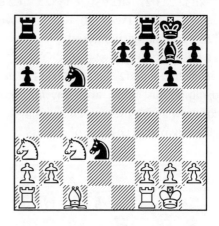

19 ♖b1 ♖ab8 20 ♖d1 ♖fd8 (or 20...♘cb4!? and ...♖fc8) **21 ♔f1 f5! 22 ♔e2 ♘ce5**

It was possibly better to win a pawn immediately – 22...♘xc1+ 23 ♖dxc1 ♘b4 24 ♘c4 ♗xc3 25 ♖xc3 ♘xa2, or to build up the pressure by 22...♘cb4!? (Stohl) 23 ♘c4 (23 ♗d2 ♖bc8) 23...♖d4! 24 ♘a5 ♘xc1+ 25 ♖dxc1 ♖c8 26 ♘b3 ♖d6 etc. But the move in the game, maintaining the tension, is also quite unpleasant for White.

23 ♘a4

A difficult choice. There is no sense in 23 ♗g5 h6! (24 ♗xe7? ♖d7), and 23 ♗e3 f4 24 ♗a7?! ♖b7 25 ♗c5 f3+! is also cheerless for White, while if 23 g3 there is the simple 23...♘xc1+ 24 ♖dxc1 ♘d3 25 ♖d1 ♘xb2.

23...♖d6

With the ideas of ...♖e6 and ...♖bd8 or ...♖b4 – Black continues playing for an attack, which in the end brings him success. 23...♘b4!? was also good.

24 ♗e3

Again a difficult choice. White would like to drive away the knight by 24 f4, but after 24...♖d4! 25 fxe5 (Stohl's move 25 ♘c5 is worse because of 25...♘xf4+!) 25...♘xc1+ 26 ♖bxc1 ♖xa4 he loses a pawn. Against the attempt to solve the problem of the a3-knight by 24 ♘c4 I was planning the spectacular 24...♘xc4 (24...♖d4!?) 25 ♖xd3 ♖xd3 26 ♔xd3 ♘a3 27 ♖a1 e5! 28 f3 (28 ♔e2 e4!) 28...e4+! 29 fxe4 fxe4+ 30 ♔e2 e3!, when White is completely paralysed.

24 g3 ♖b4 25 b3 ♖e4+ 26 ♔f1 ♘xf2! 27 ♖xd6 exd6 28 ♔xf2 ♘d3+ 29 ♔f3 ♗d4! is also dangerous, while after my *Informator* suggestion 24 b3 there is 24...♘b4!, regaining the pawn with chances of success.

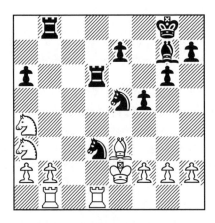

24...f4 25 ♗c5 f3+?!

My plan of attack goes into operation! True, first 25...♖d5! was more accurate, when after both 26 ♗xe7 ♖e8 27 ♗c5 ♖xc5 28 ♘xc5 ♘xc5 29 ♔f1 f3! and 26 ♗b6 f3+! 27 ♔f1 fxg2+ 28 ♔xg2 ♘f4+ 29 ♔h1 ♖xd1+ 30 ♖xd1 ♘ed3, or 26 b4 f3+! 27 gxf3 ♘f4+ 28 ♔f1 ♘xf3 29 ♖xd5 ♘xh2+ 30 ♔g1 ♘f3+ and ...♘xd5 Black has a big advantage.

26 gxf3 ♘f4+ 27 ♔e3

Consideration should have been given to 27 ♔f1!? ♖xd1+ (27...♖c6!?) 28 ♖xd1 ♘xf3: for example, 29 h3?! ♗xb2 30 ♗xe7 ♘d2+! (Stohl's move 30...♖e8 is worse in view of 31 ♗c5) 31 ♔e1 ♘e4 32 ♘c4 ♖e8 with a dangerous initiative, or 29 ♗xe7 ♘xh2+ 30 ♔g1 ♘f3+ 31 ♔f1 h5 32 ♘c4 (32 ♖d8+?! ♖xd8 33 ♗xd8 h4!) 32...♗f8! 33 ♗f6 ♖e8 – the passed h-pawn is strong, but the outcome is still far from clear.

27...♖f6

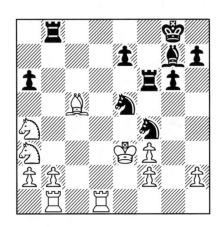

28 ♗xe7?

An oversight on the threshold of time-trouble. 28 ♗d4! was more resilient: 28...♖f5! 29 ♗xe5 ♖xe5+! (my earlier 29...♗xe5 30 ♘c4 ♖bf8 is unclear because of 31 ♖d7) 30 ♔xf4 ♖b4+ 31 ♔g3 ♖g5+ 32 ♔h3 ♖xa4 33 ♖bc1! (33 ♘c2 ♗e5! or 33 ♖d3 ♖h5+ 34 ♔g2 ♖ah4 is worse for White) 33...♖f4 34 ♖d3 ♗xb2 35 ♖c4!, and after

35...♗e5 36 ♖xf4 ♗xf4 37 ♘c4 ♖h5+ 38 ♔g4 ♖xh2 39 ♔xf4 ♖h4+ 40 ♔g3 ♖xc4 even a pawn down White would retain chances of a draw. Now things are difficult for him.

28...♘g2+ (Black also has a great advantage after 28...♖f7 29 ♖d8+ ♖xd8 30 ♗xd8 ♘fd3, but I decided to continue the attack) **29 ♔e2 ♖xf3**

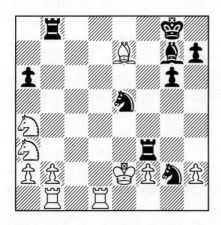

30 ♗d6

It would not have helped to play 30 ♖d8+ (30 ♗g5? ♖bf8) 30...♖xd8 31 ♗xd8 ♘f4+ 32 ♔f1 ♘g4 33 ♗b6 ♘xh2+ (33...♖h3!?) 34 ♔e1 ♘d3+ 35 ♔e2 ♘xb2 36 ♘xb2 ♖xa3 and wins.

30...♘f4+ 31 ♔f1 ♘g4! **32 ♖d2** (the rook cannot be taken: 32 ♗xb8? ♖xf2+ 33 ♔g1 ♖g2 with mate) **32...♖e8 33 ♘c4**

After 33 ♗xf4 ♖xf4 34 ♘c3(c5) ♘xh2+ 35 ♔g2 ♘f3 Black has a decisive attack.

33...♘xh2+

Apart from this obvious move there was 33...♖e4!? 34 ♗xf4 (34 b3 ♗d4!) 34...♖xc4 35 ♖d8+ ♔f8 36 ♗d6 ♖xa4 winning a piece, but after 37 h3! I would still have had to overcome technical problems: 37...♘h6 38 ♖c1 ♖a5 39 ♖cc8 ♖af5 40 ♗c5 is not altogether clear, and therefore Black does better to go into an endgame with an extra pawn – 37...♖xf2+ 38 ♔g1 ♖f6 (or 38...♖d4 39 hxg4 ♖f7 40 ♖xf8+ ♖xf8 41 ♗xf8 ♖xg4+ 42 ♔h2

♔xf8) 39 ♖f1 ♖xd6 40 ♖fxf8+ ♔g7 41 ♖g8+ ♔f7 42 ♖gf8+ ♔e6 43 ♖de8+ ♔d5 44 hxg4 ♖xg4+, or 37...♘xf2 38 ♖xf8+ ♖xf8 39 ♗xf8 ♘xh3 40 ♗h6 ♖h4 41 ♗d2 ♘f4 etc.

34 ♔g1 ♘g4

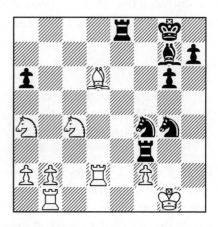

35 ♖f1?!

The final time-trouble error. 35 ♗c5 was essential, although after 35...h5 (Stohl) White would still have had a difficult position.

35...♗d4 (35...♘xf2!? would also have been decisive after 36 ♖dxf2 ♗d4 or 36 ♗xf4 ♖xf4 37 ♖fxf2 ♖xc4) **36 ♗c5**

There would have been a no less spectacular mating finish after 36 ♘c5 ♗xf2+! 37 ♖dxf2 ♖g3+ 38 ♔h1 ♘xf2+ 39 ♖xf2 ♖e1+, or a more prosaic end after 36 ♗xf4 ♖xf4 37 b3 ♖ef8, picking up the f2-pawn.

36...♖g3+ 37 ♔h1 ♖h3+ 38 ♔g1 ♘h2! (or 38...♘e5! with the same threat of ...♘f3 mate) **0-1**

With a score of 2½ out of 3 I took the lead. But in my 'black' game with Short in the 4th round I encountered for the first time the English Attack, which was still then an exotic line (1 e4 c5 2 ♘f3 d6 3 d4 cxd4 4 ♘xd4 ♘f6 5 ♘c3 a6 6 ♗e3 e6 7 ♕d2 b5 8 f3 etc.), expended a lot of time and after a time-trouble blunder on the 38th move I suffered a painful defeat. From the press: *'Short was happy: he was the first English grandmaster to defeat Kasparov'*.

The tournament situation became sharper, but not for long. In the next round, which concluded the first cycle, I was able to outwit the highly experienced Portisch.

1 d4 ♘f6 2 c4 e6 3 ♘f3 d5 4 ♘c3 ♗e7 5 ♗g5 0-0 (5...h6 – *Game No.25*) **6 e3 ♘bd7**

Portisch slightly surprised me with his choice of the classical Queen's Gambit – possibly he was afraid of allowing me a mobile pawn centre, with memories of Niksic 1983 (Game No.85 in *Garry Kasparov on Garry Kasparov Part I*).

7 ♕c2 h6

Forcing White to make up his mind.

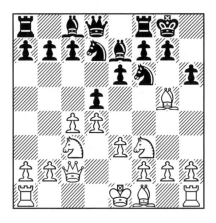

Very unclear play results from 8 h4 c5 9 0-0-0 ♕a5 10 g4 or 10 ♔b1 (Game No.33 in *Garry Kasparov on Garry Kasparov Part I*), while in the event of 8 ♗h4 c5 9 cxd5 ♘xd5 10 ♗xe7 ♕xe7 11 ♘xd5 exd5 12 dxc5 (12 ♗d3 no longer gains a tempo – the pawn

has moved from h7) 12...♘xc5 Black maintains equality.

8 cxd5!?

I had looked at this piece sacrifice a few years earlier with Yusupov and Geller. We didn't analyse it seriously, but the idea itself greatly appealed to me. And, after overcoming my hesitation (after a loss one should really play more solidly), I decided on it. The unexpected intermediate move dumfounded the maestro.

8...exd5

Played without any particular thought. Taking me 'at my word', Portisch rejected the variation 8...hxg5! 9 dxe6 fxe6 10 ♘xg5 ♘b6 11 h4! with two pawns for the bishop, a dangerous attack and at least equal chances: 11...♘bd5 12 h5 ♕e8 (12...♘xc3? 13 bxc3 is weak) 13 a3 ♔h8 14 ♗c4 c6 15 ♘e2, or 11...c5 12 h5 cxd4 13 h6 (13 0-0-0!?) 13...dxc3 14 ♖d1 ♕e8 15 hxg7 ♔xg7 16 ♖h7+ ♔g8, and here a draw results from both 17 ♖d4 (Portisch) 17...♗d7 18 ♖dh4 cxb2 19 ♖h8+ ♔g7 20 ♘xe6+! ♔f7! (but not 20...♗xe6? 21 ♖4h7+! with mate in 9 moves) 21 ♘g5+, and 17 ♗b5 ♗d7 (17...♘bd7? 18 f4! and wins) 18 ♗xd7 ♘bxd7 19 ♖xd7! ♘xd7 20 ♖h8+! ♔g7 21 ♖h7+.

And, indeed, who wants right from the opening to have to seek a defence against mate? Portisch's move is supposedly safer, but now White acquires a favourable version of the system with the bishop on f4.

9 ♗f4!

The point! Instead, if 9 ♗h4 Black replies in 'Carlsbad' style – 9...c6 followed by ...♖e8 and ...♘e4, when the move ...h7-h6 may prove useful for him.

9...c5

A quick and natural reaction. In the event of 9...c6 10 h3! against the typical 10...♖e8 11 ♗d3 ♘f8 both 12 0-0 and especially 12 0-0-0 (Marshall-Thomas, Folkestone 1933) are good, since ...h7-h6 becomes a weakening of the king's defences and the loss of an important tempo (compare with Portisch-Larsen, Game No.42 in Part III of *My Great Predecessors*). Therefore in search of counterplay Black is forced to weaken his d5-pawn.

10 ♗e2 b6 11 0-0 ♗b7 12 ♖fd1 ♖c8 13 dxc5 bxc5

Rather than a depressing position with an isolani (13...♘xc5 14 ♕f5 etc.), Portisch prefers sharper play with a hanging pawn pair.

14 a4!

With the obvious intention of a4-a5.

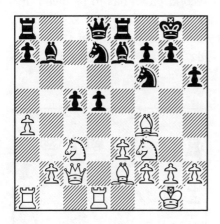

Here my opponent became perceptibly nervous and he made a serious mistake.

14...♕a5?

If Black found it psychologically difficult to decide on 14...a5 (in view of the 'eternal' weakness of the b5-point), he should have played 14...♕b6 with the idea of ...♕e6. On a5, although it blocks the a4-pawn, the queen is too distant from the key squares.

15 ♘h4!

I was terribly proud of this sudden thrust on the opposite side of the board. Exploiting the drawback to ...h7-h6 (Black does not have the reply ...g7-g6), White invades at f5 with his knight and stretches the opponent's defences.

15...♖fd8 16 ♘f5 ♗f8 17 ♘b5 (the white knights are attacking from both sides!) **17...♘e8?!**

On rapidly encountering difficulties, Portisch tries to defend the squares d6 and c7, but he weakens the defence of the d5-pawn. True, it is hard to offer Black good advice: 17...c4 18 ♘bd6 ♖b8 19 e4! with a powerful initiative, or 17...♗a8 18 ♕d2! (more accurate than the *Informator* suggestion 18 ♕c3), when both 18...♕xd2 19 ♖xd2 and 18...♕b6 19 ♘fd6 followed by a4-a5 are unpleasant.

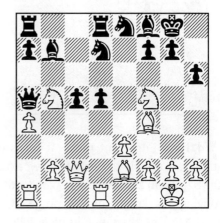

18 ♗d6!

Another surprise: both knights wanted to jump to d6, but it is a bishop jump that proves decisive! The threat is ♘e7+.

18...♘xd6

The penitential 18...♘ef6 would have lost the exchange after 19 ♘e7+ ♗xe7 20 ♗xe7 ♖e8 21 ♗xf6 ♘xf6 22 ♘d6. Material equality could still have been maintained by 18...♘df6 19 ♘e7+ ♗xe7 20 ♗xe7 ♖d7 21 ♗xc5 a6 22 b4! ♕xb4 23 ♗xb4 ♖xc2 24 ♘d4, but this endgame is extremely difficult for Black: apart from his isolani, he also has a weakness on a6, and White has two powerful bishops. Therefore Portisch preferred to give up a pawn, regarding this as the lesser evil.

19 ♘fxd6 ♖b8 20 ♘xb7 ♖xb7 21 ♖xd5 ♖db8

With the idea of somehow activating the pieces after ...a7-a6. Just six or seven moves ago Black was preparing for a protracted battle with hanging pawns – and suddenly his hopes are dashed. The phase of converting the material advantage begins.

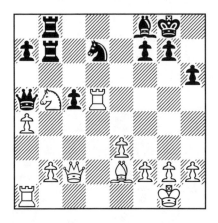

22 ♕d2! (an important move: it turns out that Black is unable to exploit the weakness of the b2-pawn) **22...♕xd2 23 ♖xd2 ♘f6**

Moving the knight out of range of the rook. If 23...♘e5 there would have followed 24 f4 ♘c6(g6) 25 ♗f3 etc.

24 ♖a2

In principle 24 ♗f3 ♖d7 25 ♖ad1 ♖xd2 26 ♖xd2 was also good, but to me it seemed useful for the moment to keep both rooks on the board: Black's activity is only temporary.

24...♘e4 25 ♖c2 ♖d7 26 g3 a5 (after 26...♖bd8, 27 a5 or 27 ♔g2 and ♗f3 is strong, and if 27...♖d2 28 b3!) **27 ♔g2 g6 28 ♗f3 ♘f6 29 ♘a3**

After making all the consolidating moves, I decided to place my knight on c4 (to attack the a5-pawn), and my bishop on b5 (to block the b-file).

29...♗d6 30 ♗c6 ♖dd8 31 ♖a1 ♗e5 32 ♗b5 ♘d5 (32...♘e4 33 ♔f3! f5 34 ♔e2 with the threat of f2-f3) **33 ♖b1 ♗d6**

In any event, White has a technically won position. If 33...♘b6, in order after 34 ♖xc5 ♗xb2! 35 ♖xb2 ♘xa4 or 35 ♘c4 ♗f6 to obtain saving chances, the simple 34 f4 ♗g7 35 ♔f3 etc. was possible.

34 ♖d2 ♘b6 35 ♖c1! (the rook exchanges after 35 ♖bd1 ♗e7 would be to Black's advantage, in view of the opposite-coloured bishops) **35...♗e7 36 ♖e2! ♖bc8 37 ♘b1**

Now, when the knight on b6 is guarding the c4-square, the white knight heads via d2 to b3.

37...♔g7 38 ♘d2 ♖a8 39 ♘b3 ♖dc8 40 ♖ec2 c4

A second pawn has to be given up – the tactical trick 40...♖a7 41 ♘xc5 ♖ac7(?) does not work, mainly because of 42 ♘e6+.

41 ♘d2 ♖a7 42 ♘xc4 ♘xc4 43 ♖xc4 ♖xc4 44 ♖xc4

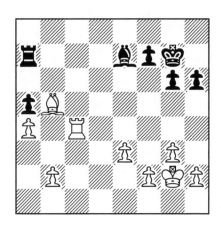

With two extra pawns and with rooks on the board, White need not fear the opposite-colour bishops. He is threatening, beginning with e3-e4, to begin advancing his kingside pawns.

44...f5 45 h3! h5 46 g4 hxg4 47 hxg4 fxg4 48 ♔g3 ♗d6+ 49 ♔xg4 ♖c7 50 ♗c6 (of course, not 50 ♖xc7+?! ♗xc7) **50...♖f7**

Portisch avoided 50...♔f6 in view of 51 f4 followed by e3-e4-e5 and ♔f3-e4-d5.

51 f4 ♔h6 52 ♗d5 ♖f6 53 ♖c1 ♔g7 54 b3

♖f8 55 ♖d1 ♝c5 56 ♖d3 ♝a3 57 ♝c4 ♝c1 58 ♖d7+ ♚h6 59 ♖e7 ♝d2 60 ♚f3

Expecting Black to capitulate at any moment, I relaxed somewhat. 60 ♖e5(e6) was better.

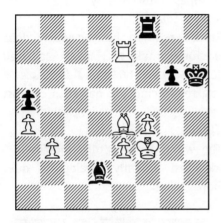

60...♝b4 (60...g5!? 61 ♖d7 ♝b4 62 ♝d3 gxf4 63 exf4 ♖h8 was more resilient) **61 ♖b7**

With the ephemeral threat of ♖xb4, but again 61 ♖e5(e6) was better.

61...♝c3 (61...g5!?) **62 ♝d3**

Here I remembered that I ought to try and win before the adjournment, and I finally set my sights on the weak g6-pawn and the vulnerability of the black king.

62...♖f6 63 ♚g4 ♝d2?! (after 63...♖d6 64 ♝c4 it would not have been possible to avoid an early morning adjournment session) **64 f5! 1-0**

The finishing stroke: both 64...gxf5+ 65 ♝xf5 and 64...♖xe3 65 fxg6 ♖f4+ 66 ♚g3 followed by ♖h7+ and g6-g7 are hopeless for Black.

A good game, and an important one in the competitive sense. With a score of 3½ out of 5 I concluded the first cycle as the sole leader.

In the 6th round I again easily, and for the third successive time, defeated Nunn, who suffered an opening disaster in the Grünfeld

(cf. Game No.13 in *Kasparov vs. Karpov 1986-1987*, note to White's 10th move). In the 7th round came a short but fighting draw with Korchnoi, and in the 8th round it was Hübner who crossed my path.

Game 24
G.Kasparov-R.Hübner
Brussels, 8th Round, 19.12.1986
Semi-Slav Defence D46

1 d4 d5 2 c4 c6 3 ♘c3 ♘f6 4 e3 e6 5 ♘f3 ♘bd7 6 ♝d3 ♝b4 (the main line of the Meran, 6...dxc4, is safer) **7 a3 ♝d6**

With his choice of a rare variation, my opponent wanted to avoid my preparation. If 7...♝a5, then 8 0-0 0-0 9 ♕c2 (Korchnoi-Hübner, 1st round; Kasparov-van der Wiel, Brussels 1987).

8 e4 dxe4 9 ♘xe4 ♘xe4 10 ♝xe4 e5 11 0-0 (11 ♝g5 ♝e7 is no better) **11...0-0**

A well-known pawn sacrifice, justified by the move a2-a3 (which weakens the light squares on the queenside).

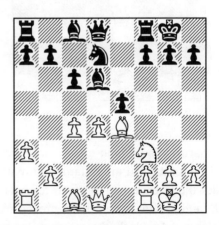

In the event of 12 dxe5 ♘xe5 13 ♘xe5 ♝xe5 14 ♝xh7+ ♚xh7 15 ♕h5+ ♚g8 16 ♕xe5 ♕d3! 17 c5 (with the pawn on a2, in the similar variation with 6...♝d6, here there would be the simple reply b2-b3) 17...♝e6 18

♗f4 ♗d5 (18...♖fd8!? – Sorokin) 19 ♖fe1 f6 20 ♕h5 ♗f7 21 ♕g4 ♖fe8 22 h3 ♕c4 (Larsen-Bisguier, San Juan 1969) or 18 ♗e3 (Nikolic-Hübner, Tilburg 1987) 18...♖fd8! the opposite-coloured bishops compensate Black for the pawn deficit and give him good drawing chances – he is not thinking of anything more.

12 ♗c2!

A novelty, devised at the board. Intuitively I sensed that White could gain the initiative, and I was not mistaken.

12...♖e8 (not all the problems were solved by 12...exd4 13 ♕xd4 ♗c5 14 ♕c3) **13 ♖e1 exd4 14 ♖xe8+ ♕xe8 15 ♕xd4 ♗e7**

White is better after 15...♗c5 16 ♕d3 ♘f8 17 b4 ♗e7 18 ♗b2 or 15...♗c7 16 ♗d2 ♘f8 17 ♖e1 ♗e6 18 ♗c3 f6 19 ♗b4 (Kupreichik-Sorokin, Blagoveshchensk 1988).

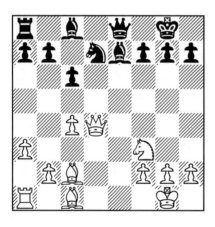

16 ♗g5

A natural developing move – in *Informator* I even attached an exclamation mark to it. But the unexpected 16 ♕e3!? followed by ♗d2 and ♖e1(d1) could have proved more unpleasant for Black (the queen on e3 both presses on the e-file, and trains its sights on the a7-pawn).

16...♗xg5?

An imperceptible, but serious mistake. The correct defence was 16...♘f8! 17 ♖e1

♗e6 18 ♕h4 ♗xg5 19 ♘xg5 h6 20 ♘xe6 ♘xe6 21 ♕e4 (21 ♗f5 ♕d8!) 21...g6 22 ♕e3 (22 h4 ♘g7!), and now not my *Informator* suggestion 22...♔h7?! 23 h4! or 22...♘g7 23 ♕c1 and ♕xh6, but 22...♘c7! 23 ♕d2 ♕f8 with hopes of full equality.

17 ♘xg5 ♘f6

Black's position has obviously deteriorated: for example, 17...♘f8 18 ♘e4 ♗e6 19 ♘d6 ♕d7 20 ♖d1 b6 21 b4 ♖d8 22 ♗e4 ♕c7 23 c5, reinforcing the powerful outpost at d6.

18 ♖d1!

The white army is fully mobilised, and Black must urgently develop his queen's bishop.

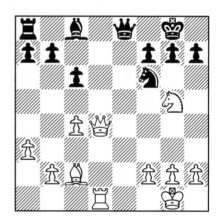

18...♗e6

Hübner decided to allow the exchange of knight for bishop and the creation in his position of a weak pawn on e6. This could not have been avoided by 18...h6? on account of 19 ♘e4! ♘xe4 20 ♕xe4 ♕xe4 (20...♗e6 21 ♕h7+) 21 ♖d8+ ♔h7 22 ♗xe4+ g6 23 g4, when Black is paralysed. But perhaps the best practical chance was 18...♗g4!? 19 ♗xh7+! (19 f3 ♗h5) 19...♘xh7 20 ♕xg4 ♘xg5 21 ♕xg5 ♕e2 22 ♕c1 ♖e8 with some compensation for the pawn.

19 ♖e1 (with the threat of 20 ♘xe6 fxe6 21 ♗f5) **19...♕d8**

After 19...♕d7 apart from 20 ♘xe6, White can also win a pawn by 20 ♗xh7+ ♘xh7 21 ♘xe6.

20 ♘xe6 fxe6 21 ♕e3 ♔h8 22 h3!

Possibly Hübner was hoping for 22 ♕xe6?! ♕d4! with definite counterplay, but it is far better to increase the pressure – Black now has a difficult position. An analogous pawn structure, with similar material, was soon to occur in two of my games with Karpov (*Game Nos.31 and 34*), but there the knight was better placed – on f8, defending the e6-pawn and the weakened light squares.

22...♕d7

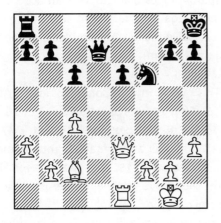

23 g4!

Combining a pawn offensive on the kingside with an attack on the e6- and a7-pawns.

23...♖e8

In avoiding the loss of the e6-pawn in variations such as 23...a5 24 g5 ♘h5 (24...♘g8 25 ♕e4) 25 ♗d1 or 23...h6 24 ♔g2 ♔g8 25 ♗g6, Black gives up his a7-pawn.

24 ♕e5?!

24 ♖d1! suggests itself: 24...♕f7 25 ♕xa7 e5 26 b3 e4 27 ♕e3 or 24...♕c7 25 ♕xa7 c5 – this looked unclear, but after 26 ♕a4! ♕f4 27 ♕b3 the queen successfully returns home. However, as before I did not want to allow Black any counterplay.

24...♕d8 25 ♔g2 ♕b6?

Hübner cracks under the pressure and misses a chance to create a last line of defence with gain of tempo – 25...♘d7! and ...♘f8.

26 ♖d1! (now the queen on b6 is out of play and Black has no defence) **26...c5**

The potential attack on the f2-point – 26...♖f8 would have been parried by the simple 27 ♖d2 or the forceful 27 ♕d6! ♖g8 (27...♖f7 28 ♕xe6) 28 g5 ♘h5 (28...♕xb2 29 ♕d3) 29 ♕e5 c5 30 ♗e4 and wins.

27 ♗a4! (unexpectedly the bishop attacks from the other side) **27...♖f8 28 ♖d6 ♕c7** (28...♕a5 29 ♗c2 was also hopeless) **29 ♖xe6 ♕f7** (a desperate attempt to confuse matters) **30 ♕xc5**

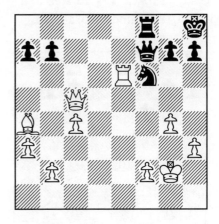

30...♘xg4 (also after 30...♘e4 the simplest is 31 ♕xf8+! ♕xf8 32 ♖xe4 b5 33 ♗xb5 ♕a8 34 f3 and ♖e8+) **31 ♕xf8+! ♕xf8 32 hxg4 1-0**

After this confident win I had 6 out of 8, and two rounds before the finish the lead over my pursuers had reached two points.

However, at this I did not calm down: in the 9th round I faced a critical, psychologically important duel with Short – I needed to gain revenge for my failure in the first cycle! Incidentally, in classical play Nigel gained only one more win against me (in the 16th game of our 1993 match), with 27 draws and 21 defeats...

Game 25
G.Kasparov-N.Short
Brussels, 9th Round, 20.12.1986
Queen's Gambit Declined D55

1 d4 e6 2 ♘f3 ♘f6 3 c4 d5 4 ♘c3 ♗e7 5 ♗g5 h6 (5...0-0 – *Game No.23*) **6 ♗xf6 ♗xf6 7 e3 0-0 8 ♖c1 c6 9 ♗d3 ♘d7 10 0-0 dxc4 11 ♗xc4 e5 12 h3**

A system which I tested in my matches with Karpov (1985 and 1986).

12...exd4 13 exd4 ♘b6 14 ♗b3 ♗f5 (weaker is 14...♗g5 15 ♖c2 ♗f5 16 ♖e2 and ♖fe1, Ribli-Short, Dortmund 1986) **15 ♖e1**

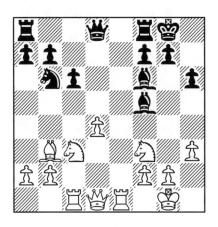

Previously White retained some advantage after 15...♖e8 16 ♖xe8+ ♕xe8 17 ♕d2 ♕d7 18 ♖e1 ♖d8 (18...a5!?) 19 ♕f4 (23rd game of the 1985 match), or 15...a5! 16 a3 ♖e8 (if 16...♕d7, then 17 ♘e5! ♗xe5 18 ♖xe5 ♖fe8 19 ♕e2, Karpov-Beliavsky, Moscow 1986) 17 ♖xe8+ ♕xe8 18 ♕d2 ♘d7?! 19 ♕f4 ♗g6 20 h4! ♕d8 21 ♘a4! h5 22 ♖e1 (22nd game of the 1986 match).

But a game played in November, M.Gurevich-van der Sterren (Baku 1986),

changed the assessment: 18...♕d7! 19 ♖e1 ♖e8 20 ♖xe8+ ♕xe8 21 ♕f4 ♗e6! 22 ♗xe6 ♕xe6 (without the moves 15...a5 16 a3 a pawn would now be lost – 22 ♕b8+ and ♕xa7) 23 ♕b8+ (23 ♘e4 ♗e7 or 23 ♕c7 ♘c4 24 ♕xb7 ♗xd4! with equality is no better) 23...♕c8 24 ♕a7 ♘c4 25 b3 ♘xa3 26 ♕xa5 ♗e7 with a quick draw.

According to Short, he didn't yet know of this improvement, and on the morning before the game he devised his own novelty. **15...♗g5** (now White does not have 16 ♖c2, but Nigel underestimated my reply) **16 ♖a1!**

Little was promised by 16 ♘xg5 ♕xg5. 'While losing time on moving his rook, Kasparov forces Black to seek an acceptable defence against the knight invasion on e5 and to solve the current problems of the g5-bishop.' (Nikitin)

16...♘d7?!

This was my opponent's idea. After 16...♗f6(f4) 17 ♘e5 ♗xe5 18 ♖xe5 or 16...a5 17 ♖e5 ♗g6 18 ♘xg5 hxg5 19 ♖c1 ♘d7 20 ♖e3 White has a minimal advantage and it is not clear why 15...♗g5 was played. But with the move in the game Black loses control over the d5-point.

17 d5! (this reaction came as a surprise to Short, and he stopped to think) **17...♖c8?**

Probably already a losing move, as was 17...cxd5? in view of 18 ♕xd5 ♗e6 19 ♖xe6! fxe6 20 ♕xe6+ ♔h8 21 ♖d1.

17...♘c5! was essential – after 18 ♗c2 ♗xc2 19 ♕xc2 and ♖ad1 or 18 ♖e5!? ♗g6 (18...g6?! 19 g4! ♘xb3 20 axb3 is dangerous for Black) 19 ♘xg5 hxg5 20 dxc6 ♘xb3 21 ♕xb3 (21 ♘d5!?) 21...bxc6 22 ♕c4(a3) White has the initiative, but Black can put up a tenacious resistance.

18 ♘d4! ♗g6

Of course, not 18...♕f6? since the reply 19 dxc6 bxc6 20 ♘xf5 ♕xf5 21 ♗c2 wins the knight.

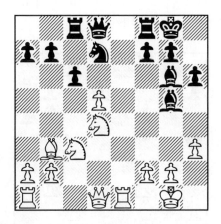

19 ♘e6!

'An unexpected turn of events! White opens the centre in very favourable circumstances. His bishop becomes enormously strong, and cracks appear in the black king's fortress.' (Nikitin)

19...fxe6 20 dxe6 ♔h7

Defending the bishop on g6. If 20...♔h8? there is the decisive 21 exd7 ♖c7 22 ♕d6! ♔h7 (both 22...♗f6 23 ♖e8! and 22...♖f6 23 ♕xc7! ♕xc7 24 ♖e8+ are bad for Black) 23 ♖ad1 etc.

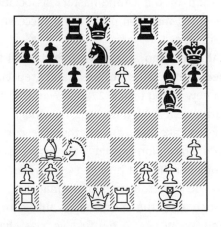

21 ♕xd7!

Accurately calculated. Now in the event of 21 exd7? ♖c7 White would have to play 22 ♗e6, when Black is saved by 22...♗f5! 23 ♗xf5+ ♖xf5 24 ♕c2 g6 and ...♖(♕)xd7 or 23

♘e4 ♗xe6 24 ♘xg5+ hxg5 25 ♖xe6 ♖xd7 26 ♕c2+ ♔g8.

21...♕b6!

A clever resource, creating the maximum difficulties for me. The ending after 21...♕xd7 22 exd7 ♖cd8 23 ♖ad1 ♗f5 (23...♗f7 24 ♗c2+) 24 ♗e6 ♗xe6 25 ♖xe6 ♖f7 26 ♖ed6 is altogether unattractive for Black.

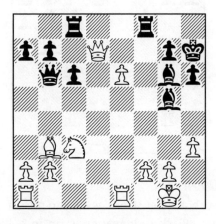

22 e7! (otherwise 22...♖fd8) **22...♖fe8**

Seeing that in the variation 22...♕xf2+ (22...♖xf2? 23 ♘a4) 23 ♔h1 ♖fe8 24 ♘e4 neither 24...♖xe4 25 ♖xe4, 24...♕xb2 25 ♘d6, nor 24...♕h4!? 25 ♘xg5+! (25 ♘d6? ♖cd8!) 25...♕xg5 26 ♕xb7 will do, Black creates the threat of winning the e7-pawn by 23...♖c7. He is literally a smidgen away from equalising.

23 ♕g4!

The only path to the goal! There is now the serious threat of h3-h4: for example, 23...♖c7 24 h4! ♖cxe7 25 ♖xe7 ♗xe7 26 h5 ♗d3 27 ♕f3 ♖d8 28 ♖d1 winning a piece, or 23...♕a5 24 h4! ♗f6 (24...♗f5 25 ♕f3!) 25 ♘e4! ♗xb2 (25...♗xe7 26 ♗c2!!) 26 ♖ad1 etc.

23...♕c5

The alternative defence 23...♗f6 (with the idea of 24 h4? h5) did not help because of 24 ♖e6! ♖c7 25 ♘e4(d5).

At this point Short looked full of optimism: now 24 h4? is parried by the simple 24...♗xe7 25 ♘e4 ♛h5. But White continues his brilliant series of forcing moves.

24 ♘e4! (24 ♗e6? ♖c7 25 ♘e4 ♗xe4 26 ♖xe4 ♖cxe7 was far weaker) **24...♛xe7**

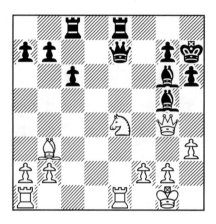

25 ♗c2!!

Such a 'quiet stroke' is easy to miss in advance. 'Black suddenly ends up in a high-tensile web of diagonal and vertical pins.' (Nikitin).

25...♖f8 (25...♖cd8 26 f4 or 25...♛e5 26 h4, and after the bishop moves – 27 ♘g5+, was equally dismal) **26 g3**

Calmly preparing h3-h4 or f2-f4. 26 h4!? ♗xh4 27 ♘g3! would have won more quickly: for example, 27...♗xc2 28 ♖xe7 ♗xe7 29 ♛e2! or 27...♛g5 28 ♗xg6+ ♔xg6 29 ♛e4+. On the other hand, now the finish of the game turns out to be even prettier.

26...♛d8

26...♗f5 would have been met by the thunderous 27 ♘d6!!, and 26...♖ce8 27 h4 ♗d2 28 ♘g5+ ♛xg5 29 hxg5 ♗xe1 30 gxh6! ♗xf2+ 31 ♔g2 ♖f6 32 ♛d7 ♖g8 33 ♗xg6+ was equally depressing.

27 ♖ad1 (or immediately 27 h4!? ♗e7 28 h5 ♗f5 29 ♘f6+) **27...♛a5 28 h4 ♗e7 29 ♘c3!**

This is more flamboyant than 29 ♘d6: up until now all White's threats have been on

the light squares, but in the end mate is given on the dark squares.

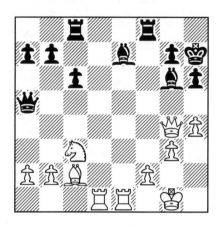

29...♗xc2 30 ♖xe7 ♖g8 31 ♖dd7 ♗f5 (31...♗g6 32 ♛d4!) **32 ♖xg7+ ♔h8 33 ♛d4 1-0**

Probably the best of my wins in this tournament.

Before the last round I was 2½ points ahead of a trio of leading rivals, and I was very happy that neither my cold coupled with fatigue, nor my involvement in the creation of the Grandmasters Association, prevented me from performing successfully in Brussels.

After playing a draw with Portisch, I finished with a 'plus five' result and drew close to a new rating peak – 2750! It was after this tournament that they began saying it was time to take bets on whether the current world champion would beat Fischer's old record. For the first time in 14 years the 2780 mark no longer seemed unattainable.

Such was the outcome of this complicated, nervy year – my first year as champion.

Winning 'to order'

International tournament in Brussels (10-24 April 1987): 1-2. **Kasparov** and Ljubojevic –

8½ out of 11; 3. Karpov – 7; 4-5. Korchnoi and Timman – 6½; 6. Tal – 6; 7. Larsen – 5½; 8-9. Torre and van der Wiel – 5; 10. Winants – 3½; 11. Short – 3; 12. Meulders – 1.

I began the fourth year of battles for the title with an unusual rapidplay match with Nigel Short (London, 4-5 February 1987). We played in white and black dinner suits on the stage of a popular rock club, and this spectacle was broadcast on commercial TV – hence the time control of 25 minutes each for the entire game: this made a total of 50 minutes, and in a program lasting an hour this left time for advertisements and commentary. I won 4-2 (with no draws). This was an entertaining, but also a highly unusual spectacle. And when my manager Andrew Page suggested organising a series of rapidplay tournaments, many fellow-grandmasters rejected the idea – it had not yet attracted the masses! It was only several years later that everyone saw the wonderful prospects available to rapid chess thanks to the appearance of electronic demonstration boards.

At that time the shortening of the time control was, indeed, an urgent question. Obvious progress in the study of the openings and the analysis of adjourned games demanded a reduction in thinking time and a longer playing session without adjournments. The classical five-hour time control (40 moves in 2½ hours with an adjournment, and then 16 moves in every hour) gave way to a six-hour control (40 moves in 2 hours plus 20 moves in an hour followed by an adjournment). When the GMA began functioning, the new control finally gained acceptance, gradually changing the pace at which chess developed.

All the indicators were that a new era was beginning in chess, and many were full of the most optimistic hopes. Those elected on to the board of the newly-formed Grandmasters Association were Garry Kasparov (president), Anatoly Karpov and Jan Timman (vice-presidents), Ljubomir Ljubojevic, Lajos Portisch, Yasser Seirawan, John Nunn and the businessman Bessel Kok (chairman and chief sponsor). The emergence of the GMA was marked by an amazing coincidence: on 15th February 1985 Campomanes cut short my first match for the world title, and exactly two years later in Brussels our Association was founded. The date of an unprecedented act of tyranny in the chess world coincided with the starting date of an organised resistance to the forces which had been behind it.

Around then there was a joint meeting, unique in its way, of the leaders of the GMA and FIDE, which discussed the conditions proposed by the Association for a new competition of leading grandmasters – a World Cup coordinated with the next three-year world championship cycle, and a common schedule of events for 1987-1990 was compiled. Subsequently, to all appearances, the Soviet Chess Federation interfered – or rather, the Sports Committee (or perhaps even another Committee), and our collaboration with FIDE did not in fact come to fruition. A pity, since it could have radically changed the entire modern map of the chess world.

From Brussels I travelled to Hamburg, where I gave a repeat clock simul' against the local Bundesliga team and gained convincing revenge (7-1) for my defeat in December 1985 (the only one I ever suffered in a simul'). A little later, in May, in a similar simul' I was able to crush the Swiss national team (5½-½).

I spent the whole of March in my native Baku: first I instructed juniors at a session of the Botvinnik-Kasparov school, and at the end of the month, during the spring school holidays, I gave simuls' with clocks in the national final of the tournament of Pioneers Palaces. Again, for the third time, I made the best score among the captains, and for the first time this secured victory for the Baku team.

In the meantime it transpired that in the autumn I again faced a match with Karpov – already the fourth since 1984! In the Candidates super-final the former champion confidently defeated Andrey Sokolov, the winner of the qualifying cycle, by 7½-3½. However, before the next match for the title, fate finally granted Karpov and me a tournament game, the first for six years. This occurred in April, at the excellent SWIFT Tournament in Brussels, organised for the second successive year by the indefatigable Bessel Kok.

The tournament was an important landmark in the establishment of the young Grandmasters Association. New technology was tried – electronic demonstration boards, first tested in my match with Karpov in London (1986), as well as the new, six-hour time control, which was later used in the World Cup tournaments. There was a marked change in the atmosphere in the auditorium: the spectators watched the games with a kind of reverence and in complete silence. Nearly all the founders of the GMA were in Brussels, and so every day we had lively discussions about *what* to do next and *how*. It was a turbulent, interesting time, full of optimism: chess was obviously moving on to a different qualitative level. True, apart from debates there was also the small matter in the evenings of 'moving the pieces'.

The field of 12 players was very strong, although uneven – the concept of super-

tournaments was only then being developed. Ten grandmasters, seven from the world's elite, and one (Short) with the reputation of a rising star, were set loose on two Belgian masters, Winants and Meulders. And, incidentally, Tal, who was working as chief consultant in the press centre and was brought in at the last minute to replace the indisposed Hübner, in the end defeated only these two. By the will of the pairings I began with wins over them, van der Wiel and Short (although I played badly against Nigel), then I had something of a skid – draws against Torre, Timman and Korchnoi, before winning with Black against Larsen (in the good old Tarrasch Defence!) to reach 6½ out of 8. Usually in 11 rounds a score of 'plus five' is quite sufficient for first place, but in this tournament Ljubojevic was playing brilliantly: by defeating Korchnoi in the 8th round, he kept level with me.

In the 9th round, in order to take first place on my own, I needed without fail to beat my rival with White. Alas, things didn't work out: Ljubojevic unexpectedly employed the Slav Defence with ...g7-g6, and I responded badly. Black achieved a comfortable game and drew easily.

My strict teacher Botvinnik wrote about this: *'The world champion still needs to improve. This was confirmed at the finish of the tournament in Brussels (1987), where Kasparov was competing with Ljubojevic. The culmination came in the 9th round, when Kasparov had White against his main rival. The game ended in a draw, and as a result Kasparov and Ljubojevic shared 1st place. This episode indicates that the present champion has not yet achieved the highest mastery in tournament play. Meanwhile, Lasker (remember, among others, his famous game with Capablanca, St. Petersburg 1914), Capablanca, Alekhine, and the author of these* lines (*I can point to my game with Keres, Leningrad 1941*) all demonstrated their ability to win "to order" at decisive moments in a tournament. Yes, Kasparov still is able to and needs to progress, but we should not be too severe on him, since there are spots even on the sun...'

But let's see what happened then in Brussels. In the next, penultimate, round I had Black against Karpov, who was a point behind me and Ljubojevic. For the ex-champion this was the last chance to interfere in the fight for 1st place: he needed to beat me (and then also Ljubojevic) in his individual games. But for me, by contrast, it was essential not to lose: both to avoid spoiling the picture of our long-standing duel, in which I was then leading by 'plus one', and to surpass Karpov – the winner of SWIFT-1986 – not only in a match, but also in a tournament. This duel was a notable event, especially before the impending match in Seville. For some reason Karpov played passively, uncertainly and got into an inferior endgame, but he nevertheless held on (Game No.25 in *Kasparov vs. Karpov 1986-87*).

When I was making my last few moves, I was already thinking about how to catch up with Ljubojevic, who that day defeated Larsen and, with 8 out of 10, burst half a step ahead. In the last round he drew with Karpov, and now I had to win 'to order' against Mikhail Tal.

Game 26
G.Kasparov-M.Tal
Brussels, 11th Round, 24.04.1987
Nimzo-Indian Defence E48

1 d4 ♘f6 2 c4 e6 3 ♘c3

'The first surprise: I had prepared for 3

♘f3 b6.' (Tal). To be honest, I didn't know exactly where to fight for an advantage, and after consulting with Nikitin I decided to go in for comparatively complicated play in the Nimzo-Indian.

3...♗b4 4 e3

'The second surprise: Kasparov once made this move against Yurtaev (Moscow 1981) and since then he had not employed it again.' (Tal). Soon I also adopted 4 ♕c2 (*Game Nos.63, 65*), whereas I had already given up the line 4 ♘f3 c5 5 g3 (cf. *Game No.13*).

4...0-0 (4...c5!? 5 ♘e2 – Game No.39 in *Garry Kasparov on Garry Kasparov Part I*) **5 ♗d3**

In an old training game between us (1st match game, Baku 1980) Tal gained equal chances after 5 ♘e2 d5 6 a3 ♗e7 7 cxd5 ♘xd5 8 g3 ♘xc3 9 ♘xc3 c5.

5...d5 (this is how my opponent played since the times of his matches with Botvinnik) **6 cxd5**

'This simple and logical move had not previously occurred in my games, which is simply amazing. Here doubts began to creep in: had all this been prepared in advance for a meeting with me? Alas, this turned out to be so...' (Tal)

6...exd5 7 ♘e2

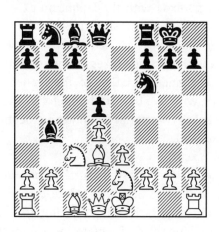

7...c5

In the aforementioned game with me, Yurtaev experienced difficulties after 7...♘bd7 8 0-0 c6 9 f3 c5 (9...♖e8!?) 10 a3!. Today, after a good thousand games have been played with this variation, 7...♖e8! 8 0-0 ♗d6(f8) is considered safe. But Tal, without any particular thought, made the most natural moves.

8 0-0 ♘c6

8...b6 9 a3 ♗xc3 10 bxc3 ♗a6 would have led to a position from the famous Botvinnik-Capablanca game (Game No.37 in Part II of *My Great Predecessors*), when I would have replied 11 f3! and ♘g3, preparing e3-e4, as I had already done against Ivanovic (Niksic 1983).

9 a3 cxd4 10 exd4!?

10 axb4 dxc3 11 b5 ♘e5 12 ♘xc3 retains a small plus, but I thought that here Black would have an easier game. However, in the event of 12...♗g4 13 f3 ♗h5? 14 ♗e2 with the threat of g2-g4 (D.Gurevich-Tal, Saint John (blitz) 1988), White already has an obvious advantage, but he is also better after 13...d4 14 ♗xh7+! ♘xh7 15 ♕xd4 ♘xf3+ 16 gxf3 (Kir.Georgiev-Spasov, Sofia 1984). The alternative is 12...♕c7(d6) or 12...♘xd3 13 ♕xd3 ♗e6.

Besides, I liked the structure that arises after 10 exd4 with the knight on e2 and a rapid f2-f3. 'What should Black do now? After the retreat 10...♗d6 there follows 11 f3, and the position takes on the contours of the exchange variation of the French Defence, with two (!) extra tempi for White. At the board I did not in fact find an acceptable plan.' (Tal).

10...♗xc3?!

Again the most natural reply. After 10...♗e7 11 f3 and ♔h1 White can calmly prepare an attack with g2-g4. But 10...♗d6! (controlling the dark squares) was nevertheless better, as played back in the games Stolberg-Botvinnik (12th USSR Championship, Moscow 1940) and Gligoric-Smyslov (Palma de Mallorca Interzonal 1970). Later Tal himself upheld this variation as White against Sax (Subotica Interzonal 1987) – 11 f3 (11 ♗g5? ♗xh2+) 11...h6! 12 ♔h1 ♘h5 (12...♖e8!?) 13 ♕e1 f5 14 ♘xd5 ♗xh2 15 ♔xh2 ♕xd5 16 ♕h4 and himself indicated 16...♕f7 with 'equality'.

11 bxc3!?

A novelty devised at the board. Black is also slightly worse after 11 ♘xc3 ♗g4 (11...♘xd4?! 12 ♗xh7+ and ♕xd4) 12 f3 ♗e6 (Porath-Pachman, Amsterdam Olympiad 1954) 13 ♗e3, but I decided to support the d4-pawn and then create an attack on the king. 'One surprise after another! It somehow escaped my memory that Kasparov was a pupil of Botvinnik, who possessed a truly encyclopaedic knowledge of opening theory. It was no wonder that the pupil proved fully worthy of his teacher.' (Tal).

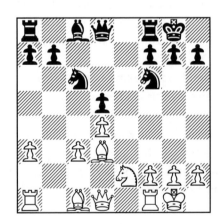

11...♘e7?!

With the obvious intention of ...♗f5, but White easily prevents this. After 11...h6 12 f3 the attack with ♔h1, ♖g1 and g2-g4 would have gained in strength. Nikitin suggested solving the problem of the c8-bishop's development by 11...♗g4, but after 12 f3 (12

♗g5 h6 13 ♗h4 ♘a5 14 f3 ♗d7 is not so clear) 12...♗h5 13 ♖b1 ♘a5 14 ♗g5 ♗g6 15 ♘f4 Black is tied down by the pin on the f6-knight and the weakness of the d5-pawn. Apparently the best is 11...♖e8!? (Savon) 12 f3 ♘a5 and ....♗d7 or 12 ♗g5 h6 followed by ...♘a5 and ....♗d7.

12 ♕c2

Of course! 12 ♗g5?! was much weaker in view of 12...♘e4.

12...♗d7?!

Black wants to develop his bishop, but 12...♘g6 was more resilient, in order after 13 ♗g5 h6 14 ♗d2 (14 ♗c1!?) to sacrifice a pawn – 14...♘e4 15 ♗xe4 dxe4 16 ♕xe4 ♖e8, although after 17 ♕d3 ♗e6 18 ♖fe1 ♖c8 19 ♘g3 the compensation for it is insufficient.

13 ♗g5!

With the threat of ♗xf6. It would appear that Tal was preparing for a positional battle after 13 f3, but White unexpectedly launches an assault on the king's fortress.

13...♘g6

Now the pawn sacrifice 13...♘e4 14 ♗xe4 dxe4 15 ♕xe4 f6 16 ♗d2 would be even less correct.

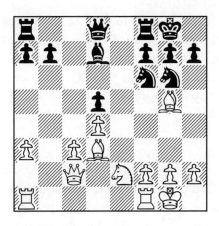

14 f4!

It turns out that White also has this plan, the idea of which I grasped quite quickly.

Without making a single serious mistake, Black ends up in a difficult position.

14...h6

Forced: in the event of 14...♖e8 15 f5 ♘f8 16 ♘f4 ♗c6 17 ♘h5 ♘8d7 18 ♖f3 the pin on the f6-knight is too unpleasant.

15 ♗xf6 ♕xf6 16 f5!

'With a powerful and virtually irresistible attack. I would have been happy to play this position with White.' (Tal)

16...♘e7 17 ♘g3

It suddenly transpires that Black has no good defence against the threat of ♘h5 and f5-f6.

17...♘c8?!

This manoeuvre of the knight to d6 is too slow, as is 17...♔h8?! 18 ♘h5 ♕g5 19 f6! gxf6 (19...♕xh5? 20 fxe7 ♖fe8 21 ♖ae1 and wins) 20 ♘xf6 ♗xf5 21 ♗xf5 ♕xf6 22 ♖ae1 ♘xf5 23 ♖xf5 ♕g6 24 ♕f2 etc. However, even after the more resilient 17...♕g5 18 ♖f3! h5 19 f6 gxf6 20 ♘f5 or 18...♖ae8 19 f6 gxf6 20 ♖af1 Black's position is extremely dangerous.

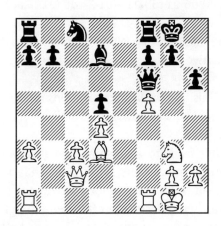

18 ♖f4?

This move suggests itself and in *Informator* I attached an exclamation mark to it, underestimating Black's possible reply, and I rejected the strongest move 18 ♖f3(!) because of the 'unclear' 18...♔h8. But in fact after 19 ♘h5 ♕g5 20 ♘f4 Black is in trouble: he has to bring his knight back – 20...♘e7, and in the event of 21 f6 ♕xf6 22 ♘g6+ fxg6 23 ♖xf6 ♖xf6 there are still chances of setting up a fortress with rook, knight and pawn for the queen. However, after the unexpected 21 ♕f2!? ♗xf5 22 ♗xf5 ♕xf5 (after 22...♘xf5? 23 ♘h3 a piece is lost) 23 ♖e1! ♘g6 (and after 23...♕d7 24 ♘e6! – the exchange) 24 ♘e6! ♕xe6 25 ♖xe6 fxe6 26 a4 these chances vanish.

18...♘d6?

Returning the favour – we both thought that this was the only move! Black would have lost ignominiously after 18...♕d6? 19 f6!! ♕xf4 (19...g6 20 ♖af1) 20 ♗h7+ ♔h8 21 fxg7+ ♔xg7 22 ♘h5+ and ♘xf4.

However, the latent computer resource 18...g5! (it is not easy for a human player to venture such a committal looking move) would have given Black a defensible position, although after both 19 ♘h5 ♕d6 20 ♖f2 f6 21 ♕b3 ♘b6 22 a4 or 21 c4!? dxc4 22 ♗xc4+, and 19 ♖f2 ♘b6 20 ♘h5 ♕c6 (20...♕d6 21 f6!) 21 ♖b1 ♖ad8 (21...♖ac8 22 ♗b5!) 22 a4 or 19...♘d6 20 ♘h5 ♕d8 21 ♕a2 ♗c6 22 h4 White would retain the initiative.

19 ♕f2!

'Finishing the last preparations for driving the black queen out of f6.' (Stohl)

19...♖fe8

This leads to a crushing defeat (again a 'natural' move!), but what should Black do instead? After the voluntary retreat 19...♕d8 there is the decisive 20 f6! ♘e8 (20...g5 21 ♕f3! and ♕h5 or 20...g6 21 ♖f1! is no better) 21 fxg7 ♘xg7 22 ♖f6!. And in the event of 19...♘e8 20 ♘h5 ♕d6 (but not 20...♕g5 21 h4! ♕xh5 22 g4 – a key idea!) 21 f6! g5 (21...g6 22 ♖f1(e1) with an irresistible attack) 22 ♗b1! (threatening ♕c2) 22...♕e6 23 ♖f5! ♘d6 24 ♘g7 ♘xf5 25 ♘xe6 fxe6 26 c4

Black does not have sufficient compensation for the queen.

Things are also very dismal for him after the more resilient 19...♔h8 20 ♘h5 ♕g5 21 h4! ♕d8 (21...♕xh5? 22 g4) 22 ♖g4 ♖g8 23 ♕f4 ♘e4 24 ♗xe4 dxe4 25 ♖e1 etc.

20 ♘h5 ♕d8

After 20...♕g5 21 h4! ♕d8 (21...♕xh5 22 g4) both 22 ♕g3 and 22 ♖g4 are strong.

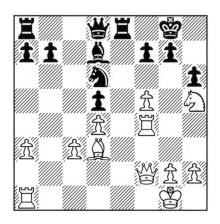

21 ♘xg7! (21 f6? no longer makes sense in view of 21...g5) **21...♘e4**

Despair. Black would have lost immediately after 21...♔xg7 22 f6+ ♔h8 23 ♕h4. But now too it all concludes with a swift attack on the king.

22 ♗xe4 ♖xe4 23 f6 ♔h7 24 ♖xe4 dxe4 25 ♕f4 ♗c6 26 ♖e1 (26 ♖f1!?) **26...♕f8 27 c4** (the immediate 27 ♘f5! and ♖e3 was also possible) **27...♕xa3 28 ♘f5! ♕f8 29 ♖e3 ♗d7 30 ♖g3 ♗xf5 31 ♕xf5+ 1-0**

This was my only tournament win against Tal.

As a result I caught Ljubojevic and shared 1st-2nd places with him, and I finished one and a half points ahead of Karpov, gaining revenge for the 1981 Moscow 'Tournament of Stars'. As for what Botvinnik said about me being unready to win decisive games, I quickly 'corrected' this, by winning in the final rounds not only against Tal, but also against Karpov in Seville 1987 (*Game No.31*), and against Spassky in Barcelona 1989 (*Game No.51*).

The day after the conclusion of the main tournament, the organisers staged a 'world blitz championship' – a grandiose double-round event. To increase the competitive intrigue, an additional match of two games was included between the players who finished first and second. The composition of the tournament was also strengthened: the Belgian masters Winants and Meulders were replaced by Sosonko and the convalescent Hübner. The twelve contestants played two successive games against one another, with White and with Black. Instead of drawing lots, the players were arranged in order of rating, with No.1 on the rating list playing first against No.12, then No.11, and so on. Thus Karpov and I were to meet at the very finish.

After an ultra-successful start (11 out of 12!) I was practically assured of a place in the first two and I reduced the tempo somewhat. Before the last round the leading trio was Kasparov – 15½ out of 20, Timman – 13, Karpov – 12. There was hardly any chance of an additional match with Karpov, since it would have taken a miracle for him to overtake Timman. Due to our weak motivation and accumulated fatigue, both my blitz games with Karpov were of very poor quality (Game Nos.26 and 27 in *Kasparov vs. Karpov 1986-87*). Luck was on my side: 1½-½.

Results of the experimental SWIFT World Blitz Championship: 1. **Kasparov** – 17 out of 22; 2. Timman – 15; 3-4. Karpov and Ljubojevic – 12½; 5. Hübner – 12; 6-7. Korchnoi and Short – 11; 8. Tal – 10½, etc. In the additional mini-match with Timman, a draw would have satisfied me (thanks to my first

place in the tournament), but, summoning my remaining strength, I nevertheless won: 1½-½.

In the next six months before the match with Karpov I limited myself to participating in another interesting experiment – a televised match-tournament of three USSR teams (Moscow, 8-10 May), with a time control of 45 minutes for a game. Leading the 'young generation' team, I scored 2½ out of 4 against Beliavsky and Tal, and my team also won. It was then, for the first time in history – a sign of the times – that nearly fifty Soviet grandmasters assembled for a meeting chaired by Botvinnik. Apart from me, among those who spoke were Tal, Geller, Polugayevsky, Razuvaev, Psakhis and many others. In a unanimously agreed resolution, those present stated that '*the structure of the chess movement in the country is out of date and requires radical reform*', they approved '*the participation of world champion Kasparov and ex-world champion Karpov in the international Grandmasters Association*', and they recommended that their colleagues should join this organisation on an individual basis.

And so, my new match with Karpov was to start on 10th October 1987 in the Spanish city of Seville. At the end of May, after returning from Barcelona, where I had been presented with what was by then my fourth chess 'Oscar', I began my preparations for the match (which were interrupted only in August for a familiarisation visit to Seville). The training sessions were held, as usual, on the banks of the Caspian Sea, at the Zagulba sanatorium.

After the 1986 match a difficult problem arose with my group of trainers, since, with the departure of Timoshchenko and Vladimirov, only three remained of those with whom I had begun the struggle: Nikitin,

Shakarov and Dorfman. Therefore in March I entered into discussions with the young Georgian master Zurab Azmaiparashvili (within a year he became a grandmaster), who immediately joined our preparation work and, in particular, helped me to master a new match opening – the English Opening. Even so, the team still lacked a strong grandmaster. At the end of August I approached Sergey Dolmatov, and, fortunately for me, he agreed to help. Sergey's arrival ensured that in Seville we would have a marked advantage in the analysis of adjourned games.

The trials which I endured in those months are described in detail in *Kasparov vs. Karpov 1986-87*. For me the match in Seville was psychologically the most difficult of all my five duels for the title with Karpov. To some extent, my win in the 1986 match had disarmed me, since it seemed like the final victory.

And in 1987, in addition to my fight with the FIDE and Sports Committee bureaucracy, I was busy with numerous other important matters: work at the junior chess school (six weeks before the match Botvinnik and I held our last joint session), trying to set up a Soviet-British chess publishing house and a chess magazine, the creating and leading of the GMA in Brussels, and the founding of a junior computer club in Moscow. Incidentally, the games in the first-ever 'Star chess' display (with a centre in Cannes), in which I played simultaneously with ten cities in various parts of the world, were transmitted from the junior computer club via a telecommunications link.

Continuing work on my autobiography *Child of Change*, which began at the end of 1986, was another distraction. As the work progressed, it was hard to shake off the feeling that the main fight for the world title

was already behind me. Not long before the match, the book was published in London, and then in another five European languages, and in Seville I arranged for it to be launched.

Numerous problems prevented me from focusing on the main thing, which was psychological preparation for the next match with Karpov. The forthcoming clash was somehow very remote from my mind, and I couldn't help wishing that I didn't have to go through with it. Why did I have play again? I'd already proved my superiority – I'd already won and then defended my world title... Although I realised that far more was at stake this time than in the previous matches, I really didn't want to play the match, and my whole being rebelled against the very thought that I must once again (for the umpteenth time!) mobilise myself for battle.

Fourth Match with Karpov

Match for the World Championship **Kasparov** – Karpov (Seville, 10 October – 19 December 1987): 12-12.

After an easily gained draw with Black at the start of the Seville match I felt the desire to engage in an immediate large-scale battle and in the 2nd game to demonstrate all I was capable of with White. But already in this game it became evident that on this occasion my nervous system was not ready for the severe pressure of a world championship match. On encountering a novelty in the English Opening, I 'fell asleep' for 83 minutes, blundered on the 20th move, forgot to press my clock on the 26th, and lost on time on the 33rd, without even managing to resign. It need hardly be said what a state of shock I was in, having at the start practically repeated Karpov's anti-record, established by him in the 8th game of the previous match. My failure in the opening was also painful and left me feeling desperately disillusioned.

However, I managed to pull myself together and by confidently gaining a draw in the 3rd game I seemed to have overcome the crisis. On the Saturday and Sunday I relaxed and prepared, tuning myself up for a large-scale battle in the 4th game. And my expectations were justified.

Game 27
G.Kasparov-A.Karpov
World Championship Match
4th Game, Seville 19.10.1987
English Opening A29

---

1 c4

Played without any doubts! We didn't prepare 1 c4 for the match in order that one novelty from the 2nd game, prepared by the opponent for his battles with Korchnoi, should scare me away from the move. Of course, the struggle with the black e3-pawn (cf. the note to Black's 9th move) contained a considerable risk, but how do you win without taking risks?

1...♘f6 2 ♘c3 e5

I think that Karpov was expecting a repetition of the opening duel (in our matches I always began by playing the main system I had prepared with White), and he did not arrive for the game empty-handed.

3 ♘f3 ♘c6 4 g3 ♗b4 5 ♗g2 0-0 (4) 6 0-0 e4 (10)

Again, as in the 2nd game, this came after some hesitation – perhaps 6...♖e8 should be played (16th game)?

7 ♘g5 ♗xc3 8 bxc3 ♖e8 (4) 9 f3! exf3?! (3)

In the press centre this exchange provoked a lively debate: many were perplexed

as to why Black should avoid the new – and better! – move 9...e3, which had been successfully tried in the 2nd game. It seems to me that the sharp position after 10 d3! d5 11 ♕b3 ♘a5 12 ♕a3 c6 13 cxd5 cxd5 14 f4 ♘c6 15 ♖b1 ♕c7 16 ♗b2 ♗g4 was not to Karpov's taste. He did not want to check what improvement the opponent had prepared instead of 17 c4?! (namely 17 ♘f3!), and already in the course of the match, with limited time for preparation, he found an interesting palliative (although he did not play 9...exf3 immediately, and somehow not very confidently).

10 ♘xf3

Pleased by my opponent's choice, I froze in anticipation of the usual reply 10...d5: 'At last I'll be able to employ my novelty!' But my joy lasted just a few seconds...

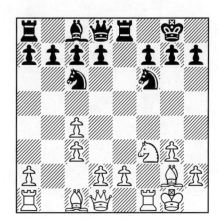

10...♕e7

An instantaneous reply, which at that time occurred rarely, since Black was happy with 10...d5 11 cxd5 ♕xd5. But it was here that I had prepared a novelty – 11 d4!, with which my 'searches' in the English Opening began. I was able to play this nearly a year later against Ivanchuk, and Black failed to cope with the new problems (*Game No.41*). Apparently in their preparations for the 4th game Karpov and his trainers had discovered this move and he sensibly decided to avoid it, doing so by preparing an interesting counter-idea.

11 e3 (4)

'Such a pawn grouping in the centre is a favourite weapon with Kasparov. These pawns and the bishops lurking behind them contain a powerful attacking potential.' (Suetin)

11...♘e5 (2)

A novelty with a deep positional point: the exchange of knights is aimed at disarming White and reducing the dynamic potential of his position. In the event of 11...d6 (Kapengut's move 11...♕c5 is little better) 12 d3 he retains active possibilities: 12...♗g4 (12...♘e5 13 ♘d4) 13 h3 ♗d7 14 e4 h6 15 ♖b1 ♖ab8 16 ♘h4 (Smyslov-Peev, Cienfuegos 1973).

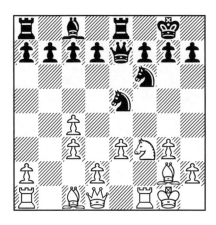

12 ♘d4! (31)

An unexpected pawn sacrifice – the knight is aiming for f5 (my favourite square for a knight). The alternatives were harmless: 12 ♘xe5 ♕xe5 13 ♖b1 (13 e4 d6! 14 d4 ♕e6) 13...♖b8 14 ♖b5 ♕e7 15 d3 d6 16 e4 ♘d7, or 12 d3 ♘xf3+ 13 ♕xf3 d6 14 e4 ♘d7 15 d4 ♖b8 16 ♖b1 b6, and there are no defects in Black's defences. And without dynamism, White's central pawns are not so much a strength, as a weakness (this also

happens with Black in the Sicilian Defence with 2...♘c6 3 ♗b5 and 4 ♗xc6 bxc6).

Therefore the only chance of exploiting Black's retarded development is to avoid the exchange of knights, even at the cost of a pawn. In addition, my move made Karpov feel uncomfortable: it would appear that he thought I would not risk giving up a pawn in an unfamiliar position when I was already one down in the match.

12...♘d3?! (19)

In aiming to eliminate the potentially dangerous bishop on c1, Karpov loses precious time. Perhaps he should have ventured 12...♘xc4 (Korchnoi would certainly have taken the pawn!) 13 ♘f5! ♕e6 14 d3 ♘d6 15 ♘d4 ♕e5 (15...♕e7? 16 e4 c5 17 ♘f3 is worse) 16 ♗d2 with excellent compensation for the pawn, or 14...♘e5 15 d4 ♘g6 or 15 e4 (Dlugy) 15...d5! 16 d4!, and White retains somewhat the better prospects. The quiet 12...d6!? 13 d3 c5 was also suitable, although here too after 14 ♘e2!? with the idea of ♘f4, e3-e4 and h2-h3 White's chances are rather better.

13 ♕e2 (34)

13 ♘f5!? was also unpleasant for Black. Where should the queen go? If 13...♕c5? there is 14 ♘h6+!. This means that the queen must keep the knight at f6 covered. However, 13...♕d8 leaves the bishop alive – 14 ♗a3! (Dlugy) 14...d6 15 ♕e2 ♘c5 16 d3 with an obvious advantage. If 13...♕e6 there is the strong reply 14 ♕e2! ♘xc1 (14...♕xc4? 15 ♘h6+ ♔f8 16 ♖xf6 gxf6 17 ♗f1! – Najdorf) 15 ♖axc1, when White's position is even better than in the game. And if 13...♕e5, then 14 ♕c2! ♘xc1 15 ♖axc1 d5 (15...d6 16 ♖f4) 16 cxd5 ♘xd5 17 e4 ♘e7 18 d4, and under the cover of his powerful pawn centre White begins preparing an attack on the kingside.

13...♘xc1 (2) **14 ♖axc1 d6 15 ♖f4!** (10)

White doubles rooks on the f-file, hoping to prevent the knight from redeploying from f6 and to gradually destroy the black king's fortress.

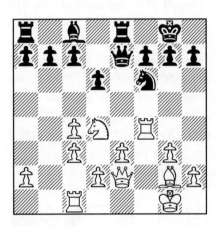

15...c6 (2)

Preparing the development of the c8-bishop. 'For carrying out a regrouping Black is all the time one tempo short: if 15...♘d7 there follows 16 ♘f5, and there is no better reply than 16...♕f8' (Makarychev). And then 17 ♖cf1 with increasing pressure. In the press centre 15...c5?! 16 ♘f5 ♗xf5 17 ♖xf5 was studied, but 'the weakening of the d5-square is fatal' (Andersson).

16 ♖cf1 (4) **16...♕e5** (18)

Prophylaxis against the capture on f6. If 16...♗e6 there could follow 17 ♖xf6! gxf6 18 ♗e4! with a dangerous attack: 18...f5 (but not 18...♗xc4? 19 ♗xh7+! or 18...♕f8?! 19 ♖f4!) 19 ♗xf5 ♗xf5 20 ♘xf5 ♕f6 21 ♕h5 (Dorfman).

In the event of 16...♗d7 nothing is given by 17 ♖xf6 gxf6 18 ♕h5, in view of 18...♔h8! 19 ♖f4 ♖g8, but 17 ♘f5 ♗xf5 18 ♖xf5 is good, as is Makarychev's suggestion 17 g4!? with the threat of g4-g5 (exploiting the fact that the bishop at d7 is occupying the knight's retreat square).

17 ♕d3! (14)

The queen joins the attack. To judge by the time spent on his reply, Karpov had underestimated this manoeuvre. It turns out that Black faces difficult problems.

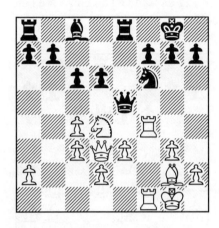

17...♗d7 (17)

Black completes his development. 17...♕h5 is too risky – 18 ♖xf6 gxf6 19 ♖xf6 merely gives White solid compensation for the exchange, but after 18 ♘f5! ♗xf5 19 ♖xf5 it becomes uncomfortable for the queen on the kingside: 19...♕g4 20 e4! or 19...♕g6 20 ♕xd6 (20 ♕d4 ♖e6 21 a4 is steadier) 20...♘e4 (not 20...♖ad8? 21 ♕f4 ♖xd2 22 ♖g5) 21 ♕f4 ♘xd2 22 ♖f2 ♖ad8 23 ♖xf7 ♕b1+ 24 ♗f1, and Black faces a battle for a draw.

In *Informator* Dorfman suggested 17...♖f8!? with the idea of 18 ♘f5 ♗xf5 19 ♖xf5 ♕e7 and ...♘d7. Then White could have chosen between the standard exchange sacrifice 20 ♖xf6!? gxf6 21 ♖f4 with quite good compensation, and 20 ♖1f4!, in order after 20...♘d7 to retain the initiative by 21 ♖e4 ♘e5 22 c5!. In addition, 18 a4 is possible, not hurrying with ♘f5.

18 ♘f5 (6) **18...♗xf5** (2) **19 ♖xf5 ♕e6**

A quick reply. If 19...♕e7, then 20 ♖1f4! is strong. Now 20...♖f8? is not possible on account of 21 ♖xf6 gxf6 22 ♖e4! ♕d7 23 ♖h4 f5 24 ♗h3 and ♗xf5, winning, nor 20...♕f8? in view of 21 ♖h4! and ♖xf6. And in the event of 20...h6 White continues to build up the pressure: 21 ♕e2 (21 ♕f1!?) 21...♔h7 (21...♘d7 22 ♖xf7 can hardly be correct) 22 e4 ♖ad8 23 d4 b6 24 ♕e3 etc.

20 ♕d4! (4)

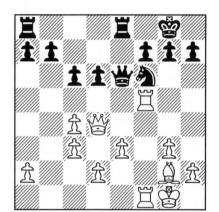

20...♖e7? (7)

With the vain hope of solving Black's problems by ...♘d7. It was psychologically difficult to decide on a second successive queen move, but 20...♕e7 was necessary. Since the white queen has left the d3-square, 21 ♖1f4 is no longer so terrible, although even here the threat of ♖xf6 condemns Black to a difficult defence. The immediate 21 ♖xf6!? gxf6 22 ♖xf6 is also interesting: for example, 22...♖ad8 23 ♗f3! or 22...♕e5 23 ♕g4+! ♔h8 (23...♔f8 24 ♖h6) 24 ♖xf7 ♖e7 25 ♖f5 ♖g7 26 ♕f3 with excellent play for the exchange – but not yet a win.

'After 20...♖e7 the press centre began buzzing like a beehive. Najdorf insistently suggested 21 ♖xf6?! gxf6 22 ♖xf6 ♕e5 23 ♖xd6 *[if 23 ♕g4+ there follows 23...♔f8! 24 ♖f5 ♕g7 25 ♖g5 ♔h8 26 ♕f4 ♖e5 – G.K.].* After heated debates it was decided that here it would have been very hard for White to convert his advantage. Kasparov's reply is much stronger.' (Suetin)

21 ♕h4! (8)

It would appear that Karpov had only expected the exchange sacrifice. Now, however, White has decisive threats.

21...♘d7 (24)

The result of an agonising think. There is nothing better: if 21...♘e8, then here too 22 ♗h3 (22...h6 23 ♖b5!); after 21...♖ae8 apart from the simple 22 ♖1f4 White now wins by 22 ♖xf6 gxf6 23 ♖xf6 ♕e5 24 ♗h3!; and it is also hopeless to play 21...♘e4 22 ♗xe4 ♕xe4 23 ♕xe4 ♖xe4 24 ♖xf7 ♖b8 25 ♖c7 ♖xc4 26 ♖ff7 ♖g4 27 ♖fd7 d5 28 ♔g2 a6 29 h3 ♖g6 30 ♖xb7 etc.

22 ♗h3! (3) **22...♘f8**

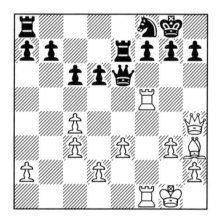

23 ♖5f3 (4)

'An accurate and rational decision – White transposes into a winning endgame, although the mass of tempting possibilities was simply dazzling!' (Suetin). And indeed, I also wanted to play for an attack: 23 ♖g5!? ♕e4 24 ♖g4 ♕e5 25 ♖f5! ♕e6 (25...♕xf5 26 ♖xg7+ and ♗xf5) 26 ♖xg7+ ♔xg7 27 ♖g5+ ♕g6 28 ♗f5 etc.

23...♕e5 (3) **24 d4 ♕e4** (2) **25 ♕xe4 ♖xe4** (3) **26 ♖xf7 ♖xe3 27 d5!?** (2)

This leads to a clear win, but 27 ♖xb7! would have been more quickly decisive: 27...♖xc3 28 ♖bf7! (with the threat of ♖xf8+ and ♗e6+; the alternative 28 ♖c7 is also good: 28...♖xc4 29 ♖cf7! or 28...♖d3 29 ♖xc6

♖xd4 30 ♗g2!) 28...g5 (28...♘g6 29 ♖c7!) 29 d5! etc.

27...♖ae8 (6)

Black would also not have saved himself with 27...cxd5 (27...♖xc3? 28 ♖xf8+) 28 ♗g2!, 27...c5 28 ♖xb7 ♖xc3 29 ♖ff7, or 27...♖b8 28 c5! dxc5 29 d6 g5 (29...♖d8 30 ♖e7! – cf. the following note) 30 ♖c7 ♖d8 31 d7 ♔g7 32 ♖c8.

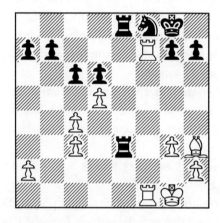

28 ♖xb7? (5)

It was a pity that in impending time-trouble I did not take my idea to its logical conclusion (yet another sign of my indifferent form!). 28 c5! dxc5 29 d6 was correct, with a straightforward win: 29...♖d8 (29...♖d3? 30 ♖xf8+ or 29...g6 30 d7 also loses) 30 ♖e7! ♖d3 31 d7! ♘xd7 32 ♗e6+ ♔h8 33 ♗xd7. Now, however, the battle continues.

28...cxd5 29 cxd5 ♖3e7! 30 ♖fb1 h5? (2)

30...♔f7! was more resilient, with the idea of 31 ♔f2 ♔f6! – here Andersson assessed the chances of White winning and of Black drawing as 'fifty-fifty'. Of course, White has numerous technical difficulties to overcome, but after 31 a4!? ♖xb7 32 ♖xb7+ ♖e7 33 ♖b8 ♖c7 34 a5 he would have advanced his pawn to a6 and could have hoped to win.

31 a4! (3) **31...g5** (2)

It is now too late for 31...♔f7 because of

32 a5 ♖xb7 33 ♖xb7 ♖e7 34 a6! (Dlugy) 34...♘g6 35 c4! ♘e5 36 c5 etc.

32 ♗f5

I did not want to allow ...g5-g4, but 32 a5!? g4 33 ♗f1 (Dorfman) was more energetic – in addition the h5-pawn is a weakness.

32...♔g7 33 a5 (4) **33...♔f6** (2) **34 ♗d3 ♖xb7** (2) **35 ♖xb7 ♖e3!**

Using the tempo granted, Karpov tries to create at least some counterplay. 35...♖e7 36 a6 ♖xb7 37 axb7 ♘d7 38 h4! was completely hopeless.

36 ♗b5 ♖xc3 37 ♖xa7 ♘g6 38 ♖d7

The immediate 38 a6! was more accurate, although even here White would still have had to demonstrate some endgame technique:

1) 38...♖c1+ 39 ♔f2 ♖c2+ 40 ♔e3! ♘e7 (40...♖xh2 41 ♖d7) 41 ♔e4 ♖xh2 42 ♖a8 ♖a2 43 ♖d8 and wins;

2) 38...♖a3 39 ♖b7 h4 40 ♔f2! hxg3+ (40...h3 41 a7 etc.) 41 hxg3 ♘e7 42 ♗c4 g4!? (42...♘f5 43 g4 ♘h6 44 ♗e2 and wins) 43 ♖b2 ♖a4 44 ♖a2 ♖xc4 45 a7 ♖c8 46 a8♕ ♖xa8 47 ♖xa8 ♘xd5 48 ♖a5 ♔e5 49 ♔e2 ♔e4 50 ♖a4+ ♔f5 51 ♖d4 ♘f6 52 ♖xd6 ♘e4 53 ♖d3 etc.

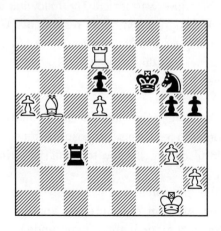

38...♘e5?

An empty blow. A paradox: starting with

35...♖e3, Karpov had about 10 minutes left to the time control, but for some reason he made all his moves at blitz speed (apparently, what told was fatigue). And in his haste he missed the best chance – 38...♔e5!, forcing White to find 39 ♖g7! ♔f6 40 ♖b7!, and if 40...♘e5 41 a6 ♗c2, then 42 h3! (Dlugy). 40...♔e5 is no longer possible because of 41 ♗e8!, while 40...♖a3 41 a6 leads to a position from the previous note. The march of the a-pawn is also decisive against other possible replies: 40...h4 41 a6 hxg3 42 a7! gxh2+ 43 ♔xh2 ♖a3 44 ♖d7, or instead 40...♖c1+ 41 ♔f2 ♖c2+ 42 ♔e3 ♘e7 43 a6 ♖xh2 44 ♗e2! ♘f5+ 45 ♔d3 ♖h1 46 a7 ♖a1 47 ♗xh5 ♔e5 48 ♔c4 ♘e3+ 49 ♔b3 ♘xd5 50 ♗e8.

In this case the game could have been not only adjourned, but most probably also resumed, since definite accuracy would still have been required of me. However, the advantage of the move 38 ♖d7 was that, by marking time for a couple of moves, White gained the opportunity to take important decisions after the time control.

39 ♖xd6+ (with two passed pawns, the win for White is obvious) **39...♔f5 40 a6 ♖a3 41 ♖d8**

This move was sealed. The following day Black resigned without resuming (**1-0**): 41...♘f3+ 42 ♔f2 ♘xh2 43 d6, or 41...♖a2 42 ♖f8+ ♔e4 43 d6 ♘f3+ 44 ♖xf3 ♔xf3 45 d7. Times: 2.38–2.22.

The score in the match became equal: 2-2. In order to regain his composure after such a painful defeat, Karpov took his first time-out.

The 5th game was extremely tense and nervy. Alas, on encountering another surprise by the opponent, I again ended up in terrible time-trouble, which decided the outcome of the battle.

> ## Game 28
> ## A.Karpov-G.Kasparov
> ## World Championship Match
> ## 5th Game, Seville 23.10.1987
> ### *Grünfeld Defence D87*

1 d4 ♘f6 2 c4 g6

I was curious to know what variation my opponent would employ after his 'limbering up' with 3 g3 (1st and 3rd games). It appeared that I was beginning to run into form, and I wanted to aim for counterplay.

3 ♘c3 d5 4 cxd5

A match novelty – the main variation! Up until then Karpov had played only 4 ♗f4 or 4 ♘f3 (which we looked at in the first instance).

4...♘xd5 5 e4 ♘xc3 6 bxc3 ♗g7 7 ♗c4 c5 8 ♘e2

We analysed this line in our preparations for the third match, but we thought that it was not the most appropriate weapon for Karpov: the positions that result here are too complicated and unclear. Besides, as Makarychev aptly commented, 'towards the mid-1970s the variation with 7 ♗c4 and 8 ♘e2 went out of fashion for a long time, its status remaining unchanged.'

8...♘c6 9 ♗e3 0-0 10 0-0 ♗g4

A worthy alternative to Smyslov's plan with 10...♕c7. The idea of the immediate bishop move to g4 belongs to Timman – earlier they played 10...cxd4 11 cxd4 ♗g4 12 f3 ♘a5, and after 13 ♗d3 ♗e6 one of the main *tabiyas* was reached, while the rare continuation 13 ♗xf7+ ♖xf7 14 fxg4 was considered harmless (cf. the note to White's 12th move). The presence on the board of the c5- and c3-pawns increases Black's defensive resources somewhat and reduces White's attacking potential.

11 f3 (I would have been quite happy with

the gambit variation 11 d5 ♘a5 12 ♗d3 c4 13 ♗c2 ♗xc3 14 ♖b1, Polugayevsky-Timman, 6th match game, Breda 1979) **11...♘a5**

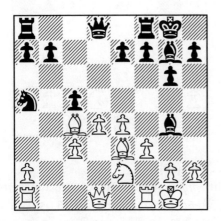

12 ♗xf7+!?

But here is a surprise – the old 'harmless continuation', revived in a new version by Igor Zaitsev.

Previously only 12 ♗d5 ♗d7 occurred, as in Timman's games with Hort (Niksic 1978), Spassky (Montreal 1979) and Polugayevsky (Tilburg 1985), or 12 ♗d3 cxd4 13 cxd4 ♗e6, transposing into the main lines. Here we had looked at both the exchange sacrifice – 14 d5 ♗xa1 15 ♕xa1 f6, and the sacrifice of the a2-pawn – 14 ♖c1 ♗xa2 15 ♕a4 ♗e6 16 d5 ♗d7 17 ♕b4 e6 (these analyses later came in useful in my games with Beliavsky and Yusupov in the 55th USSR Championship, Moscow 1988).

The capture on f7 surprised me, of course. All of us Soviet players grew up on *Kurs Debyutov* by Panov and Estrin, where in black on white it was written that 13 ♗xf7+ (after the exchange of pawns on d4) 'does not give any advantage', and 'Black's position fully compensates for the sacrificed pawn'. The same verdict was given by Botvinnik and Estrin in their monograph on the Grünfeld Defence (1979), and by Karpov

himself in the Yugoslav *Encyclopaedia of Chess Openings* (1976). And now at the board I was forced to try and understand why Karpov had nevertheless captured on f7.

12...♖xf7 13 fxg4 ♖xf1+ (3) 14 ♔xf1 (3)

Here I 'went to sleep' for more than an hour – the second longest think in the match after my 83-minute record in the 2nd game. And again I managed to find the best plan!

14...♕d6 (64)

A new direction. I decided fairly quickly not to relieve the pawn tension in the centre, but a mass of time was taken up by all kinds of doubts and hesitations, typical of an unfamiliar situation.

14...cxd4 15 cxd4 could have led to a position that had been known for a long time.

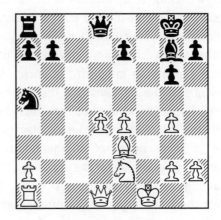

Analysis diagram

At one time they played 15...♕d7 (thinking about how to deviate from theory, I also examined both the currently fashionable 15...e5, and 15...♕b6 – 9th game) 16 h3 ♕e6 17 ♕d3 ♕c4 18 ♕d2 ♕a6! 19 ♕c2 ♘c4 20 ♕b3 ♔h8 with good counter-chances for Black (Spassky-Korchnoi, 22nd USSR Championship, Moscow 1955), or 18 ♕xc4+(!) ♘xc4 19 ♗g5 e6 20 ♖d1 b5 with equality (*Encyclopaedia of Chess Openings*).

But this last assessment seems rather

questionable: after 20 e5!? or 20 ♖b1!? with the idea of e4-e5 it is not so easy for Black to find sufficient compensation for the pawn. 19...e5 20 d5 h6 21 ♗c1 ♘d6 22 ♘g3 ♖c8 (Dlugy-Nickoloff, Toronto 1989) is hardly any better in view of 23 ♗a3! and ♖c1. And besides, instead of 16 h3 there is the logical move 16 g5!?, which had already occurred but was not yet favoured by theory.

After the immediate 14...♕d7 (or 14...♕c8, Portisch-Korchnoi, Reykjavik 1988) again 15 g5 is not bad: for example, 15...♕e6 16 e5 (shutting in the bishop at g7) 16...♕c4 17 ♔g1 ♖d8 18 ♕e1 with a complicated game (Karpov-Gavrikov, Gijon (rapid) 1988).

Today, casting my eye over the entire tree of variations which developed after 12 ♗xf7+ became popular, I come to the conclusion that the best reply was 'articulated' in this, the very first published game.

'The world champion devised a plan which exploits an important nuance – the presence of the c-pawns (for the moment the exchange on d4 has not been included). With the position more closed, Black was able to keep control of all the points of potential counterplay for the opponent, thus retaining excellent compensation for the pawn. And although many commentators saw the reason for Kasparov's defeat to be his hour-long think, I find it hard to suggest that the loser acted unwisely. The favourable character of the subsequent middlegame was worth the boldly sacrificed time.' (Makarychev)

15 e5 (11)

The opponent's hesitation was probably caused precisely by the fact that the c5- and c3-pawns had remained on the board. In the 11th game Karpov also introduced 15 ♔g1; 15 ♕a4 ♕xh2!? 16 ♕xa5 ♖f8+ 17 ♔e1 ♕h1+ 18 ♘g1 ♕xg2 (Zakharov-I.Khenkin, Smolensk 1989) is excessively sharp.

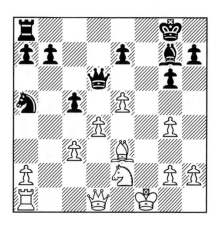

15...♕d5 (10)

In *Informator* Zaitsev recommended 15...♕e6(?!) with the idea of 16 g5 ♘c4, but 16 ♘f4 ♖f8 (16...♕c4+ 17 ♕e2) 17 ♔g1 ♕c4 18 g5! is stronger. But now after 16 ♘f4 Black has the equalising 16...♖f8 17 ♔g1 ♕e4!. The black queen controls the important light squares, and I was intending to exploit this factor, although as yet I had only a vague impression of what would happen next: the position is very unclear.

16 ♗f2 (10)

By our fifth match (1990) this variation had already been thoroughly studied, but it did not in fact occur there, although against Beliavsky (Linares 1992) I was able to demonstrate a clear-cut draw after 16 g5 ♕e4! 17 ♗f2 ♖f8 18 ♘g1 (18 ♔g1 ♕f5!) 18...♘c4 19 ♘f3 ♘e3+ 20 ♗xe3 ♕xe3 21 ♕b3+ ♔h8 22 ♖e1 ♕xg5 23 ♕xb7 ♕d2! 24 dxc5 (24 ♕xe7 ♕xc3 with equality, Onischuk-Grischuk, Poikovsky 2005) 24...♕xc3 25 ♕d5 ♗h6 etc.

16...♖f8 (12)

Probably the strongest move. However, during the match we had doubts about this, and I switched to 16...♖d8, after which Karpov tried against me 17 ♕e1 (7th game), 17 ♕c2 (Amsterdam 1988), and 17 ♕a4, which had become popular (Belfort 1988).

17 ♔g1 (5) **17...♗h6!** (1)

'Strangely enough, Black's 14th move determined the actions of the two sides up to the 20th move. White was threatening to shut the g7-bishop out of the game by g4-g5. In defending against this threat, Black, in turn, threatens to achieve domination in the centre. Thus 18 ♕d3 is weak because of 18...♘c4, intending ...♘xe5. Therefore, by renewing his previous threats, White temporarily forces his opponent to move away from the centre, i.e. to carry out an unusual, active defence.' (Makarychev)

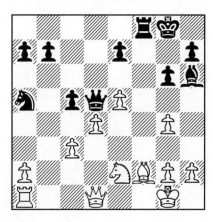

18 h4 (18)

It is not in Karpov's style to voluntarily spoil his pawn structure – 18 dxc5!? ♕xe5 19 ♕d3, but for a long time it seemed to me that this would give White an unpleasant initiative (as a result of which I stopped playing 16...♖f8): for example, 19...♕f6 20 ♖f1 e5(?) 21 ♘g3 ♕e6 22 ♘e4! (Razuvaev-Andersen, Dortmund 1992). However, after 20...♕e6! 21 ♘d4 ♕xa2 22 ♕e4 I underestimated the simple 22...♖f7 23 h4 ♕c4 with equality (it only remains for Black to bring his knight to the centre).

The course of opening theory is truly inscrutable. Had it not been for my groundless fears regarding 18 dxc5, which arose before the 7th game, it is possible that the entire

variation with 12 ♗xf7+ would have had a different fate.

18...♕f7 (2) **19 ♗g3**

The further activation of the enemy pieces has to be allowed: in the event of 19 ♕f1? (into a pin!) 19...♗d2! 20 dxc5 ♘c6 or 20 ♖d1 ♘c4 21 ♘g3 ♘e3 22 ♗xe3 ♗xe3+ 23 ♔h2 ♕xa2 Black simply dominates.

19...♗e3+ 20 ♔h2 ♕c4! (16)

An important move, but it should have been made automatically. It is now evident that the retention of the c5- and c3-pawns has been to Black's advantage.

21 ♖b1 (32)

The reckless 21 d5?! ♕xg4 22 d6 ♗f2 (Zaitsev) or 22 ♘g1 ♕e4! was dangerous, but 21 dxc5! was sufficient for a draw: 21...♕xg4 (21...♗xc5 is also not bad) 22 ♘d4 ♕xd1 23 ♖xd1 ♖d8 24 e6 ♖d5 (Lerner-Pribyl, Prague 1988) or 24 ♖b1 ♗xd4 25 cxd4 ♖xd4 26 ♗e1 ♖a4.

'21 ♖b1 is hardly a good idea. However, in assessing Karpov's decision one has to take psychological factors into account. Already in his choice of the opening variation with 12 ♗xf7+ he was aiming not only to avoid the well-trodden theoretical paths, but also, knowing Kasparov's competitive nature, to create a complicated position on the board. I think that the main thing for Karpov was to "drive" his opponent into time-trouble. There was a clash between two fundamentally different approaches to the fight – the classical and the purely competitive. At the same time Karpov was relying on his defensive skill and, of course, was taking a risk (in fact he was in the "danger zone" almost to the very end of the game). But he was very consistent in the implementation of this strategy.' (Suetin)

21...b6 (5)

Of course, not 21...♕xa2? 22 ♖a1 ♕b3 23 ♕d3 ♘c4 24 dxc5 when White wins. And after 21...♖d8 22 ♕e1! all the same Black has to play 22...b6, defending his knight.

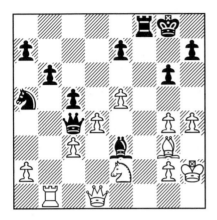

22 ♖b2? (5)

'A critical decision. White defends his a2-pawn, continuing a full-blooded struggle. As Karpov said after the game, he "all the time was in control of events and at no point did he see any serious danger for himself." I think that Karpov took into account both his opponent's shortage of time, and the psychological aspect of the struggle: considering his position to be objectively better, Kasparov spent his remaining minutes searching for ways to strengthen it.' (Makarychev)

From the standpoint of chess truth, 22 dxc5 was now necessary, with a roughly equal game after 22...♗xc5 23 ♘d4 ♕xa2 (and if 24 h5, then 24...♕d5!), or 22...♗xc5 23 ♘g1 ♕e4! (but not Zaitsev's recommendation 23...♗f2? because of 24 ♗xf2 ♖xf2 25 ♘h3 ♖f8 26 ♕d7 and wins) 24 ♘f3 ♘c4. Although the 'psychological' rook move maintains the intensity of the struggle, it does not take into account the dynamics of the position and places White on the verge of defeat. I think that Karpov underestimated the strength of my reply.

22...♕d5! (8) **23 ♕d3 ♘c4 24 ♖b1**

The critical moment of the game and of the entire initial stage of the match.

24...b5? (2)

A tactical trick which loses Black his advantage. 24...♘xe5? 25 ♗xe5 ♖f2 was incorrect because of 26 ♖g1 (this was why the rook returned to b1), while the immediate 24...♖f2 would have been parried by 25 ♗xf2 ♘xe5 26 c4! (Zaitsev).

But it is surprising that both the players and the analysts in the press centre overlooked the excellent move 24...g5!, which I discovered only after the game. Black takes control of the f4-point and intends ...♗f2!. It would be interesting to know how in this case Karpov would have 'controlled events'. 25 ♔h3 ♗f2 26 ♗xf2 (26 ♘f4 ♖xf4!) 26...♖xf2 27 ♖g1 ♘xe5 or 27...gxh4 28 ♔xh4 ♘xe5 is clearly to Black's advantage.

White would have had to find the only reply 25 ♖d1! with the sequel 25...gxh4 26 ♗xh4 ♗f2 27 ♕h3! ♕e4! 28 ♗xe7! (but not 28 ♘g3 ♕f4! 29 ♗xe7 ♘e3!, winning).

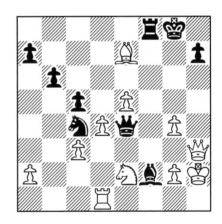

Analysis diagram

Here in *Informator* Zaitsev gave the very interesting variation 28...♖f7 29 ♗f6 ♘e3! 30 g5! (threatening perpetual check – 31 ♕c8+ ♖f8 32 ♕e6+) 30...♘g4+! 31 ♔h1 ♗xd4! 32 ♘g3! ♕f4 33 ♕h5! ♕xg3 34 cxd4 ♘f2+ 35 ♔g1 ♘xd1 36 ♕xd1 ♕e3+ 37 ♔h1 ♕xd4 38 ♕h5(?) ♕d2! 39 g6 ♖d7 'with advantage to Black'. But the computer suggests that after 38 ♕f3! ♕h4+ 39 ♔g1 or 38...♖f8 39 ♕e6 the menacing e-pawn guarantees White a draw.

This variation can be avoided by 28...♖e8 (L.Silaev, *Shakhmaty v SSSR*, 1988, No.3) 29 ♖f1 ♘xe5 30 dxe5 ♕xe5+ 31 ♘g3 ♗xg3+ 32 ♕xg3 ♖xe7, and Black is effectively a pawn up in the rook ending, but his winning chances are slight.

28...♕xe2!? also comes into consideration. The forced 29 ♕h6! ♖f7 30 e6 ♕xd1 31 exf7+ ♔xf7 32 ♕f8+ ♔e6 33 ♕xf2 ♔xe7 34 ♕h4+ ♔e6 35 ♕h6+ ♔d5 36 ♕h5+ ♔e4! (36...♔d6 37 ♕h6+) 37 ♕xh7+ ♔e3 leads to a position which I have analysed a great deal. After 38 dxc5 ♕xg4 39 c6 ♕f4+ 40 ♔h3 ♘d6 Black succeeds in converting his extra piece (41 c7? ♘f5), but with the accurate 38 g5! ♘d2 39 ♕h3+ White should be able to save the game.

In an interview after the match I claimed that 24...g5 would have won the game. This was probably an exaggeration, but the resulting difficult problems would have demanded enormous inventiveness on White's part. In my opinion, it would have been unrealistic to find all the best moves with the clock ticking away.

25 ♔h3?! (17)

It would appear that Karpov 'took me at my word' and decided that 25 ♖xb5 would not do. In fact it was a sure way to equalise: 25...♘xe5 26 ♖xc5! (of course, not 26 ♗xe5? ♖f2) 26...♘xg4+ (and not 26...♕xc5? 27 ♗xe5) 27 ♔h3 ♕e6 28 ♕c4 (28 ♕b1? ♗g1!) 28...♘f2+ with perpetual check. But now the chances are again on Black's side.

25...a6

A continuation of the light-square strategy. Georgadze in the match bulletin and Suetin in *Shakhmaty v SSSR* recommended the 'energetic' 25...b4, but after 26 cxb4 cxd4

27 ♖e1 White could have defended by keeping an eye on the newly-created passed pawn on d4.

26 ♘g1! (4)

Probably the best decision – an attempt to create at least some counterplay and 'an unexpected resource, particularly in view of the lack of time for the opponent, who of course wanted to refute this strategy.' (Makarychev)

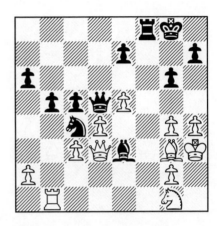

26...cxd4 (11)

'It was here that Kasparov made a mistake. No, not on the board: on this move he spent 11 minutes, when he was already seriously short of time.' (Suetin). Unfortunately, I was carried away by ideas of an attack on the king (...♕e6, ...h7-h5, ...♘d2 and so on), and after this I had just 10 minutes left for 14 moves (whereas Karpov had 34).

27 ♘f3 (22) **27...♖d8**

Black has regained the pawn with a good position, but time, time... After the reckless 27...♖xf3? 28 gxf3 ♘d2 White would have won by both 29 ♖d1 (Zaitsev), and 29 ♖e1! ♘xf3 30 ♖xe3.

28 a4!? (2)

Adding fuel to the fire. 'The best move and a psychologically interesting one, giving the game an unexpected turn. After all,

Black is in time-trouble...' (Suetin). In the press centre they were expecting 28 cxd4 ♗xd4, but here Black's chances are somewhat better: 29 ♖e1 (29 ♖d1? ♘b2!) 29...♗c5! etc.

28...dxc3

It is curious that by this point Karpov had caught up with me on the clock, and we each had less than 10 minutes for 12 moves.

29 ♕xc3

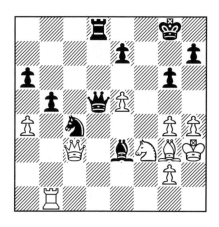

29...♕e6! (2)

A very strong move, with which Black retains hopes of an advantage. I had no desire to switch on to a drawing path by 29...♕d3.

30 ♔h2! (2)

The only move: after 30 axb5?! h5! 31 ♔h2 hxg4 32 ♘g5 ♗xg5 33 hxg5 ♘d2 White has a difficult position. Now, however, Black 'is again forced to change his plans' (Makarychev).

30...bxa4?

This almost instantaneous reply is, alas, a serious mistake, changing the character of the play. The seemingly tempting 30...♘d2? would have run into 31 ♕xe3! ♘xb1 32 axb5 axb5 33 ♕c1! ♕a2(b3) 34 ♕h6! and ♘g5, winning. In the press centre they mainly looked at the drawing variation 30...♕xg4 31 axb5 axb5 32 ♖xb5 – here the simplest is 32...♖c8.

However, 30...♖d5! (crowning Black's light-square strategy!) would have retained the extra pawn on the queenside and a clear advantage: for example, 31 axb5 axb5 32 g5 ♗b6 33 ♖a1 ♘e3. Black's pieces are still dominant, and White has no real counterplay.

31 ♖b4

For the first time since the 22nd move White can feel comfortable.

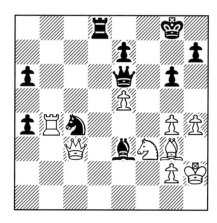

31...♘d2

'Black had based his tactical operation on this manoeuvre. The threat is 32...♘f1+ 33 ♔h3 h5. But for the moment the g4-pawn is defended by the rook along the 4th rank.' (Suetin)

32 ♖xa4 ♘f1+ (1)

I should have reconciled myself to a draw – 32...♘xf3+ 33 gxf3 ♗d2 34 ♕c4 ♕xc4 35 ♖xc4 a5 or 34 ♕a1 a5 35 ♖d4 ♖xd4 36 ♕xd4 ♗b4, but I was loathe to deviate from the planned course.

33 ♔h3 ♖d1?

Again a rapid reply 7 moves before the time control, and a completely senseless move, which simply blunders a pawn. 'In severe time-trouble even the world champion has the right to lose his bearings' (Makarychev). Which is exactly what happened! In any sort of time-trouble Black should have played 33...h5!, easily maintaining the balance: 34 ♕c4 (34 ♗e1?! ♖d5!; 34 ♕a1 ♘d2) 34...♕xc4 35 ♖xc4 ♘xg3 36 ♔xg3 a5.

'The press centre froze: everyone saw that White had 34 ♖xa6 ♕xa6 35 ♕b3+ ♔g7 36 ♕xd1 ♘xg3 37 ♔xg3 with an extra pawn and quite good winning chances. To universal surprise, Karpov played differently.' (Suetin). The ex-champion also rejected another endgame with an extra pawn – after 34 ♗f4 (winning the g5-square for the knight) 34...♗d2! 35 ♗xd2 ♘xd2 36 ♘g5 ♕b3 37 ♕xb3+ ♘xb3 38 ♖xa6.

It is probable that this advantage seemed insufficient to Karpov, and – leaving himself with just a couple of minutes for 6 moves! – he made a move that was far more dangerous and unpleasant for Black, exploiting the 'hanging' state of his pieces.

34 ♕c2! (7) **34...♖c1** (34...♖d8 35 ♕e2!) **35 ♕e2?**

A typical time-trouble error. White could have gained an almost decisive advantage by 35 ♕d3! h5 36 ♗e1 g5! (there is nothing else) 37 hxg5 ♖a1! 38 ♕c4!, transposing into an endgame with an extra pawn, which, moreover, is passed.

35...h5 36 ♗e1

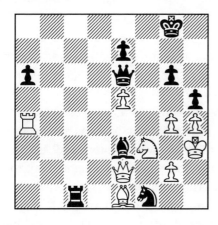

36...♕d7? (1)

Black loses control. He could have saved himself with the unexpected tactical stroke 36...♖a1!. White would have instantly had to find the only reply 37 ♕c4!, and after 37...♕xc4 38 ♖xc4 ♖c1! 39 ♖a4 hxg4+ 40 ♖xg4 ♖c6 followed by ...♗b6(a7) and ...♘e3 things would have ended in a draw.

37 ♕xa6 ♖a1??

A final blunder (and yet if the king had been on g7, this move would even have won the game!). Strangely enough, 37...♔g7 38 e6 ♕c6 still offered chances of a draw.

38 ♕xg6+ 1–0

Times: 2.29–2.28.

My state of shock after this tragic game was even stronger than after the 2nd. Again time-trouble, again serious blunders... And yet I had managed to outplay Karpov, by solving difficult opening problems at the board, and in an unexplored position finding new, very interesting ideas. And had it not been for the missed opportunities (24...g5!; 30...♖d5!), the entire match could have turned out quite differently. But, thinking only about winning, I overstepped the mark and missed even a draw, since I was not ready for an ultra-tense struggle.

Thus Karpov again took the lead: 3-2. I urgently had to compose myself and cast off the burden of negative emotions. In the next phase of the match, albeit not without my opponent's help, I managed to solve these problems. It began with a draw in the 6th game. A surprise in the opening of the 7th game again caused me to think for a painfully long time, and after a grandiose two-day battle, with difficulty I gained a draw on the 80th move. Naturally I was very pleased with that: after all, had I lost, the match score would already have been 'plus two' in Karpov's favour.

'It can be imagined how the ex-world

champion was feeling, when he arrived for the 8th game. After all, in the preceding game the bird of fortune, as though teasing him, had time after time itself flown into his hands, but he was unable to grasp it.' (Makarychev)

Game 29
G.Kasparov-A.Karpov
World Championship Match
8th Game, Seville 02/03.11.1987
English Opening A36

---

1 c4 e5 2 ♘c3 d6

Instead of the usual 2...♘f6 (*Game No.27*) or 2...♘c6, Karpov springs a surprise – a move from my 'black' repertoire. He himself had made this move only once in his early youth.

3 g3 (2)

I don't known what would have followed after 3 ♘f3 (logically, 3...f5 or 3...c5), but in the event of 3 d4 my opponent could have been using 3...exd4 4 ♕xd4 ♘f6 as a guideline (*Game No.1*).

3...c5?! (1)

'A rare and highly questionable continuation: Black sets up a powerful pawn centre, but weakens the d5-point' (Suetin). In the given version this idea is not new: Botvinnik tried it both with White against Smyslov (*Game No.109* in *Volume II* of *My Great Predecessors*), and with Black against Pachman (Moscow 1956) – 1 c4 c5 2 ♘c3 g6 3 g3 ♗g7 4 ♗g2 ♘c6, followed by ...e7-e5, ...♘ge7, ...0-0 and only then ...d7-d6. Much earlier, Karpov had also played it successfully – against Donchenko (Leningrad 1969), Barcza (Caracas 1970) and Veselovsky (Rostov-on-Don 1971).

But after 2...d6 this set-up is positionally dubious: this move order allows White

immediately, without ♖b1 and with his knight on g1, to begin an offensive on the queenside, emphasising the weakness of the d5-point (2...c5 and 3...♘c6 really is better). But the main thing is that, being a player of classical style, Karpov did not much like playing ...g7-g6 and ...♗g7 – these positions were alien to him and he handled them uncertainly. Not without reason did he avoid both 3...g6 (Levy-Karpov, Groningen 1967/68), and 'my' plan 3...f5 4 ♗g2 ♘f6 followed by ...g7-g6, ...♗g7, ...0-0 and ...c7-c6 (cf. *Game No.82*), and after the 8th game he altogether ceased such experiments.

4 ♗g2 ♘c6

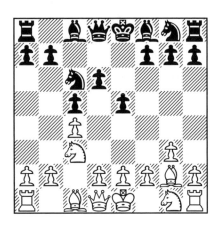

5 a3! (6)

'The game Uhlmann-Pietzsch (Gröditz 1976) went 5 e3 ♗f5 6 a3 ♘f6 7 d3 ♕d7 8 h3 g6 9 ♘ge2 ♗g7 10 ♖b1 0-0 11 b4 with the initiative for White. The world champion chooses a more active plan.' (Suetin)

5...g6 (5)

Many commentators recommended the blockading 5...a5. Makarychev said that although it was 'quite possible', it was 'clearly unaesthetic', and pointed out that in this case White would have gained a tempo compared with the variation 5 ♖b1 g6 6 a3 a5. Indeed, after 5...a5 White is no longer obliged to play ♖b1 and proceed with b2-b4.

Black has acquired a second 'hole' – the b5-point, and it is possible to continue simply 6 e3 g6 7 ♘ge2 ♝g7 8 d3 and 0-0 with a slight but enduring advantage.

Karpov did not want to give himself additional weaknesses, and he refrained from action on the queenside. But this game showed that one should not play English-cum-King's Indian set-ups using the criteria of the Queen's Gambit.

6 b4 (3)

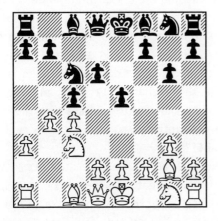

6...♝g7

Black sticks to his solid but passive plan. 6...cxb4?! 7 axb4 ♘xb4 was dangerous, as after this White has two good continuations: 8 ♕a4+ ♘c6 9 ♝xc6+ bxc6 10 ♕xc6+ ♝d7 11 ♕b7, regaining the pawn with unpleasant pressure (11...♖c8 12 ♖xa7 ♖xc4 13 ♘f3 – Dorfman), and the gambit line 8 ♘f3 or 8 ♝a3 ♘c6 9 ♘f3, when the weakness of the d6-pawn prevents Black from developing his bishop at g7.

7 ♖b1 (2)

'Now, when the pawn has already advanced to b4, this move, taking control of the b4-point and, "by X-ray", the b7-pawn, is quite appropriate.' (Makarychev)

7...♘ge7

After this move the two players began spending a lot of time on the opening, which is not surprising: this non-standard position was unfamiliar to both of us, and we were trying to play 'by logic', on the basis of general considerations.

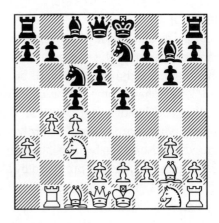

8 e3 (24)

If 8 ♘f3 there could have followed 8...f5!, hindering White's development (9 d3? e4), while 8 d3 0-0 9 ♘f3 (with the idea of 9...f5 10 ♝d2) would allow the freeing 9...cxb4 10 axb4 d5. And, so that Black should not be able to free himself (for Karpov this was the most unpleasant thing!), I decided not to weaken my control of d5 and to develop my king's knight at e2.

8...0-0 (5) **9 d3!** (5)

'After 9 ♘ge2 cxb4 [or first 9...♝e6 – G.K.] 10 axb4 ♝e6 White would have had to reckon with numerous tactical possibilities for the opponent: for example, 11 b5 ♘a5 12 d3 d5 or 11 ♘d5 b5!?. Kasparov does not intend to occupy d5 with his knight, which is a very unusual way of playing this set-up.' (Makarychev)

9...♖b8 (21)

Now in the event of 9...cxb4?! 10 axb4 ♝e6 the c4-pawn is defended and White is able to prevent ...d6-d5 by 11 b5 ♘a5 12 ♝a3.

10 ♘ge2 ♝e6 (9)

In Suetin's opinion, '10...a6 came into

consideration, and if 11 0-0, then 11...cxb4 12 axb4 b5'. However, 11 bxc5! dxc5 12 0-0 ♗f5 13 ♘e4 is stronger – White has an extra pawn in the centre and the better prospects: 13...b6 14 ♕c2 ♕d7 15 ♘2c3 etc.

11 b5?! (10)

Georgadze and Makarychev attached an exclamation mark to this move: 'In this way (rather than 11 ♘d5) White defends against ...d6-d5'. But I have come to the conclusion that the cool-headed 11 0-0 was more accurate, when Karpov would hardly have ventured 11...cxb4 12 axb4 d5, since after 13 b5 ♘a5 better chances are promised by all of 14 c5, 14 cxd5, and 14 ♗a3 dxc4 15 dxc4 ♖e8 16 c5 ♘c4 17 ♕a4.

As for 11 b5, although it does not squander White's entire advantage, it gives Black a simple and understandable game. But, paradoxically, this move, although not the best, wins the game! Here we are already in the realms of psychology, which is not directly related to the quality of moves. Karpov did not like playing with bad pieces. Indeed, the knight on a5 became a curse for him and it vegetated out of play right to the moment of capitulation...

11...♘a5

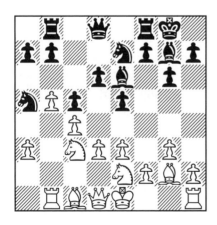

12 ♗d2!

The commentators approved of this move

for preventing 12...d5?! in view of 13 cxd5 ♘xd5 14 ♘xd5 ♗xd5 15 ♗xd5 ♕xd5 16 0-0 (but not 16 e4?! ♕d8 17 ♕a4?, as recommended by Makarychev and Suetin, because of 17...♕xd3, winning) 16...♕d8 17 ♕c2 (Dlugy) or 16...b6 17 ♗xa5 bxa5 18 ♘c3 (Dorfman) 18...♕d7 19 ♕c2 and ♖fd1 with an obvious advantage to White.

In fact 12 0-0 d5?! 13 cxd5 ♘xd5 14 ♘xd5 ♗xd5 15 ♗xd5 ♕xd5 16 ♗d2! would have led to a simple transposition of moves, but after castling the undermining move 12...a6! was possible – in the event of 13 a4 axb5 14 axb5 d5 Black would have finally freed himself (15 cxd5 ♘xd5 16 ♘xd5 ♗xd5 17 ♗xd5 ♕xd5 18 ♗d2 ♖a8 with equality), while the exchange 13 bxa6, although it retains a slight plus, releases the knight on a5 from captivity.

12...b6! (6)

Now 12...a6?! is weak because of 13 ♘d5! (with the threat of ♘xe7+) 13...♗xd5 14 cxd5 c4 15 b6 cxd3 16 ♗xa5 dxe2 17 ♕xe2 ♖c8 18 0-0 ♖c5 19 ♕d2 and ♖fc1. Therefore Black prepares ...d6-d5.

13 0-0 (4) **13...♘b7** (9) **14 e4** (14)

A radical solution to the problem. I did not play this willingly, but after 14 ♕b3 ♕d7 and ...♖fd8 all the same ...d6-d5 would have been threatened, and 15 ♘d5 ♘xd5 17 cxd5 ♗h3 would not have brought White any real gains. Now, however, he has a 'small but persistent positional advantage' (Suetin), which 'is not really so great: Black's position is solid' (Makarychev).

14...♔h8 (13)

Most of the commentators condemned this slow move and, fearing 14...f5 15 ♗g5, suggested the 'more useful' 14...h6.

15 ♕c1 (9) **15...f5** (4) **16 ♗g5** (6)

White fights for control of the key d5-square – I did not see anything better.

16...♕e8 (5)

16...♗f6 17 ♗xf6 ♖xf6 18 f4 or 16...fxe4 17 ♗xe4! ♗f6 18 ♗xf6+ ♖xf6 19 f4 would have favoured White – in the resulting play on the kingside he effectively has an extra piece.

17 ♗xe7 (3) **17...♕xe7 18 exf5**

A turning-point of the game.

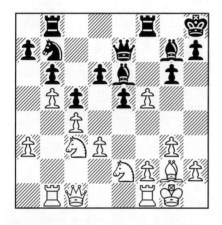

18...♗xf5? (7)

This conceding of the light squares is a positional blunder. However, this mistake is psychologically explicable: Karpov did not want to play 18...gxf5 – creating 'King's Indian' weaknesses for himself was not to his taste. It is interesting that after this the commentators recommended 19 f4(?!), ignoring the reply 19...e4! which disrupts all White's plans. I would have had to try and demonstrate an advantage for White by 19 ♘d5 ♗xd5 20 ♗xd5 ♘d8 21 ♘c3 ♘e6 22 ♗xe6 ♕xe6 23 f3 and ♘d5, but in this case Black would have got rid of his hapless knight and retained counterplay on the kingside.

19 ♘d5 ♕d7 20 ♕d2 ♘a5 (7)

According to Suetin, 'this move is the cause of Black's later difficulties – 20...♘d8 suggested itself.' Dorfman was of the same opinion, indicating the variation 21 a4 ♘f7 22 a5 ♗h6 with the idea of ...♘g5-h3+. However, 22 ♘ec3! ♗h6 23 ♕d1 ♘g5 24 h4

♘h3+ 25 ♔h2 is more accurate, killing Black's initiative on the kingside. Then White carries out a4-a5 and breaks through on the a-file.

Instead of this Karpov took the bold decision to 'stand still', endeavouring not to allow the opening of the position. Indeed, although White is completely dominant in the centre, the opportunities for breaking through are very restricted. He needs to play f2-f4, but this demands serious preparation, since it activates the bishop on g7. A phase of prolonged manoeuvring begins – White gradually strengthens his position.

21 ♘ec3 (3) **21...♖be8 22 ♘e4** (5) **22...♘b7 23 a4 ♘a5** (5) **24 h4** (3) **24...♘b7** (4) **25 ♔h2 ♖b8 26 ♖a1** (8) **26...♘a5 27 ♖a3**

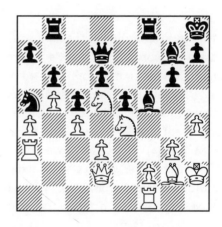

'The rook replaces the queen in guarding the b3-square, via which the black knight dreams of jumping to d4.' (Makarychev)

27...♖f7 28 ♕c3 (8) **28...♖d8** (4) **29 ♖a2 ♗h6** (3) **30 ♘g5 ♖ff8 31 ♖e2 ♗g7 32 ♕c2 ♖de8 33 ♘e3 ♗h6** (4)

33...h6 34 ♘e4 ♗e6 35 ♘c3 and ♗e4 would not have changed the character of the play.

34 ♗d5 (3) **34...♗g7** (4)

The exchange 34...♗xg5? 35 hxg5 would have substantially weakened the black king's defences and facilitated the f2-f4 advance (35...♕e7?! 36 ♘xf5 and 37 f4!).

35 ♕d1

White's pieces are harmoniously placed, and the time for decisive action is approaching.

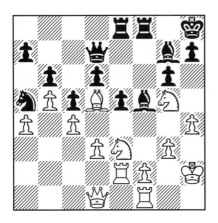

35...h6

'A serious weakening of the light squares, probably provoked by Karpov's desire to change the position before the adjournment.' (Makarychev). Dlugy was also doubtful about this move, although he noticed the strong threat of 36 ♖h1, ♔g2 and h4-h5.

36 ♘e4 ♕d8 (4)

After 36...h5 37 ♘xf5! ♖xf5 (37...gxf5? 38 ♖b2 with the threat of ♕xh5+) 38 ♘c3 ♖ff8 39 ♗e4 Black has no defence: 39...♕e6 40 ♘d5 ♖c8(b8) 41 f4 etc.

37 ♖a2? (3)

Carried away by manoeuvring, I missed an excellent opportunity to immediately create a target – 37 h5! (this was also not noticed by the commentators): for example, 37...gxh5 (37...♗xe4 38 dxe4 is also unsuitable) 38 ♘xf5 ♖xf5 39 ♖e3! h4 40 ♕g4 or 39...♕e7(d7) 40 ♖h1! and ♔g1, winning. Black can put up a tougher defence with 37...g5 38 ♘xf5 ♖xf5 39 ♖b2 ♕d7 40 ♕g4, but here too he stands badly – it is merely a question of what plan White should choose, and this question would have been resolved

in adjournment analysis.

37...♗c8! (4)

By removing this bishop from exchange, Black is able to neutralise 38 h5 with 38...g5.

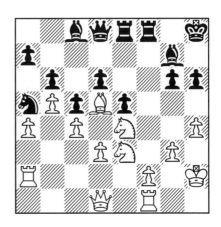

38 ♘c3

A necessary regrouping: the bishop goes to e4 (to attack the g6-pawn) and the knight to d5. After 38 ♘g2 ♕d7! the planned f2-f4 advance is hindered.

38...h5 (2)

A new weakening – but an outlet for the bishop on g7. Black also regroups, exploiting the remoteness of the white knight from g5.

39 ♗e4 ♖e6 40 ♘cd5 (4) **40...♗h6**

The control was reached, but since we had 20 minutes in hand and I did not want to seal my 41st move, I continued playing.

41 ♘g2 (2)

Preparing f2-f4. In reply Karpov also decided not to adjourn the game for the moment – and he committed a serious mistake.

41...♔g7? (5)

41...♗b7! (aiming to eliminate the knight on d5) would have made things much harder for me, since the immediate 42 f4?! no longer achieves its goal on account of 42...♗xd5 43 ♗xd5 ♖ef6 44 ♖af2 exf4 45 gxf4 ♕d7. Of course, here Karpov should have remembered about the 'Botvinnik rule' – have a good think, find the move 41...♗b7, and seal it in the envelope, taking on his clock the time remaining. In this case there would have been a lengthy adjournment session in prospect. No direct way for White to win is apparent, and I would again have had to manoeuvre, preparing a breakthrough (for example, 42 f3 ♔g7 43 ♖af2 ♗xd5 44 ♗xd5 ♖ef6 45 ♗e4 ♕d7 46 f4, although this is not yet the end of things).

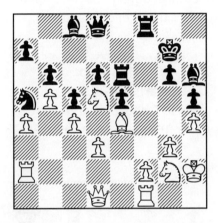

42 f4! (11)

My opponent was probably hoping that I would not enter into an open battle before the adjournment. But I had no doubts about the move chosen: Black's position is on the verge of cracking up – such a chance could not be missed! And I made the move when the five hours of play had almost expired and the time had come to adjourn the game. Karpov had to find the best reply on the stage, with his clock ticking away.

42...exf4? (7)

The sealed move, for which I was not even hoping: now Black loses very quickly. He had two ways of prolonging the resistance:

1) 42...♖ee8 43 ♖af2 (with the threat of f4-f5) 43...♗f5 (43...♗g4 44 ♕c2) 44 ♗xf5 ♖xf5 45 ♘ge3 ♖f7 46 f5 ♗xe3 (46...♖ef8 47 f6+ ♔h8 48 ♘e7 or 47...♔h7 48 ♘f5! is no better) 47 f6+ ♔h7 48 ♘xe3 e4 49 ♖f4 ♖e6 50 ♘d5, and White must win, although not

as easily as in the game;

2) 42...♗b7! (alas, with a delay of one move) 43 f5 (or first 43 ♖af2!?) 43...♗xd5 (43...♖ee8? 44 f6+!, while 43...gxf5? 44 ♗xf5 leads to the loss of the h5-pawn) 44 fxe6 ♖xf1 (44...♗xe6 45 ♖af2) 45 ♕xf1 ♗xe6 46 ♕e1! and ♘e3 with good chances of converting the exchange advantage.

The difficult defence over the entire game had evidently so tired Karpov, that he decided 'simply' to get rid of the threat of f4-f5, by playing 42...exf4. But he went from the frying pan into the fire...

43 ♘gxf4 ♖e5

43...♗xf4 was also hopeless: 44 ♘xf4 (but not Dlugy's move 44 ♖xf4? because of 44...♘xc4!) 44...♖ef6 45 ♕d2 (more subtle than 45 ♖af2) 45...♔g8 (45...♗g4 46 ♕c3! and ♖af2) 46 ♕e1! ♔g7 (the threat was ♗xg6) 47 ♖af2 ♘b3 48 ♕e3! with the threats of ♘xh5+ and ♗xg6.

44 ♘xg6! (5)

This combinative solution was accurately calculated during our analysis, although 44 ♖af2 would also have won easily.

44...♖xf1 (2) **45 ♕xf1 ♖xe4 46 dxe4 ♔xg6 47 ♖f2 ♕e8** (12)

The only move: if 47...♗g7, then 48 ♖f7!.

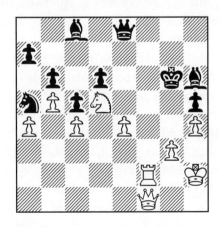

48 e5! (1)

A pretty stroke, which stunned Karpov.

The machine 'sees' it immediately, but it also indicates another, computer line – 48 ♖f6+ ♔g7 49 ♖xd6 ♕e5 50 ♖d8 ♗e6 51 ♖e8! ♘xc4 52 ♕f2! ♘d6 53 ♖e7+ ♔h8 54 ♕f6+ ♕xf6 55 ♘xf6 ♗g8 56 e5 and wins.

48...dxe5 (48...♕xe5 49 ♖e2) **49 ♖f6+ ♔g7 50 ♖d6!**

The threat of 51 ♕f6+ forces the fatal 50...♕f7 51 ♕xf7+ and ♖xh6. After thinking for nearly 10 minutes, Black resigned (**1–0**). The brief and spectacular adjournment session provoked a lengthy ovation by the spectators. The game was judged to be the best in *Informator* Volume 44. Times: 2.45–3.02.

This difficult win enabled me to again level the scores (4-4) and, it would appear, seize the initiative in the match. But, alas, my psychological problems had not gone away – moreover, in the second half of the match they began to dominate...

After two draws, Karpov lost the 11th game with a blunder on the 35th move. I think that this 'gift' did me a bad service: after finally taking the lead (6-5) I completely 'fell asleep'. I was seized by a sub-conscious desire to curtail the play and eliminate any risk. The opponent needs to win two games – let him come at me. Play was transformed into torture, and my dream was that it would all end as soon as possible. The typical syndrome of a return match! It is hardly surprising that the psychological initiative soon passed to Karpov, and after four draws I lost the 16th game with White in undistinguished fashion – on this occasion the magic of numbers did not work.

After this there followed a further six draws: 11-11! Now the fate of the chess crown was to be decided by the last two games. The anticipated full-blooded battle in Seville may not have occurred, but the

finish to the match left no one indifferent. It was an incredible, simply fantastic denouement! 'The intensity of the fight in the two unprecedentedly dramatic games at the finish exceeded anything observed in all the preceding matches for the world championship' (Makarychev).

In the 23rd game I had to mount a lengthy and tenacious rearguard action. The crisis ensued during the resumption, not long before the second time control.

Game 30
A.Karpov-G.Kasparov
World Championship Match
23rd Game, Seville 16/17.12.1987

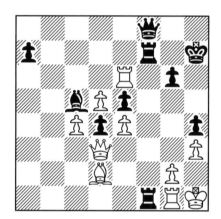

50 ♖c6

Here I suddenly became feverish, and I ceased to understand what I should do next. The result of this time-trouble panic was a 'powerful tactical stroke'.

50...♖7f3?? (2)

Completely losing control! I suddenly suffered one of the most nightmarish hallucinations in my career, and I made an error that lost immediately. I had hardly pressed the clock button, when I immediately saw the simple refutation of my move, and I remembered that we had found it at home in our adjournment analysis...

As Nikitin later reminded me, we had also examined the best reply – 50...♗b4! with the idea of 51 ♗g5?! ♗e1! or 51 ♗xb4 ♖xg1+ 52 ♔xg1 ♕xb4 53 ♕d1 ♖f4! with a draw. Karpov writes: 'However, now 51 ♖a6! is good, maintaining the pressure'. And in *Informator* together with Zaitsev he specifies: after 51...♗c5. But, in my opinion, it is simpler to play 51...♗xd2 52 ♕xd2 ♕c8 53 ♖a4 ♖1f4 or 53 ♖c6 ♕b8 54 ♕g5 ♖xg1+ 55 ♔xg1 ♕b1+ 56 ♔h2 ♕xe4 and ...d4-d3 with a draw.

51 gxf3 (3) **51...♖xf3 52 ♖c7+ ♔h8 53 ♗h6!**

'A spectacular counter, which decides the game. But the most surprising thing is that Kasparov knew about this refutation, having analysed it previously together with his seconds, but – he simply forgot about it!' (Taimanov)

'The world champion froze, then mechanically replied and turned away from the board and the auditorium...' (Makarychev)

53...♖xd3 (1) **54 ♗xf8 ♖xh3+ 55 ♔g2 ♖g3+ 56 ♔h2 ♖xg1 57 ♗xc5 d3 1-0**

Black resigned, without waiting for his opponent's reply. 'After 58 ♗e3 White gives up his bishop for the pawn, when the passed c- and d-pawns cannot be stopped' (Karpov). Times: 3.28–3.27.

A shocking end to the game. But, apparently, the match intrigue demanded such a blunder from me.

Unexpectedly, Karpov was now a point ahead (12-11), and only a draw separated him from the cherished crown. It was obvious that the title was almost lost. Even now I shudder when I recall those first few minutes after the adjournment session, the drive back, and the state of doom into which I sank. The torment of that evening would

have sufficed for an entire match. I had the feeling that I was looking into the abyss...

The day after this disaster I had White in the final, 24th game, and only a win would do. The situation at the finish in Seville was a mirror reflection of the conclusion of the 1985 match. There before the 24th game I held a one-point lead, and to retain his title Karpov needed to win. He also had White, and he launched an all-out assault, but at a critical moment through force of habit he chose a more cautious line, then went wrong, and in the end lost the game. When I was preparing for the decisive battle, I remembered that turning-point. What strategy should be chosen for White, when only a win would do? The plan for the last game had not only to take account of my own personal preferences, but also set my opponent the most difficult problems. And what could be more unpleasant for Karpov than if I were to play in his own style?

Game 31
G.Kasparov-A.Karpov
World Championship Match
24th Game, Seville 18/19.12.1987
English Opening A14

1 c4 e6 (not even contemplating plans with ...e7-e5 – *Game Nos.27, 29*) **2 ♘f3**

In turn, White avoids the hackneyed Queen's Gambit.

2...♘f6 (2) **3 g3 d5** (2) **4 b3**

Also avoiding the Catalan – 4 d4. The plan with the double fianchetto had always attracted me, although I played it very rarely. In the given instance this proved to be a psychologically successful and key decision.

4...♗e7 (7)

A hopeful sign: from the very first moves my opponent began thinking.

5 ♗g2 0-0 (3) **6 0-0** (1) **6...b6** (5)

The alternative is 6...c5 7 ♗b2 ♘c6 and then 8 cxd5 ♘xd5 9 ♘c3 (in this way I once defeated Govashelishvili, 1978) or the more complex 8 e3, as I played against Toro Sanchez (Dortmund 1980) and Sosonko (Brussels (blitz) 1987). But my opponent preferred to fianchetto his light-squared bishop.

7 ♗b2 ♗b7 8 e3

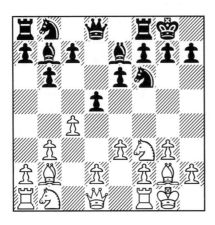

8...♘bd7 (16)

8...c5 was stronger – after 9 ♘c3 ♘c6 10 cxd5 ♘xd5 (10...exd5 11 d4) 11 ♘xd5 ♕xd5 (11...exd5 12 d4) 12 d4! (this was played in the 1960s by Botvinnik), or 9 ♕e2 ♘c6 10 ♖d1 ♕c7 11 ♘c3 ♖ad8 12 cxd5 ♘xd5 (12...exd5 13 d4) 13 ♘xd5 ♖xd5 14 d4 cxd4 15 ♘xd4 ♘xd4 16 ♗xd4 (Vaganian-Karpov, 39th USSR Championship, Leningrad 1971) White has some advantage, but under the influence of the 8th Korchnoi-Spassky match game (Kiev 1968) the main line became 9...dxc4!? 10 bxc4 ♘c6. Instead of this Karpov chose a more restrained and flexible continuation (the most 'Queen's Indian-like'), which, however, does not prevent White from deploying his pieces comfortably and obtaining the freer position.

9 ♘c3 (15)

9 ♕e2!? was probably more accurate, with the idea of 9...a5 10 ♘c3 ♘e4 11 ♖fd1

♗f6 12 d4, avoiding the exchange of bishops (Botvinnik-Stahlberg, Moscow 1956), or 9...c5 10 d3 and then ♘c3 (Polugayevsky-Petrosian, 1st match game, Moscow 1970).

9...♘e4! (11)

Threatening to exchange a pair of knights, and then also the bishops (after ...♗f6).

10 ♘e2 (3)

In order to retain as many pieces as possible, I avoided both 10 ♕c2 (Geller-Keres, Riga 1968) and 10 cxd5 (Geller-Kholmov, 37th USSR Championship, Moscow 1969).

10...a5?! (2)

A rather unKarpov-like move, creating a potential weakness for Black on b6, which in time may (and will!) become perceptible. 'Karpov waits for White to play d2-d3, in order to definitely exchange the dark-square bishops. In a different competitive situation he would possibly have preferred 10...♗f6 11 d4 c5 with an excellent game' (Makarychev). Or 'the immediate 10...c5, and if 11 d3, then 11...♗f6 12 ♕c2 ♗xb2 13 ♕xb2 ♕f6' (Taimanov).

11 d3 (18) **11...♗f6** (11) **12 ♕c2** (10) **12...♗xb2** (2) **13 ♕xb2 ♘d6**

This creates a definite lack of harmony in the placing of the black pieces, but here 13...♕f6 is no longer so good on account of 14 ♕c2 ♘ec5 15 cxd5 (not 15 d4? because of 15...dxc4) 15...exd5 16 ♘f4 with a slight advantage to White.

14 cxd5 (1) **14...♗xd5** (5)

The correct decision, maintaining a certain symmetry (in order to meet d3-d4 with ...c7-c5). '14...exd5 would have led to more complicated play, but Karpov was not interested in this' (Taimanov). Indeed, after 15 d4 c5 16 dxc5 bxc5 17 ♖fd1 White would retain some pressure.

'I think at that moment few of the world champion's supporters believed that a miracle could occur. All the more credit to him both for his play, and for the staggering persistence displayed in such a situation.' (Makarychev)

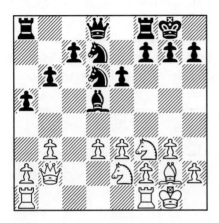

15 d4 (35)

Apparently 15 ♘f4!? ♗b7 16 d4 (16 ♘h5 is weaker because of 16...f6!) was more accurate, since it would have narrowed Black's choice: 16...c5 17 ♖ac1 ♕e7 (17...cxd4 18 ♖fd1!) 18 ♘d3 ♖ac8 19 dxc5 or 18...♘e4 19 ♘fe5 etc.

15...c5 (17) **16 ♖fd1**

'Outwardly Black's position looks quite safe, but he has not yet achieved full equality: there are obvious defects in his queenside pawn structure, and on the d-file there is a perceptible overloading of his pieces.' (Taimanov)

16...♖c8 (22)

Black reconciles himself to the exchange of his light-squared bishop for a knight. 16...♕f6? 17 ♘e5 ♖fd8 18 ♗xd5 exd5 19 ♘f4 was bad. However, 16...♕e7 suggests itself – in *Informator* I recommended answering this with 17 ♘c3 ♗b7 18 ♘a4, but after 18...c4! 19 bxc4 (19 ♘c3 ♖fc8) 19...♘xc4 20 ♕b5 ♘d6 Black has a good game. Therefore it is better to play 17 ♘f4 ♗b7 (Makarychev) 18 ♖ac1 ♖fd8 19 ♘d3, when White's chances are slightly better.

It is probable that Karpov also considered 16...c4!? – this is justified in the event of 17 bxc4 ♘xc4 18 ♕b5 ♘d6 or 17 ♘f4 b5 18 ♘xd5 exd5 19 ♘e5 ♘f6 20 a4 b4 21 bxc4 ♘xc4, but after 17 ♘c3!? White has the better pawn structure (if 17...b5, then 18 bxc4).

Therefore I would not especially criticise 16...♖c8. Black did not want to complicate the play and he was seeking clear equality – but it wasn't there, and the minor problems gradually accumulated. The doubts which tormented Karpov on almost every move cost him time and created discomfort. Indeed, White's chance was above all a psychological one.

17 ♘f4 (15) **17...♗xf3** (5)

Now this has to be played: not 17...♗e4? 18 dxc5 ♘xc5 19 ♕e5 ♘cb7 20 ♘h5 and wins, while after 17...c4?! 18 ♘xd5 exd5 19 ♘e5 White's position is simply better.

18 ♗xf3

'A long-range bishop against a knight lacking a support – this is already a serious, permanent factor.' (Taimanov). It is hardly a great achievement by White, but he undoubtedly has a small plus.

18...♕e7

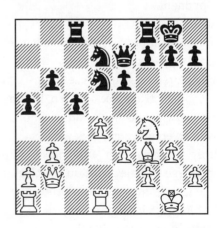

19 ♖ac1 (23)

White calmly completes his development.

19 dxc5!? was interesting, since after 19...♘xc5 (19...♖xc5?! 20 ♘d3! ♖cc8 21 ♖ac1) 20 ♕e5! (20 b4?! ♘c4!) considerable resourcefulness would have been demanded of Black: 20...♖fd8 21 ♘d5 ♕a7 22 b4! ♘a4! 23 ♖ac1 ♘e8! 24 ♖xc8 ♖xc8 25 ♗g4 ♕b8 26 ♕xb8 ♖xb8 27 ♘e7+ ♔f8 28 ♘c6 ♖c8 29 ♗f3 ♘c3 with equality.

All is also not so clear after 19 ♘h5!? c4 (as pointed out by Taimanov, 19...f6 is weaker in view of 20 ♘f4, 'intending the breakthrough d4-d5' or simply strengthening the position) 20 ♖ac1 – after all, Black has weakened himself and a different game begins. I think that, from the purely practical point of view, the optimal decision was in fact 19 ♘h5.

19...♖fd8 (1) **20 dxc5** (1) **20...♘xc5**

Perhaps Black should have exchanged a pair of rooks by 20...♖xc5!?. In the event of 21 ♘d3 ♖xc1 22 ♖xc1 e5 he has nothing to complain of, although after 21 ♖xc5 ♘xc5 22 b4 axb4 23 ♕xb4 he would still have had to display accuracy and patience.

21 b4 (1)

What else can be done? White at least discloses the weakness of the b6-pawn, by which he creates additional discomfort for the opponent.

21...axb4 (14)

'In the event of 21...♘ce4 there is the unpleasant 22 ♖xc8 ♖xc8 23 ♕d4!' (Taimanov). After 23...♘g5 (23...e5? 24 ♘d5) 24 ♗g2 ♘b5 25 ♕xb6 ♘c3 26 ♕b7! ♕xb7 27 ♗xb7 Black would have had to fight for a draw in an ending a pawn down.

After thinking over this move, Karpov overtook me in time spent on the clock, and for the last 19 moves to the control he had just 22 minutes left against my 26.

22 ♕xb4 ♕a7 23 a3 ♘f5 (5)

In a slightly inferior position Karpov looks for the simplest way to initiate exchanges.

Makarychev and Taimanov recommended the 'consolidating' manoeuvre 23...♘e8 and ...♘f6. However, in my view, after 24 ♘d3 the assessment of the position would not have fundamentally changed: 24...♘f6 25 ♘e5 ♘d5 26 ♗xd5! exd5 27 ♘d3 or 24...♘xd3 25 ♖xc8 ♖xc8 26 ♖xd3 etc. The position of the knight on f5 has its plus point – its proximity to the important d6-square.

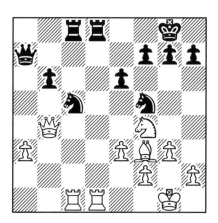

24 ♖b1 (2)

Here too 24 ♘d3 was possible, but I did not want to hurry with the exchange of my agile knight. 24 ♖b1, at the least, forces Black to go in for another minor concession – to give up the d-file.

24...♖xd1+ (3) **25 ♖xd1** (1) **25...♕c7** (2)

Preparing further simplification. If 25...♕a5, then simply 26 ♔g2.

26 ♘d3! (5)

'A cunning plan. White intends a general exchange on c5, in order to obtain a passed a-pawn against a c-pawn *[already a real trump! – G.K.]*. Although this is still a long way off, the very fact of offering an exchange of knights, sharply changing the character of the play, is psychologically very effective.' (Taimanov). And, indeed, in the ensuing time scramble Karpov began to overestimate the dangers threatening him and became nervous.

26...h6?! (3)

After this move Black had 10 minutes left. 26...♘xd3 27 ♖xd3 was unfavourable for Black (the rook is sharply activated), but the escape square for the king could have been created by 26...g6!? – with a light-squared bishop I would have been unable to exploit the weakening of the f6-square, and the position would have remained almost equal.

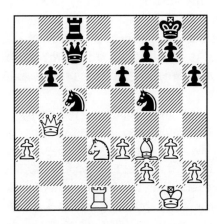

27 ♖c1 (2) **27...♘e7** (3)

27...♘xd3? loses to 28 ♖xc7 ♖xc7 29 ♕d2! etc. In *Informator* I recommended 27...♘d6, but then 28 ♘e5 is good, and if 28...f6?! (a new weakening!), then not 29 ♘c6? ♘d3! or 29 ♘d3 (Makarychev) 29...♘xd3 30 ♖xc7 ♘xb4 31 ♖xc8+ ♘xc8 32 axb4 ♘d6 with equality, but 29 ♘g6! ♘f7 30 h4 or 29...f5 30 ♘f4 ♕b8 31 h4 etc.

28 ♕b5 (2) **28...♘f5** (2)

In time-trouble Karpov decides to bring his knight back to d6. He would still have been under pressure after 28...♕a7 29 ♖c3 (but not 29 ♘xc5 ♕xa3! with equality) 29...♘f5 30 ♘e5 ♘d6 31 ♕b4.

29 a4 (4) **29...♘d6** (1) **30 ♕b1**

With the threat of a4-a5. 'Purely time-trouble play, but very elegant', as Makarychev commented.

30...♕a7 (1)

30...♕d8 31 ♘xc5 bxc5 (31...♖xc5? 32

♖xc5 bxc5 33 a5! and wins) 32 ♖d1 would have led to the desired position, dangerous for Black, with a passed a-pawn for White.

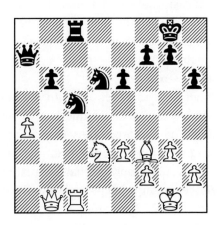

31 ♘e5!

'An excellent manoeuvre, which with Black in time-trouble set him difficult practical problems. In the first instance 32 ♘c6 is threatened.' (Taimanov). This is indeed a critical position. Karpov had already used a lot of time – here he had just three minutes left (I had twelve), but he failed to find a safe way to draw.

31...♘xa4? (1)

Allowing a decisive combination. 'A fatal mistake. By playing 31...♕xa4 32 ♕xb6 ♕a3!, Black would have emerged unscathed: 33 ♖d1 ♘ce4! 34 ♘xf7!? (34 ♗xe4 ♘xe4 35 ♕b7 ♘d6! 36 ♖xd6 ♖c1+) 34...♕a2!! 35 ♖f1 ♖c1! 36 ♗xe4 ♖xf1+ 37 ♔xf1 ♘xe4.' (Makarychev). After 38 ♕b8+ ♔h7! White is unable to convert his extra pawn because of the insecurity of his king. And if 34 ♖d4, then 34...♕c1+ 35 ♔g2 ♘xf2! or immediately 34...♘xf2! 35 ♖xd6 ♕a2!!. However, with your clock flag about to fall it is unrealistic to find all these sharp moves.

It was also acceptable to play 'again 31...♘f5' (Taimanov): for example, 32 ♘c6 (32 ♔g2 ♕a6) 32...♕xa4 33 ♕xb6 ♘d3! 34 ♖f1 ♕a3 35 ♗e4 ♔h8, holding the position.

But Karpov instinctively captured the pawn with his knight, retaining his infantryman on b6. In such situations he always 'just in case' grabbed material, if he did not see an immediate loss (remember, for example, 26...♞xa2 in the 6th game of the first match).

32 ♖xc8+ ♞xc8

Now I need to penetrate with my queen into enemy territory – the question is: where it should go to. Karpov tensely awaited my move, preparing to reply instantly: otherwise he would simply not have managed to make the remaining eight moves to the time control. I would have stopped to think, but here the chief arbiter Gijssen suddenly tapped me on the shoulder. Bending over me, he said: 'Mr Kasparov, you must record the moves'. And indeed, carried away by the play, I had forgotten to write the moves ♖xc8+ and ...♞xc8 on my scoresheet. Of course, the arbiter was obliged to remind me of the need to observe the rules, but what a moment for this to occur! Had it all turned out differently, this tap on the shoulder could have become a blow of fate. By arguably following too strictly the letter of the law, Gijssen almost changed the course of chess history...

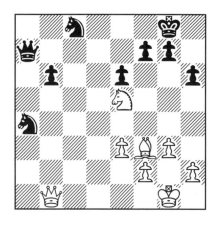

33 ♕d1??

My nervous reaction was to instantly pick up my queen – and place it on the wrong square! I overlooked a clever defensive resource for Black and did not manage to calculate the consequences of the obvious 33 ♕b5!. As it transpired, this would have won by force. After 33...♞d6 34 ♕c6 ♞f5 35 ♕e8+ ♚h7 there are two strong continuations: 36 ♞xf7 (Makarychev) and 36 ♞d7 with the idea of 36...♞c5 37 ♞f8+ ♚g8 38 ♞g6+ ♚h7 39 ♗h5! – a spectacular mating finish! It is no better to play 33...♞f8 34 ♞c6 ♕a8 35 ♕d3! g6 36 ♕d8+ ♚g7 37 ♕d4+ ♚h7 38 ♕d7 or 33...♚h7 34 ♕e8 ♞d6 35 ♕d8.

In Taimanov's opinion, 'the energetic 33 ♗h5!? would also have won the game quickly, for example: 33...♞d6 34 ♕d1! or 33...g6 34 ♗xg6!.' 33...f6 34 ♗f7+ ♚f8 is far more tenacious, and in the event of 35 ♗xe6 fxe5 36 ♕f5+ ♚e8 37 ♕xe5 (37 ♗xc8 ♕e7 is not so clear) 37...♕e7 38 ♕b5+ ♚d8 39 ♗xc8 ♚xc8 40 ♕xa4 White 'merely' reaches a queen endgame with an extra pawn, but he has the more energetic 35 ♕h7! fxe5 36 ♕g8+ ♚e7 37 ♕e8+ ♚d6 38 ♕xe6+ ♚c7 39 ♕xe5+ ♚d8 40 ♕e8+ ♚c7 41 ♗e6 b5 42 ♕xc8+ ♚b6 43 ♗d7, and although the play still retains some sharpness, it is most probable that Black cannot hold the position.

The only virtue of 33 ♕d1 was that it came as a surprise to Karpov.

33...♞e7?? (1)

'Black misses a chance opportunity to retain an advantage in this titanic duel: 33...♞c5! 34 ♕d8+ ♚h7 would have relieved him of his problems (35 ♕xc8? ♕a1+ and ...♕xe5). As sometimes happens, the chess throne is shaky when its fate is decided by seconds.' (Taimanov). 35 ♗d1 ♞e7 36 ♞xf7 ♞g6! (Makarychev) or 35...f5 36 ♕xc8 ♕a1 37 ♕d8! ♕xe5 38 ♕xb6, and also 35 ♚g2 f6 36 ♕xc8 fxe5 37 ♕c6 should lead to a draw.

For an instant Karpov was one step away from regaining the title of champion, but his hasty reply promptly deprived him of this chance.

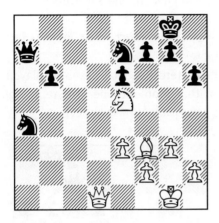

34 ♕d8+?!

A tempting move, but not the most correct – 34 ♗h5! would have given White every chance of winning: 34...♘c5 35 ♗xf7+ ♔h7 36 h4! ♕c7 37 ♕a1 (or 37 f4) and h4-h5 with a fearfully strong attack. But I played more safely.

34...♔h7 35 ♘xf7 (here after 35 ♗h5?! ♘c5! 36 ♘xf7 ♘g8 37 h4 ♕a2 White's advantage is smaller than in the game) **35...♘g6 36 ♕e8!** (1)

Undoubtedly the strongest. 36 ♘d6? was incorrect in view of 36...♕e7 37 ♕b8 (37 ♕a8 ♘c5) 37...♕f8!, transposing into a drawn ending.

36...♕e7!

In desperate time-trouble Karpov rises to the occasion – 36...♘c5? 37 ♗h5! was hopeless for Black: for example, 37...♕a1+ (37...♕a2 38 h4) 38 ♔g2 ♕f6 39 f4 with the deadly threat of 40 ♗xg6+ ♔xg6 41 ♘g5+, while if 37...♕a4, then 38 ♘g5+ hxg5 39 ♕xg6+ ♔g8 40 ♕xg5 or 38 ♕xa4 ♘xa4 39 ♗d1! ♔g8 (39...♘c5 40 ♗c2 and h2-h4-h5) 40 ♘xh6+ gxh6 41 ♗xa4 with a won endgame.

37 ♕xa4 ♕xf7 38 ♗e4 ♔g8 39 ♕b5! (1)

An accurate reply. The transposition into a queen endgame with an extra pawn suggested itself – 39 ♗xg6 ♕xg6 40 ♕b3 ♕g4 41 ♕xb6, which could then have been 'shuffled endlessly' (41...♕d1+ 42 ♔g2 ♕d5+ 43 f3 ♕d2+ 44 ♔h3 etc.). But I intuitively realised that the bishop should be retained: although it is 'of the wrong colour' (for the h8-square), it may well come in useful for an attack on the weak e6-pawn, cut off from base.

39...♘f8 40 ♕xb6 ♕f6 41 ♕b5 (2) **41...♕e7**

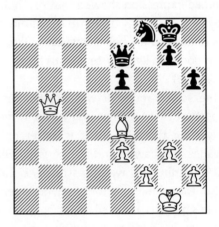

'The time scramble came to an end, and here the game was adjourned. White's extra pawn promises him winning chances. But is it possible to breach Black's defences with the play on a narrow sector of the board?' (Taimanov). My trainers and I studied the various possibilities of attack and defence, but we were unable to reach a clear verdict. The chances of a win and a draw seemed roughly equal, although in practice it is far from easy to save such an endgame against a persistent opponent. However, as it later transpired, Karpov had lost his belief in a successful outcome and he assessed his chances more pessimistically – only 30% for a draw against 70% for a loss. Thus I also had a psychological advantage.

The ovation which greeted me when I walked back on to the stage convinced me that my fans were very much in the majority. The possibility of lengthy manoeuvring, with the aim of provoking some mistake by my opponent, also made me hopeful. Karpov was depressed by the prospect of a gruelling defence: I could read this in his eyes when soon after me he came on the stage (obviously weighing on his mind was the thought that at one point he could have gained an immediate draw, instead of which he now had to defend such a repulsive position). His doomed expression showed that psychologically he had already given up the game, and this reinforced my belief in success. I was in the mood for a lengthy, tenacious fight.

42 ♔g2 (9)

The sealed move. It was psychologically important that I did not play 42 h4 immediately – for the moment it is better not to advance the pawns and to see what Black will do. Unhurried waiting strategy became one of the winning factors. In general terms, White's plan is reduced to placing his e3-pawn on e5 and then if possible exchanging queens, but where will Black place his g- and h-pawns?

42...g6 (1)

'Play was renewed, and with bated breath the chess world followed the development of events. The first few moves were made quickly. Karpov avoided 42...g5, although most of the commentators thought that this active plan of defence was the most promising.' (Taimanov). But then Black would have run into 43 f4!, which is not good for him – say, 43...♕f6 44 ♔h3 gxf4 45 exf4 etc.

And if 42...♕f6 43 h4 g5 we were intending 44 h5!? (unexpectedly the pawn moves to a square of the colour of its bishop), and then the same plan with e3-e4-e5. True, I am still not sure whether this was good enough

to win. But after the game Karpov said that he was afraid of the exchange 44 hxg5 hxg5 and the appearance of a weak g5-pawn. Therefore he took the decision to erect something resembling a fortress on the light squares and to wait.

43 ♕a5 (4) 43...♕g7 (3) 44 ♕c5 (1) ♕f7 (2) 45 h4 (2)

'It is interesting that Kasparov played h2-h4 at that moment when the reply ...g6-g5 was impossible.' (Makarychev)

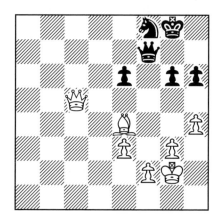

45...h5?

I remember being very surprised when Karpov weakened his defences so seriously. The point of this move is not clear. Now Black's pawn structure has lost its flexibility and it contains more targets. The degree of uncertainty has been reduced, and the play has become more concrete. Sometimes the most difficult problem in a tense situation is to maintain the tension. A player who is under positional pressure has a reflex desire to take any decision, even one that is by no means best, if only to 'lift the burden'. That is what Karpov did, avoiding the main lines of our analysis, but this was sheer capitulation, because White was not yet threatening anything and after 45...♕f6 46 ♕a7 (46 h5 g5) 46...g5 47 hxg5 hxg5 48 f3 ♘g6 it was possible to put up a tenacious defence.

'The arrangement of the pawns on g6 and h5 is the most vulnerable: now the exchange of queens is unacceptable for Black, and this factor plays a decisive role. Thanks to it White gains the opportunity to penetrate with his pieces into the opponent's territory.' (Taimanov). And, therefore, White now has a technically won position.

46 ♕c6 (9) **46...♕e7** (7) **47 ♗d3** (2) **47...♕f7** (1) **48 ♕d6** (8) **48...♔g7** (2) **49 e4!** (1)

After a series of preparatory moves I finally began the advance of my pawn to e5.

49...♔g8 (2)

In *Informator* I drew attention to 49...♕b7!? (hindering e4-e5). I think that the simplest here is 50 ♕a6!: for example, 50...♕c7 51 ♗c4 ♔f7(f6) 52 f4 or 50...♕xa6 51 ♗xa6 e5 52 ♗c4 ♔f6 53 f4 ♘d7 54 ♔f3, when the white king advances into the opponent's territory, and Black cannot do anything, since he is tied to his weak pawns.

50 ♗c4 (6) **50...♔g7** (2)

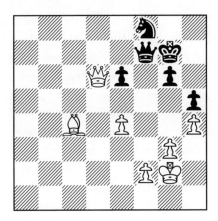

51 ♕e5+ (2)

An exploratory check: will the opponent go in for the exchange of queens?

51...♔g8 (2)

If 51...♕f6 (the best chance) there would have followed 52 ♕xf6+ ♔xf6 53 f4 e5 54 ♔f3 ♘d7 55 ♔e3 ♘c5 56 ♗d5 and ♔d2-c3-c4, winning.

52 ♕d6 (2)

After 52 f4?! ♔h7 the weakening of the white king's defences could have told.

52...♔g7 (1) **53 ♗b5** (3)

After repeating moves, I now forcibly carry out the plan with e4-e5, and the bishop heads for c6, to take control of the long diagonal.

53...♔g8 (1) **54 ♗c6 ♕a7** (23) **55 ♕b4!** (1)

Also an important prophylactic move. After 55 e5?! ♕a5! 56 ♗e4 ♕e1 the black queen would have become active. Perhaps White would still have won after 56 f4, but why voluntarily expose the king? It is better to seize control of the seventh rank with the queen and play e4-e5 at the most appropriate moment.

55...♕c7 (4) **56 ♕b7!**

'The mechanism of threatening to exchange queens operates faultlessly!' (Taimanov). Here I sensed that the win was not far off.

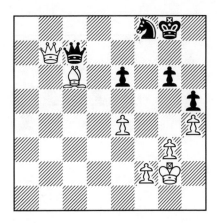

56...♕d8

Resistance would have been prolonged, but the assessment of the position would not have changed after 56...♕xb7 57 ♗xb7 e5 58 f4, when the white king embarks on an out-flanking manoeuvre – Black's downfall is caused by the weakness of his g6- and h5-pawns.

57 e5! (11)

Now there will no longer be an endgame with knight against bishop; White completely controls the situation and Black is practically in zugzwang. Karpov thought for a long time...

57...♕a5 (45)

The ending after 57...♕d3 58 ♗e8 ♕f5 59 ♕f3! ♔g7 60 ♕xf5 exf5 61 ♔f3 ♘e6 62 ♔e3 is won 'on auto-pilot', since all the black pawns are on light squares and it is very easy for the white king to break through.

58 ♗e8! (1) **58...♕c5** (the only move) **59 ♕f7+** (2) **59...♔h8 60 ♗a4** (1)

But now things are decided by the manoeuvre of the bishop to e4, after which the kingside pawns fall.

60...♕d5+ (3) **61 ♔h2** (1) **61...♕c5** (or 61...♘h7 62 ♗c2 ♕xe5 63 ♕e8+) **62 ♗b3** (2) **62...♕c8** (1) **63 ♗d1** (1) **63...♕c5** (1) **64 ♔g2** (1)

Here the ex-champion thought for 8 minutes...

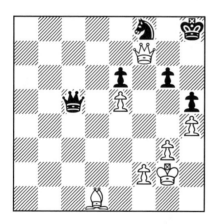

'White cannot be prevented from further and now decisively strengthening the placing of his pieces, and Karpov conceded defeat. (**1–0**) The great battle was crowned by an unforgettable finale!' (Taimanov). 13 pieces remained on the board – the last winning factor!

'Karpov did not bother to check whether his opponent would fall into a stalemate trap, and he immediately congratulated Garry Kasparov. After 64...♕d5+ 65 ♗f3 ♕c5 66 ♗e4 ♕a3 White cannot play 67 ♗xg6?? ♘xg6 68 ♕xg6 because of 68...♕f3+!! He must play 67 ♔h3! ♕b4 68 f3 ♕b8 69 f4 [*the immediate 69 ♗xg6 is simpler – G.K.*] 69...♕d8 70 ♗xg6 ♘xg6 71 ♕xg6 ♕xh4+! 72 ♔g2!, and the black queen runs out of checks' (Makarychev). And if 66...♕b4, then 67 ♗xg6?? ♘xg6 68 ♕xg6 is not possible in view of 68...♕b7+ 69 ♔h2 ♕g2+!!, but 67 ♔h2 ♕c5 68 ♔h3! etc. decides matters. The terrible thing is that at the board I did not see this stalemate! But neither did Karpov, as otherwise he would have tried to exploit this unique chance.

Times: 3.39–4.17.

That was undoubtedly the loudest and most prolonged (roughly 20 minutes) ovation I had ever been awarded outside of my own country. The theatre walls were shaking, and Spanish TV interrupted the broadcast of a football match to switch to the conclusion of our duel. I had done that which Karpov failed to do in 1985: by winning the last game, I had drawn the match (12-12) and retained my title. Now I could enjoy three quiet years at the chess summit.

As I left the stage of the Lope de Vega Theatre, I embraced Litvinov and joyfully cried: 'Three years! I've got three years!' Alas, those years until the following title match flew past quickly, although they also contained a mass of events...

Chapter Two

At the Peak of My Career

The Dispute continues

Four-Cycle Match-Tournament in Amsterdam (12–28 May 1988): 1. **Kasparov** – 9 out of 12; 2. Karpov – 6½; 3. Timman – 5½; 4. van der Wiel – 3.

Immediately after the Seville match with Karpov I announced my tournament plans: 'I want to play. I will play as much as I am able. I am reaching the age when I am obliged to try and realise my full potential, to achieve the maximum I can in the game.'

But apart from this I also had plenty of other obligations, connected in particular with the international Grandmasters Association (GMA), which was setting up the World Cup, and with the creation of an independent union of USSR chess players. Engrossed in these various problems, for nearly five months I did not take part in any competitions, with the exception of the FIDE knock-out blitz championship in the Canadian city of Saint John (19-20 February 1988), from which I was eliminated in the quarter-final. Tal: *'The world champion was either tired, or he did not manage to acclimatise –*

at any event, that confident Kasparov, who a year ago easily won the blitz tournament in Brussels, was not present here.'

In mid-May I at last plunged into tournament play – and immediately came a clash with Karpov, with not just one game, but a whole mini-match! Together with Jan Timman and John van der Wiel, we took part in a four-cycle match-tournament of four grandmasters in Amsterdam, where we were assisted by our regular trainers: Karpov by Igor Zaitsev, and I by Alexander Nikitin.

Nikitin: *'The idea of the organisers was that the event should as though continue the Seville match of the two great "Ks" against the background of a contest between the two leaders of the Dutch team and a kind of USSR-Holland match.'* In addition, Bessel Kok, the sponsor of the match-tournament, was favourably disposed towards Timman and wanted to give him an opportunity to prove himself in mini-matches with the two strongest players on the planet.

Zaitsev: *'The drawing of lots was highly unusual. About three weeks beforehand, each of the four was invited to guess the exchange rate of the Dutch Guilder against the American Dollar on 12th May 1988. The most far-sighted proved to be van der Wiel, who was exactly right – 1.825. Then came Timman, Karpov and Kasparov. It was in this order that they chose their numbers in the tournament table (more precisely, the world champion had to take what was left). Once again displaying insight and far-sighted modesty, van der Wiel chose number 4 (within a couple of weeks this "prognosis" of his was also confirmed), Timman chose number 2, and Karpov, voluntarily condemning himself to two Blacks at the start, selected 3. Kasparov was left with number 1, to his satisfaction.'*

Yes, I took this to be a good sign – it was hard to imagine that the No.1 would remain unclaimed. But they all had their own reasons: perhaps Timman would not object to finishing second, while Karpov wanted to have White against me in the first cycle. This next encounter of the champions was undoubtedly the main intrigue of the match-tournament, and it created great interest, and not only in the chess world.

In the first two rounds we both defeated van der Wiel and drew with Timman, and in the 3rd round we drew with each other. In the meantime Timman defeated van der Wiel and finished the first cycle level with me and Karpov on 2 out of 3. The status quo was not changed by the drawn 4th round. Then I again met Karpov (so that no one should play three successive games with the same colour, the organisers interchanged the order of the rounds – the 5th with the 6th and the 11th with the 12th), and my win in this incredibly dramatic game (Game No.2 in *Kasparov vs. Karpov 1988-2009*) largely decided the outcome of the entire event. Zaitsev: *'That day tournament fortune erected a barrier in Karpov's path towards first place.'* Nikitin: *'After this dramatic win*

Kasparov sharply improved his play and became irresistible.'

Indeed, after receiving this boost, in the third cycle I beat both the Dutch grandmasters, which further strengthened my leading position. The 7th round game with John van der Wiel opened the second half of the match-tournament.

Game 32
G.Kasparov-J.van der Wiel
Amsterdam, 3rd Cycle,
7th Round, 21.05.1988
Queen's Indian Defence E12

---

1 d4 ♘f6 2 c4 e6 3 ♘f3 b6 4 a3

Remembering our game in Graz (1981), I again, as in the 1st round, chose my favourite set-up with this particular move order – 4 ♘c3 allows 4...♗b4 (*Game Nos. 9-11, 18, 20*).

4...♗b7

Reverting to classical lines. In that earlier game after 4...c5 5 d5 ♗a6 6 ♕c2 ♕e7?! (6...exd5 – Game Nos.32, 68 in *Garry Kasparov on Garry Kasparov Part I*) I successfully employed a novelty – 7 ♗g5 exd5 8 ♘c3! ♗xc4 9 e4!, while our 1st round game went 4...♗a6 5 ♕c2 ♗b7 6 ♘c3 c5 7 e4 cxd4 8 ♘xd4 ♗c5 9 ♘b3 ♘c6 10 ♗g5 a6 11 0-0-0 ♕c7 12 ♔b1 0-0-0?! 13 ♕d2 (13 ♘xc5!?) 13...d6?! 14 f3 h6 15 ♗f4 ♘e5 16 h4! ♔b8 17 h5 with a stable advantage for White.

5 ♘c3 d5 6 cxd5 ♘xd5 7 ♕c2 c5

Later the best reply was deemed to be 7...♘xc3 8 bxc3 (8 ♕xc3 h6!) 8...♗e7 9 e4 0-0 10 ♗d3 c5 11 0-0 ♕c7(c8), but not 7...♘d7?! 8 ♘xd5! exd5 9 ♗g5!, which occurred in the 32nd game of my first match with Karpov.

8 dxc5! (this is what I was planning to play in that game) **8...♗xc5 9 ♗g5 ♕c8**

Complete happiness is not promised by any of 9...♗e7 10 ♘xd5!, 9...f6 10 ♗d2, and

9...♕c7 10 ♖c1 f6 11 ♘xd5 ♗xd5 12 e4! (Vyzhmanavin-Novikov, Tashkent 1984).

10 ♖c1 (gradually creating pressure on the c-file) **10...h6 11 ♗h4 a5**

White also has some advantage after 11...0-0 12 ♘xd5 exd5 13 e3 (Yusupov-Chernin, Tunis Interzonal 1985).

12 ♘a4! (an important manoeuvre, forcing the b8-knight to take up a passive position) **12...♘d7**

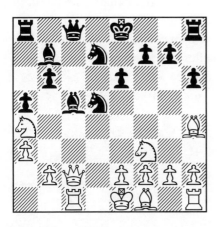

13 e4!

Instead of the restrained 13 e3 (Salov-Timman, Belgrade 1987) – a novelty! Although this idea had already been briefly mentioned in the Soviet chess press, I had my own analysis, and I was pleased that at last I was able to make use of it.

13...♘c7?

Confusion. 13...♘5f6?! 14 ♗xf6! gxf6 (14...♘xf6 15 ♘xc5 bxc5 16 ♗b5+ ♔e7 17 ♘d2) 15 ♗b5(e2) was also not good for Black, but after 13...♘f4 14 ♗g3! (14 ♕d2 g5 15 ♗g3 ♕c6, tried by some correspondence players, is unclear) 14...♘h5 15 ♗b5 or 15 ♘xc5 it is more difficult for White to retain the initiative.

14 ♘xc5! bxc5

Black is forced to create weak pawns in his position: 14...♘xc5? loses a piece after 15 b4 axb4 16 axb4 ♗xe4 17 ♕b2.

15 ♗e2 ♗a6 (White is also better after 15...e5 16 0-0 ♘e6 17 ♗g3) **16 0-0 0-0 17 ♖fd1 f6**

An attempt to restrict White's dark-square bishop by ...e6-e5 and then activate the c7-knight via e6(b5). 17...♖e8?! 18 ♗xa6 ♘xa6 (18...♖xa6? 19 ♕d3) 19 ♕a4 is altogether depressing.

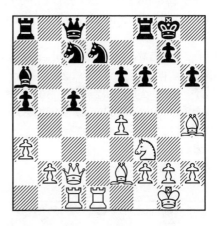

18 ♗c4

Preventing the suggested plan. It was also tempting to play 18 e5!? f5 (an almost forced reply) 19 ♗e7 ♖e8 20 ♗d6 ♘d5 21 ♘h4! or 18 ♗g3!? ♗xe2 (18...e5?! 19 ♘h4! ♘e6 20 ♗g4 ♘d4 21 ♖xd4! is worse) 19 ♕xe2 ♖f7 (19...e5?! 20 ♘h4!) 20 ♗d6 with a serious advantage.

18...♗xc4 (18...♖f7?! 19 ♗a2! and ♗g3) **19 ♕xc4 ♖f7?!**

19...♖b8 was more resilient, in the hope of 20 ♖d2 ♖f7, but here too after 20 ♗g3! ♖xb2 21 ♘d4! things are not easy for Black: 21...♖f7 22 ♘xe6 ♘xe6 23 ♕xe6 ♕b7 24 h3 (and if 24...♖e2, then 25 ♖d5), or 21...cxd4 22 ♕xd4 ♖b7 23 ♕xd7 e5 24 ♕xc8 ♖xc8 25 f4! ♖f8 26 fxe5 with an extra pawn.

20 ♗g3 e5 (blocking the bishop, but allowing a knight invasion at f5) **21 ♘h4! ♕e8** (not 21...♕a6? because of 22 ♕xf7+! ♔xf7 23 ♖xd7+) **22 ♘f5 ♕e6 23 ♕e2!**

The correct decision: with the queens on

White has an obvious advantage, his queen being needed more on the kingside, where an attack is imminent. In the event of 23 ♕a4?! ♖b8! 24 ♘d6 ♘b6 25 ♕xa5 ♖d7 26 ♕a7 ♘a6! 27 ♕xa6 ♖xd6 or 24 ♕xa5 ♘b5 25 b4 ♘d4 26 ♘xd4 cxd4 Black would become more active and gain some compensation for the pawn.

23...♖b8 24 ♖d6 (24 ♘d6! was more forceful, killing the counterplay with ...♘b5-d4)
24...♕e8

Not 24...♕b3?! 25 ♕g4!, when Black is lost: 25...♔h7 26 ♘xg7! ♕xb2 27 ♖cd1 ♘f8 28 ♘f5 ♘e8 29 ♖6d2 ♕b6 30 ♕h5, or 25...♔h8 26 ♘xh6! gxh6 27 ♖xd7 ♕xb2 28 ♖cd1 ♖xd7 29 ♕xd7 and h2-h3.

25 ♖cd1

25 f4?! ♘b5! was premature.

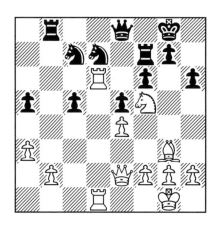

25...♘f8?

Probably the decisive mistake. 25...♔h7? was also weak in view of 26 ♕h5!: for example, 26...♖xb2 27 h3 ♖b7 28 ♖6d3! (threatening ♘d6) 28...♘b5 29 ♖b3 ♘f8 30 a4, or 26...♘b5 27 f4! ♘d4 28 fxe5 ♘xe5 29 ♗xe5 ♘xf5 30 exf5 fxe5 31 ♕g6+ ♔h8 32 f6 ♕f8 33 fxg7+ ♕xg7 34 ♕e4 with good winning chances. However, 25...♘b5 26 ♕g4 ♔h8 was more resilient, in order after 27 ♖a6 ♕g8! 28 ♖xa5 ♘d4 to continue the resistance a pawn down.

26 f4! (now White's attack gathers pace)
26...♘b5

Black would have lost ignominiously after 26...♘g6? 27 ♕h5! ♘xf4 28 ♗xf4 exf4 29 ♕g6 etc. But the battle would merely have been prolonged by 26...exf4 27 ♗xf4 ♘ce6 (after 27...♘fe6(?), suggested by me in *Informator*, 28 ♗xh6! is even more effective) 28 ♗xh6! gxh6 29 ♘xh6+ ♔g7 30 ♘xf7 ♕xf7 31 ♖f1 or 31 ♖1d3, with rook and two pawns for a pair of knights and a continuing attack.

27 fxe5! (of course!) **27...♘xd6?!**

'Reflex' time-trouble play. However, 27...fxe5 28 ♖6d5 ♘d4 (28...♘d7? 29 ♕g4!) 29 ♘xd4 cxd4 30 ♗xe5 etc. was also hopeless.

28 ♘xd6 ♕a4 29 ♘xf7 ♖xb2 (despair) **30 ♘xh6+! ♔h7**

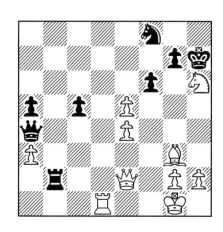

31 ♕h5

Expecting my opponent's immediate capitulation, I relaxed slightly and made a move which, although not bad, is not the most lethal. In the event of 31 ♕f3!? or 31 ♕g4! it would all have concluded far more quickly.

31...g6 32 ♕f3 ♔xh6 33 ♖f1 (in the time scramble for some reason I did not take the pawn – 33 exf6!) **33...♕d4+ 34 ♔h1 ♘h7 35 exf6 ♘xf6 36 ♗f4+**

Time, time... 36 e5! ♘h7 37 e6 or 36...♘g4 37 ♕f8+ ♚h5 38 h3 would have been immediately decisive.

36...♚g7 (36...♚h7 37 ♗g5!) **37 ♗g5** (and again 37 e5! would have won on the spot: 37...♘e4 38 ♗h6+!) **37...♖b6 38 ♕h3?**

Some kind of nightmare – blundering away the e4-pawn! There was a simple win by 38 ♕f4! and h2-h4.

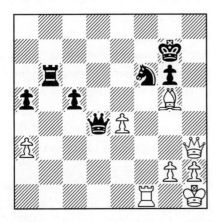

38...♚g8?

With his flag about to fall, van der Wiel missed 38...♕xe4! – here I would still have had to work hard after 39 ♕c3 ♕d4 40 ♕xa5, 39 ♗h6+ ♚h7 40 ♗f8++ ♚g8 41 ♗xc5, or 39 ♚g1!? ♕d4+ 40 ♗e3 ♕e4 41 ♕h6+ ♚g8 42 ♗xc5 ♖b2 43 ♕g5 ♕g4 44 ♕xg4 ♘xg4 45 ♖f8+ ♚g7 46 ♗d4+ ♚xf8 47 ♗xb2, and the bishop with the extra pawn overcomes the knight.

39 ♕c8+ ♚g7 40 ♕c7+ ♘d7 41 ♕f4

Not yet knowing that the first time control had passed, I overlooked the radical 41 ♕d8! ♖e6 42 ♗e7! ♖xe4 43 ♗f8+ ♚h7 44 ♖f7+ ♚g8 45 ♖g7+ ♚h8 46 ♗xc5+ ♚xg7 47 ♗xd4+ ♖xd4 48 h3 with an easy win.

41...♕c4 42 h3 (a long-awaited escape square!) **42...♕e6 43 ♖d1** (43 ♗h6+!) **43...♖c6 44 ♖d8! ♘b6?!**

The dash to the queening square – 44...c4?! 45 ♗xa5 c3 did not work because of

46 ♗xc3+! ♖xc3 47 ♖xd7+ ♕xd7 48 ♕e5+ and ♕xc3, while if 44...a4, then 45 ♗a5 ♕e7 46 ♗c3+ ♚h7 47 e5 ♖a6 48 ♕c4 ♖e6 (48...♖a7 49 e6) 49 ♕xa4 etc.

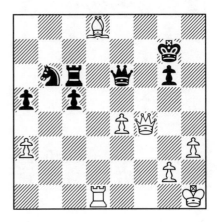

45 ♖f1

Ignoring 45 ♗xb6! ♖xb6 46 ♕c7+ ♚h6 47 ♖d7. But as it was, Black resigned (**1-0**): he is practically in zugzwang (45...♘d7 46 ♗xa5).

And the game with Jan Timman played the following day was later called the best in the tournament.

> *Game 33*
> **G.Kasparov-J.Timman**
> Amsterdam, 3rd Cycle,
> 8th Round, 22.05.1988
> *Slav Defence D18*

1 d4 d5 2 ♘f3 ♘f6 3 c4 c6 4 ♘c3 dxc4

I did not expect from my opponent this solid defence – Timman was playing the Slav for virtually the first time. I had to tune myself up for painstaking work with the accumulation of small advantages.

5 a4 ♗f5 6 ♘h4

Back in 1981, I played 6 e3 e6 7 ♗xc4 ♗b4 8 0-0 ♘bd7 9 ♘h4 or 9 ♕b3. But later I switched to 6 ♘e5 – and achieved success:

6...♘bd7 7 ♘xc4 ♘b6?! 8 ♘e5 ♘bd7?! 9 ♕b3! (Kasparov-Timman, Riga 1995).

6...♗c8

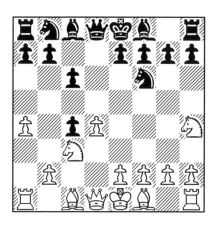

7 ♘f3

After some thought I rejected the variation 7 e3 e5 8 ♗xc4! exd4 9 exd4 ♗e7 10 0-0, which I was then in the process of studying and which came to the fore a few months later (Kasparov-Tal, Reykjavik 1988; Kasparov-Hübner, Barcelona 1989).

7...♘f5 8 e3 (reverting to a well-tried set-up) **8...e6 9 ♗xc4 ♗b4 10 0-0 ♘bd7 11 ♕b3**

11(9) ♕e2 or 11(9) ♘h4 (*Game No.97*) has also occurred several times in my games.

11...a5 12 ♘a2 ♗e7 13 ♘h4

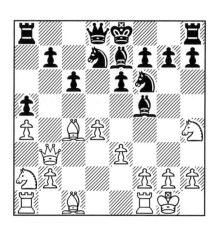

A position which was familiar to me from the 49th USSR Championship (Frunze 1981).

13...♗g6

The alternative is 13...♗e4!? 14 ♘c3 ♘b6, as Kupreichik played against me, and then also Nikolic (Reykjavik 1988), or 14...♗d5 (Beliavsky-Khalifman, 54th USSR Championship, Minsk 1987).

14 g3

14 ♕xb7 ♖b8 (15 ♕xc6? ♗e4) leads to a draw. Sometimes White plays the immediate 14 ♘xg6 hxg6 15 ♘c3 (now after 15 ♕xb7 ♖b8 the capture 16 ♕xc6? is bad because of 16...♖b6 17 ♕f3 ♕c7 – a double attack!), but more often he waits for Black to castle kingside, to avoid opening up the rook on h8. This is a rather unpretentious set-up: White prepares to meet ...c6-c5 or ...e6-e5, hoping to exploit the advantage of the two bishops, but Black has a solid position.

14...♕c7

14...♗h5 comes into consideration, but as yet no one has dared to sacrifice the b7-pawn. In Frunze Beliavsky tried 14...♕c8 against me, and Dolmatov – 14...♕b6, and in both cases after 15 ♘c3 White retained somewhat the better chances.

15 ♘c3 0-0 (15...♗h5 16 f3 is questionable) **16 ♘xg6 hxg6 17 ♖d1** (with the intention of ♗d2 and ♖ac1) **17...♗b4**

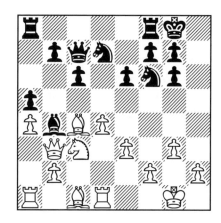

A novelty of not the highest quality – the developing 17...♖ad8!? is more useful. But after 17...e5 (Tukmakov-Beliavsky, also Frunze 1981) 18 ♕c2! (threatening ♕xg6) 18...exd4 19 exd4 ♘b6 20 ♗b3 ♔h7 21 ♖e1 White has some pressure. Apparently Black does better to aim for ...c6-c5.

18 ♕c2

Suddenly 18 ♗d2 seemed to me to be too modest, and I began preparing e3-e4, in order then to develop the c1-bishop to a more active position.

18...♖ad8

18...♖fd8, not weakening the a5-pawn, was more accurate. 18...c5!? was also interesting, with the idea of 19 d5 ♘e5! (but not the *Informator* suggestion 19...♗xc3? 20 dxe6!) 20 ♘b5 ♕e7 21 dxe6 ♘xc4 22 ♕xc4 ♕xe6 or 21 d6 ♕d7 22 ♗e2 ♕c6, maintaining approximate equality.

19 ♘a2! (it is too early for 19 e4 because of 19...e5 with equality, Gleizerov-Tischbierek, Biel 2011) **19...♗e7 20 ♗d2** (20 e4?! e5!) **20...♕b6**

Now 20...e5?! is dangerous in view of 21 ♘c1! and ♘b3 (in addition ♕xg6 is threatened), but again 20...c5!? came into consideration – after 21 ♗f1(e2) ♕b6 or 21 ♘c3 cxd4 22 ♘b5 ♕b6 23 exd4 ♘b8 White's advantage would be largely symbolic.

21 ♖ac1

The first critical moment.

21...♘d5?!

Unexpectedly helping the opponent to carry out e3-e4 (with gain of tempo!) and to seize the initiative. Black should have either 'stood his ground' with 21...♖fe8, or decided on 21...c5, since after 22 ♕b3 ♕xb3 23 ♗xb3 b6 24 ♔g2 (24 ♘c3 e5!) 24...e5 or 22 ♗c3!? cxd4 23 ♗xd4 ♗c5 24 ♗c3 ♖c8 White's achievements are slight.

22 e4 ♘5f6

22...♖c8 23 ♗e2 or 22...♘b4 23 ♘xb4 (exchanging the 'bad' a2-knight) 23...♗xb4 24 ♗e3 ♕c7 25 d5 etc. is hardly any better.

23 ♗e2!

A good, provocative move. I wanted to prevent ...e6-e5 by 23 ♗f4, but then after 23...♘b8! Black becomes somewhat more active. The d2-bishop will be useful on e3!

23...e5?!

Timman succumbs to the provocation, for the moment not sensing that this advance is merely to the advantage of the white bishops. The lesser evil was 23...c5! 24 ♗e3 ♕c6 with an inferior, but still defensible position: for example, 25 f3 b6 26 b4 axb4 27 ♘xb4 ♕b7 etc.

24 ♗e3 exd4 (if 24...♕c7, then 25 d5! is unpleasant) **25 ♗xd4 ♕c7** (after 25...c5 26 ♗e3 and ♘c3 the weakness of the b5- and d5-squares is perceptible) **26 f4**

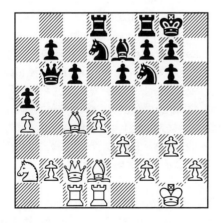

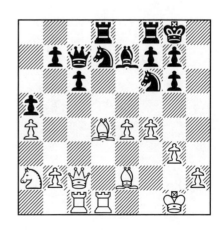

Thus, White has complete domination of the centre, to where he only needs to carefully bring up his reclusive knight, after which he will begin a decisive attack.

26...g5?!

In a difficult situation Timman tries to complicate matters, but this weakening of his king's defences merely hastens the end.

27 e5! ♞d5

27...♞e8 28 ♔h1! c5 29 ♕e4 was no better, while after 27...gxf4 28 exf6 ♗xf6 29 ♔g2 Black does not have serious compensation for the piece.

28 ♕e4! (setting up the attacking ♕+♗ battery with gain of tempo: at the same time ♕xd5 is threatened) **28...♞7b6**

28...♞5b6 would not have saved Black in view of 29 ♗d3 (the 'lateral' 29 ♗h5 gxf4 30 e6! is also strong) 29...g6 30 f5 ♞xa4 31 fxg6 ♞dc5 32 gxf7+ ♖xf7 33 ♕g6+ ♖g7 34 ♗c4+ ♔h8 35 ♕f5 with a powerful attack.

29 ♗d3 g6

After 29...f5?! 30 exf6 ♞xf6 White wins by both 31 ♗xf6 ♗xf6 32 ♕h7+ ♔f7 33 fxg5, and 31 ♕e6+ ♔h8 32 ♗g6 or 32 ♕h3+ ♔g8 33 ♗xf6 etc. I thought that in any case the end was close, but it all turned out to be not so simple...

30 f5 f6!

Belated resourcefulness.

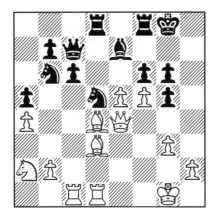

31 fxg6 f5 32 ♕e2 ♔g7

32...♞f4(?) does not work, in the first instance on account of 33 gxf4 ♖xd4 34 ♕h5!. And if 32...g4 the most accurate is 33 ♖f1!.

'It appears that Black has succeeded in erecting a barrier between the white pieces and his king. However, as a result of the clever tactical exchanges which soon ensue, the last word remains with the commander of the white pieces.' (Zaitsev)

33 ♕h5 (the 'quiet' 33 ♗b1!? is also good) **33...♖h8 34 ♕f3 ♞f4!?**

Not wishing to suffer after 34...f4 35 ♗e4 ♕c8 36 g4, Timman launches a desperate counter-attack.

35 ♗xf5 ♖xd4! 36 ♖xd4 ♕xe5 37 ♖e4! **♗c5+ 38 ♔h1 ♕xf5** (if 38...♕xb2, then 39 ♕c3+! ♕xc3 40 ♖xc3 and wins) **39 gxf4** **♗d6**

The alternatives were also insufficient: 39...g4 (39...♖h3? 40 ♖xc5) 40 ♕d3!, and 39...♞d7 40 ♕d3!, when if 40...♖f8 or 40...♕d5 – 41 ♖d1!.

40 ♕c3+! ♔xg6 41 ♕d3!

'After this Black's temporary counter-initiative dies away and the end is close.' (Zaitsev)

41...♗e7 42 fxg5 (the flamboyant 42 ♖c5?! was worse in view of 42...♞d5) **42...♕d5 43** **♕e2** (43 ♕c2! was even stronger) **43...♖h4** **44 ♞c3 ♖xe4 45 ♞xe4**

The endgame after 45 ♕xe4+ ♕xe4+ 46 ♞xe4 ♞xa4 47 b3 is also won.

45...♞xa4 46 ♖d1 ♕e6 47 ♕c2! ♕f5 48 **♕xa4 ♕f3+ 49 ♔g1 ♕g4+** (there is also no perpetual check after 49...♗c5+ 50 ♞xc5 ♕e3+ 51 ♔g2 ♕e2+ 52 ♔g3 ♕e3+ 53 ♔g4 ♕e2+ 54 ♔f4 etc.) **50 ♔f2 ♕f4+ 51 ♔e2** **♕g4+ 52 ♔d3 ♗b4** (52...b5 53 ♕c2!) **53 ♕c2** **♕f3+ 54 ♔d4 ♔g7 55 ♔e5! 1-0**

This win brought me a double joy – both creative and competitive. As a result it also enabled me to win my mini-match with Timman, which at that time was not easy, even for the world champion, and it practically decided the question of the match-tournament winner.

In the next round Karpov had White against me, and this was his last attempt to join the fight for first place, but things ended in a draw. This was the position after the third cycle: Kasparov – 6½ out of 9; Karpov – 5; Timman – 4; van der Wiel – 2½. Effectively the fight for the allocation of the places was already decided. In the 10th round I beat van der Wiel, while Karpov drew with Timman, and my lead increased to two points.

And then came the concluding duel of the champions, already our 127th encounter. Although Karpov had achieved a relatively modest objective – finished ahead of Timman in the fight for second place, the game, as always, was an important one for both of us. I wanted to gain a win which was not 'dubious' (as in the second cycle), but 'clean' – to show everyone that I could also play differently.

> ### Game 34
> **G.Kasparov-A.Karpov**
> Amsterdam, 4th Cycle,
> 11th Round, 26.05.1988
> *Caro-Kann Defence B17*

1 e4

In Seville I played this only twice, and both times I stumbled against the Caro-Kann, but I had not given up hope of breaching this 'concrete' defence.

1...c6 2 d4 d5 3 ♘d2 dxe4 4 ♘xe4 ♘d7 5 ♘g5

Avoiding 5 ♘f3 ♘gf6 6 ♘g3 e6, as in our game from the 2nd cycle. In the 8th round van der Wiel played 5 ♗d3 against Karpov,

but after 5...♘df6! 6 ♘g5 ♗g4 7 ♘1f3 ♗h5 8 c3 e6 9 ♕b3 ♕c7 10 ♘e5 ♗d6 Black equalised. For the 1990 match I also prepared the variation 5 ♗c4 ♘gf6 6 ♘g5 e6 7 ♕e2 ♘b6 8 ♗b3, which I was able to employ only later (*Game No.85*).

5...♘gf6 (6) **6 ♗d3**

A fresh idea for that time (compared with the usual 6 ♗c4), to which attention was drawn after a fine win by Geller over Meduna (Sochi 1986).

6...e6 (6...h6?! 7 ♘e6!) **7 ♘1f3**

7...♗d6

A solid move, in contrast to the incautious 7...♕c7?! 8 ♕e2 (threatening ♘xf7) 8...h6 9 ♗g6! hxg5 10 ♗xf7+! ♔d8 11 ♘xg5 (van der Wiel-Karpov, Amsterdam 1987), or 7...h6?! 8 ♘xe6!: for example, 8...♕e7 9 0-0 fxe6 10 ♗g6+ ♔d8 11 ♗f4 (11 c4!?), as in Geller-Meduna and also in the memorable game Deep Blue-Kasparov (6th match game, New York 1997), or 8...fxe6 9 ♗g6+ ♔e7 10 0-0 ♕c7 11 ♖e1 ♔d8 12 c4! ♗b4 13 ♖e2 (Wolff-Granda, New York 1992), and everywhere White has powerful compensation for the piece.

8 0-0 (7)

The main line later became 8 ♕e2 h6 9 ♘e4 ♘xe4 10 ♕xe4 – the modern *tabiya* of the variation, which I began studying before the 1990 match. Here my opponent initially played 10...♘f6 11 ♕e2 (11 ♕h4 ♔e7!?, Kamsky-Karpov, Dortmund 1993) 11...b6 12 ♗d2 ♗b7 13 0-0-0 ♕c7 (right up to his 8th match game with Kamsky, Elista 1996), and then 10...c5, or, most often, 10...♕c7 11 ♕g4 ♔f8, avoiding the unclear 11...g5 (Kasparov-Kamsky, Linares 1994) or 11...♖g8 (Kasparov-Anand, Linares 1998).

At the board I also considered the more aggressive 8 ♕e2, but in the end I decided to castle. The position was new, and in the existing competitive situation I decided to play simply for a small plus – it is clear that here White cannot gain any serious advantage.

8...h6 9 ♘e4 ♘xe4 10 ♗xe4 0-0 (6)

In view of Black's intention to attack the centre (by ...c6-c5 or ...e6-e5), this is more accurate than 10...♘f6 or 10...♕c7 with the idea of ...b7-b6, ...♗b7 and ...0-0-0.

11 c3!? (5)

Amazingly, 11 c4 e5 12 ♗c2 would have led to almost the same position as in my game with Hübner, where in the end White obtained the same advantageous balance of forces: bishop against knight with a weak pawn on e6 (*Game No.24*).

True, Karpov would have had two trumps: my a-pawn would still have been on a2 and, far more important, his h-pawn would already have been on h6 – a useful move! Black effectively has an extra tempo compared with the variation 1 d4 d5 2 c4 c6 3 ♘c3 ♘f6 4 ♘f3 e6 5 e3 ♘bd7 6 ♗d3 ♗d6 7 e4 dxe4 8 ♘xe4 ♘xe4 9 ♗xe4 0-0 10 0-0 h6 11 ♗c2 (as played long ago by Steinitz in his matches with Chigorin and Lasker) 11...e5 – here it is White to move, and after 12 ♖e1 exd4 13 ♕xd4 ♗c5 14 ♕c3 a5 15 a3 ♘f6 16 ♗e3 (16 ♗xh6!? gxh6 17 ♖ad1 is sharper, with an attack) 16...♗xe3 17 ♖xe3 he retains the initiative (Kasparov-Deep Blue, 4th

match game, Philadelphia 1996).

Therefore here 11 c4 has little point. Of course, with moves such as 11 c3 not much can be achieved, but even so accurate play is demanded of Black.

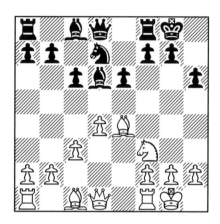

11...e5 (4)

In the only previous game Bellin-Thipsay (Swansea 1987) Black switched to passive defence – 11...♕c7 12 ♗c2 ♖e8?! 13 ♕d3 ♘f8. But later equality was gained by 11...♘f6 12 ♗c2 c5 (Smirin-Kharitonov, Podolsk 1990) or 11...c5 12 ♗c2 (according to Karpov, 12 dxc5 ♘xc5 13 ♗c2 ♕c7 14 ♕e2 is better for White, but after 14...b6! Black is okay) 12...♕c7 13 ♖e1 ♖d8 (Kamsky-Karpov, Tilburg 1991).

The opponent's novelty did not catch me unawares, since revolving in my mind was the set-up from my aforementioned game with Hübner.

12 ♗c2 (5) **12...♖e8 13 ♖e1 exd4** (6) **14 ♖xe8+ ♕xe8 15 ♕xd4 ♕e7?!** (5)

15...♕e2?! would have led in a round-about way to the same thing after 16 ♗d2! ♗c5 17 ♕h4 ♕e7 18 ♕g3! (18 ♗g5 ♕e2) 18...♗d6 19 ♗f4 ♗xf4 20 ♕xf4. And 15...♗e7?! 16 ♗f4 (of course, not 16 ♗xh6?! gxh6 17 ♖e1 ♘f8 18 ♕e3 ♗e6 19 ♕xh6 because of 19...♕d8! and ...♗f6) 16...♗f6 (Karpov, Zaitsev) is weak in view of 17 ♕d6!

♕e7 (17...♘f8 18 ♗xh6) 18 ♖e1, when Black faces a difficult struggle for a draw.

However, 15...♗c5! 16 ♕h4 ♕e7 (not 16...♗e7? 17 ♕g3) was better, maintaining approximate equality: 17 ♕xe7 ♗xe7 18 ♗f4 ♘f6 19 ♖e1 ♗f8 or 17 ♗g5 (a recommendation of Karpov and Zaitsev) 17...♘f6! with the idea of 18 ♗xf6 ♕xf6, intending ...♗e6 and ...♖e8.

But, to all appearances, Karpov also considered 15...♕e7 to be acceptable.

16 ♗f4! (5)

The same motifs are evident as in my games with Hübner and Deep Blue: the exchange of the dark-squared bishops, the development of the queen's rook with gain of tempo, and the aim of obtaining light-squared bishop against knight with the better pawn structure.

16...♗xf4 (8)

Black should perhaps have gone into a slightly inferior position with the bishops on – 16...♗c5!? 17 ♕d3 ♘f8 or 17 ♕d2 ♘f6, when it is unclear how serious White's initiative is. However, for the moment Black is still within the zone of equality.

17 ♕xf4 ♘f8 (17...♘f6?! is worse: 18 ♖e1 ♗e6 19 ♘d4 etc.) **18 ♖e1 ♗e6** (but not 18...♘e6? 19 ♕e4 g6 20 h4!: for example, 20...♕f6 21 h5 gxh5 22 ♖e3!) **19 ♘d4**

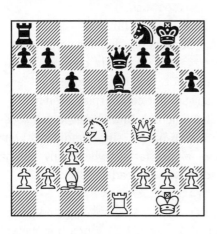

19...♖d8?!

19...♖e8! (with the idea of 20 ♗b3 ♕d8) was stronger – this recommendation of Karpov and Zaitsev was soon put into practice: 20 g3 (20 ♘f5? is refuted by the amusing 20...♗xf5 21 ♖xe7 ♖xe7) 20...♕d8 21 ♖d1?! ♗h3 22 ♘f3 ♕e7 23 ♕d6 ♕e2, and it was now White who had to seek a way to equalise by 24 ♕d3 (Smirin-Khalifman, Moscow 1989). 21 ♘xe6 ♖xe6 is correct, and now either 22 ♖xe6 ♘xe6 23 ♕e3 (Khalifman), or 22 ♖d1 ♕e7 23 b4 and then ♗b3. It is probable that this too is a draw, but Fischer with White would have played on for a long time in an attempt to win. Thus even after the best defence Black would have faced certain trials.

20 h4!

This does not signal the start of an attack, but is a link in the strategic plan. White takes away the g5-square from the opponent and thereby further cramps the movement of the black pieces.

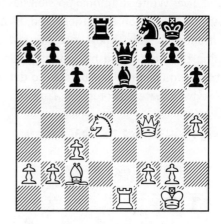

20...♕c5?! (10)

Another small concession. Karpov does not sense the danger and he loses time. 20...♕d6 at once was preferable (Karpov, Zaitsev), and after 21 ♘xe6 ♘xe6 22 ♕e4 ♔f8 (22...♘f8!?) 23 g3 (Ulibin-Giorgadze, Simferopol 1988; 23 ♕h7?! ♕d2!) 23...♕e7 White's advantage would have been rather smaller.

21 ♖e3! (15)

One of my patent methods: the rook is threatening to join the attack on the king along the third rank.

21...♕d6 (19) **22 ♘xe6 fxe6?**

Hanging over the board is the spectre of the 24th game of the match in Seville: Karpov goes in for the same pawn structure, and with almost the same balance of forces – without the rooks it would be identical!

Of course, 22...♘xe6 23 ♕e4 ♘f8 was more resilient (if 23...♔f8?, then 24 ♕h7! is unpleasant). Although after 24 g3 all the same Black's position is worse (White has gained several tempi and he can attack the f7-point), it is as yet too early to attach a '±' sign. After the exchange of the heavy pieces the situation will begin to resemble the ending of the 10th game of the 1986 match, where there was also a light-squared bishop against a knight – true, without the c-pawns. Whom does their presence favour? I think that it gives White additional possibilities.

After 22...fxe6, on the other hand, Black's position is already almost lost. Karpov was hoping that by placing his knight passively at f8 he would somehow be able to defend, but why create chronic weaknesses for himself?

23 ♕g4 (9) **23...♕d2 24 ♗b3!**

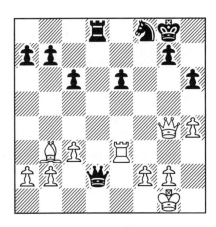

24...♔h8

It transpires that 24...♕xb2? is bad in view of 25 ♖g3! ♕b1+ 26 ♔h2 ♕h7 27 ♗c2! ♕h8 28 h5, practically forcing 28...g5 29 hxg6 ♖d7 30 ♕f4 or 29...♔g7 30 ♗b3 with a decisive advantage for White.

25 ♖e2 ♕d6 26 g3

With the weak pawn on e6 the only question is whether White will succeed in converting his advantage. The main thing is not to rush: this is the most terrible thing for the opponent, since it is possible for White to alternate between various plans.

26...a6 27 ♔g2

Not rushing with 27 ♗xe6?! ♘xe6 28 ♖xe6, since after 28...♕d1+ 29 ♕xd1 ♖xd1+ 30 ♔g2 ♖d2 Black easily gains a draw in the rook ending.

27...♖e8 28 ♖e3 ♖e7 29 ♖f3 ♖d7 30 ♕h5

Exploiting the opponent's forced passivity, White gradually improves the placing of his pieces.

30...♕e7 31 ♕e5

31 g4!? came into consideration, with the threat of a direct attack on the king: for example, 31...♔g8 32 g5 hxg5 33 hxg5 g6 34 ♕g4 ♕d6 35 ♖f6 ♖e7 36 ♕e4(f3), and White has an obvious advantage. But in the fourth hour of play I did not want to weaken my king's defences and determine the position too much.

31...♖d8 32 a4 b5 (8)

A questionable decision, typical of Karpov's manner of play in cramped positions: he did not like being 'squeezed' and he usually sought counterplay even at the cost of strategic risk. Thus here he weakens the a6- and c6-pawns, since he did not want to allow a4-a5 (after which any endgame would have been bad for Black).

33 ♕e4 (6) **33...♕c7 34 ♖f4** (7)

Later 34 axb5 was suggested with the idea of 34...axb5?! 35 ♕b4!, but the strong reply 34...cxb5! would have made things more difficult for White: for example, 35 ♗a2 ♕d7 36 b4 ♔g8 37 ♗b3 ♖c8.

34...c5 35 ♕f3 ♕d6

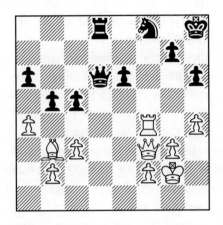

36 axb5

Again there was some sense in maintaining the pawn tension, to retain the a4-a5 resource: after 36 ♕b7!? Black would have faced a difficult defence. However, even after the text it is no easier.

36...axb5 37 ♖f7 ♖b8?! (6)

Maintaining the b-pawn, but the lesser evil was 37...c4 38 ♗c2 ♔g8 39 ♖b7 ♖d7!, when 40 ♖xb5?? is not possible because of 40...♖f7 (41 ♕e4 ♕d2). 40 ♖xd7?! is unclear: 40...♘xd7! 41 ♗g6 ♘e5 42 ♕a8+ ♕f8 43 ♗h7+ ♔f7 44 ♕a7+ (44 ♕b7+ ♔f6 with the threat of ...g7-g6) 44...♕e7 45 ♕b8 ♔f6 46 ♗e4 ♕d7. But after, say, 40 ♗e4 sooner or later Black would have lost a pawn: 40...♕e5 41 ♕e3! ♔f7 42 ♖b6 etc, or 40...♖xb7 41 ♗xb7 (threatening ♕c6) 41...♕d2 (if 41...b4, then 42 ♕e4 is possible) 42 ♗c6 ♕xb2 43 ♗e8 ♕a3 44 ♕f7+ ♔h7 45 ♗xb5 ♕a5 46 ♗c6 ♕f5 47 ♕xf5+ exf5 48 ♔f3 ♔g6 49 ♔e3, picking up the c4-pawn and winning.

38 ♖a7?

In the heat of the battle I missed the forceful 38 ♕g4! ♕e5 39 f4 ♕e4+ 40 ♔f2 g6 (40...♘g6 41 ♕xe6 or 40...♕h7 41 f5! exf5 42

♕f4 etc. does not help) 41 ♕f3 ♕xf3+ 42 ♔xf3 with a won ending.

38...b4 39 ♗c2 (this appealed to me more than 39 cxb4 cxb4 40 ♕e4 ♔g8 41 ♗c4)

39...bxc3 40 bxc3

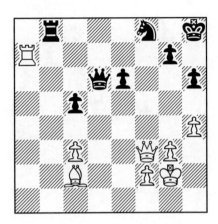

40...♕e5?

40...♖d8! was more resilient, with the idea of ...♖d7 (and if 41 ♗b3, now 41...♕e5). However, Karpov, apparently remembering Seville, did not want to initiate the exchange of rooks and, being in slight time-trouble, with his last move before the time control he simply centralised his queen.

41 ♖f7 (13)

Again I unhurriedly manoeuvre, assuming that White's advantage will not run away. Meanwhile, 41 c4!, the move suggested by Karpov and Zaitsev, would not only have increased it, but also led to the almost forced win of the c5-pawn, and with it the game: 41...♖d8 42 ♖f7 ♔g8 43 ♕b7 ♕d4 (the queen cannot be maintained on this square) 44 ♕e7! ♖c8 (44...♖b8 45 ♖f4) 45 ♔h2 ♖a8 46 ♖f4 ♕d8 47 ♕xc5 etc.

41...♘h7 (9) **42 ♕g4**

Again 42 c4! was strong, with the sequel 42...♕d4 43 ♖f4 ♕b2 (43...♕d7 44 ♕h5!) 44 ♗xh7 ♔xh7 45 ♕e4+ ♔h8 46 ♕xe6, and this time White has a won heavy piece endgame.

42...♔g8 43 ♖e7? (the correct way was 43 ♖a7 ♘f8 44 ♕f3, when after 44...c4 45 ♕f7+ ♔h8 46 ♕c7 the c4-pawn is lost, but otherwise White reverts to the plan with c3-c4) **43...♘f8 44 ♕f3**

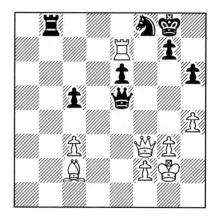

44...c4! (9)

An excellent chance! 'Exploiting the fact that White did not play a timely c3-c4 and has not taken control of the very important d5-square.' (Zaitsev). Karpov is hoping to exchange his e6- and c4-pawns for the pawn on c3 and gain a draw with two pawns against three on the same wing.

45 ♗e4 (8)

White has acquired a new target – the c4-pawn, and I decided to aim for the exchange of rooks, in order to then win this pawn with the bishop and obtain the 'Seville structure' in pure form. It has to be said that the analogy with the ending of the 24th game of the 1987 match clearly weighed on both players.

After 45 ♗a4 (with the intention of ♖e8) 45...♕d5!? Black would have retained better saving chances. But it was possible to begin the pursuit of the c4-pawn while keeping the rooks on – 45 ♖a7!?, in order after 45...♕d5 46 ♗e4 ♕e5 47 ♖a4 (or 45...♖c8 46 ♗e4 ♖b8 47 ♖a4) 47...♖c8 48 ♖a6 ♕f6 49 ♕xf6 gxf6 50 ♖c6! to transpose into a technically won endgame with bishop

against knight. Therefore 45...♖d8!? is a more resilient defence, with the idea of 46 ♗e4 ♘d7! or 46 ♕f7+ ♔h8 47 ♕e7 ♖c8 48 ♕b7 (48 ♕b4 ♕d5+) 48...♖d8 49 ♕c7 ♕d5+ 50 ♔g1 ♖d7.

45...♔h8 (6) **46 ♗c6 ♘h7** (9) **47 ♕f7** (6) **47...♘f8** (9) **48 ♖e8** (11)

Achieving the desired exchange – and reducing Black hopes of eliminating the c3-pawn. 48 ♗e8 ♘h7 49 ♕xe6 ♕xc3 would have led to this immediately – after 50 ♖c7 or 50 ♗f7 White would have won the c4-pawn, but not the game. Obsessed by the 'Seville syndrome', I thought that without the rooks White's position should be won.

48...♖xe8 49 ♗xe8

It is clear that the c4-pawn is doomed, and the fact that the Seville e3-pawn has moved to c3 should seemingly be only to White's advantage.

49...♘h7! (7)

A strong move – the knight is activated even at the cost of a pawn. 'Although Black has managed to get rid of the terrible rook on the 7th rank, nevertheless for the moment it is only a question of obtaining practical saving chances' (Zaitsev), and Karpov was once again in time-trouble...

50 ♗d7 ♘f6 51 ♗xe6

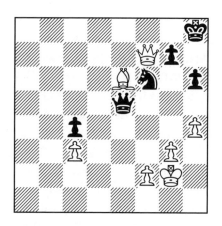

51...h5?

Also the 'Seville syndrome': with his pawn on h5 it becomes unacceptable for Black to exchange queens (it is curious that this important moment is not mentioned by Karpov and Zaitsev in their commentary). The best chance was 51...♔h7!. After 52 ♗xc4 ♕xc3 53 ♕e6 ♕d4 the win for White is problematic. And in the event of 52 h5!? ♕e4+ 53 ♔h2 ♕c2 it is possible to exchange the queens, but after 54 ♕g6+ ♕xg6 55 hxg6+ ♔xg6 56 ♗xc4 ♔f5 or 54 ♕a7 ♕e4 55 ♕e3 ♕xe3 56 fxe3 ♘xh5 57 ♗xc4 ♔g6 Black retains hopes of saving the ending a pawn down.

52 ♗xc4 ♕e4+

White's task has become much easier. If 52...♕xc3 he wins by 53 ♕f8+ ♔h7 54 ♕c5! (with the threat of ♗g8+) 54...♔h6 55 ♕g5+ ♔h7 56 ♗f7 or 54...♕d2 55 ♕f5+ ♔h8 (55...♔h6? 56 ♗f7) 56 ♗f7 ♕d1(e2) 57 ♗g6, picking up a second pawn.

53 ♔h2 ♔h7?

'The time deficit and the fatigue, caused by having to conduct a difficult defence, make themselves felt. 53...♕f3 was necessary, after which the world champion was intending 54 ♕f8+! with the sequel 54...♔h7 55 ♕c5 ♘e4 56 ♗d5 ♕xg3+! (this entire variation was given by Karpov immediately after the game) 57 fxg3 ♘xc5 58 ♗f3! (an important nuance, to which Kasparov draws particular attention – for a time the black king is restricted to playing a very modest role) 58...♔h6 59 ♔g2 g5 60 c4! *[but not 60 ♔f2? ♘a4 61 c4 ♘b2 62 ♗e2 ♘xc4 63 ♗xc4 gxh4 with a draw – G.K.]*. Now Black can play either 60...gxh4, or, as Karpov suggests, the immediate 60...♔g6, which is probably rather more cunning, since the g5-pawn covers the f4-square in the event of the white king invading. This would have left Black with definite practical chances, although the overall evaluation of the end-game is obviously unfavourable for him.' (Zaitsev)

And, indeed, White gradually wins by activating his king and exploiting the weakness of the h5-pawn: 60...♔g6 (things are not changed by 60...gxh4 61 gxh4 or 60...♘a4 61 ♔f1!, and it is not possible to give up the knight for the c-pawn) 61 ♔f2 ♘e6 62 ♔e3 ♘g7 63 ♗e4+ (or 63 ♔e4) 63...♔f6 64 ♔d4 ♘e6+ 65 ♔d5 etc. – Black is unable to prevent the advance of the c4-pawn to the queening square.

By playing 53...♔h7, Karpov wanted to break out with his king, but after this move White immediately parries all the opponent's threats.

54 ♕e6! ♕f3 55 ♕e1 (it is all over: Black is two pawns down) **55...♘g4+ 56 ♔g1 ♕c6 57 ♗d3+ g6 58 ♕e7+ ♔h6 59 ♗e4 ♕b6 60 ♕f8+ ♔h7 61 ♕f7+ ♔h6 62 c4 ♕a6** (12)

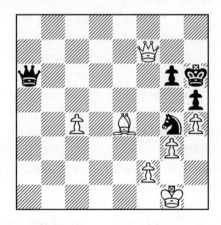

'Of course, it was also possible to resign, but it is typical for a human player to hope for a miracle. Suppose White were to play 63 ♕f8+ ♔h7 and only now 64 c5? Will not the stalemating mechanism operate after 64...♕a1+ 65 ♔g2 ♘e3+! (66 fxe3? ♕h1+! 67 ♔f2 ♕f1+ 68 ♔xf1 – stalemate)? Alas, on closer examination of this illusion it transpires that after 66 ♔f3! ♕d1+ 67 ♔f4 ♘d5+ (67...♕g4+ 68 ♔e5 ♘c4+ 69 ♔f6 with mate) it self-destructs by 68 ♔e5 ♕a1+ 69 ♔e6 ♘c7+ 70 ♔d7.' (Zaitsev)

63 c5 1-0

An interesting game, full of instructive analogies with two of my previous wins – this never occurred again in my career.

The situation before the last round was highly unusual: I was on '+6', whereas the other contestants had not more than 50%. Something similar had already occurred with me at the super-tournament in Brussels (1986), where only Korchnoi, by winning in the last round, climbed to '+1'. Here with a final effort Karpov reached '+1', and he took 2nd place, 2½ points behind me.

Nikitin: *'The world champion's victory in Amsterdam was complete and impressive. He won all three mini-matches, did not lose a single game, scored more wins than all the others put together, and by a big margin won the prize for the most aggressive player. Garry now has an optimal manner of play, and the correct approach to preparation. What is evident is his striving for interesting play in every game, and for intensive work at the board, as Fischer used to do. Garry has remained above all a creator, a researcher; the main thing for him is the richness of the play, which (he firmly believes this!) also ensures the necessary number of points.'*

Almost 'The Tournament of my Life'

Second World Cup Tournament (Belfort, 12 June – 4 July 1988): 1. **Kasparov** – 11½ out of 15; 2. Karpov – 10½; 3. Ehlvest – 9; 4–7. Ribli, Hübner, I.Sokolov and Spassky – 8; 8. Short – 7½; 9. Speelman – 7; 10–13. Ljubojevic, Andersson, Nogueiras and Beliavsky – 6½; 14–16. Hjartarson, Yusupov and Timman – 5½.

Two weeks after Amsterdam, Karpov and I again met, when we arrived in the French town of Belfort for the second stage of the World Cup. The initial tournament in April, in which I did not take part, was confidently won by my arch-rival (1. Karpov – 11 out of 16; 2. Salov – 10; 3–5. Ljubojevic, Beliavsky and Nunn – 9½, etc.), and now everyone was awaiting a fierce direct confrontation between us.

I should remind you that the two-year series of the first World Cup consisted of six big (16-18 participants) super-tournaments with the classical time control: in 1988 – Brussels, Belfort and Reykjavik, and in 1989 – Barcelona, Rotterdam and Skellefteå. The 25 strongest grandmasters in the world took part – each played in four of the six tournaments, and the three best results were added up. One representative of each of the organising countries had the right to play without his score counting. For the unification of the tournaments the points scored were always counted out of 16 games (if in fact fewer were played, arbitrary draws were added) and to these points were added: for 1st place – 17 points, for 2nd place – 16, for 3rd – 15, and so on. Karpov and I were due to meet twice, and after lengthy discussions the choice fell on Belfort and Skellefteå – the peak of intrigue, the final stage!

I arrived in Belfort after a short training session in Zagulba (where I was assisted by Gurevich and Psakhis) and, inspired by my Amsterdam triumph, I was intending to continue my sequence of successful performances. At the demand of the organisers, semi-forced pairings were made – such that Karpov and I would play each other as near as possible to the finish. The pairings had to be made several times, until our game fell in the penultimate, 14th round.

Karpov began with a loss against Sokolov, whereas I won against Yusupov, who suddenly gave up a pawn in a drawn ending.

Then I defeated Nogueiras, drew with Ribli and Hübner, and in the 5th round with the black pieces I overcame Jan Timman – who later failed in the race, but in those days was still full of high hopes.

1 d4 ♘f6 2 c4 g6 3 ♘c3 d5 4 ♗f4 ♗g7 5 e3 c5 6 dxc5 ♕a5 7 ♕a4+ ♕xa4 8 ♘xa4 0-0

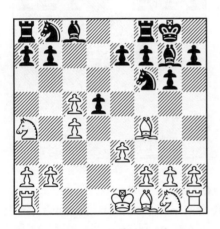

A fresh move, which I had already tried against Timman in the fourth cycle of the match-tournament in Amsterdam. In the second cycle I chose 8...♘e4 (8...♘a6 or 8...♗d7 is also played) 9 f3 ♗d7 10 fxe4 ♗xa4 11 cxd5 ♗xb2 12 ♖b1 ♗c3+ 13 ♔f2 ♘d7 14 ♖c1 (14 ♘e2!?) 14...♘xc5 15 ♔f3 ♗b4 16 ♖c4 ♗b5! 17 ♖xb4 ♗xf1 18 ♘e2 ♗xe2+ 19 ♔xe2, and White retained slightly the better endgame.

Knowing how my opponent stuck to his opening principles, I was almost certain that the variation would be repeated.

9 ♘f3

After the natural 9 ♖c1 ♗d7 10 ♘c3 dxc4

11 ♗xc4 Black has not only 11...♘a6 (Salov-Korchnoi, Brussels 1988), but also a promising exchange sacrifice – 11...♖c8 12 b4 a5 13 b5 a4! 14 ♘d5 ♘xd5 15 ♗xd5 ♗xb5 16 ♗xb7 ♘a6 17 ♗xa8 ♖xa8 18 ♘e2 ♗b2, when it is now White who has to seek equality (Rashkovsky-Dvoirys, Elista 1996).

9...♘e4 10 ♗e5

Little is promised by 10 cxd5 ♗d7: for example, 11 ♗d3 ♗xa4 12 ♗xe4 ♘d7 (Novikov-Lputian, Blagoveshchensk 1988) or 11 c6 bxc6 12 ♗c4 c5! 13 ♗d3 ♗xa4 14 ♗xe4 ♘d7 15 d6 ♖ae8 with equality (Dreev-Ivanchuk, London (rapid) 1995).

10...♗d7 11 ♘c3 ♘xc3 12 bxc3 dxc4 13 ♗xc4 ♖c8

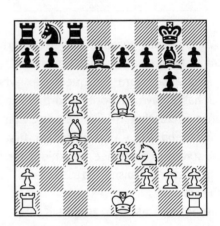

14 ♗d4

And here is a novelty. In our recent Amsterdam game Timman played 14 ♗d5, but after 14...♗c6 15 ♗xc6 ♖xc6 16 ♗xg7 ♔xg7 17 ♖b1 ♖c7 18 ♘d4 ♘a6 Black did not experience any problems.

14...e5!

The correct reply. If 14...♘c6, then 15 ♖b1! e5 16 ♖xb7 ♗e8 17 ♖b1 exd4 18 cxd4 with three strong central pawns for the piece. After the game Timman and I discussed this position and came to the conclusion that it is rather more pleasant for White.

15 ♗xe5 ♖xc5 16 ♗xg7 ♔xg7 17 ♗b3

Black also has no problems after 17 ♘d2 ♘c6 18 ♗b3 (18 ♖c1 ♖d8!) 18...♗f5 or 18...♘a5 (but not 18...♖xc3? 19 ♘e4), inevitably regaining the pawn.

17...♖xc3 18 0-0

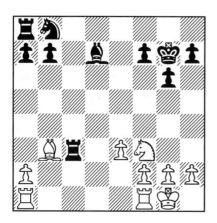

White already needs to exercise a certain caution. It was hardly right for him to take his king away from the queenside, where Black has a pawn majority and there is the chance of creating an outside passed pawn. 18 ♔d2 and ♖hc1 was better, or first 18 ♘e5, trying to exchange the knight for the dangerous black bishop (18...♗e8 19 ♘c4! with equality).

18...♘a6! 19 ♘e5 ♗e8! 20 ♗d5 ♖c7!

Black temporarily retreats, in order to establish his knight on c5 and begin the advance of his a- and b-pawns, whereas White has no good counter-plan. The hasty 20...♘c5 would have allowed the exchange of the active rook – 21 ♖ac1 ♖xc1 22 ♖xc1, and after 22...♖d8! 23 ♖xc5 b6 24 ♖c7 ♖xd5 25 f4 or 24 ♘c6 ♗xc6 25 ♖xc6 ♖xd5 26 g4 it would all have ended in a draw.

21 ♖ab1 ♘c5 22 e4 ♖d8 (prophylaxis against f2-f4, but the immediate 22...♖ac8! was more accurate, not fearing 23 f4 in view of 23...b6 with the idea of ...♘a4-c3) **23 ♖fc1**

If 23 f4?!, then 23...♖e7 with the threat of ...f7-f6 is good, as is 23...f6 24 ♘f3 ♖e7 (my

Informator suggestion 24...f5(?!) is unclear because of 25 ♖bc1) 25 f5 ♗f7 26 ♗xf7 ♔xf7 27 fxg6+ ♔xg6, winning a pawn.

23...♖dc8

The immediate 23...b5 was weaker because of 24 ♘d3 ♖dc8 25 ♘xc5 ♖xc5 26 ♖xc5 ♖xc5 27 ♔f1 with a probable draw. Here Timman sensed that his position might become worse, and he grew nervous.

24 g4

Pseudo-activity, which later rebounds on White. 24 ♘c4!? was more solid.

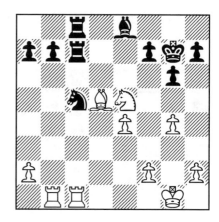

24...f6

It was perhaps more promising to play 24...b5!? 25 g5 f6 26 gxf6+ ♔xf6 27 f4 ♘a4 or 27 ♘g4+ ♔g5 28 ♘e3 ♘d3.

25 ♘f3

It was sounder to stabilise the position by 25 ♘c4!? (but not 25 ♗xb7? ♖b8!) 25...♖d8 (25...♘xe4 26 ♖xb7 with equality) 26 ♘e3 b6 27 f3, when White is close to equalising.

25...b6 26 ♘d4

Timman was hoping that the knight manoeuvre to d4 would give him some counterplay, but in Black's position there are no real targets to attack.

26...♗d7 (26...♗f7!?) **27 f3 ♘d3!**

In White's position, on the other hand, there are weaknesses, and in addition his pawn wedge e4-f3-g4 is stuck on light squares, which will be uncomfortable in the event of a bishop endgame. But with the rooks on, Black develops c-file pressure.

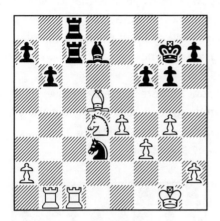

28 ℤxc7

In view of the fact that, with every exchange, the threat of Black creating an outside passed pawn on the queenside is strengthened, 28 ℤd1!? ♞f4 29 ♔f2 also came into consideration.

28...ℤxc7 29 ℤd1 ♞f4 30 ♔f2 ♔f8

White's position is continuing to deteriorate gradually. After 30...♞xd5 31 exd5 ♔f7 32 ♔g3 it would have been easier for him to gain a draw.

31 ♗b3

If 31 ♔e3!? Timman was afraid of 31...♞xd5+ 32 exd5 ℤc5. In *Informator* I evaluated this position in Black's favour on the basis of 33 ♔e4(?) ♔e7, but after 33 ♞c6(b3) things are not so clear. It would seem more sensible to fix the white pawns – 31...g5, but then there could follow 32 ♞e2 ♞xe2 33 ♔xe2 (with the idea of h2-h4 and ℤh1) 33...ℤc2+ 34 ♔d3! ℤxh2 35 ℤc1 and ℤc7 with counterplay, apparently sufficient for a draw.

31...♔e7 32 ♞e2?!

Getting rid of the annoying black knight merely aggravates White's difficulties. If 32 ♔e3 g5 did not appeal to him, he should

have chosen 32 h4! h6 33 h5!? g5 34 ♞f5+ ♗xf5 35 exf5, remaining with a long-range bishop against a knight, shut in on f4.

32...♞xe2 33 ♔xe2 ℤc3! (not 33...g5?! 34 h4! with equality) **34 h4 h6**

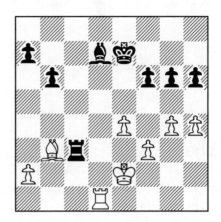

35 e5?

Forced over the course of the last fifteen moves to solve small, unnerving problems, Timman got into serious time-trouble and, cracking under the strain, unexpectedly gave up a pawn. But what should he have done instead?

Transposing into a bishop ending by 35 ℤd5 (or 35 ℤd2 g5) 35...♗c6 36 ℤd2 g5 37 hxg5 hxg5 38 ℤc2? was fatal in view of 38...♗b5+! 39 ♔f2(d2) ℤxc2+ 40 ♗xc2 ♗c4 and ...♔d6-e5, while against the attempt to break through in the centre – 35 ♔f2 a5 36 ℤe1 b5 37 e5 both 37...a4 and 37...f5 are promising. Perhaps the best chance consisted in 35 ℤg1!? b5 36 g5 fxg5 37 hxg5 h5 38 f4 and f4-f5 or 35...♗e6 36 ♗xe6 ♔xe6 37 a4 ℤa3 38 h5 g5 39 ℤc1! ℤxa4 40 ℤc7(c8), hoping to save the rook endgame a pawn down.

35...♗b5+ (35...fxe5! 36 ℤd5 ℤc5 37 ℤxc5 bxc5 would have restricted White's choice) **36 ♔f2 fxe5 37 ℤd5** (37 ℤe1 was more resilient) **37...ℤc5 38 ℤxc5 bxc5 39 g5** (39 ♔e3 g5!) **39...hxg5 40 hxg5**

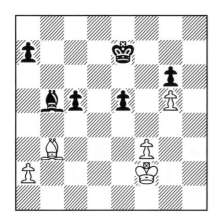

40...♗d3!

The threat is ...c5-c4 and ...♔e6-f5xg5.

41 ♗g8 ♗f5 42 ♗b3 ♗e6 43 ♗c2 ♗xa2 44 ♗xg6 a5 45 ♔e3 a4 0-1

A decent, strictly professional game: by positionally outplaying one of the world's leading grandmasters in a quiet endgame, I once again demonstrated that my style had become far more diverse.

With 4 out of 5 I took the lead, but after three draws – with Speelman, Spassky and Hjartarson (when I had an absolutely won position!) – Jaan Ehlvest moved half a point ahead. The World Cup tournaments were his finest hour, especially Belfort, where he played with great energy and invention.

In the 9th round the pursuit of the leader began. Playing Black against Ljubomir Ljubojevic, to raise my competitive tone I chose one of the most risky Sicilian set-ups.

> ### Game 36
> **L.Ljubojevic-G.Kasparov**
> World Cup, Belfort
> 9th Round, 25.06.1988
> *Sicilian Defence B81*

1 e4 c5 2 ♘f3 e6 3 d4 cxd4 4 ♘xd4 ♘f6

(more often I used to avoid the Keres Attack with 4...♘c6) **5 ♘c3 d6 6 g4 ♘c6**

The first game of my 1984/85 match with Karpov went 6...h6, but that is what nearly all Ljubojevic's previous opponents had played, and so I had prepared the plan with kingside castling.

7 g5 ♘d7 8 ♖g1

Soon a more accurate move order appeared – 8 ♗e3 ♗e7 9 h4 0-0 10 ♕h5! and 0-0-0, not wasting time on ♖g1.

8...♗e7 9 ♗e3 0-0

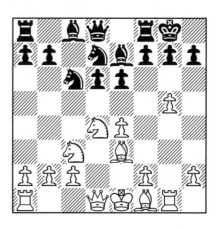

Of course, White's impending pawn storm is very dangerous (I remembered 9...a6 10 h4 0-0 11 h5, Kasparov-Polugayevsky, Moscow 1979), but Black has counterplay and, besides, in such sharp positions I felt very much at home. And, incidentally, that was why initially I underestimated White's offensive potential in the English Attack (6 ♗e3 a6 7 f3, ♕d2, 0-0-0 and g2-g4), regarding it simply as an analogue of the Keres Attack with the inclusion of f2-f3. But this is a fundamentally different set-up: the f3-pawn reinforces the centre, allowing the g- and h-pawns to go into battle.

10 ♕d2

10 h4 is also played, as well as 10 ♕h5, but here this lunge is no longer so good: 10...g6 11 ♕h6 (11 ♕e2?! ♘xd4 12 ♗xd4

♗xg5, Kudryashov-Kasparov, Moscow 1979) 11...♘de5 12 0-0-0 f6 13 gxf6 ♗xf6 with approximate equality (Kengis-Murugan, Gausdal 1991).

10...a6 11 0-0-0 ♘xd4 12 ♗xd4 b5 13 f4 (13 a3!?, Shamkovich-H.Olafsson, Lone Pine 1979) **13...b4 14 ♘e2**

14 ♘a4?! is weaker in view of 14...♕a5! 15 b3 ♗b7.

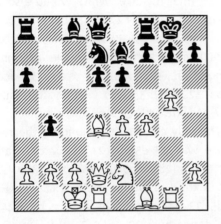

14...♕a5

Stepping on to an unexplored path. 14...e5 15 ♗e3 exf4 (Espig-Schöneberg, Weimar 1968) 16 ♘xf4! is better for White, but consideration should be given to 14...♗b7!? 15 f5 ♕a5 16 f6 ♗d8 with double-edged play: 17 fxg7 ♖e8 18 ♔b1 ♗xe4 or 17 ♔b1 g6 18 ♗g2 ♖c8 etc.

15 ♔b1!

After 15 a3?! ♖b8 16 ♔b1 e5 17 ♗a7 (17 ♗e3? ♘c5) 17...♖b7 18 axb4 ♖xb4 or 15...e5!? 16 ♗e3 ♖b8 17 f5 ♘c5 18 f6 ♗d8 19 ♕xd6 bxa3 20 b4 a2! 21 ♗xc5 ♕xc5 22 ♕xc5 a1♕+ 23 ♔d2 ♕b2 the initiative passes to Black.

15...e5?! (15...♘c5 is better, although after 16 ♗g2 White's chances are slightly preferable) **16 ♗f2?!**

16 ♗e3 (with the threat of f4-f5) 16...♘c5 17 ♗g2! would have given a clear opening advantage: for example, 17...g6 (17...♗b7 18

f5!) 18 f5 gxf5 19 exf5 ♗xf5 20 ♘g3! ♗e6 21 ♗d5 or 17...♗e6 18 b3 exf4, and now 19 ♗xf4 (Dvoiris-Sherbakov, Chelyabinsk 1989) 19...♖ac8! is unclear (Stohl), but after 19 ♘xf4! ♖ac8 (19...♗xg5? 20 ♗f3!) 20 h4 Black has problems.

16...♘c5

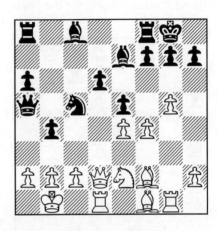

17 ♕e3?!

This finally loses the initiative, which was still appreciable after 17 ♗g2! with the same threat of f4-f5. With the bishop on f2 Black has more tactical chances, but he does not equalise with 17...♗e6 18 b3 exf4 (18...g6 19 f5!) 19 ♘xf4 ♘a4?! 20 bxa4 ♗xg5 21 e5! ♕xa4 22 ♗d5 ♗xd5 23 ♕xd5 ♖ac8 24 ♕e4 ♗xf4 25 ♖xd6 g6 26 ♗d4! ♖c4 27 ♖f1! ♗h6 28 e6 f5 29 ♕e2 or 19...♗xg5?! 20 ♗f3 f6 21 h4 ♗xf4 22 ♕xf4 ♖ac8 23 ♗d4 with an attack, or with 17...exf4 18 ♘xf4 ♗xg5 19 e5! dxe5 20 ♗xa8 ♗xf4 21 ♕d6 ♘e6 22 ♗b6 ♕b5 23 ♗e4, when the rook outweighs the knight and pawns.

17...♗e6 18 ♘c1

In the event of 18 b3 g6! White is no longer threatening f4-f5 and if 19 ♕f3 there is the reply 19...d5!? 20 ♖xd5 (20 exd5?! ♗f5 – Stohl) 20...♗xd5 21 exd5 e4 or 19...♖ad8!? (20 f5? d5!).

18...exf4 19 ♕xf4 ♖ac8 (19...♕c7!? with the idea of ...a6-a5-a4) **20 ♗d4** (20 ♘b3! is safer)

20...♖fe8

Black could have immediately launched a counter-attack by 20...♕c7! 21 ♖d2 a5.

21 ♘b3! ♕a4

Equality would more simply have been maintained by 21...♕c7!?, almost forcing 22 ♗xc5 dxc5 23 ♕xc7 ♖xc7 24 ♗xa6 ♖a8 25 ♗b5 g6 with excellent play for the pawn.

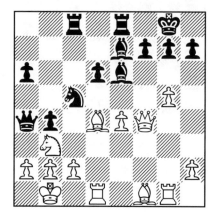

22 ♗f6?!

Showy, but ineffective. 22 h4 ♕c6 would have led to a complicated, roughly equal game – thus the attempt 23 ♗xc5 dxc5 24 ♘a5 is parried by 24...♕c7! (better than 24...♕a4 25 ♘c4, as given by me in *Informator*) 25 ♕xc7 ♖xc7 with equality.

22...♗f8 23 ♖g3?!

White continues on his reckless course. He should have urgently brought his bishop back – 23 ♗d4, although after 23...a5 (with the intention of ...♕c6) the loss of time begins to tell and White's position becomes unpleasant.

23...♕c6

'Emphasising the weakness of the e4- and c2-squares.' (Polugayevsky). White is forced to exchange on c5.

24 ♘xc5 dxc5! (now threatening ...c5-c4 and ...b4-b3) **25 ♗e5**

25 c4? bxc3 26 ♗xc3 ♗xa2+! was completely bad for White (Stohl). Shutting in the bishop on f6 by 25 e5?! also did not work in view of 25...c4 26 ♗g2 ♕b5 27 ♗e4 b3! with a crushing attack.

25...c4 26 ♗d6

A use has finally been found for the unfortunate bishop: with its help the d-file is blocked. If 26 c3 (Stohl) or 26 ♗e2, then 26...♕a4! is strong.

26...b3! 27 c3?

The final mistake. White would also not have been saved by 27 ♗xf8? bxc2+ 28 ♔xc2 ♕a4+ 29 ♔c1 c3! 30 ♖xc3 ♖xc3+ 31 bxc3 ♕xa2! (more accurate than the *Informator* suggestion 31...♖xf8) 32 ♗d3 (32 ♗d6? ♗b3) 32...♗b3! 33 ♗b1 ♕a1 34 ♖d3 ♗a2 or 33 ♖e1 ♖xf8 34 ♕c7 ♗e6 and wins.

The only chance of prolonging the resistance was 27 e5! bxc2+ 28 ♔xc2 – after 28...♕a4+ (28...♕b6!?) 29 ♔c1 ♖b8 30 ♖a3 (30 ♗xb8?! ♖xb8 31 ♕d4 ♕xa2 32 ♗h3 ♗d5! 33 ♗f5 g6 34 ♗b1 ♕a1 35 b4 ♕a4! is too dangerous) 30...♕b5 31 ♖d2 ♗xd6 32 exd6 ♗f5 Black has an obvious advantage, but for the moment there is no forced win.

27...♖cd8! (it would appear that Ljubojevic was hoping for 27...bxa2+ 28 ♔a1, but a severe disappointment awaited him) **28 e5 ♗xd6** (or immediately 28...♖xd6!) **29 exd6**

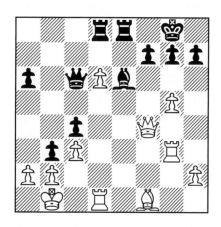

29...♖xd6!! (an insidious blow!) **30 ♖c1**

The rook is taboo because of the back rank:

30 ℤxd6? ♗f5+ 31 ♔c1 bxa2, or 30 ♕xd6?
♗f5+ 31 ♔c1 (31 ♔a1 ♕xd6) 31...bxa2 32
♕a3 ♕e4 33 ♗d3 ♕f4+, mating.
**30...♕c5 31 ♔a1 ℤed8 32 ℤe3 ℤd1 33 ℤe1
ℤxe1 34 ℤxe1 ♕a5 35 a3 ♕d5**

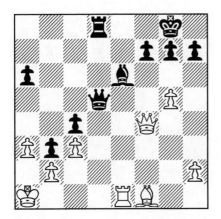

'Strategically it is all over: the white king
is completely stalemated.' (Polugayevsky)
36 ♗e2 g6 37 h4 ♕d2 38 ♕f1 (after 38
♕xd2 ℤxd2 the creation of a passed pawn
on the kingside is quickly decisive) **38...♗h3!
39 ♕g1 ℤe8 0-1**
'A typical Sicilian attack, excellently conducted by Black.' (Polugayevsky)

Despite this win, I did not in fact catch the
leader, who that day defeated Beliavsky.
After nine rounds the positions were: Ehlvest
– 7 (!); Kasparov – 6½; Karpov – 5½. And in
the 10th round the attention of the spectators was especially focused on the Karpov-
Ehlvest and Kasparov-Andersson games.

> *Game 37*
> **G.Kasparov-U.Andersson**
> World Cup, Belfort
> 10th Round, 26.06.1988
> *Queen's Gambit Declined D36*

1 d4 ♘f6 2 c4 e6 3 ♘c3

Earlier against Andersson I employed both
3 ♘f3 (Game No.61 in *Garry Kasparov on
Garry Kasparov Part I*), and 3 g3 (*Game No.2*).
3...d5 (Ulf avoids 3....♗b4, as he played
against me in Moscow 1981 and later in
Skelleftea 1989) **4 cxd5 exd5 5 ♗g5**
In this branch of the 'Carlsbad' White can
advantageously develop his king's knight on
e2.
5...c6 (5....♗e7 – *Game No.45*) **6 ♕c2 ♗e7**
6...♘a6 7 e3, as in my games with Ljubojevic (Madrid (rapid) 1988) and Ivanchuk
(Wijk aan Zee 1999), is hardly any better for
Black.
7 e3 ♘bd7 8 ♗d3
If 8 ♘f3, then 8...♘h5 9 ♗xe7 ♕xe7 10
0-0-0 ♘b6 11 h3 g6 12 g4 ♘g7 13 ♗d3 ♗e6
is possible, with the intention of ...0-0-0
(Kasparov-Smyslov, 55th USSR Championship, Moscow 1988).
8...0-0
Four months later my opponent solved his
opening problems by 8...♘h5 9 ♗xe7 ♕xe7
10 ♘ge2 g6 11 0-0-0 ♘b6 12 ♘g3 ♘g7
(Kasparov-Andersson, Reykjavik 1988), and
at Barcelona 1989 I changed my move order
(6 e3 – *Game No.51*).
9 ♘ge2 ℤe8 10 0-0 ♘f8

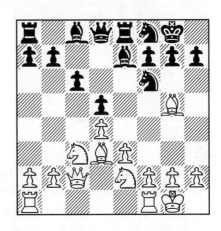

11 f3!
This plan of creating a mobile pawn cen-

tre stems from an old Botvinnik-Keres game: 11 ♖ab1 ♗d6?! 12 ♔h1 ♘g6 13 f3! ♗e7 14 ♖be1 etc. (Game No.43 in Part II of *My Great Predecessors*). Against Beliavsky (Moscow (rapid) 1987) I tried 11 a3 g6 12 b4 ♘e6 13 ♗h4 a6 14 f3! ♘g7 15 ♗f2! h5 16 h3 and also successfully carried out e3-e4.

11...♗e6

White is better after 11...c5?! (a typical reaction to the threat of e3-e4) 12 ♗xf6 ♗xf6 13 dxc5 and ♖ad1. But 11...♘g6 has been more often played, and when it transpired that after 12 e4 dxe4 13 fxe4 ♗e6 Black is okay (14 ♖ad1 ♘g4! or 14 h3 c5! 15 d5 ♗d7), 12 ♖ad1! came to the fore: for example, 12...h6 13 ♗xf6 ♗xf6 14 ♗xg6 fxg6 15 e4 g5?! 16 e5 ♗e7 17 f4 gxf4 18 ♘xf4 with the initiative (Kasparov-Barua, Internet 2000).

12 ♖ae1 (12 ♖ad1!? is also popular) **12...♖c8**

Completing the mobilisation of the forces. The alternative is the immediate 12...♘6d7 (Kir.Georgiev-van der Sterren, Lugano 1987).

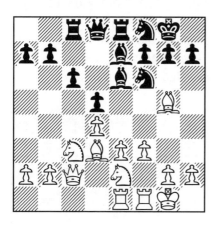

13 ♔h1 ♘6d7

Now if 13...c5 there would have followed 14 dxc5 and ♘d4. I did not expect this from Andersson, since without particular need he did not like creating an isolani for himself.

14 ♗xe7 ♖xe7 (14...♕xe7!?, Lutz-Yusupov, Tilburg 1993) **15 ♘f4**

Hindering ...c6-c5 and continuing to prepare e3-e4. Less was promised by 15 f4 ♘f6 (15...f5!?) 16 f5 ♗d7 17 e4 dxe4 18 ♘xe4 ♘xe4 19 ♗xe4 f6, or 15 e4 dxe4 16 fxe4 c5 17 d5 c4! 18 dxe6 fxe6 19 ♗xc4 ♖xc4.

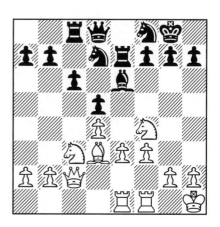

15...♖c7?!

The start of an unwieldy counter-plan of pressure on the enemy centre. 15...♘f6 16 ♕d2 ♖d7 was more natural (but not 16...♕d6?! 17 e4 dxe4 18 fxe4 ♕xd4? 19 e5 and wins, or 16...b5?! 17 e4, Bareev-Asrian, New York 1998), although after 17 b4 White is ready to mount an offensive on all parts of the board.

16 ♕f2

Not rushing to determine the position earlier than necessary. In the event of 16 e4 dxe4 17 fxe4 it would be simpler for Black to defend: 17...♘b6 18 ♕f2 ♘g6 etc.

16...♘f6?! (the second link of the dubious plan) **17 e4**

'The white pieces are ideally placed – it is time to carry out the thematic advance.' (Polugayevsky)

17...dxe4 18 fxe4 ♖cd7

The concluding link of the plan, which is seemingly more appropriate for Black than 18...♘g4 19 ♕g1 (a benefit of the move ♔h1), 18...♗c8 19 e5, or 18...♘g6 19 ♘xe6 ♖xe6 20 e5. But now White suddenly carries out a breakthrough at the most fortified point.

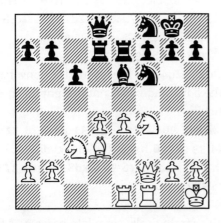

19 d5! cxd5 20 ♗b5

This attack in conjunction with my 22nd move was apparently underestimated by Andersson. After 20 exd5? ♗xd5! White simply loses a pawn.

20...♖c7

Only practical saving chances were offered by the sacrifice of the exchange for a pawn: 20...dxe4 21 ♗xd7 ♕xd7 (21...♖xd7? 22 ♘fd5 ♖e6 23 ♘xe4! and wins) 22 ♘xe4 ♘xe4 23 ♖xe4 ♗xa2 24 ♖xe7 ♕xe7 25 ♕xa7 ♗c4 26 ♖c1 ♕e4 27 ♕f2, or 20...d4!? 21 ♗xd7 ♗c4! (21...♖xd7 22 ♘cd5) 22 ♗f5! dxc3 23 ♖g1 cxb2 24 ♕xb2 and e4-e5.

21 exd5 ♗d7

Hoping to exchange the bishops and neutralise the passed d-pawn. It was no better to play 21...♗f5 (21...♘xd5? 22 ♖d1) 22 ♕xa7 or 22 d6!? ♖xe1 (22...♕xd6 23 ♖d1 ♕c5 24 ♘fd5! winning the exchange) 23 dxc7 ♖xf1+ 24 ♕xf1 ♕d6 (24...♕xc7? 25 ♘fd5!), when my *Informator* suggestion 25 ♗c4 is questionable on account of 25...♗c8, but after 25 ♘h5! ♗c8 (25...♘g4?! 26 ♕f4! ♕c5 27 h3) 26 ♘xf6+ gxf6 27 ♘e4 ♕xc7 28 ♘xf6+ ♔h8 29 ♘d5 ♕e5 30 ♕xf7 White is a sound pawn to the good.

22 ♗e2!

An important resource, enabling a pawn to be won: White is threatening both ♕xa7, and d5-d6 (the awkward placing of the black rooks!). Far weaker was 22 ♗xd7 (and not 22 ♕xa7?! ♖xc3! or 22 d6? ♖xe1 23 ♖xe1 ♖xc3! 24 ♗xd7 ♘c4) 22...cxd7 23 ♕xa7 ♖xe1 24 ♖xe1 g5 25 ♘d3 b6 26 ♕a3 ♘xd5 27 ♘e5 ♕e8! with a probable draw.

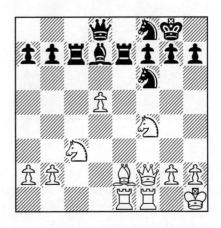

22...♖c8

After 22...♘e4 23 ♕xa7 ♘d6 (23...♘xc3? 24 d6!) 24 ♗d3 Black also has no compensation for the pawn.

23 ♕xa7

For safety's sake I decided simply to grab material, although 23 d6!? ♖e5 24 ♕d4! and ♘fd5 was also tempting, with powerful pressure.

23...b6! (cutting off the queen; 23...♘e4 24 ♕d4! – Stohl) **24 ♕a6?!**

This could have allowed Black some counterplay. 24 d6! was more accurate: 24...♖e5 25 ♗f3 ♖a5 26 ♕b7 (Stohl) 26...♖b8 27 ♕c7 or 26...♘e6 27 ♘xe6 ♗xe6 28 ♖d1 with an overwhelming advantage.

24...♘e4?!

An answering error in approaching time-trouble. 24...♘g6! was more resilient. After this I gave 25 ♕d3 in *Informator* with the evaluation '±', but after 25...♘xf4 26 ♖xf4 b5! things are not so clear. 25 ♘xg6 hxg6 26

♗f3 (Stohl) or 26 ♕d3! is stronger, although here too Black's resources are not yet exhausted.

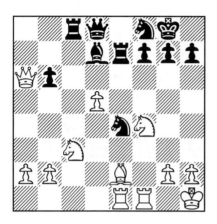

25 d6!

By sacrificing his passed pawn in the centre, in return White creates a pair of connected passed pawns on the queenside, and Black's position becomes untenable.

25...♘xd6 (25...♖e5? 26 ♘xe4 ♖xe4 27 ♘d5 and wins) **26 ♘fd5** (26 ♘cd5! and ♕xb6 was more forceful, imposing the exchange of queens)

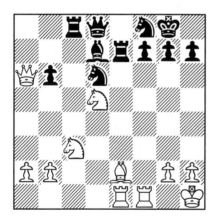

26...♖e5?!

White's task could have been made more difficult by 26...♖e6 27 ♕xb6 ♕g5 (Stohl; 27...♕h4 28 ♕f2!), but after 28 ♗f3! ♘c4 29 ♕f2 the win is merely a matter of time.

27 ♕xb6 ♘f5

Equivalent to capitulation. However, it was also hopeless to play 27...♗c6 28 ♕xd8 ♖xd8 29 ♗f3 or 27...♕xb6 28 ♘xb6 ♖ce8 29 ♖d1 ♖8e6 30 ♘xd7 ♘xd7 31 a4 etc.

28 ♕xd8 ♖xd8 29 ♗d3

Or 29 ♗g4!?. In any event, the conversion of the advantage does not present any great difficulty.

29...♖xe1 30 ♖xe1 ♘g6 31 a4 ♔f8 32 a5 ♘d4 33 ♗xg6 hxg6 34 ♖d1 ♘e6 (34...♖e8 35 h3) **35 ♘b6 ♗c6 36 ♖xd8+ ♘xd8 37 b4 ♘e6 38 b5 1-0**

This strategically complete game was the second in a series of five successive wins. It enabled me to again take the lead in the tournament, since that day Ehlvest lost to Karpov. The situation in the race intensified: Kasparov – 7½ out of 10; Ehlvest – 7; Karpov – 6½.

In the 11th round I had Black against Alexander Beliavsky. Our games always took an uncompromising course and began with critical disputes in topical opening systems.

> *Game 38*
> **A.Beliavsky-G.Kasparov**
> World Cup, Belfort
> 11th Round, 27.06.1988
> *Grünfeld Defence D97*

1 d4 ♘f6 2 c4 g6 3 ♘c3 d5 4 ♘f3 ♗g7 5 ♕b3 dxc4 6 ♕xc4 0-0 7 e4 ♘a6 8 ♗e2 c5 9 d5 e6 10 ♗g5

My opponent decided to catch me unawares with a rare continuation, after being unsuccessful in the main lines approved in my matches with Karpov (1986 and 1987): 10 0-0 exd5 11 exd5 ♗f5 12 ♗f4 (if 12 ♖d1 or 12 ♗e3, then 12...♕b6! is good) 12...♖e8 13 ♖ad1 ♘e4 14 ♘b5 (14 ♗d3 ♗xc3! 15

bxc3 b5, M.Gurevich-Kasparov, 55th USSR Championship, Moscow 1988) 14...♛f6 15 d6 (15 ♗d3 ♗d7!, Ivanchuk-Dorfman, Lvov 1988) 15...♗d7 16 g3 g5 17 ♗e3 h6, and it is already White who has problems (Beliavsky-Kasparov, Moscow 1987).

And here I did indeed sink into thought, endeavouring to recall the correct reaction to White's aggressive plan.

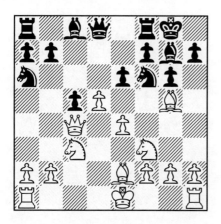

10...exd5 11 ♘xd5 ♗e6 (natural, although 11...♛a5+ 12 ♗d2 ♛d8 is also acceptable, Farago-Dorfman, Budapest 1988) **12 0-0-0** (a serious challenge!) **12...♗xd5!**

It is sensible to get rid of such a powerful knight.

13 ♖xd5 ♛b6

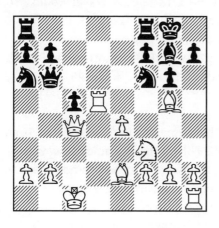

14 ♗xf6

If 14 ♖d2 Black equalises with the reply 14...♛c6!: for example, 15 ♘e5 ♛xe4 16 ♗xf6 ♛xc4+ 17 ♗xc4 ♗xf6 18 ♘xf7 ♖xf7 19 ♖d7 ♖af8 20 ♖xb7 ♔g7 21 ♖xf7+ ♖xf7 22 ♗xf7 ♔xf7.

14...♛xf6 15 e5

Beliavsky made these well-known moves quite quickly.

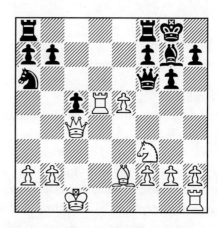

15...♛f5!

A strong novelty. 15...♛e7 16 ♖hd1 is better for White (Flear-Korchnoi, Lugano 1988), whereas now the harmonious coordination of his pieces is disrupted, and this clearly disturbed Beliavsky.

16 ♗d3 (this has to be played on account of the threat of ...♗h6+) **16...♛c8**

16...♛e6! 17 ♖d6 ♛e7 would have caused White more problems, but on the other hand after the 'modest' move in the game he begins to lose control.

17 ♖d1?!

In *Informator* I recommended 17 ♖d6(?!), overlooking the reply 17...♛c7! with the threat of ...♗xe5 and the better chances for Black. In fact, equality would have been secured by 17 ♗e4! b5 18 ♛e2 ♖b8 19 ♖d6 c4 20 ♖c6, forcing 20...♘c7.

17...b5! 18 ♛h4 (18 ♛xb5? ♘c7) **18...♘b4**

The counterplay spring quickly uncoils, and White has to be extremely accurate.

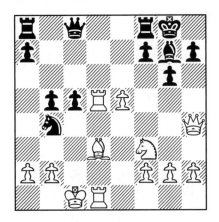

19 ♗xg6?

A faulty combination! While Beliavsky was considering it, I suddenly sensed that this was what he would play: it was evident that with every minute his desire was strengthening to 'display his brilliant combinative mastery'. And to save time I worked out in advance a five-move variation with a final sacrifice of the black queen...

Of course, it was essential to play 19 ♖d6! c4 20 ♗e4 (20 ♔b1? ♘d3+!), parrying the attack after both 20...♕c5 21 a3 (21 ♗xa8? c3!) 21...♘d3+ 22 ♔b1 ♗xe5 23 ♖d7 ♗xb2 24 ♗xg6! h5! 25 ♗xd3, and 20...c3! 21 ♖1d4! (21 a3? c2! 22 axb4 cxd1♕+ 23 ♔xd1 ♖b8 is bad for White) 21...cxb2+ 22 ♔xb2 ♕c5 23 a3 ♖fc8 24 axb4 ♕c3+ 25 ♔a2 a5 26 ♖d8+ ♗f8 27 ♖xc8 ♖xc8 28 ♖d8 ♕c4+ 29 ♔a1 a4 30 ♖xc8 ♕xc8 31 ♔b2 ♕c4 32 ♗c2 a3+ 33 ♔xa3 ♕xc2 34 ♕d4, when things head for a draw.

19...fxg6 (not 19...hxg6?? 20 ♘g5 ♖e8 21 ♖d7 and wins) **20 ♖d7 ♕e8!** (the prelude to a refutation of the combination) **21 ♖e7**

21 a3 ♘c6 or 21 ♖1d6 ♖xf3! was also unsuitable.

21...♗h6+!

The overloading of the white queen tells. White would still have had some chances after 21...g5?! 22 ♕xg5 ♕g6 23 ♕xg6 hxg6

24 ♖dd7 ♗h6+ 25 ♔b1.

22 ♔b1 (22 ♖d2 g5!) **22...♖d8!** (exploiting an unusual weakness of the back rank!) **23 ♖d6**

After rejecting 23 ♖e1 because of 23...g5! or 23...♕c6! 24 a3 (24 ♕xh6 ♖d1+!! 25 ♖xd1 ♕e4+ with a smothered mate) 24...g5! 25 ♘xg5 ♕g6+ 26 ♘e4 ♘d3 and wins, Beliavsky looked happy with his position.

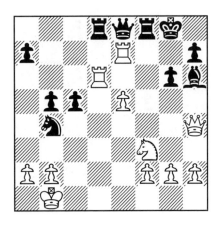

23...♕c6!

But here is the surprise: 24 ♖xc6? ♖d1 mate or 24 ♕xh6? ♕e4+!. After placing my queen on c6, I experienced an enormous amount of aesthetic pleasure, but the same could not be said about my opponent.

24 a3 (24 ♕g4 ♖xd6 25 exd6 ♖f6 26 d7 ♖d6 27 ♖e8+ ♗f8 28 d8♕ ♕xe8! would also not have helped) **24...♖xd6 25 exd6 ♕xd6 26 axb4 cxb4 27 ♕e4 b3 0-1**

In view of 28 ♕e6+ (otherwise Black has a deadly attack) 28...♕xe6 29 ♖xe6 ♖c8 30 ♖e1 ♖c2.

That same day Karpov defeated Timman, while Ehlvest made a quick draw with Short. The leading positions were now: Kasparov – 8½ out of 11, Ehlvest and Karpov – 7½.

In the 12th round I won against Ehlvest, and he dropped out of the fight for first place. And in the 13th round I gained revenge against Nigel Short for my defeat in Brussels in an English Attack.

1 e4 c5 2 ♘f3 d6 3 d4 cxd4 4 ♘xd4 ♘f6 5 ♘c3 a6 6 ♗e3 e6 7 f3 ♗e7

7...b5 8 ♕d2 ♘bd7 9 g4 h6 10 0-0-0 ♗b7 11 ♗d3 (11 h4!?) 11...♘e5 12 ♖he1 was the sharp position reached in our game from the first cycle of Brussels 1986, and after 7...♘bd7 8 g4 h6 9 h4 – from our rapidplay match (London 1987). On this occasion I had prepared a different deployment of my forces.

8 ♕d2 ♘c6 9 g4 0-0 10 0-0-0

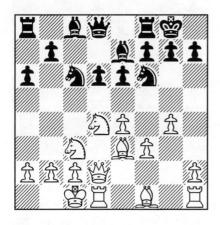

10...♘d7

With the idea of ...♘de5 and ...♘a5-c4. I should remind you: at that time I thought the position on the board was simply a Keres Attack with the 'insipid' move f2-f3, and that Black could do virtually as he pleased. Thus six weeks later, in the 55th USSR Championship, I tried 10...♖b8 against Khalifman. And it was only after this that I realised how hard

it was to fight against the English Attack by copying the classical methods of play in the Keres Attack, and I switched to 10...♘xd4 11 ♗xd4 b5.

11 h4 ♘de5 12 ♘xc6?!

For this move, made after a long think, Short was strongly criticised: why reinforce Black's position in the centre? If 12 ♕f2 I was planning 12...♘a5 (12...♗d7 is better), but after 13 ♔b1 ♘ac4 14 ♗c1 White's chances are slightly better. And soon 12 ♕g2! also appeared, supporting the pawn storm with g4-g5, h4-h5 and g5-g6.

12...bxc6 13 ♗e2 ♖b8

After the exchange on c6 things have become easier for Black: this and his following reply are quite obvious.

14 g5 d5

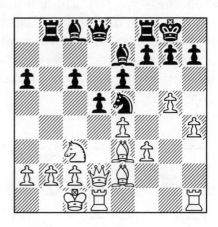

Black increases his influence in the centre and creates the grounds for various tactical operations. The weakening of the c5-square is unimportant.

15 ♗a7

This routine trick with the manoeuvre of the bishop to d4 does not bring White any benefits, although little was also promised by 15 ♔b1 ♗b4 or 15 f4 ♘d7 16 h5(f5) ♕a5. After the logical 15 ♘a4!? there is the satisfactory reply 15...♕c7!? 16 h5 (16 f4 ♖b4!) 16...dxe4 17 fxe4 ♖b4 with counterplay.

15...♖b7 16 ♗d4 ♘d7 17 exd5 cxd5!

After 17...exd5 18 ♗xa6 Black's compensation for the pawn is more problematic: 18...♖b8 19 ♗xc8 ♕xc8 20 h5 or 18...♖xb2?! 19 ♘xd5! ♖b8! (19...♖xa2? is weak: 20 ♘xe7+ ♕xe7 21 ♗c4 ♖a4 22 ♗b3) 20 ♘xe7+ ♕xe7, and here apart from 21 ♗b2 ♖xb2! 22 ♔xb2 ♗xa6 (or 22...♕e5+ 23 c3 ♗xa6 24 ♕xd7 ♖b8+ 25 ♔c2 ♕a5 with equality) 23 ♕xd7 ♕b4+, with at least perpetual check (24 ♔c1 ♕a3+ 25 ♔d2 ♕a5+), White has the resource 21 ♕e3! ♕xe3+ 22 ♗xe3 with the better endgame.

18 f4

After 18 ♗xa6 the sacrifice 18...♖xb2! works, with a powerful attack in the event of 19 ♔xb2?! (19 ♗xc8? ♖b8!) 19...♗xa6 20 f4 ♕a5, so that White has to play 19 ♘xd5! ♖b8! 20 ♘xe7+ ♕xe7 21 ♗b2 (this is now the only move: 21 ♕d3?! e5!) 21...♖xb2! 22 ♔xb2 ♗xa6 23 ♕xd7 ♕b4+ 24 ♔c1, when Black can force a draw – 24...♕a3+ 25 ♔d2 ♕a5+ or retain some initiative by 24...♗e2.

18...♕a5

A turning-point in the battle.

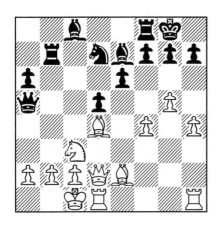

19 ♕e3

This is not yet a mistake, but it overlooks Black's clever manoeuvre in response. 19 h5! was more energetic: 19...♕a3! (19...♗a3? 20 ♘xd5! or 19...♘b8?! 20 ♗d3! is worse) 20

♗b5! ♕b4! (20...♕d6 21 ♗a4!) 21 a3 ♕d6 22 ♗xd7 ♗xd7 23 b4 or 22 ♗d3 e5 23 fxe5 ♘xe5 24 ♖dg1 with chances for both sides.

19...♘b8!

On seeing this move (with the unexpected threat of ...♘c6xd4), Nigel was unable to hide his disappointment. He became rattled and began to 'flounder'.

20 f5?

Neither 20 g6? hxg6! 21 h5 ♘c6 nor 20 h5? ♘c6 21 h6 g6 22 ♗g7 ♖d8 was any good. Only 20 ♕e5! f6 21 gxf6 ♗xf6 22 ♕d6!, preventing both ...♘c6 and ...♕b4, would have maintained approximate equality.

20...♘c6 21 f6 (not 21 ♗xg7? ♗c5! and ...♔xg7) **21...♘xd4**

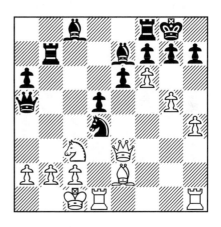

22 ♖xd4?

This exchange sacrifice proves to be a fatal mistake. After 22 fxe7?! ♘xe2+ 23 ♕xe2 ♖xe7 (23...♖e8!?) 24 h5 (24 ♘xd5? ♖b7! 25 ♘c3 ♕b4) 24...d4 White would have lost a pawn without any compensation.

However, 22 ♕xd4! ♗c5 23 ♕e5 was more resilient, gaining a brief respite. Then Black could immediately force the transition into a better endgame – 23...♕c7 (or 23...♕b6 24 ♘a4 ♕d6) 24 ♕xc7 ♖xc7, or continue playing for an attack – 23...g6 24 ♔b1 (24 h5? ♕c7!) 24...♕b6 25 ♘a4 ♗d6!

26 ♕d4 ♕c7 or 25 b3 ♗d6 26 ♕d4 ♕c7 (although 26...♕xd4 27 ♖xd4 ♗e5 28 ♖d3 ♖c7 29 ♘d1 ♗b7 etc. is also promising).

22...♗c5 23 fxg7 ♖d8!

After 23...♖e8?! 24 ♖hd1 the win is far less clear, since in the variation 24...♕b4 (24...♗d7!?) 25 b3 e5? (25...♗d7!) White is saved by 26 ♘xd5!.

24 ♖hd1

A semblance of reinforcement. If 24 ♗d3 there would have followed 24...♕b6 (only not 24...♕b4?? 25 ♗xh7+!) 25 ♗xh7+ ♔g7! (25...♔xh7? 26 ♘a4) 26 ♕e5+ ♔xh7. Objectively it was better to get rid of the pin – 24 ♕d3(d2), but after 24...♗xd4 25 ♕xd4 ♕b6! 26 ♕f6 e5! all the same Black would have won: 27 b3 ♕xf6 28 gxf6 ♖c7 29 ♔b2 ♗b7 etc.

24...♕b4! 25 b3

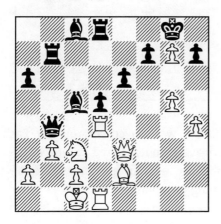

25...e5! (a flamboyant final touch; White suffers decisive loss of material) **26 ♕xe5**

Or 26 ♖xb4 ♗xe3+ 27 ♔b1 ♖xb4 28 ♘xd5 ♖d4 29 ♘xe3 ♖xd1+ 30 ♗xd1 ♖d4 and wins.

26...♕xc3 27 ♖xd5 ♕xe5 28 ♖xe5 ♗a3+ 29 ♔b1 ♖xd1+ 30 ♗xd1 ♖d7! 31 ♗g4 ♖d4 32 ♗f3 ♔g7 33 h5 h6 34 gxh6+ ♔xh6 35 ♖a5 ♗b4 (35...♖f4!?) **36 ♖e5** (if 36 ♖a4 the simplest is 36...♗c3) **36...f6 37 ♖e8 ♗f5 38 ♖h8+ ♔g5 39 ♖b8 ♗a3 40 h6 ♖d2 0-1**

Five wins in a row! As for Karpov, in the 12th and 13th rounds he had to be satisfied with draws, and before the game between us everything was practically decided: with 10½ out of 13, I was leading my rival by two points. However, our games were always keenly contested, whatever the tournament situation.

What operated here was the factor which I call the 'five victory curse'. The point is that, until Wijk aan Zee 1999, where I 'bagged' 7 out of 7, five successive wins was always the limit for me. Even in Tilburg 1989, one of my very best tournaments, after five wins I was quite unable to play as Black against Sax, and I was saved only by his peaceableness. After five successive wins I usually 'cracked'! And that is what happened on this occasion. After losing the necessary concentration, I played what was probably one of my worst games, which in the end proved to be Karpov's only tournament win against me in the history of our meetings (Game No.6 in *Kasparov vs. Karpov 1988-2009*).

Before the last round the fight for first place had unexpectedly sharpened: now Karpov was just a point behind me. However, in the purely competitive sense the outcome of the tournament seemed predetermined, since on the last day I had White against Sokolov, whereas my rival had Black against Spassky.

However, the World Cup stimulated a fight not only for first place, but also for the maximum result. In addition, a new landmark in my forward advance was Fischer's legendary rating of 2780, and every point brought me closer to the goal. I endeavoured to assess objectively the standard of my play in Belfort, and I came to the conclusion that it was at a fairly high level, giving me grounds for aggressive aims in the decisive game. A draw with me would practically guarantee Andrey Sokolov a place in the top five, and I was expecting to have to overcome a solid defensive set-up. But surprises began from the very first moves.

Game 40
G.Kasparov-A.Sokolov
World Cup, Belfort
15th Round, 3.7.1988
English Opening A19

1 c4 (after looking through a number of set-ups at home, in the end I chose my Seville weapon) **1...♘f6 2 ♘c3 e6**

Andrey had not played this since his youth, obviously not wishing to dispute the sharp variations after 3 e4. But why did he go in for sharp play in the last round?

3 e4 (5)

Of course, 3 d4 or 3 ♘f3 is safer, but I had great belief in my powers and I did not hesitate for long.

3...c5 (1)

Adding fuel to the fire. I expected the more solid 3...d5, which my opponent had once employed. The determination and speed with which the c-pawn was advanced mark Sokolov out as a subtle psychologist.

4 e5 ♘g8 5 ♘f3 (1)

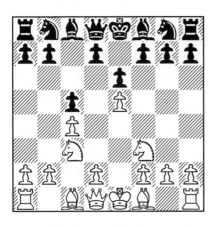

5...♘c6 6 d4 cxd4 7 ♘xd4 ♘xe5 8 ♘db5 a6 9 ♘d6+ ♗xd6 10 ♕xd6 f6 11 ♗e3 ♘e7 12 ♗b6 ♘f5

My trainers and I analysed this topical position before the match in Seville and we had worked out a new idea.

13 ♕c5!?

13 ♗xd8 ♘xd6 14 ♗c7 ♔e7 15 c5 ♘e8 or 13 ♕b4 ♘c6 14 ♕c5 ♕e7 15 0-0-0 ♕xc5 16 ♗xc5 d6 (Korchnoi-Timman, 4th match game, Brussels 1991) leads to an endgame which is far less attractive than the middle-game as regards playing for a win.

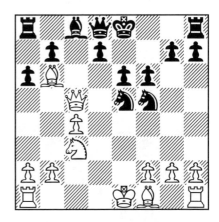

All this was played very quickly. Each of the players endeavoured to emphasise his confidence – and his knowledge of the opening variation.

White is a pawn down, while Black has a lack of space for developing his pieces and only dim prospects for their participation in the forthcoming battle. It will be hard for Black to coordinate his pieces, and only the absence of pawn weaknesses in his position makes things unclear.

13...d6 (19)

White's last move, known from one old game in the 29th volume of *Informator* (R.Hernandez-Am.Rodriguez, Havana 1980), apparently came as a surprise to my opponent. He rejected the as yet altogether unknown 13...♕e7!?, to which White could either reply 14 ♕a5 (suggested by me in *Informator* and first tried in Miles-Y.Grünfeld, Philadelphia 1989), or go in for the exchange of queens – 14 ♕xe7+ (Karpov-Ribli, Reggio Emilia 1989/90) with sufficient compensation for the pawn.

14 ♕a5 ♕e7 (14...♕d7!? – *Game No.75*) **15 0-0-0 0-0 16 f4 ♘c6** (16...♘f7?! 17 ♗d3 was weaker, but later 16...♘g6!? 17 g3 ♗d7 was tried) **17 ♕a3**

White has almost completed the mobilisation of his forces and he has created the positional threat of 18 g4, while Black still has little space and no convenient squares for his pieces.

17...e5

17...h5!? 18 ♗d3 e5 came into consideration, although after 19 ♘d5 ♕f7 20 ♖hf1 White would retain the initiative: 20...exf4 21 ♖xf4 ♘fe7 22 ♕xd6 ♗g4 23 ♘xe7+ ♘xe7 24 ♖e1 ♖ae8 25 h3! (25 ♕c7 ♘g6) 25...♘c8 26 ♕b4 ♖xe1+ 27 ♕xe1 ♘xb6 28 hxg4 ♘d7 29 ♖d4 etc.

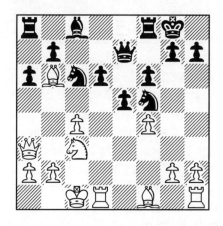

18 g4!

A new move, suggested by Amador Rodriguez, instead of 18 c5?! ♕f7!, which occurred in the aforementioned Havana game. Now Black's position becomes extremely dangerous.

18...♘fd4 (6)

Rodriguez recommended 18...♘h6 19 ♘d5 ♕d7 with an 'unclear' assessment, but after 20 h3 exf4 (20...♘f7 21 f5!) 21 ♘xf4 ♘f7 22 c5 a difficult defence again awaits Black.

19 ♘d5 (3) **♕f7** (8)

Here Sokolov wasted too much time (and, incidentally, at the end he was in serious time-trouble). To convince himself that there was no choice, two minutes would have sufficed: after 19...♕d7 (not giving up the d6-pawn) 20 f5! Black cannot extricate himself, and therefore he is forced to return the material for the sake of counterplay.

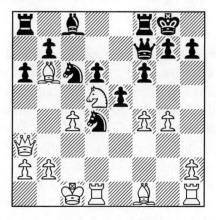

20 f5! (23)

The conclusion of Rodriguez's variation with a '±' assessment. But playing for a bind demands accurate calculation.

20...g6! (to avoid suffocating, Black has to go in for a sharpening of the play) **21 ♖g1?!** (3)

Craving an attack, but 21 ♕xd6! was both stronger, and more practical: 21...gxf5 22 ♗xd4 ♘xd4 (22...exd4 23 ♗g2!) 23 ♘b6 ♗e6 (after 23...♖a7 both 24 ♗g2! with the threat of ♗d5 and 24 ♖xd4 exd4 25 ♗d3 are good, with prospects of success) 24 ♘xa8 ♖xa8 25 gxf5 ♗xf5 26 b3, and Black does not have sufficient compensation for the exchange.

21...gxf5 22 g5!

After making this paradoxical move I began strolling about while awaiting my opponent's reply. Here the honoured guest of the tournament, Mikhail Botvinnik, appeared in the hall, and he immediately asked me: 'Which variation of the Sicilian Defence did you play?'

22...♔h8? (18)

22...♕g7? was altogether bad: 23 ♕e3! f4 24 gxf6 fxe3 25 ♖xg7+ ♔h8 26 ♗xd4 ♘xd4 27 ♖xd4! ♖xf6 (27...exd4? 28 ♗d3 with mate) 28 ♖xh7+ ♔xh7 29 ♘xf6+ and ♖xd6.

Earlier I thought that 22...fxg5 was also weak in view of 23 ♖xg5+ (23 ♗xd4 exd4!) 23...♔h8 24 ♕xd6, and if 24...♗e6?, then 25 ♖xd4! ♖ad8 (25...exd4 26 ♗xd4+) 26 ♕c5! ♘xd4 27 ♕xd4! with a spectacular rout. But then in the computer era I discovered the variation 24...♘f3! 25 ♖g2 (25 ♖g3 ♘xh2) 25...♗e6 with extremely intricate play. 24 ♖xd4!? exd4 25 ♕xd6 is more insidious, with the idea of 25...♖g8 26 ♖xg8+ ♔xg8 27 ♗g2!, but after 27...f4 28 ♘f6+ ♔g7 29 ♘h5+ ♕xh5 30 ♗xc6 bxc6 31 ♗xd4+ ♔f7 32 ♕f6+ ♔e8 33 ♕xc6+ ♔f7 34 ♕xa8 ♕f5, after giving up a pawn, thanks to the opposite-coloured bishops Black retains every chance of a draw.

23 gxf6?! (31)

At the moment when I began thinking about the position (with what to capture on f6?), there was a burst of applause in the hall and the unoccupied players went up to the board where Karpov was playing Spassky. Although Karpov's position from the opening had been somewhat inferior, I was in no doubt that he would save the game. 'A draw there?' I asked Short, who was walking past. 'No, Spassky blundered a bishop' Nigel replied.

Karpov had suddenly caught me on number of points scored and my individual

triumph in the tournament was in question. After with difficulty restoring my equanimity and concentration, I resisted the temptation to offer a draw. However, I decided to act as safely as possible and it was only for this reason that I rejected the tempting and, apparently, better continuation 23 ♘xf6! (after which Stohl gave the 'unclear' 23...♗e6 24 ♕xd6(?) ♗xc4, but 24 ♗xd4!? ♘xd4 25 g6 is far stronger, or the immediate 24 g6! hxg6 25 ♕h3+ ♔g7 26 ♘h5+ ♔g8 27 ♘f4! exf4 28 ♕h6 ♘e5 29 ♗xd4 ♕h7 30 ♕xf4 with a powerful attack), choosing a quieter path with clear guidelines.

23...♗e6 (3) **24 ♕xd6** (2)

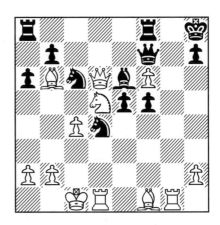

24...♗xd5 (7)

The only move. 24...♖ac8? would have lost ignominiously after 25 ♖g7 ♕h5 (while after 25...♖ae8? the correct reply is 26 ♖xb7!) 26 ♖xd4! ♘xd4 27 ♗xd4 ♗xd5 28 f7!!, or 24...♖g8? 25 ♖xg8+ ♖xg8 26 ♗xd4! exd4 (26...♖d8 27 ♕xd8+! and ♗xe5) 27 ♖e1! ♗c8 28 ♗d3.

25 cxd5 ♕xf6 (not 25...♖ad8? because of 26 ♗xd8 and ♖g7!) **26 ♕xf6+ ♖xf6**

Thus Black has avoided major problems and is hoping to save an inferior endgame. However, the long-range bishops and the strong passed pawn in the centre give White grounds for playing for a win.

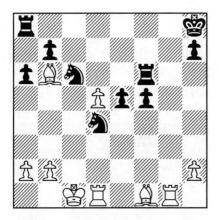

27 ♔b1! (2)

The point of White's idea: wherever the black knight goes, he wins back the pawn and retains the initiative.

27...♘d8

Not an easy choice. 27...♘e7? would be fatal after 28 ♗c7! ♘f3 (28...♘g6? 29 ♖xg6) 29 ♖g3 e4 30 d6 ♘c6 31 d7 ♖ff8 32 ♗c4!, or 27...♘b4? 28 ♗c7! (more forceful than my *Informator* suggestion 28 ♗xd4) 28...♖e8 29 ♗g2 (29 ♗c4!? – Stohl) 29...♖f7 (29...♖g6 30 d6!) 30 ♗xe5+! ♖xe5 31 ♖xd4 a5 32 a3 ♘a6 33 d6. However, there were two other lines:

1) 27...♘a7!? 28 ♗c7 (28 ♗c5!?) 28...♖e8 29 ♗c4! (Stohl's variation with 29 d6 ♖f7 is more harmless) 29...♘c8 30 ♖ge1 ♘f3 31 ♖e3 e4 32 ♗e2 or 30 ♗xe5 ♖xe5 31 d6! ♖f8 32 ♖xd4 ♖e4! 33 ♖xe4 fxe4 34 d7 ♘b6 35 ♗e6 ♖d8 36 ♖d1 e3 37 ♗g4, and White has only a minimal plus;

2) 27...♘b8!? (getting rid of the annoying bishop on c6) 28 ♗xd4 exd4 29 ♖xd4 ♘d7 30 ♗h3, and again White's advantage is not great, even if equality is still a long way off,

Sokolov quickly decided to block the pawn with a ...♘d8-f7-d6 manoeuvre, but he had overlooked a venomous reply.

28 ♗c5! (3) **28...♖c8?!** (8)

Alas, 28...♘f7? is not possible in view of 29 ♖xd4! b6 30 ♗e7 and wins. Upset by the

unexpected deterioration in the situation, Andrey misses a chance to put up a stubborn resistance after 28...b5 29 ♖g3 or 28...b6 with the idea of 29 ♗e7 ♖f7 30 d6 (there is no point in playing 30 ♗d6 ♘f3 31 ♖g3, as in the game, because of 31...♘b7!) 30...♘8c6 31 ♗c4 (31 ♗g5 h6!) 31...♖xe7 32 dxe7 ♘xe7 33 ♖ge1 b5! 34 ♖xe5 ♘dc6 35 ♗d5 ♖d8 with equality, but 30 ♗b4!? is better, or even 29 ♗xd4!? exd4 30 ♖e1! ♘f7 31 ♗xa6.

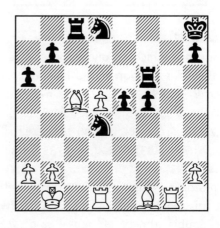

29 ♗e7 (2)

One of the bishops has become rampant, and the other is awaiting its hour. Black is unable to coordinate his pieces.

29...♖f7 (3)

After 29...♖h6 30 d6 ♘8c6 31 ♗c4 (threatening ♗d5) 31...♖g6 32 d7! ♘xe7 33 dxc8♕+ ♘xc8 34 ♗d5 Black has insufficient compensation for the exchange. 29...♖g6 30 ♖xg6 hxg6 31 ♗f6+ ♔g8 32 ♗xe5 ♘f3 33 ♗g3 is also depressing for him.

30 ♗d6! (4) **30...♘f3 31 ♖g3 e4** (3)

Possibly the lesser evil was 31...♖d7 32 ♖xf3 ♖xd6 33 ♖xf5 ♘c6 34 ♗g2 (34 ♗e2 ♘d4 35 ♖xe5 ♘xe2 36 ♖xe2 ♖c7 is unclear) 34...♖e8 35 ♗e4 ♖d7 36 ♖h5 ♘d4. Instead, Sokolov again does not exchange my dark-squared bishop, which is capable of creating mating threats.

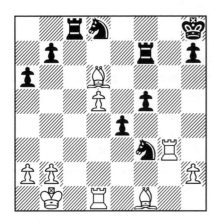

32 ♗e2? (3)

An error which no one noticed. After 32 ♗f4! Black's position would have remained critical: 32...h5 (32...♖g7? 33 ♗h3) 33 ♖h3 ♔g7 34 ♖xh5 ♖f8 35 ♗h3 ♔g6 36 ♖h6+ ♔g7 37 ♗g2!, or 32...h6 33 ♗e2 ♖d7 (33...♔h7 34 ♖h3) 34 ♗xf3 exf3 35 ♖xf3 etc.

32...♖f6? (3)

In Stohl's opinion, 32...♖d7(?) was better, but this would have lost to 33 ♗b4! (with the double threat of ♗c3+ and ♗xf3) 33...♘e5 34 ♖g5 or 33...♘h4 34 ♗h5!.

After 32...♖g7, which is indeed better, I had prepared the following finish: 33 ♗xf3 ♖xg3(?) 34 ♗xe4! ♖e3 (34...♖g5 35 ♗e7 ♖h5? 36 ♖g1!) 35 ♗xf5 ♖c4 36 b3 etc. However, 33...♘f7! is correct: for example, 34 ♗e7 ♖xg3 35 ♗xe4 fxe4 36 hxg3 ♖c7 37 d6 ♖d7 or 34 ♗f4 ♖xg3 35 ♗xg3 (35 ♗xe4 fxe4 36 ♗xg3 ♖d8!) 35...exf3 36 d6 ♔g7 37 d7 ♖g8 with a probable draw.

33 ♗f4! (5)

Alternatively, 33 ♗e7! ♖g6 34 ♗xf3 ♖xg3 35 ♗xe4! ♖g7 36 ♗xf5 ♖xe7 37 ♗xc8 and wins. Having miraculously survived, the bishop becomes ferociously strong. The battle is essentially decided – the mopping-up has begun.

33...♖g6 (33...♘f7 34 ♗xf3 exf3 35 d6! ♖d8 36 d7 f2 37 ♖f3 etc. was also hopeless) **34**

♗xf3 (2) **♖xg3** (1)

Stohl wrongly attached a question mark to this move: in the event of 34...exf3 35 ♖xf3 Black would have lost his f-pawn and would have been quite unable to cope with the passed d-pawn.

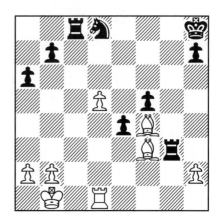

35 ♗xe4! (an example on the theme of bishop domination: if 35...♖g7, then 36 ♗xf5 is decisive, or if 35...♖g4 – 36 ♗e5+ ♔g8 37 ♗xf5) **35...fxe4 36 hxg3 ♔g7** (36...♘f7?! 37 d6! ♔g7 38 d7) **37 ♖d4**

With the fall of the e-pawn Black's last hopes disappear. But in severe time-trouble Sokolov fights to the last bullet.

37...♘f7 38 ♖xe4 ♖d8 39 ♖e7 ♖xd5

According to Stohl, 39...b5 40 d6 ♔f8 (40...♔g8 41 ♖e6!) was more resilient, but after 41 ♖a7! ♘xd6 42 ♖xa6 another pawn would soon have been lost.

40 ♖xb7 h5 41 ♖a7 a5 (12) **42 a4!** (5)

The time scramble was over, and in view of the inevitable loss of the a5-pawn, Black resigned (**1-0**).

An interesting game, which had everything – an opening novelty, a complicated middlegame, some instructive 'questionable decisions' and an elegant finish.

For the third successive time (following the agonising 12-12 in Seville) I finished ahead of my eternal opponent in a tournament battle. In the second half of the event Karpov defeated his two main rivals and achieved a brilliant result – 5½ out of 7, but this did not suffice for first place, only because I scored 6 out of 7, and altogether 'plus eight'! The Belfort tournament could have been one of the best in my career, had it not been for the painful loss to Karpov...

As everyone expected, the main contenders for the Cup were the 12th and 13th world champions. After Amsterdam and Belfort my rating approached ever closer to the cherished 2780 mark. Karpov also endeavoured not to fall behind: after beginning the year 1988 at 2715, he concluded it on 2750, a record high for him.

USSR Champion for the Second Time

55th USSR Championship Premier League (Moscow, 25 July – 19 August 1988): 1–2. **Kasparov** and Karpov – 11½ out of 17; 3–4. Yusupov and Salov – 10; 5–6. Eingorn and Ivanchuk – 9½; 7. Yudasin – 9; 8. Beliavsky – 8½; 9–13. Ehlvest, Smyslov, Gavrikov, A.Sokolov and Vaganian – 8; 14. Khalifman – 7½; 15–16. Smirin and M.Gurevich – 7; 17–18. Malaniuk and Kharitonov – 6.

Three weeks after Belfort, the star-studded 55th USSR Championship in Moscow was wedged in between the solid list of international super-tournaments. This was the last in history to attract the entire cream of Soviet chess. Apart from the participants in the Candidates matches and talented young players, four world champions of different eras began the event – Kasparov, Karpov, Smyslov and Tal (true, after the first round the last named withdrew on account of illness and was replaced by Eingorn), while a fifth, Botvinnik, performed the role of chief arbiter.

Here too there was a tough battle between me and Karpov for the championship, although, of course, we also had other rivals – in particular, Valery Salov, Alexander Beliavsky and Artur Yusupov. By present-day standards the length of the tournament – 17 rounds – was a genuine marathon!

Tal: *'Initially it seemed that the tradition "he came, he saw, he conquered" would be observed. In the first three rounds the clear dictator of fashion, the clear choir leader, was the world champion. His two wins were highly spectacular and instructive. Moreover, the one over Ivanchuk had a very curious psychological background...'*

Indeed, I started well: after a draw with Yusupov I won prettily against the 19-year-old Lvov player Vassily Ivanchuk. This was a significant duel: at 25 years of age I crossed swords for the first time with one of the brightest leaders of the new wave (Ivanchuk, Gelfand, Anand, etc). Dorfman had once told me about his compatriot: he said that they had a lad who was mowing down everyone in turn. By the time of our meeting Ivanchuk was already a champion and prize-winner in many junior championships, the winner of the 55th USSR Championship First League, a strong New York Open and the Barcza Memorial in Debrecen.

Game 41
G.Kasparov-V.Ivanchuk
55th USSR Championship
2nd Round, Moscow 27.07.1988
English Opening A29

---

1 c4 ♘f6 2 ♘c3 e5 3 ♘f3 ♘c6 4 g3 ♗b4 5 ♗g2 0-0 6 0-0 e4 7 ♘g5 ♗xc3 8 bxc3 ♖e8 9 f3!

'Everyone was asking: if Kasparov goes in for a variation (the 2nd and 4th games of the match in Seville), which is not favoured by opening theory, does this mean that there is something in it? Various conjectures were put forward, but they were obscure and vague. Ivanchuk confidently, without a hint of doubt (as indicated by the chess clock), went in for this variation. Ivanchuk's boldness staggered me: it was clear that "Kasparov & Co." had prepared something.' (Tal)

9...exf3?!

9...e3 is nevertheless better (cf. *Game No.27*, note to Black's 9th move), but Vassily replied without thinking. Incidentally, he prepared for the championship of the country at a training session with Karpov (apparently the ex-champion needed to stock up on new chess ideas, with which Ivanchuk was simply overflowing). Noticing that Karpov was following my game with unfeigned interest, I realised that he was seeking the clearest way to equalise.

10 ♘xf3 d5

The main move, which had an excellent reputation. Karpov himself chose against me the rare 10...♕e7 and after 11 e3 he experienced some problems (*Game No.27*). But now he wanted to see what I had up my sleeve. And my reply also followed at blitz speed.

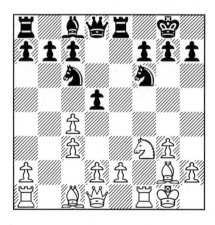

11 d4!

At last I employed my novelty, prepared for the Seville match, with which my 'searches' in the English Opening began. Black was happy with 10...d5 11 cxd5 ♕xd5 (but not 11...♘xd5?! 12 e4!, Uhlmann-Smyslov, Hastings 1972/73) – deprived of his pawn base in the centre, in return he obtained active piece play: 12 d4 ♕h5 (Ribli-Vasyukov, Camaguey 1974), or 12 ♘d4 ♕h5 13 ♘xc6 bxc6 14 e3 ♗g4 (Sigurjonsson-Smyslov, Reykjavik 1974; Uhlmann-Makarychev, Amsterdam 1975).

11...♘e4!

Ivanchuk continued playing at blitz speed, endeavouring to dishearten me, but that didn't happen! Apart from the knight move, which is now the main one, I had also extensively analysed 11...dxc4 12 ♗g5 and 11...h6 12 cxd5, and everywhere, without taking any great risk, White retained the initiative. Moreover, the resulting quite unconventional positions were very much to my taste – their dynamic nature resembled the g2-g3 variation in the Nimzo-Indian Defence, which I had successfully tried in the second and third matches with Karpov.

12 ♕c2!

Trusting in my home analysis, I maintained the same rapid-fire as my opponent. The weaker 12 cxd5 ♘xc3 13 ♕d2 ♘xd5 14 e4 ♘f6 15 e5 ♘e4 16 ♕e3 f5 leads to equality (Vaisser-Janjgava, Uzhgorod 1988).

12...dxc4

Later 12...♗f5 13 ♘h4! was also tried, but why not take the pawn? If Black can manage to consolidate in the centre, things will be difficult for White. But nevertheless there is a possibility of disturbing the knight on e4.

13 ♖b1!

The key move: by attacking the b7-pawn, the rook hinders the development of the bishop on c8, and in some cases it is threatening via b5 to support the action in the centre or on the kingside. 13 ♘e5 ♘xe5 14 ♕xe4 suggested itself (this was probably also analysed by my opponents), but here Black could have fought for equality by 14...♘g4 15 ♕f4 f6 or 14...f5 15 ♕d5+ ♕xd5 16 ♗xd5+ ♘f7.

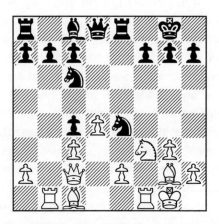

13...f5?! (8)

A risky weakening of the king's citadel. If 13...♕e7 White has the promising 14 ♘d2 (Hodgson-Naumkin, Amantea 1995) or 14 ♘e5! ♘xe5 15 ♗xe4 ♘g4(g6) 16 ♗d5.

13...f6! is more solid: 14 ♘e5! (little is given by 14 ♘h4 ♕e7 15 ♘f5 ♗xf5 16 ♖xf5 ♘d8), when White is better after 14...fxe5? 15 ♗xe4 ♗h3 (or 15...exd4 16 ♗xh7+ and ♗g6!; 15...h6? 16 ♗xh6!) 16 ♗xh7+ ♔h8 17 ♗g6! ♕d5 (17...♗xf1? 18 ♕f5!, while if 17...exd4? then 18 ♖b5! ♗e5 19 ♕e4!! is prettily decisive) 18 ♖f3 exd4 19 ♗xe8 ♖xe8 20 ♕g6 ♕e6 21 ♕xe6 ♖xe6 22 ♖f8+ ♔h7 23 ♖b5! or 17...♖e6! 18 ♗f5! ♗xf5 19 ♕xf5 ♖f6 20 ♕e4 etc. But, after 14...♘xe5! 15 ♗xe4 ♘g6 (from the early 1990s this variation was tested by correspondence players) 16 ♗xb7 (16 ♖f2 c6!) 16...♗xb7 17 ♖xb7 c5 18 e3 ♕c8 Black has an acceptable game.

14 g4! (7)

On seeing this unexpected move, Vassily nervously flinched and sank into agonising thought. What I had played was obviously

not in his analysis! It suddenly transpired that Black faced serious dangers, and Ivanchuk's ardent expression somehow immediately faded.

14...♕e7 (46)

A difficult choice. After 14...♘d6 15 ♗g5! (David-Polak, Olomouc 1995) or 14...g6 15 ♗f4! (Smirin-Avrukh, Groningen 1996) White's initiative more than compensates for the pawn deficit. He is also better after 14...fxg4 15 ♘e5! ♘d6 16 ♘xc6 bxc6 17 e4, while 15...♘xe5? 16 ♗xe4 ♘g6 17 ♗xg6 hxg6 18 ♕xg6 is altogether ruinous for Black: 18...♕d7 (even worse is 18...♖e7? 19 ♗a3 or 18...♕e7? 19 ♖b5, Lesiege-Zugic, Montreal 2001) 19 ♖b5!! (but not my *Informator* suggestion 19 d5(?) because of 19...a5!) 19...♖e6 (Black cannot play either 19...♕xb5? 20 ♖f7 or 19...♕e6? 20 ♕h5) 20 ♕h5 ♕e8 21 ♗a3! with an attack that does not die away even after the exchange of queens.

15 gxf5 (28) **15...♘d6?**

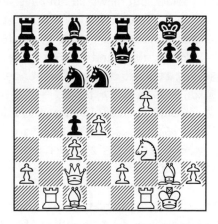

Unable to compose himself after such an abrupt turn of events, Vassily commits a decisive mistake. The obvious 15...♗xf5 was necessary, when after 16 ♘g5! (the weaker 16 ♘e5 ♘xe5 17 ♖xf5 ♘g4! allows Black to equalise) 16...♗g6 (or 16...g6?!) 17 ♗xe4 ♗xe4 18 ♘xe4 ♕xe4 19 ♕xe4 ♖xe4 20

♖xb7 Black merely has an inferior endgame.
16 ♘g5! (8)

Now White simultaneously has several strong concrete threats.

16...♕xe2 (16...h6 17 f6! or 16...♘d8 17 ♗d5+ ♔h8 18 f6! was fatal, but otherwise there follows e2-e4) **17 ♗d5+** (7) **17...♔h8 18 ♕xe2 ♖xe2 19 ♗f4**

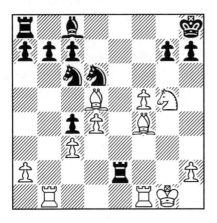

19...♘d8 (13)

Now Black comes under a spectacular mating attack, but he would not have saved the game by 19...♗xf5 20 ♗xd6 ♗xb1 21 ♘f7+ and mate in two moves, 19...♘xf5 20 ♘f7+ ♔g8 21 ♘d8+ and ♘xc6, 19...♘e7 20 ♗f3 ♖xa2 21 ♗xd6 cxd6 22 ♖be1, or 19...h6 20 ♗xd6 hxg5 21 ♗xc7 etc.

20 ♗xd6 cxd6 21 ♖be1! ♖xe1 22 ♖xe1 ♗d7 23 ♖e7 ♗c6 (or 23...h6 24 f6!) **24 f6! 1-0**

In view of 24...♗xd5 25 ♖e8+ ♗g8 26 f7 ♘xf7 27 ♘xf7 mate.

This interesting miniature was the product of one of my best novelties. After this opening catastrophe Karpov finally learned what had been awaiting him in reply to 10...d5, while Ivanchuk suffered for about a further six years when playing against me with Black. Tal: *'The elegance with which Kasparov conducted the attack is impressive. My tastes differ to those of the prize jury.*

Kasparov's combination in his game with Smirin was very good, but the meeting with Ivanchuk... To put it crudely, I too could have done the same against Smirin.'

In the 3rd round I won quite a nice Grünfeld with Black against Gurevich. But then, as Tal put it, I 'rather lost my way'. My 'white' game in the 4th round with Sokolov affected my fighting mood. After catching my opponent in a variation of the English Opening (also prepared for Seville), I emerged a pawn up – and suddenly I simply blundered it away! I then had to fight for a draw in an inferior position. After this vexing lapse there followed draws with Gavrikov, Smyslov, Karpov (Game No.5 in *Kasparov vs. Karpov 1988-2009*), Malaniuk and Ehlvest!

A series of six successive draws – previously this had occurred with me only in the 47th USSR Championship (1979), and also in rounds 4-9. It was time to accelerate! In the 10th round I defeated Kharitonov and reached '+3'. At this point Salov was leading with 7 out of 10, pursued by the two 'Ks' and Beliavsky on 6½. In the 11th round Salov lost to Yudasin, I shared the point with Beliavsky, and Karpov beat Gurevich to burst half a step ahead. The battle for the lead became intense in the extreme.

For the 12th round game with the 20-year-old Belorussian master Ilya Smirin I arrived in a very fighting mood. Ilya was another talented representative of the new wave, a pupil of the well-known theoretician and trainer Albert Kapengut. Soon he became a grandmaster, moved to Israel and played successfully in many Olympiads and international tournaments. Being a dangerous tactician, Smirin did not appear to be a very comfortable opponent: after all, with Black he employed my favourite opening – the King's Indian Defence, and I had to fight as though against myself.

Game 42
G.Kasparov-I.Smirin
55th USSR Championship
12th Round, Moscow 10.08.1988
King's Indian Defence E97

1 ♘f3 ♘f6 2 c4 g6 3 ♘c3 ♗g7 4 e4 d6 5 d4 0-0 6 ♗e2 e5 7 0-0 ♘c6 8 d5 ♘e7 9 ♘d2

In the late 1980s this line supplanted even 9 ♘e1 (*Game Nos.58, 64, 77*), and it was only from the mid-1990s that 9 b4 came into fashion.

9...a5 10 a3 ♘d7 11 ♖b1 f5 12 b4

It was after my games with Gavrikov and Smirin from this 55th USSR Championship that the rapid development of this variation began.

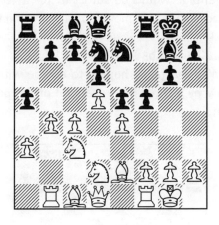

12...b6?!

This merely creates a new target for White to attack. 12...♔h8! is better, as I played in the 5th round against Gavrikov, not yet imagining what to do next. Black's problem is to overcome the crowding of his pieces, and soon I devised the plan with ...♔h8 and ...♘g8, which later became the main line (*Game No.80*).

13 f3 f4

Black begins preparing a typical attack on the king with ...g6-g5-g4, assuming that

White's offensive on the queenside is not so terrible for him. After 13...♔h8 14 ♕c2 the move ...b7-b6 looks to be a waste of a tempo, and also 13...♗h6 14 ♘b3 ♗xc1 15 ♕xc1 does not eliminate the threat of c4-c5.

14 ♘a4

14 ♘b3 axb4 15 axb4 g5 16 c5 (Bönsch-Vogt, Glauchau 1987) or 14 ♕c2 g5 15 ♘b5 ♖f7 16 c5! bxc5 17 bxc5 ♘xc5 18 ♘b3 (Dautov-Bokan, Sverdlovsk 1989) comes into consideration, but I thought that the d2-knight would be more useful on c4.

14...axb4 15 axb4 g5 16 c5 ♘f6 17 cxd6 (not 17 c6? h5, when the play is all one way) **17...cxd6 18 b5**

This move with the threat of ♘c4 and ♗a3 seemed to be very strong, but Black has an adequate defence.

18...♗d7 19 ♘c4 ♘c8 20 ♗a3 ♘e8

The first critical moment.

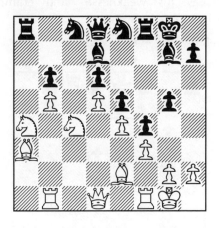

21 g4!

Realising that White's activity on the queenside has come to a standstill (the manoeuvre of the knight from a4 to c6 or the bishop from a3 to f2 is too slow), and that Black is about to play ...h7-h5 and ...g5-g4, I decided to try and stifle the opponent's attack.

21...fxg3?!

Annotating the game in *Informator*,

Nikitin and I considered this capture to be the only move and we condemned 21...h5 in view of 22 h3 hxg4(?) 23 hxg4. However, 22...♖f7! and ...♗f8 was correct, with unclear, double-edged play.

Smirin's striving to open the game on the kingside is understandable, but after the removal of the pawn from f4 White's dark-squared bishop is sharply activated, and in addition e3 becomes a potential transit square for the knight, which is dreaming of reaching f5.

22 hxg3 g4! 23 ♗c1!

A timely switching of the bishop to the main part of the battlefield. After 23 fxg4 ♖xf1+ 24 ♔xf1 (24 ♗xf1 ♘f6!) 24...♕g5 25 ♔g2 ♘f6! 26 ♘c3 ♘xg4 or 25 ♔g1 ♕g6!, intending ...♕xe4, ...♘f6xg4 and ...♗h6, the opponent's plan would have been justified. Now, however, Black's attack comes to a halt, whereas his weaknesses and cramped position are perceptible.

23...gxf3 24 ♗xf3

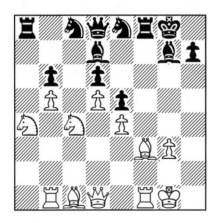

24...♘f6

White has the advantage after 24...♖b8 25 ♗e3, keeping the b6-pawn under fire (the *Informator* recommendation 25 ♗g4(?!) ♖xf1+ 26 ♔xf1 is less good because of 26...♘f6! 27 ♗xd7 ♕xd7). But 24...♕c7!? is probably better – after 25 ♕b3 ♗h3 26 ♖f2

♘f6 27 ♗g5 ♘g4 28 ♗xg4 ♗xg4 29 ♖bf1 White's advantage is not so appreciable.

25 ♗g5 (here too 25 ♗e3!? or 25 ♖f2!? is somewhat stronger, and only in the event of 25...h5 – 26 ♗g5!) **25...♖a7**

Again 25...♕c7!? was better.

26 ♖f2 (26 ♕b3!? ♖b7 27 ♕e3 h6 28 ♗h4! was also interesting) **26...♖b7 27 ♖b3** (27 ♗e3!?) **27...♖a7?!**

Incautiously weakening the b6-pawn. 27...♕e8 would have retained a more or less defensible position: for example, 28 ♗xf6 ♖xf6 29 ♗h5 ♕d8 30 ♖xf6 ♗xf6 31 ♗g4 ♗g5.

28 ♖b1

Doubting whether after the tempting 28 ♘axb6!? ♘xb6 29 ♘xb6 ♕xb6 30 ♗e3 ♕a5(b7) 31 ♗xa7 ♕xa7 32 b6 White's advantage would be sufficient for a win, I decided to repeat moves to gain time on the clock.

28...♖b7 29 ♖b3 ♖a7?!

Was Ilya really hoping to escape with a draw by a three-fold repetition of the position?

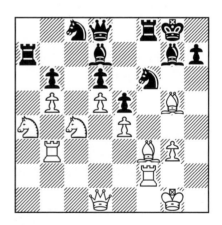

30 ♖b4!?

'This rook has carried out an enormous amount of prophylactic work in this game. Now it simultaneously defends three white pieces, freeing the queen to take part in the attack.' (Nikitin). Again 30 ♘axb6!? came into consideration, but I was afraid of selling my advantage too cheaply and preferred to increase the pressure.

30...♔h8?!

30...♕e8? did not work because of 31 ♘axb6 ♘xb6 32 ♘xb6 (32...♗xb5? 33 ♗xf6! and ♗h5, winning), but the passive 30...♖b7 was more resilient.

31 ♕f1!

'A strong manoeuvre, switching the weight of the battle to the kingside. Though defended many times, the f6-knight suddenly turns out to be in a desperate position.' (Nikitin)

31...♗xb5?!

It was already too late for 31...♖b7? in view of 32 ♗h5! h6 33 ♗h4 or 32...♖c7(a7) 33 ♘ab2 with the lethal threat of ♖b3-f3, while moves such as 31...♔g8 or 31...♖a8 might be described as merely awaiting the execution. And, after some thought, Smirin decided that it was 'better to die standing than to live on his knees'.

32 ♖xb5 ♖xa4

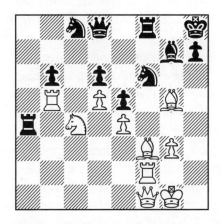

33 ♗g2

Everyone approved of this infiltrating move: it is clear that White has powerful compensation for the pawn. And only the intervention of the computer brought to light a far from obvious alternative – 33 ♗d1!? ♖a1 34 ♘e3, when Black has no satisfactory defence against the threat of ♖bb2 and ♘g4 (if 34...h6, then 35 ♗h4).

33...h6 34 ♗h4 ♕e8!

'Without this move the battle would have lost its point: passive defence was equivalent to resignation.' (Nikitin)

35 ♗xf6! ♖xf6 (alas, if 35...♕xb5?, then 36 ♗xg7+ and ♖xf8 is decisive) **36 ♖xf6 ♕xb5 37 ♖e6!**

'Here none of the watching grandmasters could suggest an effective continuation of White's attack. I thought that Garry would force a draw by 37 ♖f8+ ♗xf8 38 ♕xf8+ ♔h7 39 ♕f7+.' (Nikitin). And, indeed, 39 ♗h3? does not work because of 39...♕c5+ 40 ♔g2 ♖a2+ 41 ♔h1 ♖a1+.

And the tempting 37 ♗h3!? would have been parried by 37...♕c5+ 38 ♔h1 ♖a1! 39 ♕xa1 ♗xf6 40 ♕f1 ♔g7 41 ♗xc8 b5! 42 ♘xd6 ♕xd6 43 ♕xb5 ♕a3, when in view of the opposite-colour bishops and the open position of his king, White is unable to convert his extra pawn.

37...♔g8!

There is nothing else: 37...♖xc4? 38 ♕f7! ♖c1+ 39 ♔h2 and ♖e8+.

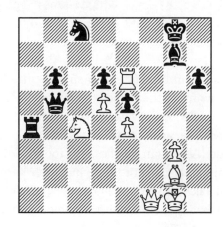

38 ♗h3?

With this plausible move, strangely

enough, White squanders his entire enormous advantage! I discovered an amazing way to win only with the help of a computer – 38 Bf3! Rb4 (38...Wxc4 39 Be2!, 38...Ra2 39 Be2! and 38...Ra7 39 Bh5! Re7 40 Kg2! are also bad for Black) 39 Bd1!! with an irresistible attack on the light squares: 39...Rb1 40 Wf3 and then Wh5 (and if 40...Rxd1+ 41 Wxd1 Wxc4, then 42 Re8+ Kh7 43 Wf3), or 39...h5 40 Kh1! Rb1 (40...h4 41 gxh4!) 41 Wf3 Wd7 42 Kg2! b5 43 Ne3. But to mentally find *such* a line at the board just before the first time control...

38...Rxc4?

In severe time-trouble Smirin loses control of the position and overlooks the sudden, uncommonly pretty inclusion of the h3-bishop in the attack. 38...h5! was essential – it is doubtful whether White has anything stronger than 39 Ne3 Wxf1+ 40 Bxf1! Rxe4 41 Nf5 Bf8 42 Re8 Ne7! 43 Nxe7+ Kf7 44 Rxf8+ Kxf8 45 Nf5 (Stohl) 45...h4 with equality, or 42 Bb5! Re1+ 43 Kg2 Rc1! 44 Re8 Kf7, and with accurate defence Black overcomes his slight difficulties.

39 Rxh6!! Bxh6 (39...Wc5+ 40 Kh1 Rc1 41 Be6 mate!) **40 Be6+ Kh8 41 Wf6+ 1-0**

In view of 41...Kh7 (41...Bg7 42 Wh4+) 42 Wf7+ Bg7 43 Bf5+ Kh8 44 Wh5+ Kg8 45 Be6+ Kf8 46 Wf7 mate. The auditorium erupted in a storm of applause.

This win brought me a special prize 'for the swiftest attack' and enabled me to catch the leader, Karpov, who had made a quick draw. We were joined by Salov, who defeated Vaganian. In the 13th round I overcame Yudasin with Black, but both Karpov and Salov also won their games. The leading trio had 9 points, with Yusupov and Beliavsky on 7½.

In the 14th round came my clash with Salov, which was of colossal competitive importance. Despite the apparently calm, even course of events, the underlying intensity of the struggle was very great. In the fifth hour of play I was able to set my opponent some problems, and on the 40th move, the last before the time control, now deep in the endgame, he made a decisive mistake.

Since that day Karpov made a quick draw, for the first time in the tournament I became the sole leader. But here my traditional 'curse of five wins' told (although in rounds 10-14 I scored 'just' 4½ out of 5): at the finish I did not find the strength to win even one of my three remaining games (with Khalifman, Vaganian and Eingorn). And as a result Karpov caught me, by easily winning in the 16th round against his army club-mate Malaniuk.

Mikhail Tal: *'Many are saying: "How badly Kasparov played!". Karpov knew that "+6" would be sufficient. Incidentally, this was the ex-champion's expected score according to his rating. So that "only" +6 for the world champion is an excellent advertisement for the championship of the country! After all, Kasparov did not play worse than in Amsterdam or Belfort. It was simply that there he didn't have the same opponents. But now everyone was clinging on "for dear life". The fact that to maintain his rating Kasparov had to score +8 indicates that most Soviet players are rather under-rated... After all, this was a high result. And the fact that the winners finished 1½ points ahead of their nearest rivals indicates that on this occasion victory was gained by them with an obvious superiority.'*

Now, according to the regulations, on 22nd August an additional match of four games for the title of USSR champion between Karpov and me should have begun (and with a score of 2-2 – play to the first win). And on 19th August the drawing of lots even took place. Karpov drew the white pieces in the first game, but he did not want to play. After a scandal, described in detail in *Kasparov vs. Karpov 1988-2009*, this match did not in fact take place. In the autumn the Plenum of the Soviet Chess Federation (for which read: the State Sports Committee) decided to award USSR championship gold medals to both grandmasters.

Difficult Autumn in Reykjavik

Third World Cup Tournament (Reykjavik, 1–27 October 1988): 1. **Kasparov** – 11 out of 17; 2. Beliavsky – 10½; 3. Tal – 10; 4–5. Hjartarson and Ehlvest – 9½; 6–8. Timman, Sax and Yusupov – 9; 9–11. Andersson, Speelman and Nunn – 8½; 12–13. Nikolic and A.Sokolov – 8; 14. Ribli – 7½; 15–16. Portisch and Spassky – 7; 17. Korchnoi – 6½; 18. Petursson – 6.

The autumn super-tournament in Reykjavik, with cold and penetrating sea winds, was for Iceland the most important sporting and cultural event since the time of the legendary Spassky-Fischer match (1972). This was a kind of battle of the dinosaurs from the classical chess era: Korchnoi, Tal, Portisch and Spassky himself, plus Karpov's generation – Timman, Andersson, Ribli, Sax and Beliavsky. The feeling of living chess history was further intensified when the policeman who in 1972 had guarded Fischer arrived at the new opera theatre, where we were playing.

There was an incident at the start of the tournament: because of a strike by baggage handlers at Amsterdam airport, many of the participants lost their suitcases. However, gradually they turned up – thus my case arrived two days after the start. There were no computers or internet, there were no entertainments in small, peaceful Reykjavik, (the rapid leap in the development of Iceland was to occur later), and we simply played chess.

This marathon tournament – 17 games! – went very badly for me. Before the event I was unable to relax normally and create the necessary reserve of nervous energy. Even so, after beating Andersson in the 2nd round and Hjartarson in the 6th, at the one-third distance I was in the leading group: Tal – 4½ out of 6; Beliavsky and Kasparov – 4.

But in the 7th round a disaster occurred: after convincingly outplaying Andrey Sokolov with Black in a Scheveningen, I first squandered a big advantage, and on the 37th move I left my queen en prise!

Tal: *'A sensation! The distraught Kasparov was still sitting at the board, when Spassky came up to console him: "Don't be upset, Garry! These things happen – yesterday I also made a terrible blunder...". "When I blunder my queen at the age of 50, it will also be nothing terrible", Garry replied. The favourite's unexpected mishap has imparted a piquant flavour to the tournament battle. Everyone was expecting one of the world champion's famous spurts, but it has clearly been delayed.'*

This painful defeat was followed by two draws. In my 9th round game with Tal I had an enduring advantage, but in a pawn endgame with my hasty 34th move I lost quite good practical winning chances. True, in the 10th round I beat Korchnoi, but then I again stalled, gaining only draws against Nunn, Spassky and Beliavsky.

It was quite logical that in the first thirteen rounds I managed with great anxiety (mainly because of missed opportunities) to reach only +2, a pitiful score for my rating and title. Together with Timman, Nunn and Hjartarson I was half a point behind the leaders – Beliavsky, Tal and Ehlvest.

At times I felt that I had no strength left,

and it was not clear thanks to what I could make a finishing spurt. But on the eve of the 14th round, friends phoned from Moscow and informed me of the details of another surprise, which the USSR State Sports Committee had prepared for me.

Averbakh: *'Exploiting Kasparov's absence from Moscow, on 22nd October the State Sports Committee hastily arranged an extraordinary pre-election plenum of the Chess Federation, at which Vitaly Sevastyanov was again elected chairman. The new praesidium also included a number of supporters of ex-world champion Karpov. In this way the State Sports Committee once again demonstrated how little account it took of the world champion's opinion.'*

The intrigues of my opponents encouraged me. Suddenly I acquired the additional strength and competitive malice that was so needed. And I found my form!

Game 43
J.Timman-G.Kasparov
World Cup
14th Round, Reykjavik 22.10.1988
King's Indian Defence E88

1 d4 ♘f6 2 c4 g6 3 ♘c3 ♗g7

Up until then Timman had not gained an opening advantage when I chose the Grünfeld Defence. But here I wanted to avoid his home preparation and I chose the King's Indian, which was familiar to me from childhood and where there is more risk for both sides.

4 e4 d6 5 f3 (my opponent's main weapon) **5...0-0 6 ♗e3 e5**

A surprise! Earlier I played 6...♘c6, including against Timman (Moscow 1981; Bugojno 1982), while once I surprised Beliavsky with the gambit 6...a6 7 ♗d3 (7 ♕d2 ♘c6 – *Game*

No.91) 7...c5 (Game No.81 in *Garry Kasparov on Garry Kasparov Part I*). 6...♘bd7 with the idea of ...c7-c5 is also possible (*Game No.68*).

7 d5 (7 ♘ge2 – *Game Nos.90, 98*) **7...c6**

A more dynamic move than the old 7...♘h5 8 ♕d2 f5, which I later tried against Karpov (Game No.28 in *Kasparov vs. Karpov 1988-2009*) and Timman (*Game No.84*).

8 ♗d3 (8 ♕d2 – *Game No.92*) **8...b5?!**

My first experience in this variation, which I later repeated against Gulko (Linares 1990). 8...cxd5 9 cxd5 ♘h5 10 ♘ge2 f5 is more solid, as I played against Timman (Paris (rapid) 1991) and Karpov (Game No.36 in *Kasparov vs. Karpov 1988-2009*).

9 cxb5

Timman took the pawn very confidently (he had already played this), although the restraining 9 a3! is stronger. Because of this move, which became widely known after the game Ivanchuk-Piket (Tilburg 1989), in the end I gave up 8...b5.

9...cxd5 10 exd5

Here I had a serious think: what to do next?

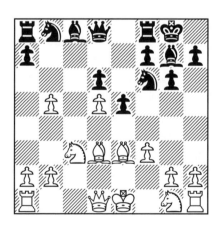

The *Encyclopaedia of Chess Openings* of that time assessed the position after 10...♗b7 and ...♘b8-d7-b6 as 'unclear'. But after 11 ♘ge2 Black is rather a long way from this assessment: 11...♘xd5?! 12 ♘xd5

♗xd5 13 ♘c3 ♗b7 14 ♗e4 or 11...♘bd7, and now 12 ♗c2 a6 13 bxa6 (Timman-Quinteros, Bled/Portoroz 1979) 13...♗xa6! 14 0-0 (14 b4?! e4!) 14...♘b6 15 ♗b3 ♕c7 is indeed unclear, but after 12 0-0! ♘b6 (12...♘xd5?! 13 ♘xd5 ♗xd5 14 ♘c3 ♘b6 15 ♗xg6!) 13 ♗g5 ♘bxd5?! 14 ♘xd5 ♗xd5 15 ♗xf6! ♕xf6 16 ♗xg6 White has an obvious advantage.

However, at the board a reckless idea immediately occurred to me, and after thinking for some 40 minutes I convinced myself that at the least it was interesting and practically correct.

10...e4!

At that time this was a little-known continuation. Black unmasks his 'main strength' – the g7-bishop, and here this fully justifies his insignificant loss. Besides, the audacious pawn break – into a three-fold attack! – stunned Timman.

11 ♘xe4

Of course, not 11 ♗c2? (van der Sterren-Scheeren, Amsterdam 1980) 11...exf3! and ...♖e8. However, Black had to reckon with two other possibilities:

1) 11 ♗xe4 ♘xe4 12 ♘xe4!? (nothing is given by 12 fxe4 ♕h4+! 13 ♔f1 f5 or 13 ♔d2 ♗xc3+ and ...♕xe4) 12...f5! (stronger than Stohl's variation with 12...♖e8 13 ♘e2 f5 14 ♗g5!) 13 ♘c3 ♖e8 14 ♔f2 a6! with sufficient compensation for the material deficit: 15 ♘ge2 ♖xe3! 16 ♔xe3 axb5 17 a3 ♕b6+ 18 ♔d2 ♘d7 19 ♔c2 ♗a6 etc;

2) 11 fxe4!? ♘g4 12 ♕d2 (12 ♗f4 a6!) 12...f5 13 ♘f3 (13 ♘ge2?! fxe4! 14 ♗xe4 ♘d7 is weaker), when Black faces a choice:

a) 13...♗xc3?! 14 bxc3 fxe4 15 ♗xe4 ♕e7 (my *Informator* suggestion 15...♖e8(?) is bad because of 16 ♘g5!) 16 h3! ♘xe3 17 ♕xe3 ♗f5 18 0-0! ♕xe4 19 ♕h6! ♕e7 20 ♖ae1 ♕g7 21 ♕xg7+ ♔xg7 22 ♘d4 with powerful compensation for the piece;

b) 13...♘xe3! 14 ♕xe3 f4 15 ♕f2 ♘d7 16 0-0 ♘e5 17 ♘xe5 ♗xe5, when 18 ♘e2?! (Agdestein-Maki, Gjovik 1985) is inaccurate in view of 18...f3! 19 gxf3 ♗h3, but also after 18 ♔h1! (18 ♗e2 g5!) 18...♕f6 the active play on the dark squares and kingside compensates for the missing pawns.

This all seemed too risky to Timman and, as usual in his duels with me, he played as safely as possible.

11...♘xd5 12 ♗g5

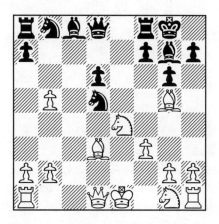

12...♕a5+

In my commentary made soon after the game I condemned 12...♕b6(!?) because of 13 ♕d2 ♘d7 14 ♗c4, 'driving the knight from the centre and comfortably completing development'. But later I went in for this in the aforementioned game with Gulko, and after 14...♘5f6 15 ♘xf6+ (15 ♘xd6 ♘e5!) with 15...♘xf6! 16 ♘e2 ♖e8 I could have gained full compensation for the pawn (alas, when calculating the variation 17 ♗h4 d5 18 ♗f2 ♕e6 19 ♗d3, I overlooked the strong blow 19...♘e4!).

13 ♕d2 ♕xd2+ (the exchange of queens is the point of Black's plan) **14 ♗xd2!**

If 14 ♔xd2 the simplest is 14...h6 15 ♗h4 ♗xb2 16 ♖b1 ♗e5 with equality, but 14...♘d7!? is also interesting – Black has no reason for complaint.

14...♗xb2

In avoiding the complications, White has been deprived of his material plus. The gambit line 14...a6!? 15 ♘xd6 ♗e6 promised only equality, and with my characteristic optimism I was already hoping for more.

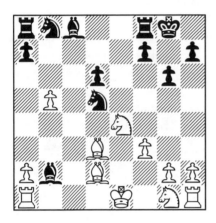

15 ♖b1

15 ♖d1!? ♘d7 16 ♘e2 was more accurate (after 16 ♘xd6?! ♗a3! White is dangerously behind in development), after which Black can play 16...♘7b6 (16...♘e5? 17 ♗h6) 17 ♘xd6 ♗e6 with compensation for the pawn (Razuvaev–Lautier, Paris 1989), or 16...♗a3 17 ♗c1 ♗b4+ 18 ♔f1 ♘7b6 19 a3 ♗c5 20 ♘xc5 dxc5, maintaining approximate equality.

15...♗g7

Not seeing any need to defend the 'unappetising' d6-pawn. However, 15...♗e5!? 16 ♘e2 ♘d7 also made sense, provoking the weakening f3-f4.

16 ♘e2

White completes his development. Perhaps 16 ♘xd6 should nevertheless have been preferred, if only to vacate the e4-square for the bishop. After 16...♗e6 17 ♘e2 ♘d7 the play becomes more lively, but Black's activity is merely sufficient for comfortable equality.

16...♘d7

Black aims above all to activate his pieces as much as possible (by ...♘e5), and to restrict the opponent's pieces. I rejected the obvious 16...♗e6 largely because of 17 ♘g5 ♘d7 18 ♘xe6 fxe6 19 0-0 (Muir-Vogt, Bern 1990), fearing that I would not manage to derive much from this position with defects in my pawn structure.

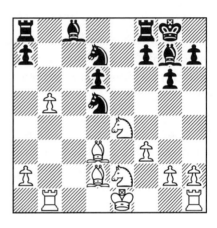

17 ♘xd6

A responsible move: now White has to play very accurately. However, in any case Black has an excellent game: 17 ♖c1 ♘e5 18 ♗b1 a6! or 17 ♗c2 ♘c5! and ...♗e6. I thought that 17 ♔f2 ♘e5 18 ♗c2 was more solid, with the idea of 18...♘c4 19 ♖hd1 or 18...♗f5 19 g4!?.

17...♘c5 18 ♗c2 (18 ♗c4?! ♘b6 was inaccurate, but 18 ♗e4!? was quite suitable)

18...♗e6 19 ♘e4

Despite his extra pawn, White's position is rather unpleasant – to the problem of evacuating his king is added the uncoordinated state of his pieces: 19 ♔f2?! ♖ad8 20 ♘e4 ♘xe4+ 21 ♗xe4 ♘f6! or 19 0-0?! ♖fd8 20 ♘e4 ♘xe4 21 ♗xe4 (21 fxe4 ♘b6!) 21...f5 22 ♗c2 ♘b6 23 ♗g5 ♖e8! with the initiative. If 19 a4 there was the good reply 19...♘b6 20 a5 ♘c4 21 ♘xc4 ♗xc4 22 ♔f2 ♖fe8, and if 19 ♖c1 – 19...♖fd8 20 ♗b1 ♖xd6 21 ♖xc5 a6 etc.

19...罝ac8

Imperceptibly Black has gained complete control over the centre of the board. And Timman flinched in the face of the slowly increasing pressure.

20 0-0?!

Incorrectly taking the king away from the defence of the minor pieces. If 20 ♘g5 there is the simple 20...♗d7, but 20 ♔f2 was better, or else a line soon tested in a correspondence game – 20 a4 ♘xe4 21 ♗xe4 f5 22 ♗d3 罝fd8, still with roughly equal chances (23 a5! ♘c3!). But after castling, White's difficulties increase.

20...♘xe4 21 ♗xe4 f5 22 ♗d3

In *Informator* I attached a question mark to this move, and in the magazine *Shakhmaty v SSSR* I added: 'A serious mistake, with severe consequences. White decided against the exchange 22 ♗xd5 ♗xd5, although this was his only chance of retaining equality.' However, in fact this exchange would have been to the advantage of Black, with his pair of powerful bishops dominating the entire board: 23 ♘c1 (23 罝fc1 ♗xa2) 23...♗c4 24 罝d1 罝fd8, or 23 a4 罝c2 24 罝fd1 ♗a2 25 罝bc1 罝b2 etc. Whereas after the retreat of the bishop it is more difficult for him to capitalise on his advantage.

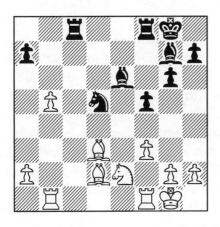

22...♘b6!

Now all the central squares are under fire by Black, and it is difficult for the white pieces to find strong points. Both ...♗xa2 and ...罝fd8 are threatened.

23 ♘c1?!

Awkward prophylaxis. If 23 罝bc1, then 23...罝cd8! is unpleasant. But it was better to return the extra pawn by 23 ♗e3!? ♗xa2 (23...罝fd8 24 罝fd1) 24 罝bc1! 罝xc1 (24...罝ce8 25 ♔f2) 25 罝xc1 罝d8 26 ♗b1 with decent chances of a draw.

23...罝fd8 (White's position is deteriorating step by step) **24 ♗g5 罝d7 25 罝e1**

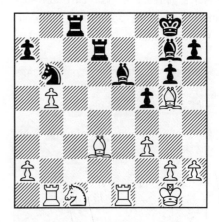

25...♔f7?!

An imperceptible error. The modest 25...♗f7! with the same threat of ...罝xc1 would have posed White more problems: both 26 ♗f1? ♗d4+ 27 ♔h1 ♗c3 and 26 ♗e3?! ♘a4! are weak, and therefore he has to go in for the variation 26 罝e7 罝xe7 27 ♗xe7 ♘d5 28 ♗g5 ♘c3 29 罝b4 h6 30 ♗d2 (30 ♗h4?! ♘xb5!) 30...罝d8 31 ♗xc3 ♗xc3 32 罝b1, still with hopes of saving the game.

26 ♗e2?!

Returning the favour. The incautious king move to f7 presented White with a latent tactical resource – 26 ♗f1! ♗d4+ 27 ♔h1 ♗c3 28 ♘d3! ♗xa2 (28...♗xe1?! 29 ♘e5+ ♔g7 30 ♘xd7) 29 罝bc1! ♔g7 (29...♗xe1 30

♘e5+ ♔g7 31 ♖xc8 and ♘xd7) 30 ♖e2!
♗b3!, and Black's advantage is altogether
slight.

26...h6

If 26...♘a4, then 27 ♗e3! ♘c3 (27...♖e8
28 ♗f2) 28 ♖b4 with the saving idea of b5-
b6. The immediate 26...♘d5!? looked tempting – then 27 ♘b3(?) ♘c3 28 ♖b2 would
have encountered the double attack
28...♘e4!, but there is the far more resilient
27 ♖d1 ♘c3 28 ♖xd7+ ♔xd7 29 ♖b3 ♘xe2+
30 ♘xe2 ♖c2 31 ♔f1 ♖xa2 32 ♗f4 and b5-
b6 with equality.

27 ♗h4 ♘d5

Black's pressure is threatening, but
White's defensive possibilities are still far
from exhausted.

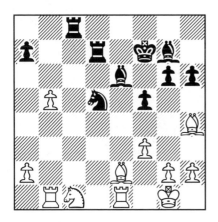

28 ♗d1?

With time-trouble approaching, White
collapses. 'It should have been possible to
hold on by giving up a pawn: 28 b6(?!) axb6
29 ♗b5' I wrote in 1988, but after 29...♖a7
White's position is unenviable. On the other
hand, after 28 ♘b3! ♘c3 29 ♖b2 f4 Black's
advantage is not so clear. Now, however, a
crisis quickly ensues.

28...♗d4+!

An elegant solution to the problem, although 28...♘c3 29 ♗b3 ♗xb3 30 ♖xb3
♗d4+! 31 ♔f1 (31 ♗f2 ♗xf2+ and ...♘d1+)

31...g5 32 ♗g3 f4 was also sufficient.
29 ♗f2 (there is nothing else: 29 ♔f1 ♘e3+!
or 29 ♔h1 ♘c3! and ...g6-g5) **29...♗xf2+ 30
♔xf2 ♘c3 31 ♗b3 ♗xb3 32 ♖xb3 ♘d1+!**

This knight has had an amazing career!
Black's domination in the centre has extended to all 16 squares on the c- and d-files
– and has become absolute. Now White is
obliged to give up the exchange.

33 ♖xd1 ♖xd1 34 ♘d3 ♖d2+ 35 ♔e3 ♖xg2

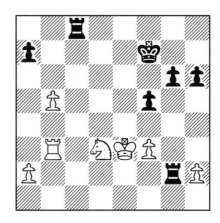

The battle is essentially over. 35...♖xa2!
would have won more simply: 36 b6 ♖e8+
37 ♔f4 axb6 38 ♖xb6 ♖xg2 or 36 g3 ♖xh2
37 ♖a3 ♖c7 38 ♘e5+ ♔g7. But in the time
scramble I slightly lost my grip and prolonged the game for another ten moves.

36 ♖a3 ♖e8+ 37 ♔d4 ♖e7 38 ♘e5+ ♔f6
(38...♔g7!?) **39 ♘c6** (39 ♖a6+ ♖e6!)
**39...♖d7+ 40 ♔c4 ♖c2+ 41 ♔b4 ♖xh2 42
♖a6 ♔g5 43 a4 h5 44 ♖xa7 ♖xa7 45 ♘xa7**

And White resigned (**0-1**), without waiting for the obvious 45...h4 or 45...♖b2+ 46
♔c3 ♖b1 47 ♔c2 h4!.

A difficult win, which was awarded the
brilliancy prize. That same day Beliavsky
defeated Tal and became the sole leader – 9
out of 14. Ehlvest and I had half a point less,
with Tal and Hjartarson a further half point
behind.

In a time scramble in the next round I scored an equally difficult win over Sax – and I caught Beliavsky, who drew with Korchnoi. Hot on our heels were Ehlvest and Tal, who beat Timman.

It need hardly be said how enormously important was the clash of the leaders in the 16th, penultimate round. I had Black against one of my contemporaries – the Estonian grandmaster Jaan Ehlvest, one of the heroes of the World Cup battles.

Tal: *'That year Ehlvest had completed a course at the Psychology Faculty of Tartu University, and it was very interesting to see how, in accordance with the knowledge gained, he would plan his game. With White you can try playing actively, even riskily, but when your opponent is the world champion, this to a large degree compensates for the white pieces. It was obvious that in this game Kasparov would not be satisfied with a draw: only a win would do for the champion! What will be the first move? If 1 e4 there automatically follows 1...c5, while if 1 d4 the Grünfeld or the King's Indian is possible. Jaan had plenty to think about even before the 1st move.'*

Game 44
J.Ehlvest-G.Kasparov
World Cup
16th Round, Reykjavik 24.10.1988
English Opening A28

---

1 c4

'Kasparov thought for several minutes. He was looking more at the ceiling than at the board, obviously trying to remember which variation had occurred more rarely than others in Ehlvest's games.' (Tal)

1...♘f6 2 ♘c3 e5 3 ♘f3 ♘c6

I had not expected Ehlvest to play the Eng-lish Opening and in turn I decided to surprise him by improvising: I had not previously employed the variation with ...e7-e5, ...♘c6 and ...♗b4. However, the Seville match with Karpov had given me a good knowledge of its subtleties.

4 e3

After some thought Jaan rejected the usual 4 g3 (*Game Nos.27, 41*) and chose a set-up where exact knowledge is not required and for some time White can make solid moves based on general considerations.

4...♗b4 5 ♕c2 0-0

5...♗xc3 6 ♕xc3 ♕e7 is steadier, excluding ♘d5.

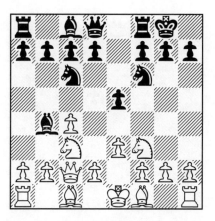

6 d3?!

'This decision can probably be called dubious.' (Tal). White rejects any ambitious opening pretentions in favour of simple development.

Black's immediate castling is risky in view of 6 ♘d5! ♖e8 7 ♕f5! d6 (7...♗e7 8 ♘xe5 ♘b4 9 ♘xb4 did not gain acceptance, Kasparov-Romanishin, 46th USSR Championship, Tbilisi 1978) 8 ♘xf6+ gxf6 (8...♕xf6 9 ♕xf6 gxf6 is also played) 9 ♕h5 d5 (9...e4!? 10 a3 exf3, Lerner-Romanishin, Kiev 1978), when first 10 cxd5 ♕xd5 was tried (Keene-Korchnoi, Montreux 1977; Timman-Portisch,

Montreal 1979; Korchnoi-Karpov, Amsterdam 1987), and then 10 &d3!? e4 11 cxd5 became fashionable, with double-edged play.

6...&e8 7 &d2 &xc3 (in order to play ...d7-d5, Black does not begrudge giving up bishop for knight) **8 &xc3 d5 9 cxd5 &xd5**

Black has achieved a comfortable Sicilian structure with reversed colours. 'A Sicilian Defence has nevertheless arisen, but not in the usual version. And it quickly transpired that the psychological duel had been won by Kasparov.' (Tal).

10 &e2 &f5!

It would appear that this well-known move, provoking e3-e4, confused Ehlvest.

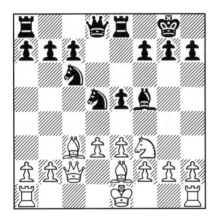

11 &d1

11 e4 is more critical, with the idea of 11...&xc3 12 bxc3 &g4 13 0-0 (Taimanov-G.Kuzmin, 42nd USSR Championship, Leningrad 1974). Instead, I was intending to launch into a maelstrom of complications – 11...&f4!? 12 exf5 &d4 13 &xd4 exd4 14 &g1 &d5! with very sharp play and good compensation for the piece: 15 &d2 &xg2+ 16 &f1 &h4 or 15 0-0-0 &xa2 16 &f3! (better than 16 g3?! &a1+ 17 &d2 &a5+ 18 &c1 &e5!) 16...&a1+! (but not 16...&e5? 17 &c4!, and not 16...c5? 17 &c4!, as in a half-forgotten game from the 1985 East German

Correspondence Championship) 17 &b1 &a5, when it is risky to play 18 g3?! (18 &h3? &e2+) 18...&e5! (Stohl) 19 gxf4 &c5+ 20 &c2 &xc2+ 21 &xc2 &xf5 (the queen and pawns are superior to the rook, knight and bishop) or 19 &d2 &e1+ 20 &d1 &c5+ 21 &d2 &e5! and ...&b4+ with an attack, while if 18 &e4, then 18...c5! and ...c5-c4 is strong. Therefore 18 &c2! (Stohl) is correct, forcing a draw by repetition – 18...&a1+ and ...&a5.

Taking me 'at my word', Jaan decided to avoid such chaos and to maintain the solidity of his pawn chain. If 11 0-0, then 11...&d(c)b4 has been played (while Stohl recommended 11...&d6!?), whereas now the knight move to b4 has no point.

11...a5

Standard Sicilian restriction. 11...&e7 12 0-0 e4 or 12...&ad8 with equality has also occurred.

12 0-0 &e7

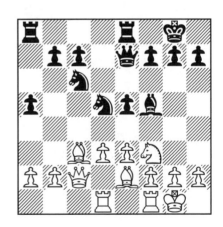

13 a3

13 e4?! is anti-positional – 13...&db4! 14 &b1 &g4. It would seem that the move in the game is not necessary, but it is also unpromising to play 13 &b3 &e6! 14 &a4 (14 &xb7?! &a7! and ...&eb8) 14...&d7, when White has to lose time defending against ...&d4!.

13...a4 (a thematic move, fixing the opponent's pawn pair) **14 ♗e1**

Now 14 e4?! is weak in view of 14...♘xc3 15 bxc3 ♗e6. To create the threat of e3-e4 Ehlvest withdraws his bishop to e1 (on d2 the bishop would block the d-file and take away this square from the knight). But this is rather passive, and 14 ♖fe1!? or 14 ♖c1!? (14...e4 15 ♘d4 with equality) was more advisable.

14...♗g6

Maintaining the tension: now White has to forget about e3-e4. He would have been quite satisfied with 14...e4 15 dxe4 ♗xe4 16 ♕c4.

15 ♕c4 (15 ♘d2?! ♘f4!, but the 'Sicilian' move 15 ♖c1! was better, with the idea of 15...♖ed8 16 ♕c5 or 15...e4 16 dxe4 ♗xe4 17 ♕c5 with equality) **15...♖ed8**

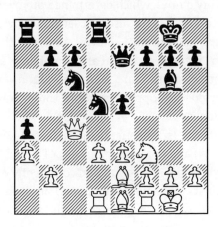

16 ♘d2?

Careless. White directs his knight via the route d2-e4-c5, overlooking Black's reply. In *Informator* I recommended 16 d4(?!), but here White is slightly worse after 16...e4 17 ♘d2 f5 (not 17...♘f4?! 18 exf4 ♘xd4 19 ♘b1!) or 16...exd4!? 17 ♘xd4 ♘e5 18 ♕c1 c5 19 ♘b5 c4 20 ♘c3 ♗d3. The balance would have been maintained more forcefully by 16 ♕h4 (Stohl) or 16 h3.

16...♘d4!!

A bolt from the blue. Intuitively I sensed that the knight sacrifice was an excellent opportunity to exploit the extreme congestion of the white pieces.

17 exd4 ♘f4 18 ♗f3 ♖xd4

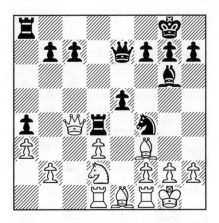

19 ♕b5?

Stunned by such a sharp change of scene, Ehlvest makes a decisive mistake. 19 ♕c3! was essential, although here too Black could have fought for an advantage: 19...♗xd3 20 g3 ♘h3+! (20...♘d5!?) 21 ♔h1 (21 ♔g2 ♖ad8 – cf. 19...♖ad8) 21...♖ad8 22 ♗g2 ♗xf1 23 ♗xf1 ♕d7 24 ♖c1 ♘xf2+ 25 ♗xf2 ♖xd2 26 ♔g1 c6, or 19...♖ad8 20 g3 (20 ♖c1?! ♘xd3) 20...♘h3+! (my *Informator* suggestion 20...♖xd3 is unclear because of 21 ♕a5!) 21 ♔g2 (now 21 ♔h1? is not possible on account of 21...♖xd3!) 21...♗xd3 22 ♔xh3 ♗xf1+ 23 ♘xf1 ♖xd1 24 ♗xd1 ♖xd1, and in both cases the rook and pawns are rather stronger than the two minor pieces.

19...c6 20 ♗xc6 (to save his queen, White has to return the material: 20 ♕b6? ♖a6) **20...bxc6 21 ♕xc6 ♕d8!**

The most accurate reply. Black's heavy pieces achieve coordination and White's position becomes hopeless.

22 ♘f3 ♖d6 (22...♖c8!? was equally good) **23 ♕b5**

The white queen feels very uncomfortable:

235

23 ♕b7? ♖b6 or 23 ♕c4(c2) e4!.

23...♖d5 (23...♗h5! is quicker) **24 ♕b4**

If 24 ♕b7 I earlier gave 24...♗xd3, but the strongest is 24...♗h5! (Stohl) 25 ♔h1 e4, when White suffers a major loss of material.

24...e4

Here many roads lead to Rome.

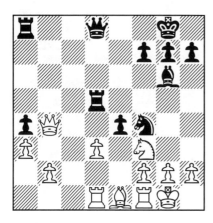

25 ♗c3

In time-trouble Jaan blunders a piece, but 25 ♘d2 also fails after 25...♕h4! (with the threat of 26...♘e2+ 27 ♔h1 ♕xh2+! and ...♖h5 mate) or 25 ♖d2 ♘xd3 etc.

25...♘e2+ 0-1

A third successive win! However, still level with me was Beliavsky, who beat Nunn, while Tal, who made a draw, was now a point behind us. In the last round I was unable to beat Nikolic with White, but thanks to Beliavsky's unexpected loss to Spassky (who after the opening offered a draw!) I nevertheless took sole first place. The powerful finishing spurt also enabled me to maintain my 2760 rating, and to lead Karpov by two points on the sum of the World Cup tournaments.

Directly from Reykjavik I travelled to Cologne, where I played an exhibition minimatch of four games with Vlastimil Hort with a time control of 60 minutes each. The prize for my 2½-½ victory was the first car I had ever owned – a Mercedes 300E.

'Heavy Artillery'

28th World Chess Olympiad (Thessaloniki, 12–30 November 1988): 1. USSR – 40½ out of 56; 2. England and 3. Holland – 34½; 4–5. USA and Hungary – 34; 6. Yugoslavia – 33½; 7–11. Philippines, China, Cuba, Argentina and Israel – 33, etc. (altogether – 107 teams). The winning team comprised **Kasparov** (8½ out of 10), Karpov (8 out of 10), Yusupov (6 out of 10), Beliavsky (7 out of 10), reserves Ehlvest (4½ out of 7) and Ivanchuk (6½ out of 9).

At the 1988 Olympiad in the Greek city of Thessaloniki the USSR team had far fewer problems than in 1986 and 1980. On the top two boards Karpov and I scored +13 in twenty games, which determined our overall success. We were also not let down by the young debutants – Ehlvest and Ivanchuk, who increased the team's mobility and fighting spirit. In fourteen rounds we granted our opponents only three drawn matches!

At the start our team defeated Syria (3½-½) and the Philippines (3-1). I joined the battle in the 2nd round and confidently won against Torre with Black. And in the 3rd round came the match with Argentina, where I was opposed by the 31-year-old Daniel Campora, quite a solid grandmaster.

> *Game 45*
> **G.Kasparov-D.Campora**
> World Chess Olympiad
> 3rd Round, Thessaloniki
> 15.11.1988
> *Queen's Gambit Declined D35*

1 c4 ♘f6 2 d4 e6 3 ♘c3 d5 4 cxd5 exd5 5

♗g5 ♗e7 (5...c6 – *Game Nos.37, 51*) **6 e3 0-0**

Another way of handling this variation involves 6...h6 7 ♗h4 0-0 8 ♗d3 b6 (Game No.80 in *Garry Kasparov on Garry Kasparov Part I*), and also 8...c6 or 8...♘bd7 with the idea of ...c7-c5, as played against me in some simultaneous displays.

7 ♗d3 ♘bd7 8 ♘ge2 ♖e8 9 ♕c2

9 0-0 is also interesting: 9...♘f8 10 b4!? a6 (10...♗xb4? 11 ♗xf6 gxf6 12 ♘xd5! ♕xd5 13 ♕a4) 11 a3 c6 12 ♕c2 g6 13 f3 ♘e6 14 ♗h4 (Kasparov-Short, 15th match game, London 1993) 14...a5!? 15 b5 c5 with double-edged play.

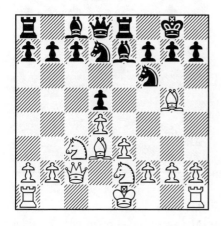

9...♘f8

9...c6 10 0-0 ♘f8 11 f3 could have led to a position from my Belfort game with Andersson (*Game No.37*). Campora chooses a more subtle plan: Black saves a tempo on ...c7-c6, in order to play ...c7-c5 in one go if the opponent castles queenside.

10 0-0-0 (after a little thought I nevertheless stuck to my principles) **10...♗e6**

Again ignoring the traditional 10...c6 (10...h6 11 ♗f4!) 11 h3 a5 12 g4 b5 etc.

11 ♔b1 (useful prophylaxis) **11...♘g4**

This standard exchange of the dark-squared bishops involves a loss of time. 11...♘e4 12 ♗xe7 ♘xc3+ 13 ♘xc3 ♕xe7 14 f4 also favours White. 11...♖c8!? 12 ♘f4 is

more consistent, and now not 12...c6?! 13 ♘xe6 fxe6 14 f4 (Vladimirov-Klovans, Frunze 1988), but 12...h6 (to answer ♘xe6 with ...♘xe6) followed by ...c7-c5(c6).

12 ♗xe7 ♕xe7 13 ♘f4 ♘f6 14 f3! (preparing both e3-e4, and, most importantly, a pawn storm with g2-g4) **14...c5**

Black carries out his intention. If 14...♘g6?!, both 15 g4, as given by me in *Informator*, and 15 ♘xe6!? ♕xe6 16 ♘b5 are unpleasant.

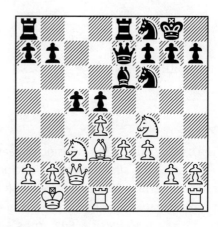

15 g4

Some advantage is promised by 15 dxc5 ♕xc5 (Stohl's move 15...♖ac8 is worse in view of 16 g4! ♕xc5 17 ♕d2) 16 ♕f2 (nothing is given by 16 ♘cxd5?! ♕xc2+ 17 ♗xc2 ♘xd5 18 ♘xd5 ♗xd5 19 ♖xd5 ♖xe3 with equality) 16...♖ad8 17 g4, but I wanted to deny Black any definite counterplay.

15...cxd4

White also attacks in the event of 15...c4 16 ♗f1 ♘g6 17 ♘xe6 ♕xe6 18 g5 ♘h5 19 f4 ♘e7 20 ♗e2 or 18...♘d7 19 h4 ♘e7 20 e4.

As a lesser evil Nikitin suggested 15...c4 16 ♗f1 ♕d6 (but not 16...♕d7? 17 e4! dxe4 18 d5 ♗xg4 19 fxg4 ♕xg4 20 ♘fe2!) 17 g5 ♘6d7 18 h4 ♖ab8, when he gave the questionable 19 ♘xe6(?!) fxe6 20 e4 b5. 19 h5 b5 20 g6 (Stohl) 20...h6 or 20...♘f6 is also unclear. However, the move 19 ♕h2! is stronger, preventing 19...b5(?) in view of 20 ♘fxd5!, winning a pawn in the event of 19...♗f5+(?!) 20 ♔a1 ♖xe3 21 ♘cxd5 ♖ee8 22 ♗xc4, and retaining the initiative after 19...♘b6 20 e4.

16 exd4 ♕d6 17 ♕d2 a6

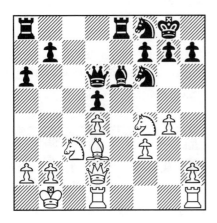

18 ♘ce2!?

'The cavalry raid on the kingside increases the threats and simultaneously excludes Black's counterplay on the queenside' (Gipslis). Campora was apparently expecting the direct 18 h4 b5 19 g5(?!) ♘6d7 20 h5 ♘b6 with chances for both sides (to Stohl's move 21 ♕h2 there is the good reply 21...♖ad8). However, in the event of 19 ♕h2! (with the threat of g4-g5 and ♘fxd5) 19...♕c6 20 ♖c1 or 19...b4 20 ♘a4 in this case too Black has problems.

After some thought, I decided to advance not my h-pawn, but my f-pawn, in order to disturb the bishop on e6, which has cemented together Black's defences.

18...♖e7

An attempt to double rooks on the e-file – it is not easy to suggest a more sensible plan for Black. For instance, 18...♘6d7?! is premature on account of 19 ♘h5! and ♖hg1 with an escalating attack. Even so, 18...b5 (Stohl) was preferable.

19 ♘g3 ♘g6

Alas, if 19...♖ae8, then 20 ♘xe6! ♖xe6

(20...fxe6 21 g5 ♘6d7 22 f4!) 21 ♘f5 followed by h2-h4-h5 and g4-g5 is strong.

20 ♘g2!

This knight retreat came as an unpleasant surprise to my opponent. Any exchange of minor pieces would bring Black considerable relief (thus, after 20 ♘xe6 ♖xe6 he has the f4-point under control).

20...♘d7 21 ♖hg1 ♖ee8

Essential. On this occasion 21...♖ae8?! was unsuitable in view of 22 ♘e3! ♘h4 23 ♕f2 f6 24 f4 etc.

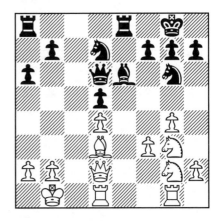

22 ♖df1!

Another unforeseen 'quiet' move, which quickly overwhelmed Campora. After 22 ♘f5 (22 ♘h5 ♘b6!) 22...♗xf5 23 gxf5 ♘e7 24 ♘f4 ♔h8! Black's defences are solid. However, now f3-f4-f5 is threatened, with White sacrificing his g4-pawn in order to open the g-file.

22...♘gf8?

Equivalent to capitulation, as was 22...♖ac8? 23 f4! ♗xg4 24 f5 ♘e7(f8) 25 ♘f4! or 22...♘b6? 23 f4! ♗xg4 24 f5 ♘e7(f8) 25 ♕g5!. But there was the far more resilient 22...♘e7 23 f4! ♘f6! (23...♗xg4?! 24 h3! ♗xh3 25 ♖h1 is dangerous for Black) 24 f5 (24 ♘e3 ♗d7!) 24...♗d7 25 g5 ♘e4 26 ♗xe4 dxe4 27 ♘xe4 ♕c6! 28 ♘g3 ♘d5, when it is hard for White to convert his extra pawn, or

22...♛b6, after which I would not have chosen 23 f4?! (on account of 23...♝xg4 24 f5 ♛xd4! 25 fxg6 hxg6 with three pawns for the piece and sharp play), but 23 ♝c2! and then f3-f4.

23 ♘e3!

A dangerous attack would also have been given by 23 ♘h5!? ♛e7 (23...♘g6 24 h3 and f4-f5) 24 f4! ♘f6 (24...♝xg4?! 25 ♖e1 ♛d6 26 ♘xg7!) 25 ♘xf6+ ♛xf6 26 g5 ♛d8 27 f5 etc.

23...♚h8 (23...♛f4?! was weak in view of 24 ♘h5 ♛h6 25 f4) **24 ♘h5!**

Preventing the d7-knight from returning to f6. However, White also has a big advantage after 24 f4!? f6 25 h4 or 24...♘f6 25 f5 ♝d7 26 g5 ♘e4 27 ♝xe4! (better than my *Informator* suggestion 27 ♘xe4 dxe4 28 ♝c4 ♝b5!) 27...dxe4 28 ♘c4 ♛c7 29 ♖c1 etc.

24...g6

Comparatively best, unlike 24...f6? 25 ♘f5 ♝xf5 26 gxf5! ♖e7 27 ♖g4 and ♖fg1.

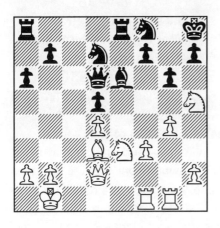

25 f4!

But not 25 ♘f5? ♝xf5 26 gxf5 gxh5 27 ♛g5 ♘g6!. Now, however, the white pieces are ideally placed for the landing of a decisive blow and, in the words of Gipslis, 'their strength is literally doubled'.

25...gxh5 26 f5 h4 (26...♘g6 27 fxg6 fxg6 28 gxh5 was even worse) **27 fxe6 fxe6**

(27...♛xe6 28 ♘f5) **28 g5!** (opening the way for the knight) **28...♖e7**

If 28...♘g6, then 29 ♝xg6 hxg6 30 ♛f2 ♖e7 31 ♘g4 ♖h7 32 ♘f6! ♝xf6 (32...♖f8 33 ♛e3) 33 gxf6 ♖g8 34 ♖g4 with an easy win.

29 ♘g4 (29 g6!?) **29...♖g7**

After the desperate 29...♛b6 30 ♛f4 e5 31 ♘xe5 ♘xe5 White would have won by 32 ♛f6+! ♝xf6 33 gxf6 ♖e6 34 dxe5 ♖xe5 35 f7 ♘e6 36 ♖g4 ♖f8 37 ♖fg1. The more resilient 29...e5!? was also hopeless: 30 ♘h6! e4 31 ♘f5 ♛e6 32 ♘xe7 ♛xe7 33 ♝e2 etc.

30 ♘h6 ♛b6?!

This leads to a crushing defeat, but 30...♛e7 31 ♖e1! (Stohl) would also not have saved Black.

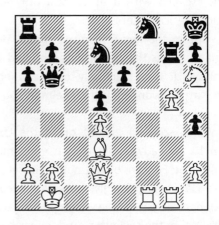

31 g6! hxg6 32 ♘f7+ ♚g8 33 ♛h6! ♖h7 (33...♖xf7 34 ♝xg6 ♖xf1+ 35 ♖xf1 ♘f6 36 ♝f7+! ♚xf7 37 ♛xf6+) **34 ♖xg6+ ♘xg6 35 ♛xg6+ ♖g7 36 ♛h6**

Mate is inevitable, and Black resigned **(1-0)**.

A very tense battle with castling on opposite sides. In a game with an opponent of inferior class there is always the temptation to play quietly, but here I had an enormous desire to play sharply and brilliantly.

As a result we crushed Argentina (4-0) and the next day also Romania (3½-½), when I won a sharp King's Indian with Black against Gheorghiu. *'It was the energy and enormous drive of the world champion that enabled our team to confidently forge ahead after a rather sluggish start, and to predetermine the final outcome of the event. Kasparov played the greater part of his games with Black, but he invariably aimed for a win'*, our captain Sergey Makarychev wrote at the time. He was echoed by the captain of the USSR women's team, Aivar Gipslis: *'I have never seen the world champion so determined, convincing, full of ideas and energetic in their implementation.'*

In the 5th round I outplayed Hjartarson with Black in a sharp Sicilian, but my opponent escaped with a draw, and our team struck the Icelanders a blow with the 'tail': 3-1. But in the key 6th round match with England it was the champions who had the final word: I spectacularly crushed Short, and Karpov won against Speelman. Again 3-1!

With a score of 20 out of 24 the USSR team had already drawn away from its main rivals – the English, by 4½ points. In second place (17½), surprisingly, were the Swedes, who had defeated the strong Hungarian team 3-1. In the seventh round we probably relaxed somewhat after a series of convincing victories: our clash with Sweden ended only in a draw (that day I did not play). But the following day, thanks to my win over Ljubojevic, we were able to beat the solid Yugoslav team (2½-1½).

After eight rounds the leading positions (USSR – 24½ out of 32; USA and Sweden – 21½; England, Hungary, Holland – 20½) heralded a gripping battle for the silver and bronze medals. But first the question of the gold medals had to be conclusively settled, and in 9th round came the crucial USSR-USA match.

From the press: *'The last few rounds have shown that the fighting spirit of the Americans is growing. Therefore in the match with them the Soviets put out their strongest team. The tone was again set by the "heavy artillery" – the world champion and the ex-champion.'*

Makarychev: *'Kasparov is famed worldwide as an opening expert. But for the game with the 28-year-old grandmaster Yasser Seirawan he was especially keyed up, remembering the painful defeat against the leader of the Americans in Dubai. "Today I must decide the game within 25 moves" the world champion declared, when I called in on him with the "red volume" of the Yugoslav Encyclopaedia of Chess Openings, which he had requested for preparation. On the board stood the position depicted in the following diagram.'*

Game 46
G.Kasparov-Y.Seirawan
World Chess Olympiad
9th Round, Thessaloniki
22.11.1988
Queen's Gambit Accepted D21

---

1 d4 d5 2 ♘f3 c5 3 c4 dxc4 4 ♘c3!?

It was this continuation that I had prepared, leaving to one side the set-ups with 4 e3 ♘f6 5 ♗xc4 e6 or 4 d5 e6 5 ♘c3 exd5 6 ♕xd5 ♕xd5 7 ♘xd5 ♗d6 8 ♘d2 ♘e7 9 ♘xc4 ♘xd5 10 ♘xd6+ ♔e7 11 ♘xc8+ ♖xc8 which were well known to my opponent.

4...cxd4

If 4...♘f6 there would have followed 5 d5 e6 6 e4 exd5 7 e5 ♘fd7 8 ♗g5 (little is promised by 8 ♕xd5 ♘b6 9 ♕xd8+ ♔xd8, Torre-Seirawan, London 1984) 8...♗e7 9 ♗xe7 ♕xe7 10 ♘xd5 ♕d8, and here 11 ♗xc4 suggests itself (Beliavsky-Seirawan,

2nd match game, London 1984), but I was planning the fashionable 11 ♕c2!? – this would be played against Seirawan by Yusupov (Rotterdam 1989).

5 ♕xd4

An important positional nuance: after the exchange of queens, because of his somewhat retarded development, Black has problems with the defence of his queenside.

5...♕xd4 6 ♘xd4 ♗d7?!

A loss of a tempo. The prophylactic 6...a6?! is also weak on account of 7 ♘d5!. However, it is better to play 6...e5 7 ♘db5, when 7...♔d8(?!) 8 ♗g5+ f6 (8...♘f6 9 ♘d5!) 9 ♗e3 ♘c6 10 0-0-0+ ♗d7 11 g3 favours White (Becker-Lokvenc, Vienna 1921), but after 7...♘a6! 8 e4 ♗e6 9 ♗e3 ♘f6 10 f3 ♗b4 Black is close to equalising (Magerramov-Sermek, Tilburg 1994).

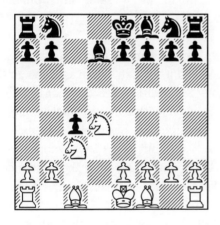

Yasser had already played the text move against H.Olafsson (Dubai Olympiad 1986), and after 7 e4 ♘c6 8 ♘xc6 ♗xc6 9 ♗xc4 e6 he easily gained a draw: 10 f3 ♗c5 11 ♔e2 ♘f6 12 ♗e3 ♗xe3 13 ♔xe3. Also 10 ♔e2 a6 11 ♗e3 ♘f6 (Korchnoi-Seirawan, Roquebrune (rapid) 1992) or 10 ♗e3 a6 (Shirov-Anand, Paris (rapid) 1992) does not impress.

7 ♘db5!

In our days it is rare to see a novelty as early as the 7th move! It was devised at an express analysis before the game. Sergey Makarychev, who was alongside, later recalled: 'The speed of the concrete analytical work was impressive. But I was even more surprised when two hours later Seirawan did indeed play the difficult variation with 6...♗d7.'

7...♘a6

After 7...♔d8 later White successfully played 8 ♗e3 ♘c6 9 0-0-0 ♘f6 10 g4! (Krasenkow) 10...e6 11 h3! (Khalifman-A.Grünfeld, Pardubice 1994), but 9...♔c8!? 10 h3 h5 11 g3 ♘f6 12 ♗g2 g6 is more solid. On the other hand, White retains a solid plus with 8 ♘a3!? e5 9 ♘xc4 or 8...♘c6 9 e4 – the insecure placing of the black king is felt.

8 e4 ♘f6

In the event of 8...e6 9 ♗xc4 ♖c8 10 ♗e2 ♘b4 11 ♘xa7 ♖xc3 12 bxc3 ♘c2+ 13 ♔d2 ♘xa1 14 ♗b2 (if 14 ♘b5, then 14...♗e7 15 f3 ♘h6!? is not bad), it is dangerous to play 14...♗c5?! 15 ♘b5 ♗xf2 16 ♘d6+ ♔e7 (Magerramov-Psakhis, Groningen 1993) on account of Psakhis's suggestion 17 ♗a3!, but after 14...♘f6 15 f3 ♗d6! 16 ♗xa1 (or 16 g3 h5 17 ♘b5 ♗b8 and ...h5-h4 with counterplay for the pawn) 16...♔e7 17 ♘b5 ♖a8 18 ♘xd6 ♖xa2+ 19 ♔e3 ♔xd6 20 c4 ♔e7 White has only a slight advantage (Zakharevich-Vaulin, Yekaterinburg 1997).

9 f3

A safe restricting move. 9 ♗xc4!? ♖c8 10 ♗e2 ♘b4 11 ♘xa7! ♖xc3!? (11...♖c5 12 0-0!) 12 bxc3 ♘c2+ 13 ♔d2 ♘xa1 14 f3 g6 (Yuferov-Maljutin, Moscow 1989) 15 ♔d3! or 14...e6 15 ♘b5! is more energetic, regaining the piece and retaining an extra pawn (which, it is true, is difficult to convert). However, I did not want to allow the opponent even a hint of counterplay.

9...♗xb5

Exchanging bishop for knight, in order to gain time for development. Later 9...e5 10

♗e3 (Seirawan was concerned about 10 ♗g5 ♗e6 11 0-0-0 ♗e7 12 ♗xf6 gxf6 13 ♔b1, but 11...♗c5! is better) 10...♗e6 was tried, obtaining a position from the note to Black's 6th move with an extra tempo for White(!) and not fearing 11 ♗xa7 ♗b4 12 ♗f2!? or 11 a3!?.

10 ♘xb5 e5

11 ♗e3

Black's position is also slightly worse after 11 ♗d2!? or 11 a3!? ♗c5 12 ♗xc4 ♖c8 13 ♔e2, but with careful defence he should be able to hold out.

11...♗b4+ 12 ♔f2 ♔e7 13 ♗xc4 ♖hc8 14 ♖ac1 ♗c5! (simplifying the play and depriving the opponent of the advantage of the two bishops) **15 ♖hd1**

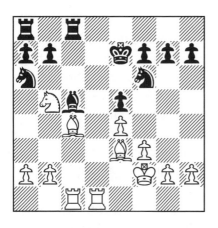

There is a temporary defect in Black's position – one of his rooks is tied to the a7-pawn, and White is looking for a way to exploit this factor.

15...♗xe3+

After my *Informator* suggestion 15...♖c6 White would have retained the initiative by 16 ♗d5 ♘xd5 17 exd5 ♗xe3+ 18 ♔xe3 ♖b6 19 a4 ♖d8 20 ♖c4 etc.

16 ♔xe3 ♘e8

It was more natural to evict the knight from b5 – 16...♘c7!? with the idea of 17 ♘d6 ♘cd5+! 18 ♗xd5 ♘xd5+ 19 ♔f2 ♔xd6 20 ♖xd5+ ♔e6 21 ♖cd1 ♖c6 with equality (Seirawan) or 17 ♘c3 ♖d8. And after 17 g3!? ♘xb5 18 ♗xb5 White's only remaining trump would have been the 'Fischer bishop'.

Not seeing how to extract any benefit from the unexpected retreat of the knight from f6 to e8, I sank into prolonged thought...

17 ♗b3

17 ♗d5 is parried by 17...♖xc1 18 ♖xc1 ♘b4!, and if 19 ♗xb7, then 19...♖b8 20 ♖c8 ♖xb7! 21 ♖xe8+ ♔xe8 22 ♘d6+ ♔d7 23 ♘xb7 ♘xa2 with a drawn knight endgame. Also nothing was given by 17 f4 exf4+ 18 ♔xf4 ♘ac7!, but 17 b3!? was more shrewd, for the moment avoiding the exchange of rooks: 17...♘ac7 18 ♘xc7 ♖xc7 (18...♘xc7? 19 ♗xf7!) 19 ♖d5 f6 20 ♖cd1 or 17...♘b4 18 a3 ♘c6 19 ♗d5 with persistent pressure.

17...♖xc1

Black also somehow holds on after 17...♘c5 18 ♗d5! (18 ♖d5 ♘xb3 19 ♖xe5+ ♔f8! 20 ♖xc8 ♖xc8 21 axb3 ♖c2 with equality) 18...a6: for example, 19 ♘c3 ♖ab8 20 b4 ♘e6 21 ♗xe6 ♔xe6 22 ♘a4 ♘d6 23 ♘c5+ ♔e7 24 ♖d5 f6 25 ♖cd1 ♖c6 (Seirawan) or 19 ♘a3 ♘f6 20 ♘c4 (20 ♖c3!?) 20...♘xd5+ 21 exd5 ♘d7 22 f4 f6.

18 ♖xc1 f6

Yasser waits to see what White will do.

After the active 18...♞b4 there could have followed 19 ♖c5 or 19 a3 ♞c6 20 ♗d5, retaining some pressure.

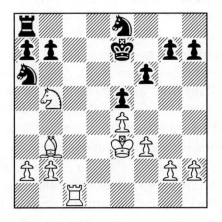

19 a3

Of course, not 19 ♗d5?! ♞b4 when Black equalises. The study-like 19 ♗a4!? is more interesting, preventing the e8-knight from escaping to d6: 19...♞d6?! (19...b6? 20 ♗b3!) 20 ♞xd6 ♚xd6 21 ♖d1+ ♚e6! 22 ♗d7+! ♚e7 23 ♗f5! with the threat of ♖d7+ winning a pawn, or 19...g6?! 20 a3! ♞d6 21 ♞xd6 ♚xd6 22 ♖d1+ ♚e6 23 b4 with an obvious positional superiority. However, after 19...♞b4 20 ♞c7 ♖c8! 21 ♗xe8 ♞c6 22 ♗xc6 ♖xc7 and ...bxc6 Black would reach a slightly inferior, but tenable rook endgame.

19...♞d6! (not 19...♚d8? 20 ♗e6! – Seirawan) **20 ♗d5!**

'Kasparov sacrifices two minor pieces for rook and pawn, foreseeing that without strong points on the queenside it will be difficult for the black knights to coordinate their actions.' (Gipslis). 'It is not clear whether this endgame is won or drawn, but it is not easy for Black to play, and Seirawan suffers a collapse within literally a few moves.' (Makarychev).

20...♞xb5

The following alarms could have been avoided by a far from obvious pawn sacrifice

– 20...♖b8!? 21 ♞xa7 ♚d7! (21...♖a8? 22 ♞c8+!) 22 a4 ♞c7 (Seirawan), when even the 'Fischer bishop' would hardly have helped White to convert his material plus.

21 ♗xb7 ♞bc7!

21...♞ac7?! was weaker: 22 ♗xa8 ♞xa8 23 ♖c8 ♞b6? 24 ♖c5! a6 (24...♞d4 25 ♖c7+ – Seirawan) 25 ♖c6 ♞a4 26 b3 and ♖xa6, or 23...♞bc7 24 ♚d3!, and Black cannot avoid the loss of material.

22 ♗xa8 ♞xa8 23 ♖c8 ♞b6

In *Informator* I incorrectly recommended 23...♞6c7(?!), overlooking that this was a position from the note to Black's 21st move (24 ♚d3! etc). But 23...♞8c7!? 24 b4 ♚d7 25 ♖f8 (25 ♖g8 ♞e8, cutting off the rook) 25...♚e7 came into consideration, and if 26 ♖c8 ♚d7 with a repetition of moves (Seirawan).

24 ♖g8! ♚f7 25 ♖h8

This agile rook unnerves Black: he has to watch out both for the attack on his kingside pawns, and for White's threat to create a passed pawn on the queenside.

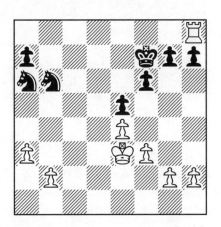

25...♞c5

Missing an opportunity to immediately set up an impregnable fortress by 25...♞c4+ 26 ♚e2 ♞xb2 27 ♖a8 ♞c5 28 ♖xa7+ ♚f8 and ...♞ba4 (Seirawan). However, it is not yet curtains for Black...

26 ♖b8! ♔e7 27 b4 (there is nothing better) **27...♘c4+?**

The fatal effect of time-trouble! It was essential to play 27...♘cd7! 28 ♖b7 ♘c4+ 29 ♔d3 ♘xa3 30 ♖xa7 ♘b5 31 ♖a5 (suggested by me in *Informator*) 31...♘d6 (Seirawan) or 31...♘d4, gaining a draw.

28 ♔e2 ♘d7 29 ♖g8! (an elegant diverting manoeuvre) **29...g5** (or 29...g6, but not 29...♔f7 30 ♖a8!) **30 a4**

The surviving a-pawn quickly becomes passed. The threat is ♖a8.

30...a5 31 bxa5

Also the result of time-trouble. Seirawan attached an exclamation mark to this move, but 31 ♔d3! would have led more quickly to the goal: 31...♘b2+ (31...♘d6 32 bxa5 ♘c5+ 33 ♔c3!) 32 ♔c2 ♘xa4 33 ♖g7+ and ♔b3, or at once 33 ♔b3 ♔f7 34 ♖d8! ♔e7 35 ♖h8!.

31...♘xa5

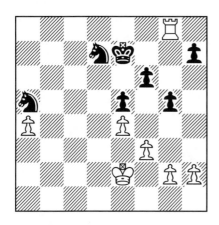

32 ♖a8 (32 ♖g7+ ♔e6 33 ♖xh7 ♘c6 34 g3! and h2-h4 was also good, creating a second passed pawn on the h-file) **32...♘c6 33 a5 ♔d6 34 g3**

34 a6! ♔c7 35 ♖h8 was more forceful, winning the h-pawn followed by g2-g3 and h2-h4.

34...h5 (alas, 34...♘c5 35 a6 ♘e6 36 a7 ♘c7 37 ♖f8! ♘xa7 38 ♖xf6+ and ♖h6 was hopeless) **35 h4?**

But this is already a serious error. 35 a6! ♔c7 36 h4 gxh4 37 gxh4 ♔b6 38 ♔e3 and ♖h8xh5 was correct.

35...gxh4 36 gxh4 ♘c5! 37 a6 ♔c7?

Returning the favour (Yasser's time-trouble was more acute). Black could have unexpectedly saved himself by 37...♘e6! 38 ♖h8 (if 38 ♔e3, then 38...♘c7! 39 ♖h8 ♘xa6 40 ♖xh5 ♔e7 41 ♖h7+ ♔f8 with a draw) 38...♘f4+! (38...♘c7? 39 ♖xh5 ♘xa6 40 ♖h7! and h4-h5) 39 ♔f2 ♔c7! 40 ♖f8 ♔b6 41 ♖xf6 ♔b5, and the position is a fortress (42 ♔e3 ♘g2+ and ...♘f4), or 39 ♔e3!? ♔c7 (after 39...♔c5 40 ♖b8! ♘g2+ and ...♘xh4-g6 Black remains the exchange down, but he would appear to have a draw) 40 ♖f8 ♘g2+ (now 40...♔b6? 41 ♖xf6 ♔b5 is bad because of 42 ♖xf4) 41 ♔f2 ♘f4 42 ♖xf6 ♘b4 43 ♖f7+ ♔b8 44 ♖b7+ ♔a8 45 ♔e3 ♘xa6 46 ♖e7 ♘g2+ 47 ♔e2 ♘c5 48 ♖xe5 ♘e6! – yet another fortress, and this time a fairy-tale one!

38 a7

The preparatory 38 ♔e3! (Seirawan) was more accurate.

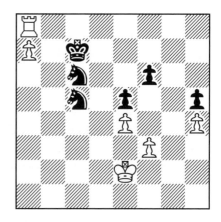

38...♘b7?

A final error with the flag about to fall, but also after 38...♔b6 (38...♔b7? 39 ♖c8!) 39 ♖h8 ♔xa7 40 ♖xh5 ♔b6 41 ♖h8! or 40...♘d4+ 41 ♔e3 ♘ce6 42 ♖h8! followed by the advance of the h-pawn White would have won.

Without waiting for the obvious 39 ♖c8+ and a8♕, Black resigned (**1-0**).

An uneven but gripping game. I managed to level my individual score with Seirawan (and to reach 6½ out of 7!), and our team won this important match: 2½-1½. The same day England defeated the Swedes 3-1 and finally moved into second place, 3½ points behind us.

In the 10th and 11th rounds the USSR team drew with Hungary (I shared the point with Portisch) and Holland (without me), and the English slightly reduced the gap. But then we made a powerful finishing spurt: by beating Denmark 3-1 (I miraculously held out with Black against Curt Hansen) and Bulgaria (I won against Kiril Georgiev, gaining revenge for my loss in February in the world blitz championship), we secured first place a round before the finish, and 'for a treat' there we crushed Czechoslovakia 3½-½! That day I did not play, but Karpov converted a minimal positional advantage in an ending with Ftacnik, with the game finishing at nearly two in the morning.

The battle for silver and bronze did, indeed, prove dramatic. Before the last round the English had 33 points, with the Hungarians, Americans and Dutch on 32. After great adventures the Hungary-USA match ended in a draw. The Dutch unexpectedly took the lead against England – 2-1, and everything was to be decided by the Nunn-van der Sterren game, where Black had an advantage. But Nunn obtained a draw, and this suited the English: with the same number of points as the Dutch, they had the superior tie-break score, and they won the silver medals for the third successive Olympiad! The Dutch received medals for the second

time in history (in Haifa 1976 they took the silver, but then there were no teams from USSR, Hungary, Yugoslavia etc).

I again achieved the best result on board 1 (+7=3) and, taking account of the strength of opponents, the absolutely best result at the Olympiad. As a result of this busy tournament year my rating reached the 'pre-Fischer' mark of 2775.

A week after the Olympiad battles I gave a simultaneous display with clocks against the French team in the Parisian suburb of Évry (4½-1½). Then I took part in an unusual GMA event – a rapidplay charity match between a team of Soviet grandmasters and a team from the rest of the world (Madrid, 14-18 December): eight against eight on the Scheveningen system. We won 32½-31½. For our team the best result (5½ out of 8) was achieved by myself and Gurevich, and for our opponents – Korchnoi. This match was a symbol of the great changes occurring in the USSR. Indeed, for the first time Soviet chess players were allowed to travel abroad not under the direction of the State Sports Committee!

Birthday Present

Fourth World Cup Tournament (Barcelona, 30 March – 20 April 1989): 1–2. Ljubojevic and **Kasparov** – 11 out of 16; 3. Salov – 10; 4. Korchnoi – 9½; 5–6. Hübner and Short – 9; 7. Nikolic – 8; 8–12. Vaganian, Yusupov, Ribli, Spassky and Beliavsky – 7½; 13. Speelman – 7; 14–15. Hjartarson and Seirawan – 6½; 16–17. Illescas and Nogueiras – 5½.

The next stage of the World Cup took place in beautiful Barcelona, in the grand hall of the Royal Palace, where at one time Christopher Columbus was feted when he returned from his historic voyage. My preparations for the super-tournament were very chaotic – in March 1989 I got married for the first time, and we celebrated this event in both Moscow and Baku. In addition, as usual, I had the burden of public responsibilities. And although I arrived in Barcelona after a training session, with a supply of fresh ideas, I proved to be not altogether ready for a fierce battle.

After drawing No.1 in the pairing list, in the first round I was free (since the 18th contestant Mikhail Tal had to miss the tournament through illness), and in the second round I went in for a sharp opening duel with Ribli in the Vienna Variation of the Queen's Gambit. It appeared that White had gained an advantage, but with accurate defence Ribli equalised. A drawn endgame was reached, but just before the time control, in a time scramble, I suddenly blundered and could have lost by force. Fortunately, my opponent did not notice this: he was fully satisfied with a draw.

In the 3rd round I had Black against Artur Yusupov, games with whom were always of a crucial nature. Nikitin: *'The first half of the tournament proved unusually difficult for Garry and was spent largely in a battle with himself. Many of his games constituted a parade of missed opportunities. In this respect the most noteworthy was the game with Yusupov.'*

Game 47
A.Yusupov-G.Kasparov
World Cup
3rd Round, Barcelona 2.4.1989
King's Indian Defence E92

---

1 ♘f3

Before this we had met three times in tournaments in 1988, invariably at the start, and each time I had the black pieces. In Belfort 1 d4 ♘f6 2 ♘f3 g6 3 ♘c3 d5 was tested, and in Moscow and Reykjavik – 1 d4 ♘f6 2 c4 g6 3 ♘c3 d5. Now it was the turn of the King's Indian Defence, which had become my main weapon with Black.

1...♘f6 2 c4 g6 3 ♘c3 (3 g3 – *Game No.66*) **3...♗g7 4 e4 d6 5 d4 0-0 6 ♗e2 e5 7 d5**

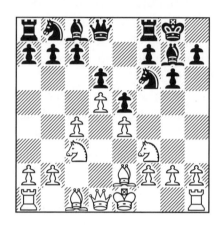

Artur had employed the Petrosian Variation from his early years, and it was only in the 1990s that he switched to 7 0-0 (cf. *Game No.77*, note to Black's 13th move).

7...a5 (7...♘bd7 – cf. Game No.10 in *Garry Kasparov on Garry Kasparov Part I*, note to White's 5th move) **8 ♗g5** (8 ♗e3 – *Game No.78*) **8...h6 9 ♗h4 ♘a6 10 ♘d2 ♕e8**

An alternative is 10...♗d7 11 0-0 ♘c5 (Kramnik-Kasparov, Munich (blitz) 1994).

11 0-0 ♘h7 12 a3 ♗d7

In an old game with Veingold (Moscow 1979) I played 12...f5 immediately, but after 13 exf5 (13 f3 ♗d7 is steadier, Kramnik-Kasparov, Paris (rapid) 1995) 13...♗xf5 14 g4! ♗d7 15 ♘de4 a4 16 f3 b6 17 ♗d3 I experienced some discomfort. 13...gxf5!? 14 ♗h5 ♕d7 is not so clear, although in this case the c8-bishop is temporarily shut in.

13 b3 (mechanically preventing ...a5-a4; later both 13 ♘b5 and 13 ♔h1 were played) **13...f5!?**

The main line with 13...h5 14 f3 ♗h6 15

♖b1 was well known to Yusupov and had occurred several times in his games.

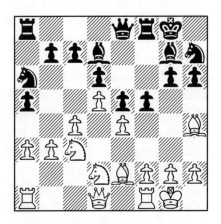

14 exf5 gxf5!?

14...♗xf5 was considered obligatory and acceptable for Black: 15 g4 (not 15 ♘de4? ♗xe4 16 ♘xe4 ♖f4 winning a piece) 15...e4! 16 ♖c1 e3 (16...g5!? 17 gxf5 gxh4 18 ♘dxe4 ♖xf5, Palatnik-Gofshtein, Iraklion 1992) 17 gxf5 exd2 18 ♕xd2 ♘c5 (Yanvarjov-Plisetsky, Moscow 1981) or 17 fxe3 ♕xe3+ 18 ♗f2 ♕g5 (I.Khenkin-Shirov, Borzhomi 1988).

But at the board I devised an interesting idea with an exchange sacrifice, and after a long think I risked putting it into effect. 'When the demonstrator moved the pawn to f5, I did not believe my eyes.' (Nikitin). Artur was also very surprised by my choice.

15 ♗h5 ♕c8 (the remoteness of Black's heavy pieces is alarming after 15...♕b8 16 ♗e7 ♖c8 17 ♕c2!? and ♖ae1)

16 ♗e7 ♖e8!

'The world champion's calmness indicated that he had not blundered the exchange' (Nikitin). An unusual idea: in the King's Indian a rook is far more often given up for the dark-squared bishop. But here, in the absence of the opponent's light-squared bishop, the knight on a6 can comfortably establish itself at d3, and also the tactical nuances in the position are in Black's favour.

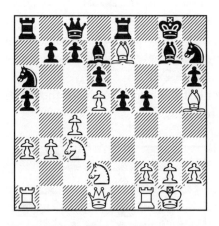

17 ♗xe8 (17 ♗h4 e4!?) **17...♕xe8 18 ♗h4 e4** (the g7-bishop has begun operating at full strength) **19 ♕c2**

With the idea of ♖ae1(d1). Sharp play also results from 19 ♖c1 ♘c5 20 ♖c2 (20 ♕e2 ♕g6!) 20...♘f8 21 ♘e2 ♘g6 22 ♗g3 ♘d3 (Naumkin-A.Kuzmin, Moscow 1989).

19...♕h5 (now apart from 19...♘c5, there is the possibility of including the a8-rook in the battle with gain of tempo) **20 ♗g3** (20 g3?! ♘c5 and ...♘g5 is really too clumsy) **20...♖f8**

The threat of ...f5-f4 forces White to determine his pawn structure.

21 ♗f4

During the game we both thought that this move was forced, but later, in my hotel room, I came to the conclusion that 21 f4!? (depriving the knight on h7 of the g5-square) was sounder, although even here after 21...♘c5 22 ♖fd1 (given by me in *Informator*) 22...♖e8!? Black has powerful compensation for the exchange (23 ♘f1 e3!).

21...♕g4! 22 g3 ♘g5!

Again White faces a difficult choice.

23 ♔h1

One would like to exchange the annoying knight – 23 ♗xg5(?!), but after 23...hxg5 Black has a dangerous initiative: 24 ♖ae1 ♘c5 (24...♕h5!?) or 24 f3 ♕h3 (24...exf3!?) 25 ♖ae1 (25 fxe4? ♗d4+! 26 ♔h1 f4 27 e5?

♗f5 and wins) 25...♗d4+ 26 ♔h1 e3 27 ♘db1 f4 etc.

23...♘f3 (threatening ...♕h5) **24 ♖ac1** (defending the c3-knight, in order to play ♘xf3) **24...♘c5**

At last the knight heads for the cherished d3-square.

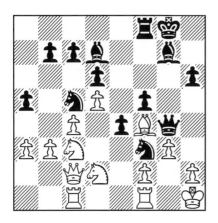

25 ♘xf3

In the event of 25 ♕d1?! ♘d3 White would have had to return the exchange and switch to a difficult defence: 26 ♘xf3 (26 ♖c2? ♘fe1! and wins) 26...♘xc1 27 ♗xc1 exf3 28 ♕d3 ♗e5 29 ♖g1 ♕d4 30 ♕xd4 ♗xd4 31 ♘d1 ♖e8.

25...♕xf3+ 26 ♔g1 ♘d3 27 ♕d2

The best move. 'The queen and c1-rook must defend the knight, and the bishop cannot move because of the deadly ...f5-f4.' (Nikitin). After 27 ♘e2?! the cool-headed 27...♔h7! is good, with the ideas of ...♖g8, ...♗b2(f6) and ...♗e8-h5, while if 27 ♕e2?! – 27...♘xf4! 28 gxf4 (28 ♕xf3? ♘h3+! 29 ♔g2 exf3+ 30 ♔xh3 f4+ 31 ♔h4 ♗f6+ or 31 g4 h5 leads to the downfall of the white king) 28...♕xf4 with a pawn for the exchange and an attack: 29 f3 e3 or 29 ♕e3 ♕h4 30 ♕g3 ♕e7 etc.

27...♗d4!?

'The banal "a move in the style of the world champion" is fully appropriate here.

Black does not fritter away his advantage but strengthens his position to the maximum.' (Nikitin). After 27...♘xc1 28 ♖xc1 the position is materially and positionally equal (28...h5 29 h4), but I wanted more.

28 ♖c2?!

Again 28 ♕e2?! was insufficient on account of 28...♘xf4! 29 gxf4 (29 ♕xf3? ♘h3+!) 29...♕xf4, when if 30 ♔h1 the most promising is 30...♗e8!. However, roughly equal chances would still have been retained by 28 ♘b5! (Stohl), with the idea of 28...♗b6 29 ♖c3 (without loss of tempo!), or 28...♗xb5 29 cxb5 ♖f7 30 ♖c4, when after 30...♖g7 (30...♗c5 31 ♖c3!) 31 ♗e3! ♘xf2 32 ♗xf2 ♖xg3+ 33 hxg3 ♕xg3+ Black has no more than perpetual check.

28...♔h7!

Vacating the g8-square for the rook.

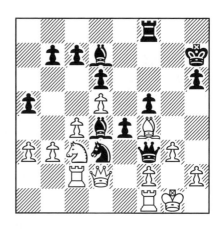

29 h3?

Probably a decisive mistake (as was 29 ♕e2(d1)? ♘xf4!). It was essential to play 29 ♘b5, driving away the bishop from d4. Now White would be satisfied with 29...♗xb5?! 30 cxb5 ♗c5 (30...♖f7?! 31 ♗e3!) 31 ♕d1! or 29...♗c5 (Stohl) 30 ♘xc7 ♖g8 31 ♖c3! with the intention of ♖xd3, but with the accurate 29...♗b6! 30 ♖c3 ♖g8 Black retains the initiative: 31 c5!? ♗xc5 32 ♘xc7 h5! etc.

29...♖g8 30 ♔h2 ♕h5!

Yusupov was expecting 30...♞xf4 31 ♕xf4 ♕d3 32 ♘e2! ♝e5 (32...♕xc2? is weak in view of 33 ♘xd4 and ♘xf5, while if 32...♝c5, then 33 ♕d2 ♕xb3 34 ♖c3 or 33...♝xa3 34 ♖b1) 33 ♖d2! ♕xb3 34 ♕e3! a4 35 ♖c1 with chances for both sides. The unexpected return of the queen sets White very difficult problems: the deadly 31...♞xf4! 32 ♕xf4 ♝e5 is threatened.

31 ♘d1?

A time-trouble blunder. It was also bad to play 31 ♕d1? (31 ♕e2? ♕g6) 31...♞xf4 32 gxf4 ♕h4 33 ♕d2 ♝e8! (more forceful than Stohl's move 33...♝c5), or 31 ♖cc1? ♞xf4 32 gxf4 (32 ♕xf4 ♝e5) 32...♕f3 33 ♖g1 ♝xf2 34 ♖xg8 ♔xg8 and wins. The only way to avoid an immediate rout was 31 ♘e2 ♝xf2 32 ♘g1, although after 32...♝c5 Black has a pawn for the exchange and an attack.

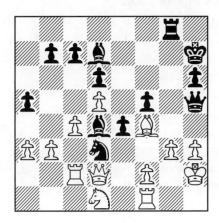

'Here I noticed that the world champion had suddenly lost his bearings and his ability to calculate. Although he had just four minutes left on his clock, this was quite sufficient to conclude the attack. But Garry couldn't see anything! He endeavoured to calculate at least some variations, but his mental computer had stopped. So he switched to "manual control", and started making moves on general grounds.' (Nikitin)

31...♘e5?

How could I forget about the main threat?! After the simple 31...♞xf4! 32 ♕xf4 (or 32 gxf4 ♕g6! with a quick mate) 32...♝e5 33 ♕e3 f4 White would have had to resign.

32 f3?!

Stohl rightly condemns 32 ♝xe5? ♝xe5 33 ♕e2 ♕g6 34 ♔h1 f4 and wins, but he is wrong to attach an exclamation mark to the text move: after it White is again on the edge of a precipice. 32 ♖c3! ♝xc3 33 ♕xc3 was more resilient, after which Black could develop his initiative by 33...♘d3 34 ♕d2 a4, 33...♘f3+ 34 ♔g2 a4, or 33...♕e2 34 ♘e3 ♘f3+ and ...♘d2.

32...♘d3?

It is a pity that I did not find 32...♕xf3! with a won endgame after 33 ♖xf3 ♘xf3+ 34 ♔g2 ♘xd2 35 ♖xd2 ♝c5 and a spectacular rout after 33 ♝xe5 ♕xf1 34 ♝xd4 f4! 35 g4 ♝xg4! 36 hxg4 ♖xg4 37 ♕f2 ♕xd1 38 ♖d2 ♕xb3! (not 38...♖h4+? 39 ♕xh4 ♕xd2+ 40 ♝f2! e3 41 ♕e7+ with perpetual check).

33 ♘e3?

A time-trouble comedy of errors! 33 fxe4! was essential, although after 33...fxe4 34 h4 ♕g6 35 ♘b2 (35 ♕g2? ♝g4) 35...♖e8 or 34 ♕g2 (my *Informator* recommendation) 34...e3! 35 ♘xe3 ♘xf4 36 ♖xf4 ♝xe3 37 ♖e4 ♝g5 the chances are on Black's side.

33...♘xf4 34 gxf4

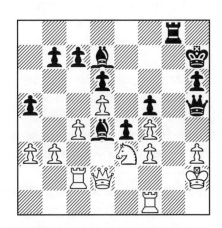

34...♗b6??

A complete black-out! There was an immediate win by 34...♕h4! 35 ♕xd4 (35 ♕e1(f2) ♕xf4+) 35...♖g3! with unavoidable mate.

'The champion's victory over one of the candidates for the world title could have become a genuine brilliancy. Alas, at the moment when the wonderful canvas was practically concluded, at the very end of the round the artist crossed out everything with a few dabs of black paint – and in horror seized his head in his hands.' (Nikitin)

35 ♕f2! (parrying the attack and retaining the extra exchange) **35...♕g6?!**

The dabs continue. 35...♗c5 was more resilient.

36 ♖e2! (36 fxe4 fxe4 37 f5 ♕g5 38 ♖e2 ♕h5! is not so clear) **36...♗c5?**

And here 36...♕h5! 37 ♖ee1 ♖e8 was preferable.

37 fxe4 fxe4 38 f5? (an error in reply – 38 ♕g2! was correct) **38...♕h5 39 ♖d2 ♖g5?**

It was obviously not my day! After 39...♕g5! Black could have successfully resisted.

40 ♕f4 ♕e8?! (40...♗xe3 41 ♕xe3 ♗xf5 was essential, although after 42 ♖g2! White should be able to convert his material advantage) **41 ♘g4!**

The time scramble was over, and Black resigned (**1-0**). My only loss against Yusupov, and a most painful one.

In the 4th round I drew with Seirawan (after missing what appeared to be a certain win), in the 5th I beat Korchnoi (cf. *Game No.77*, note to White's 9th move), and then I confined myself to draws with Hübner and Hjartarson.

Gipslis: *'The battle in Barcelona was notable for its great tension and fervour. The author of the rapidly changing scenario was* undoubtedly the world champion Garry Kasparov. After stalling at the start he developed full speed, beginning only from the 8th round.'

Before my game with Nigel Short the gap between me and the leaders had already become critical: Ljubojevic – 5½/7; Short – 4½/7; Yusupov – 4/6; Hübner and Hjartarson – 4/7; Korchnoi – 3½/7; Kasparov and Salov – 3/6.

Game 48
G.Kasparov-N.Short
World Cup
8th Round, Barcelona 8.4.1989
English Opening A20

1 c4 (I quite often played this against Nigel) **1...e5 2 g3 d6 3 ♗g2 g6**

The avoidance of 3...♘c6 allows White to make an unexpected pawn thrust in the centre, changing the character of the play intended by Black.

4 d4!? exd4

After 4...♘d7 the game switches to King's Indian lines, while in the event of 4...♗g7 Black has to reckon with 5 dxe5 dxe5 6 ♕xd8+ ♔xd8 7 ♘c3 with a favourable ending for White. And so Short preferred to concede the centre.

5 ♕xd4 ♘f6 6 ♘c3!

The most accurate way to develop the pieces, which I found at the board. It is pointless playing 6 ♗g5 ♗g7 7 ♕e3+ ♔f8! with the idea of ...h7-h6 or 6 ♕e3+ ♗e7!? (Korchnoi-Arnason, Reykjavik 1987), and the white queen may soon come under attack by the black pieces.

6...♗g7

The alternative is 6...♘bd7, but not 6...♘c6? 7 ♗xc6+ bxc6 8 ♗g5 ♗e7 9 ♘e4 and wins (Gulko-Benjamin, Modesto 1995).

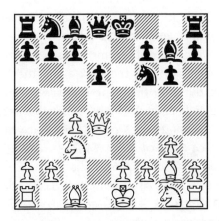

7 ♕e3+ ♕e7

Here avoiding the queen exchange by 7...♔f8 promises White somewhat the better chances: for example, 8 ♘f3 ♘bd7 9 0-0 h6 10 b3 ♔g8 11 ♗b2 ♔h7 12 ♖ad1 (Ribli-Mokry, Vienna 1991).

8 ♕xe7+

The pawn grab 8 ♘b5?! ♘a6 9 ♘xa7 is unfavourable because of 9...♗e6! 10 ♘c6 (10 ♗xb7? ♘g4) 10...♕d7 11 ♘d4 ♘g4 12 ♕d2(f4) ♘c5 etc.

8...♔xe7 9 b3!?

A strong move and, as it later transpired, a new one. Earlier 9 ♗g5 was played, after which 9...c6 is good, and later – 9 ♘h3 ♗xh3!? 10 ♗xh3 ♘a6 11 ♗g2 c6 12 ♖b1 ♖he8 13 0-0 ♘d7 14 ♗g5+ f6 with equality (Korchnoi-Smyslov, Beer Sheva 1990).

9...a5?!

This turns out to be both the loss of a tempo, and weakening. Also nothing was given by 9...♘e4?! 10 ♘d5+ ♔d8 11 ♖b1 ♗f5 (11...♘c3? 12 ♗b2) 12 g4! c6 (not 12...♘c3? 13 gxf5 ♘xb1 14 f6 ♗f8 15 ♘f3!) 13 gxf5 cxd5 14 ♘h3 gxf5 15 ♘f4 with some advantage for White.

9...c6 10 ♗b2 (Arkhipov-Blatny, Kecskemet 1992) 10...♘a6 was better, but I was considering the more aggressive 10 ♗a3!? a5 11 ♖d1 or 10...♘e4?! 11 ♘xe4 ♗xa1 12 ♘xd6!

♔f6! 13 f4 and ♘f3 with a dangerous initiative. As we can see, despite the exchange of queens, it is still a middlegame position. Therefore the king should have been removed from the centre – 9...♖e8! and ...♔f8, not weakening the position and retaining approximate equality.

10 ♗b2 c6

Again 10...♖e8! is better, since 11 ♘d5+ need not be feared in view of 11...♘xd5 12 ♗xg7 ♘b4! 13 ♔d2 f6.

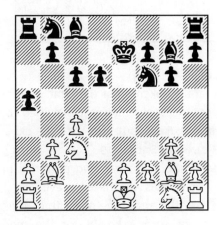

11 ♘a4!

Probing the weaknesses in the opponent's position and including the b2-bishop in the play.

11...♗e6?!

Another small error. 11...♘bd7 and ...♘c5 was correct, not fearing the doubling of the pawns after ♘xc5 and ...dxc5. In this case White's advantage would be comparatively slight.

12 ♘f3 ♘bd7 13 ♘d4 ♖hc8

If 13...h5, then 14 h3(h4). And 13...♘c5 would now allow the unpleasant 14 ♘xc5 dxc5 15 ♘xe6, with the perceptible advantage of the two bishops.

14 0-0 ♖ab8

Black has managed to complete his development, but he has been left without any counterplay and with a weak pawn on d6.

White can calmly intensify the pressure.

15 ♖ac1 ♘e8 16 ♖fd1

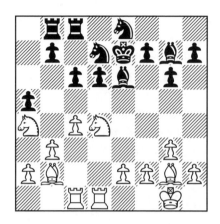

16...c5?

A fatal weakening of the light squares. It is possible that initially Short had been planning 16...b5, but after 17 cxb5 cxb5 18 ♘c3 ♗xd4 (18...b4?! 19 ♘cb5 is worse) 19 ♖xd4 White again has two powerful bishops. And yet this was the lesser evil.

17 ♘b5 (this promises more than the exchange of such a knight for the modest bishop on e6) **17...♗xb2 18 ♘xb2 ♘b6 19 ♘c3** (19 ♖c3!?)

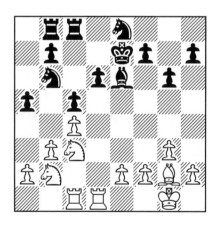

19...♘a8?!

An artificial manoeuvre. 19...♖d8 20 ♖d2 ♘c7 21 ♖cd1 a4!? 22 ♘bxa4 ♘xa4 23 ♘xa4 b5 24 cxb5 ♘xb5 was more resilient, with

some hopes of holding out a pawn down.

20 ♘ba4! (the white knights are completely dominant) **20...♘ec7 21 ♖d2**

In *Informator* I recommended 21 ♖d3, in order to also use the rook along the third rank, but after this there is a pawn sacrifice – 21...b5!? 22 ♘xb5 ♘xb5 23 ♗xa8 ♖xa8 24 cxb5 ♖ab8 25 ♘c3 c4 26 bxc4 ♖xc4 or 22 cxb5 c4 23 bxc4 ♗xc4 24 ♖e3+ ♔f8 25 b6 ♘xb6 26 ♘xb6 ♖xb6 27 ♘a4 ♖b4 28 ♘b6 ♖xb6 29 ♖xc4 ♖b1+ 30 ♗f1 d5 31 ♖c2 d4 32 ♖a3 ♖bb8 33 ♖xa5 ♘e6 34 ♖xc8+ ♖xc8 with drawing chances.

21...♗d7 (now 21...b5? does not work because of 22 cxb5 ♘xb5 23 ♗xa8!) **22 ♘e4 ♘e8**

Black is almost stalemated after 22...♗xa4 23 bxa4 ♘e8 (or 23...♖d8) 24 ♖b1.

23 ♘ac3 ♗c6 (23...b5? was again bad: 24 ♘xb5 ♗xb5 25 cxb5 ♖xb5 26 ♘c3! ♖bb8 27 ♗xa8 ♖xa8 28 ♘d5+ and ♘b6) **24 ♖cd1 ♖d8**

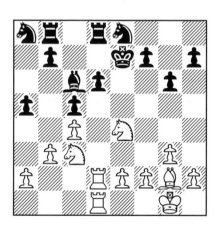

25 g4

Starting to set up a bind on the kingside. My *Informator* recommendation 25 a4 is hardly any better, since the threat of ...a5-a4 is really not so serious.

25...♘ac7

Perhaps Black should have tried to sharpen the play by 25...a4!? 26 ♘xa4 (26

♖d3!?) 26...♗xa4 27 bxa4 ♘b6, although after 28 ♖c1! ♘xa4 29 ♖d3! with the idea of ♖e3(a3) his position would remain difficult. **26 a4!** (denying the opponent even a hint of counterplay) **26...♘e6 27 e3 h6 28 f4 ♖d7 29 h4 ♖bd8 30 ♘g3**

The outcome is practically decided: Black has no way of opposing White's systematic offensive.

30...♘6g7 (30...♘f6?! 31 f5 or 30...♘6c7 31 g5 is also not very comforting) **31 ♘d5+** (31 ♗h3!?) **31...♔f8 32 ♔f2 ♘e6 33 g5 hxg5 34 hxg5 ♘6c7**

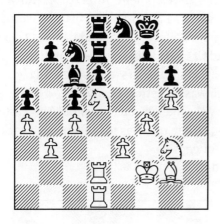

35 ♗h3!

'35 ♘f6 also looked attractive' (Gipslis), but after 35...♘xf6 36 gxf6 d5 White's advantage would have diminished. 35 ♘xc7!? ♖xc7 36 e4 was tempting, but the move in the game is more forceful.

35...f5! (35...♘e6 36 ♘e4 was altogether unappealing) **36 gxf6 ♖h7 37 ♘xc7 ♘xc7?!**

Possibilities of resistance would still have been retained by 37...♖xc7! 38 ♗g2! ♘xf6, although after 39 ♗xc6 (more accurate than 39 ♖xd6 ♘g4+ 40 ♔g1) 39...♖xc6 40 e4 ♔e7 41 e5 Black's chances of saving the game are close to nil.

38 ♗g2 ♘e8 (38...♖h2? 39 ♔g1!) **39 ♗xc6 bxc6 40 ♔g2** (the soundest) **40...♖b8 41 ♖d3 d5**

41...♖hb7 would not have saved Black: 42 ♘e4 ♖xb3 43 ♖xb3 ♖xb3 44 ♔f3 ♖b4 (44...♔f7 45 ♘xd6+) 45 ♖h1!, and if 45...♔g8 then 46 ♖h8+! ♔xh8 47 f7.

42 cxd5 cxd5 43 ♖xd5 ♖xb3 44 ♘e4! ♖xe3

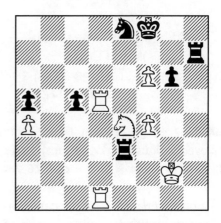

45 ♖e5!

The final touch. 45 ♘g5? was wrong in view of 45...♖e2+ 46 ♔f3 ♖hh2! with a draw.

45...♖h5!? 46 ♖e6

46 ♘xc5 ♖exe5 47 ♘d7+! (avoiding a cunning trap: 47 fxe5? ♘xf6! 48 ♖f1 ♖g5+ 49 ♔h3 ♖h5+ with a draw) 47...♔f7 48 fxe5 ♔e6 49 ♔f3 would also have been decisive.

46...♖e2+ (46...♖hh3 47 ♖a6!?) **47 ♔f3 ♖hh2 48 f7! ♖hf2+** (48...♘g7 49 ♖d8+, and mate) **49 ♘xf2 ♖xe6 50 fxe8♕+ ♔xe8 51 ♖c1 1-0**

This win made me optimistic. Although I became slightly unwell and in the next round with Black I was unable to gain more than a draw against the leader Ljubojevic, there was every indication that I was running into form.

Gipslis: '*These comparative failures could not dampen Kasparov's fighting spirit, and did not cool his burning desire to win. On the board the world champion created complicated, dynamic positions, in which he found unusual ways of developing his initiative.*'

Noteworthy was the 10th round game with one of the title contenders at that time, the 32-year-old English grandmaster Jonathan Speelman.

Game 49
G.Kasparov-J.Speelman
World Cup
10th Round, Barcelona 11.04.1989
Modern Defence A42

1 d4 d6 2 e4 g6 (at that time Speelman employed various 'quirky' set-ups) **3 c4 e5 4 ♘f3 exd4 5 ♘xd4 ♗g7 6 ♘c3 ♘c6 7 ♗e3 ♘ge7**

In a blitz preparation for the game, in this well-known position I suddenly wanted to play sharply, and without much thought at the board I boldly advanced my rook's pawn.

8 h4!?

In my opinion, this move of Bilek's is no worse than the usual 8 ♗e2.

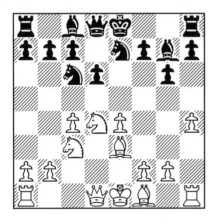

8...h6?!

8...0-0?! would have been rash in view of 9 h5. Now if h4-h5 there is ...g6-g5, and in addition the g5-square is taken under control, but the kingside has been weakened. 8...h5 is more popular, or else 8...f5 9 h5 fxe4 10 hxg6 (10 ♘xe4 ♘f5 11 ♗g5 ♕d7

12 ♘b5!? is also interesting, Hoeksema-Hartoch, Dieren 2005) 10...hxg6 11 ♖xh8+ ♗xh8 12 ♘xe4, and now not 12...♗f5?! 13 ♘xf5! gxf5 (13...♘xf5 14 ♗g5) 14 ♕h5+ ♔d7 15 0-0-0 with an attack (M.Gurevich-Speelman, Antwerp 1993), but 12...d5!? (Kramnik-Mamedyarov, Moscow 2007).

9 ♗e2! (more accurate than 9 ♕d2 f5) **9...f5**

A typical attack on the centre. After 9...0-0 10 ♕d2 White is ready to begin storming the king's defences.

10 exf5?!

This reply suggests itself, but it assists Black's development. After 10 ♘xc6! ♘xc6 (10...bxc6 11 ♗d4) 11 ♕b3 his king would be in great danger – if 11...♘d4, then 12 ♗xd4! ♗xd4 13 ♖d1 with a powerful initiative.

10...♘xf5 11 ♘xf5 ♗xf5 12 ♕d2 (12 g4 ♗e6 was no better) **12...♕d7**

With the obvious intention of castling long. White now has to build up an attack on the queenside.

13 0-0

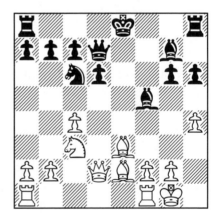

13...0-0-0!

Black boldly sharpens the play and intends to launch a counter-offensive, by sacrificing a pawn with ...g6-g5. At this point Speelman was very happy with his position.

14 b4!

Aiming to get there first! The seemingly

useful 14 ♘d5 would have been an empty threat in view of 14...g5! – if 15 b4? the prosaic 15...♗xa1 and ...♕g7! is now good.

14...♘xb4

A radical defence against b4-b5. However, 14...♔b8 15 b5 ♘e7! would have been safer (but not 15...♘e5?! 16 ♘d5).

15 ♘b5!

Sacrificing the a1-rook for the sake of an attack. It would appear that this decision stunned my opponent.

15...♘c2?

A serious mistake. 15...♗xa1? 16 ♕xb4 was also unsuitable: for example, 16...♗e5 17 ♘xa7+ ♔b8 18 ♗f3 c5 19 ♕a3 ♕c7 20 g4! or 16...a6 17 ♘a7+ ♔b8 18 ♗f3 c5 19 ♕b6 ♗c3 20 ♘c6+ ♔c8 21 ♖c1 ♖de8 22 ♘a7+! ♔b8 23 ♗f4! with a swift rout.

The knight could have been either withdrawn – 15...♘c6, although after 16 ♗f3 White's threats are highly unpleasant, or defended: after 15...c5? 16 ♖ad1 the weakness of the d6-pawn is fatal, but the unexpected 15...a5! (this move was not seen by any of the commentators) 16 ♖ac1 (16 a3?! ♘c6) 16...♖he8 would have maintained the dynamic balance – White merely has compensation for the pawn.

feated Speelman psychologically: the knight leap to c2 turns out to be a fatal loss of time. The frontal attack 16 ♕a5? would have been parried not only by my *Informator* suggestion 16...♘xe3 17 ♕xa7 ♕c6 18 ♕xe3 ♕c5, but also by the cool-headed 16...♗xa1! 17 ♘xa7+ ♔b8 18 ♘b5 ♕g7 19 ♗f3 ♔c8 etc.

16...d5?

Desperation. There was no salvation after any of 16...♗xa1 17 ♘xa7+ ♔b8 18 ♖b1! c5 19 ♘c6+ ♔c8 20 ♕a5 ♘b4 21 ♖xb4, or 16...♘xa1 17 ♘xa7+ ♔b8 18 ♕a5 ♗e5 (18...c6 19 ♘b5!) 19 ♖e1! (an ambush!) 19...♖de8 (19...c6 20 ♗b6 or 19...♕g7 20 ♘c6+! ♔c8 21 ♗f4!! is also bad) 20 ♘b5 ♕g7 21 ♗b6!, 16...♘xe3 17 ♕xe3 ♖de8 (17...♗xa1? 18 ♕xa7 ♕g7 19 ♕xb7+ ♔d7 20 ♖e1! ♖c8 21 ♘xd6!) 18 ♕xa7 ♘d8 19 ♖ad1, 16...c5 17 ♘xa7+ ♔b8 18 ♖ab1!, and 16...♕e7 17 ♗xb7+! ♔d7 (17...♗xb7 18 ♘xa7!) 18 ♖ad1, when Black's days are numbered.

But 16...♖de8! 17 ♘xa7+ ♔d8 18 ♗xb7 ♖xe3 19 fxe3 ♗xa1 was more resilient, although after 20 g4! White would regain the piece, retaining every chance of winning.

17 ♗xd5 (the battle is decided: White's attack is irresistible) **17...♘xa1** (17...♕f7 18 ♖ac1!) **18 ♘xa7+ ♔b8**

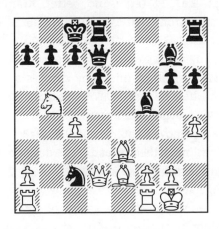

16 ♗f3!!

This quiet, intuitively found move de-

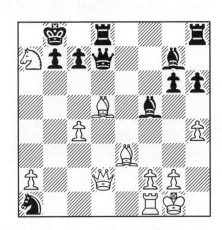

19 ♕b4 (19 ♕a5!?) **19...♕xd5** (19...c5 20

♗f4+! would have led to mate) **20 cxd5 ♘c2 21 ♕a5**

Or 21 ♘c6+!? ♔c8 22 ♕a5.

21...♘xe3 (21...♘d4 22 ♖d1) **22 fxe3 ♖he8 23 ♘b5** (23 ♘c6+!?) **23...♖xd5 24 ♕xc7+ ♔a8 25 ♕a5+ 1-0**

Inspired by this spectacular miniature, in the next round against Beliavsky I risked repeating the sharp line of the Scheveningen from the 24th game of the 1985 match. This was a very difficult and nervy game. On the 18th move my opponent improved on Karpov's play, launching a fierce assault on the kingside. In reply I carried out an experimental counter-stroke in the centre and could have lost a pawn. But Beliavsky delayed, upon which Black seized the initiative, in a time scramble sacrificed the exchange, and won with a direct attack on the king.

Finally I joined the leading group: Ljubojevic and Short – 7½/11; Kasparov – 6½/10; Salov – 6/10. And for the 12th round 'white' game with my rival and contemporary Valery Salov I arrived in the most fighting mood possible, especially since it was played on the 13th April, my birthday. To mark the occasion, before the start of play the organisers presented me with a cake with candles, which I successfully blew out.

> ### Game 50
> ### G.Kasparov-V.Salov
> World Cup
> 12th Round, Barcelona 13.04.1989
> *English Opening A34*

1 ♘f3 ♘f6 2 c4 b6 3 ♘c3 c5

Four months later in Skelleftea, Salov successfully solved his opening problems in a Queen's Indian Defence – 3...e6 4 g3 ♗b7 5 ♗g2 ♗e7 6 d4 ♘e4 7 ♗d2 ♗f6 etc. But here

he prefers a 'hedgehog' set-up.

4 e4 d6 5 d4 cxd4 6 ♘xd4 ♗b7 7 ♕e2!?

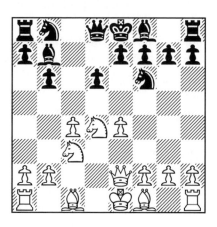

I didn't have a deep knowledge of this set-up, but at the board I remembered this original queen move, introduced by Korchnoi. White far more often plays 7 f3, and sometimes 7 ♗d3 (Dorfman-Salov, Nikolaev 1983).

7...♘bd7

White's idea is revealed after 7...♘c6 8 ♘xc6 ♗xc6 9 ♗g5 and 0-0-0 (Korchnoi-Gheorghiu, London 1980) or 7...g6 8 g3 ♗g7 9 ♗g2 0-0 10 0-0 followed by ♖d1.

And if 7...e6 the sharp 8 g4!? is possible, or the quiet 8 g3 ♗e7 (8...♘c6 9 ♘xc6 ♗xc6 10 ♗g2 ♗e7 11 0-0 is no better, Kramnik-Adams, Groningen 1993) 9 ♗g2 a6 10 0-0 ♕c7 11 ♗e3 ♘bd7 12 ♖ac1 ♖c8 13 b3 ♕b8 14 ♗d2 0-0 15 g4!? (Korchnoi-Csom, Rome 1981). Instead of this Salov chooses a risky plan where he first develops his queenside.

8 g3 (if 8 g4, apart from 8...h6 the usual 'Dragon' move 8...g6!? is good) **8...♖c8**

It is nevertheless better to develop the kingside first – 8...e6 9 ♗g2 ♗e7 etc.

9 ♗g2 a6?!

Overestimating the safety of his king's position in the centre. Correct was 9...e6 10 0-0 ♕c7 11 b3 ♗e7 or the immediate 10...♗e7, with the idea of 11 e5 ♗xg2 12 exf6 ♗xf6! 13 ♔xg2 ♗xd4 14 ♘b5 ♗e5, not fearing 15 f4 a6, 15 ♘xa7 ♖c5, or 15 ♖d1 0-0.

10 0-0 ♕c7?!

Now Black heads for the scaffold – he openly provokes the thematic sacrifice of the white knight. True, his position was also worse after superior replies: 10...e6 11 ♘xe6! fxe6 12 e5! ♗xg2 13 exf6 ♕xf6 14 ♔xg2 ♗e7 15 ♖e1, or 10...g6 11 ♖d1 (11 ♗g5!?) 11...♕c7 12 b3 e6 13 ♗a3! (Salov-Yudasin, St. Petersburg 1997).

11 b3 e6

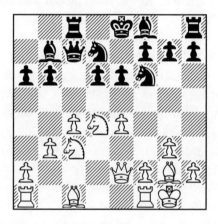

12 ♘d5!

Without hesitation! 'After the inaccuracies committed by Black his position must be judged to be lost, since the acceptance of the piece sacrifice leads to a situation where he is completely helpless, and after the retreat of the queen White gains an overwhelming lead in development. The battle loses its sharpness, but it is very instructive to follow how Garry develops the initiative granted to him.' (Salov)

12...♕b8

Salov replied quite quickly – probably on pragmatic grounds: the move ...♕b8 is part of his set-up, and no great harm from the d5-knight is immediately apparent. In the event of 12...exd5 13 exd5+ ♔d8 (13...♘e5?

14 f4 or 13...♗e7?! 14 ♘f5 is worse) I would have played the simple 14 ♗b2 (although 14 a4!? is also interesting). It is hard for Black to move anything, while White prepares an attack with practically no risk.

13 ♖d1

The commentators, myself included, awarded this move an exclamation mark, although 13 ♖e1!? was a worthy alternative, with the idea of 13...g6 14 e5! dxe5 15 ♘xf6+ ♘xf6 16 ♗xb7 ♕xb7 17 ♕xe5 ♗e7 18 ♗h6 ♖c5 19 ♕e2 ♖g8 20 h4, when Black cannot breath freely (20...♖h5 21 ♗g5 h6 22 ♗xf6 ♗xf6 23 ♘xe6! ♖e5 24 ♕g4 etc).

13...g6

After 13...exd5?! 14 exd5+ ♔d8 15 ♘c6+ ♗xc6 16 dxc6 ♘c5 17 b4, in the words of Salov, 'Black's position is tragic'. But perhaps after 13...e5 14 ♘xf6+ ♘xf6 15 ♘f5 g6 16 ♘h6! (my *Informator* move 16 ♗g5 is worse because of 16...♘g8!) 16...♘g8 17 ♘xg8 ♖xg8 his suffering would have lasted somewhat longer.

The reply 13...g6 rather surprised me: I hadn't seen any acceptable defence for Black, and suddenly the threat of ...♗g7 and ...exd5 had appeared. I had to select a way of retaining my advantage.

14 ♗g5!?

'Again very accurately played' (Salov). Just in case I decided to win a pawn. 14 ♗a3!? looked tempting, with the pretty idea 14...♗g7? 15 ♘f5!, but 14...e5 would have complicated the situation. In analysis after the game we also looked at the creative 14 ♗h3 ♗g7 15 ♗xe6!? fxe6 16 ♘xe6 ♔f7 17 ♘g5+ ♔f8 18 ♗a3, and came to the conclusion that 'precisely in this case Black would have had a chance of defending' (Salov).

14...♗g7

14...exd5? 15 exd5+ ♗e7 16 ♘c6! ♗xc6 17 dxc6 ♘e5 18 f4 etc. would have been even more catastrophic than before.

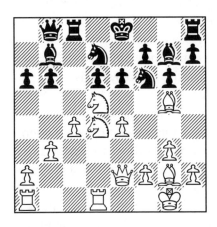

15 ♗xf6! ♘xf6

15...♗xf6? would have led to a difficult position after 16 ♘xf6+ ♘xf6 17 e5! ♗xg2 (17...dxe5? 18 ♗xb7 ♕xb7 19 ♕xe5 ♕e7 20 ♘c6! or 19...♔e7 20 ♘xe6! fxe6 21 ♖xd6 is hopeless for Black) 18 exf6 ♗h3. Here Salov and I considered 19 ♕e3 ♕b7 20 f3 with a big advantage, but Stohl's recommendation 19 ♕e4! is even stronger, when 19...h5 (19...0-0? 20 ♕h4) 20 ♖d2, and 19...♕a8 20 ♕xa8 ♖xa8 21 ♘c6, winning material, are both bad for Black.

16 ♘xb6 ♖d8?

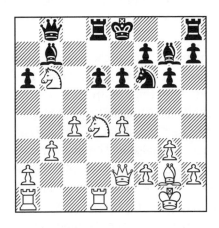

Valery fails to withstand the fierce pressure, and he allows another tactical stroke. 16...♖c7! was essential, retaining control of the c6-square and threatening ...♗xe4. Then

with 17 ♘a4! White would have had to begin the patient conversion of his extra pawn, for which Black would have had some compensation in the form of his long-range dark-squared bishop.

17 e5!

'This forces a win' (Salov). We both saw this thematic move, but we assessed its consequences differently. Indeed, my opponent had overlooked something.

17...♗xg2

17...dxe5 was objectively more resilient: 18 ♘c6 ♗xc6 19 ♗xc6+ ♔e7 20 c5! e4! (the only chance: 20...♕c7? 21 ♕xa6 and wins) 21 ♕xa6 (to all appearances 21 b4!? is also sufficient) 21...♘g4 22 ♖d7+ ♖xd7 23 ♘xd7 ♕c7 24 ♖d1! e3! 25 fxe3 ♘xe3 26 ♖d3 ♘f5 27 ♕a4! ♗d4+ 28 ♖xd4 ♘xd4 29 ♕xd4 ♕xc6 30 ♕xh8 ♕xd7 31 ♕c3, and White has a won queen endgame – 31...♕d1+ 32 ♔f2 ♕h1 33 a4! ♕xh2+ 34 ♔e1! ♔d7 35 b4 ♔c8 36 b5, but what a lengthy procedure this would have been!

Now, however, my task is simplified.

18 exf6 ♗xf6 19 ♘xe6!

'I think it was Reuben Fine who wrote that in such positions a combination is as natural as a baby's smile.' (Salov)

19...fxe6 (19...♗xa1 20 ♘xd8+ ♔xd8 21 c5!)
20 ♕xe6+ ♗e7

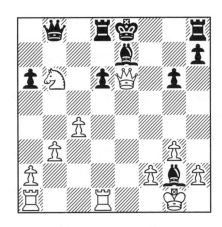

21 c5!!

'I have to admit: at this moment I was still hoping to reach an inferior endgame after 21 ♖e1 ♕b7 22 ♕xe7+ ♕xe7 23 ♔xg2, in which Black's chances of a draw are very good. The reality proved much more bleak.' (Salov)

21...♗b7 (also after 21...dxc5 22 ♔xg2 Black has no defence) **22 ♖e1 ♕c7 23 c6!**

The culmination of White's destructive attack.

23...♗xc6 (if 23...♗c8 the simplest is 24 ♕f6 ♖f8 25 ♕g7) **24 ♖ac1! ♖d7 25 ♘xd7** (25 ♕e3!? was rather more forceful, but I immediately began the mopping-up) **25...♕xd7**

'This is no longer a defence, but simply a joke.' (Salov)

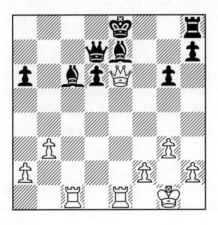

26 ♕c4!

Black's last hope was for a bad rook endgame: 26 ♖xc6(?!) ♕xe6 27 ♖xe6 ♔d7 28 ♖xe7+ ♔xc6 or 26 ♕xe7+ ♕xe7 27 ♖xe7+ ♔xe7 28 ♖xc6 a5.

26...♗b7 27 ♕c7 ♖f8 (or 27...♗d5 28 ♕b8+) **28 ♕b8+ ♔f7 29 ♖c7!**

And in view of the upcoming major loss of material, Black resigned (**1-0**).

This game was judged the best both in the tournament, which brought me a special

prize of 1,000 dollars, and in the 47th volume of *Informator*. '*After playing through it*', Valery Salov wrote at the time, '*again and again I am convinced that it is perceived not as a meeting between two strong grandmasters, which in the end determined their places in the tournament table, but more like a textbook example on the theme: "Attack on a king caught in the centre". Or even worse – simply as a present for the world champion, who that day celebrated his 26th birthday. Who after this game will believe that Kasparov was in poor form in Barcelona? What then can be said about me?*'

After this third successive win I was already established in the leading trio: Ljubojevic – 8½/12; Short – 8/12; Kasparov – 7½/11. But here came the traditional slump in my play, the result of which was three draws – with Vaganian, Nikolic and Nogueiras. Two rounds before the end of the tournament, my chances of first place had almost evaporated: Ljubojevic – 10½/15; Kasparov – 9/14; Salov, Korchnoi, Short and Hübner – 8½/14.

In the 16th round Ljubojevic was free, while I was able to beat Illescas with Black (incidentally, the last two rounds were interchanged, so that at the finish it was Illescas, the home representative, who was free), and now I was only half a point behind the leader. Close behind me was Salov, who had beaten Hübner.

And then came the final, 17th round. Ljubojevic, who played splendidly in Barcelona, decided not to tempt fate and he quickly concluded peace with Short. In a flash Salov and Korchnoi also agreed a draw. I had White against Boris Spassky. Nikitin: '*Garry had to solve a very difficult problem. The fact that he came on to the stage with the firm intention of beating Spassky, against whom he had previously never won, was* known, I think, by all the participants.'

Gipslis: *'The game between the champion and the ex-champion proved decisive. All the other games of the round ended in draws – and in order to catch the leader, Kasparov had to win "to order".'*

Game 51
G.Kasparov-B.Spassky
World Cup
17th Round, Barcelona 19.04.1989
Queen's Gambit Declined D35

1 d4 ♘f6 2 c4 e6 3 ♘c3 d5 4 cxd5 exd5 5 ♗g5 c6 (5...♗e7 – *Game No.45*) **6 e3** (6 ♕c2 – *Game No.37*) **6...♗e7**

After 6...♗f5 7 ♕f3 ♗g6 8 ♗xf6 ♕xf6 9 ♕xf6 gxf6 Black has a dreary but acceptable endgame (an example: Tal-Spassky, Sochi 1973). On this occasion the ex-champion produced a different idea.

7 ♗d3 ♘bd7 8 ♘ge2!?

White is not in a hurry to play ♕c2, as he has Botvinnik's plan in mind – 8...♘f8 9 f3 or 8...0-0 (or first 8...h6 9 ♗h4) 9 0-0 ♖e8 10 f3, which later occurred both in simultaneous and rapid games of mine.

8...♘h5

Played under the influence of my games with Smyslov (55th USSR Championship, Moscow 1988) and Andersson (Reykjavik 1988), in which White did not achieve anything from the opening (cf. the notes to *Game No.37*). I was expecting this move, since Spassky was being helped by Andersson himself, who had flown to Barcelona for the end of the tournament.

The relieving move 8...♘e4 also promises White a minimal advantage: 9 ♗xe7 ♘xc3 (not 9...♕xe7?! 10 ♗xe4 dxe4 11 ♘g3, winning a pawn) 10 bxc3 ♕xe7 11 ♕c2 ♘f6 12 0-0 0-0 13 c4.

9 ♗xe7 ♕xe7

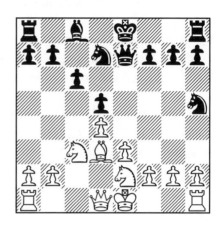

10 g4!?

This was my preparation – an immediate seizure of space on the kingside. The usual 10 ♕c2 would have led to a well-known position from the aforementioned game with Andersson, which went 10...g6 11 0-0-0 ♘b6 with roughly equal play.

10...♘hf6 11 ♘g3 (with his queen on d1, White can manage without 11 h3) **11...h6**

Later it became more popular to defend with 11...g6 12 g5 (12 ♕f3!?) 12...♘g8 13 h4 h6 (Yakovich-Grosar, Sochi 1989), or 11...♘b6 12 g5 (12 h3 ♗e6 is equal, Gelfand-Karpov, Cap d'Agde (rapid) 1998) 12...♘g8 13 h4 g6 and ...h7-h6 (Vyzhmanavin-Kharitonov, Helsinki 1992).

12 h3

White supports the obstructing pawn on g4, in order then to decide where to play his queen and what to do with his king. The alternative is 12 ♘f5 ♕f8 (Speelman-Andersson, Reykjavik 1991).

12...♘b6 13 ♕d2 ♗d7

An important moment: 13...♘c4 14 ♗xc4 dxc4 15 e4 would have led to unclear play, but Spassky did not like such a position with Black – he preferred to have a mobile pawn centre himself.

14 b3 g6 15 a4

In Seirawan's opinion, the immediate 15 f3 followed by e3-e4 was more logical, but I decided first to inhibit the opponent's activity on the queenside.

15...a5 (or 15...♘c8 16 f3) **16 f3 h5**

Black wants to fix the kingside pawns, but I am unsure about the advisability of this decision. Perhaps the simple 16...0-0 was better.

17 g5 ♕d6!

Beginning a regrouping, which to me seems correct. 17...♘h7 is passive – after 18 h4 0-0 19 ♘ce2 there is scope for the activation of the white pieces, whereas Black's are rather restricted.

18 ♘ge2 ♘g8 19 e4 ♘e7

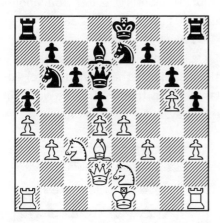

20 ♕f4!

Nikitin: 'The decision of a mature Master.' Seirawan also praised this move – a voluntary exchange of queens! However, there is no other way to fight for even a slight advantage.

20...♕xf4

In *Informator* I condemned 20...♕b4(!?) because of 21 ♔f2, but wrongly so: after 21...0-0 Black would have retained the queens and hopes of active counterplay. But Spassky happily simplified the position, assuming that in the endgame it would be easier for him playing against me.

21 ♘xf4 0-0 22 ♘ce2! (but not 22 h4 because of the undermining move 22...f6!) **22...h4!?**

Fixing the h3-pawn and depriving the g5-pawn of support. Now 22...f6? would have run into 23 gxf6 ♖xf6 24 e5. However, 22...♔g7 was steadier, and if 23 h4, then even 23...dxe4 24 fxe4 ♗g4, setting up pressure on the pawn centre.

23 ♘g2 ♔g7 24 ♔d2

If 24 ♘xh4 ♖h8.

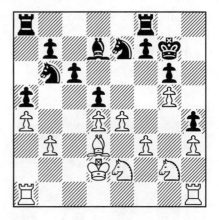

24...dxe4?

Here conceding the centre is a mistake: without control of the g4-square, the d4- and e4-pawns are invulnerable. 24...f6?! was also weak: 25 gxf6+ ♔xf6 (25...♖xf6? 26 e5 ♖f7 27 ♖ag1! or 26...♖xf3 27 ♘xh4 ♖xh3 28 ♖xh3 ♗xh3 29 ♖g1 is worse) 26 e5+ ♔f7 27 ♘xh4 ♖h8 28 ♘g2 ♗xh3 29 ♘gf4 ♗f5(d7) 30 ♖ag1 with an obvious advantage.

Perhaps Spassky was afraid of the bind after e4-e5, but the benefits of this advance are unclear. Therefore the waiting move 24...♖h8 should have been preferred: for example, 25 ♘ef4 ♖ad8 26 ♖ac1 ♘a8 27 ♘e3 ♗e6 with a solid enough position.

25 fxe4 (now White has an easy and pleasant game: he has acquired the f-file and some good squares) **25...♖ad8 26 ♖af1**

With the threat of ♖f4xh4. It is probable

that 26 ♘xh4!? ♖h8 27 ♘f3 ♗xh3 28 ♘f4
♗c8 29 ♔c3 and ♘e5 was even better, with
a highly favourable endgame.

26...♖h8 27 ♘e3 (changing plan, since if 27
♖f4 there is the reply 27...♖h5) **27...♖h5 28
♖fg1 ♗c8** (28...♗e6!? or 28...♘ec8!? was
better) **29 ♔c3 ♖hh8 30 ♘f4 ♖d6**

30...♘a8? 31 ♘c4 b6 32 ♖f1 etc. was altogether too passive.

31 ♗c2?

A serious delay. After 31 ♘c4! ♘xc4 32
bxc4! White's mobile pawn centre would
have become terribly strong: for example,
32...♖hd8 33 d5 cxd5 (33...c5? 34 ♖b1) 34
cxd5 ♗d7 35 ♖b1 b6 36 ♗b5 ♖c8+ 37 ♔d4
♗xb5 38 axb5 and ♖hc1.

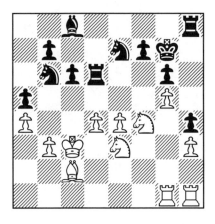

31...♘a8?

As a result of Black's tiring defence and
time-trouble, he blunders the a5-pawn. My
error would have been best exploited by
31...f5! 32 ♘c4 (32 gxf6+ ♖xf6 is equal)
32...♘xc4 33 bxc4 fxe4 34 ♖e1 ♖f8 35 ♖xe4
♘f5 36 ♖d1 ♖f7, obtaining a perfectly
defensible position.

32 ♘c4 ♖dd8 33 ♘xa5 ♘c7 34 ♖f1

As it is said in such cases, 'the rest is a
matter of technique'. My eyes were slightly
dazzled by the mass of possibilities. 34 ♖g2
or 34 ♖h2 was good, as was 34 ♘c4
(34...b5?! 35 ♘e5!), or 34 ♗d3 and ♗e2. The

move played was only slightly inferior.

34...b5!?

Shutting in the knight on a5. After losing
a pawn, Spassky as though woke up and
began resisting desperately, looking for the
slightest opportunity to make it harder for
White to win. But I, in turn, remembered
how once I had failed to win two completely
won positions against the ex-champion
(Game Nos.58 and 87 in *Garry Kasparov on
Garry Kasparov Part I*), and I endeavoured to
rid myself of any premature thoughts of
victory.

35 ♖f3 ♖hf8

35...b4+? 36 ♔xb4 ♖xd4+ 37 ♔c3 c5 38
♖hf1 was hopeless for Black. However, even
the more resilient 35...♗a6!? would not have
eased his lot after 36 ♖g1! ♗a8 37 b4.

36 ♖hf1 bxa4 37 bxa4 f6

If 37...f5 White could have replied 38 exf5
or 38 gxf6+! (as in the previous note). For an
instant Spassky thought that he was gaining
counterplay, but this was a mirage.

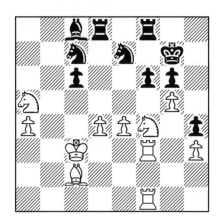

38 ♘xg6!

'After Black's mistake on the 31st move,
Kasparov has literally torn his position to
pieces' (Gipslis). This stroke is, indeed, both
more forceful and much more flamboyant
than 38 gxf6+ ♖xf6 39 ♘h5+ gxh5 40 ♖xf6
♘cd5+! 41 exd5 ♘xd5+ 42 ♔c4! (but not my

Informator suggestion 42 ♔b2(?) ♘xf6 43 ♘xc6 ♖d6 44 ♖g1+ ♔f8 with a probable draw) 42...♘xf6 43 ♖g1+ ♔f8 44 ♘xc6 ♖d6 45 ♔c5 ♖d5+ 46 ♔b6 ♗d7 (46...♗xh3 47 a5) 47 ♗b3 ♖d6 48 ♖c1 and a4-a5, winning.

38...♘xg6 39 gxf6+ ♔h6 40 ♘xc6 ♖d6 41 d5

'The four passed pawns more than compensate White for the sacrificed knight, and in addition the black pieces lack coordination. Spassky finds the best practical chance: with a counter exchange sacrifice he breaks up the chain of white pawns in the hope of dealing with them one at a time.' (Nikitin)

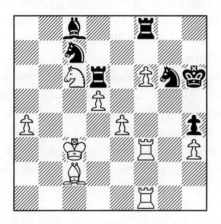

41...♖xc6+!?

There was little comfort in 41...♗b7 42 ♘d4 and ♘f5+ or 41...♗a6 42 ♘e7 ♗xf1 (42...♘xe7 43 fxe7 ♖e8 44 ♖f6+ etc.) 43 ♘f5+ ♔g5 44 ♘xd6 ♗g2 (44...♖xf6 45 ♘f7+!) 45 ♖f5+ ♔h6 46 ♗d1!, and the curtain comes down.

42 dxc6 ♘e6 (if 42...♘e5, then 43 ♖3f2 ♘xc6 44 f7 or 43...♗xh3 44 ♖h1 ♗g4 45 ♖xh4+ ♔g5 46 ♖h1 and wins) **43 e5!?**

At the cost of a pawn, White opens the way for his bishop and denies the opponent any chances of a blockade. 43 ♖f5 or 43 ♗b3 was also good.

43...♘xe5

White would have won just as quickly and

elegantly after 43...♘g5 44 ♖e3 ♗xh3 (or 44...♗e6 45 ♔b4! etc.) 45 ♖xh3! ♘xh3 46 e6, decisively breaking through to the queening square.

44 ♖e3! ♘g6 (44...♘xc6 45 ♖e4!) **45 f7!** (with the terrible threat of ♖f6) **45...♘gf4**

If 45...♔g7 the simplest is 46 ♗xg6!? ♔xg6 47 a5, when Black's defences crumble.

46 ♗b3 ♔g7 47 ♖e4 ♖xf7

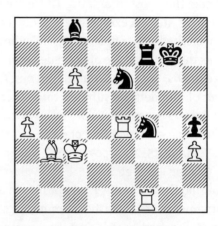

48 ♗xe6! ♘xe6 49 ♖xf7+ ♔xf7 50 ♖xh4 ♔e7 51 ♖h8 ♗a6 52 h4! 1-0

It is not possible to stop all the pawns.

This was my first ever win against Spassky, after two losses and four draws. The outcome of the game distressed Ljubojevic, with whom I shared 1st place: I had the better tiebreak and the organisers awarded me the special prize for the tournament winner. But in the battle for the World Cup the games with Illescas did not count, and the winner of the stage nevertheless became Ljubomir Ljubojevic, who achieved the greatest success in his chess career.

Of course, I was happy to have managed to overcome the crisis at the start and to achieve a solid points reserve before the concluding stage of the Cup in Skelleftea, where I was facing a decisive direct battle with Anatoly Karpov.

In June, in Rotterdam the penultimate, fifth stage of the World Cup was held; this was due to give an answer to the question: would Karpov manage to take first place and score a minimum of 10½ out of 14 against the contestants who counted, in order to catch me before Skelleftea? This tournament promised to be one of the most brilliant in Karpov's career, but in fact it probably became the most dramatic. The ex-world champion started excellently – 5 out of 6, then reached 9½ out of 12 (!), including 9 points that counted. He only needed to make three draws, but – his strength ran out. As a result of blunders, he suffered three successive defeats – against Salov, Ljubojevic and Nunn – and conceded first place (1. Timman – 10½ out of 15; 2. Karpov – 9½; 3. Vaganian – 9; 4. Nunn – 8½, etc.).

During these months I did not play in any tournaments, but in the summer I conducted a 'return match' in Evry – a repeat simultaneous display with clocks against the French team. The opposition line-up was much stronger: Renet was playing on board 1, and the trainer was none other than Spassky. However, I won by the same score (4½-1½), beating Renet with White and Kouatly with Black – in a memorable King's Indian with a positional piece sacrifice.

Missed Opportunities

Sixth World Cup Tournament (Skelleftea, 12 August – 2 September 1989): 1–2. Karpov and **Kasparov** – 9½ out of 15; 3–5. Portisch, Seirawan and Short – 8½; 6–7. Salov and Sax – 8; 8–9. Nunn and Andersson – 7½; 10–12. Hübner, Ribli and Tal – 7; 13. Ehlvest – 6½; 14–15. Nikolic and Korchnoi – 6; 16. Vaganian – 5.

Before the last, Swedish stage of the Cup, I had two first places and one second (83

points), while Karpov had one first and two second (80½). Thus Karpov could still achieve overall success, if he were to take clear first place in Skelleftea and score 11 out of 15 (again '+7'!), and finish a point ahead of me. This looked an ultra-difficult task, and yet in Rotterdam, after conducting 12 rounds brilliantly, he had achieved this mark, and if it had not been for the three losses... It was clear that Karpov's collapse in Rotterdam had practically ensured my victory in the Cup, provided only that I did not suffer a similar collapse. This thought preyed on my sub-conscious, and, although my preparation was very good, I involuntarily began thinking that now the main thing was not to overdo things and not to leave anything *en prise*.

At the start the ex-champion drew with Black against Sax, while with White I crushed Korchnoi, who went wrong in the opening. By the will of the pairings (on this occasion there were no 'Belfort experiments'), the arch-rivals met as early as round 2, with Karpov once again having the white pieces. After choosing the King's Indian Defence I soon seized the initiative (cf. *Game No.80*, note to White's 14th move), but in my opponent's severe time-trouble I missed some excellent winning chances.

Nikitin: *'This draw did both players a bad service. For a long time Karpov was unable to play a more or less normal game, under the impression of his opponent's obvious superiority, while Garry was tormented by his errors on the 35th and 37th moves. In this tournament the world champion's superiority over his opponents was more obvious than ever before: only in two games did they worthily withstand the onslaught, whereas in a good dozen games his advantage varied between '±' and '+−'. But at decisive moments, during the third or fourth hour, there were short-*

term (for two or three moves) slumps in the champion's play; his calculating machine switched off, and his intuition stopped working. He had to spend a mass of effort, so as not to lose confidence in himself.'

Indeed, on the number of missed opportunities this was one of my record tournaments! Tal: *'Kasparov should have scored a couple of extra points, or perhaps even more.'* Fortunately, Karpov too did not play very brilliantly in Skelleftea: apparently the trauma received in Rotterdam had not yet healed. Therefore on this occasion we did not have such a tense race as, say, in the previous year's USSR Championship.

In the 3rd round I met Robert Hübner, and after a mistake by my opponent I already had a completely winning position by the 20th move, but I was unable to apply the finishing touch.

Game 52
G.Kasparov-R.Hübner
World Cup
3rd Round, Skelleftea, 15.08.1989

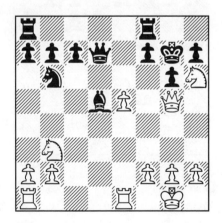

White is threatening both ♖ad1 and ♘c5(d4), with a terribly strong attack against the weakened black king. None of

these replies will do: 19...♖ae8? 20 ♘g4!, 19...♕d8? 20 ♘f5+ ♔h8 21 ♘e7 ♘d7 22 ♘c5!, or 19...♗xb3? 20 ♕f6+ ♔xh6 21 ♖e4! ♗d1 22 f3 ♗xf3 23 gxf3 ♕h3 24 ♖d1! c5 25 ♖h4+ ♕xh4 26 ♕xh4+ and f3-f4-f5.

19...f6?

In his confusion Hübner failed to find the only defence – 19...♗e6!, hobbling the knight on h6 and then forcing the exchange of queens: for example, 20 ♘c5 (20 ♖ad1 ♘d5) 20...♕d8 21 h4! ♘d5 22 ♖ad1 (22 g3!?) 22...♕xg5 23 hxg5, and White has merely a slightly better endgame.

20 exf6+ ♖xf6 21 ♖e7+

In my surprise I also became somewhat confused and instantly seeing the tactical stroke with the win of queen for rook and bishop, I was unable to resist the temptation. Meanwhile, White had another three (!) ways to win:

1) 21 ♘g4 ♖f5 22 ♕h4! ♕d6 (22...♖e8 23 ♕h3! and ♕c3+) 23 ♘d4 ♖f7 24 ♖ad1 ♕f8 25 ♘e6+ ♗xe6 26 ♖xe6 with the threat of ♕h6+ and ♘e5. White has a big advantage, but I had not calculated as far as a clear win, although after 26...♖e8 27 ♕h6+ ♔h8 28 ♖xe8 ♕xe8 29 ♕c1! the black king is in deadly danger;

2) 21 ♘c5 ♕d6 22 ♖e7+ (in my calculations I became obsessed with this variation, which is similar to the game continuation) 22...♔h8 23 ♖e6! ♖xe6 24 ♘f7+ and ♘xd6, or 22...♕xe7 23 ♘f5+ ♖xf5 24 ♕xe7+ ♖f7 25 ♕e5+ ♔g8 26 ♖e1 with a technically won position, although there is a difficult conversion phase in prospect;

3) 21 ♘d4! (alas, this leap of the 'reserve' knight to the critical f5-square was something that I glanced at only fleetingly) 21...♗e6 (there is nothing else) 22 ♖ad1 ♘d5 23 ♖e5 c6 24 ♖de1 (pointed out by Hübner in *Informator*), and Black can resign: 24...♗f7 25 ♘hf5+ ♔g8 26 ♖xd5, or 24...♖e8

25 ♘df5+ ♚f8 26 ♖xd5. When after the game I was shown this possibility, I was horrified.

21...♕xe7 22 ♘f5+ ♖xf5 23 ♕xe7+ ♖f7 24 ♕e5+ ♚g8 25 ♘c5 c6 26 b3?!

Again not the strongest move! The exchange of knights, easing Black's defence, should have been avoided. Then White would have been able to include his knight in the attack or force its exchange for the bishop. Hübner recommended 26 ♘e4, assuming that after 26...♗xe4 27 ♕xe4 ♘d5 28 ♖e1 and b2-b4-b5 Black would be unable to hold out. But the most unpleasant for him was 26 ♕c3!? followed by ♖e1, f2-f3 and ♘d3-e5(f2).

26...♘d7! 27 ♘xd7 ♖xd7 28 ♖d1 (28 h4 or 28 ♖e1 was also not bad, but in any case the win is no longer easy) **28...a5 29 h4 ♖f7**

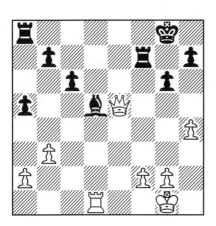

30 ♖d4 (30 h5! was more energetic) **30...♖f5 31 ♕e1 b5 32 ♖d3?**

The culmination of my imprecise play: now Black gets rid of his weak a5-pawn. 32 f3 was correct.

32...a4! (of course!) **33 ♖e3 axb3 34 axb3 ♖af8 35 f3 h5**

And White was unable to breach this fortress – draw on the 61st move (½-½).

These painful draws with Karpov and Hübner as though set the tone for my performance in the tournament. True, in the next round I won with Black against Short, who played too timidly in a Queen's Pawn Opening, and I caught the leader – Salov (3 out of 4). But then things again stalled.

In the 5th round I had a technically won ending against Andersson, but with my hasty 29th moved I immediately contrived to squander my entire enormous advantage. In the 6th round came a fighting Sicilian draw with Sax. In the 7th round I completely outplayed Mikhail Tal, and had a decisive material advantage, but in my opponent's desperate time-trouble I blundered a piece (apparently, for the first time in my serious games).

> ### Game 53
> ### **G.Kasparov-M.Tal**
> ### World Cup
> ### 7th Round, Skelleftea, 20.08.1989

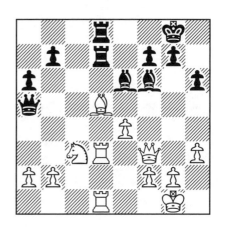

28...♗xc3?

Already a pawn down and with his flag wavering, Tal overlooked my interposed reply. 28...♕c7(b6) was more resilient.

29 ♗xe6! ♖xd3 30 ♕xf7+ ♚h8 31 ♖xd3

'White's position is completely won, but I

was in such time-trouble that I simply did not manage to resign.' (Tal)

31...♗f6

31...♗xb2 was also hopeless: 32 ♖d5! (the most energetic) 32...♕e1+ (32...♕b6 33 g4! and g4-g5) 33 ♔h2 ♖b8 34 ♗f5! ♕c1 (34...♕xf2 35 ♕g6) 35 g3 ♕c2 36 ♔g2 ♕c6 37 ♖d7 ♕f6 38 ♖xb7.

32 ♖xd8+ (here too 32 ♖d5! ♕e1+ 33 ♔h2 ♖b8 34 ♖f5! ♗xb2 35 ♕c7 or 34...♗h4 35 g3 was more forceful) **32...♕xd8**

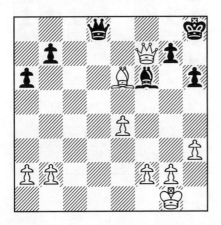

33 ♕xb7??

A nightmare! 33 b3 or 33 g3 (33...♗xb2 34 ♕xb7) would have won easily.

33...♕d1+ 34 ♔h2 ♕d6+ 35 g3 ♕xe6 36 b3 (fortunately, for the piece White has three pawns) **36...♕d6**

'How I reached the 40 move mark, I don't know – perhaps it was my Riga blitz training. It was also amazing that in the remaining moves to the time control I blundered only one pawn – this was sufficient for a draw.' (Tal)

37 ♔g2 ♗d4 (37...♔h7!?) **38 h4 ♕f6** (38...h5!?) **39 f4 ♕d6 40 e5 ♕c5** (40...♕g6 with a draw) **41 ♕xa6 ♕d5+** (41...♕c2+!?) **42 ♔h2 ♕f3** (42...♗c5!?) **43 ♕c8+ ♔h7 44 ♕c2+ ♔h8 45 ♕g2 ♕d3! 46 h5** (or 46 b4 ♗c3! 47 a3 ♔g8 with a draw) **46...♗c5**, and a draw (½-½) on the 61st move.

After this dramatic game there followed a short draw with Salov, a good strategic win with Black against Portisch (Game No.44 in *My Great Predecessors Part III*), and fighting draws with Nunn and Ehlvest.

Four rounds before the finish Karpov and I were unhurriedly leading, with just 7 points out of 11. In a tense game from the 12th round with Rafael Vaganian, who two months later was to become USSR champion, I was able to employ one of my opening ideas for Seville.

Game 54
G.Kasparov-R.Vaganian
World Cup
12th Round, Skelleftea,
26.08.1989
English Opening A33

1 c4 c5 2 ♘f3 ♘f6 3 ♘c3 ♘c6 4 d4 cxd4 5 ♘xd4 e6 6 g3 ♕b6 7 ♘db5

At that time this was a rare, little-explored move, and earlier I had employed the usual 7 ♘b3 (Game Nos.28 and 30 in *Kasparov vs. Karpov 1975-1985*).

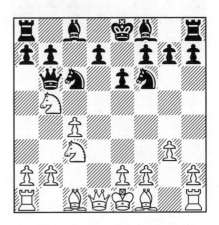

7...d5

If 7...♗c5 there would have followed 8 ♗g2! – White is clearly better after

8...♗xf2+!? 9 ♔f1 ♘g4 10 ♕d6! (as in the source game Lipinski-Schinzel, Poland 1978), and Black also does not equalise with 8...a6?! 9 ♘d6+ ♔e7 10 ♘de4 or 8...d5 9 0-0.

But after the strongest reply 7...♘e5! Black has no reason for complaint:

1) 8 ♗g2 a6 9 ♕a4 (9 ♗e3?! ♕a5!, D.Byrne-Geller, Moscow 1955), and now not 9...♗c5?! (Vaganian-Dvoirys, 56th USSR Championship, Odessa 1989) 10 ♗f4!, but 9...♖b8 10 ♗e3 ♗c5 11 ♗xc5 ♕xc5 12 ♕a3 b6! 13 ♘d6+ ♔e7 14 ♕xc5 bxc5 15 ♘xc8+ ♖hxc8 16 b3 d5! 17 cxd5 c4 with equality (Timman-Alterman, Pula 1997);

2) 8 ♗f4 (8 ♗e3?! ♕c6) 8...♘fg4 9 ♕a4 (this replaced the earlier 9 e3 a6! of Anand-Leko, Wijk aan Zee 1996) 9...g5! 10 ♗xe5 ♕xf2+! 11 ♔d1 ♘xe5 12 ♘c7+ ♔d8 13 ♘xa8 ♕d4+ 14 ♔c2 ♘xc4, gaining a draw (Carlsen-Dominguez, Linares 2009).

Instead of this Vaganian decided to follow the game Tukmakov-Mikhalchishin (51st USSR Championship, Lvov 1984), but he ran into a novelty.

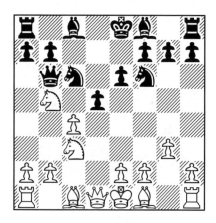

8 ♗g2!?

The aforementioned game went 8 ♗e3 d4! 9 ♘xd4 ♕xb2 10 ♘db5 ♗b4 11 ♕c1 ♕xc1+ 12 ♖xc1 0-0 with equality. By 11 ♗d2!? ♘d4! 12 ♖c1 ♘xb5 13 cxb5 White could still have fought for an advantage, but

9...♗c5! is simpler, practically forcing 10 ♘a4 ♗b4+ 11 ♘c3 ♗c5 with a draw.

8...d4 9 ♘a4 ♕a5+ 10 ♗d2 ♗b4

Also after 10...♕d8 11 e3! e5 (not 11...dxe3?! 12 ♗xe3 ♗b4+ 13 ♘bc3) 12 exd4 exd4 13 0-0 (H.Olafsson-Gligoric, Palma de Mallorca 1989) or 12...a6 13 ♘bc3 ♘xd4 14 0-0 ♗e7 15 h3 White retains appreciable pressure.

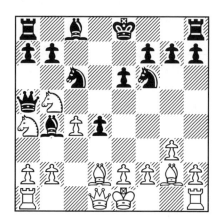

11 ♘c5!

The only way! In the event of 11 ♗xb4 ♕xb4+ 12 ♕d2 ♕xd2+ (12...♕xa4? 13 b3 and wins) 13 ♔xd2 ♔e7 Black would have got away with a slight fright.

11...0-0 (11...a6? 12 ♘d6+ ♔e7 13 ♘cxb7 and 11...♖b8?! 12 ♘d3 are weak alternatives) **12 ♘d3!**

An ideal place for the knight. After 12 0-0 ♗xd2 (12...e5!?) 13 ♘b3 ♕b6 14 ♕xd2 e5 15 ♘d6 ♕c7 (my *Informator* suggestion 15...♗e6(?!) is worse because of 16 f4!) 16 c5 ♘e8 17 ♘b5 ♕e7 18 f4 (18 e3 ♗e6!) 18...a6 19 ♘a3 ♗e6 and ...♗xb3 Black is close to equality.

12...♗xd2+ 13 ♕xd2 ♕xd2+ (if 13...♕d8, then 14 c5!) **14 ♔xd2 ♖d8 15 c5** (with the intention of ♘d6) **15...♘e8 16 ♘a3**

And now the knight goes to c4 via a3. 16 f4 f6 17 ♖hc1!? with the idea of ♖c4 was also interesting.

16...f6 17 f4 ♗d7

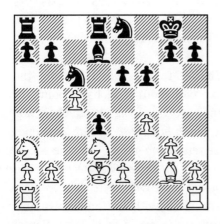

18 ♘c4

18 ♖hc1!? (then ♖c4 and ♘c2) again came into consideration, as well as 18 b4!? at once, with the initiative after all of 18...♖ab8 19 b5 ♘e7 20 ♖ab1!, 18...a6 19 ♘c4 and 18...♘c7 19 ♘c4 and a2-a4. The move in the game allows Black an additional possibility, which Vaganian exploits.

18...♖ab8 19 b4 ♘e7 20 a4 ♗c6?!

Trying to ease the defence by an exchange of bishops. Even so, the prudent 20...a6 was preferable, and if 21 ♘a5, then 21...♘c6.

21 ♗f3?!

A loss of precious time. The simple 21 ♗xc6! would have given White an enduring advantage: 21...♘xc6 22 b5 ♘e7 23 ♖hb1 or 21...bxc6 22 b5! cxb5 23 axb5 ♖xb5 24 ♖xa7, when the passed c-pawn is very strong.

21...a6

Reverting to the correct plan. Both 21...♖bc8?! 22 b5!, and 21...♗xf3?! 22 exf3 followed by ♖he1 and b4-b5 were advantageous to White.

22 ♖hb1 ♘c7 23 ♘d6 (23 ♘f2!?) 23...♘f5?!

It was better to tackle the d6-knight with 23...♘c8!, since in the event of 24 ♘xc8 ♖bxc8 White's advantage is altogether slight. I would probably have had to bring back my knight – 24 ♘c4 and direct the d3-

knight via f2 to e4.

24 b5

It made sense to spoil the opponent's pawn chain – 24 ♘xf5!? exf5 (isolating and condemning the d4-pawn to its fate), and only then to carry out the cherished 25 b5: for example, 25...axb5 26 ♗xc6 bxc6 27 ♘b4 bxa4 28 ♘xc6 ♖xb1 29 ♖xb1, and Black faces a gruelling defence.

24...axb5

A difficult choice. The immediate exchange of the bishop looked tempting – 24...♗xf3 with the idea of 25 ♘xf5 ♗xe2!, when it suddenly transpires that swift pawn breaks do not work: 26 c6?! ♗xd3 27 ♔xd3 exf5 28 b6 ♖dc8!, or 26 ♘e7+?! ♔f7 27 b6 ♘d5! 28 c6 ♗xd3 29 ♔xd3 ♔xe7 30 c7 e5. But after 26 b6! ♘d5 27 ♘d6 White would nevertheless have retained the initiative: 27...♗f3 28 a5! or 27...♗xd3 28 ♔xd3 e5 29 fxe5 fxe5 30 ♔e4! (with excellent compensation for the exchange after 30...♘c3+ 31 ♔xe5 ♘xb1 32 ♖xb1).

25 axb5?!

Strangely enough, this natural capture loses White the greater part of his advantage. 25 ♗xc6 bxc6 26 ♘xf5 exf5 27 ♘b4 (transposing into the variation from the note to White's 24th move) or 25 ♘xb5!? ♗xf3 26 ♘xc7 was more promising.

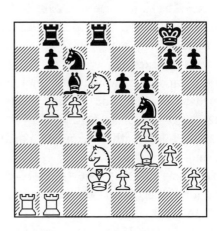

25...♘xd6?

A fatal mistake: Vaganian cracks under the strain of a lengthy defence. It was essential to play 25...♗xf3 26 ♘xf5 ♗xe2 (26...exf5? 27 exf3, and if 27...♘d5, then 28 ♖c1! is strong), and now nothing is given by either 27 b6 ♘d5 28 ♘xd4 ♗xd3 29 ♔xd3 e5 or 28 ♘d6 ♗f3!, or 27 ♘e7+ ♔f7 28 b6 ♗xd3 (not 28...♘e8? 29 ♘c6! and wins) 29 ♔xd3 ♖d7 30 bxc7 ♖xc7 31 ♘d5 exd5 with equality.

True, with the opening of the a-file White would have acquired the fantastic resource 27 c6!! ♗xd3 (if 27...♘d5?, then 28 ♘e7+! ♘xe7 29 c7 winning the exchange: 29...♗f3 30 ♘c5! etc.) 28 ♔xd3 exf5 29 b6! ♖dc8 30 bxc7 ♖xc7 31 ♖a6! ♔f7 32 ♖ab6, but after 32...♔e7 33 cxb7 (33 ♖xb7 ♖bc8 is equal) 33...♖d7 it is not apparent how Black's position can be breached.

26 bxc6!

With the elimination of the f3-bishop's opponent, the battle enters the technical phase: White will inevitably create a passed pawn and win a pawn.

26...♘c4+ 27 ♔c1 (27 ♔e1!? was also good: 27...bxc6 28 ♘b4 or 27...b5 28 cxb6 ♖xb6 29 ♖xb6 ♘xb6 30 ♘c5) **27...bxc6 28 ♖xb8 ♖xb8 29 ♖a4!**

A useful interposition, although also after 29 ♗xc6 ♖b3 30 ♖a7 ♘b5 31 ♗xb5 ♖xb5 32 ♖d7 ♘a5 (32...e5?! 33 c6!) 33 ♔c2 Black cannot save the game.

29...♘e3 30 ♗xc6 e5

Desperation. It would also not have helped to play 30...♖d8 31 ♖a7 ♘ed5 32 ♔d2!? or 32 ♘e1!? ♖b8 (32...♔f8 33 ♘f3) 33 ♘c2 e5 34 ♔d2 with a victorious march by the king.

31 fxe5 fxe5 32 ♘xe5 ♘e6 33 ♖a5! ♖c8 34 ♔d2! (on this occasion I was accurate to the end) **34...♔f8 35 ♔d3 ♔e7** (35...♖c7 36 ♗a4!) **36 ♖a7+ ♔f6 37 ♘d7+ ♔g5** (37...♔e7

38 ♘b6+) **38 ♗f3 ♘f5 39 h4+ ♔g6 40 ♖a6 ♔f7 41 ♗d5 ♖e8 42 ♘e5+ ♔f6 43 ♘f3**

And in view of the further loss of material, Black resigned (**1-0**).

Thanks to this win I became the sole leader with 8 out of 12, half a point ahead of Karpov. Nikitin: *'The world champion was very much hoping to win at least one of his three remaining games – and he was close to victory in all three. First he played a mind-boggling game with Yasser Seirawan.'*

The clash with the ambitious American grandmaster was a crucial one. Remembering our encounters at the previous two Olympiads, we were both aiming to win!

Game 55
Y.Seirawan-G.Kasparov
World Cup
13th Round, Skelleftea,
27.08.1989
Modern Benoni A65

1 d4 ♘f6 2 c4 g6 3 ♘c3 ♗g7 4 e4 d6 5 ♗e2 0-0 6 ♗g5

At that time Yasser regularly employed the Averbakh Variation. Although I had 6...♘bd7 (Game No.76 in *Garry Kasparov on Garry Kasparov Part I*) and 6...♘a6 in my armoury, I decided to reply by taking my opponent's games into account.

6...c5 7 d5 h6 (7...b5?! – Game Nos.58, 67 in *Garry Kasparov on Garry Kasparov Part I*) **8 ♗e3**

Alburt once chose against me 8 ♗f4 e6 9 dxe6 ♗xe6 10 ♗xd6 (Game No.28 in *Garry Kasparov on Garry Kasparov Part I*), but here there is also 8...♕b6.

8...e6 9 ♕d2 exd5 10 cxd5

This leads to a fashionable Modern Benoni set-up. If 10 exd5 Black has more than one option – say, 10...♘g4 11 ♗xg4 ♗xg4 12 ♗xh6 ♖e8+ with sharp play (Podgaets-Bronstein, Tbilisi 1973), or 10...♘h7 11 h3 ♖e8 12 ♘f3 (12 ♗d3 b5!) 12...♗f5 13 ♗d3 (Dydyshko-Kasparov, Minsk 1978) 13...♘e4 with equality.

10...♖e8 11 f3 (3)

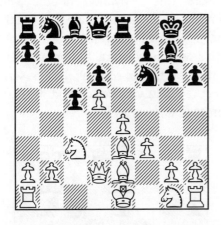

It is curious that a well-known position from the Sämisch Variation has arisen, in which instead of the normal ♘ge2 White has played ♗e2.

11...h5! (5)

Of course, not 11...a6? (Seirawan-Am.Rodriguez, Toluca Interzonal 1982) because of 12 ♗xh6!, when 12...♘xe4? 13 ♘xe4 ♕h4+ 14 g3 ♕xh6 15 ♘f6+ is bad for Black. And after the passive 11...♔h7 White plays 12 a4 or, most often, 12 g4 (Seirawan-Scheeren, Wijk aan Zee 1983).

12 a4! (2)

The prelude to an interesting regrouping. White has a problem with the development of his g1-knight – if ♘h3 there follows ...♗xh3 (for this reason Black is not in a hurry to play ...♘bd7).

12...a6 (5)

Also a logical and useful move. 'This position was on the magnetic set in Garry's room, when he was leaving for the game.' (Nikitin). 12...♘a6 is also not bad, but then

the white knight easily comes into play: 13 ♗b5 ♗d7 14 ♘ge2 (Seirawan-R.Byrne, Berkley 1984).

13 a5 (19)

If 13 h4, then 13...♘h7!, forestalling ♘h3 and provoking the weakening move g2-g3. I had also studied 13 ♗g5 ♕a5 14 ♖a3 ♘h7! (14...♘bd7?! 15 ♘h3, Seirawan-Bouaziz, Hamburg 1982) 15 ♗f4 ♕c7 with complicated play.

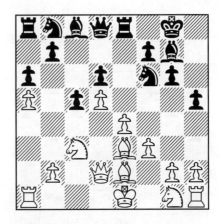

13...♘h7!? (4)

It was this move, which had not yet occurred in grandmaster play, that I was relying on. Of course, my opponent was ready for 13...b5 14 axb6 ♕xb6 – in the well-known game Christiansen-Marin (Szirak Interzonal 1987) after 15 ♗d1 ♘bd7 16 ♘ge2 ♘e5 17 b3 a5 this led to a double-edged battle.

14 ♗d1 (10)

The point of White's plan: the bishop vacates the e2-square for the knight. If 14 ♘a4!? Seirawan recommended 14...f5(?!) 15 ♘b6 ♖a7, but after 16 ♕c2! White's chances are somewhat better. 14...♘d7! is more correct: 15 ♘h3 b5 16 axb6 ♘xb6 17 ♘f2 ♘xa4 18 ♖xa4 ♖b8 19 ♘d1 (or 19 ♖a2) 19...f5 with sufficient counterplay.

14...♘d7 (4) **15 ♘ge2** (2) **♘e5 16 b3**

By parrying the threat of ...♘c4, White

blocks the bishop's access to the desired a4-square. However, 16 ♗b3 b5(b6) was no better.

16...♕h4+ (31)

Seirawan was afraid of 16...f5, judging Black to be better after 17 ♗c2 fxe4 18 ♗xe4 c4! (another recommendation by Yasser – 18...♘f6 is worse because of 19 ♗c2!), but after 19 0-0 cxb3 20 ♗d4 White soon regains the pawn and does not experience any problems.

17 ♗f2 ♕f6

With the transparent threat of ...♕xf3!.

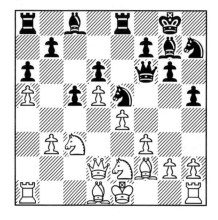

18 ♕e3 (8)

A rather artificial manoeuvre. After the natural 18 0-0 White did not like 18...♘g5! (not 18...♕xf3? 19 ♗xc5! or the questionable 18...h4 19 f4!? ♘g4 20 ♗e1), although 19 ♗e3 (19 ♔h1? ♘gxf3! and wins) 19...♘gxf3+ 20 gxf3 ♘xf3+ 21 ♖xf3 ♕xf3 22 ♘f4 ♕xe3+ 23 ♕xe3 ♗d4 leads to a roughly equal endgame.

18 ♗e3 will also do, inviting a repetition of moves – 18...♕h4+ (Seirawan). I thought that the sharp 18...h4?! was acceptable, with the idea of 19 h3 ♘xf3+?! 20 gxf3 ♕xf3 21 ♖g1 ♕xh3, but after the sudden 22 ♘f4 ♕d7 23 ♗h5! White would seize the initiative.

18...h4! (6) **19 h3** (6) **g5! 20 0-0** (8) **♗d7** (10)

Black calmly completes his development. Things were unclear after 20...♘h6 (Spassky) 21 ♗e1 g4 22 f4, or 20...♘f8 (Nikitin) 21 ♗e1 ♘g6 22 ♗d2 ♗h6 23 ♘a4.

21 ♔h1 (5)

Here too 21 ♗e1!? came into consideration.

21...♘f8 (the activation of the knight strengthens the dark-square blockade) **22 ♗g1** (3) **♘fg6 23 ♗h2?!** (2)

This seemingly logical bishop manoeuvre (control of the f4-square!) has a serious defect. 23 ♗c2 was better, and if 23...♘f4, then 24 ♘xf4 gxf4 25 ♕d2.

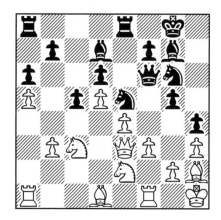

23...c4?! (7)

Activity on the wrong wing: here Black has no advantage in force! Nothing real was promised by 23...♗b5 24 ♗c2 ♖e7?! 25 ♘xb5 axb5 26 f4!, or 23...♗h6 24 ♗c2 ♘f4?! 25 ♘xf4 gxf4 26 ♕d2. But I could have landed an insidious blow, not noticed by the commentators: 23...g4! 24 f4 (24 hxg4? ♘xg4) 24...♘f3!, forcing 25 ♖xf3 (25 gxf3?! g3! with an attack) 25...gxf3 26 ♕xf3 ♗b5, and although White has knight and pawn for the exchange, his position is unpleasant.

24 ♖b1 (3) **♖ac8** (24...♖ec8!?) **25 ♕a7!** (11)

Yasser immediately creates counter-threats. Nevertheless, the position remains dynamically balanced.

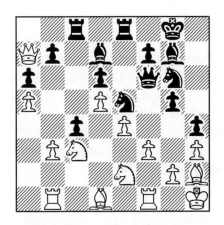

25...♘f4?! (10)

Too slow. It was time to launch an attack – 25...g4! 26 hxg4 ♗xg4! (26...♘xg4?! 27 ♗g1) with very sharp play in most of the variations:

1) 27 ♘d4? h3! 28 g3 ♘d3 29 ♘ce2 ♖xe4 or 29 ♗g1 h2! and wins;

2) 27 ♘g1?! (Seirawan attaches two exclamation marks to this move, analysing only the reply 27...♘d3) 27...cxb3! 28 ♖xb3 ♘c4 or 28 ♘ce2 ♗d7 with the initiative for Black;

3) 27 ♗c2 cxb3! 28 ♗xe5 (28 ♗xb3? h3! 29 fxg4 hxg2+ 30 ♔xg2 ♕g5!) 28...♘xe5 29 ♗xb3 ♗d7 30 ♕xb7 h3 31 g3 ♕g6 with excellent compensation for the pawn;

4) 27 ♘f4 ♗xf3!? (27...cxb3 and ...♘c4 is less exacting) 28 ♘h3!? cxb3 29 ♘a4 ♘f4 (29...♕d8!?) 30 ♗xf3 ♘xh3 31 ♗g4 ♘xg4! 32 ♖xf6 ♖c2! with a pretty draw;

5) 27 ♕g1 ♗h5! 28 bxc4 ♘xc4 29 ♖xb7 ♘d2! 30 e5! ♖xe5! 31 ♗xe5 ♕xe5 32 ♖f2 ♗h6 and here Black has good play for the exchange.

26 bxc4 (6)

In the event of 26 ♗xf4 gxf4 27 ♕xb7 (27 bxc4!?) 27...♖b8! 28 ♕xa6 ♖a8 29 ♕b6 ♖eb8 30 ♕d4 ♖xa5 Black has sufficient compensation for the pawn. He also has every chance of holding on after 26 ♕xb7 ♖b8! 27 ♕a7!? (27 ♕xa6 ♕e7! 28 ♗g1 ♘xh3!) 27...♘xe2 28 ♘xe2 ♗b5 29 ♘c3 cxb3 30 ♘xb5 axb5 31 ♗xb3 ♖a8 etc.

26...♘xc4 (Seirawan expected 26...♖xc4? 27 ♖xb7 ♗c8 28 ♖c7! with an obvious advantage to White) **27 ♖xb7?** (7)

Not wishing to exchange the dark-square bishop, but 27 ♗xf4! gxf4 28 ♖xb7 ♖a8 29 ♕f2 ♖e7 30 ♖g1 with the idea of ♗a4 would have given White the better chances (30...♘xa5 31 ♖b4!).

27...♘d2! (3) **28 ♖g1?** (6)

28 ♖e1? ♘xg2! or 28 ♖f2? ♖a8 29 ♕b6 ♘d3 was also bad. Therefore 28 e5! dxe5 29 ♘e4 ♘xe4 30 fxe4 ♗b5 31 ♗g1 was necessary, going on to the defensive.

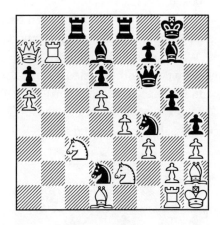

28...♘xh3!! (10)

A cold shower: having miraculously remained alive, this knight lands a crushing blow. All Black's other replies would have lost, whereas this one wins: the knight cannot be taken and the trapping of the queen by 29...♖a8 30 ♕b6(e3) ♘c4 is threatened.

29 e5!?

The best practical chance (in the event of the mechanical 29...dxe5?! 30 ♖xd7 ♖a8(?) 31 ♕e3 ♘c4 White has the counter-blow 32 ♘e4! ♕f5 33 ♕c3 ♘xg1 34 ♖c7). Later, on a flight from Skelleftea to Brussels, I analysed this position with Seirawan, Korchnoi and Nikitin, and an apparently more resilient defence was found with the sacrifice of the queen for two minor pieces – 29 ♖xd7 ♗a8 30 ♕b6 ♘c4 and now:

1) 31 gxh3 ♘xb6 32 axb6 ♕xf3+ 33 ♖g2 ♕xh3! (more accurate than 33...♗xc3, analysed by Seirawan in *Informator* and in his book *Chess Duels: My Games with the World Champions*) 34 ♖xd6 ♗xc3 35 ♖c6 ♗g7! 36 ♘g1 ♕d3 37 ♗c2 ♕b5 38 ♖xg5 a5! or 34 ♖c7 ♖ac8! 35 ♘g1 ♕e3 36 ♗g4 ♖xc7 37 bxc7 ♕c5! – the queen and pawns should tip the scales in Black's favour;

2) 31 ♖f1!? ♘xb6 32 ♖xd6 (32 axb6? ♘f4 and wins) 32...♕e7! 33 ♖xb6, and here we only looked at 33...♘f4(?), which after 34 ♘xf4 (the immediate 34 d6! is even better) 34...gxf4 35 d6 or 34...♗xc3 35 d6 and ♘d5 gives White every chance of saving the game. However, with the elegant 33...♗xc3! 34 ♗d6 (34 ♘xc3 ♘f4 and wins) 34...♘f2+! 35 ♖xf2 ♗xa5 36 ♗xe7 ♗xb6 37 ♖f1 ♖xe7 Black could obtain a won endgame.

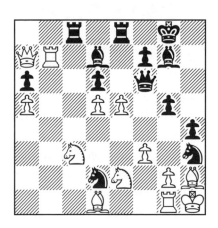

29...♖xe5?

'An impulsive decision, typical of Kasparov's time in Skellefteå.' (Nikitin). And, indeed, I was obliged to find 29...♕f5! with the previous threat of ...♖a8. Neither 30 gxh3? ♕xf3+ nor 30 ♖xd7? ♕xd7! will do,

and the new possibility 30 e6 does not save White in view of 30...♖a8! 31 exd7 ♖ed8! 32 ♕b6 ♘c4. In this remarkable position White also does not have real compensation for the queen: 33 ♖f1 ♘xb6 34 axb6 g4! or 33 gxh3 ♘xb6 34 axb6 ♕xf3+ 35 ♖g2 ♗xc3 36 ♘xc3 ♕xc3 37 ♖xg5+ ♔h8 38 ♖h5+ ♔g7 39 ♗g4 ♕e1+ 40 ♔g2 (40 ♗g1 a5) 40...♕d2+ 41 ♔h1 a5, and matters are decided by the modest a-pawn.

30 ♖xd7 (3) **♘xg1** (1)

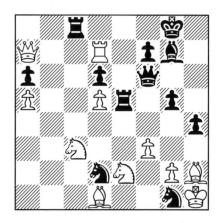

31 ♕xg1?! (1)

Yasser wrongly attaches an exclamation mark to this move. He should have taken the rook – 31 ♗xe5!, and after 31...♕xe5 32 ♕(♔)xg1 White would have remained with an extra piece, which, it is true, would not have brought a win on account of the open position of his king:

1) 32 ♔xg1 g4! (32...♖xc3? 33 ♖e7!) 33 fxg4 ♕f6! 34 ♕f2 ♕xf2+ 35 ♔xf2 ♗xc3, or 33 ♖e7 ♕f5 34 ♘e4 gxf3 35 ♘xd2 fxe2 36 ♗xe2 (36 ♖xe2 ♖c1 is equal) 36...♕f4! 37 ♘f3 ♖c1+ with perpetual check;

2) 32 ♕xg1! (this is slightly better) 32...h3 33 ♖a7! ♕f5! 34 ♕e3 g4 35 ♘g3 ♕e5 36 ♕xe5 ♗xe5 37 f4! ♗xf4! 38 ♗xg4 hxg2+ 39 ♔xg2 ♖xc3, nevertheless achieving a draw.

It should be said that the events took place in a severe time scramble: each player had roughly five minutes left on his clock.

31...♖ee8?!

A sensible retreat (31...♖e7? 32 ♖xd6 ♕f5 33 ♗c6! was much worse), but lurking in the position was another combination – 31...♘xf3! 32 gxf3 ♕xf3+ 33 ♕g2 ♕f5! 34 ♗xe5 ♗xe5 with the double threat of 35...♕xd7 and, most importantly, 35...h3!. Despite his two extra pieces, White has to give back a rook to try and gain a draw: 35 ♘e4 ♕xd7 36 ♕xg5+ ♔f8 37 ♕xh4 or 37 ♘f4 (Seirawan) 37...♕b5 38 ♔g2.

32 ♖xd6 ♕f5 (apart from ...♗xc3, Black is threatening ...h4-h3, which should guarantee him a draw) **33 ♗a4!** (2)

Finally the bishop ends up where it wanted to go back in the opening. If 33 ♖c6, then 33...h3!.

33...♕d3?

Alas, an incorrect sacrifice, but in my panicky haste I thought it was the only chance. If 33...♖ed8? 34 ♖xd8+ ♖xd8, then 35 ♗c7! was decisive. 33...♗xc3 34 ♗xe8 ♖xe8 35 ♘xc3 looked dangerous (although it would appear that 35...h3! saves Black).

I also did not see any defence after 33...♖e7! 34 ♖c6! – if 34...♖ce8(?) 35 d6! etc. However, it was here that Black could have maintained the balance – 34...♖xc6 35 ♗xc6, and now not 35...♗xc3? 36 ♘xc3 ♘xf3 37 d6!! ♖e1 38 d7 ♖xg1+ 39 ♗xg1 ♕xa5 40 ♗xf3 when White wins, but 35...♘xf3! immediately, for example:

1) 36 d6 ♖xe2 37 ♗xf3 ♖d2! 38 ♕e3 ♗xc3 39 ♕xc3 ♖d3 40 ♕c6 (40 ♕b2 ♖xf3!) 40...♔g7 41 ♗e2 (41 ♕b7 h3!) 41...♖b3! 42 ♗g1 h3! 43 g3 ♕e5! 44 d7 h2! 45 d8♕ hxg1♕+ 46 ♔xg1 ♖xg3+ 47 ♔h1 ♖h3+ with perpetual check;

2) 36 ♕b6 h3 37 d6 hxg2+ 38 ♔xg2 ♖xe2+ 39 ♘xe2 ♘xh2 40 ♔xh2 ♕e5+ 41 ♘g3 ♕xd6 and ...♗e5, or 36...♗xc3 37 ♕d8+ ♔g7 38 ♕xe7 ♘xh2 39 ♔xh2 ♗xa5 40 ♕e3

(40 d6 ♗b4!) 40...♗c7+, again saving the game a piece down.

34 ♗xe8 ♖xe8 35 ♖c6 h3 (2)

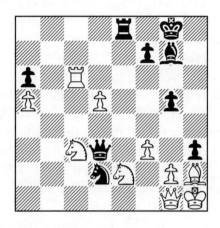

36 ♗g3?

A time-trouble error in reply. For many years Seirawan thought he could have won by 36 ♕f2(?!) ♗e3(?) 37 ♖c8+ ♔h7 38 ♕g3, or 38 ♘g1, or 38 ♗f4!, but then he discovered 36...hxg2+! 37 ♔xg2 (37 ♕xg2?! ♘xf3 is equal) 37...♘c4! with compensation for the piece. I think that after 38 ♕g3 g4! 39 ♗g1 f5 40 ♗f2 (40 ♖xa6 ♘e5!) 40...gxf3+ 41 ♕xf3 ♕xf3+ 42 ♔xf3 ♘e5+ 43 ♔f4 ♘xc6 44 dxc6 ♔f7 45 ♗d4 ♗h6+ 46 ♔xf5 ♖c8 and ...♖xc6 Black would have had good drawing chances.

On the other hand, the fearless 36 gxh3! would have led to a win: 36...♗xc3 37 ♖xc3! ♕xe2 38 ♕xg5+, or 36...♘xf3 37 ♕g2 ♘xh2 (37...f5 38 d6!) 38 ♔xh2 ♕e3 (38...♗e5+ 39 ♔h1) 39 ♖c4! etc.

36...hxg2+

The storm has passed. Black would also have equalised with 36...♗xc3!? 37 ♘xc3 hxg2+ 38 ♕xg2 ♘xf3 39 ♕h3 ♘d2 or 39...♕d4 40 ♔g2 g4.

37 ♕xg2 (2) **♘xf3** (1) **38 d6**

Although by now I sensed that I would save the game, this pawn thrust concerned me. Later Yasser suggested 38 ♕f2(?!), but

this is weak on account of 38...♕h7+! 39
♔g2 (39 ♗h2? ♗e5) 39...g4, when White has
to overcome some problems: 40 ♕f1! ♗xc3
41 ♖xc3 (41 ♘xc3? ♖e1!! and wins)
41...♕e4! 42 ♔f2 ♘d2 43 ♕d1 ♕xd5 44
♕a4! with hopes of defending.

38...♖e6

38...♕h7+?! was no longer so attractive in
view of 39 ♗h2! ♘xh2 (39...♗e5? 40 d7! and
♖c8) 40 ♕xh2 ♕f5 41 ♕g2 ♔f8 42 ♖c4,
although it is hard for White to convert his
plus. But the problems would have been
more easily solved by 38...g4! 39 ♕f1 ♕f5 40
♔g2 ♗xc3 41 ♖xc3 ♕d5 with a draw.

39 ♕f2

The transition into an endgame was more
dangerous for Black – 39 ♖c8+! ♔h7 40 ♕f1
g4 41 ♕b1 ♕xb1+ 42 ♘xb1 ♖xe2 43 d7
♗f6, and here I would have had to work a
little to reach the haven of a draw: 44 d8♕
♗xd8 45 ♖xd8 ♖a2 46 ♗c7 ♖c2! 47 ♗f4
♖a2, or 44 ♘c3 ♖d2 45 ♘e4 ♖d1+ 46 ♔g2
♗e7 47 ♘d6 ♖d5 etc.

39...g4

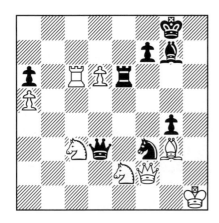

40 ♖c8+

With his flag about to fall, Yasser decided
to deprive my queen of the h7-square. 40
♔g2 was slightly more dangerous, since only
40...♖h6! with the idea of 41...♘e1+! 42 ♔g1
♘f3+ leads to an immediate draw.

40...♔h7 (1) **41 ♘f4** (37)

The time control was reached, and my
opponent gradually realised that White has
nothing: 41 ♔g2 ♖h6 or 41 ♗f4!? ♗h6!.

41...♖h6+ (1) **42 ♔g2 ♘e1+!** **43 ♔g1** (43
♕xe1? ♕f3+) **43...♘f3+ 44 ♔g2 ♘e1+ ½-½**

'A grandiose battle! Fantastic chaos! And
excellent training material.' (Nikitin)

In the next round I played without enthusiasm, not greatly believing that I could
engage Zoltan Ribli in a large-scale battle.
The Hungarian grandmaster endeavoured
to extinguish the slightest sharpness from
the battle, although he did this not altogether correctly. In the fourth hour of play
another rare instance in my games occurred:
I did not notice a decisive, very pretty combinative stroke!

> *Game 56*
> **G.Kasparov-Z.Ribli**
> World Cup
> 14th Round, Skelleftea,
> 28.08.1989

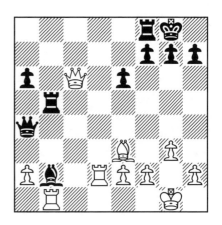

25...♗d4??

Expecting a peace agreement, for an instant Ribli let his vigilance slip and he de-

cided to force exchanges in an elegant way. 25...♗c3! 26 ♖dd1 ♗f6 was correct.

26 ♖xb5

After making this move, without thinking I offered a draw (½-½)! Before we had time to sign the scoresheets, Vaganian rushed up and quietly exclaimed: 'Rook dee eight!' I immediately understood – after 26...♗xe3 27 ♖d8!! (the weakness of the back rank!) 27...♕xb5 (27...♖xd8 28 ♖d5!!) 28 ♕d6! ♗xf2+ 29 ♔xf2 ♕f5+ 30 ♔g1! (30 ♔g2? ♕d5+!) 30...♕b1+ 31 ♔g2 ♕e4+ 32 ♔h3 ♕f5+ 33 g4 ♕f1+ 34 ♔g3 White would escape from the checks and win: 34...♕g1+ 35 ♔f3 ♕f1+ 36 ♔e3 ♕h3+ 37 ♔d4! e5+ 38 ♔d5! ♕g2+ 39 ♔c5 ♕g1+ 40 ♔c6. But, alas, this was fated not to happen.

Nevertheless, before the final, 15th round, I was still half a point ahead of Karpov. I outplayed Nikolic with Black, but on the 25th move I missed a very real winning chance (again it was observed by Vaganian), and although I tormented my opponent until the 68th move, in the end I had to reconcile myself to a draw. But on the same 68th move Karpov overcame the resistance of the hard-to-beat Andersson – and he caught me at the very last moment.

Nikitin: *'Thus the two eternal opponents, playing in completely different styles, arrived at the tournament finish with identical results. Each of them fought mainly with himself, and both in their own way deserved the favour of Caissa: the one for the rich creative content of his games, and the other for his mighty fighting spirit.'*

Of course, for me this '+4' was an indifferent result, but the main thing was that it was sufficient for victory in the World Cup. After the series of exhausting matches, I had shown that I was also the strongest in tournament play. The combined lead achieved by me and Karpov over the other contestants comprised almost a whole tournament (never again would the world see such an imposing superiority of the 'two Ks'): 1. **Kasparov** – 83; 2. Karpov – 81; 3. Salov – 68½; 4. Ehlvest – 68; 5. Ljubojevic – 66½; 6. Nunn – 65½; 7–8. Beliavsky and Short – 63½; 9–10. Hübner and Timman – 57½, etc.

In the World Cup a marked improvement in the financial and organisational conditions was achieved. These gripping but cumbersome tournaments, each lasting more than three weeks, went down in history as the last 'monsters' of the classical chess era. After the GMA the maximum number of contestants in such events became 14 (as in the current FIDE Grand Prix, which is largely copied from the World Cup), with 10 the most common number. Therefore, even now, one has to be impressed by the scale of the events conducted then – over the course of just two years! – and united in a single system: six all-play-all super-tournaments and four grandmaster qualifying 'Swisses' (Belgrade, Moscow, Palma de Mallorca and Moscow).

Many thought that 'both organisationally and materially the GMA was ready to take over from the weakening hands of FIDE the conducting of the world championship cycle.' It is a great pity that this did not happen and that a second World Cup did not take place: in the early 1990s an internal conflict, skilfully stirred up from outside, led to the break-up of the Grandmasters Association (details of this are given in *Kasparov vs. Karpov 1988-2009*).

Fischer's Record is Broken!

Double-round super-tournament in Tilburg (14 September – 3 October 1989): 1. **Kasparov** – 12 out of 14; 2. Korchnoi – 8½; 3–4. Ljubojevic and Sax – 7; 5. Ivanchuk – 6½; 6–7. Agdestein and Hjartarson – 5½; 8. Piket – 4.

The traditional tournament in Tilburg began just two weeks after Skelleftea. I did not manage to rest and prepare properly: on returning from Brussels, where the closing ceremony of the World Cup took place, I set off to the USA on GMA business. But, as is apparent, in the last stage of the World Cup I 'warmed up' well: in Tilburg I managed to win practically all the games in which I had winning chances.

Although I arrived at the tournament feeling slightly unwell and without a trainer (Nikitin managed to get out of the USSR only for the start of the second half), I was in a fighting mood. I very much wanted to gain revenge for the failure in Tilburg 1981 and, by scoring a minimum of 11 out of 14, to surpass Fischer's ancient rating record (2780). And at the same time to finish ahead of the young Vassily Ivanchuk – the triumphant winner of Linares 1989 (ahead of Karpov!), who by that time was already the No.3 rated player in the world. The expected rivalry between us imparted a particular colouring to the tournament. Korchnoi predicted victory for Ivanchuk, and this was also hinted at by Genna Sosonko and Botvinnik: *'If Ivanchuk is playing in a tournament, I know who will win the tournament, but I myself will not say.'* This infuriated me: had they really forgotten that the world champion could also play quite well? I had been challenged, and I decided to demonstrate everything I was capable of.

To start with I made a psychologically difficult, but good move: I repacked my bags and moved from the comfortable, out of town De Parel Hotel, where the participants were accommodated, to a small family hotel in the centre. By secluding myself, I was able to create an ideal working atmosphere – I did much analysis, fulfilled the role of trainer myself, and passionately played chess.

In the first round I was paired with White against the new hope of Dutch chess, the 20-year-old grandmaster Jeroen Piket (he had replaced Timman, who was preparing for his Candidates match with Speelman). At the opening ceremony Sosonko asked me whether I was happy with the pairings, and I replied that I was already thinking what to play against Piket – 1 d4, or more probably 1 c4. With a laugh Genna enquired: 'But aren't you up to playing 1 e4?' He knew full well that Piket might employ the sharp Dragon Variation. His 'aren't you up to' comment urged me on, and the following day I in fact chose 1 e4. When he arrived for the round, Sosonko was extremely surprised to see on the monitor a smoothly-played Yugoslav Attack (I never played 9 ♗c4 either before or after this game!).

Game 57
G.Kasparov-J.Piket
Tilburg, 1st Round, 15.09.1989
Sicilian Defence B78

1 e4

The reversion to this move began in the summer, at a regular training session in Zagulba. For eighteen months I had managed with the material accumulated during my preparations for the matches with Karpov, especially the one in Seville, where I mainly played 1 c4. And after 1 e4 we had looked only at the main lines of the Ruy Lopez, the Petroff and the Caro-Kann. However, at this training session I began studying the popular Sicilian set-ups, including the Dragon Variation.

1...c5 2 ♘f3 d6 3 d4 cxd4 4 ♘xd4 ♘f6 5 ♘c3 g6

A surprise: earlier Piket had nearly always played 5...♘c6. But I was not too alarmed, since I was already familiar with the new trends in the Dragon, and I accepted the challenge.

6 ♗e3 ♗g7 7 f3 ♘c6 8 ♕d2 0-0 9 ♗c4 ♗d7 (9...♘xd4?! – Game No.52 in *My Great Predecessors Part IV*) **10 h4**

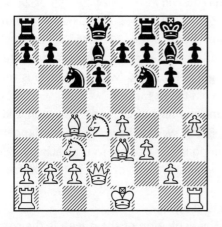

The fashion of the 1970-1980s. Nowadays the flexible 10 0-0-0 ♘e5 11 ♗b3 ♖c8 12 ♔b1! is more topical, and if 12...♘c4, then 13 ♗xc4 ♖xc4 14 g4!, preventing ...h7-h5: White retains both control over the centre, and prospects of an attack on the king.

10...♘e5 11 ♗b3 ♖c8 12 0-0-0 ♘c4

I had also studied the radical move 12...h5!, which was introduced into top grandmaster practice by Miles and Sosonko, and which later, largely thanks to its surprise effect, brought me success in my world championship match with Anand (1995). For details, see *Revolution in the 70s* (pp.104-121).

13 ♗xc4 ♖xc4 14 h5 ♘xh5 15 g4 ♘f6 (one of the best known Dragon *tabiyas*) **16 ♗h6**

Following the old game Geller-Korchnoi (4th match game, Moscow 1971). The insidious 16 ♘de2 (Karpov-Korchnoi, 2nd match game, Moscow 1974) was no longer considered dangerous for Black in view of 16...♖e8! (cf. Game No.67 in *My Great Predecessors Part V*). This reply is also good after the most

subtle move 16 ♔b1!? (in the 1990s Anand played this).

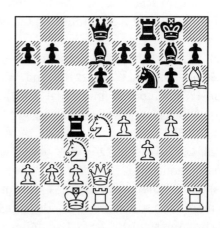

16...♘xe4! 17 ♕e3 (if 17 ♘xe4?! ♖xd4 18 ♕h2, then, if there is nothing better, 18...♗e5 19 ♕h4 ♖xe4!? 20 fxe4 ♕b6 21 c3 ♖c8 with excellent play for the exchange) **17...♖xc3! 18 bxc3 ♘f6 19 ♗xg7 ♔xg7 20 ♖h2**

Continuing Geller's plan. Little is promised by 20 ♕h6+ ♔h8! with the idea of ...♖g8 or 20 ♘e2 ♕a5!, and 20 ♘b3 or 20 ♖h4 (Tseshkovsky-Miles, Wijk aan Zee 1989) is no better.

I had known the Geller-Korchnoi game since childhood: we analysed it in lessons at the chess section of the Baku Pioneers Palace. At that time, despite his broken pawns, White's position looked very threatening, but later games showed that without great difficulty (and in not just one way!) Black could parry the attack, retaining two pawns for the exchange and a flexible pawn structure.

20...♖h8

Perhaps not the strongest move, but a perfectly competent one. I will mention three other possibilities:

1) 20...♕a5 (if 20...♕c7?!, then 21 ♕xe7 ♕xc3 22 ♕xd6 is unpleasant) 21 ♘b3 (21 ♕xe7 ♕a3+! and ♖e8) 21...♕a3+! (Korchnoi

played 21...♕xa2?! and after 22 ♕xe7 ♕a3+?! 23 ♔b1 ♖e8 24 ♕xd6 ♕xd6 25 ♖xd6 he reached a somewhat inferior endgame) 22 ♔b1 ♖e8!, protecting the base pawn on e7;

2) 20...♖g8 (the most popular) 21 ♘e2 ♗c6 (but not 21...♕a5? 22 g5 and ♕xe7, Short-Ernst, Subotica Interzonal 1987) 22 ♘g3 ♔f8 23 c4 (Nunn-Ljubojevic, Amsterdam 1988) 23...♕a5! or 23 g5 ♘d5 24 ♕xa7 ♘xc3 25 ♖d3 ♘b5 26 ♕e3 ♕a5! with dynamic equality;

3) 20...e5 (the rarest) 21 ♘f5+ (this gives no more than a draw, but 21 ♘e2 ♕a5 is also unpromising) 21...♗xf5 22 gxf5 ♕c7 23 ♕h6+ (23 ♕xa7?! ♕xc3) 23...♔g8 24 ♕g5 ♔g7! 25 ♖dh1 ♖h8 26 ♕h6+ ♔g8 with sufficient counterplay.

21 ♘b3

After some thought I did not find anything promising for White after 21 ♘e2 ♗c6 or 21 ♖dh1 e5!? 22 ♘b3 ♗c6 with the idea of ...h7-h5 – and I made a new move.

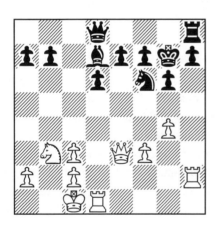

21...♗c6

This weakens Black's control of f5, which White promptly exploits. If 21...b6 I thought that 22 ♖e1 was very strong (22 ♔b2 h5!?), but now I see that after both 22...e5 23 ♕h6+ ♔g8 24 ♖d2 ♕e7 25 g5 ♘e8 (25...♘h5!?) 26 f4 e4, and 22...♖e8 23 ♕h6+ ♔g8 24 ♘d2 d5

25 c4 ♕c7 26 cxd5 ♕c3! Black is quite alright.

Even the immediate 21...h5 was not so bad, since my *Informator* suggestion 22 g5(?!) ♘h7 23 f4 has been successfully parried in practice by 23...♗g4 (23...b6 24 ♕d4+ f6 will also do) 24 ♖e1 e5 or 24...♖e8. 22 gxh5 ♘xh5 23 ♕xa7 is better, although even here after 23...♗c6 it is unclear whether White can gain any real advantage. **22 g5! ♘h5 23 f4** (with the obvious intention of f4-f5) **23...♖e8**

In the event of 23...♕d7?! 24 ♘d4 and f4-f5 Black would have been in danger of coming under a dangerous attack (24...♕g4? is weak in view of 25 ♕xe7 ♕xf4+ 26 ♖hd2!).

24 f5 ♕b6!

The activation of the queen is the correct way of curbing White's aggression.

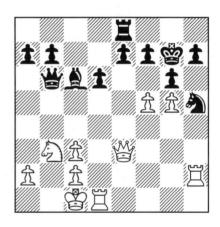

25 ♘d4!

Maintaining the tension. After 25 ♕xb6 axb6 26 ♘d4 ♗d7 I would have had to forget about an attack and play an equal endgame.

25...♕c5

25...♕a5 (but not 25...♔g8? 26 ♖xh5! gxh5 27 g6 and wins) was equally safe: 26 ♘xc6 bxc6 27 f6+ ♔g8 (now 27...♔f8? 28 ♖xh5! gxh5 29 g6! is bad for Black) 28 fxe7

♕xa2 with equality.

26 ♖e1 ♗d7!

For the moment Piket defends impeccably. 26...♔g8? would have been met by an unexpected offer to exchange queens – 27 ♘xc6!. Had he declined, Black would have lost: 27...♕a3+? 28 ♔d2 bxc6 29 fxg6 hxg6 30 ♖xh5! gxh5 31 g6 ♕c5 32 ♕h6! ♕f2+ 33 ♖e2 ♕f6 34 gxf7+ ♔xf7 35 ♕h7+ ♔f8 36 ♖g2 or 27...♕xc6? 28 fxg6 hxg6 29 ♖xh5! gxh5 30 g6 (with the same threat of ♕h6) 30...d5 (Black is not saved by either 30...♕g2 31 ♖g1, or 30...fxg6 31 ♕e6+ ♔h7 32 ♕f7+ ♔h6 33 ♖e6) 31 gxf7+ ♔xf7 32 ♖f1+ ♔g7 33 ♕e5+ ♔h6 34 ♕f4+ ♔h7 35 ♕f7+ ♔h6 36 ♖g1.

27...bxc6? 28 ♕xc5 dxc5 29 ♖h4! etc. was also bad. However, the forced 27...♕xe3+ 28 ♖xe3 bxc6 would also not have promised Black an easy life: 29 c4! (not the inaccurate 29 f6?! e6 30 c4 h6!) 29...♘g7 30 fxg6 hxg6 31 ♖eh3! (via the third rank the rook breaks into the opponent's position) 31...♘h5 32 ♖a3! ♖a8 33 c5! with good winning prospects.

27 ♕f3

27 ♖f2 ♔g8! was unclear.

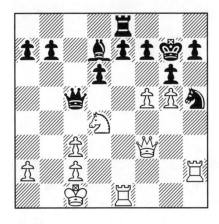

27...♗c6?!

Previously I attached an exclamation mark to this move, but I overlooked some-

thing. 27...b5? is premature in view of 28 ♔b1! (this defence against ...♕xg5+ creates the threat of ♖xe7!) 28...b4 29 fxg6 fxg6 (29...hxg6 30 ♖f2! ♕c4 31 ♖e4) 30 ♖xh5! gxh5 31 ♕xh5, or 28...♔g8 29 ♖he2! ♔f8 (29...d5 30 ♖e5) 30 ♖h1! ♔g8 31 fxg6, and now 31...hxg6 32 ♖xh5 gxh5 33 ♕xh5 (after 29 fxg6 hxg6 30 ♖xh5? gxh5 31 ♕xh5 Black would be saved by 31...♕xc3 – the e1-rook is attacked, whereas now if 33...♕xc3 there is the decisive 34 g6!) is bad for Black, as is 31...fxg6 32 ♖f2 (not 32 ♖xh5? gxh5 33 ♕xh5 ♕d5 with equality) 32...♕c4 33 ♖xh5! gxh5 34 ♕xh5 ♕d5 35 ♖f5! e5 36 g6 or 32...♔h8 33 ♕f7 ♕c4 (33...♕e5 34 ♖hf1) 34 ♖e1! and wins.

However, after 27...♔g8! Black would have avoided the immediate tactical threats and retained a defensible position.

28 ♕e3?!

Missing a chance opportunity to destroy Black's defences with the spectacular 28 ♖xe7! (28 ♘xc6 bxc6! is weaker) 28...♖xe7 (28...♗xf3? 29 ♘e6+!) 29 f6+ ♔f8 30 fxe7+ ♔e8 (30...♖xe7 31 ♖e2+ ♔f8 32 ♕e3!) 31 ♕e3! and ♖e2 with a dangerous initiative, or 29...♔g8 30 fxe7 ♕xg5+ 31 ♖d2 ♕xe7 32 ♘xc6 bxc6 33 ♕xc6 and ♕xd6 with hopes of converting the exchange advantage.

28...♗d7 29 ♕f3 ♗c6?! (a tacit draw offer) **30 ♕f2?!**

In avoiding the repetition of moves, I again did not see 30 ♖xe7! and I played without any concrete aim – simply hoping for the chance possibility of sacrificing the exchange on h5.

30...♔g8

The balance would have been more simply maintained by 30...♕xc3!? 31 ♖xe7 ♖xe7 32 f6+ ♔f8 33 fxe7+ ♔e8! 34 ♘xc6 bxc6 or 31...♕a3+ 32 ♔d1 ♖xe7 33 f6+ ♔f8 34 fxe7+ ♔xe7 35 ♘xc6+ bxc6 36 ♕d4 – in *Informator* I assessed this position in favour of

White, but after 36...♕xa2 37 ♖e2+ ♔d7 there appears to be no way to gain an advantage (38 ♕e3 ♕a1+ 39 ♔d2 ♕a5+ etc).

31 ♖e3 (for the moment defending the c3-pawn) **31...♗d5?**

An imperceptible time-trouble mistake: Black cuts off his queen from the defence of the kingside. For the same reason it was dangerous to play 31...♕a3+?! 32 ♔d2 ♕xa2 33 ♕e2! (33...♘f4? 34 ♕g4 ♘h5 35 ♖xh5! etc.), but the cool-headed 31...♗d7! 32 ♕f3 ♗c6 or 32 ♕e1 (my *Informator* recommendation) 32...d5! would have retained a double-edged situation.

As soon as my opponent placed his bishop on d5, immediately I intuitively sensed that now the sacrifice on h5 was probably correct, and I did not especially calculate any variations. Indeed, was it possible to calculate them to the end with the clock ticking mercilessly away?

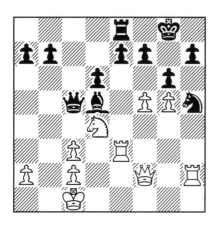

32 ♖xh5!

The preparatory 32 ♕e2 was also tempting, but you should not expect too much of a good thing. It should be said that this is a not altogether usual 'Dragon' exchange sacrifice (as Fischer said: pry open the h-file, sac, sac... mate!): here after the best defence the king escapes to the queenside.

32...gxh5 33 ♕h4 ♕c4?

Piket cracks. Also 33...♗g2? 34 ♕xh5 or 33...♔h8? 34 ♕xh5 was obviously bad, but he could have played more strongly:

1) 33...♗c6 34 ♕xh5 ♗d7 35 ♕h3!! (a very pretty, quiet move: after defending the f5-pawn, White is threatening to switch his rook to the h-file) 35...e6 (35...d5 36 ♕h6! e5 37 ♖h3 also fails to save Black) 36 g6! fxg6 37 fxg6 h5 (37...hxg6 38 ♖g3! ♔g7 39 ♕g4 or 38...♖f8 39 ♖xg6+ ♔f7 40 ♕h7+ ♔e8 41 ♖g7! etc. leads to a crushing attack) 38 ♕h4! ♔g7 39 ♖f3! ♕e5 40 ♖f7+ ♔xg6 41 ♖xd7 ♕g5+ 42 ♕xg5+ ♔xg5 43 ♔d2 with a won ending;

2) 33...e5 34 ♕xh5 ♔f8 (the only chance: if 34...♕a3+?, then 35 ♔d2! ♕a4 36 g6! fxg6 37 fxg6 ♕d7 38 ♘f5! with an irresistible attack) 35 f6! ♖c8 (35...♖d8 36 g6!!) 36 ♕xh7 ♔e8 37 g6 ♔d7 38 ♕h3+ ♔c7 39 ♘b3! ♕c4 (39...♗xb3 40 axb3! fxg6 41 ♖g3) 40 g7 ♗e6 41 ♕g2 or 39...♕a3+ 40 ♔b1! fxg6 41 ♕h7+ ♔b8 42 ♕e7, and Black cannot hold out.

34 ♕xh5

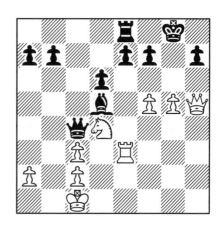

The murderous ♖h3 or g5-g6 is threatened, and if 34...♖c8, then first 35 ♕h6!. The further resistance is pointless.

34...♕f1+ 35 ♔b2 e5 (35...♗g2 36 g6!) **36 ♕h6!** (with the threat of f5-f6) **36...♔h8 37 g6! fxg6 38 fxg6 ♖e7 39 ♖f3!** (the decisive interference move) **39...♕c4 40 ♕f8+ 1-0**

In the 2nd round I drew with Black against Ljubojevic, and before the 3rd round Sosonko asked whether I was 'up to' playing 1 e4 again. And I played this against Sax's Sicilian, choosing the Keres Attack in the Scheveningen – and crushing my opponent in 30 moves.

Nikitin: *'Such a successful change of "opening tune" was unexpected only at first sight. Behind these results of Kasparov is a great deal of preparatory work, thanks to which he has acquired colossal opening erudition and, breaking with usual patterns, he no longer remembers a variation, but simply knows whether or not it is good. Keeping in mind the typical techniques in different types of positions, he is able to play anything he wants without mistakes and preparation.'*

After a draw with Korchnoi I was leading together with Ivanchuk (3 out of 4). In the 5th round I had to play Ivanchuk. And when Genna asked his favourite question regarding 1 e4, with a smile I replied 'Not up to it!' True, after playing 1 d4, from the opening I did not achieve anything, but Vassily played uncertainly, went wrong on the 35th move, and soon resigned. After this he literally 'floundered', scoring just half a point in the next four rounds.

Now I was sharing the lead with Korchnoi (4 out of 5), and was very optimistic about my chances of taking first place. And, indeed, at the end of the first cycle Korchnoi made two draws, whereas I beat Hjartarson with White and Agdestein with Black. The game with Agdestein was a critical one for me – before it I said to myself: if I win it, I will do everything possible to break Fischer's rating record.

It was in this mood that I went along to my 'black' game with Jeroen Piket, which opened the second half of the tournament. The opening in it was fully predictable.

Game 58
J.Piket-G.Kasparov
Tilburg, 8th Round, 24.09.1989
King's Indian Defence E99

1 d4 ♘f6 2 ♘f3 g6 3 c4 ♗g7 4 ♘c3 0-0 5 e4 d6 6 ♗e2 e5 7 0-0 ♘c6 8 d5 ♘e7 9 ♘e1 (9 ♘d2 – *Game Nos.42, 80*) **9...♘d7**

Impeding the typical c4-c5 break. Later I also tried 9...♘e8.

10 ♗e3

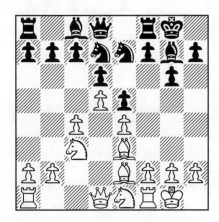

Piket was very fond of this set-up and he gained a number of wins in it, although 10 ♘d3 f5 11 ♗d2 was more popular (*Game No.64*).

10...f5 11 f3 f4 12 ♗f2 g5

The main *tabiya* of the variation. There are mutual flank attacks in prospect, with Black's seemingly the more dangerous: he has the white king in his sights. But if White can set up a solid defence, his breakthrough on the queenside followed by play against the exposed black king will be more important.

13 b4

Straightforward play. 13 ♘d3 is rather slow and has long been in the shade: 13...♘f6 14 c5 ♘g6 15 ♖c1?! (15 a4!) 15...♖f7! 16 ♖c2 ♗f8! (Game No.29 in *My*

Great Predecessors Part IV), while after 13 ♘b5 (Game No.39 in *My Great Predecessors Part V*) the defence 13...b6! was found. Later Korchnoi brought to the fore 13 a4 (*Game No.77*), and then also 13 ♖c1.

13...♘f6 14 c5 ♘g6 15 cxd6 cxd6 16 ♖c1 (with the positional threat of ♘b5-c7-e6) **16...♖f7 17 a4**

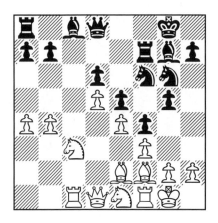

17...♗f8!

A method of play which is known from the classic games Najdorf-Gligoric (Mar del Plata 1953), and Taimanov-Najdorf (Zurich Candidates 1953). But before this my opponent had only encountered 17...b6, after which he sacrificed a pawn – 18 a5!? (and won against Nijboer and Douven, Hilversum 1989), or 17...h5 18 a5 ♗d7 19 ♘b5 ♗xb5 20 ♗xb5 g4 21 ♔h1 g3 22 ♗g1 gxh2 23 ♗f2 h4 (23...a6!?, Burgess-Watson, Plymouth 1989) 24 ♔xh2 ♘h5 and then:

1) 25 ♖g1 ♘g3 26 a6 bxa6 (26...♗f8! with the idea of ...♖h7 and ...h4-h3 is correct) 27 ♗xa6 ♗f8?! (27...♖b8 is better) 28 ♘d3?! (28 ♕c2! and ♗c8! would have given an obvious advantage) 28...♖h7 29 ♗e1 h3 30 gxh3 ♕h4 31 ♘f2 ♔h8? (31...♗e7! and ...♗d8-b6 was essential) 32 ♖c8! ♖xc8 33 ♗xc8 ♗e7 34 ♘h1! ♕h6 35 ♗e6 ♘f8 36 ♗g4, and White won (Piket-Paneque, Adelaide 1988);

2) 25 a6! (an improvement) 25...b6 26

♘d3 ♗f6 27 ♖g1 ♖g7 28 ♗e1 h3 29 gxh3 ♗h4 30 ♗xh4 ♘xh4 31 ♖xg7+ ♔xg7 32 ♘f2 ♔h8?! (32...♖c8 or 32...♘g3 was more resilient) 33 ♘g4 ♘g6 34 ♕c2! ♕h4 35 ♖g1 ♘e7 36 ♗d7! and White won (Piket-Pieterse, Holland 1989).

However, for the moment Black can manage without ...h7-h5, by supporting the ...g5-g4 advance with his pieces and leaving the h5-square free for his knight.

18 a5

If 18 ♘b5?!, then immediately 18...g4! (the e4-pawn has been left without defence), when 19 ♘xa7? g3! or 19 ♗xa7? ♗d7 20 ♗f2 g3! 21 hxg3 fxg3 22 ♗xg3 ♘h5 etc. is bad for White.

18...♗d7!

18...♘e8? is too passive: 19 ♘b5! a6 20 ♗b6 ♕f6 (Novak-Grivas, Athens 1989) 21 ♘a7! ♗d7 22 b5, and White's attack gets there first.

19 ♘b5?!

Going along with Black's plan. At the board I was more afraid of the subtle prophylactic move 19 ♔h1!?. As later games showed, in this case after my *Informator* suggestion 19...♕e8(?!) White has the unpleasant 20 ♘c2! h5 21 ♘a3 g4 22 ♘cb5 with serious threats, and it is better to play 19...♖g7! 20 ♘b5 (20 ♗b5 g4!, D.Gurevich-Gruenberg, New York 1991; after Stohl's move 20 ♘c2 there is the quite good reply 20...♘h8!? with the idea of ...g5-g4 and ...♘f7-g5) 20...g4 21 ♘xa7 (21 ♘c7 g3!) 21...g3 22 ♗b6 ♕e8! 23 ♖c7 (Burgess-Badea, Prestwich 1990) 23...♘h4! and ...♕h5 with double-edged play.

19...g4!

Only this energetic move is a novelty: Black does not have time to protect his valuables on the queenside! 19...♗xb5?! 20 ♗xb5 g4 (after 20...h5 21 ♘d3 g4 22 ♕e2 the exchange of the light-squared bishop is also felt) 21 fxg4! ♘xe4 22 ♗d3 is to White's advantage, when his bishop becomes strong (Brinck-Claussen–Hvenekilde, Copenhagen 1984).

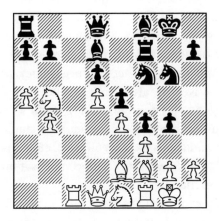

20 ♘c7

This move suggests itself (20...♖c8? 21 ♘e6!). After 20 fxg4?! (previously I incorrectly attached an exclamation mark to this move) 20...♘xe4 21 ♘c7 Black is better after both 21...♖c8 22 ♘e6 ♖xc1 (but not the *Informator* suggestion 22...♕f6? 23 ♖xc8 ♗xc8 because of 24 ♕c2!, winning) 23 ♘xd8 (23 ♕xc1?! ♗xe6) 23...♖xd1 24 ♗xd1 ♖e7 25 ♗xa7 ♘c3 with a favourable endgame, and 21...♗a4!? 22 ♕xa4 ♖xc7 23 ♖xc7 ♕xc7 with a promising middlegame.

20 ♘xa7 g3! 21 ♗b6 is more interesting, when 21...gxh2+? 22 ♔xh2 ♕e7 is bad in view of 23 ♖h1! ♘h5 24 ♔g1 ♘g3 25 ♖h2. Therefore I recommended 21...♕e7 – after 22 h3? ♗xh3! 23 gxh3 ♕d7 and ...♕xh3 Black has a decisive attack, and also 22 ♘b5?! ♘h5! (the key threat) 23 ♔h1 (23 h3? ♕h4 and ...♗xh3!; 23 hxg3? fxg3! and wins) 23...gxh2 24 ♗f2 ♗xb5 25 ♗xb5 ♘g3+ 26 ♗xg3 fxg3 or 25...♗h6!? with the idea of ...♗g5-h4 does not promise White an easy life. 22 ♘c6 (Stohl) 22...bxc6 23 dxc6 gxh2+ 24 ♔xh2 ♗e6 and ...♘h5! is also dangerous. However, after 22 ♗b5! (exchanging this

'blunt' bishop for its powerful opponent) 22...gxh2+ 23 ♔xh2 ♘h5 24 ♗xd7 ♕xd7 25 ♘d3 ♘g3 26 ♖e1 ♘h4 27 ♘f2 Black still has to demonstrate that he has full compensation for the pawn.

This can be avoided by 21...♕e8!: for example, 22 b5 ♘h5 (23 ♖c7?! ♕d8!) or 22 ♕c2 ♖g7! with very complicated play and good practical chances against the vulnerable white king.

20...g3!

Black's main trump in connection with ...♘h5. While the g2-f3-e4-d5 chain remains unbroken, 20...♗a4? 21 ♕xa4 ♖xc7 22 ♖xc7 ♕xc7 is ineffective in view of 23 ♘d3 and ♖c1, or 23 ♕c2 with the idea of 23...♕d7 24 fxg4! ♘xg4 25 ♗xg4 ♕xg4 26 ♘f3.

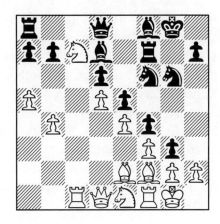

21 ♘xa8?

This resembles panic. White was obliged to accept the pawn sacrifice and seek his chances in a difficult defence. Had Piket been 10 years older, that is probably what he would have done. After 21 hxg3 to fight for an advantage I would have had to make several energetic and exact moves – 21...fxg3! (after 21...♘h5? 22 g4! the attack comes to a standstill) 22 ♗xg3, when Black faces a choice:

1) 22...♗h6 – earlier I thought that this was the best reply. In the event of 23 ♘xa8?!

♘h5! 24 ♗f2 (24 ♗h2? ♗e3+) 24...♗xc1 (my previous suggestion 24...♘gf4(?) was wrong because of 25 ♖c3!, a discovery by correspondence players) 25 ♕xc1 ♘gf4 in connection with ...♕g5 and ...♖g7 Black has dangerous threats. But his aggression is curbed by both 23 ♖c2 ♘h5 24 ♗f2, and 23 ♘e6! ♗xe6 24 dxe6 ♖g7 25 ♖c2! (Stohl's move 25 ♖c3 invites 25...d5!?), and although the position remains rather unclear, White's chances are somewhat better;

2) 22...♘h5! (as recent games have shown, this is more promising) 23 ♗f2 (23 ♗h2? is weak in view of 23...♗h6 24 ♖c3 ♗f4!) with another division:

a) 23...♘gf4 24 ♘e6! (24 ♘xa8? is fatal in view of 24...♕g5! 25 g4 ♘h3+ 26 ♔h2 ♘5f4 27 ♘g2 ♕h6! 28 ♗h4 ♘xg2 29 ♔xg2 ♕xh4 30 ♕e1 ♘f4+ 31 ♔g1 ♕h3 32 ♖f2 ♕g3+ 33 ♔h1 ♗h6!) 24...♗xe6 (24...♕f6!? – cf. 23 ♘e6) 25 dxe6 ♖g7 26 g4 ♕f6! 27 ♘d3 ♗e7 or 26 ♗c4 ♔h8! 27 g4! ♖g6, and both sides have chances;

b) 23...♗h6!? (the most interesting) 24 ♖c3 (24 ♖c2 ♘gf4!?) 24...♗f4! 25 ♘xa8 ♕g5! 26 g4?! (if 26 ♗c4, then 26...♗h6! 27 ♗xa7 ♘g3 28 ♔f2 ♗g5! and ...f4) 26...♕h6! 27 ♘d3 ♗h2+! 28 ♔xh2 ♘hf4+ 29 ♔g1 ♕h3 30 ♘e1

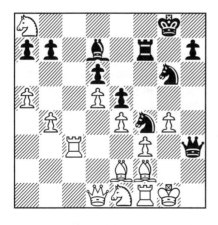

Analysis diagram

30...♘h8!! (the charming point of this unique position: the threat is ...♖f6-h6 and ...♘f7-g5) 31 ♕d2 ♖f6! 32 ♕xf4 exf4 33 ♘g2 ♖h6 34 ♗e1 (after 34 ♗h4 the knight changes route: 34...♘g6! 35 ♗e1 ♕h2+ 36 ♔f2 ♖h3 37 ♖g1 ♘h4! 38 ♔f1 ♘xf3! and wins) 34...♕h2+ 35 ♔f2 ♘f7! 36 ♖g1 ♘g5! and 0-1 (Bobel-Hauff, internet 2009).

Apparently 23 ♘e6! at once is safer, when Black is okay after both 23...♕f6 24 ♗h2 ♗h6 25 ♖c3 ♕h4 or 24 ♗f2 ♘gf4 25 ♗c4 ♕g6! with approximate equality, and also the audacious 23...♗xe6!? 24 dxe6 ♘xg3 25 exf7+ ♔h8! with sufficient compensation for the exchange.

By capturing the rook, White cuts off his king's retreat and condemns it to its fate.

21...♘h5!

A very strong rejoinder, which was underestimated by Piket: he was hoping to defend after 21...gxf2+ 22 ♖xf2 ♕xa8 23 ♗c4.

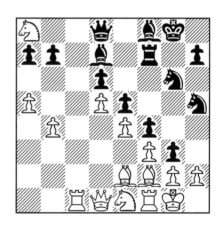

22 ♔h1

To get rid of the g3-pawn, White gives up his bishop. The simple-minded 22 ♗xa7 would have allowed Black to conclude the battle with a series of direct blows: 22...♕h4 23 h3 ♗xh3! 24 gxh3 (24 ♖f2 ♗d7!) 24...♕xh3 25 ♖f2 gxf2+ 26 ♔xf2 (26 ♗xf2? ♖g7) 26...♕g3+! (my earlier 26...♘h4(?) 27 ♗f1 ♕h2+ 28 ♘g2 ♖g7 is weaker on account of 29 ♔e2! ♘xg2 30 ♔d3 ♘e3 31 ♕d2) 27 ♔f1 ♘h4 28 ♘c2 ♘g2! and wins.

22...gxf2 23 ♖xf2 ♘g3+! (a new wave of the attack: the knight cannot be taken because of mate) **24 ♔g1 ♕xa8**

The outcome is decided, since now Black has also a material advantage (the simple ...♘xe2+ is threatened).

25 ♗c4 (25 b5 ♕d8!) **25...a6!**

A very important link in Black's winning plan: his queen comes into play with decisive effect along the a7-g1 diagonal.

26 ♕d3

A difficult choice: White would also have lost after both 26 hxg3 fxg3 27 ♖a2 ♕a7+ 28 ♔f1 ♖f4! 29 ♔e2 ♖h4 30 ♘c2 ♖h2, and the desperate 26 ♘d3 ♕a7 (threatening ...♖g7, ...♘h4 and ....♖h3!) 27 ♘c5!? dxc5! 28 d6 cxb4 29 ♕d5 ♘h8! 30 ♕xe5 ♗g7 31 ♕g5 h6! 32 ♕d8+ ♔h7 33 hxg3 ♖f8 or 31 ♕e7 ♘e2+ 32 ♔f1 ♘xc1 33 ♕xd7 ♕d4.

26...♕a7 27 b5 (allowing a pretty finish, but if 27 ♖cc2, then 27...♗e7! and ....♗h4, winning) **27...axb5 28 ♗xb5**

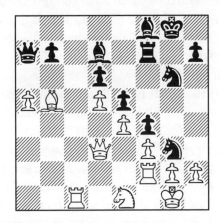

28...♘h1! 0-1

The other knight was dreaming of jumping via h8, but in the end this one jumped to h1!

This game appealed to both the specta-

tors, and the players. The successful swift attack reminded me of the days of my chess youth. Happy memories!

Before the next game with Ljubomir Ljubojevic I had 7 out of 8 and was in the mood to fight not so much for first place in the tournament, as for the conquering of a sky-high rating peak.

Game 59
G.Kasparov-L.Ljubojevic
Tilburg, 9th Round, 25.09.1989
Bogo-Indian Defence E11

1 d4 ♘f6 2 c4 e6 3 ♘f3 ♗b4+ (avoiding the main set-ups) **4 ♗d2 ♗xd2+ 5 ♕xd2 0-0 6 g3**

After 6 ♘c3 d5 7 e3 ♕e7 on one occasion I was unable to breach Andersson's defences (Lucerne Olympiad 1982).

6...d5 7 ♗g2 ♕e7 8 0-0 ♖d8

They began playing this after my win against Petrosian in the variation 8...dxc4?! 9 ♘a3! (Game No.69 in Garry *Kasparov on Garry Kasparov Part I*).

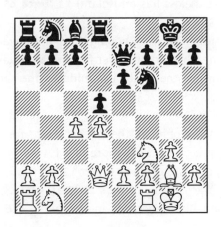

9 ♕c2

Against Timman (Belgrade 1989) I tried 9 ♖c1 c6 10 ♕e3 ♗d7 11 ♘bd2 ♗e8 12 ♘b3 (before this Timman himself played 12 a3)

12...♘bd7 13 ♘a5 ♖ab8 14 ♖ab1, also with a minimal advantage.

9...♘a6

Robatsch's rare move instead of the well-known 9...♘c6!? 10 ♖d1 or 10 cxd5 exd5 11 ♘c3.

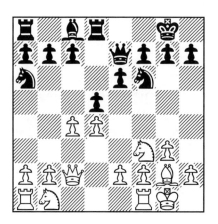

10 a3!?

After the aforementioned game with Petrosian I understood how to play such positions: the main thing is not to rush and to do everything to restrict the opponent's active possibilities.

10...dxc4 (after 10...c5!? 11 cxd5 exd5 Black nevertheless has an isolani) **11 ♕xc4 c5 12 dxc5 ♕xc5**

Ljubojevic was hoping that in the endgame it would be easier for him to equalise than in the 'Catalan' middlegame after 12...♘xc5 13 ♘c3.

13 ♘bd2!?

In my opinion, the correct route for the knight: on c4 it has more of a future. Nothing real was given by either 13 ♕h4 ♗d7! or 13 ♕xc5 ♘xc5 14 ♘c3 ♗d7 15 ♘e5 ♗e8, when Black succeeds in defending (16 b4 ♘b3 or 16...♖ac8!?).

13...♗d7 14 b4 ♕xc4

Consistent, at the least: with his 'bad' knight on a6 Black does not even contemplate 14...♕b6 15 ♖fc1 or 14...♕h5 15 ♘e4

♘xe4 16 ♕xe4 ♗c6 17 ♕f4.

15 ♘xc4 ♗b5 16 ♖fc1

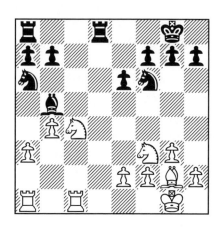

White completes the mobilisation of his forces. 16 ♘fe5?! was premature because of 16...♘d5! 17 ♖fc1 f6 18 ♘d3 ♖ac8, when White's pressure evaporates. But now he has a small plus – mainly thanks to the better placing of his pieces.

16...♖ac8?

This obvious move (development with gain of tempo!) proves to be a serious mistake. I also considered other continuations:

1) 16...♘d5?! 17 ♘d4 (17 e3!?) 17...♗xc4 18 ♖xc4 ♘b6 19 ♖cc1! ♘xb4 (19...♖xd4? 20 ♗xb7) 20 ♘xe6 fxe6 21 axb4 with a persistent initiative;

2) 16...♖ab8! 17 e3! (less is promised by 17 ♘a5!? ♗xe2 18 ♘xb7! ♖xb7 19 ♘d4 ♖bd7 20 ♘xe2 ♘c7 21 ♘d4 ♖xd4 22 ♖xc7 ♖4d7) 17...♘c7!, and my *Informator* suggestion 18 ♘d4 is not so clear in view of 18...♗xc4 19 ♖xc4 ♘ce8, and therefore 18 ♘ce5!? ♘cd5 19 ♘d4 ♗e8 20 ♖c5 and ♖ac1 is more energetic, retaining pressure on the queenside.

17 ♘fe5

17 ♘a5!? was also very tempting, but I found another way of exploiting the poor position of the knight on a6.

17...b6

17...♖c7 18 ♘a5 b6 19 ♘ac6 was unpromising. After immediately removing his pawn from the attack on it, Ljubojevic was planning ...♘b8-c6(d7) and he thought that he was about to solve all his problems.

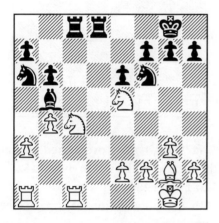

18 ♗b7! (the start of an unexpected multi-move operation) **18...♖c7** (there is no choice: after 18...♖b8? 19 ♗xa6 ♗xa6 20 ♘c6 White wins) **19 a4! ♘xb4** (19...♗xc4? 20 ♗xa6!) **20 axb5 ♖xb7 21 ♘d6!**

White has to act energetically, as otherwise his attack with a small army will peter out: 21 ♖a4?! ♘bd5 22 ♘d6 ♖e7 23 ♘c6?! (23 ♖c6 is better) 23...♖xd6 24 ♘xe7+ ♘xe7 25 ♖xa7 ♘g6!, and Black is okay (26 ♖cc7 ♘f8! 27 ♖xf7? ♘8d7! and wins).

21...♖e7 22 ♘c8!

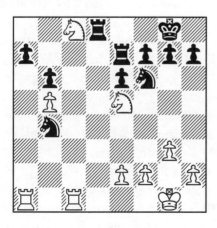

Regaining the pawn and retaining the initiative. By pinning his hopes on a far-advanced passed pawn – 22 ♘c6!? ♘xc6 23 bxc6 ♘d5 24 ♘b5 a5 25 c7 ♖c8 26 ♖c6! f5 (26...♘xc7? 27 ♖ac1) 27 ♖ac1 (threatening f2-f3 and e2-e4) 27...g5! 28 g4! White could also have condemned Black to an unpleasant defence.

22...♖ee8?

The rook should not have been moved off the seventh rank – 22...♖b7 23 ♘xa7 g5 was more resilient, and after 24 ♘ac6 ♘xc6 25 bxc6 ♖c7 26 ♖ab1 or 24 ♖c4 ♖a8 (24...♘bd5?! 25 ♘ac6 and e2-e4) 25 ♖c8+ ♖xc8 26 ♘xc8 ♘bd5 27 ♘d6 ♖c7 28 ♔g2 White's advantage is smaller than in the game.

23 ♘xa7

Now the b6-pawn is weak and the threat of ♘ac6 has increased in strength – from here the knight will paralyse Black's defences, and an exchange on c6 will give White a deadly dangerous passed pawn.

23...♘bd5

Of course, not 23...♘fd5?! 24 e4 ♘f6 25 ♘ac6 ♘xc6 26 bxc6 and wins (26...♘xe4 27 ♘c4!). However, the alternatives were also bad: 23...♖a8 24 ♖c4! ♖e7 25 ♖a4 g5 26 ♖c8+! ♖xc8 27 ♘xc8 ♖c7 28 ♘xb6 or 26...♖e8 27 ♖c7! ♘bd5 28 ♖xf7, and 23...♖d2 24 ♔f1 (threatening ♘c4) 24...♖a2 25 ♖xa2 ♘xa2 26 ♖c6! or 24...♘e4 25 ♖a4! ♖b2 26 ♘ac6, and in each case White wins.

24 ♘ac6

Justifiably regarding my position as won, I relaxed and lost the necessary concentration. The most correct strategy was to continue restricting the mobility of the black pieces: 24 f3! ♘d7 (24...♖a8 25 e4 ♘b4 26 ♘ec6! or 25...♘e7 26 ♖a6! is no better) 25 ♘c4 ♘c5 26 ♖a3! f5 27 ♘xb6 or 25...♖a8 26 e4 ♘b4 27 ♘d6 ♖f8 28 ♘c6 ♖xa1 29 ♖xa1 ♘d3 30 ♘e7+ ♔h8 31 ♖a7 ♘3c5 32 ♖c7, and Black will die from suffocation (32...f5 33 ♘ec8! with the threat of ♘xb6).

24...♖a8!

The only chance.

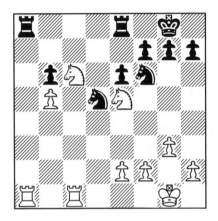

25 ♘c4?

And this already an obvious error. Only 25 ♖a6! (threatening f2-f3 and e2-e4) 25...♘e4 26 ♘c4 would have retained real chances of success: for example, 26...♘ec3?! 27 ♖ca1 ♖xa6 28 bxa6 ♖a8 29 a7 b5 30 ♘d6 ♘xe2+ 31 ♔f1 ♘ec3 32 ♔e1! or 26...♘c5 27 ♖xa8 ♖xa8 28 ♘xb6 ♘xb6 29 ♖xc5 with an extra passed pawn.

25...♘e4?

Continuing the parade of mistakes (and yet previously I attached an exclamation mark to this move!). If 25...♘c3? there was an elegant win by 26 ♖xa8 ♘xe2+ 27 ♔f1 ♘xc1 28 ♖a1! (but not the *Informator* suggestion 28 ♘xb6(?) ♖xa8 29 ♘xa8 ♘d3 30 b6 ♘c5 31 ♘a5, in view of 31...♔f8 and ...♘fd7 with a probable draw) 28...♘b3 29 ♖a3 ♘c5 30 ♘d6, when 30...♖f8? fails to 31 ♘e7+ ♔h8 32 ♘xf7+! ♖xf7 33 ♖a8+.

However, 25...♖xa1 26 ♖xa1 ♘c7! would have given Black every chance of a draw: 27 ♘a7 (the b5-pawn has to be defended) 27...♘fd5 28 ♖a3(c1) f5 or 27 ♘d6 ♖a8 28 ♖xa8+ ♘xa8 29 ♘e5 ♔f8! with the idea of 30 ♘d(e)xf7 ♔e7 and ...♘c7xb5.

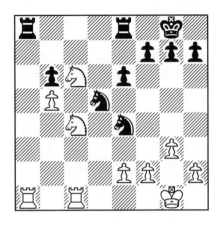

26 ♔f1? (alas, I again overlooked 26 ♖a6! – cf. the note to White's 25th move) **26...♖xa1 27 ♖xa1 ♘c7! 28 ♘a7!**

With difficulty White seeks a chance to continue the fight.

28...♖d8?

A time-trouble error. 28...♘c3?! was also inaccurate: 29 ♘d6 ♖d8 30 ♖c1! ♘3d5 (30...♖xd6?! 31 ♖xc3 ♘e8 32 ♖c8 ♔f8 33 ♖b8) 31 ♘dc8! or 29...♖a8 30 ♖c1! ♖xa7 31 ♖xc3 ♔f8 32 e4. In *Informator* I recommended the passive 28...♖b8(?!), but after 29 f3! ♘c3 30 ♘d6 ♖a8 31 ♖a3 ♘b1 (31...♘3d5?! 32 ♘c4) 32 ♖d3 White holds the initiative (32...♖xa7? 33 ♘c8!).

But by making a simple escape square – 28...g6!, Ljubojevic could have reached the haven of a draw: 29 ♘xb6 ♖b8 30 ♘d7 ♖b7 31 f3 ♘xb5 or 29 ♖a3 ♖d8! 30 ♔g2 ♖d1 31 ♖e3 (31 ♘xb6 ♖b1!) 31...♘c5 32 ♘xb6 ♖a1! 33 ♖e5 ♖xa7 34 ♖xc5 ♖b7 35 ♘c4 ♘xb5.

29 ♘xb6 ♘c3 30 ♖a5! ♖d1+ 31 ♔g2 ♖b1

If 31...♘xe2 32 ♘c4 ♖g1+ White could have decided matters not with my *Informator* suggestion 33 ♔f3(?!) ♘d4+ 34 ♔e4 (34 ♔e3? ♖d1! with a draw) 34...♘b3 35 b6 on account of the unclear 35...♘a6!, but by the accurate 33 ♔h3! ♘f4+ 34 ♔g4 and b5-b6.

Black would also have lost after 31...h5 32 ♘c4 ♖b1 33 b6 ♘7d5 34 ♘c8! ♖xe2 35 h4!

♘d4 (35...f6 36 ♖a7) 36 ♖a6 ♘c6 37 ♘8d6!, forcing 37...♘xb6 38 ♖xb6 ♖xb6 39 ♘xb6 – he is not able either to construct a fortress or to exchange all the pawns.

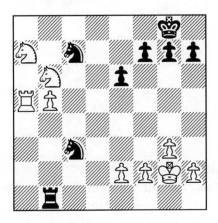

32 ♘d7!

Another unpleasant surprise: because of the weakness of the back rank, Black does not have time to capture the passed pawn – 32...♘3xb5 33 ♘xb5 ♖xb5 34 ♖a7! ♘e8 35 ♖a8 and wins.

32...f6

After other escape squares – 32...g6 or 32...h5, the quickest way to the goal was 33 b6 ♘7d5 34 ♘b5! ♘xb5 35 ♖a8+ and b6-b7-b8♕, winning the exchange and the game. **33 b6 ♘7d5 34 ♘c8! ♘xe2 35 b7! ♖g1+ 36 ♔h3 ♘ef4+!?** (the last chance: 37 gxf4?? ♘xf4+ 38 ♔h4 g5+ 39 ♖xg5+ fxg5 mate) **37 ♔g4 h5+ 38 ♔f3**

The checks have come to an end, and Black resigned (**1-0**).

A fifth successive win – and 8 out of 9! Playing the next day with Black against Sax, I felt extremely tired, but, fortunately for me, my opponent was peaceably inclined and he accepted a draw as early as the 16th move. Then, after a free day, I defeated Korchnoi and drew with Ivanchuk, after missing a chance of gaining an obvious advantage on the emergence from the opening. I reached 10 out of 12, and at the finish two draws would have sufficed, but again I defeated Hjartarson and Agdestein.

From the press: *'Kasparov operated like a well-regulated machine. He scored 6 out of 7 in each half of the tournament, won all seven "White" games and all the mini-matches (three by a clean score), and employed several novelties. After achieving a phenomenal result for a tournament of this standard (plus 10!), he exceeded Robert Fischer's rating record by roughly 15 points. To mark this, at the closing ceremony he was crowned with a special wreath.'*

From my interview with the magazine *New in Chess*: 'I feel I've done something very important for chess. Fischer's name now belongs to the past. His achievements were great, but now an active chess player has the record. It must help the further development of chess. It's a relief for chess. The door is open!'

Sky-high Peak

International Tournament in Belgrade (14–28 November 1989): 1. **Kasparov** – 9½ out of 11; 2–3. Timman and Ehlvest – 6½; 4–5. Yusupov and Ljubojevic – 6; 6. Hjartarson – 5½; 7–8. Agdestein and Kozul – 5; 9–10. Nikolic and Short – 4½; 11. Popovic – 4; 12. Damljanovic – 3.

I happily accepted an invitation to the super-tournament dedicated to the 1111th anniversary of Belgrade, since I have always played successfully in Yugoslavia, and after my Tilburg triumph, reinforced by a victory in New York over the computer Deep Thought (2-0), I was experiencing a special mental surge. This tournament was the focus of the chess world's attention, not only because of the strong line-up (three quarters of the participants had appeared in the World Cup, and five in the Candidates matches), but mainly because many were excited by the question as to whether I would be able to exceed my recent rating record (2793), and achieve the unthinkable mark of 2800. According to preliminary calculations, for this I would have to score 8½ out of 11.

With the aim of justifying the fans' hopes, I fought under the motto: 'I am going for the record!' True, in the 1st round I was again paired with Black against Yusupov, and my Grünfeld produced only a quiet draw on the 22nd move. I scored my first win in the 2nd round, in which I met one of the 'home' players, the 30-year-old grandmaster Petar Popovic.

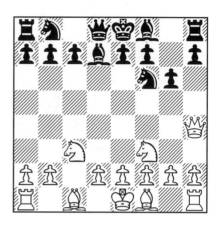

> ## Game 60
> ## G.Kasparov-P.Popovic
> Belgrade, 2nd Round, 15.11.1989
> *English Opening A16*

1 ♘f3 ♘f6 2 c4 g6 3 ♘c3 d5 4 cxd5 ♘xd5 5 ♕a4+

After discovering in my preparations that my opponent employed the Grünfeld and that against the 'English' move order he chose a questionable variation, I decided to try and demonstrate this at the board.

5...♗d7 (nowadays 5...♘c6!? 6 ♘e5 ♕d6 7 ♘xc6 ♕xc6 8 ♕xc6+ bxc6 is also fashionable) **6 ♕h4 ♘f6**

A strange retreat. After 6...♗c6 7 ♕d4! (7 g3 ♗g7 is equal, Korchnoi-Kasparov, Brussels 1987) 7...f6 8 e4 ♘xc3 9 bxc3 ♕xd4 10 ♘xd4 White merely has a slightly better endgame (Kasparov-Kouatly, Evry (simul') 1988). But I considered the most logical to be the exchange 6...♘xc3, which I had studied before my matches with Karpov.

7 e4!?

This had not previously been played against my opponent. White had unsuccessfully tried both 7 d3 (C.Hansen-Popovic, Dortmund 1988) and 7 ♘e5 (Marjanovic-Popovic, Zlatibor 1989), as well as the more aggressive 7 d4 ♗g4 (a distinctive version of the 'Grünfeld') 8 ♗g5 (8 e4 ♗xf3!, Adamski-Popovic, Naleczow 1984) 8...♗xf3! 9 exf3 (9 ♗xf6 exf6 is weaker, Gheorghiu-Popovic, Novi Sad 1982) 9...♗g7 10 ♗c4 h6 11 ♗e3 (Ribli-Popovic, Subotica Interzonal 1987), or 9 gxf3 ♗g7 10 ♖d1 (Panchenko-I.Sokolov, Belgrade 1988).

7...♗g4

With the same idea of 8 d4 ♗xf3!. White is clearly better after 7...♗g7 8 d4 ♗g4?! (8...h6 is stronger) 9 ♘e5! ♗c8 10 ♗e3 (Khalifman-Shterengas, Leningrad 1983). If 7...c5, then 8 e5 ♘h5 9 ♗c4 is strong, while after 7...♘c6 I had prepared 8 e5 ♘g4 (if 8...g5, then 9 ♕xg5 ♖g8 10 ♕e3 ♘b4 11 ♕e2!) 9 d4 (9 ♗e2!?) 9...♘b4 10 h3 ♘c2+ 11 ♔d1 ♘xa1 12 hxg4 with sharp, non-standard play, which is what I was after.

8 ♘e5!?

And here is a novelty: White avoids the spoiling of his pawn structure and wants to create a powerful centre. 8 e5 ♗xf3! 9 gxf3 ♘d5 is perfectly acceptable for Black.

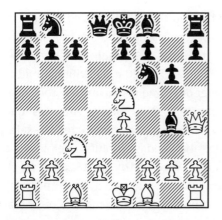

8...♗e6 9 f4 (the second link of my plan) **9...♗g7 10 ♕f2**

The third, key link – and an unexpected one for a routinely-thinking player: without completing his development, White makes what is already a third move with his queen, in order to play d2-d4. The premature attack 10 f5?! gxf5 11 exf5 ♗xf5 12 ♗c4 would have been refuted by 12...e6! (12...♗g6 13 d4 ♘c6 is also possible, Milanovic-Popovic, Vrnjacka Banja 2005) 13 0-0 0-0 14 d4 ♘c6 or simply 14...♘e4.

10...0-0

The immediate 10...♘c6 allows 11 ♗b5. Without preparatory analysis Popovic did not venture with the pawn sacrifice 10...c5! 11 ♕xc5 ♘fd7 12 ♘xd7 ♕xd7 with quite good compensation, or the risky 10...♘g4 11 ♘xg4 ♗xg4 12 f5! ♘c6! (12...gxf5?! 13 h3 ♗h5 14 exf5 f6 15 d4 is worse) 13 h3! ♘b4! 14 hxg4 ♘c2+ 15 ♔d1 ♘xa1 with intricate play – in *Informator* I recommended 16 ♖h3, but after 16...c6! and ...♕b6 Black is perfectly okay (White will have to pay dearly for the capture of the knight on a1), and therefore 16 ♗c4!? is more accurate, or 16 ♕c5!? with the idea of b2-b4 and ♗b2.

11 d4 ♘c6!

It is now dubious to play 11...c5?! 12 d5 ♗c8 13 ♗e2!, or 11...♘g4?! 12 ♘xg4 ♗xg4

13 ♗e3, reinforcing the centre. And if 11...♘bd7, then 12 ♗e2 or even 12 ♘f3 is good, emphasising the awkward placing of the enemy minor pieces.

12 ♘xc6 bxc6

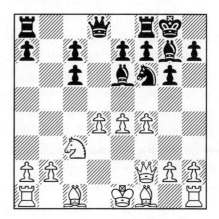

13 h3!?

An ambitious decision: I was not satisfied with a small plus after the quiet 13 ♗e2 ♘g4 14 ♗xg4 (14 ♕g3!?) 14...♗xg4 15 ♗e3.

13...♕b8?!

This mobilisation plan (...♖d8, ...♕b4 and ...♖ab8) is too slow. 13...♘e8?! is passive: 14 ♗e3 (14 e5?! f6!) 14...♘d6 15 g4!, and if 15...♘c4, then 16 ♗xc4 ♗xc4 17 h4! (more forceful than my *Informator* suggestion 17 0-0-0) and h4-h5 with an attack. However, the natural 13...♖b8!? (not removing the pressure on the d-pawn) would still have retained almost equal chances: 14 ♗e2 (14 ♗d3?! c5! 15 d5 c6!) 14...♖b4 15 e5 ♘d5 or 14 ♗e3 c5! 15 ♖d1 c6 16 dxc5 ♕a5, and although Black's position is slightly worse, nothing terrible for him is apparent.

14 ♗d3!

14 ♗e2 also favours White, since 14...c5(?) 15 d5 ♘xe4 16 ♘xe4 ♕b4+, as given by me in *Informator*, does not work because of 17 ♔f1! ♗xd5 18 ♘xc5. However, the move in the game is stronger.

14...♖d8 15 ♗e3

Not falling for 15 0-0? ♘g4! 16 hxg4 ♗xd4 17 ♗e3 ♗xc3 18 bxc3 (18 f5? ♕xb2!) 18...♖xd3 19 f5 ♗c4 with equality.

15...♕b4

Previously I criticised this move, a logical one in its own way, and gave preference to the active 15...c5 16 d5 c4!, but after 17 ♗b1! (17 ♗xc4? ♕b4!) 17...♗c8 (not 17...♗d7?! 18 e5 and especially not 17...♖xd5? 18 exd5 ♘xd5 19 ♘xd5 ♖xd5 20 0-0 ♕xb2 21 ♕xb2 ♗xb2 22 ♗e4 and wins) 18 0-0 White has a persistent initiative. He is threatening a2-a4(a3) and ♗a2xc4, and if 18...e6 19 dxe6 ♗xe6 there is the impending f4-f5.

16 0-0 ♖ab8

Not 16...♖xd4? 17 a3! (17 ♗xd4? ♘xe4!), when the forced queen sacrifice 17...♕xc3 18 bxc3 ♖xd3 is obviously insufficient: 19 e5 (19 ♕e2!? ♖xc3 20 ♗d4 is more subtle, or 19...♗c4 20 ♕f3) 19...♘e4 20 ♕e2 ♗c4 21 ♗f2 ♘xc3 22 ♕b2 and wins.

17 ♖ab1

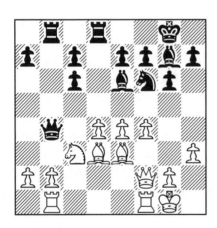

17...♘e8?

Catastrophic: Popovic provokes e4-e5, but he is unable to exploit the resulting weakness of the light squares. 17...♗c4! was essential, and although after 18 ♗xc4 ♕xc4 19 ♕c2(f3) or 18 a3 ♕b3 19 ♗c2 ♕b7(b6) 20 ♖fe1 White has a big advantage, at least Black's pieces are normally developed.

18 e5

Shutting the e8-knight and the g7-bishop out of the game, and at the same time threatening f4-f5 (after the sharp 18 f5!? gxf5 19 d5 cxd5 20 exf5 White would be in danger of selling his advantage too cheaply). It transpires that Black, with his glaring pawn 'holes', has overestimated the safety of his position and is absolutely helpless.

18...f5 (18...c5 19 d5 or 18...♗c4 19 ♗xc4 ♕xc4 20 ♖bc1 was also dismal) **19 ♖fc1**

A sound positional move. Consideration could also have been given to the sharp 19 d5!? cxd5 20 ♗xa7 ♖a8 21 ♗b5! or 20 ♗c5 ♕b7 21 ♗xe7 ♖dc8 (21...♖d7 22 ♗a3) 22 ♘a4 etc, but 19 g4! fxg4 20 f5! was best.

19...♗f8 20 b3

White gradually intensifies the pressure, preparing ♘a4 (the natural follow-up to ♖fc1), and quite reasonably assuming that he has no reason to rush.

20...♘g7 (20...♗d5 21 ♘xd5! cxd5 22 ♖c6 ♖b6? 23 ♗d2, trapping the queen) **21 ♘a4 ♗d5 22 ♘c5** (22 ♗d2!? ♕a3 23 ♖c5) **22...♕b6 23 b4 e6 24 ♘a6** (or 24 ♕d2! with the threat of a2-a4-a5) **24...♖bc8 25 a4 ♕b7 26 ♕f1 ♕a8** (26...♘h5 27 ♔h2 ♗e7 28 ♗c4!) **27 ♗c4 ♗e4 28 ♖b2 ♔h8 29 ♗d3 ♗d5 30 ♔h2 ♗e7 31 ♖bc2 ♖d7?!**

Time-trouble! 31...♕b7 was more resilient.

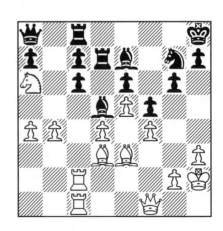

32 b5 (destroying Black's defences) **32...cxb5 33 ♘xc7 ♕b7 34 ♘xd5 ♖xc2 35 ♖xc2 ♖xd5 36 ♗xb5 ♖d8 37 ♕c1 ♕e4 38 ♖c3** (38 ♖c7!?) **38...h6?** (a blunder, but 38...♕d5 39 ♖c7 was also hopeless) **39 ♗c6 1-0**

A highly unusual opening battle!

In the 3rd round I beat Damljanovic, and in the 4th round I spectacularly outplayed Timman, sacrificing two pieces for a rook, and then also a rook, but in a sharp time scramble I missed a win, and the game was drawn on the 48th move.

After this I was leading together with Short – 3 out of 4. The very strong Yugoslav grandmaster, the 39-year-old Ljubomir Ljubojevic, who was a point behind us, arrived for his 5th round game with me in a most aggressive mood.

Game 61
L.Ljubojevic-G.Kasparov
Belgrade, 5th Round, 19.11.1989
Sicilian Defence B96

1 e4 c5 2 ♘f3 d6 3 d4 cxd4 4 ♘xd4 ♘f6 5 ♘c3 a6 6 ♗g5 (6 ♗e2 – *Game No.7*; 6 ♗e3 – *Game Nos.39, 100*; 6 ♗c4 – *Game No.99*) **6...e6 7 f4 ♕c7**

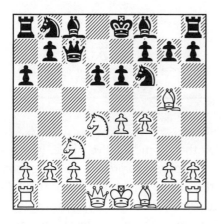

A move which I had tried a few times, although already the radical 7...♕b6 was also in my arsenal (*Game No.67*).

8 ♕e2!?

A rare continuation, but I was ready for it: a month earlier in Tilburg this was played against me by Ivanchuk. 8 ♗xf6 gxf6 is steadier (e.g. Yudasin-Kasparov, 49th USSR Championship, Frunze 1981). But in what was then the main line with 8 ♕f3 b5 9 0-0-0 b4! 10 e5 ♗b7 11 ♘cb5 (11 ♕h3 dxe5!) 11...axb5 12 ♗xb5+ after 12...♘fd7? 13 ♘xe6! fxe6 14 ♕h3 ♔f7 15 f5 ♗e4 16 fxe6+ ♔g8 17 ♕b3 I suffered a painful defeat at the hands of Krum Georgiev (Malta Olympiad 1980), but 12...♘bd7! 13 ♕h3 b3! is correct – I found this idea in a joint analysis with Tukmakov (the source game for 'the rest of the world' was Kosten-Kuligowski, London 1981).

8...♘c6!? (at that time this appealed to me more than 8...♘bd7 9 0-0-0, transposing into the 7...♘bd7 8 ♕e2 variation) **9 0-0-0 ♘xd4**

White is better after 9...♗e7 10 ♘xc6 bxc6 (10...♕xc6?! is worse: 11 e5 dxe5 12 fxe5 ♘d5 13 ♗xe7 ♘xe7 14 ♕h5! with the idea of ♗d3 and ♘e4, or 13...♘xc3 14 bxc3 ♔xe7 15 ♕g4! ♗d7 16 ♗c4 with an attack) 11 e5 dxe5 12 ♕xe5! (Hracek-Wojtkiewicz, Warsaw (Zonal) 1990).

10 ♖xd4 ♗e7

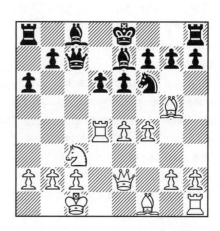

In my game with Ivanchuk I thought about this move for quite a long time, fearing the 11 e5 break, but I came to the conclusion that things are more or less normal for Black.

11 g3

A novelty! The prophylactic 11 ♔b1 is also possible, while Ivanchuk chose the immediate 11 e5 dxe5 12 fxe5 ♘d5 13 ♗xe7, and after 13...♘xe7 14 ♘e4 0-0 15 ♕h5?! (15 ♘d6 is equal) 15...♘g6 (15...♘f5!?) 16 ♘g5?! h6 17 ♘f3 I could have seized the initiative with 17...♖d8!.

The variation 11 g4!? h6 (11...0-0!? – Stohl) 12 ♗h4 g5 (12...e5!?) is more topical: for example, 13 e5! dxe5 14 ♖c4! ♕b8 (14...♕a5!? 15 fxg5 ♘d7 16 ♗g2 hxg5 17 ♗e1!) 15 fxg5 hxg5 16 ♗g3! ♘d7 17 ♗g2 b5 18 ♖c6 b4 with sharp play (Naiditsch-Swiercz, Budva 2009), but 18 ♖d4! is stronger: 18...b4 (18...f6 19 ♖dd1!) 19 ♖xd7! bxc3 20 ♖xe7+ ♔xe7 21 bxc3 f6 (21...♗b7?! 22 ♗xe5 ♕a7 23 ♗d4 ♕b8 24 ♖f1! with an attack) 22 ♗xa8 ♕xa8 23 ♖f1 ♕b8 24 ♕f2 ♖f8 25 h4!, retaining the better chances.

11...♗d7!

Urgent development. After 11...b5?! 12 ♗g2 White is threatening e4-e5: 12...♗b7 (Stohl recommends 12...♖b8(?!), allowing 13 e5! dxe5 14 fxe5 ♘d5 15 ♕d2!) 13 ♖hd1 0-0 (13...♖c8 14 ♔b1) 14 ♗xf6! gxf6 (Black has to spoil his pawns: 14...♗xf6? 15 e5 wins) 15 f5 with a clear advantage.

12 ♗g2 h6

It is useful first to push back the bishop, in order to have the resource ...g7-g5 and ...0-0-0. Here all my opening anxiety disappeared: Black has a solid position.

13 ♗h4 ♗c6 14 f5?

A typical move, but in the given instance inappropriate (as is 14 e5?! ♗xg2 15 ♕xg2 dxe5 16 fxe5 ♕xe5 17 ♕xb7 0-0!). If 14 ♖hd1 I was planning 14...g5! 15 fxg5 hxg5

16 ♗xg5 ♖xh2 and ...0-0-0. 14 ♕d2 is more cautious, although after 14...0-0 15 ♖d1 (15 ♗xf6?! ♗xf6 16 ♖xd6 ♗xc3 17 bxc3 ♗d5!) 15...♖ad8! and ...b7-b5 Black is also okay.

14 ♖c4!?, which occurred later, is little better: 14...♕b6 15 a3 (Ljubojevic-Xu Jun, Novi Sad Olympiad 1990) 15...0-0! 16 ♖d1 ♖ac8 or 15 e5 ♗xg2 16 ♕xg2 dxe5 17 fxe5 ♘d5! (threatening ...g7-g5) 18 ♗xe7 ♘xe7 with equality (Luther-Sadler, Altensteig 1992).

14...0-0 15 ♖hd1

White is not ready for sharp advances: after 15 g4? there is the counter 15...♘xe4!, while if 15 fxe6? the fearless 15...g5! is possible – in *Informator* I condemned this because of 16 ♘d5 ♗xd5(?!) 17 exd5 gxh4 18 ♖xh4 with compensation for the piece, but after 16...♘xd5! 17 exd5 ♗b5 18 ♕d2 fxe6 19 dxe6 ♗f6 no particular compensation is apparent.

15...b5!

With the obvious threat of ...♖ab8 and ...b5-b4.

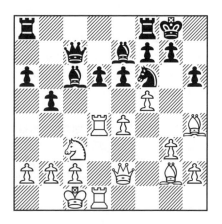

16 g4

Another pseudo-active move, which was probably played to provide an escape square for the bishop on h4. The quiet 16 a3 ♖ab8 or 16 ♔b1 ♖ab8 is also unpromising.

Therefore I recommended 16 fxe6 fxe6 17

♗xf6!, but 17...♖xf6! (stronger than my previous 17...♗xf6) 18 e5! dxe5 gives Black somewhat the better chances: 19 ♗xc6 ♕xc6! (instead of 19...exd4?! 20 ♘d5! exd5 21 ♗xd5+ ♔h8 22 ♗xa8, Hector-Parligras, German Bundesliga 2009) 20 ♖d7 (20 ♕xe5 ♖f2) 20...♖f7 21 ♔b1 b4 22 ♘e4 a5, although with his knight on e4 White should not have any particular problems. On the other hand, the interposition of 16...g5! would appear to refute the capture on e6: 17 ♘d5 (17 ♗h3!? ♔h8!) 17...♘xd5! 18 exd5 ♗e8, and it is unlikely that White will find sufficient compensation for the piece.

16...e5?!

16...♘xe4? no longer works – after 17 ♗xe7 ♘xc3 18 bxc3 ♕xe7 the bishop on c6 is *en prise*. But 16...♖ab8! was more subtle.

bit line 18 exd5! ♗xb4 19 ♗xf6 ♗xc3 is stronger, with two interesting possibilities:

1) 20 bxc3 ♗xd5 21 ♗xd5 gxf6 22 ♗xa8 ♖xa8 23 ♔b2, maintaining the balance, or 20...gxf6 21 dxc6 ♖ad8 22 ♗d5! – White's position resembles an impregnable fortress;

2) 20 dxc6 ♗xb2+ (20...gxf6 21 bxc3 – cf. above) 21 ♔xb2 gxf6 22 g5!! ♕e7 (22...hxg5 23 ♖d7 ♕b6 24 ♕h5 and ♗d5, or 23...♕a5 24 ♗d5 and ♕h5 leads to perpetual check) 23 gxf6 ♕xf6 24 ♗e4 ♖ac8 25 ♕f2, and again the powerful passed pawn compensates White for the exchange deficit.

17...b4 18 ♗xf6 (there is nothing else) **18...bxc3! 19 ♗xe7 cxb2+ 20 ♔b1** (White would have quickly succumbed to the attack after 20 ♔xb2? ♕xe7 21 ♖xd6 ♖fc8 etc.) **20...♕xe7**

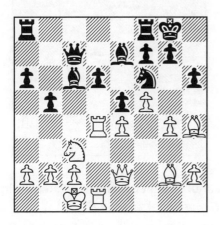

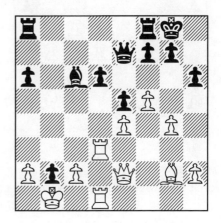

17 ♖4d3?!

The sacrifice of the exchange for a pawn – 17 ♗xf6? exd4 18 ♗xd4 is incorrect in view of 18...b4 19 ♘d5 ♗xd5 20 exd5 ♗g5+ and ...♖fe8. And 17 ♖4d2?! b4 18 ♘d5 is rather weak on account of 18...♗xd5! 19 exd5 a5 with the threat of ...a5-a4-a3.

17 ♖b4(!) d5 also looked dangerous for White – if 18 ♖b3, then 18...d4 19 ♘d5 ♗xd5 20 exd5 ♖ac8 21 ♗xf6 ♗xf6 22 ♗e4 ♗h4 followed by ...♕d6, ...♖c5 and ...♖fc8, increasing the pressure. However, the gam-

21 ♖xd6?

The decisive mistake. 21 f6! gxf6 22 ♕d2! ♔g7 23 ♖h3 ♖h8 24 ♕xd6 was essential, with hopes of saving an inferior ending.

21...♖fc8!

Intending ...♗b5-c4. 'The difference in the strength of the bishops is now obvious.' (Gipslis). White's defences are creaking.

22 ♖1d2 (22 c4 also did not help: 22...♗a4 23 ♖1d2 ♖ab8 with the threat of ...♗c2+!) **22...♗b5** (22...♖ab8!? with the idea of 23 ♕xa6 ♗b5 24 ♕a3 ♗c4, winning) **23 ♕e3**

In *Informator* I gave 23 ♕d1 ♖ab8 24 ♗f1 as more resilient, but after 24...♗a4! (with the threat of ...♗xc2+) 25 ♖6d5 ♔h7 or 25 ♖xa6 ♕b4 26 ♗d3 ♖c3 White cannot hold out for long.

23...♖ab8 24 ♖b6 (or 24 f6 ♗c4! with the threat of ...♗xa2+!) **24...♗c4! 25 ♖d1**

25 ♖dd6? ♕xd6! or 25 c3? ♕a3! was even worse. 25 ♖xb2 (25 ♔xb2? ♕g5!) 25...♖xb2+ 26 ♔xb2 ♕b4+ 27 ♔c1 ♖b8 or 25 ♖b3 ♗xb3 26 cxb3 a5 27 ♖xb2 a4 was also hopeless.

25...♖xb6 (the alternative was 25...♕c7 26 ♖xb8 ♗xa2+! 27 ♔xa2 ♖xb8 or 25...♗xa2+ immediately) **26 ♕xb6 ♕a3 27 ♕xb2**

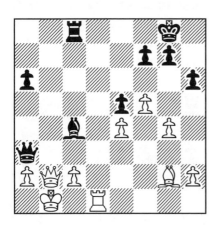

27...♗xa2+!?

Forcibly transposing into a won rook endgame. 27...♕e3 was also decisive, threatening ...♕e2, and if 28 c3 – 28...♗e2!.

28 ♔a1 (the only move) **28...♕a4 29 ♕xa2**

29 ♖d2? ♕a5! or 29 ♖c1? ♗c4+ 30 ♔b1 ♖c5 was bad for White. The rest is clear without any commentary.

29...♕xa2+ 30 ♔xa2 ♖xc2+ 31 ♔b3 ♖xg2 32 ♔c4 ♖xh2 33 ♔d5 f6 34 g5 hxg5 35 ♔e6 g4! 36 ♖d8+ ♔h7 37 ♔f7 ♖h5

Or 37...♖b2(c2). White resigned (**0-1**).

After then beating Ehlvest and Kozul, I reached 6 out of 7. In my 'white' 8th round game with Hjartarson I played the opening uncertainly and, after overcoming some difficulties, I gained an advantage only in the time scramble just before the first control, then I won a pawn – and missed a pretty win with my incorrect 45th move.

In the 9th round I had another 'Sicilian skirmish' with Nigel Short, which led to a curious ending.

Game 62
N.Short-G.Kasparov
Belgrade, 9th round,
24/26.11.1989

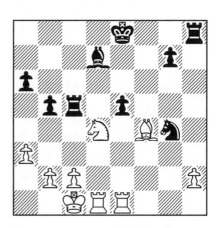

30...0-0! (another example of late castling – cf. *Game No.12*) **31 ♘b3 ♖xc2+!**

This sacrifice of the exchange for a pawn is the only way of creating full-scale counterplay.

32 ♔xc2 ♗f5+ 33 ♔c3 exf4 34 ♖d2

Protecting the h2-pawn. White could have maintained equality, albeit not without some difficulty, by 34 ♘d4 ♘xh2 (34...♘f2 35 ♖a1!) 35 ♘xf5 ♖xf5 36 ♖e8+ ♔f7 37 ♖h8 ♘g4 38 ♖d7+ ♔g6 39 ♖g8, or 36 ♖d8+ ♔f7 37 ♖d7+ ♔f6 38 ♖d6+ ♔g5 39 ♖e7 g6 40 ♖ee6 etc.

34...♖c8+?!

Dubious. Black should not have driven the

enemy king towards his own pawns. But too little was promised by 34...f3 35 ♘c5 ♗g6 36 ♖f1 or 34...♘e3 35 ♘c5! a5 36 h4.

35 ♔b4 ♘e3 36 ♖c1! ♖xc1 37 ♘xc1 f3 38 ♔c5?!

Time-trouble confusion. After 38 ♘b3! ♘g4 39 ♘d4 ♗e4 40 ♘xf3! ♗xf3 41 ♔a5 and ♔xa6 it is Black who would have had to save the game.

38...♘g4

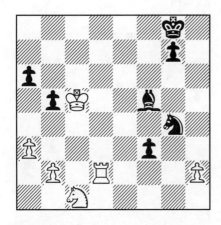

39 ♘e2!?

With his flag about to fall, Short gives up his knight for the dangerous passed pawn, not wishing to suffer after 39 ♘d3 ♗xd3! 40 ♖xd3, although here too White would have gained a draw: 40...♘xh2 41 ♖d2 ♘g4 42 ♖d4! (but not immediately 42 ♖d1? ♘e3 43 ♖d2 g5!, when Black wins) 42...♘e5 43 ♖d1! and ♔d4, or 40...f2 41 ♖f3 ♘e5! 42 ♖xf2 ♘d3+ 43 ♔b6 ♘xf2 44 ♔xa6 ♘d1 45 ♔b5 ♘xb2 46 a4 ♘xa4 47 ♔xa4.

39...fxe2 40 ♖xe2 ♔f7 41 ♔b6

In *Informator* I criticised this 'greedy' move and recommended the safe 41 b4 ♗d3 42 ♖a2 with a draw (42 ♖g2 ♘e5 43 ♖g3 will also do). But as yet there is nothing terrible for White.

41...b4! (a good practical chance) **42 axb4?!**

White would unexpectedly have lost after 42 ♖d2?! b3! 43 ♔xa6 ♗c2! 44 a4? ♘e5 45

a5 ♘d3 etc. Therefore 42 ♖g2! was correct, with an easy draw.

42...♗d3 43 ♖g2 ♘e5

There now commences a lengthy struggle with slightly the better chances for Black – the win is problematic because so few pawns remain. In my career I have played far more often with a rook and pawn against two minor pieces, but here we have an 'exception to the rule'.

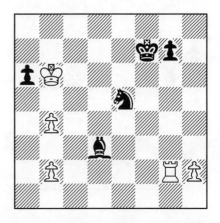

44 ♔c5 (44 h4!?) **44...♗b5 45 ♔d4 ♘d3 46 ♔c3 ♔f6 47 ♖g3 ♘f4 48 ♖g4 ♘e6 49 ♔d2** (49 h4!?) **49...g5 50 ♔e3 ♔f5 51 ♖g3**

The rook would have had more freedom after 51 ♖g2!? ♘f4 52 ♖d2 or 51...♘d8 52 ♖f2+ ♔g4 53 ♖f8 ♘c6 54 ♖e8.

51...♘f4 52 ♖f3 ♔e5 53 ♖g3 (53 ♔d2!?) **53...♘d5+ 54 ♔f2 ♔f5 55 ♖f3+ ♔g4 56 ♖g3+ ♔h4 57 ♔f3** (57 ♖b3?! g4 58 ♔g1 ♘f4 and ...♘d3) **57...♘f6**

My earlier optimistic recommendation 57...♗d7 58 ♔e4 ♘f6+(?!) is refuted by 59 ♔d4! with the idea of 59...♘g4 60 ♖g2 ♔h3 61 ♖g3+ ♔xh2 62 ♖f3 with a draw. 58...♘xb4 is better, since after the *Informator* suggestion 59 ♔e5 there is the unpleasant 59...♗b5(a4), but here too after 59 ♖b3! ♘c6 60 ♖b6 a5 61 ♖b7 or 59...a5 60 ♖c3 ♗c6+ 61 ♔f5 g4 62 ♖a3 a4 63 ♔f4 White should be able to hold on.

58 ♔g2 ♘h5 59 ♖e3 ♘f4+ (59...♔g4!?) 60 ♔g1

A concession. 60 ♔f3 was more solid: 60...♗c6+ (60...♘h3 61 ♖e5!; 60...♘d3 61 ♖e7!, aiming to exchange the h- and g-pawns) 61 ♔f2 ♗d7!? 62 ♖c3! (not now 62 ♔f3 ♘h3 63 ♖e5 ♘e6!) 62...♔g4 63 ♖g3+ ♔f5 64 ♖c3 with a probable draw.

60...♔g4 61 ♖g3+ ♔f5 62 ♖f3

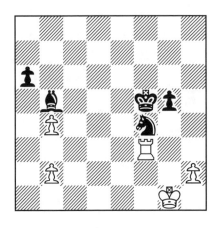

62...g4

62...♔e4 was hardly any better: 63 ♔f2 ♘d3+ 64 ♔g3 ♘xb4 (64...♘xb2 65 ♖f8 ♘c4(d3) 66 ♔g4! ♘e5+ 67 ♔xg5 ♘f3+ 68 ♔f6 ♘xh2 69 ♔e6 with a draw) 65 ♖f8! etc.
63 ♖e3 (of course, not 63 ♖f2? ♗e2 and wins) **63...♘d5**

If 63...♘d3 there is 64 ♖e7! ♘xb2 65 ♔f2, aiming to eliminate the g4-pawn.
64 ♖b3 ♔f4 (it is hard to believe that 64...♔g5 and ...♔h4 is any more promising) **65 ♔f2**

Not 65 ♔g2? ♘e3+ 66 ♔f2 ♘d1+ 67 ♔g2(e1) in view of 67...♗c4! and ...♘xb2.
65...♘f6 66 ♖a3 ♘e4+ 67 ♔g2 ♗e2 (I also studied 67...♘d2, but after 68 ♖a1 White has something resembling a fortress) **68 ♖b3** (68 ♖a1!? ♗b5 69 ♖c1) **68...♗f1+ 69 ♔g1 ♗c4** (69...♗b5!? and ...♘d2 was more accurate) **70 ♖a3 ♘g5 71 ♖c3 ♗d5 72 ♖a3 ♗e4?!**

Losing practically all the advantage, which would still have been retained by 72...♘f3+ 73 ♔g2 ♘e5+ 74 ♔g1(f2) ♗c4.
73 ♔f2! ♗b7 74 ♖d3?!

An answering error in the second time scramble. The accurate 74 ♖a5! ♘e4+ (74...♘f3 75 b5) 75 ♔g1 ♘d6 76 ♖a1(h5) would have given a fairly simple draw.
74...♘h3+ 75 ♔e1 (or 75 ♔f1 ♗e4 76 ♖a3 ♗c6!) **75...♗c6! 76 ♖d4+ ♔f3 77 ♖d3+ ♔e4 78 ♖g3 ♔f4**

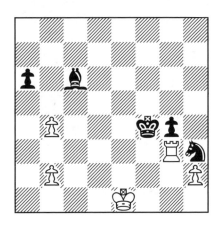

79 ♖a3?

With his flag again about to fall, Short loses a highly important tempo and the h2-pawn. Only the immediate 79 ♖c3 ♗b5 80 ♖c7(c8) ♔e3 (80...♔f3 81 ♖c3+) 81 ♖g7(g8) would have allowed him to fight for a draw.
79...♗b5 80 ♖c3 (80 ♖b3? ♘g5 81 ♔f2 ♘f3 82 ♔g2 would have run into 82...♗f1+! 83 ♔h1 g3 84 hxg3+ ♔xg3 and wins) **80...♘g5 81 ♖c8?!**

81 ♖c7 was more resilient, in order to parry 81...♔e3?! with 82 ♖e7+!. After 81...♘f3+ 82 ♔f2 ♘xh2 83 ♖f7+ ♔g5(e4) Black would still have had some work to do. Now, however, it all concludes quickly.
81...♔e3! 82 ♖h8 (82 ♖c3+ ♗d3) **82...♘f3+ 83 ♔d1 ♗e2+** (83...♔f2!) **84 ♔c2 ♘xh2!?**

84...♔f2 would also have won, but I had already seen the final position, in which because of zugzwang White has to allow his opponent to get rid of his 'bad' rook's pawn. **85 ♖xh2 g3 86 ♖h3** (86 ♖g2 ♔f3) **86...♔f2 87 ♔d2 g2 88 ♖h2 ♗b5 89 ♖h6 g1♕ 90 ♖f6+ ♔g2 91 ♖g6+ ♔f1 92 ♖xg1+ ♔xg1 93 ♔e1 ♔g2 94 ♔d1 ♔f3 95 ♔d2 ♔e4 96 ♔c3 ♔e3 97 ♔c2 ♔e2 98 ♔c1 ♗d3 99 b3 ♔e1 100 ♔b2 ♔d2 101 ♔a1 ♔c2 102 ♔a2 ♔c1 103 ♔a1** (or 103 ♔a3 ♔b1 104 ♔a4 ♔b2 etc.) **103...♗b1!**

Zugzwang! In view of the forced 104 b5 axb5 White resigned (**0-1**).

Before the resumption of this game I won, again with Black, against Agdestein – and ahead of schedule I reached the cherished 8½ points, which promised a rating of 2800. But, as is well known, one's appetite improves during the meal... In the concluding round I was opposed by the second strongest Yugoslav (now Bosnian) grandmaster, the 29-year-old Predrag Nikolic.

Game 63
G.Kasparov-P.Nikolic
Belgrade, 11th Round, 27.11.1989
Nimzo-Indian Defence E35

---

1 d4 ♘f6 2 c4 e6 3 ♘c3 ♗b4 4 ♕c2

I began playing this in 1988, setting aside both 4 ♘f3 (*Game Nos.3, 6, 13*), and 4 e3 (*Game No.26*).

4...d5 5 cxd5

I already had experience in the variation 5 a3 ♗xc3+ 6 ♕xc3 ♘e4 7 ♕c2 – Kir.Georgiev (Thessaloniki Olympiad 1988) and Renet (Evry (simul') 1989) were unable to hold out after 7...c5 8 dxc5 ♘c6 9 cxd5 exd5 10 ♘f3, while Nikolic (Barcelona 1989) went in for 7...e5 8 e3 exd4 9 cxd5 ♕xd5 10 ♘f3 ♘c6 11 ♘xd4 ♕xc2 12 ♘xc2 and held a somewhat inferior endgame. On this occasion I decided to employ a different plan, which I had successfully tried in Tilburg against Korchnoi.

5...exd5

Later the following line came to the fore: 5...♕xd5 6 e3 (6 ♘f3 ♕f5!, Beliavsky-Romanishin, Groningen 1993) 6...c5 7 a3 (Kasparov-Nikolic, Moscow Olympiad 1994) or 7 ♗d2 (Kasparov-Anand, both 2nd match game, New York 1995, and Frankfurt (rapid) 1999).

6 ♗g5 (it is rather early for 6 a3?! – Game No.25 in *My Great Predecessors Part IV*) **6...h6 7 ♗h4**

I had studied this position for quite a long time, which in the end produced good results.

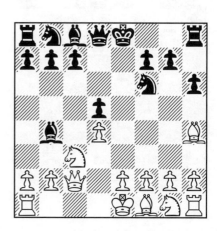

7...g5

For some reason Nikolic avoided the usual 7...c5 (*Game No.65*) and chose a new, strategically risky continuation.

8 ♗g3 ♘e4 9 e3 c6?!

Black hopes to calmly complete his development and defend his ragged kingside, in particular his backward h6-pawn. Alas, the dynamics of the position do not allow him time for such 'solid' moves. The correct approach is 9...h5 10 f3 ♘xg3 (not including 10...♗xc3+?! 11 bxc3, Bacrot-Smyslov, 2nd match game, Albert 1996) 11 hxg3 ♕e7 – this is the present-day fashion.

10 ♗d3 ♘xg3 11 hxg3 ♗e6 12 a3

12 f4 suggested itself, but first I set my opponent a choice: either to exchange his b4-bishop (which is undesirable), or retreat it, but to where?

12...♗f8

In order by ...♗g7 to support the weakened part of the battlefield. If 12...♗d6, apart from my *Informator* suggestion 13 0-0-0 ♘d7 14 ♘f3 and e3-e4, 14 f4!? is good, or, as in the game, 13 f4!.

13 f4!

The threat of f4-f5 prevents the natural development of the knight at d7.

13...gxf4

The g5-pawn cannot be maintained. After

13...♗g7 14 ♘f3 and 0-0-0 it is difficult for Black to find a useful developing move. His defence is also not eased by 13...♗g4 14 ♘f3 ♗xf3 (avoiding 14...gxf4 15 ♘e5!) 15 gxf3 gxf4 16 gxf4 ♘d7 17 0-0-0 ♘b6 18 e4! etc.

14 gxf4 ♗g4 15 ♗f5!

15 ♘f3 or 15 ♘h3!? would also have given an enduring advantage. However, I immediately began play aimed at exploiting the weakness of the light squares and the h6-pawn.

15...♗xf5 (15...♖g8 16 ♗xg4 ♖xg4 17 ♘f3 ♘d7 18 0-0-0 was hardly any more attractive) **16 ♕xf5 ♘d7 17 e4! ♕f6**

Also in another endgame – after 17...dxe4 18 ♘xe4 ♕e7 (otherwise White has a fearfully strong attack) 19 ♘f3 ♕e6 20 ♕xe6+ fxe6 21 ♔f2 Black would have faced a difficult struggle for a draw.

18 ♕xf6 ♘xf6 19 e5

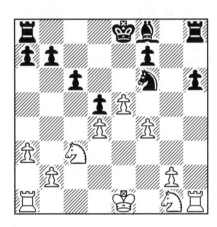

Now Black is cramped and the chronic holes on the kingside leave him little hope of saving the game.

19...♘d7 (or 19...♘g4 20 ♔e2 followed by ♔f3 and ♘ge2-g3) **20 ♘ge2 ♘b6 21 b3 ♖g8?!**

21...a5 22 a4 f6 was more resilient, at least getting rid of one of the weak pawns.

22 ♔f2 ♔d7

After 22...f6 in *Informator* I gave 23 e6(?),

which loses almost White's entire advantage in view of 23...♔e7! 24 f5 ♖g5 25 ♘g3 ♘c8 26 ♖h5 ♘d6 27 ♖ah1 ♗g7 etc. 23 ♔f3! is correct, with the ideas of g2-g4 and ♘g3-f5, and if 23...a5, then 24 ♘a4! ♘xa4 25 bxa4 is now strong.

Therefore here too 22...a5!? 23 a4 f6 was better, although the inclusion of the moves ...♖g8 and ♔f2 is to White's advantage.

23 ♘g3! ♖c8 (the undermining move 23...f6? is ruled out by 24 ♘h5) **24 ♔f3** (or 24 ♘f5!? ♖g6 25 ♔f3) **24...c5?!**

An active attempt, which merely hastens the end.

25 dxc5 ♖xc5 26 ♘ce2 (26 ♘ge2! was even better, followed by pressure on the d5-pawn and g2-g4) **26...♖c6**

Nothing was given by 26...♖c2 27 a4 ♖b2 28 ♖hb1! ♖c2 29 ♖c1 ♖b2 30 ♖ab1 ♖a2 31 ♘c3 ♖d2 32 ♖d1 and wins.

27 ♖hc1 (27 ♘h5(f5) or 27 a4! was no worse) **27...♖xc1** (27...♖cg6 28 ♖d1!?) **28 ♖xc1 ♗xa3 29 ♖a1 ♗c5**

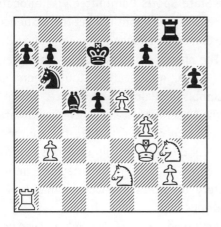

30 ♘f5!?

30 ♖xa7 would also have won – the desperate 30...♘c4!?, hoping for 31 ♖xb7+ ♔c6 32 bxc4 (32 ♖xf7?? ♘d2 mate) 32...♔xb7 33 cxd5 ♖d8 with drawing chances, is parried by the accurate 31 ♖a2! ♘e3 (otherwise ♘f5) 32 ♖a5! ♗b6 (32...b6 33 ♖a7+ ♔c6 34

b4!, but not 34 ♖xf7?? ♘c2! with the threat of ...♘e1 mate) 33 ♖b5 ♖g6 34 f5 ♖c6 35 ♘f4 and wins.

Instead of this excitement I preferred to pick off the h-pawn and create a powerful pawn phalanx.

30...♖a8 31 ♘xh6 ♔e6 32 g4 a5 33 ♖c1! ♘d7

If 33...♖c8 the simplest is 34 ♘f5 and ♖h1-h6+(h7) followed by the advance of the pawns.

34 ♘c3 (here too 34 ♘f5! with the threat of ♘ed4+ was simpler) **34...♖a6 35 ♖e1**

35 ♘f5 or 35 g5 would also have been decisive, but I wanted to exclude even the incorrect sacrifice 35...♘xe5.

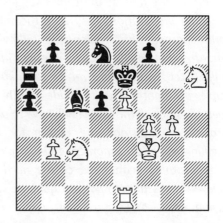

35...d4?!

Equivalent to capitulation, although the alternatives were also bad: 35...♘b6?! 36 f5+ ♔e7 37 e6! or 35...♗b4 36 f5+ ♔e7 37 ♘xd5+ ♔f8 38 ♘xb4 ♖xh6 39 g5! ♖h3+ 40 ♔g4 ♖xb3 41 ♘d5 ♖b5 42 ♘f6!.

36 f5+ ♔e7 37 ♘d5+ ♔f8 38 e6 (or 38 ♘xf7! ♘b6 39 ♘c7 and wins) **38...fxe6 39 fxe6 ♘b8 40 ♘f5 ♘c6 41 g5**

And in view of the inevitable breakthrough of the e- and g-pawns, Black resigned (**1-0**).

And so, after finishing 3 points ahead of

my closest pursuers, I reached the sky-high rating mark of 2805 – this was comparable to a long jump of nine metres! Taking inflation into account, my Belgrade achievement was almost comparable to my 2851 super record, attained in 1999.

Nikitin: *'To be honest, I didn't believe that Garry could reach 2800 in such a short time. But the incredible happened: with all his chess and non-chess disadvantages, although burdened with a mass of problems, a dozen major matters and hundreds of minor ones, after his customary jocular lamentation about poor health and a complete lack of energy, he already reached the 2800 mark by the end of 1989! I happened to be helping him in Tilburg, and at the time I suggested discussing preparations for the forthcoming world championship match the following year. After thinking for about a minute, Garry replied: "Let's wait until I return to Baku. A couple of months won't decide anything, especially since all the same I will have to play Karpov." I understood the reason for his unwillingness at that moment to build plans for the coming year: freed of the need to achieve some vitally important goal, he was playing easily and, above all, very confidently.'*

My appearance in Belgrade coincided with some concerts by the famous cellist and conductor Mstislav Rostropovich, a fanatical chess enthusiast and a long-standing supporter of Korchnoi. *'Sometimes I even dream chess'*, said the great musician, *'but I play very badly. No, I tell a lie: in my childhood I was a champion! True, of the entrance to our block, and this included girls...'* We found time to meet together. Rostropovich showed me his unique Stradivarius cello, and I showed him a few of my games.

Those months are memorable for the enormous democratic changes in Eastern Europe: the fall of the notorious Berlin Wall (which, incidentally, I publicly predicted back in 1987), the 'velvet revolution' in Czechoslovakia... The situation also changed in the USSR – one only has to mention the speeches by the disgraced academic Sakharov at the congress of peoples deputies!

The changes also affected Soviet chess. In November 1989, as a counter to the dominance of the State Sports Committee, an inaugural meeting of the independent Union of USSR Chess Players was held, and I was elected President. And at a December meeting of the country's chess players, in place of Sevastyanov the chairman of the Soviet Federation became Vladimir Popov, a minister in the Russian Federation government. This victory was unexpected: 109 of the 148 delegates voted against the State Sport Committee's protégé – a terrible blow to the authorities! Soon Krogius was pensioned off, and the Chess Administration of the State Sports Committee was altogether done away with (but not yet the influence of the Committee itself).

The chess year concluded with a grandiose GMA qualification tournament and assembly in Palma de Mallorca, where on 18th December 1989 the Grandmasters Association decided to take the running of the world championship under its control. It appeared that from that day the genuine history of professional chess might begin, and yet...

At the very end of December I was voted the top USSR sports person of 1989. In an interview regarding this I also said that in the forthcoming title match I would like to meet Karpov again: 'After all, I have not once won a match against him convincingly. I think this is the only thing that I have not yet managed to do in chess'.

After the Escape

International Tournament in Linares (17 February – 4 March 1990): 1. **Kasparov** – 8 out of 11; 2. Gelfand – 7½; 3. Salov – 7; 4. Ivanchuk – 6½; 5. Short – 6; 6–7. Gulko and Yusupov – 5½; 8. Beliavsky – 5; 9–11. Spassky, Illescas and Portisch – 4; 12. Ljubojevic – 3.

For me and those close to me 1990 was a critical year and probably the most difficult in my life. In my native Baku, to where I flew from Moscow on 6th January, there was great unrest: in connection with the conflict in Nagorno-Karabakh, anti-Armenian hysteria burst our everywhere. Two days later my mother and I, with Shakarov and Tsaturian, set off to one of our regular training sessions in Zagulba.

I will never forget 'black Saturday', the 13th of January. It was a beautiful sunny day and over the sea there was a rainbow, but in Baku mass pogroms were beginning on an unprecedented scale – seizures of flats, robberies, rapes and brutal murders. It was impossible to believe this, but people were attacked and beaten to death with iron bars, burned alive and thrown out of upstairs windows. Many Azeris saved their Armenian friends from being killed, but others, seeing the inactivity of the police and the army, were afraid to come to their aid.

My Moscow friends insisted on my immediate return, but I refused to fly out without my relatives and I racked my brains over how to save them. My aunt Nelli barely escaped the pogromists who broke into her flat, and a cousin of mine had to be freed from the headquarters of the Azerbaijan Popular Front. The telephone rang day and night. Acquaintances begged: 'Save us, save us!' My relatives and friends with their families reached Zagulba, where about 60 people assembled.

But even there it was not safe. The protection assigned to us by the authorities consisted of just two KGB officers, armed with pistols, whereas the pogromists had not only knives and iron bars, but also automatic rifles. At some point the telephone link was suddenly severed, and we were cut off from the outside world in a kind of trap.

It was then that a headquarters was set up in Moscow to save the 'Kasparov group', directed by Popov, the chairman of the USSR Chess Federation. He set up a special telephone link with Zagulba, and Boris Rogatin, the leader of the Soviet sports trades union, gained government permission to send a special plane to Baku. To fly to Moscow in the usual way was unrealistic, and not only because of the cancellation of flights and the deficit of tickets: at the approaches to the airport Azeri patrols were committing outrages. The expense of the rescue operation, including the admission of the refugees, was borne by the Union of USSR Chess Players and Moscow business acquaintances of mine.

The night before the flight, friends helped me to travel secretly to my home in Baku. This was a risky, even reckless step (the house was in the centre of the town), but I very much wanted to say farewell to my native home, which I was leaving for ever.

Our TU-134 left Moscow during the day on 17th January, and landed in Baku at dusk, at the very far end of the airfield (although the airport was held by paratroopers, the boarding was kept secret). It was to there by some half-forgotten track that we also approached – in two buses and two cars. Nikitin: *'How they managed to avoid meeting the Azeri patrols was a professional secret of the special forces, who assured Moscow that the safety of the Kasparov group on the way to the airport would be guaranteed.'* The boarding of the plane took no more than ten minutes: people had escaped from Baku virtually without any possessions. When everyone had sat down, I counted about a dozen free seats and together with the assistants I allocated them to mothers with children who were languishing in the waiting hall.

It was late in the evening that we landed in Moscow. Indescribable grief was etched on the faces of the people who descended from the plane on to the snowy ground. Some were even led out by hand, and some were in light indoor clothing. The terrible fate of refugees awaited them, a position in which many thousands of Armenians found themselves. It was easier for me than for others: my wife Maria lived in the capital. But her small two-room flat in a five-storey block built in Khrushchev's time could not even accommodate my mother, and I took on the job of making arrangements for my relations.

'Our flight was like something out of a film', I said at the time to a journalist from the Spanish newspaper *El Pais*. 'I picked up 60 people and miraculously saved their lives: travelling to the airport was a real adventure. Excuse me, but now I am in such a mental state that I am unable to give a political analysis.' Other words of mine were published in the press around the world: 'That which you have seen on television is nothing compared with what I have had to endure.'

In Moscow, with the help of Politburo member Alexander Yakovlev (who, I should remind you, saved me from disqualification in the summer of 1985) I obtained a meeting with Mikhail Gorbachev, and on 20th January, after the belated entry of Soviet troops into Baku, for a long time I talked to him, explaining how I saw things. Alas, this was in vain. Troops occupied the city, in order to save not the Armenians (there were none left in Baku), but the communist regime.

This was the plan from the very start... Soon I returned my Communist Party card to the Azerbaijan State Sports Committee, where I was registered, with a letter explaining why I was leaving this organisation. Then in the spring I took a very active part in the creation of the Democratic Party of Russia, and at the end May I was elected its deputy chairman. Thus unexpectedly – in the year of a world championship match! – my political activity began and Moscow became our second home.

Strangely enough, a month after the January tragedy I made a worthy debut in the leading Spanish event in Linares, although I had neither the strength nor the time to prepare seriously for this popular super-tournament. At last I was able to make the acquaintance of the well-known organiser Senor Luis Rentero – the owner of the Hotel Anibal, where we played and lived. Having secured a big prize fund, he imposed on the players an obligatory condition: not to agree a draw earlier than the 40th move.

In the absence of Karpov (in March he won the final Candidates match against Timman), my main rivals were considered to be the winner of the previous year's tournament, Vassily Ivanchuk, the third prize-winner in the World Cup, Valery Salov, and the victor at the recent GMA qualifying tournament, the 21-year-old Belorussian (now Israeli) Boris Gelfand – against whom I was paired with black at the start. A gripping battle ensued...

Game 64
B.Gelfand-G.Kasparov
Linares, 1st Round, 18.02.1990
King's Indian Defence E99

1 d4 ♘f6 2 c4 g6 3 ♘c3 ♗g7

Without hesitation! 'It was very interesting to cross swords for the first time with the world champion – especially with White, and in the very first round. I anticipated a King's Indian Defence – a fighting opening, which was also in my repertoire. And, indeed, a very tense battle ensued.' (Gelfand)

4 e4 d6 5 ♗e2 0-0 6 ♘f3 e5 7 0-0 ♘c6 8 d5 ♘e7 9 ♘e1 (9 ♘d2 – *Game Nos.42, 80*) **9...♘d7 10 ♘d3** (10 ♗e3 – *Game Nos.58, 77*) **10...f5 11 ♗d2 ♘f6 12 f3**

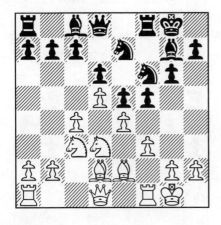

12...♔h8

After not much thought I made Geller's flexible move, vacating g8 for the knight. Although earlier I played only 12...f4 – and in Reggio Emilia (1991/92) I also played this against Gelfand, but instead of the usual 13 c5 g5 (Game No.21 in *Garry Kasparov on Garry Kasparov Part I*), there followed 13 g4 (killing the attack with ...g6-g5-g4) 13...g5 14 b4 h5 15 h3 ♔f7 with double-edged play.

13 ♖c1

If 13 b4 there can follow 13...♘eg8 14 c5 ♗h6 (Malaniuk-Gelfand, 56th USSR Championship, Odessa 1989) or 13...c6!? (Bareev-A.Kuzmin, Moscow 1989).

13...c5

Hampering White's offensive. 13...c6 14 ♗e3!? a6! is also not bad (Gelfand-Topalov, Amsterdam 1996; Gelfand-Nijboer, Wijk aan Zee 1998). But it was in the variation with ...c7-c5 that I had prepared something.

14 g4

Counter-prophylaxis.

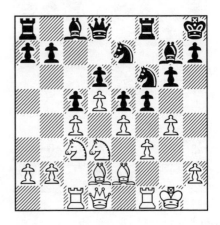

This position was judged to favour White: he succeeded in suppressing the opponent's counterplay on the kingside and in retaining the initiative on the queenside after both 14...♗d7 (14...h6 15 h4!) 15 a3 (Taimanov-Geller, 41st USSR Championship, Moscow 1973) or 15 ♘f2 (Ftacnik-Geller, Sochi 1977), and 14...♘eg8 15 ♔g2! (Ftacnik-Nunn, Vienna 1986).

14...a6! (an important improvement) **15 ♘f2**

Now if 15 ♔g2(?!) there is 15...b5! – the e4-pawn is rather weak! 'White does not want to play 15 a4 (if only because of 15...a5), and he is forced to spend a tempo on defence, but after this he does not succeed in securely reinforcing his kingside.' (Gelfand)

15...h6!

The point of my novelty – counterplay against the weaknesses in the opponent's position. 15...♗d7 is too sluggish: 16 a3 ♘eg8 17 b4 (Ftacnik-Ost Hansen, Esbjerg 1982).

16 h4 (not wishing to allow 16...fxg4 17 fxg4 g5 and ...♘g6-f4!, Boris goes in for a forcing variation with a pawn sacrifice) **16...fxg4 17 fxg4 ♘eg8** (aiming at the h4-pawn) **18 ♔g2 ♘h7 19 ♖h1 ♗f6**

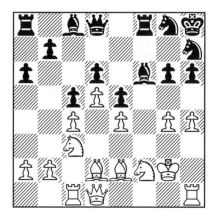

20 g5!

It is not possible to keep the kingside closed – 20 ♔g3?! (20 h5? ♗h4) 20...♘xh4+! 21 ♖xh4 ♖xf2, when 22 ♗xh6? ♘xh6 23 ♖xh6 ♕f8 24 ♕d2 ♗xg4! is bad for White, while after 22 ♕h1 ♕f8 or 22 ♗f3 ♗d7!? (22...b5 or 22...♘g5 23 ♔xf2 ♘xf3 will also do) 23 ♖h1 ♖xd2 24 ♕xd2 b5 Black has an excellent game.

20...hxg5 21 h5!

White is essentially forced to give up a pawn, but in return he opens the h-file and gains use of the strong-point g4.

21...♕e8?

21...♘e7 was much safer, but I did not want to block the f6-bishop's path to d8 and I was afraid of 22 ♗g4, but needlessly: after 22...♕e8! the situation would have remained completely unclear.

22 b4!

Again Boris quickly hit on the correct line. If 22 ♕a4 he looked at 22...b5!? (22...♗d7? 23 hxg6!) 23 cxb5 ♗d7, whereas I was considering 22...♕f7. '22 ♗g4 would have given sufficient compensation for the pawn, but the energetic move in the game seemed more tempting to me.' (Gelfand)

22...cxb4

If 22...b6, then 23 ♕a4! is now very strong: for example, 23...♕f7 (again 23...♗d7? 24 hxg6! will not do) 24 bxc5 bxc5 25 ♕c6 ♗e7 26 ♖cf1 or 23...♘e7 24 ♕xe8 ♖xe8 25 ♘a4 ♖b8 26 ♖b1 ♗d7 27 bxc5 ♗xa4 28 cxd6 ♘f5 29 exf5 gxf5 30 ♗e3 with winning prospects.

23 ♘a4 (threatening ♘b6; after 23 ♕a4? bxc3 24 ♕xe8 ♖xe8 25 hxg6 ♘e7! 26 ♖xh7+ ♔g8 27 ♖xc3 ♘xg6 Black simply has an endgame with an extra pawn) **23...♗d8 24 ♗xb4 ♗d7!?**

A tactical trick: 24...♖f6 25 hxg6 ♕xg6 26 ♗h5 ♕g7 27 c5! is really too unpleasant.

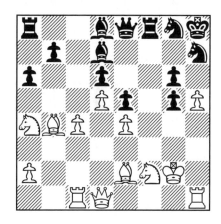

25 hxg6?

Gelfand took me 'at my word' and rejected 25 ♗xd6! because of 25...♗xa4, although after 26 ♕d3! (we hadn't seen this; the *Informator* move 26 hxg6(?) is weak because of 26...♕xg6! 27 ♗xe5 ♗f6 28 ♕d4 ♗xe5 29 ♕xe5+ ♕g7 with equality) 26...♖f4 (26...♖xf2+ 27 ♔xf2 ♗f6 28 ♖b1 b5 29 c5 is no better) 27 hxg6 ♕xg6 28 ♗xe5+ ♘gf6 29 ♗xf4 gxf4+ 30 ♔f1 ♕g5 31 ♖b1 or 28...♗f6 29 ♗xf4 gxf4+ 30 ♔f1 ♕g7 31 ♖b1 the armada of passed pawns would have promised White every chance of success.

25...♕xg6 (now the black queen is activated and the d6-pawn is defended – the storm has passed!) **26 c5?**

Seemingly a pretty move – but not without reason is it said that mistakes come in pairs. 26 ♗h5! was correct (26 ♗g4?! ♗xg4 27 ♕xg4 b5! is less good), and in the event of 26...♕f6 27 ♘d3 g4 28 ♕e2! (28...♗xa4?! 29 ♖cf1) or 27...♖h6 28 ♕c2! White has some advantage, although 26...♖xf2+! 27 ♔xf2 ♕xe4 would give Black sufficient counterplay: 28 ♕f3 ♕xf3+ (28...♕d4+!? 29 ♔g2 g4 30 ♕e2 ♗f5! is sharper) 29 ♗xf3 ♗xa4 30 ♗xd6 ♘gf6 31 ♗xe5 ♔g8 with equality.

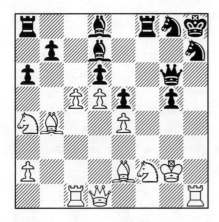

26...g4?

It was my turn to be tempted by pretty threats. After 26...♘gf6! the e4-point comes under fire and Black seizes the initiative: 27 ♗d3?, 27 ♕c2? or 27 ♘c3? is bad in view of 27...g4 and ...g4-g3, and the desperate piece sacrifice is hardly correct – 27 ♗h5?! ♘xh5 28 ♕xh5 ♕xh5 29 ♖xh5 ♗e8! (the immediate 29...♗xa4 is less clear in view of 30 c6! bxc6 31 ♗xd6 ♔g8 32 ♘g4). All that remain are moves with the c-pawn:

1) 27 cxd6 ♘xe4 28 ♘d3 g4 29 ♗e1 ♕xd6 30 ♕b3 ♖f3! with a powerful attack, or 28 ♗e1 ♘xf2 29 ♗xf2 ♕e4+ 30 ♗f3 ♖xf3 31 ♕xf3 ♕xf3+ 32 ♔xf3 ♗xa4, and the activity of the white pieces does not compensate for the lost material;

2) 27 c6 ♘xe4 28 ♘d3 (not 28 ♘xe4?

♕xe4+ 29 ♗f3 ♕xb4 30 cxd7 g4 or 28 cxd7? ♖xf2+ 29 ♔g1 ♕f7 30 ♗e1 ♕f4!) 28...bxc6 29 dxc6, and if 29...♗e6 30 c7 ♗d5 White saves the game with 31 ♔g1! ♕g3 32 ♘xe5! dxe5 (32...♕e4 33 ♗f3) 33 ♗xf8 ♗xh1 34 c8♕! ♖xc8 35 ♖xc8 ♕e4 36 ♗g7+! ♔xg7 37 ♕d7+ ♔h6 38 ♕h3+, but after 29...♗c8! Black has the advantage:

a) 30 c7?! (30 ♕e1 ♕f5!) 30...♗b7! 31 cxd8♕?! ♘c3+! 32 ♔g3 ♘xe2+ 33 ♕xe2 ♖axd8 or 31 ♔g1 ♗e7 32 ♕c2 g4 33 ♘xe5 dxe5 34 ♗xe7 ♕f7! with crushing threats;

b) 30 ♗h5 (comparatively the best chance) 30...♕g8! 31 ♖c2 (31 ♕e2?! g4 32 ♕xe4 ♗f5 33 ♕c4 ♗e6 and wins) 31...a5 32 ♗a3 ♘ef6 etc.

27 c6! (the only way!) **27...g3** (27...♗e8!?) **28 ♘d3** (a cool-headed reply) **28...bxc6 29 dxc6**

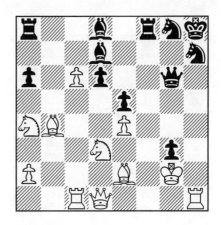

29...♖c8!

After making this move, I inwardly rejoiced: Black's position looked excellent. Gelfand: 'A move of enormous strength, which, frankly speaking, I had overlooked. I thought that White had seized the initiative (29...♕xe4+? 30 ♗f3), but the world champion had seen further. Now 30 cxd7? ♖xc1 31 ♘xc1 ♖f2+ or 31 ♕xc1 ♕xe4+ is bad for White. I had to switch to finding a way to save the game.'

30 ♗f3

30 ♗xd6! would have more reliably maintained equality: for example, 30...♕xd6 31 cxd7 ♖xc1 32 ♘xc1 ♕c6! 33 ♘d3 ♕xe4+ 34 ♗xf3 ♖xf3 35 ♕xf3 ♕xa4 or 30...♕xe4+ 31 ♗f3 ♖xf3 32 ♕xf3 ♗xc6 33 ♗xe5+ ♗f6 with further simplification and a probable draw.

30...♖xf3!

Far more aggressive than the submissive 30...♗xc6 31 ♘xe5! dxe5 32 ♗xf8 ♗xa4 33 ♕d6! (33 ♕xa4? ♖xc1) 33...♕xd6 34 ♗xd6 ♖xc1 35 ♗xe5+ ♗f6 36 ♗xf6+ ♘gxf6 37 ♖xc1 ♘g5, reaching the drawing haven.

31 ♕xf3 ♗g4

It was still possible to fight for an advantage by 31...♗xc6! 32 ♘c3 ♔g7 33 ♕xg3 ♘g5 with excellent compensation for the exchange.

32 ♕xg3 ♕xe4+

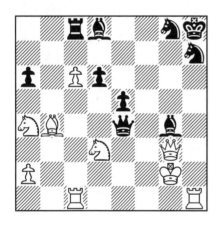

33 ♔g1!

Despite his time-trouble, Gelfand plays accurately. In *Informator* I recommended ♔h2(?), not noticing the strong reply 33...♗f3! 34 ♘f2 ♕xb4 35 ♕xf3 ♕xa4, winning.

33...♘gf6

33...♗f3 34 ♘f2 ♕xb4? (34...♕f5 is equal) 35 ♕xf3 ♕xa4 was no longer possible on account of 36 ♖xh7+! ♔xh7 37 ♕f5+. And 33...♗f5 34 ♗xd6 ♕d4+ 35 ♕f2 ♕g4+ 36

♕g2 ♕d4+ would only have led to a draw.

34 ♗xd6! (White has to hurry: ...♘h5 was threatened) **34...♕d4+**

The capture 34...♖xc6?! 35 ♖xc6 ♕xc6 was weaker in view of 36 ♗xe5! (instead of 36 ♘xe5, as given in *Informator*) 36...♕xa4 37 ♘f2 ♔g8 38 ♖h4!. And the complications after 34...♕xa4 35 ♗xe5 (35 c7? ♕d4+ and ...♕xd6) 35...♗b6+ 36 ♘f2! ♖xc6 (36...♔g8 37 c7 is no better) 37 ♖xc6 ♕xc6 38 ♕xg4 ♗xf2+ 39 ♔h2 ♕c2 40 ♔h3 would also have ended in a draw.

35 ♘f2 ♕xd6

'Black's activity is very dangerous, although in analysis after the game we were unable to find an advantage – everywhere White found the only moves to defend.' (Gelfand)

36 ♘xg4 ♕d4+

36...♘xg4 37 ♕xg4 ♗b6+! 38 ♘xb6 ♖g8 was simpler, with unavoidable perpetual check.

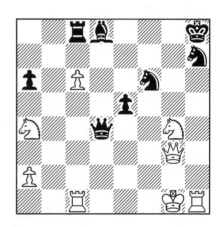

37 ♘f2

The attempt to squeeze out more – 37 ♘e3!? would have been parried by 37...♘e4! 38 ♖xh7+ (38 ♕h3 ♘g5!) 38...♔xh7 39 ♕h3+ ♔g7 40 ♖d1! (an insidious reply!) 40...♘g5!, maintaining equality: 41 ♕d7+ (41 ♕g3 ♕f4) 41...♕xd7 42 ♖xd7+ ♔f8 43 ♘d5 ♘e6.

37...♕xa4 38 ♕xe5 ♖c7

Black needlessly delays 38...♖xc6, after which the most accurate was 39 ♖xh7+! ♔xh7 40 ♕h2+ with the idea of 40...♔g7?! 41 ♕g2+ and ♖xc6, but 40...♘h5! (the last move before the time control!) 41 ♕xh5+ ♔g7 is correct, with a draw.

39 ♖h2

In severe time-trouble Boris played solidly, but passively. 39 ♖d1!? ♖g7+ 40 ♔f1 was more interesting, forcing 40...♕c4+! (again the last move before the time control!) 41 ♕e2 ♕xe2+ (41...♕g8 42 ♖d6 is more dangerous) 42 ♔xe2 ♗b6 with a draw.

39...♖g7+ (39...♖xc6!? – cf. the note to Black's 38th move) **40 ♖g2 ♗c7 41 ♕f5** (of course, not 41 ♕e6? ♕f4!) **41...♕xa2**

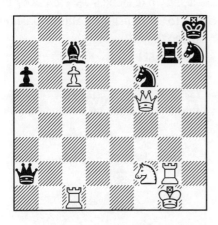

Forcing the exchange of the heavy pieces. White would not have been concerned by 41...♖xg2+ 42 ♔xg2 ♔g7 43 ♕e6 ♕f4 44 ♖c4.

42 ♕c8+ ♕g8 43 ♕xg8+ ♔xg8 44 ♖xg7+ ♔xg7 45 ♘d3 ½-½

Gelfand: '*At the closing ceremony this game was declared "the most brilliant in the tournament" and a prize was awarded – a sculpture weighing roughly 50 kilos. It was impossible to lift it. Garry, laughing, said to me: "Take it, take it". But I realised that,*

firstly, I would be unable to drag the statue home, and secondly, I had absolutely nowhere to put it – it would take up half the flat, not less. In the end we tossed a coin – and, fittingly, it was the world champion who won.'

In the 2nd round I won a game of very uneven quality against Short: both of us were only just running into form. But in the 3rd round I scored quite a good King's Indian win over Portisch, who aimed only to retain equality and was punished for his passivity.

My next opponent was the ex-world champion Boris Spassky, a person with an inimitable sense of humour. He arrived for the game in ceremonial dress, with a bow tie and, as he shook my hand, declared: 'A meeting with the world champion is a festive occasion for any grandmaster!'

> ## Game 65
> ### G.Kasparov-B.Spassky
> Linares, 4th Round, 21.02.1990
> *Nimzo-Indian Defence E35*

1 d4 ♘f6 2 c4 e6 3 ♘c3 ♗b4

On this occasion, instead of 3...d5 and his 'Carlsbad sufferings' (*Game No.51*), Spassky chooses the flexible Nimzo-Indian Defence, hoping to improve Black's play in the variation which brought me wins over Korchnoi (Tilburg 1989) and Nikolic (Belgrade 1989).

4 ♕c2 d5 5 cxd5 exd5 6 ♗g5 h6 7 ♗h4 c5 (7...g5 – *Game No.63*) **8 dxc5**

One of the *tabiyas* of that time (it is rash to play 8 0-0-0? ♗xc3! etc – Game No.39 in *My Great Predecessors Part II*).

8...♘c6

After 8...0-0 9 e3 ♘bd7 10 ♗d3 ♕a5 11 ♘e2 ♗xc3+ 12 ♕xc3 ♕xc3+ 13 ♘xc3 ♘xc5 14 ♗c2 Korchnoi found himself in a permanently inferior endgame. Black also had problems in the main line with 8...g5 9 ♗g3 ♘e4 10 e3 ♕a5 11 ♘e2 ♗f5 (the alternative is 11...♘c6 12 a3! ♗f5 13 ♕c1, Kasparov-Timman, Novgorod 1995) 12 ♗e5! 0-0 13 ♘d4 ♗g6?! 14 ♘b3 ♘xc3 15 ♗xc3! (Kasparov-Short, 9th match game, London 1993).

9 e3 g5 10 ♗g3 ♘e4 11 ♘f3 ♕f6

At the time this was considered the best reply, but then they all turned to 11...♕a5 12 ♘d2 and now 12...♗xc3 13 bxc3 ♕xc3 14 ♕xc3 ♘xc3 15 f3 ♗f5 with an acceptable ending (Korchnoi-Portisch, Amsterdam 1990) or 12...♘xc3 13 bxc3 ♗xc3 14 ♖b1 ♕xc5! (14...a6? 15 ♗d6, Glek-Yuferov, Moscow 1989) 15 ♖b5 ♕a3 16 ♖b3 ♗xd2+ 17 ♕xd2 ♕a5 (Spassky-Fischer, 10th match game, Yugoslavia 1992) 18 ♕xa5! ♘xa5 19 ♖b5 b6 20 h4, when Black nevertheless has problems (Dreev-Khairullin, Moscow 2009).

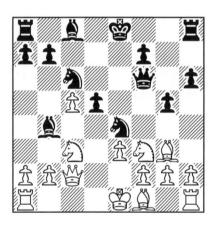

A game played six months before this, Gelfand-Balashov (56th USSR Championship, Odessa 1989) went 12 ♖c1 ♗f5?! 13 ♗d3 h5?, and here White could have landed the powerful stroke 14 ♘d4!, since 14...♘xd4 15 exd4 ♕xd4 is bad on account of 16 0-0 ♗xc3 (16...♘xg3 17 ♖fd1!! and wins) 17 bxc3 ♕f6 (17...♕xc5 18 ♗e5!) 18 ♗xe4 ♗xe4 19 ♕b3 etc. True, after 12...♗g4 13 ♗e2 0-0 14 0-0 ♗xc3 15 bxc3 ♘xc5 Black is comparatively okay.

12 ♗b5!

I had prepared this strong novelty the previous year, and its hour had finally arrived. The effect of it was such that the move 11...♕f6 disappeared from serious use, although, as we will see, the position is still full of life.

On encountering this unexpected bishop move, Spassky sank into painful thought. His elated mood quickly evaporated.

12...♘xc3?!

The first minor concession. Sounder was 12...0-0 (but not 12...♘xg3? 13 hxg3) 13 0-0, and now 13...♘xc3?! 14 bxc3 ♗xc5 (14...♕xc3? 15 ♕a4! ♗d7 16 ♖ac1 ♕a3 17 ♕c2 is even worse) 15 ♘d4 ♗d7 16 ♕b3 ♖ad8 17 ♗e2(d3) favours White, but after 13...♗xc3! 14 bxc3 ♘xc5 15 ♘d4 ♗d7 Black is close to equalising (Lahlum-Gashimov, Tromso 2007).

13 ♗xc6+ bxc6?!

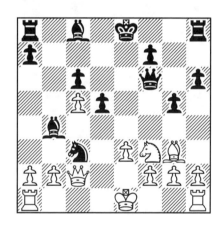

A second step towards the precipice: Spassky did not yet fully appreciate how dangerous his position had become. 13...♕xc6 14 bxc3 ♗xc5 was a better try, although after 15 h4!? g4 16 ♘e5 ♕a6 17 ♖d1 White would have retained the initiative.

14 a3! g4?

And this attempt to sharpen matters

proves fatal! It was essential to play 14...♗f5 15 ♕d2 ♗xc5 (after 15...♘e4?! 16 ♕xb4 Black does not have compensation for the pawn), and if 16 ♗e5! – either 16...♘e4 17 ♗xf6 ♘xd2 18 ♔xd2 ♖g8 19 ♖hc1 ♖g6 with a difficult but not yet altogether hopeless endgame, or 16...♕e7! with chances of holding out after 17 ♕xc3(!) 0-0 or creating counterplay in the event of 17 ♗xh8(?!) ♘e4 18 ♕c1 g4 19 ♘d4 ♗d7 20 b4 ♗d6 21 ♘f5 (21 ♘xc6 ♕h4! 22 g3 ♕h3) 21...♗xb4+! 22 ♔e2 ♕g5 23 ♘g3 ♘xg3+ 24 hxg3 ♗e7.

15 ♗e5!

A knock-out blow. Apparently Black was hoping to save the ending with opposite-colour bishops that arises following 15 ♘d4?! ♗xc5 16 ♕xc3 ♗xd4! or 15 axb4?! gxf3 16 ♕xc3 ♕xc3+ 17 bxc3 fxg2 18 ♖g1 ♗h3.

15...♘e4+ 16 axb4 ♕f5 17 ♗xh8 gxf3

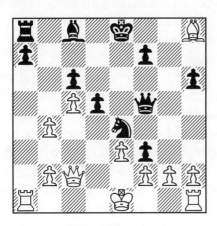

18 ♖g1!

I was terribly proud of this unusual, and at the same time solid move, which does not allow the opponent any chances of confusing matters. But the computer suggests White could also have won with 18 gxf3!? (even the 'wild' 18 g4?! ♕xg4 19 0-0-0 is not so bad) 18...♕xf3 19 ♖g1, when the best reply 19...♗g4 does not help in view of 20 ♖a6 (20 b5!?, 20 ♗e5!?)

20...♘xf2 21 ♗d4 ♘e4 22 ♖xc6 ♖b8! 23 ♖f1! ♕h3 24 ♖f4 ♕h4+ 25 ♔f1 ♗h3+ 26 ♔e2 ♗g4+ 27 ♔d3 ♕e1 28 ♖xh6 ♖xb4 29 ♖xe4+! dxe4+ 30 ♔xe4 ♗e6 31 c6 ♕h1+ 32 ♔f4 ♕d5 33 ♕e4.

18...♕g4

Slightly confused by my reply, Spassky missed a more resilient defence – 18...fxg2, and if 19 ♖xg2, then 19...♕f3 20 ♖g1 (20 ♖g8+ ♔e7 21 ♖g1 is no better) 20...♗g4, transposing into a sharp position from the previous note. However, I could have denied the opponent counterplay on the light squares: 19 ♕e2!? ♕h3 (19...♘g5 20 f4!) 20 f3! ♕h4+ (20...♘g5 21 0-0-0) 21 ♔d1 ♗h3 22 ♔c1, gradually converting the material advantage.

19 ♕d1! (a pretty manoeuvre with the simple threat of ♕xf3) **19...♘g5 20 ♕d4! ♘e4 21 ♕e5+ ♗e6 22 ♕f4**

By threatening the exchange of queens, White nevertheless picks up the f3-pawn.

22...♕g6 23 ♕xf3 (23 ♗d4!?) **23...f6 24 ♕f4 ♔f7 25 f3 ♘g5**

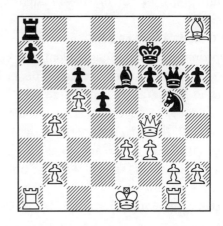

26 ♔d2! ♕f5 27 h4 ♕xf4 28 exf4 ♘h7 29 g4

And Black finally resigned (**1-0**).

This was my last tournament game with the 10th world champion. Our fierce chess battles concluded with the score +2–2=4.

Thus, I reached 3½ out of 4 – but Gelfand had the same number of points! In the next round 'by tradition' I was paired with black against Artur Yusupov, a recent semi-finalist in the Candidates cycle.

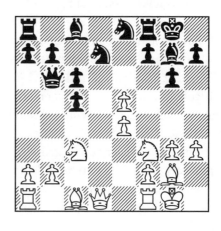

Game 66
A.Yusupov-G.Kasparov
Linares, 5th Round, 23.02.1990
King's Indian Defence E69

1 ♘f3 ♘f6 2 c4 g6 3 g3

On this occasion, instead of 3 ♘c3 ♗g7 4 e4 d6 5 d4 (*Game No.47*), Yusupov chooses a more solid set-up, guessing that his opponent will be eager to avenge his painful defeat in Barcelona.

3...♗g7 4 ♗g2 0-0 5 d4 d6

Earlier in such cases I used to reply 5...c6 and ...d7-d5 or immediately 5...d5 (as in our Belgrade game), but now I decided to play the King's Indian with ...♘bd7, which I had begun preparing for my next match with Karpov.

6 0-0 ♘bd7 7 ♘c3 e5 8 h3

In Linares 1992 our game went 8 e4 c6 9 ♗e3, and after 9...♘g4 10 ♗g5 ♕b6 11 h3 exd4 12 ♘a4 ♕a6 13 hxg4 b5 14 ♗e7 ♖e8 15 ♗xd6 bxa4 16 e5 c5! 17 b4! cxb4 18 ♕xd4 (18 ♖b1! is stronger) 18...♗b7 19 ♖ae1 (19 ♖fe1!?) 19...♖ac8 20 c5? ♕b5 21 ♕f4 ♗xf3 22 ♗xf3 ♘xc5 I was also able to seize the initiative.

8...c6 9 e4 ♕b6 (the alternative is 9...♖e8) **10 c5!?**

With this quickly played reply Artur surprised me: at that time 10 ♖e1 or 10 d5 was usually played. But later it was the sharp 10 c5 that killed many players' liking of the variation with 9...♕b6.

10...dxc5 11 dxe5 ♘e8

12 ♘a4

After 12 ♗g5(e3) White has to reckon with 12...♕xb2, while if 12 ♕c2, then 12...♕c7 or 12...♘c7 is not bad. But the most dangerous line for Black is considered to be 12 e6!? fxe6 13 ♘g5: for example, 13...♘e5 14 f4 ♘f7 15 ♘xf7 ♗d4+! 16 ♔h2 ♖xf7 17 e5 ♘c7 18 ♘e4 ♘d5 with complicated play – White has full compensation for the pawn (Shirov-Kasparov, Linares 1993).

12...♕a6!

If 12...♕b4?! White has the unpleasant 13 ♗d2! ♕xe4? (13...♕c4!?) 14 ♖e1 with a winning attack (which has been demonstrated more than once since 1983 by the Bulgarian grandmaster Nino Kirov). If 12...♕c7, then 13 e6!? fxe6 14 ♘g5 gains in strength (Modr-Karlik, Czechoslovakia 1992). It is more difficult to cast doubts on 12...♕b5 and ...♘c7 – this was played against Yusupov by Dolmatov (12th match game (rapid), Wijk aan Zee 1991), Damljanovic (Belgrade 1991), and Ljubojevic (Linares 1993).

13 ♗f4

Not a very lethal novelty. Black's defences are also solid in the event of 13 ♕c2 b6! (13...c4 14 e6! fxe6 15 ♗e3) 14 ♗f4 ♘c7 (Soppe-Servat, Argentina 1989). And the variation I suggested in *Informator*, 13 ♗g5 b5 14 ♘c3 ♘c7 15 ♗e7 ♖e8 16 ♗d6 ♘e6!

(previously 16...♕b6 had occurred) was later tested in Hübner-Kasparov (Dortmund 1992), where after 17 a4 (Hübner's recommendation 17 ♕d2(?!) is weak because of 17...♘d4!) 17...b4 18 ♘e2 ♕a5! and ...♗a6 a double-edged battle ensued.

13...♘c7 14 ♕c2 ♘e6

Already here we were both playing spontaneously, and I felt that Black's chances were not worse: he can contemplate ...b7-b5, ...c5-c4 and ...♘dc5-d3. White has an outpost at d6, but for the moment he can only establish a rook there, and it is liable to be attacked by Black's minor pieces.

15 ♖fd1 ♖e8

15...b5!? 16 ♘c3 ♖e8 or 16...c4 17 ♖d6 ♕b7 18 ♖ad1 ♘dc5 19 ♗f2 ♕c7 is more accurate, with complicated play (Adianto-Wojtkiewicz, New York 1991).

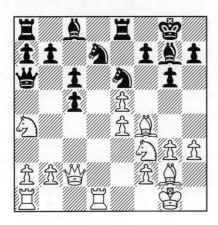

16 ♖d6

A blank shot. White could have tried to exploit my minor error by 16 b3!? with the idea of ♘b2.

16...♕a5

Again 16...b5!? was better: 17 ♘c3 (17 ♖xe6?! ♖xe6 18 ♘xc5 ♘xc5 19 ♕xc5 is hardly correct in view of 19...♕b6 or 19...♖e8 and ...♗e6) 17...♗f8 18 ♖dd1 c4 or 18...♘xf4 19 gxf4 c4.

17 ♖ad1?!

This routine developing move hands Black the initiative. The only way to fight for it was 17 b3!: for example, 17...♘xf4 18 gxf4 ♗f8 (my *Informator* suggestion 18...♗h6(?!) is questionable because of 19 ♖ad1! ♕c7 20 ♘g5 or 20 ♕d2) 19 ♘b2! ♕c7 (19...♗xd6 20 ♘c4) 20 ♖ad1 ♗xd6 21 exd6 ♕d8 22 e5 with enduring compensation for the exchange.

17...♘b6! 18 ♘xb6 (18 ♘c3 ♘c4 19 ♘6d3 b5 was also unattractive, although this was the lesser evil) **18...axb6 19 a3 ♕a4**

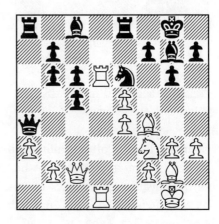

It is clear that White has lost the opening duel: the a8-rook comes into play on the a-file, the c8-bishop is also thereby 'developed', and, most importantly, Black is threatening to begin advancing his queenside pawn majority.

20 ♕e2?!

20 ♕d2! was more resourceful – in *Informator* I rated Black's chances very optimistically after 20...♕xe4 21 ♘d4 ♕xd4 22 ♖xd4 ♘xd4, but for the rook, knight and pawn it is difficult to overcome the queen. Therefore it is better to play 20...♗f8!? 21 ♗h6! ♗e7! (after 21...♗xd6 22 exd6 ♗d7 23 ♘e5 ♘f8 24 ♗xf8 ♖xe5 25 ♗e7 White has quite good play for the exchange) followed by ...b6-b5.

20...b5 (the advance begins!) **21 ♕e3** (after my *Informator* suggestion 21 h4 both 21...b4

and 21...♘xf4 22 gxf4 ♗g4 are strong)
21...b4 22 axb4 ♕xb4 23 ♖6d2

White is forced on to the defensive: if 23
b3, then 23...♖a3 24 ♖6d3 b6! and ...♗a6.
23...♖a2 24 ♖b1 (24 b3 ♖a3 or 24 ♕e2 b6!
also does not look good) **24...c4**

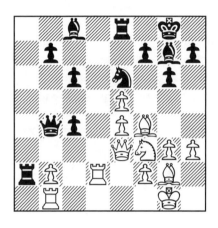

25 ♖c2

It is already hard to offer White any good
advice – it is not apparent how he can
oppose the advance of the black pawns: 25
♗f1 b5 26 ♘d4 (26 ♕b6 ♖a6!) 26...♘xd4 27
♕xd4 g5!, or 25 ♖c1 ♖xb2 (25...b5 26 ♖cc2)
26 ♖xb2 ♕xb2 27 ♖xc4 ♘xf4 28 gxf4 ♗e6
etc.

25...b5

My usual relaxation in an overwhelming
position. 25...♖d8! was more forceful – after
this in *Informator* I gave 26 ♗f1 b5 27 ♗g5
as 'unclear', but after 27...♘xg5 28 ♕xg5
♕a5(f8) Black has a clear advantage.

26 ♗h6

The exchange of the e6-knight by 26 ♘d4
would have done little to ease White's
position: for example, 26...♘xd4
(26...♘xf4!?) 27 ♕xd4 ♕e7 28 ♖d6 ♗xe5 29
♕xc6 ♗xf4 30 gxf4 ♕d7! or 26...♗f8!? 27
♘xe6 (27 ♘xc6? ♕a4 and wins) 27...♗xe6
28 ♕c1 ♕c5, also with winning chances.
26...♕c5! (26...♖d8!?) **27 ♕c1**

The exchange of queens would have been

fatal for White, but now he loses a pawn.
27...♘d4 28 ♗xg7 (28 ♘xd4 ♗xh6)
28...♔xg7 29 ♘xd4 ♕xd4 30 b3?! (desperation) **30...♖xc2 31 ♕xc2 c3**

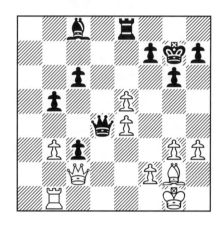

It is simply not possible to defend against
such a passed pawn.
32 ♖d1 (if 32 b4 c5!, creating a pair of connected passed pawns) **32...♕c5!**

With the threats of ...b5-b4 and ...♖xe5.
32...♕xe5?! was inaccurate in view of the
reply 33 b4!, although even here after
33...♕f6! and ...c6-c5 Black would have
retained the advantage.

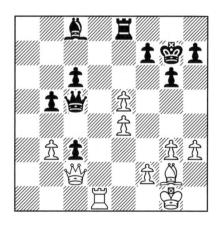

33 b4!? ♕xb4 34 ♖d3 c5 35 ♖xc3 (Artur has
found a way of getting rid of the c3-pawn,
but new troops move up to replace it) **35...c4
36 f4 ♕c5+ 37 ♔h2 ♖d4**

Again 37...♖d8! with the idea of 38 ♕c1 ♖d4 was more forceful.

38 ♖f3 b4!? (38...♗b7 or 38...♖d8 would have won without difficulty, but I was striving for brilliancy) **39 ♕a4!**

Has Black really blundered, overlooking this double attack?

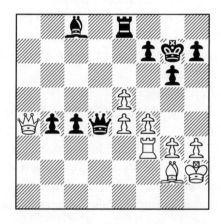

39...c3!! (no, it was not a blunder, but precise calculation!) **40 ♖xc3**

40 ♕xe8 ♕d7! 41 ♕xd7 ♗xd7 with the threat of ...c3-c2 was also hopeless. Although a whole rook down, Black inevitably queens one of his pawns:

1) 42 ♖d3 ♗e6! 43 f5 gxf5 44 exf5 ♗xf5 45 ♖f3 c2 46 ♖f1 ♗d3! (simpler than 46...b3 47 ♗d5 b2 48 ♖xf5 ♔f8!, but not 48...c1♕? 49 ♖xf7+ ♔g6 50 ♖f6+ with perpetual check) 47 ♖c1 b3 and ...b3-b2;

2) 42 e6 ♗xe6 43 f5 (43 ♖f1 b3 etc) 43...♗c4! 44 f6+ ♔g8! 45 ♗f1 ♗xf1 46 ♖xf1 c2 47 ♖a1 h5 48 e5 b3 49 ♖a8+ ♔h7 50 e6 c1♕ 51 exf7 ♕d2+, picking up the rook.

40...♗d7! 41 ♖c4! ♗xa4

Transposing into a technically won ending. 41...♕xc4 42 ♕xd7 ♖e6! was more immediately decisive, but this demanded some calculating.

42 ♖xd4 ♖b8 43 ♗f1 (43 ♗f3 ♗c2 44 ♗d1 b3 45 ♔g2 ♗b1! or 45 g4 ♖c8! would also not have saved White) **43...♗c2!**

The final precise touch: for the b-pawn White has to give up his bishop.

44 ♗c4 (of course, not 44 ♗d3 b3 45 ♗xc2 bxc2 46 ♖c4 ♖b2) **44...b3 45 ♗xb3**

Or 45 ♖d7 b2 46 ♗a2 (46 ♗xf7 ♔f8) 46...♖a8 47 ♖xf7+ ♔h8 48 e6 ♖xa2 49 e7 ♗a4 and wins.

45...♖xb3 46 g4 ♖e3 47 f5 gxf5

Avoiding a little trap: 47...♖xe4? 48 f6+! ♔h6 49 ♖xe4 ♗xe4 50 e6! ♗d5 (it is even possible to lose: 50...fxe6? 51 g5+! ♔xg5 52 f7) 51 e7 ♗c6 52 h4! g5 53 h5, with a drawing fortress.

48 exf5 ♖xe5 49 ♖d2 ♗a4 50 ♔g3 ♖e3+ 51 ♔h4 ♗b5 52 ♖d5 ♗d3

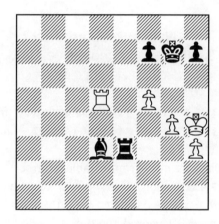

Since the h1-square is of the same colour as Black's bishop, he has no problems in converting his extra piece. Only he must not succumb to 52...♗f1?! 53 f6+! ♔f8 (53...♔xf6? 54 ♖f5+; 53...♔g6? 54 ♖g5+) 54 ♖d8+ ♖e8 55 ♖d1 ♗b5 56 ♔g5, prolonging the resistance.

53 ♖c5 h6 54 ♖c3 ♖f3 55 ♖b3 ♗e2 56 ♖b2 (or 56 ♖xf3 ♗xf3 57 ♔g3 ♗d1 58 ♔f4 f6 59 h4 h5! 60 g5 ♗c2, winning the f5-pawn and the game) **56...♗f1 57 ♖h2 ♔f6 58 ♖h1 ♔e5 59 ♖h2 f6! 60 ♖h1 ♔e4! 61 ♖h2 ♔f4! 62 ♖h1 ♗g2 63 ♖h2 ♖g3**

And in view of 64 ♔h5 ♖xh3+, White resigned (**0-1**).

After this win I had 4½ out of 5, but Gelfand was still level with me! True, in the next round both leaders showed signs of fatigue: Boris with White ruined a completely won game against Short, and I, also with White, was unable to beat Ljubojevic – the game did not go well right from the opening.

Still, I had finally burst half a point ahead, but in the 7th round I had to play Vassily Ivanchuk with Black. He was just a point behind me and, of course, was burning with the desire to justify his reputation as one of the tournament favourites, and at the same time gain revenge for previous failures.

Game 67
V.Ivanchuk-G.Kasparov
Linares, 7th Round, 25.02.1990
Sicilian Defence B97

1 e4 c5 2 ♘f3 d6 3 d4 cxd4 4 ♘xd4 ♘f6 5 ♘c3 a6 6 ♗g5 e6 7 f4 ♕b6 (7...♕c7 – *Game No.61*) **8 ♕d2**

Black is quite comfortable after 8 ♘b3 ♗e7 9 ♕f3 ♘bd7 10 0-0-0 ♕c7 11 g4 b5 12 ♗xf6 ♘xf6 13 g5 ♘d7 14 a3 ♖b8 (Topalov-Kasparov, Novgorod 1997) or 11 ♗d3 b5 12 a3 ♖b8 (Leko-Kasparov, Linares 2001).

8...♕xb2

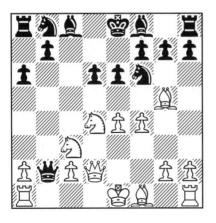

9 ♖b1

9 ♘b3 ♕a3 10 ♗xf6 gxf6 11 ♗e2, which became fashionable after the 11th game of the Spassky-Fischer match, was a variation that I tried it in my youth with White, and later it was unsuccessfully played against me by Short (c.f. Game No.18 in *Garry Kasparov on Garry Kasparov Part I*).

9...♕a3 10 f5 (10 e5 – Game No.121 in Part II and Game No.67 in Part IV of *My Great Predecessors*) **10...♘c6 11 fxe6 fxe6 12 ♘xc6 bxc6 13 ♗e2**

After 13 e5 dxe5 14 ♗xf6 gxf6 15 ♘e4, instead of Fischer's 15...♗e7, I had prepared a continuation which was tried back in 1980 by the Danish master Poulsen and recommended to me in 1986 by Magerramov: 15...♕xa2! 16 ♖d1 ♗e7 17 ♗e2 0-0 18 0-0 ♖a7! (an example: Vallejo-Kasparov, Moscow 2004).

13...♗e7 14 0-0 (14 ♖b3 ♕a5!) **14...0-0 15 ♖b3** (15 ♔h1 ♖a7!) **15...♕c5+**

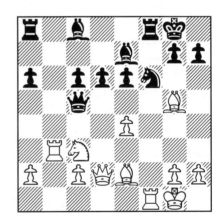

16 ♗e3

The present-day fashion is for 16 ♔h1 d5!? 17 e5 ♘d7 18 ♖xf8+ ♔xf8 19 ♗e3 ♕a5 20 ♗g4 (Ivanchuk-Grischuk, Dagomys 2010), and here the analysts recommend 20...♕c7!? with chances for both sides.

16...♕e5 17 ♗f4 (17 ♗d4 ♕a5 18 ♗b6 ♕e5 ½-½, Short-Kasparov, Novgorod 1995)

17...♛c5+ 18 ♔h1 ♞g4! 19 h3 (19 ♗xg4 e5)
19...e5 20 ♞a4 ♛a7 21 ♗c4+

21 hxg4 exf4 22 ♞b6 ♗e6 23 ♞xa8 ♗xb3
24 axb3 ♛xa8 is hardly any better for White
(Ivanchuk-Grischuk, Nice (rapid) 2010).

21...♔h8 22 hxg4 exf4 23 ♞b6

All these well-known moves were made
very quickly.

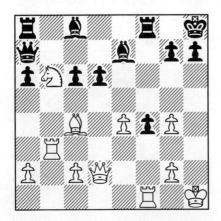

Earlier 23...♖b8 had occurred: 24 ♖xf4
♗d7 (not 24...♖xb6? 25 ♖xf8+ ♗xf8 26 ♛f2!,
or 24...♖xf4 25 ♛xf4 ♖xb6? 26 ♛f7!) 25
♞xd7 ♛xd7 26 ♖f5! (26 ♗xa6 ♛e6! is not so
clear, Enders-Stohl, Kecskemet 1989)
26...♖xb3 27 cxb3 with a minimal advantage
for White (Spraggett-A.Sokolov, 5th match
game, Saint John 1988), which does not
disappear even after the better move from
correspondence play – 26...♛a7!?.

23...d5!

A novelty! 'This game demonstrates the
direction in which chess thinking is moving.
In the quiet of a player's study, interesting
forcing variations are analysed, and new
continuations are found even after the
twentieth move.' (Gipslis)

24 exd5 cxd5

Here Vassily thought for the first time
(with what to capture on d5?). From this
point both players began thinking for an
agonisingly long time over nearly every
move – and in just ten moves they ended up
in severe time-trouble.

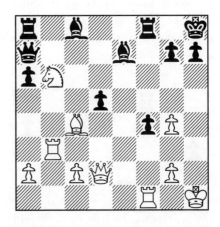

25 ♗xd5

White cannot be satisfied with 25 ♛xd5?!
♗b7 26 ♛h5 f3! (my *Informator* suggestion
26...♖ad8 is weaker because of 27 ♗d3
♖xd3! 28 cxd3 f3 29 ♔g1! g5!? 30 d4! ♗f6 31
gxf3 ♗xd4+ 32 ♔g2 ♗xb6 33 ♛h6 ♗c5 34
♖d1 ♗a8 35 ♖d8! with equality) 27 gxf3
♖ad8 with a dangerous attack (28 ♔g2?
♖d2+ 29 ♖f2 ♖xf2+ 30 ♔xf2 ♗e4!), and 25
♞xd5 ♗xg4 26 ♞xe7 ♛xe7 27 ♖xf4 ♛e5 is
equivalent to agreeing a draw.

25...♖b8 26 ♞xc8 (26 ♖xf4? ♖xb6 27 ♖xf8+
♗xf8 28 ♛f2 no longer works because of
28...♖h6+) **26...♖bxc8**

The resulting position is objectively close
to a draw, but the presence of the heavy
pieces and opposite-coloured bishops im-
parts a latent tension and sharpness. A 'war
of nerves' commences.

27 ♖h3!?

Eager to win, Ivanchuk aims to be the first
to create threats to the enemy king. Nothing
was given by the plausible 27 ♖xf4 (27 c4
♛d7!) 27...♖xf4 28 ♛xf4 ♖f8 29 ♖b7 (my
earlier recommendation 29 ♛c1(?!) is worse
in view of 29...♛f2!, but 29 ♛e5(e3) firmly
maintains the balance) 29...♛c5! (29...♛xb7
30 ♛xf8+ ♗xf8 31 ♗xb5 a5 is more tedious,

with equality) 30 ♖b8! ♗d8! 31 ♗f7 (but not 31 ♖c8? ♕e7 32 ♕g3 ♕d7 33 ♖c5 ♗e7 and wins – Stohl) 31...♕xc2 32 g5 (not blundering with 32 ♕d6? ♕c1+ 33 ♔h2 ♕c7 and wins) 32...♕c5(d3) 33 g3 with an obvious draw.

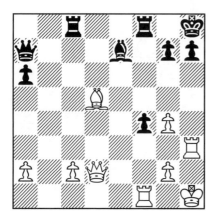

27...♕b6!

There is not a lot of choice. If 27...♕c7, then 28 ♕d4! is unpleasant, while simply making an escape square with 27...h6 did not appeal to me because of 28 ♖xf4 ♗g5 (28...♗d6!?) 29 ♖xf8+ ♖xf8 30 ♕e2!? (not 30 ♕xg5 ♖f1+ 31 ♔h2 ♕g1+ 32 ♔g3 ♕f2+ with perpetual check), and although after 30...♕d7 Black is not losing, there is no reason for him to concede the initiative. Therefore I decided to activate my queen.

28 ♖e1

This time the capture 28 ♖xf4? is bad because of 28...♕b1+ 29 ♔h2 ♗d6 30 ♖xh7+ ♔xh7 31 ♗e4+ ♔h8 32 ♕xd6 ♖xf4 33 ♕xf4 ♕b8! (Stohl). But in later correspondence play 28 ♕d3 h6 29 c4 ♖ce8 or 28 c4 ♗g5 29 ♕c2 h6 was tried, in each case with equality.

28...♗g5

Another discovery by modern correspondence players: it is simpler to neutralise the pressure on the e-file – 28...♖ce8! 29 ♕e2 (29 ♖e5? ♗c5!; 29 ♖e6?! ♕d8!) 29...h6 with equality.

29 ♖e6

This looks energetic, but 29 ♖e5!? ♕f6 30 ♕e1 was more unpleasant for Black, when he is forced to defend by 30...h6 31 c4 ♖b8 or 30...f3 31 ♖xf3 ♗f4.

29...♕d8!

Of course, there is no sense in aiming for a draw and suffering after 29...♕b1+?! 30 ♔h2 ♕xc2 (30...♕b8? 31 ♖xh7+! or 30...h6? 31 ♖hxh6+! leads to mate) 31 ♕xc2 ♖xc2 32 ♗e4 and the capture on h7.

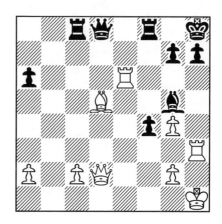

30 c4!?

Ivanchuk does not even think of curtailing the battle by 30 ♖d6 ♕xd6 31 ♖xh7+ ♔xh7 32 ♗e4+ ♔g6 33 ♗xg6+ ♔xg6 34 ♕d3+ with perpetual check, or 30 ♕d3 ♗h4 31 ♗e4 (31 ♖e5? ♕f6!) 31...♕xd3 (31...♖f6!? 32 ♖e5!) 32 ♗xd3 g5, intending ...♖fe8 with equality.

30...♖b8?!

I decided to activate the rook which was keeping an eye on the c4-pawn. The nervy 30...f3?! was unfavourable in view of 31 ♕d3 fxg2+ 32 ♔xg2 ♗h4 33 ♖f3 ♕g5 34 ♕d4! – thanks to the energy of White's pieces, his chances are better, despite the open position of his king. However, the immediate blocking of the h-file would have easily maintained equality: 30...♗h4! 31 ♕d3(c2) ♖e8 or 31 ♕e2 ♖b8.

31 ♕d3?!

A small favour in return. Black would have been set more problems by 31 ♕e1!? ♖e8 32 ♕e4 h6 33 ♖b3 ♖xe6 34 ♕xe6 ♖xb3 35 axb3 ♗e7 36 ♔g1.

31...♗h4

31...h6 was also good, and if 32 c5 ♖b5 with equality. In time-trouble I was afraid of 32 ♕g6 with the threat of ♗e4, but 32...♗h4! would extinguish the attack: 33 ♗e4 ♕d1+ 34 ♔h2 ♗g3+ with perpetual check.

32 ♗e4

The attempt 32 c5 would now be parried by 32...♖e8! (32...♖b5?! 33 ♕c2!) 33 ♖xe8+ ♕xe8 34 ♗e4 ♕e7 35 c6 (35 g5 ♖d8 and ...♕xg5) 35...g6 36 c7 ♖c8 37 g5 ♗xg5 38 ♗xg6 h6.

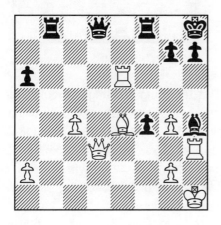

32...♕g5!?

With my flag almost about to fall, I poured fuel on the fire, by avoiding the exchange of queens and a probable draw after 32...♕xd3 33 ♗xd3 g5 or 32...♖f6 33 ♖e5 ♕xd3 (or 33...♖d6) 34 ♗xd3 g5.

This was a risky decision: by giving up his h7-pawn, Black exposes his king.

33 ♗xh7?!

An instantaneous reply, and not the best. White is slightly worse after 33 ♕d1 ♖fe8 or 33 ♗f5 ♖be8. But 33 ♕e2! ♖fe8 34 ♗d3 (not

34 ♗xh7? ♖xe6 35 ♕xe6 f3! 36 ♖xf3 ♔xh7 37 ♕e4+ ♕g6 and wins) 34...♖xe6 35 ♕xe6 would in turn have perplexed Black, although there is 35...g6 36 c5 ♔g7 37 c6 ♕c5! with equality.

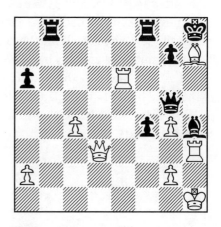

33...♖fd8?!

This natural move does not change the evaluation of the position, but, taking into account my opponent's desperate time-trouble, I missed a definite winning chance – 33...f3!, for example:

1) 34 ♖xf3? (or 34 gxf3? ♖fd8! 35 ♕f1(e2) ♔xh7) 34...♖xf3 35 gxf3 ♗g3! 36 ♔g1 ♕c5+ or 35 ♕xf3 ♔xh7, and White cannot hold out a piece down (36 ♔h2 ♕c5! 37 ♕e4+ ♔g8 38 ♖xa6 ♕c7+ 39 ♔h1 ♗g3);

2) 34 ♗f5? (an ineffective interference move) 34...♕c1+ 35 ♔h2 ♕f4+ 36 ♔h1 fxg2+ 37 ♔xg2 ♕f2+ 38 ♔h1 ♖b2 39 ♕f3 ♖b1+! 40 ♗xb1 ♖xf3 41 ♖e8+ ♖f8 42 ♖xf8+ ♕xf8 43 ♖xh4+ ♔g8 and wins;

3) 34 ♗e4! (the only saving move!) 34...f2 35 ♕f1 ♕xg4, and in *Informator* I gave only the losing line 36 ♗f3? ♕xh3+! 37 gxh3 ♖xf3 38 ♖e4 (38 ♔h2 ♖bf8!) 38...g5! 39 ♔g2 ♖g3+ 40 ♔h2 ♖f8 (...♖g3 is threatened, and 41 ♖g4 ♖e3! or 41 ♕a1+ ♔g8 42 ♖e7 f1♘+! is hopeless for White), overlooking 36 ♔h2! (again the only move!) 36...♖f4 (36...♖bd8 37 ♗d5!) 37 ♖g6! (not 37 ♗d5? ♕f5 38 ♖ee3

g5!) 37...♕h5 38 ♗d3 or 37...♕h5 38 ♖e6 with a draw.

34 ♕c2

This retreat has only one practical drawback: it allows the dangerous ...f4-f3 breakthrough. After 34 ♕f1? ♔xh7 35 ♕e1 ♔g8! the weakness of White's back rank causes his downfall (36 ♖xh4 ♖b1!), but he could easily have maintained equality by 34 ♕e2!? ♔xh7 (34...f3? 35 ♕xf3! ♔xh7 36 ♕g3) 35 ♖e5 ♕h6! 36 ♖h5 ♖b1+ and ...♖dd1 (Stohl), or 34 ♕f5! ♖d1+ 35 ♔h2 ♗g3+ 36 ♖xg3 fxg3+ 37 ♔xg3 ♕xf5 38 ♗xf5 ♖c1.

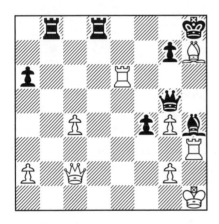

34...f3! (better late than never!) **35 ♖xf3?**

Strangely enough, in *Informator* I did not attach a question mark to this move, but gave only 35 gxf3? ♖d2 and wins. Meanwhile, with 35 ♗f5! White could have forced a draw: 35...♖b2! (but not 35...♖d2? 36 ♕b3! fxg2+ 37 ♔g1 and wins) 36 ♕xb2 ♖d1+ 37 ♔h2 ♕f4+ 38 g3 ♖d2+ 39 ♔h1! ♖d1+ with perpetual check (Stohl). 35 ♗e4 would also have done, but in this case, apart from the drawing 35...♖b2, Black could have maintained the intensity of the battle by 35...♖d2!? 36 ♕c1 f2 37 ♖f3 ♔g8.

35...♖d2 (now White is in a desperate position, but – the things that happen in time-trouble...) **36 ♕e4**

It was equally bad to play 36 ♕g6 ♖d1+

37 ♔h2 ♕c1! 38 ♖e8+ ♖xe8 39 ♕xe8+ ♔xh7 40 ♕h5+ (40 ♕e4+ g6 41 ♖f7+ ♔h6 42 g3 ♕c3!) 40...♕h6: for example, 41 ♕xh6+ ♔xh6 42 ♖h3 ♔g5 43 g3 ♖d2+ 44 ♔g1 ♔xg4! 45 ♖xh4+ ♔xg3 or 41 ♕f5+ g6 42 ♕f7+ ♕g7 43 ♕e6 ♕d4! (rather more accurate than the *Informator* suggestion 43...♕c7+) 44 ♕f7+ ♔h6 etc.

36...♖d1+ 37 ♔h2

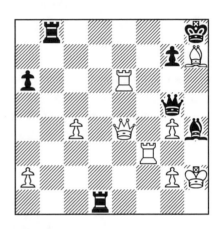

37...♖e1?

This tempting exchange of rooks, leading to the win of the bishop, proves to have a flaw, as does 37...♗f2? 38 ♖e8+! (38 ♖h3? ♖h1+!) 38...♖xe8 39 ♕xe8+ ♔xh7 40 ♖h3+ ♗h4 41 ♕e4+ g6 42 g3 with a draw. Only 37...♕c1! was decisive, forcing 38 ♖e8+ (cf. the previous note).

38 ♕f5 (or 38 ♕c6 ♖xe6, but not 38...♔xh7? 39 ♖xe1 ♗xe1 40 ♕e4+ ♔g8 41 ♕e6+! ♔h7 42 ♕xe1 ♕xg4 43 c5 and wins) **38...♖xe6 39 ♕xe6 ♔xh7 40 ♕e4+ g6**

The flippant 40...♔g8? would have led to an unexpected catastrophe after 41 ♖f5!. And in the event of 40...♕g6?! 41 ♕f4 and ♖h3 (Stohl) White would have regained the bishop with a guaranteed draw.

The natural block with the pawn was the last move before the time control, but neither player knew this, since we had both long since given up recording the moves!

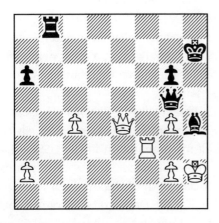

41 ♖h3?

In the time scramble Vassily misses the only move 41 ♖f7+!, when it is now Black who has to save the game: 41...♔g8! (but not my *Informator* suggestion 41...♔h6? 42 ♕d4 ♖g8 43 g3! ♕d8 44 ♖d7! ♕b8 45 ♕d2+! ♗g5 46 ♕g2 ♗h4 on account of the mating line 47 g5+! ♔xg5 48 ♕d2+ – Stohl) 42 ♕e6! ♔h8 43 g3 ♕h6 44 ♔g2 ♗g5 45 ♕e5+ ♔g8 46 ♕d5 ♔h8 (there is nothing else) 47 ♕e5+ with a draw.

41...♔g7 42 ♕d4+ ♔g8 43 ♕e4 (or 43 g3 ♕f6) **43...♕f6!**

43...♖d8!? 44 ♖b3 ♗f2 45 g3 ♗c5 would also have been decisive. But in reply to 43...♕f6 White resigned (**0-1**), after deciding not to look for chances after 44 ♖f3 ♕d6+ 45 g3 ♔g7 46 ♖d3 ♕e7! (instead of 46...♗xg3+?! 47 ♖xg3, as given in *Informator*) or 45 ♔h3 ♔g7! (45...♗g5? 46 c5! with a draw) 46 c5 (46 ♔xh4 g5+!) 46...♖h8!.

A very complicated game. Ivanchuk, like Gelfand in the 1st round, played sharply for a win against me – the leaders of the young generation did not tremble before the world champion! This was the first time I had encountered this approach during more than three years of tournament play. It was a battle of a different level of intensity, and I

had to solve some fundamentally new problems.

After this win I reached 6 out of 7 and I began to think about further increasing my rating. But in the 8th round, after initiating risky gambit play in the opening (cf. *Game No.43*, note to Black's 12th move), I suffered a disaster in my game with Gulko – and I was promptly caught by Gelfand, who beat Spassky. And then my winning drive as though evaporated: there followed protracted draws in favourable endings with Salov and Beliavsky.

Gipslis: *'The joint leadership was maintained to the last day, when Kasparov again demonstrated his wonderful fighting qualities. He scored the only win (over Illescas) and secured the first prize – not only eight thousand dollars, but also a Suzuki jeep.'*

Ivanchuk: *'It was quite right that the world champion won. I would mention first of all Kasparov's splendid opening preparation, and also his ability and desire to fight to the end.'*

Match with Psakhis

Six-game training match: **Kasparov**–Psakhis (La Manga, 13-21 July 1990): 5-1.

In the spring of 1990 I was faced with a serious question of how to prepare for the world championship match. For the first time in many years I was unable to hold my training sessions in Zagulba. All my life I had regularly prepared in the same place, in familiar surroundings. Daily runs along the banks of the Caspian Sea, intensive swimming, regular games of football and tennis – after such training I did not have to fear any physical stress. In an instant I had been deprived of all this, and I felt completely unsettled.

Before each previous match for the world

championship I had determined the necessary level of work to be one hundred days. On this occasion it was barely possible to scrape together 60 training days, but these were far from those untroubled days that I had previously spent on the Caspian Sea. Pre-match problems were closely interwoven with other vitally important problems. The war was waged simultaneously on several fronts. This included help to my relatives and friends, who were in a calamitous situation. It included the general crisis in the country, and my involvement in political life. This is what Nigel Short said about this in the London *Independent*: *'To launch into the whirlpool of Soviet politics four months before the start of a match with Karpov – this is crazy! Garry should realise that you can't kill two birds with one stone'.*

There was also the conflict in the Union of USSR chess players, the split in the GMA Board, problems with the match itself, which was divided between America and Europe, and troublesome training sessions, held abroad. All this was very difficult and unsettling. I did not have sufficient time, or nervous energy, or tranquillity.

To this day I am astonished at how, in view of all these factors, I managed to prepare for the match. In March, in addition, my long-standing trainer Alexander Nikitin, unhappy with the emergency re-allocation of duties, left the team. Nevertheless, with the help of my mother, who became my main manager, I succeeded in organising training sessions and in carrying out a considerable amount of chess work.

The first session took place in March to April at the Trades Union base in Pestov on the outskirts of Moscow, to where I had occasionally gone to relax since the time of the first match (1984/85), where the first session of the Botvinnik-Kasparov school

was held (1986), and where I had lived temporarily after the enforced flight from Baku. Alexander Beliavsky joined me, and we analysed the Ruy Lopez a great deal – in the match for the crown these analyses came in very useful.

But here it became conclusively clear that it would be impossible to productively carry out all my preparation in the USSR – I was too often distracted, literally torn into parts by officials both of the Union of chess players, and of the Democratic Party then being created. Interrupting the fruitfully begun work on chess, I plunged headlong into the organisation of the GMA's final qualifying tournament and spent 20 precious days on this. And in May I also had to find time to fly to Paris and win a rapid chess knock-out tournament. 'I am not even thinking about Karpov', I said then in an interview. 'Now everyone is joking that the match will be lost by the one who plays worse. Strictly speaking, neither of us is studying chess seriously at the moment. I have endeavoured to plan a program of preparation, but in the USSR it is very difficult to prepare for such a match, and so I will prepare abroad.'

It should be said that, for the first time, I myself had to bear all the financial expenditure for preparing for the match, since for two years I had had no dealings with the USSR State Sports Committee. But, following Soviet tradition, my opponent dutifully continued to hand over the lion's share of his prizes to the State Sports Committee, and the latter paid part of his expenses. But Karpov too was no longer satisfied with this compulsory system, to judge at least by a remark of his in an interview given before the match in *Der Spiegel*: in the Soviet Union *'for the moment everyone is controlled by people, who take money from honest people as though they had stolen it.'*

My second long training session began on 15th June in the Spanish seaside resort of La Manga, immediately after a grandmaster rapidplay Swiss held not far away in Murcia and a dramatic GMA assembly, at which the world championship remained under FIDE control and I resigned as president (and then I flew to New York for two days: in the interests of the autumn match, I had to give a TV interview there). At the same time the first session of the international chess 'Kasparov Academy' was also held, and at the opening ceremony I said that for the first time in ages I was able to think about nothing but chess, and I was beginning intensive preparations for the match. But in fact in La Manga, which in some ways reminded me of my native Zagulba, initially I simply tried to recover from the various shocks which had liberally befallen me in the first half of the year.

Not by accident, my training team comprised people who were well known to me: the strong grandmasters Mikhail Gurevich, Sergey Dolmatov (he joined us later, since until the middle of July he was playing in the Interzonal Tournament), and Zurab Azmaiparashvili, as well as two masters – the novice Gia Giorgadze and the old-timer Alexander Shakarov, who looked after the opening card index.

Unfortunately, at the summer session a break also could not be avoided: from 3-10 July I flew on business to Prague and Hamburg. In Prague I took part in a conference 'The peaceful way to democracy', and I interviewed the well-known dissident Vladimir Bukovsky for the newspaper *Demokraticheskaya Rossiya*.

On returning, I did not restrict myself to analytical work, and, remembering the successful experience of the mid-1980s, I played a six-game training match with the two-times USSR champion Lev Psakhis, who was by then already an Israeli citizen. He was not chosen accidentally: Lev had the deserved reputation of being a solid grandmaster with great creative potential and an active positional style of play. Being 'in debt' to Psakhis since the 49th USSR Championship (1981), I was eager to gain revenge for that distant loss in our only tournament game – and in this frame of mind I arrived for the first game.

Game 68
L.Psakhis-G.Kasparov
Training Match
1st Game, La Manga 13.07.1990
King's Indian Defence E81

1 c4 g6 2 e4 (preventing the Grünfeld, although in any case I was intending to play the King's Indian) **2...♗g7 3 d4 d6 4 ♘c3 ♘f6 5 f3 0-0 6 ♗e3**

A slight surprise: Psakhis usually employed the set-up with 6 ♗g5 c5 7 d5. I had not encountered the classical Sämisch Variation for more than eighteen months and, not wishing to go along with the opponent in the main lines with 6...e5 (*Game Nos.43, 84, 90, 92, 98*), from the depths of my memory I extracted a rare continuation.
6...♘bd7 (6...a6 – *Game No.91*) **7 ♗d3**

The 3rd game went 7 ♘h3 c6 8 ♕d2 e5 9 d5 cxd5 10 cxd5 a6 11 ♘f2 ♘h5 12 ♘d3 f5 with double-edged play. In my opinion, the main line with 7 ♕d2 c5 8 ♘ge2 or 7 ♘ge2 c5 8 ♕d2 is more promising, to which Black replies 8...a6, since after 8...cxd4?! 9 ♘xd4 White has an enduring advantage: for example, 9...♘c5 10 ♗e2 ♗d7 11 0-0 a6 12 b4 ♘e6 (12...♘a4!?) 13 ♘b3 ♖c8 14 ♖ac1 etc (Kasparov-Wagner, internet (blitz) 1998).

7...c5 8 ♘ge2 (with the bishop on d3 the move 8 d5 loses all its point in view of 8...♘e5 and ...e7-e6) **8...cxd4 9 ♘xd4 e6!**

'Black carries out the central break ...d6-d5 and solves his difficulties.' (Geller)

10 0-0 d5 11 exd5 exd5 12 ♗f2 (or 12 ♕d2 ♘e5 13 c5 ♘fd7, Timman-Smirin, Oviedo (rapid) 1993) **12...♘e5 13 c5**

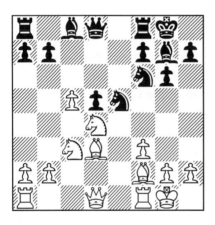

13...♘fd7!

A new, non-routine manoeuvre. 13...♘h5 14 ♘ce2 ♕g5 15 ♔h1 ♗d7 16 ♖c1 ♖fe8 is also acceptable (Gheorghiu-Sznapik, Prague Zonal 1985; Razuvaev-Lerner, Moscow 1987), but instead of this Black gives up his weak d5-pawn, sharply changing the character of the play.

14 ♗e2

On encountering a surprise, Psakhis tries to preserve his bishop and capture in the most convenient way. The direct 14 ♘xd5?!

is unfavourable because of 14...♘xc5 15 ♗e4 b6!, while 14 ♘b3 allows the equalising 14...♘xd3 15 ♕xd3 d4. A journey by the knight into the enemy position – 14 ♘db5 a6! 15 ♘d6 also runs into 15...d4! 16 ♗xd4 (16 ♘ce4? ♘xd3! and ...♘xc5) 16...♘xf3+ 17 ♕xf3 ♗xd4+ etc, and 14 ♘de2 into 14...b6!? 15 cxb6 ♘xb6 16 b3 ♕g5. Black also has good play after the blockading 14 ♘a4 (14 b4?! a5!) 14...♘xd3 15 ♕xd3 ♘e5 16 ♕c2 b6!?.

14...♘xc5 15 ♘db5 b6!

It would appear that Lev underestimated this reply: now White has some problems.

16 ♘xd5?!

A difficult choice: after 16 ♕xd5 ♗b7 17 ♕xd8 ♖fxd8 Black has a favourable ending, while if 16 b4 there is the unpleasant 16...d4! (16...♘e6 17 ♕xd5 is equal) 17 bxc5 dxc3 18 ♘xc3 ♘d7! or 17 ♗xd4 ♘e6 18 ♗e3 ♘c6.

16...♗f5!?

This reinforcement of the knight base on d3 further unsettles the opponent. 16...♗b7 suggested itself, and if 17 ♘bc3 (17 ♘dc3 ♘ed3 or 17...♕g5), apart from the variations with 17...♖c8 which I gave in *Informator*, the immediate 17...♗xd5!? is also strong: 18 ♕xd5 ♘ed3 or 18 ♘xd5 ♘ed3 19 ♗xd3 ♕xd5, winning a pawn.

17 ♘d4

Things do not look good after 17 ♘bc3 ♘cd3 or 17 ♗xc5 bxc5 18 ♖c1 c4!? (18...♘d3 19 ♗xd3 ♕xd5 20 ♗xf5 ♕xf5 21 ♘d6 ♕e6 22 ♘c4 ♖ad8 23 ♕a4 ♗d4+ 24 ♔h1 ♖fe8 is also good) 19 ♗xc4 ♖c8! 20 b3 ♘d3 (my earlier preference 20...a6 21 ♘d4 ♗d3 is unclear in view of 22 ♘e2!) 21 ♖c2 ♘b2 22 ♖xb2 ♗xb2 23 ♕e2 ♗e6, when White does not have full compensation for the exchange.

But the paradoxical quiet move 17 ♖e1!? came into consideration: for example, 17...♘cd3 18 ♗xd3 ♘xd3 19 ♘e7+ ♔h8 20 ♘xf5 gxf5 21 ♗h4 ♕xh4 22 ♕xd3 ♖ad8 23

♕e2 a6 24 ♘c3 ♗d4+ 25 ♔h1 ♖g8 26 ♖ad1 with hopes of extinguishing Black's slight activity.

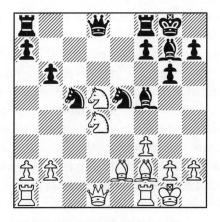

17...♗d3! 18 ♗xd3 ♕xd5!?

And this unexpected capture was the last straw for my opponent, who was expecting 18...♘cxd3 19 ♘c6! ♘xc6 (19...♕d6!?) 20 ♕xd3 ♗xb2 21 ♖ad1 ♘e7 22 ♕b3 ♘xd5 23 ♕xb2 or 21 ♖ae1 ♗g7 22 ♕b5 ♖c8 23 ♖d1 ♕d6 24 a4 ♕a3 25 ♖fe1 with quite good counterplay for the pawn.

19 ♗c2?

The worst of the three possible bishop moves, removing White's control over the c4-square. Let us consider the other two:

1) 19 ♗e2?! ♖fd8 20 ♘b3 (20 ♕c2?! ♖ac8 is extremely risky) 20...♘cd3 21 ♗h4 ♖d6 22 f4 ♘c6 23 ♗f3 ♕c4 24 ♕e2 ♖c8 25 ♖ad1 ♘cb4 with a continued initiative for Black;

2) 19 ♗b5!, and in the event of 19...a6 20 ♗e2 ♖fd8 21 ♘b3 ♘xb3 (21...♘cd3 22 ♗xb6) 22 ♕xd5 ♖xd5 23 axb3 b5 24 ♖fe1 White is okay, while if 19...♖fd8 he can hope to achieve equality with 20 ♘c6! ♕xd1 21 ♖axd1 ♘xc6 22 ♗xc6 ♖ac8 23 ♖xd8+ ♖xd8 24 b4 or 24 ♗xc5 bxc5 25 b3 etc.

19...♖ad8 20 ♕e2

It is no longer apparent how loss of material can be avoided: 20 ♕b1 (20 f4?! ♘c4) 20...♘ed3! 21 ♗xd3 ♗xd4 22 ♗e2 (22 ♗b5

♘e6) 22...♕e5!, while after the 'active' 20 b4 two replies are strong: 20...♘ed3 21 ♗xd3 ♗xd4 22 bxc5 ♗xa1 23 ♕xa1 ♕xd3 24 cxb6 axb6 25 ♗xb6 ♖c8, and 20...♘c6 21 bxc5 ♘xd4 22 cxb6 (22 ♖b1 bxc5 or 22 ♗e4 ♕c4! 23 ♗d3 ♕xc5 is no better) 22...♘xc2 23 ♕xc2 ♗xa1 24 ♖xa1 axb6 25 ♗xb6 ♖d6(c8) with a technically won ending.

20...♖fe8

An ambush! After the hasty 20...♘c4? White would have got away with a slight fright: 21 ♗e4! ♕d7 22 ♖ad1 ♘xe4 23 fxe4 ♕c8 24 b3, almost equalising.

21 ♖fe1

The attempt to block the e-file by 21 ♗e4? is strongly met not only by the *Informator* suggestion 21...♘xf3+ 22 ♗xf3 ♖xe2 23 ♗xd5 ♗xd4! etc, but also by 21...♘xe4! 22 fxe4 ♕c4, winning.

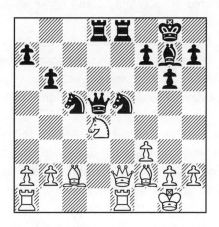

21...♘xf3+! 22 ♕xf3 ♖xe1+ 23 ♖xe1 ♗xd4 24 ♕xd5 ♖xd5

The resulting ending with an extra pawn for Black is of a technical nature.

25 ♖e2?

In time-trouble White gives up a second pawn and loses, although 25 b4 ♗xf2+ 26 ♔xf2 ♖d2+ 27 ♖e2 ♖xe2+ 28 ♔xe2 ♘e6 or 25 ♗xd4 ♖xd4 26 ♖e2 f5 27 ♔f2 ♔f7 28 ♔e3 ♖d6 was unlikely to help either.

25...♗xb2 26 ♗xc5 (with the faint hope of

exploiting the opposite-coloured bishops) **26...♖xc5 27 g3 b5 28 ♔g2 ♗e5 29 ♗b3 a5 30 ♖f2 ♖c7 31 ♖e2 ♗c3 32 ♖e8+ ♔g7 33 ♖b8 a4 34 ♗d5 ♖c5**

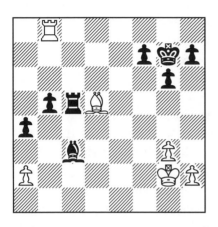

35 ♗e4

If 35 ♖d8 b4 36 ♖d7 there would have followed 36...♖xd5! 37 ♖xd5 b3 38 a3 ♗b2 or 38 axb3 a3.

35...b4 (with the threat of 36...b3! 37 axb3 a3, as a result of which my opponent overlooked a double attack) **36 ♗c2?**

In view of 36...♗e5 White resigned (**0-1**).

After this confident win there followed two very complicated draws. In the 2nd game with White in a hybrid of the Nimzo-Indian and the Queen's Indian I reached a strategically dangerous position – my initiative disappeared, but my weak pawns remained (*Game No.18*, note to White's 11th move), and I was obliged to save myself. In the 3rd game I again employed the King's Indian, but then I went wrong and equalised only with difficulty. And it was only by calmly outplaying my opponent in the 4th game that I achieved a decisive turning point. In the 5th game I was able to build up a crushing attack with Black, and by the 6th Lev was demoralised and he yielded without any particular resistance. The three succes-

sive wins produced an unexpectedly resounding match victory (+4 =2), which did not reflect the intensity of the battle.

The Spanish part of my preparations concluded on 1st August. And the third, September session was held in the USA, to the north-east of New York, by the Atlantic Ocean – I rented a villa on the picturesque island of Martha's Vineyard. My helpers lived here in turn, and our studies were more intensive and prolonged. But the thirty days of work and relaxation were, of course, very little in order to then successfully endure three months of exhausting struggle...

In view of the lack of time for thorough preparation, I decided that I needed to summon all my strength and try to crush the opponent at the very start of the match – I was planning, so to speak, a blitzkrieg. I set myself the aim of striving for the most forceful and complicated play, with both White and Black, so that Karpov should not have the slightest respite. Thus I radically changed my approach compared with the previous matches, especially the one in Seville, where the emphasis was placed on the white pieces, in order to play as solidly and soundly as possible with Black. I thought that the time had come to engage Karpov in a real battle.

Pinning my hopes on a blitzkrieg, a couple of weeks before the start of play I stopped all chess activity and simply relaxed, ran, swam, and played badminton and tennis.

Fifth Match with Karpov

World Championship Match **Kasparov** – Karpov (New York – Lyon, 7 October 1990 – 2 January 1991): 12½-11½.

After the tragic events in Baku in January 1990, I realised that it was impossible to live in the country and consider myself its citizen – and not try to avert the impending catastrophe. I was convinced that the following year the political concept 'USSR' would no longer exist, and as a mark of solidarity with my compatriots who were protesting against the communist regime, I made a written declaration about my refusal to play the match under the Soviet flag and my intention to appear under the Russian tri-colour. And on 3rd October at a joint press conference of the match contestants I once again expressed this view and, anticipating the opposition of FIDE and my opponent, I specified: 'I am not asking for a large Russian flag to be displayed – I will simply place a small one on the chess table' (one was urgently stitched by my mother for this aim).

Naturally, Krogius, the leader of Karpov's delegation, protested, and then the organisers found a compromise: they removed the flags from the chess table, but on my name-plate was drawn a white, blue and red square, and alongside Karpov's name – a red square with a hammer and sickle. It appeared that at this the problem was resolved, but my opponent (in the person of the State Sports Committee) did not calm down and he began a tenacious battle against the depiction of the Russian flag on my name-board...

After a confident draw at the start I was in good spirits before the next, 'white' game. For it my trainers and I had once again glanced over possible replies to 1 e4 and tried to lay traps over the entire perimeter.

> *Game 69*
> **G.Kasparov-A.Karpov**
> World Championship Match
> 2nd Game, New York 10.10.1990
> *Ruy Lopez C92*

1 e4 (1) **1...e5** (2)

As it later transpired, Karpov had given up his main move – 1...c6 (*Game Nos.34, 85*) for the entire match.

2 ♘f3 ♘c6 (2...♘f6 – *Game Nos.76, 95*) **3 ♗b5** (3 d4 – *Game Nos.70, 71, 81, 88*) **3...a6**

Before the match Beliavsky and I even briefly discussed the 'Berlin Wall' – 3...♘f6 4 0-0 ♘xe4 5 d4 ♘d6 6 ♗xc6 dxc6 7 dxe5 ♘f5 8 ♕xd8+ ♔xd8: might not the opponent be attracted by the early exchange of queens? In Alexander's opinion, it was not in Karpov's style to go immediately into a slightly inferior endgame. Indeed, the Berlin Wall had only just been destroyed, and the time to erect it anew had not yet come...

4 ♗a4 ♘f6 5 0-0 ♗e7 6 ♖e1 b5 7 ♗b3 d6 8 c3 0-0 9 h3 ♗b7 (2)

And so, once again the Zaitsev Variation. As an 'emergency landing' the ex-champion later chose 9...♘d7 10 d4 ♗f6 (*Game No.72*).

10 d4 ♖e8 11 ♘bd2 ♗f8 12 a4 (2)

My favourite plan, as opposed to 12 a3 (*Game No.8*) and other moves (cf. *Revolution in the 70s* pp.243-256).

12...h6 (12...♕d7 – Game Nos.50, 57 in *Kasparov vs. Karpov 1975-1985*) **13 ♗c2 exd4** (2) **14 cxd4 ♘b4 15 ♗b1**

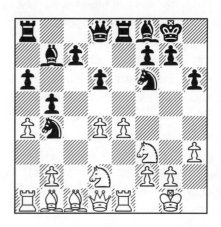

15...bxa4 (2)

One of two continuations regularly employed by Karpov. After this game he was to give preference to the main move 15...c5, which was tested back in the 1986 match (*Game Nos.16, 17, 74*).

To be honest, after 9...♝b7, 13...exd4 and especially 15...bxa4 I felt pleased, since I had not expected such an abrupt turn by my opponent in the direction of maximum activity, and, correspondingly, maximum risk when playing Black – this was a pleasant surprise. And, in addition, it was precisely in this branch that I had a 'bomb' prepared...

16 ♖xa4 a5 17 ♖a3!

This was first played by Sax, and then by me against Beliavsky in the Moscow Inter-zonal Tournament (1982). The rook prepares to switch along the third rank to the centre (to e3), or to the kingside (to g3, after the knight moves from f3).

17...♖a6

An interesting 'symmetric reply': the rook is ready to come into play along the sixth rank – in variations with ...d6-d5, with ...c7-c5 and the exchange on c5, or with the e4-e5 breakthrough and ...d6xe5. Of course, we were expecting this move: Karpov always played it, avoiding 17...g6 18 ♖ae3 (Sax-Beliavsky, Moscow Interzonal 1982), or 17...♛d7 18 ♘h4 (Ehlvest-Beliavsky, 51st USSR Championship, Lvov 1984).

18 ♘h2 (7)

Two continuations remained off-screen: both the incautious 18 ♘h4?! ♘xe4! 19 ♘xe4 ♝xe4 20 ♝xe4 d5 21 ♖ae3 ♖ae6 with equality (Timman-Karpov, 1st match game, Kuala Lumpur 1990), and 18 ♖ae3 a4 19 ♘f1 d5 20 e5 ♘e4 (Balashov-Karpov, 50th USSR Championship, Moscow 1983) or 19 ♘h4 (19 ♘h2!?) 19...c5 20 dxc5 dxc5 21 ♘f5 (Timman-Karpov, 5th match game, Kuala Lumpur 1990) 21...g6! (Krogius).

18...g6

An instantaneous reply, which was not surprising: this move had already been successfully tried by the ex-champion in two games the previous year.

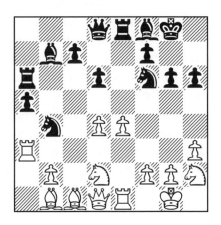

Now after the hasty 19 e5?! dxe5 20 dxe5 (J.Horvath-Razuvaev, Sochi 1987) Black easily equalises with 20...♘d7, 20...♖ae6, and 20...♛d5 21 ♘hf3 ♖ae6! 22 ♖ae3 ♝c5! 23 exf6 ♝xe3 24 fxe3 ♖xe3 etc.

19 ♘g4 also promises little in view of 19...♘xg4 20 hxg4 (Klovans-Podgaets, Riga 1988) 20...♝c8, intending ...♝g7, ...d6-d5 and ...c7-c5 (So.Polgar-Liss, Rishon le Ziyyon 1996), or 20 ♛xg4 c5! 21 dxc5 dxc5 22 e5 ♛d4 (22...♖d6!?) 23 ♛g3 ♖ae6 with equality (Hjartarson-Karpov, 5th match game, Seattle 1989).

White is slightly better, although Black again has no particular problems after the expansive 19 f4 d5 (19...c5 is interesting, and if 20 d5, then 20...♖a7! with the idea of ...♝a6 and ...♝g7) 20 e5 ♘e4 21 ♘g4 c5! 22 ♘xe4 dxe4 23 dxc5 ♝xc5+ 24 ♝e3 ♝f8 (Ivanchuk-Karpov, Linares 1989).

However, I had in mind a completely different, atypical plan.

19 f3! (2)

Finally I had the good fortune to employ a novelty, which had awaited its hour since the first match (1984/85). The idea of f2-f3 in such positions was suggested at the time by Timoshchenko. And this idea, when put into effect, made a strong impression on the experts in the press centre and the numerous commentators on the match! Razuvaev: 'White strongly supports his central e4-pawn, and three black pieces – the rook on e8, knight on f6 and bishop on b7 – are left without work.' This also applies to the rook on a6: in view of its intentions, my strictly prophylactic move proves simply ideal.

Judging by Karpov's reaction, the modest 19 f3 came as an unpleasant surprise, and he began experiencing discomfort. This was a rare occurrence in our games, when with the first unexplored move I was able to set my opponent serious problems. It is not surprising that after this game the variation almost disappeared from tournament play (although, as we will now see, the situation is still far from clear).

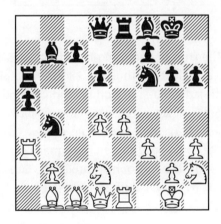

19...♕d7?! (10)

The queen will not be best placed at b5. After deviating from the correct course, within five (!) moves Black ends up in a lost position. Meanwhile, he had a choice of three natural continuations:

1) 19...d5 (the thematic move) 20 e5 ♘d7 21 f4 c5, and here White should not play 22 e6?! ♖axe6 23 ♖xe6 ♖xe6 24 f5 (Timman), since 24...♖a6 or even 24...♖e7 parries the attack, but 22 ♘df3! cxd4 (22...♘c6 23 f5) 23

♘xd4 ♘c6 24 ♗e3! ♗xa3 25 bxa3 – I found this exchange sacrifice during joint analysis with Beliavsky and I was very proud of my discovery. After 25...♘xd4 26 ♗xd4 there is the threat of f4-f5, and at the board the black player will find it hard to defend against the direct attack – provided only that it is a human, not a machine! The position looks extremely dangerous for Black (and what the mighty bishop on d4 is worth!), despite the computer assessment of 'equal';

2) 19...♗g7 20 ♘c4 ♗c8! (an unexpected move – immediately after the game Timman and I gave only 20...♕a8?! 21 d5!) 21 ♗d2 (but not 21 ♘xa5?! c5!), and White still retains some advantage: for example, 21...♘h5 22 ♗e3! d5 23 ♘xa5 c5 24 ♘b3 cxd4 25 ♘xd4 dxe4 26 fxe4 ♖d6 27 ♘hf3 ♘c6 28 ♘xc6 ♖xd1 29 ♘xd8 ♖xe1+ 30 ♘xe1 ♖xd8 31 ♘d3 etc;

3) 19...c5!? (apparently best; Seirawan suggested 19...c6 with the idea of 20 ♘c4?! d5, but after this, and after 19...♕b8, 20 ♘df1 is correct) 20 d5 (cutting off the rook on a6) 20...♕e7! with the threat of ...♗xd5. Here Beliavsky and I analysed 21 ♖ae3 and ♘c4, but 21 ♖f1!? also leads to complicated play, in which, in my view, White's chances are objectively better: for example, 22...♗g7 22 ♘c4 ♘h5 (exploiting the weakening of the g3-square) 23 ♘g4!? ♘g3 24 ♘xh6+ ♔h7 25 ♘g4 ♘xf1 26 ♕xf1 ♖aa8 27 f4 with the initiative and a pawn for the exchange.

I think that Karpov's choice was also influenced by purely practical considerations: he may have avoided 19...d5 or 19...c5 because the opponent would certainly have mainly studied these, and, besides, the Modern Benoni-type positions arising after 19...c5 20 d5 were not to the taste of the ex-champion. However, he underestimated my 21st move.

20 ♘c4 (21) **20...♕b5** (3)

'Karpov takes his queen to b5, for one thing to cover the a-pawn, but after this White turns his attention to another weak pawn in the enemy camp.' (Timman)

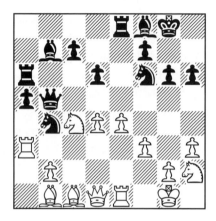

21 ♖c3! (2)

The prelude to a rather harmonious arrangement of the pieces. Now it is hard for Black to carry out the freeing ...d6-d5 because of ♘a3 (with gain of tempo!) and e4-e5.

21...♗c8 (10)

Karpov goes totally on to the defensive, but what else was there to do? 21...d5 22 ♘a3 ♕b6 23 e5 ♘d7 24 ♗e3 is clearly advantageous to White: for example, 24...c5 25 dxc5 ♗xc5 26 ♖xc5! ♘xc5 27 ♘g4 or 24...a4 25 f4 c5 (25...♘c6 26 ♖e2) 26 f5 with a strong attack. In the event of 21...♖c6 22 ♘a3 ♕b6 23 ♗e3 Black is again at a deadlock: if 23...d5, then 24 e5 ♘d7 25 f4 ♖xc3 26 bxc3 ♘c6(a6) 27 f5!, breaking through to the king at the cost of the knight on a3.

In these variations, under the cover of his protected centre, White successfully storms the king's fortress, exploiting the remoteness of the black queen from the main part of the battlefield. The attempt to bring it home immediately – 21...♕d7 with the idea of 22 ♗e3? d5! 23 ♘e5 ♕d8! with equality

(Timman) could have run into 22 ♗f4 (22 ♘a3!?), when 22...d5 23 ♘e5 ♕d8 is no longer so good in view of 24 ♘eg4, with an attack on the h6- and c7-pawns. Besides, it was psychologically difficult to play ...♕b5-d7 almost immediately after the move ...♕d7-b5.

22 ♗e3 (6)

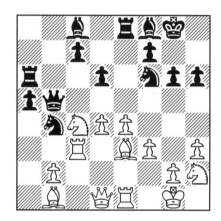

22...♔h7?! (29)

The fruit of agonising hesitation. This defence against the threat of 23 ♘a3 and ♕c1 (with a double attack on h6 and c7) hinders ...d6-d5, since after ♘e5 the f7-pawn is attacked. 22...♕b8 was more shrewd, when White could have chosen the equally shrewd ♘a3 or the unsophisticated 23 ♕c1 d5 (23...♔h7?! 24 ♘g4!) 24 ♘d2 dxe4 25 fxe4 and ♗f2, maintaining his dominance in the centre.

22...h5!? 23 ♕d2 ♕b8 with the idea of ...d6-d5 was also preferable, and if 24 ♘a3 (24 d5 c6!), then 24...♘d7 25 ♘f1 c5, nevertheless agreeing to a 'Modern Benoni' after 26 d5, although the queen stands worse at b8 than in the variation 19...c5 20 d5 ♕e7.

23 ♕c1 (15)

Renewing the threat of ♘a3. 23 ♕d2 was also good.

23...c6? (3)

This weakening of the d6-pawn places

Black on the verge of defeat. However, he already had a difficult choice: 23...c5 24 dxc5 dxc5 25 ♘g4 etc weakens the position too much, and 23...♗c6 24 ♘a3 ♕b7 25 d5 or 23...♕b8 24 ♘g4 (24 ♕d2!?) 24...♘xg4 25 hxg4 ♗g7 26 ♕d2 followed by ♔f2 and ♖h1 is also unpromising.

24 ♘g4 (19)

A typical Spanish manoeuvre, but in the given instance 24 ♗f4!? was no less strong – and if 24...♖d8, then 25 e5! ♘fd5 26 ♘xd6 or 26...dxe5 26 ♘xe5.

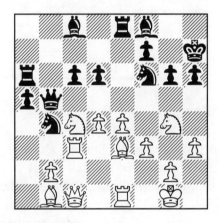

24...♘g8?! (10)

Objectively the losing move, but – 'the most natural: the knight exchange 24...♘xg4 25 hxg4 would have been a serious positional concession, since after the regrouping ♔f2 and ♖h1 it would have been even more difficult to defend the h6-pawn' (Vasyukov). However, after this exchange White at least has no forced way to win:

1) 25...d5 26 ♘e5 (there is also the standard 26 ♘a3!? ♕b6 27 e5 followed by f3-f4-f5) 26...dxe4 27 ♘xf7 ♘d3 28 ♗xd3 exd3 29 ♖d1 ♗e6 30 ♘e5, and Black loses a pawn, and therefore 26...♕b7 27 ♗f2 is more resilient, with 'simply' an advantage for White;

2) 25...♗e6 26 ♘a3! (Timman considered only 26 ♔f2) 26...♕b8 27 ♔f2 ♗g7 28 ♕d2,

and Black's defence is difficult: 28...♖h8 29 ♖h1 ♔g8 30 ♘c4 or 28...g5 29 d5! ♗d7 30 ♗d4 etc.

24...♗xg4 is also insufficient: 25 hxg4 d5 (25...♘d7 26 ♗f4!) 26 ♘a3 ♕b8 27 e5 ♘d7 28 f4 etc.

Here again I stopped to think. White has an overwhelming position, and, of course, I wanted to find a decisive continuation of the attack. But I was dazzled by the mass of tempting possibilities. I immediately saw a sharp variation with a sacrifice of two minor pieces for a rook and pawn, calculated it, and came to the intuitive conclusion that White's slight material deficit would be more than compensated by the enormous activity of his pieces.

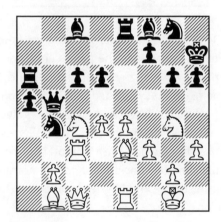

25 ♗xh6! (16)

'A spectacular move. When I received the moves through Teletext my first thought was that Kasparov had simply slipped up. Later I realised that in true Kasparov style the World Champion was looking for ways to translate his positional superiority into an offensive against the black king.' (Timman)

In the opinion of Timman and other commentators, 25 ♗f4!? would have led more simply to the goal. At the board I saw this move and I realised that it would be too depressing to reply 25...♕b8 or 25...♗xg4 26 hxg4, and that after 25...♖d8 there was the breakthrough 26 e5! dxe5 27 ♘gxe5. But I preferred a more unexpected and dynamic development of events.

25...♗xh6 (2) **26 ♘xh6 ♘xh6 27 ♘xd6 ♕b6 28 ♘xe8** (4)

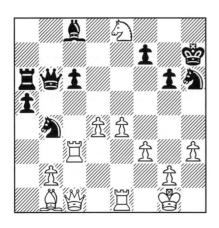

On seeing that White will lose his knight on e8, the experts in the press centre took a sceptical view of my combination, and for some reason they decided that at this point I had offered a draw, and Karpov was deciding whether or not to play on. Geller even wanted to take bets with Najdorf that peace would now be concluded, and the normally venturesome Don Miguel would not take him on.

28...♕xd4+ (22)

After a long think Karpov convinced himself that there was nothing better: after 28...♕d8 29 d5! ♕xe8 30 d6 (by no means the only move) the avalanche of white pawns supported by the heavy pieces is bound to sweep away everything in its path. Thus he preferred to eliminate a dangerous pawn, but now one of the rooks invades the black position along the opened file.

29 ♔h1 ♕d8 30 ♖d1! (8)

I reached this position in my calculation of 25 ♗xh6! and I assessed it as won. Indeed, the coordination of the black pieces is com-

pletely destroyed, whereas White's queen and both rooks are very strong. My intuition did not let me down: later analysis confirmed the correctness of my assessment.

30...♕xe8 31 ♕g5

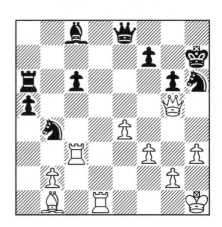

31...♖a7 (8)

If 31...♘g8, then 32 ♕h4+! ♔g7 33 ♖d8 ♕e6 34 f4 and wins. Timman also rejected 31...♗d7 in view of 32 ♖c5 (32 f4 is also good) and recommended the 'best defence 31...♕e6 – Black gets ready to chase the enemy queen from her dominant position as quickly as possible.' However, after 32 ♖d8! nothing comes of this: 32...f6?! (32...♖a7 leads to a position from the game) 33 ♕f4 ♘f7 34 ♕c7 ♖a8 35 ♗d3! ♘xd3 36 ♖cxd3 and wins.

32 ♖d8 (3) **32...♕e6 33 f4** (3) **33...♗a6** (13)

Black would have lost immediately after 33...♖d7 34 f5! or 33...f6 34 ♕c5! ♖d7 35 f5! gxf5 36 ♖xc8 ♖d1+ 37 ♔h2 ♕xc8 38 ♕e7+ ♔g8 39 ♖g3+ ♘g4+ 40 hxg4 fxg4 41 ♕xf6 ♕d7 42 e5 ♖xb1 43 ♕g6+ and ♕xb1.

34 f5! (3)

The greedy 34 ♕xa5 would have allowed Black a respite after 34...♕e7 (Timman) or 34...♕f6.

34...♕e7 (10) **35 ♕d2!** (4) **35...♕e5** (5)

Hoping to maintain the queen in its central position, but this does not prove possible.

The alternatives were also hopeless: 35...c5 36 ♖g3, 35...♘d5 36 fxg6+ fxg6 37 exd5 ♕xd8 38 ♗xg6+!, and 35...♘g8 36 fxg6+ fxg6 37 e5 etc.

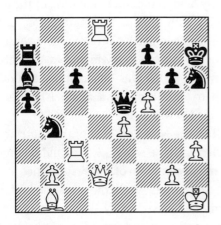

36 ♕f2! (3)

Pretty geometry: with gain of tempo the queen ensures the invasion of the rook on c5. White is completely dominant, and Black cannot avoid decisive loss of material.

However, I had a rich choice of ways to win: 36 ♖f3 with the idea of f5-f6 was also decisive, as was the devil-may-care 36 ♖g3!? ♕xg3 (36...♖e7 37 ♖g5!) 37 ♖h8+! ♔g7 (37...♔xh8 38 ♕xh6+ ♔g8 39 f6, mating) 38 ♕xh8+ ♔f6 39 ♖e8 ♘d3 40 ♗xd3 ♗xd3 41 fxg6 with an irresistible attack.

36...♕e7 (2)

Or 36...♖b7 37 ♖c5! ♕f6 38 fxg6+, combining mating threats and the 'gathering of the harvest'.

37 ♕d4 ♘g8 (if 37...f6, then 38 fxg6+ ♔g7 39 g4!) **38 e5**

The end is close. Karpov made his last few moves before the time control with his flag about to fall.

38...♘d5 39 fxg6+ (12) **39...fxg6 40 ♖xc6 ♕xd8 41 ♕xa7+** (41 ♖xg6 was more forceful) **41...♘de7 42 ♖xa6 ♕d1+ 43 ♔g1 ♕d2 44 ♕f1**

Here the arbiter was preparing to produce

the envelope for the recording of the adjourned position, but Black resigned (**1–0**). Times: 2.23–2.30.

This game was voted the best in the 50th volume of *Informator*. After such a convincing win I assumed that I was on the correct path, but already in the 3rd game my lack of adequate preparation for the match was revealed. Emerging unscathed after a recklessly played opening, I gained a big advantage, but suddenly I began to drift and I missed an excellent chance to score a second successive win.

At a meeting of the appeals committee, which took place after the adjournment session of the 3rd game, my opponent's protest against my appearing under the Russian flag was conclusively upheld. From then on not only were the miniature flags removed from the chess table, but even their depictions on our name-boards! There was nothing to be done, but from the next day I began arriving for play with a Russian badge on my jacket lapel – this was a silent demonstration on my part.

I again began the next game in an ultra-optimistic key, 'shining' with superficial and devil-may-care play, but I had to struggle to gain a draw. The crazy 4th game once again, following the 2nd, confirmed that Karpov, like myself, had also decided to fight 'flat out' with Black, not avoiding sharp play.

In the 5th game there was a comparatively quiet draw. But the 6th took a nervy and very uneven course. After hastily winning a pawn, Karpov again began playing slightly worse than me in a complicated middlegame, and White not only extricated himself from a difficult position, but after time-trouble mistakes by the opponent he could even have set him insoluble problems. But I also went wrong, and Black saved himself. This game, as though developing the pattern of the 3rd and 4th, clearly showed that my play was steadily deteriorating. Two serious mistakes at critical moments were loud warning signals, which I failed to heed.

The weight of accumulated negative emotions obviously made itself felt in the 7th game, when on the 27th move I made virtually the worst blunder of my career, overlooking an elementary tactical stroke. The match score became equal: 3½-3½. It became clear that my blitzkrieg strategy had failed.

I very much wanted to get even in the next game, the 8th – and I went along to it with only victory on my mind! However, in matches for the world championship the desire to win is not enough – you must also have a good feeling for your condition. It was precisely this quality in me that was blunted: I didn't yet realise that the terrible blunder in the previous game was not an accident, but the consequence of excessive nervous tension, which would not go away. And as a result, the 8th game, which promised to become a brilliant one, almost ended woefully for me. With difficulty I managed to gain a draw on the 84th move.

Karpov was dismayed, and the psychological initiative appeared to have passed to me. But the 9th game, played the day after the exhausting adjournment session of the 8th, showed that I was still a long way from emerging from the crisis. Of course, I was happy with a draw: for me it was the desired result. But the first employment in this match of the Grünfeld Defence proved unsuccessful – Karpov had an overwhelming advantage and he lost it only on the threshold of time-trouble.

In the 10th game the condition of the two players at this stage of the match was reflected as in a mirror: a draw was agreed as early as the 18th move. In the 11th game I reverted to the King's Indian – the result was a pretty and again very tense draw, which opened a new chapter both in opening theory, and in the understanding of the laws of play with unbalanced material (cf. *Game No.87*, note to Black's 14th move). In the 12th game I was close to a win, but at the critical moment, alas, I was let down by a sudden rush of indecision, and again I had to be satisfied with a draw.

Thus the New York half of the match concluded with the score 6-6. It would be unjust for me to complain of this result, since in the last six games, with the exception of the 11th, I had played badly.

For intrigue and intensity of the battle, the Lyons half of the match was at least the equal of the first. It is curious that in our previous matches not one of the 13th games had produced a definite result. On this occasion too the tradition was not broken. But in my next, 'white' game, there was a surprise awaiting Karpov as early as the third move – I gave the Spanish a respite!

Game 70
G.Kasparov-A.Karpov
World Championship Match
14th Game, Lyons 26.11.1990
Scotch Game C45

---

1 e4 e5 2 ♘f3 ♘c6 3 d4 (1)

The Scotch Game, which had long been forgotten at the top level (with the exception of rare experiments by Ljubojevic and Timman), was unexpectedly revived a century later in a match for the world championship! Here we were helped by the two-week break – during this time we were able to refresh the treatment of this ancient opening, which we had begun examining back in the summer in

Murcia, and the idea of employing it became firmly fixed in my mind back in the spring training session in Pestov. And our efforts were not in vain: in the next ten years I scored a good dozen wins in the Scotch (and another couple in the romantic Evans Gambit!).

3...exd4 (5) **4 ♘xd4 ♘f6** (5)

The expected reply: this is what Karpov had twice played against Timman. Something had also been prepared against Black's other main move – 4...♗c5 (*Game No.88*).

5 ♘xc6!

After 5 ♘c3 ♗b4! 6 ♘xc6 bxc6 7 ♗d3 d5 8 exd5 cxd5 9 0-0 0-0 10 ♗g5 c6 Black is okay, as shown by the entire history of the variation, from Steinitz-Zukertort (2nd match game, New York 1886) to Deep Blue-Kasparov (5th match game, Philadelphia 1996).

5...bxc6

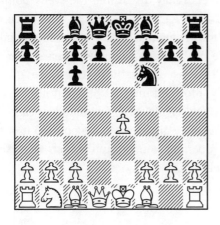

6 e5 ♕e7 7 ♕e2 ♘d5

After the rare 7...♘g8 (Mieses-Lasker, Hastings 1895) Sveshnikov has played and recommended 8 b3, but I prefer the unpretentious 8 ♘c3(d2).

8 c4 (3)

At one time there were serious arguments about White's best eighth move, but in the end the position after 8 c4 became the main *tabiya* of the variation.

8...♗a6 (2)

After this reply Black had not experienced any problems. The alternative is 8...♘b6 (*Game No.71*).

9 b3 (1)

Back to the sources! In the 20th century 9 ♘d2 had occurred, or else 9 ♕e4, allowing both 9...♘b6 10 ♘c3 ♕e6 (Ljubojevic-Spassky, Montreal 1979) or 10 ♘d2 0-0-0 11 c5?! ♗xf1 12 cxb6 ♗a6 13 bxa7 ♔b7 14 ♘b3 f6! (Timman-Karpov, London 1984), as well as 9...♘f6 10 ♕e2 ♘d5 11 ♘d2 (transposing into the same variation) 11...0-0-0 (11...f6 or 11...g6 is also not bad) 12 ♕e4 ♘b6 13 a4?! d5! 14 cxd5 ♗xf1 15 d6 ♖xd6 (Timman-Karpov, Amsterdam 1985), and Black has a comfortable game.

After studying these games by Karpov, I hit on a new idea for White with a double fianchetto, noticing that in this case Black's light-squared bishop is severely restricted. I also took into account the peculiarities of my opponent's style. Karpov does not like to create pawn weaknesses in his position, but here, in order to free himself, he would have to undermine my e5-pawn – and after ...f7-f6 his pawn chain on the kingside would be broken up, while after ...d7-d6 he would have problems with his queenside pawns. In addition, after castling long the black king does not feel altogether comfortable.

Black's counterplay is based on the fact that the white king has remained in the centre. He needs to act very energetically, and this factor also seemed to me to be unpleasant for my opponent, since sharp play was not fully in accordance with his style. And although on this occasion Karpov confidently coped with the unaccustomed problems, later he experienced serious difficulties in the Scotch and he lost two games to me – the 16th of the present match, and a year later in Tilburg. Later he even switched to 4...♗c5 and only many years later did he again revert to the ill-starred (for him) 4...♘f6.

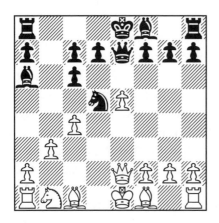

9...0-0-0 (25)

Naturally, we had also examined other possible replies:

1) 9...g6 (at that time a rare move, which enjoyed a surge in popularity beginning in 1990) 10 f4!? – this weapon was fired a year later (*Game No.81*; there 9...g5!? is also seen);

2) 9...f6, and if 10 ♗b2, then 10...♘f4 11 ♕e3 (11 exf6 ♘d3+!, Ljubojevic-Ivkov, Bugojno 1978) 11...fxe5 12 ♗xe5 ♘g6 13 ♗xc7 ♕xe3+ 14 fxe3 ♗c5 15 ♘c3 ♗xe3 with equality (Sveshnikov). Therefore I was planning 10 ♗a3, in order after 10...♕xa3 11 exf6+ ♔f7 12 ♘xa3 ♗b4+ 13 ♕d2 ♖he8+ 14 ♗e2 ♗xd2+ 15 ♔xd2 ♘xf6 16 f3 to restrict myself to a minimal plus: I thought that it would be unpleasant for Karpov to defend a position with three pawn islands and a passive bishop on a6;

3) 9...♕h4?! – this was considered the main reply to 9 b3 and was given a '!' in view of 10 a3(!) ♗c5(?!) 11 g3 ♗xf2+ 12 ♕xf2 ♕e4+ 'etc'. Say, 13 ♔d2?! ♕xh1 14 ♗g2 ♕xh2 15 cxd5 cxd5 16 ♘c3, and here apart from 16...♗b7 (Morozevich-V.Ivanov, Moscow 1992), both 16...d4 and 16...♖b8 are also good. But at the training session in Murcia I

found an important subtlety – 13 ♔d1! ♕xh1 14 ♘d2!, for example:

a) 14...f5 15 ♔c2!, and Black faces very difficult problems: if 15...f4 16 gxf4 ♘xf4, then 17 ♗b2 and e5-e6;

b) 14...♘c3+ 15 ♔c2 ♘e4 16 ♘xe4 ♕xe4+ 17 ♗d3 ♕xe5?! 18 ♗b2 ♕g5 19 h4 ♕h6 20 ♖e1+ ♔f8 21 ♗c3, and Black is the exchange and a pawn up, but – a unique situation! – he has no acceptable move. 17...♕g4 18 ♗f5 ♕h5 19 h4 f6 20 exf6 gxf6 is more resilient, but after 21 ♗b2 0-0 22 g4 ♕f7 23 ♖g1 White's chances are better (as was confirmed in practice).

In an attempt to improve Black's defence after 10 a3, we analysed 10...♘f4 11 ♕e4 ♘g6, and here 12 ♕xh4 ♘xh4 13 ♘d2 is not bad, but I preferred 12 ♕e3.

I remember being puzzled as to why Karpov did not play 9...♕h4. Had he and his trainers really discovered the weak point in the widely-accepted chain of moves? Or did he intuitively decide to avoid a highly probable nasty trick? A couple of years later the well-known theoretician Lev Gutman joyfully informed me that he had found a sure way for White to gain an advantage (13 ♔d1! etc) – and indeed, he pointed it out in an opening monograph which was soon published.

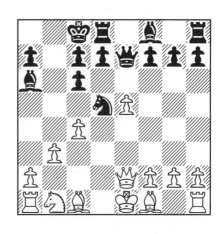

10 g3!

The point of White's idea is the sacrifice of the e5-pawn. Previously he had often fought feverishly for its existence and, going on to the defensive, had lost the initiative. But now, while the opponent spends time on the winning of the pawn, White plays for a lead in development, aiming to exploit the defects in the enemy king's shelter and the 'clogged state' of the bishop on a6.

Curiously, in the autumn of 1881 the diagram position became the subject of heated debates in the press between the strongest players of that era – Steinitz and Zukertort. It all began with the source game Blackburne-Zukertort (12th match game, London 1881), where after 10 ♕e4?! ♘f6 11 ♕e2 ♖e8 (11...♘g4!? 12 f4 ♕e6) 12 f4? (12 ♗b2 was correct) Black could have won a pawn by 12...d6! (Steinitz).

There was an equally heated discussion about 10 ♕b2?! ♘b6 11 ♗e2 (11 ♗e3 ♖e8 12 f4 f6! is hardly any better) 11...♖e8 12 ♗f4 (12 f4 f6! with the idea of 13 exf6 ♕e4!) 12...g5 'with great effect' – a recommendation of Zukertort and Hoffer in *Chess Monthly*, which was tested in practice one hundred years later (!): 13 ♗g3 ♗g7 14 ♘c3 f5 (14...♔b8!?) 15 f4 gxf4 16 ♗xf4 ♗xe5 17 ♗xe5 ♕xe5 18 0-0? (18 0-0-0 d5!) 18....♕d4+ 19 ♔h1 ♖xe2!... 0-1 (Ljubojevic-Seirawan, Wijk aan Zee 1986).

10 ♗b2 is more natural – now White is better after 10...♖e8 11 ♕d2 ♘b6 12 ♗e2 (Morozevich-Karpov, Dagomys 2008), but 10...♕g5! (Blackburne-Zukertort, 14th match game, London 1881) leads to mind-boggling play; a recent example is Smeets-Adams (London 2008).

10...♖e8 (13)

This obvious, solid move was the one that we looked at in the first instance. Two sharper continuations appeared in the next year or two: 10...g5, and in the event of 11 ♗a3 (Azmaiparashvili), 11...♘b4! 12 ♗b2 ♗g7 13 ♗g2 (13 ♗h3 ♖he8) 13...♘d3+! 14 ♕xd3 ♗xe5 Black has an excellent game (Macieja-Karpov, 2nd match game, Warsaw (rapid) 2003), but 11 ♗b2! is better, or 10...f6!? 11 ♗g2 fxe5 12 0-0 e4 13 ♕d2!? ♘f6 14 ♕a5 ♔b7 15 ♗f4! (Pavasovic-Jenni, Leipzig 2002) or 12...♘f6 13 ♘c3! (13 ♗a3 ♕e6 suits Black, Morozevich-Huzman, Amsterdam 1995) 13...♕e6 14 ♖e1 with chances for both sides.

11 ♗b2 f6

By 11...♘b6 Karpov could have transposed into the game Mieses-Teichmann (Hastings 1895), but in it after 12 ♗h3! f6 13 0-0 (13 e6!?) White attained a more favourable position, since the black knight has voluntarily moved out of play.

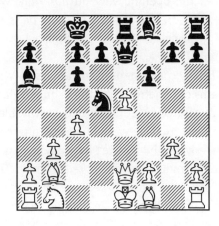

12 ♗g2

Only this is a genuine novelty. In the little-known game Czerniak-Johannessen (Nice Olympiad 1974) after 12 f4? fxe5 13 fxe5 ♕g5! 14 ♘d2 ♗b4 (14...♘e3!?) Black seized the initiative.

I made the bishop move almost without thinking, since it was the main one in our analysis. But today the immediate 12 ♕d2! seems more promising to me, forcing 12...♘b6 (an achievement by White), and now not Morozevich's move 13 a4 because of 13...♕b4!, but 13 ♗h3! and 0-0. Black's position looks extremely dubious: his king is in danger, and his knight at b6 and bishop at a6 are out of play. It cannot be ruled out that before the 16th game it was this possibility that did not appeal to Karpov.

12...fxe5 (6) **13 0-0** (3)

Counting on gaining good compensation for the pawn. In *Informator* Azmaiparashvili recommended 13 ♘d2 g6 14 0-0-0 ♗g7 (14...♗h6 15 ♔b1) 15 ♘e4 with the idea of ♕d2-a5, but Black has two less clear replies – 13...♘f6 or 13...h5 (Rublevsky-V.Mikhalevsky, Vilnius 1995).

13...h5 (9)

The start of a series of very good moves. 13...♘f6 was also possible (to which I would have replied 14 ♘d2), but: 'Karpov has played the opening very purposefully, won the battle in the centre, and now he is the first to launch an attack.' (Sveshnikov)

14 ♕d2 (2)

The key component in the analysis: White dreams of penetrating with his queen via a5 to a7 and of creating threats to the black king. Now 14 ♘d2 would have been unclear in view of 14...h4 15 ♖fe1 hxg3 16 hxg3 ♕f6! (not Azmaiparashvili's recommendation 16...♕g5 17 ♘f3 ♕h5 because of 18 ♘xe5) and ...♕h6. But 14 ♖e1 could have led merely to a transposition of moves (14...♘f6 15 ♕d2 – cf. the following note) or to the regaining of the pawn and a roughly equal endgame.

I had spent just 10 minutes on my opening moves, while Karpov had already used more than an hour. But soon it was my turn to stop and think.

14...♘f6 (2) **15 ♕a5** (15)

Strictly following the plan, although 15 ♖e1 came into consideration: for example, 15...♕c5 16 ♘c3 h4?! 17 ♘a4 ♕b4 18 ♗xb4

♗xb4 19 ♖xe5 with a somewhat better ending (Dembo-Husari, Budapest 2003).

15...♗b7!

'After 15...♔b7? 16 ♗a3 ♕e6 17 ♗xf8 ♖hxf8 18 ♘c3 all the same the bishop cannot be maintained at a6.' (Shirov). Say, 18...e4 19 ♖ae1! d5 20 ♖d1, and Black is in trouble.

16 ♗a3 (of course, not immediately 16 ♕xa7? because of 16...♕c5) **16...♕e6** (12)

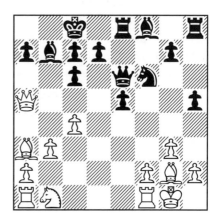

17 ♗xf8 ♖hxf8 (4)

'Karpov played safely – towards the centre. 17...♖exf8 looked tempting, and if 18 ♕xa7, then 18...♕g4 19 ♘a3 h4 20 ♘c2 ♕h5 with a powerful initiative, but after 18 ♖e1! it is not apparent how Black develops his play, whereas White gains chances on the queenside.' (Sveshnikov)

But in my opinion, 18 ♖e1? is refuted by 18...♘g4 19 f3 ♕d6!. The correct move is in fact 18 ♕xa7, since if 18...♕g4 White relieves all the threats by 19 ♘d2!? h4 20 h3 ♕d4 (20...♕e2 21 ♘f3! hxg3 22 ♖ae1! favours White) 21 ♕xd4 exd4 22 ♘f3 with somewhat the better ending. The immediate 18...h4 suggests itself, but then 19 a4! hxg3 20 a5! – at this our Lyons analysis concluded, with the optimistic conclusion: after 20...♖xh2(?) 21 a6 (Azmaiparashvili) or 20...gxh2+?! 21 ♔h1 d5 22 a6 White is close to a win.

And only modern computers have shown that after the cool-headed, truly inhuman move 20...♚d8! (or even 20...♘e4!? 21 a6 ♚d8!) Black would have saved himself: 21 fxg3 (21 ♕xb7? ♘g4) 21...♘g4! 22 ♘c3 ♕h6! 23 ♖xf8+ (23 h4? g5!) 23...♖xf8 24 h3 c5! 25 ♕xb7 (25 ♕xc5? d6) 25...♕e3+ 26 ♚h1 ♕xc3 27 ♖f1 ♖xf1+ 28 ♗xf1 ♘e3 or 28...♕e1 with a draw.

18 ♕xa7 (3)

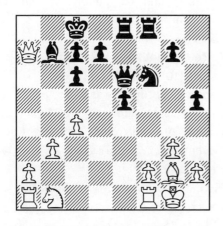

18...♕g4! (19)

This unexpected defensive resource found by Karpov (19 a4?! ♕d4!) forced me to think for a long time. It is clear that White must develop his knight, but to where?

19 ♘a3!? (53)

Planning ♘c2-e3(b4). Of course, I wanted more than 19 ♘c3(d2) ♕d4 20 ♕xd4 exd4, or the unclear 20 ♕a5.

19...h4! (7)

'Karpov has no intention of defending passively and he aims quickly to create threats against the white king' (Geller and Lein). If 19...♕d4?! White could have played 20 c5! ♘e4! (20...♕b4? 21 ♘c4; 20...d5? is even worse in view of 21 ♖fd1 ♕c3 22 ♘c4!, winning) 21 ♗xe4 ♕xe4 22 ♖ae1! (22 ♘c4 d5!) 22...♕b4 23 ♘c4 e4 24 ♘a5 ♖f5 25 ♘xb7 ♕xb7 26 ♕a4 with some advantage.

20 ♘c2 (urgently to the aid of the king!)

20...h3! (4) **21 ♗h1** (2) **21...♘e4!** (2)

Here I was seized by a slight horror. 'The white king, surrounded by its own pieces, has suddenly ended up in a mating net.' (Geller and Lein)

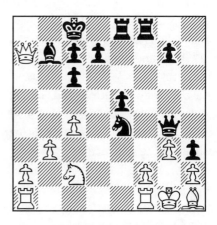

Many commentators remarked that it was bad to play 22 f3? ♘xg3! 23 ♖f2 (23 fxg4? ♘e2 mate) 23...♕g6 24 hxg3 ♕xg3+ 25 ♚f1, but here for some reason they gave only 25...c5(?) 26 ♕xc5 ♗xf3 27 ♗xf3 e4? (Suetin, Sveshnikov; 27...♖xf3 is necessary), overlooking 28 ♕a7 c6 29 ♗xe4 and wins, or 25...e4(?) 26 fxe4 ♕d3+ 27 ♚g1 ♖f6 28 ♕e3 ♖g6+ 29 ♚h2 ♕d6+ (Geller and Lein), although after 30 e5! ♖xe5 31 ♖d1! ♕e7 (31...♖d5+ 32 ♖f4!) 32 ♕d3 Black does not have sufficient compensation for the piece. 25...d6!? is correct, with the idea of ...c6-c5, or 25...d5! with an irresistible attack.

After gathering my thoughts, I found a way to neutralise Black's threats with the aid of a desperate march by the a-pawn.

22 a4! (10)

'Each does his own thing' (Sveshnikov). 'The threat of a4-a5-a6 obliges Black to force matters' (Geller and Lein). It is probable that 22 ♘e3 was also acceptable, but after 22...♕g6! (if 22...♘c3, then 23 ♕xb7+! ♚xb7 24 ♗xc6+ and ♘xg4) 23 ♖ad1 ♖f6 all the same White's only chance would be 24 a4!.

22...♞c3 (15)

With the obvious threat of ...♞e2 mate. 'Despite approaching time-trouble, Karpov plays accurately. 22...♞d2(?) suggests itself, but this would have lost after 23 a5! ♞f3+ 24 ♝xf3 ♛xf3 25 ♞e1!' (Sveshnikov). 22...♜f3? was also bad: 23 ♞e3! ♞c3 24 ♜ae1 ♛h5 (24...♛e4 25 ♛a5!) 25 a5 c5 26 a6 ♝c6 27 ♛xc5 and wins.

23 ♜ae1 (10)

'The only way' (Suetin). And, indeed, 23 f3? did not work because of 23...♞e2+! (23...c5?? 24 ♛xb7+!) 24 ♚f2 ♛g6 (Azmai-parashvili) or the spectacular 23...♛e4!?.

However, White had the more ambitious move 23 ♜fe1!? – Azmaiparashvili, who suggested it in *Informator*, gave the variation 23...♞e2+ 24 ♚f1 ♞d4 25 ♞xd4 ♛xd4 26 ♛xd4 exd4 27 ♜xe8+ ♜xe8 28 ♜e1 ♜f8 29 f4! g5 30 ♚f2 gxf4 31 g4 f3(?) 32 c5! with the better ending. But after 31...c5 32 ♝f3 d6 or 29...c5 it is hard for White to hope for success.

And besides, Black had the reply 23...♛f5, leading to double-edged play: 24 ♜ac1 ♞a2 25 ♝e4 ♛f6 26 a5 ♚d8! or 24 a5 ♚d8! (the 'crazy' 24...♛xc2 25 a6 d5 26 axb7+ ♚d7 is also possible, with the idea 26 ♛c5 e4! 27 ♜a6 ♜f6).

23...♞e2+ (2) **24 ♜xe2 ♛xe2 25 ♞b4!** (3)

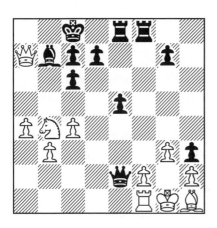

The only move – and a sudden change of plan: instead of the pawn, it is the knight that is aiming for a6.

25...d5!? (3)

Here everyone recommended a spectacular continuation suggested by the computer *Mephisto*: 25...♜f3! 26 ♞a6 (26 a5? ♜xb3) 26...♚d8! 27 ♛xb7 ♜xf2! 28 ♜xf2 ♛e1+ 29 ♜f1 ♛e3+ with perpetual check. But why should Black be thinking only of a draw? The position is still completely unclear, and Karpov continues fighting for a win.

26 cxd5 (4)

Of course, not 26 a5? ♛d2! and wins.

26...cxd5 (10) **27 ♝xd5** (25)

A logical capture. It was bad to play 27 a5? ♛b5! or 27 ♜c1? ♛d2! 28 ♛c5 ♜f7! (Geller and Lein) 29 ♞xd5 ♚b8!, winning. And in the event of 27 ♞xd5?! ♛a6! 28 ♛c5 ♛d6 'nothing is clear' (Tal).

Here I had fourteen minutes left, and Karpov had five.

27...♝xd5 28 ♞xd5 ♛c2!

'Not only defending against the mate, but also keeping the c6- and c1-squares under control.' (Sveshnikov)

29 ♛a6+ (2) **29...♚d7 30 ♞e3** (1)

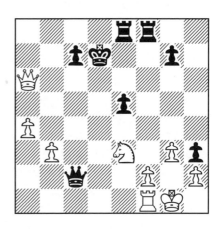

30...♛e4!

'But now Black must keep the white knight on a tight rein. By skilful manoeuvres he

restrains White's attack.' (Suetin). 30...♕xb3
31 ♖d1+ ♔e7 32 ♕g6 ♖f7 33 ♕h5 c6 34
♕xh3 ♕e6 would have led to approximate
equality, but Karpov did not want to give up
his strong h3-pawn. Instead, he again continues the fight.

31 ♖c1 (2)

With the enemy king exposed, the knight
and pawn are quite sufficient compensation
for the rook. Apparently it was simpler to
play 31 ♖d1+!? ♔e7 32 ♖c1 (Azmaiparashvili), 32 ♕a5 (Gurevich) or 32 ♕f1! ♖d8 33
♖e1 (Geller and Lein). But I did not want to
drive the black king to the shelter on g8.

31...♖b8! (2)

With just three minutes left on his clock,
Karpov continues playing for a win! 31...♕f3
32 ♕f1 ♖e6 was perfectly safe.

32 ♕f1!

First and foremost White must 'remove
the thorn' – capture the h3-pawn. The
unexpected return of the queen provoked
applause in the press centre, but Karpov did
not become flustered and with a smile he
captured a pawn with his rook.

32...♖xb3 33 ♕xh3+ (2) **33...♔d8** (1)

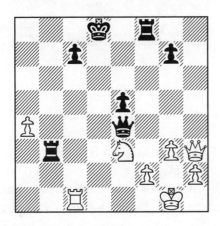

34 ♕h5 (3)

The equalising 34 ♖d1+ ♖d3 35 ♖xd3+
♕xd3 36 ♕h4+ ♔c8 37 ♕g4+ ♕d7 38 ♕e4
was good, but I wanted to retain my rook.

Here I too had just four minutes left...

34...♔c8

Safely played. White would have been set
more problems by 34...♕f3! 35 ♕g5+! ♕f6
36 ♖d1+ ♔c8 37 ♕g4+ ♔b8, but even here
after 38 ♖f1 or 38 ♕e2 he should be able to
hold out.

35 ♕d1! (1)

Centralisation with gain of tempo is the
most correct decision. After 35 ♕e2? ♖b1!
the role of the extra exchange would have
increased. Geller and Lein suggested 35 ♘c4
'with chances of an attack', but after
35...♕d4! 36 ♕e2 ♖bf3 37 ♖f1 e4 38 ♘d2
♕d3 it is only Black who has chances.

35...♖xe3!

In time-trouble this is the most practical
decision, forcing a draw. 35...♖b2? 36 ♕d6!
would have been fatal, while 35...♖d3 (Shirov) 36 ♕c2 or 35...♖b6 36 a5 was unclear.

**36 fxe3 ♕xe3+ 37 ♔h1 ♕e4+ 38 ♔g1 ♕e3+
39 ♔h1 ♕e4+ 40 ♔g1** (1) **40...♖d8** (1)

Here the game was adjourned, and I
sealed **41 ♕c2**. The following day, on White's
proposal, a draw was agreed without resuming (½–½). Times: 2.31–2.29.

This was probably the best of the drawn
games in the match (along with the 11th).
The character of the play in the Scotch

appealed to me, although I was also disappointed that my novelty did not produce any real result.

But this was nothing compared with the disappointment felt by Karpov after the 15th game. To some extent it was a turning-point in the match: a very serious error in opening preparation placed me on the verge of disaster, but my opponent was unable to achieve an apparently certain win. What Karpov squandered was not some chance opportunity, but an enormous advantage, gained for free from the opening, and he did not even manage to adjourn the game in a better position. This was a very painful lapse, after which the psychological initiative swung my way.

I began the next game, the 'trademark' 16th (normally in our matches it produced a decisive result), in an optimistic mood, not even suspecting that it would last three evenings and more than a hundred moves...

Game 71
G.Kasparov-A.Karpov
World Championship Match
16th Game, Lyons 1/2/4.12.1990
Scotch Game C45

1 e4 e5 (2) **2 ♘f3 ♘c6 3 d4**

The second act of the fascinating 'Scotch experiment'.

3...exd4 4 ♘xd4 ♘f6 (4...♗c5 – *Game No.88*) **5 ♘xc6 bxc6 6 e5 ♕e7 7 ♕e2 ♘d5 8 c4 ♘b6** (1)

Instead of 8...♗a6 (*Game No.70*) Karpov chooses a less common move, which was mentioned back in the first editions of the famous *Handbuch*, tested in the late 19th century, and revived in the middle of the 20th. Its drawback is the passive position of the knight, but it is hard for White to extract

any concrete benefit from this. 8...♘b6 is also played at the present time, including by some strong players (such as Adams and Karjakin).

To be honest, we expected that the opponent would avoid repeating the dangerous variation for Black from the 14th game, either in this way or by 8...♗a6 9 b3 ♕h4 (after which a trap had been prepared – cf. *Game No.70*, note to Black's 9th move). After all, Karpov did not know whether the Scotch had become my main weapon, or was only a temporary interruption between Spanish games, and he is unlikely to have spent all his time on it when preparing for the game. Most probably he simply looked for a way of avoiding a potentially unpleasant position.

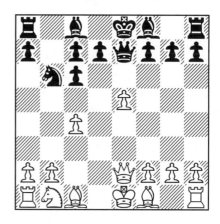

9 ♘d2 (11)

At that time the theory of this variation was still almost virgin territory. Later I successfully tried the more modern 9 ♘c3 ♕e6 (9...a5 10 ♗d2) 10 ♕e4 ♗b4 (10...g6 11 f4 is also played, or 10...♗a6 11 b3 0-0-0 12 ♗b2, Kasparov-Adams, internet (rapid) 2000) 11 ♗d2 ♗a6 12 b3 ♗xc3 13 ♗xc3 d5 14 ♕h4! (an improvement, which I devised in 1993 before the match with Short; 14 ♕f3 dxc4 15 ♗e2 0-0 is equal, Ljubojevic-Spassky, Montreal 1979) 14...dxc4 15 ♗e2 ♘d5, for example:

1) 16 ♗d4 c5 17 ♗xc5 ♘c3 18 ♗xc4 ♕xe5+ 19 ♗e3 ♘e4 20 0-0 ♗xc4 21 bxc4 0-0 22 ♖fe1 with some advantage to White (Kasparov-Adams, Sarajevo 1999), but 16...♕f5 (Morozevich-Piket, internet (blitz) 2000) or 16...♘e7!? is more accurate;

2) 16 ♗xc4 g5! 17 ♕d4 (little is promised by 17 ♗xd5 ♕xd5! 18 ♕xg5 ♖d8 19 ♕g4 h5 20 ♕f3 ♕xf3 21 gxf3 ♖g8, Stovsky-Karjakin, Pamplona 2004) 17...♗xc4 18 ♕xc4 ♘f4 19 ♕xe6+ ♘xe6 (19...fxe6 20 g3) 20 0-0-0 ♔e7 21 ♖he1 ♖hd8 22 ♖xd8 ♖xd8 23 ♖e4 with the better endgame (Kasparov-Timman, Wijk aan Zee 2000), but 18...0-0-0! is stronger (Baklan-Piket, Bundesliga 2000).

It was the novelty of the Scotch positions that created problems for Karpov and other grandmasters. In the Spanish, play was mainly built on patterns long known, whereas in the Scotch Black immediately had to make a difficult choice between various ways of developing his pieces, and initially many were simply dazzled. In any case Black's position is left with defects of some kind, and therefore he has to seek an acceptable balance of minuses and pluses. Thus, although he revealed a new idea after 8...♘b6, Karpov did not have a clear-cut equalising prescription and later he acted largely by intuition.

9...♕e6 (7)

Black has also tried 9...♗b7, 9...a5, and 9...d5!? (or 9...d6, which, however, allows 10 c5!?) 10 exd6 (suppose White does not capture en passant?) 10...cxd6 11 b3 ♗g4! 12 f3 (after 12 ♕xe7+ ♗xe7 with the idea of ...0-0 and ...d6-d5 Black's activity compensates for his inferior pawn structure) 12...♗e6 13 ♗b2 d5 14 cxd5 ♘xd5 15 0-0-0 ♕g5 (15...a5!? – Beliavsky) 16 h4!? (16 ♕a6 ♘b4!, Rublevsky-Beliavsky, Herzeg Novi 2000) 16...♕e3 with chances of maintaining the balance (Rublevsky-Beliavsky, Novi Sad

2000; Fritz-Karjakin, Bilbao 2004).

But Karpov, without delving into all these subtleties, made a solid move with his queen, which at one time was introduced by Gligoric.

10 b3 (2)

The main line.

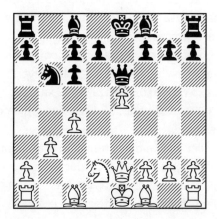

10...a5 (6)

Quite a good novelty, albeit one criticised by Geller and Lein. They, like Spassky in the match bulletin, recommended the tested 10...♗e7 11 ♗b2 0-0 12 ♕e4 d5 with equality (Bednarski-Gligoric, Havana 1967). Black can also be satisfied with 12 g3 d5 (Oll-Gildardo Garcia, New York 1997), but 12 0-0-0 is sharper, with the idea of 12...d5 13 exd6 cxd6 14 ♕f3 d5 15 ♗d3 ♕h6 16 cxd5 cxd5 17 ♔b1!, creating pressure on the isolated d5-pawn with the threat of an attack on the kingside (Ivanchuk-Almasi, Monte Carlo (rapid) 2001).

Perhaps the clearest way to equalise is 10...♗b4!? 11 ♗b2 0-0 12 0-0-0, and now in the event of 12...d5 13 exd6 ♕xd6 14 ♘f3 (to Anand's suggestion 14 ♕e3 there is the sound reply 14...♕a3) 14...♕h6+ 15 ♕e3 ♕xe3+ 16 fxe3 ♖e8 (Kasparov-Piket, Dortmund 1992) 17 ♘d4! ♗g4 18 ♗e2 ♗xe2 19 ♘xe2 ♖xe3 20 ♘d4 White has a slightly better endgame, but 12...♕e7! 13 ♔b1 ♗a3

14 ♗c3 ♗b4 is more solid, with equality (Rublevsky-Beliavsky, Vrnjacka Banja 1999) or 13 ♘e4 ♖e8! (Zelcic-Sermek, Pula 2001).

11 ♗b2 (10) **11...♗b4?!** (16)

A significant inaccuracy. 'The leitmotif of the plan with ...a7-a5 is play against the b3-pawn. 11...a4 is more logical, securing the post at b4 for the bishop' (Sveshnikov). Spassky also suggested this, but there were other opinions.

Polugayevsky: 'Possibly, Kasparov would have simply replied 12 ♗c3.' However, after 12...axb3 13 axb3 ♖xa1+ 14 ♗xa1 ♗b4 15 ♕e3 0-0 16 ♗e2(d3) d6 Black has a comfortable game.

Geller and Lein examined 12 ♕e3 ♗b4 13 ♗d3 d6(!): 'Here 14 0-0? does not work in view of 14...a3 15 ♗d4 c5. But 14 0-0-0 is advantageous to White: now if 14...a3 the bishop may retreat to a1, while after 14...dxe5 15 ♕xe5 Black has a difficult ending.' However, 14...axb3 15 axb3 d5! is far stronger, seizing the initiative (Fogarasi-Varavin, Kobanya 1992). There only remains the modest 14 exd6 ♕xe3+ 15 fxe3 cxd6 with equality.

Therefore if 11...a4 I was later planning to play 12 ♕e3 ♗b4 13 ♗e2!? with hopes of retaining a small plus.

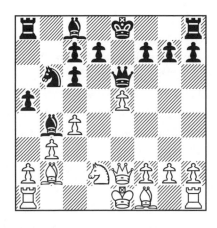

12 a3! (7)

Aiming to gain the advantage of the two bishops, which is especially perceptible in an open position.

12...♗xd2+ (12)

After 12...♗c5 White has the unpleasant 13 ♕e4! with the idea of ♗d3 and 0-0 (Spassky), and if 13...♕h6, then first 14 ♕c2. 'Perhaps 12...♗e7 would have been better' (Sveshnikov), but then after 13 ♕e3 Black is completely deprived of counterplay on the queenside (13...a4 14 b4! or 13...c5 14 a4!) and he is left with a 'bad' knight on b6. He would all the time be faced by precisely those inferior endings which Karpov was in fact aiming to avoid.

13 ♕xd2 (2)

A strategically unusual position has arisen, one which, strangely enough, we had reached at home in our preparation, since the moves 10...a5 11 ♗b2 ♗b4 looked quite natural and predictable.

13...d5? (9)

'An impulsive move, indicating a serious failure of nerve.' (Gurevich). This premature opening of the centre aggravates Black's difficulties. He had three more restrained continuations:

1) 13...a4 14 c5 ♘d5 15 b4, and after 15...♗a6 16 ♗xa6 ♖xa6 17 0-0 and f2-f4 or 15...0-0 16 ♖d1 with the intention of ♗c4, 0-0 and f2-f4 White's chances are better: the knight at d5 looks well-placed, but the a4- and d7-pawns are weak, and the undermining of the e5-pawn will merely increase the power of the bishop on b2. Black also has no counter to the opponent's pawn offensive on the kingside. Therefore Spassky recommended the blockading 15...f5, but this too is insufficient in view of 16 ♗c4 ♗a6 17 ♗a2! (Geller and Lein) or 16 ♖d1!? (with the idea of 16...♗a6? 17 b5 ♗b7 18 ♗c4);

2) 13...0-0 – the most natural reply: now in the event of 14 a4 or 14 f4 Black has more

grounds for 14...d5. The commentators drew attention to other possibilities for White:

a) 14 c5 ♘d5 15 ♗c4 ♗a6 16 0-0 ♖fb8 with counterplay on the b-file (Geller and Lein) or 16...♗xc4!? 17 bxc4 ♘e7 with an unclear position;

b) 14 ♗e2 d5(?) 15 exd6 cxd6 16 0-0(?!) a4 17 ♕c3(?) f6 'with a complicated game' (Sveshnikov), but 17 ♕d4 is stronger, to say nothing of 16 ♕d4!, when Black is in trouble. Apparently he should seek counter-chances after 14...a4 15 c5 ♘d5 16 b4;

c) 14 0-0-0!?. On c1 the king is very safely sheltered and, in the opinion of Geller and Lein, 'the threat of the f-pawn's advance places Black in a difficult position – if 14...♗a6 there follows 15 f4 or 15 a4(!)'. A pawn storm of the king's fortress is also imminent after 14...a4 15 c5 ♘d5 16 b4 ♗a6 17 f4 or 14...c5 15 a4 ♗b7 16 ♗d3 with the idea of f2-f4-f5 (here the knight on b6 is also offside, and after 16...d5 17 exd6 the bishop on b2 is activated), and again Black has no real counterplay;

3) 13...♗a6 – when there follows 14 a4, but then 14...d5 15 cxd5 ♕xd5 16 ♗xa6 ♖xa6, and after the exchange of queens Black merely has a somewhat inferior endgame.

A difficult choice. If 14...♕xd5 there is the very unpleasant 15 ♕c2!. Even so, 14...♘xd5 was better, remaining with doubled pawns on the c-file: in the event of 15 ♗c4 (Sveshnikov) 15...♕g6! 16 0-0 ♗f5 Black would have halted the opponent's attack, but after 15 ♗d3! 0-0 16 0-0 again f2-f4-f5 would have been threatened.

15 ♖c1 (3)

Now White's advantage is close to decisive.

15...0-0 (21)

15...a4? 16 ♖xc7 axb3 did not work because of 17 ♗b5+ ♗d7 18 ♕b4. If 15...c6?! both 16 ♕c2 0-0 17 ♗d3 and 16 ♗e2 are strong, as is even the immediate 16 f4. After 15...♖a7 I suggested 16 a4 in *Informator*, but White has the more energetic 16 ♗d3! 0-0 17 0-0 a4 18 b4 ♘c4 19 ♗xc4 dxc4 20 f4, when he has a powerful attack with opposite-coloured bishops.

Realising that with passive defence Black had little chance of holding out, Karpov took a decision that was typical for him: he sacrificed a pawn in the hope of 'muddying the water' – creating counterplay, by exploiting White's lag in development.

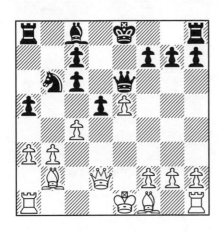

14 cxd5 (7) **14...cxd5** (9)

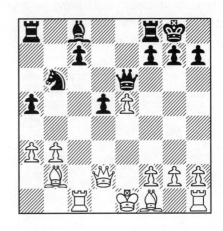

16 ♖xc7 (10)

Of course! Geller and Lein recommended the reckless 16 ♗d3(?!) a4 17 0-0(?) axb3 18 f4, ignoring 18...♘c4! 19 ♗xc4 dxc4, when it is unclear how White should conduct the attack: after 20 f5 ♕b6+ 21 ♔h1 ♗a6 22 f6 h6! he gets nowhere.

16...♕g6 (10)

16...d4 (Spassky) was another dubious recommendation, for example:

1) 17 ♕xd4 ♕xb3 18 ♗e2 ♗e6 (18...♗a6? 19 e6!) 19 ♖b7 ♖ab8 20 ♖xb8 ♖xb8 21 0-0 ♘c4(a4) 'with excellent drawing chances' (Geller and Lein), but 19 ♗d1!, suggested by me in *Informator*, is better, aiming to retain the a-pawn;

2) 17 ♗xd4 ♖d8 18 ♗e2 ♕xb3 19 0-0! (Geller and Lein give only the unclear 19 ♕b2 ♕xb2 20 ♗xb2 ♘d5 21 ♖c2 ♘f4) 19...♗e6 (19...♕xa3? 20 ♕f4) 20 ♕e3 ♕xe3 21 fxe3! ♘d5 22 ♖c5 with an overwhelming advantage for White: he must win the a5(a4)-pawn, and with it the game.

And 16...a4 would have been answered not by 17 ♗b5(?) axb3 18 ♖c6 ♘c4 (Sveshnikov), but 17 b4! ♕g6 18 f3, reaching a position which could also have occurred in the game.

17 f3 (5)

'It would appear that with this move White only defends his g2-pawn and takes control of e4, but in fact Kasparov's idea is deeper and more interesting.' (Gurevich)

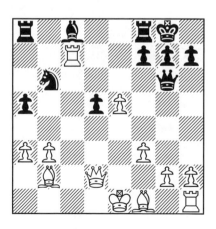

17...♗f5? (1)

17...a4!? (Geller and Lein) 18 b4! ♗e6 was more resilient, with the idea of 19...♘c4 20 ♗xc4 dxc4, pinning hopes on the opposite-coloured bishops, although even here White is a pawn up with a big advantage.

18 g4! (16)

In provoking the weakening advance g2-g4, Karpov underestimated this energetic move, driving the bishop from its active position.

18...♗b1 (18...♗xg4? 19 ♖g1 or 18...♗e6 19 ♗d3 was completely bad) **19 ♗b5!** (21)

Development with gain of tempo (♖c6 is threatened). My lengthy hesitation was caused by the mass of tempting possibilities – from 19 ♗d4 to 19 h4 ♖fc8 20 h5.

19...♖ac8 (4) **20 ♖xc8 ♖xc8 21 0-0** (3)

The pawn is poisoned: 21 ♕xa5? ♕h6!. But now White has a technically won position. However, in anticipation of a quick win, I gradually relaxed my concentration and stopped looking for the best moves, whereas Karpov, by contrast, began resisting desperately.

21...h5 (18)

21...♖c2 would have run into 22 ♕d4 ♕h6 23 ♖f2, winning (Gurevich).

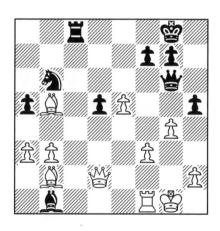

22 h3 (10)

The exchange of queens is to White's advantage, so consideration should have been given to 22 ♕d4!? hxg4 23 ♕xg4 ♕xg4+ (23...♗f5 24 ♕xg6 and ♖c1) 24 fxg4 ♗c2 (24...♗e4 25 ♖c1!) 25 ♗d4 with a won endgame: 25...♖b8 26 g5! ♗xb3 27 g6 fxg6 28 e6.

22...hxg4 (7) **23 hxg4** (1) **23...♗c2!**

Latching on to the b3-pawn. Again 23...♖c2? did not work because of 24 ♕d4 ♕h6 25 ♖f2 (Geller and Lein) 25...♖xf2 26 ♔xf2 ♕h2+ (26...♕h4+ 27 ♔g2) 27 ♔e1, when the checks come to an end. And after Sveshnikov's suggestion 23...♗f5, the simple 24 ♖f2 is good.

24 ♕d4!? (7)

Powerful centralisation of the queen, preventing 24...♗xb3? in view of 25 e6!. 24 ♖e1!? was also strong, with the same idea 24...♗xb3? 25 e6! (25...fxe6 26 ♕e3, winning a piece), or if 24...♕e6, then 25 ♗a6!.

24...♕e6 (by contrast, the black queen is forced to perform the role of blockader) **25 ♖f2** (2) **25...♖c7** (3)

Skilful defence: Black prepares the manoeuvre ...♘d7-f8, reinforcing his king's defences. After 25...♗xb3 there would not have followed 26 ♖h2? ♗c4!, but the spectacular 26 ♗d3!, and if 26...g6 27 ♕f4! with an irresistible attack: 27...♘c4 (27...♗c4? 28 ♗f5!) 28 ♗d4 ♔f8 29 ♖h2 ♔e8(e7) 30 ♖h6 etc.

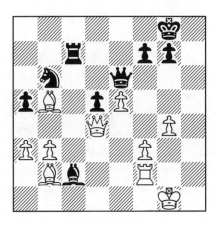

26 ♖h2 (7)

This attacking move suggests itself: the rook on the h-file looks menacing. In Gurevich's opinion, it was better to set about converting the extra pawn by 26 ♗c3 ♗xb3 27 ♗xa5 ♖c1+ 28 ♖f1 ♖xf1+ 29 ♗xf1, but after 29...♘c4 30 ♗c3 ♗a4 31 ♗d3 g6 the a3-pawn is dead, and White is in danger of selling his advantage too cheaply. Whereas 26 ♕e3!? (Spassky) 26...♘d7 (26...a4? 27 ♕g5 wins) 27 a4 ♘f8 28 ♗c3 should have brought him success.

26...♘d7 (6)

Of course, not 26...♗xb3? 27 ♕d3 and wins.

27 b4

Removing the pawn from attack. Sveshnikov, as well as Geller and Lein, rightly thought that this was an inaccuracy, making the conversion of the advantage more difficult. White had some other promising continuations:

1) 27 f4!? – this move with the idea of 27...♕xg4+? 28 ♖g2 ♕e6 29 ♗xd7 ♕xd7 30 ♖xg7+ ♔f8 31 ♖g5!, winning, was criticised by me in *Informator* because of 27...f5, but here too after 28 ♗d3! ♗xd3 29 ♕xd3 ♘c5 30 ♕b5 fxg4 31 ♖c2 White is in charge. 27...♗xb3 28 ♗xd7 ♖xd7 (28...♕xd7 29 e6!) 29 f5 ♕c6 30 ♕e3 ♗c2 31 ♕h3 ♕b6+ 32 ♔f1 ♕h6 33 ♕xh6 etc is also bad for Black. 27...♗e4! 28 f5 ♕e7 is more resilient, although after 29 ♗e2! (with the threat of f5-f6) 29...♕g5 30 ♗d1 Black's defence is difficult;

2) 27 ♗c4!? ♗e4 (after 27...dxc4 28 ♖xc2 White wins) 28 ♗e2! 'followed by f3-f4' (Sveshnikov), and if 28...♗c2, then 29 b4 is now obviously very favourable;

3) 27 a4! (the most forceful) 27...♘f8 (27...♗xb3? 28 ♕d3) 28 ♗a3 (28 b4!?), and 'after 28...♗xb3 (28...♘g6 29 ♗d6 ♖c8 30 ♗a6 ♖c6 31 ♕a7 or 30...♗xb3 31 ♗xc8

♕xc8 32 ♕e3) 29 ♗xf8 *[29 ♕e3! – G.K.]*
29...♖c1+ 30 ♔g2 ♖c2+ 31 ♔g3 ♖xh2 32
♗xg7 White wins.' (Geller and Lein)

And, indeed, 27 b4 was one of the errors
that delayed the win. But White's advantage
is so great, that it would seem he can allow
himself more than one way of converting it.

27...axb4 28 axb4 (8) **28...♘f8** (2) **29 ♗f1** (1)

Gurevich, along with Geller and Lein,
thought this was another inaccuracy and
suggested instead 29 ♗e2 with the threat of
f3-f4-f5. Then after 29...♗b3 (29...♕e7 30 b5
and wins), apart from 30 ♗d3, White would
have had the resource 30 f4!?, and if
30...♗c4, then 31 f5 ♕e7 32 ♕c3! ♖c6
(32...♗xe2? 33 ♕h3) 33 ♗d1 ♖b6 34 ♕d4!
with a winning attack.

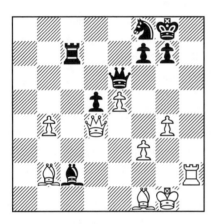

29...♗b3! (8) **30 ♗d3!** (6)

Parrying the threat of ...♗c4. Unexpectedly the position has become one where
tempi are important, and White has to play
actively, as otherwise the open position of
his king will begin to tell.

The last few moves were already made in
a time scramble: after them I had ten minutes left to the control, and Karpov six.

30...♗c4 (not 30...g6? 31 g5 with the terrible
threat of ♕h4) **31 ♗f5**

Geller and Lein gave the variation 31 ♗b1
♕a6 32 ♕d2 ♗a2(?) 33 b5 ♕a4 'with saving

chances', but after 34 e6! fxe6 35 ♗xa2
♕xa2 36 ♖h8+! ♔xh8 37 ♗xg7+ and ♕xa2
there are no chances. However, after
31...♕e7 32 ♕d2 ♘g6 the position is little
different from the one reached in the game,
and in addition White has to reckon with
31...f6.

31...♕e7 (1) **32 ♕d2 ♖c6**

'A good prophylactic move' (Geller and
Lein). If 32...♖a7?! White would have won by
33 ♖h5! (with the threat of ♕h2) 33...♖a6
(33...g6 34 ♖h6) 34 ♕h2 ♖h6 35 ♖xh6 gxh6
36 ♗c3 etc. But 32...♖b7! 33 ♗c3 ♖a7 (with
the threat of ...♖a2) 34 ♗b1 ♖a3 was more
resilient.

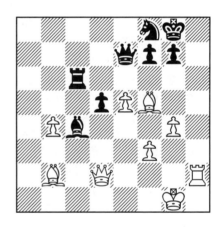

33 ♗d4

33 ♔g2! was more accurate, with the
main threat of ♕e1-h1. 33 ♖h5 (33...g6 34
♖h6) was also good, as was 33 ♖h3, condemned by me in *Informator* because of
33...♕a7+, but after 34 ♔h1 ♖a6 35 f4 or 34
♔g2 ♖a6 35 ♖h1 and ♔g3 Black is in trouble. At any event, the win here is no longer
elementary, but demands accurate calculation and a certain inventiveness. With the
help of his two active bishops, White can
combine various threats – both along the
diagonals, and along the h-file, as well as f3-
f4-f5 and also in some cases b4-b5.

33...♖a6 34 ♗b1 (1)

A time-trouble defence against ...♖a2 and the best move. After 34 ♕c3 ♘e6 (34...♘g6? 35 e6) 35 ♗h7+ ♔f8 36 ♗c2 with the threat of ♖h8 mate, Black holds on with 36...♔g8 37 ♗e3 ♕d7! (38 f4? d4).

34...♖a3

If 34...♘g6 (Sveshnikov) White has the decisive 35 ♖h5! ♖a3 36 ♔f2 ♖b3 37 ♗c5 etc, while after 34...♖a4 he has the strong reply 35 ♗c2! ♖xb4 36 ♖h5!. We have to give Karpov his due: in an extremely difficult position he has managed to create counterplay almost literally out of nothing.

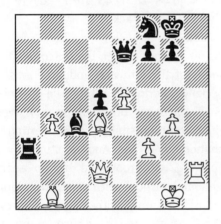

35 ♖h3 (4)

35 ♖h5! was stronger: for example, 35...♖b3 (35...♖xf3? 36 ♕h2) 36 ♗c2 ♕xb4 37 ♕f2! ♘g6 38 ♗xb3 ♕xb3 39 ♕e3 or 35...♘g6 36 ♔f2 ♖b3 37 ♗c5 ♕e8 38 ♗c2 ♖b2 39 ♕c1 ♖a2 40 ♔g3 – the king has found a relatively safe shelter, and there is nothing to prevent White from converting his advantage.

35...♖b3 (1)

Sveshnikov condemned this move, suggesting instead 35...♘g6(?) 36 ♗xg6 fxg6 37 e6 ♖a6 (but not 37...♕xe6 38 ♖h8+! ♔f7 39 ♕f4+ with mate, or 37...♖d3 38 ♕f4 and wins), but after 38 ♕h2! it is time for Black to resign (38...♖xe6 39 ♖h8+ ♔f7 40 ♕b8 etc).

36 ♗c2 ♕xb4 (1) **37 ♕f2!**

'The threats of ♕h4 and e5-e6 (in view of the fact that nearly all the black pieces are on the queenside) give White the advantage.' (Sveshnikov)

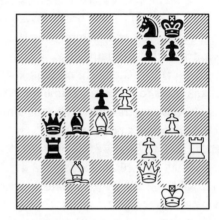

37...♘g6!

A brilliant exchange sacrifice in the time scramble. 37...♘e6(?) 38 ♕h4 ♔f8, given by me in *Informator*, would have lost to 39 ♗xb3 ♗xb3 (39...♕xb3? 40 ♗c5+) 40 ♗f2 (Geller and Lein), then ♕h8+ and so on.

38 e6! (1)

A rapid, purely intuitive reply, without a detailed calculation of its consequences. After the obvious 38 ♗xb3 both 38...♕xb3 39 ♕d2 and 38...♗xb3 39 f4 are hopeless, but I was afraid of the intermediate move 38...♘f4!, 'when Black acquires counterchances' (Sveshnikov): for example, 39 ♖h1 ♕xb3 40 ♔h2 ♕d3 41 ♖a1 ♗a6 42 ♗e3 ♘e2!. Interesting tactical play, but nevertheless after 43 ♗g5! d4 44 ♕e1 White would have retained hopes of converting his exchange advantage.

38...♖b1+

The only move: if 38...♘f4? White gives mate by 39 ♖h8+! ♔xh8 40 ♕h4+.

39 ♗xb1? (1)

At the decisive moment I faltered, and I hurriedly grabbed the rook. In the event of

39 ♔h2! things would have been difficult for Black: 39...♖c1? 40 ♗xg6 fxg6 41 ♕e3! or 40...♕d6+ 41 ♗e5! ♕xe5+ 42 f4. In *Informator* I assessed 39...♖e1 40 exf7+ ♔xf7 as being in his favour, but after 41 ♗xg6+ ♔xg6 42 ♕c2+ ♔f7 43 ♕f5+ ♔e7 44 ♔g3! (if instead 39...♖f1 had been played, 44 ♕g5+! would be good) White wins the g7-pawn, and with it the game.

And 39...♕d6+ (Gurevich) 40 ♕g3 ♕xg3+ 41 ♔xg3 leads to a won endgame for White – his bishops together with the rook simply tear the opponent's position apart:

1) 41...♖c1 42 ♖h2! ♖e1 43 exf7+ ♔xf7 44 ♖h7 ♘e5 45 f4 ♘c6 46 ♖xg7+ ♔f8 47 ♗f6 or 42...♗b5 43 ♗xg6! (to create a passed pawn) 43...fxg6 44 ♖b2 ♗a6 45 ♖b6! ♗c8 46 ♖d6 ♔f8 47 ♗e3! ♔e7 48 ♖b6 ♖c7 49 ♗g5+ ♔f8 50 ♔f4;

2) 41...♖b8 42 ♖h1! (42 ♖h5!?) 42...♖e8 (42...♘f8 43 e7) 43 ♖e1 ♗b5 44 ♖b1 ♗c4 45 exf7+ ♔xf7 46 ♖b7+ ♘e7 47 g5! ♗a6 48 g6+ ♔f8 49 ♖c7(a7).

39...♕xb1+ 40 ♔h2 (1) **40...fxe6**

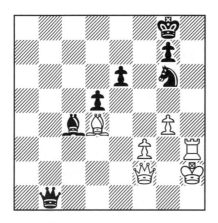

The time scramble came to an end, and I immediately realised what I had done: I had squandered nearly all of my enormous advantage. Again, for the umpteenth time! Here the game was adjourned. In a state of semi-shock I began considering my secret

move, and I soon concluded that now there were winning chances only in the endgame.

41 ♕b2! (13)

Despite all the negative emotions, common sense suggested to me that with the queens on – say, after 41 f4 ♕e4 42 ♔g3 e5 43 fxe5 ♗e2! etc – Black would easily gain a draw. The next day there followed:

41...♕xb2+

The only move: ♗xg7 was threatened, and if 41...♕e1?, then 42 ♕b8+ ♔f7 (42...♘f8 43 ♖h8+!) 43 ♕c7+ ♘e7 44 ♕f4+ ♔e8 (otherwise it's mate: 44...♔g8 45 ♖h8+ or 44...♔g6 45 ♖h6+) 45 ♖h8+ ♔d7 46 ♕b8 with a winning attack.

42 ♗xb2

As far as I remember, the outcome of our analysis of this unusual endgame was not especially cheering for White. The position is probably a draw, but even so it is worth seeking some possibilities of converting the exchange advantage. And we studied ways of playing with rook and bishop against knight and bishop (with opposite-coloured bishops), not only with pawns, but even without them (today the computer has shown that here the stronger side wins). It is not easy for Black to defend, but when the pawns become immobilised, the fifty-move drawing rule may come to his aid. It is hard to say what caused it, but the adjournment session went very well for me.

42...♘f4

'After 42...e5 43 ♖h5 d4 the reply 44 f4? is bad in view of 44...d3, but 44 ♔g3 comes into consideration' (Sveshnikov), or 43 ♗c1 ♔f7 44 ♔g3 and ♖h2.

43 ♖h4 (1) **43...♘d3 44 ♗c3** (44 ♗a3 d4 45 ♔g3 e5 is no better) **44...e5** (5)

Up to here we played quite quickly.

45 ♔g3 (4) **45...d4** (5).

Voluntarily fixing the pawn chain. The line 45...e4?! 46 fxe4 (46 ♖h5 e3!) 46...♘c5! 47

♔f3! favours White, but 45...♔f7 was not bad. **46 ♗d2 ♗d5** (4) **47 ♖h5** (2) **47...♔f7** (18)

A noteworthy fact: the resumption had only just begun, and Karpov was already spending considerable time in thought. If Black had prevented the rook from going to h8 by playing 47...♗c4, it would have invaded his position by 48 ♖h1 and ♖a1-a7.

48 ♗a5 (3)

Trying to approach the e5-pawn with the bishop, and then to attack the g-pawn with the rook, in order to somehow break up Black's defensive construction and at an appropriate moment carry out the undermining f3-f4, after which the remaining black pawns can be dealt with. However, the extremely limited material greatly hinders White, and without the opponent's 'help' he probably cannot achieve anything.

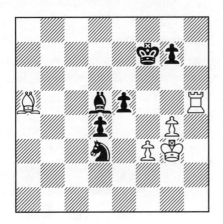

48...♔e6 (4)

For some reason Sveshnikov condemned this natural move, thinking that 'in the event of 48...♗b3 49 ♖h8 (49 ♗c7!? g6) 49...♘c5 50 ♖b8 ♗d1 Black could have put up a tenacious resistance.' But after the waiting move 51 ♖a8 he has no fewer problems than in the game.

49 ♖h8 (6)

49 ♗c7 (with the idea of 49...g6 50 ♖h8) was hardly any better. After 49...♗c6 50 ♖g5

♔f6 51 f4 a draw can be gained by 51...exf4+ 52 ♗xf4 ♘xf4 (52...g6 53 ♖a5 ♔e6 54 ♗c7 is not so clear) 53 ♔xf4 d3 54 ♖f5+ ♔e6 55 ♔e3 ♗e8! and ...♗g6. The outcome is the same after 49...♗c4!? 50 ♖g5 ♔f6 51 f4 exf4+ 52 ♗xf4 ♘xf4 53 ♔xf4 ♗e6 54 ♖b5 g5+! (55 ♖xg5 d3 with a draw). But after 49...♔f6 50 f4! (in *Informator* I gave only 50 ♖f5+ ♔e6 51 ♖f8) 50...exf4+ 51 ♗xf4 ♘xf4 52 ♖f5+ ♔e6 53 ♔xf4 ♗b3 54 ♖c5 Black has a less favourable version of the ending bishop and pawn against rook.

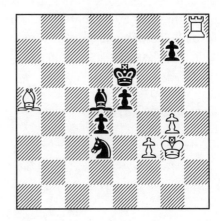

49...♘b2?! (6)

'At this moment of the game I assessed White's winning chances at 40 per cent' (Spassky). '49...e4? was weak because of 50 ♖e8+, but 49...♗c6 was possible' (Sveshnikov), or 49...♔f6. Karpov's attempt to transfer his knight to c4 is dubious, since now not only Black's knight but also his king moves away from the kingside, and White is able to regroup successfully.

50 ♖e8+ (3) **50...♔d6** (50...♔f6? 51 ♗d8+) **51 ♗b4+** (6) **51...♔c6 52 ♖c8+** (52 ♖xe5? ♘d3) **52...♔d7**

Of course, not 52...♔b5? 53 ♗f8 with the threat of ♖c5+ or ♗xg7.

53 ♖c5 ♔e6 54 ♖c7

The black king has returned to e6, but during this time White has increased his advantage, having sharply activated his rook and prepared f3-f4.

54...g6 (15)

My first achievement: 'Black has not managed to maintain his pawn on g7' (Sveshnikov). Perhaps beforehand Karpov had been intending the gambit line 54...♘c4(?) 55 ♖xg7 d3 with an interesting draw in the event of 56 ♖g6+ ♔f7 57 ♖a6 d2 (I gave a detailed analysis of this in *Informator*), but here noticed that after 56 ♖e7+! ♔f6 57 f4! Black is unable to coordinate his pieces and he loses: 57...e4? 58 f5 d2 59 ♔f4 with the threat of 60 g5 mate, 57...exf4+ 58 ♔xf4 d2?! (despair: 58...♘b6 59 g5+ and ♗d2 is hopeless) 59 g5+ ♔g6 60 ♗xd2 ♘xd2 61 ♖d7, or 57...d2 58 g5+ ♔g6 59 ♗xd2 ♘xd2 60 ♖xe5 etc.

55 ♖e7+ ♔f6 56 ♖d7 (16)

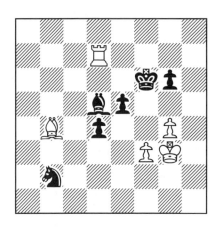

56...♗a2

Both 56...♗f7? 57 g5+ ♔g7 58 ♗e7 (Suetin) and 56...♗e6? 57 ♗e7+ ♔f7 58 ♖c7 ♘c4 59 ♗g5+ (Polugayevsky) are bad for Black, as is 56...♘d3? 57 ♖xd5 ♘xb4 58 ♖d6+ ♔g5 (58...♔f7 59 f4) 59 ♖b6 ♘d3 60 ♖e6! ♔h6 61 ♔h4 ♔g7 62 ♔g5 etc.

57 ♖a7 (22) 57...♗c4 (16)

A curious moment. After 57...♗d5 Geller and Lein give a seemingly winning variation with the fall of the g-pawn: 58 ♗e7+(?!) ♔e6

59 ♗g5 ♘c4 60 ♖g7 d3 61 ♖xg6+ ♔f7 62 ♖f6+ ♔g7 63 ♖a6 d2 64 ♗xd2 ♘xd2 65 ♖d6 ♘f1+ 66 ♔f2 ♗c4 67 ♖d1 ♘h2(?) 68 ♔g2. However, after 67...e4! 68 fxe4 ♘h2 Black saves his knight and the game (69 g5 ♔g6 70 ♖g1 ♗e6 71 ♔e3 ♘g4+ 72 ♔f4 ♘f2). Moreover, 60...♔d6!? 61 ♖xg6+ ♔c5 62 ♗e7+ ♔b5 63 ♖h6 d3 64 ♖h1 d2 65 ♖b1+ ♔a4 66 ♗g5 e4! 67 fxe4 ♗xe4 68 ♖a1+ ♔b5 (threatening ...♗c2) 69 ♗xd2 ♘xd2 etc also leads to a draw.

Therefore after 57...♗d5 the correct continuation is 58 ♖a6+! ♔f7 59 g5 or 58...♗e6 59 ♗d2 with winning chances.

58 ♗a5? (22)

A quite understandably long think (a second successive one of 22 minutes!) at the start of the third time control. I was trying to find the plan that was the most dangerous for Black. But as a result, from the several tempting bishop moves (58 ♗e7+, 58 ♗f8, 58 ♗d2) I chose the worst! And yet White also had some cunning moves with his rook – in particular 58 ♖b7!? with the idea of 58...♗d5 59 ♖b6+! or 58...♘d3 59 ♗e7+ ♔e6 60 ♗g5.

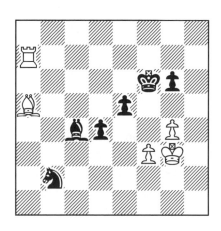

58...♗d3? (7)

Also a serious error, not noticed by anyone. Sveshnikov gave two other replies, after which, in his opinion, 'White would have gained a decisive advantage':

1) 58...♗e2(?) 59 ♗d8+(?) ♔e6 60 ♖a2 'and wins', but after 60...♘c4! Black forces a draw: 61 ♖xe2 d3 62 ♖e1 d2 63 ♖d1 ♘e3 64 ♖xd2 ♘f1+ and ...♘xd2. True, 59 ♖c7! ♘c4 (59...♘d3 60 ♗d2) 60 ♗b4 ♘e3 61 ♖c6+ ♔f7 62 ♗d2 does indeed retain chances of success;

2) 58...♘d3(!) 59 ♗d8+ ♔e6 60 ♖g7 ♘f4 61 ♗g5 'and wins', but here too after 61...d3! 62 ♖e7+ ♔d6 the position is a draw. Black also holds on after 60 ♖e7+ ♔d6 61 ♖g7 ♘f4 62 ♗a5 ♗d3, while if 59 ♗d2, then 59...g5! (for example, 60 ♖a4 ♗b5 61 ♖a8 e4! etc).

Yes, after 58...♘d3 I would possibly have been unable to breach Black's defences. But since the 49th move Karpov had been aiming to reach c4 with his knight, which is why he vacated this square by 58...♗d3. However, now White's long-planned undermining move f3-f4 becomes strong.

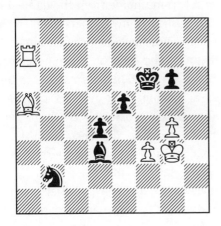

59 f4! (2)

It is not altogether clear whether there is a win after 59 ♗c7 ♘c4 60 ♖a6+ ♔e7 61 ♖c6 e4 62 ♗b6 ♘xb6 63 ♖xb6 exf3 64 ♔xf3 ♗c2.

59...exf4+?! (5)

If not Black's previous move, then this one was definitely the decisive mistake! 59...e4?

60 ♗b6 was even worse. 59...♔e6 was essential, after which there is a choice between 60 ♖a8 ♘c4 61 ♗b4 and the more forcing 60 fxe5 ♘c4! 61 ♗c7! ♘xe5 62 ♖a5 with quite good chances of converting the extra exchange, although White would still have had a fair amount of work to do.

60 ♔xf4 (1)

The rest is comparatively simple, since Black inevitably loses one of his pawns – either d4, or g6.

60...♗c2 (1)

60...♘c4 61 ♖a6+ ♔f7 62 ♗b4 will not do, nor the more resilient 60...g5+ 61 ♔g3 ♘c4 62 ♗d8+ ♔e6 63 ♗xg5 ♗c2 64 ♖c7 and wins. Suetin and Sveshnikov considered 60...♔e6 to be better, but after 61 ♗b6! ♔d5 62 ♖d7+ ♔c6 63 ♖xd4 it is time for Black to resign (63...♔xb6 64 ♖b4+ and ♖xb2).

61 ♖a6+ ♔f7 (2) **62 ♔e5** (5) **62...♘d3+** (13)

Here the d-pawn's fate is no longer a consideration, so Karpov tries to create something resembling a fortress. 62...d3 63 ♖a7+ ♔e8 64 ♔e6 ♗b3+ 65 ♔f6 or 62...♘c4+ 63 ♔xd4 ♘xa5 64 ♖xa5 followed by g4-g5 and so on was completely hopeless.

63 ♔xd4 ♘f2 (1) **64 g5**

This move, cutting off the black king, suggests itself and I made it quickly, not taking the trouble to think, since I was sure that in the remaining time I would be able to solve all the problems at the board. But: 'In this position Karpov recommended 64 ♖c6!, disrupting the coordination of the black pieces: 64...♗a4 (otherwise a piece is lost) 65 ♖c7+ ♔e6 66 g5, when the knight cannot return to its own territory.' (Geller and Lein)

64...♗f5 (1) **65 ♗d2** (2) **65...♔e7 66 ♔d5** (1) **66...♘e4** (4) **67 ♖a7+** (1) **67...♔e8** (1) **68 ♗e3 ♘c3+** (1) **69 ♔e5 ♔d8 70 ♗b6+ ♔e8 71 ♖c7** (3) **71...♘e4 72 ♗e3 ♘g3** (6) **73 ♗f4** (9)

After arranging everything 'in the proper

way', I again began thinking over my moves: it transpired that it was not so easy to find a decisive plan.

73...♘h5 (5)

In the event of 73...♘e4?! 74 ♖c4 ♘f2 75 ♗g3 the knight becomes a 'non-returner'.

74 ♖a7 (5) **74...♔f8** (1)

This retreat initially stupefied me. I was expecting the king to run to the queenside, whereas on the kingside I was hoping to checkmate it without any great difficulty.

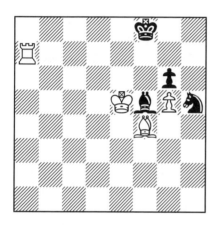

Gradually I calmed down and step by step I began working out a winning plan, which consisted of three parts: 1) the white bishop is established on e5; 2) the white king penetrates to d8 and Black's is driven to f7; 3) the white king breaks through to e7(e8), and Black is either mated or he loses material.

75 ♗h2 (6) **75...♘g7** (1) **76 ♗g1** (1) **76...♘h5 77 ♗c5+ ♔g8** (2) **78 ♔d6** (12) **78...♔f8** (1) **79 ♗d4** (1)

With the intention of ♗e5. But here I was not yet sure of success, and in order to check everything properly I decided to drag things out until the time control on move 88 and again adjourn the game.

79...♗g4 (1)

The knight is tied to h5, as 79...♘f4 merely hastens the end: 80 ♗g7+ ♔e8 81 ♖e7+ ♔d8 82 ♗f6 or 80...♔g8 81 ♗e5 etc.

80 ♗e5 (18)

The first part of the plan is fulfilled. The second, technically more difficult part is carried out by White with exaggerated lack of haste.

80...♗f5 (1) **81 ♖h7** (1) **81...♔g8** (2) **82 ♖c7 ♔f8** (3) **83 ♔c6** (2) **83...♔g8** (4) **84 ♖e7** (4) **84...♔f8** (3) **85 ♗d6** (2) **85...♔g8** (2) **86 ♖e8+ ♔f7 87 ♖e7+** (2) **87...♔g8 88 ♗e5** (1) **88...♔f8** (1)

Here the game was adjourned for the second time – the only instance of this over our five matches.

89 ♖a7 (54)

The sealed move. Of course, I thought about it for no more than a couple of minutes, and not almost an hour – it was simply that, by the rules of that time, if one of the contestants wanted to adjourn the game before the expiry of the playing session, he was obliged to take all the remaining time on his clock.

On returning home from the game, I immediately showed my trainers the plan I had found. The position was not so complicated as to enlist the help of a computer (such 'help' was reported in the press, but in those years a machine was not yet capable of solving such a problem – cf. the letter by Frederic Friedel to *64* 1991 No.4). It only remained for us to refine the shortest way to the goal in terms of moves.

However, the next day, 3rd December, we were due not to resume this game, but to play the next one, the 17th. And here, in order to be in the lead before the start of it, I decided to take my second time-out. This questionable decision had both pluses and minuses. Today it seems to me that I should have immediately turned up for the 17th game, since the existence of such an adjourned position would have psychologically affected Karpov more than me. However, it is easy to criticise myself twenty years later, and at the time I was tired out after the very difficult adjournment session. Moreover, I was not having an easy time in my 'black' games.

A day later the 16th game was finally concluded.

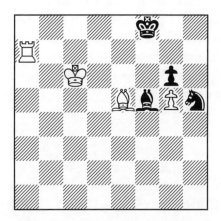

I should remind you that the last pawn advance had occurred on the 64th move and the fifty-move rule would come into force on the 114th. Thus I had 25 moves left in which to achieve the win, but thirteen proved sufficient, and on them I spent just four minutes on the clock.

89...♗g4 (7) 90 ♔d6 ♗h3 (12)

Little would have been changed by 90...♗f5 91 ♖a3!, for example:

1) 91...♔e8 92 ♖e3 ♔f7 93 ♔c7 ♗e6 94 ♔d8 ♗d5 95 ♗b2 ♘f4 96 ♖e7+ ♔g8 (96...♔f8 97 ♗a3!) 97 ♖a7 ♘d3 98 ♗c3 ♔f8 99 ♖d7 ♗c4 100 ♖d6 or 93...♔e6 (to freedom!) 94 ♗h2+ ♔d5 95 ♖e7 ♗c2 96 ♔d8 ♗a4 97 ♖e5+ ♔d4 98 ♖e6 ♗c2 99 ♔e7, reaching the g6-pawn;

2) 91...♔f7 92 ♖e3, and 92...♗e6 (92...♗c2 93 ♔d7) 93 ♔c7 ♔e7 94 ♗b2! ♘f4?! (94...♔f7 95 ♔d8) 95 ♗a3+ ♔f7 96 ♖f3 is bad for Black, as is 92...♗g4 93 ♔c7 ♔e6 94 ♗h2+ ♔d5 95 ♖e7 ♗f5 96 ♔d8 and ♔e8-f7 or 94...♔f7 95 ♔d8 ♗e6 (95...♘g7 96 ♖e7+

♔f8 97 ♗d6!) 96 ♖a3 ♗c4 (96...♘g7 97 ♖a7+ ♔f8 98 ♗d6+ and ♔e7) 97 ♖a7+ ♔e6 98 ♔e8, winning the g6-pawn or a piece (98...♔f5 99 ♖a5+).

91 ♖a3! ♗g4 92 ♖e3 ♗f5 (15) 93 ♔c7 ♔f7 (6) 94 ♔d8 (1)

The second stage of the plan has been completed. Now the white king wants to break through to e7(e8).

94...♗g4 (1)

After 94...♔e6 the black king would avoid perishing in the corner, but would be driven away from its own pawn: 95 ♗h2+ ♔d5 96 ♔e8 ♔d4 97 ♖e1 ♔d5 98 ♔f7 followed by the switching of the rook to the sixth rank (or to g8) and ♖xg6.

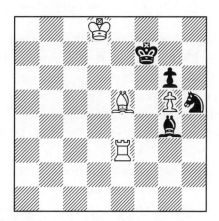

95 ♗b2!

An important nuance: in order to drive the king into the corner, the stalemated knight has to be released. I think that Karpov was taken aback by the rapidity and extreme precision of my play, and some observers were also surprised (apparently it was this that gave rise to rumours about 'computer assistance').

95...♗e6 (4)

If 95...♘f4, then 96 ♖e7+ ♔g8 (96...♔f8 97 ♗a3!) 97 ♔e8 ♘e6 98 ♖f7 with unavoidable mate.

96 ♗c3 ♗f5 (1) 97 ♖e7+ ♔f8 (1) 98 ♗e5 (1)

98...♗d3 (2) **99 ♖a7 ♗e4** (2) **100 ♖c7** (1)
100...♗b1 101 ♗d6+ ♔g8 (12)

The agonising think was not about this natural move, but the next one...

102 ♔e7 (1)

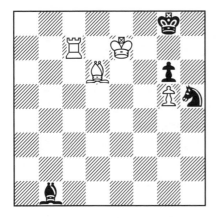

The conclusion of the third part of the plan. Black resigned (**1–0**), realising that after 102...♗f5 103 ♗e5 or 102...♘g7 103 ♖c8+ ♔h7 104 ♗e5 there was no way he would last out without a single capture until the cherished 114th move. Times: 6.23–5.54.

This was not only the most protracted game in our matches, but also the longest game with a positive result in the entire history of world championship matches.

Thus, after eight successive draws and much suffering, I again managed to take the lead: 8½-7½. Alas, the following day I suffered a set-back in the Grünfeld Defence, and the scores became equal. But, although the loss of the 17th game was very painful, I still had the feeling that as soon as I stopped leaving pieces *en prise*, the scales would tip in my favour.

In the next 'white' game, reckoning that we had already hoodwinked the opponent enough with Scotch problems, I decided to revert to the Ruy Lopez, where we had some fresh ideas. But Karpov again got his novelty in first, for the umpteenth time destroying the myth about my overwhelming superiority in opening preparation. Incidentally, at this game nearly all the directors of the Grandmasters Association were present (a meeting and a press conference of the GMA Board took place in Lyon). In the auditorium one sensed an unusual excitement and the expectation of something out of the ordinary. Would the extraordinary events of the 1986 match be repeated, when after winning the 16th game I suffered three successive defeats?

> ### Game 72
> **G.Kasparov-A.Karpov**
> World Championship Match
> 18th Game, Lyons 8/9.12.1990
> *Ruy Lopez C92*

1 e4 e5 (1) **2 ♘f3 ♘c6 3 ♗b5 a6 4 ♗a4 ♘f6 5 0-0 ♗e7 6 ♖e1 b5 7 ♗b3 d6 8 c3 0-0 9 h3 ♘d7** (1)

For the fourth and last time, instead of 9...♗b7.

10 d4 ♗f6 11 a4! (2) **11...♗b7** (1) **12 ♘a3** (1)

More promising than 12 axb5?! (6th game) or 12 ♗e3 (8th game).

12...exd4 (1) **13 cxd4 ♘b6!?** (3)

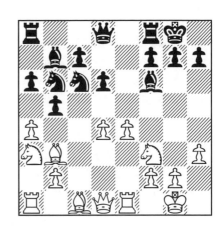

And here is the novelty, of a higher quality than 13...♘a5 (12th game), after which I had prepared 14 axb5! axb5 15 ♗c2! b4 16 ♘b5!. But now I had to have a substantial think.

14 ♗f4! (46)

'Simple, solid play, without any guile, but at the same time thematic. The threat is 15 axb5 axb5 16 ♘xb5 with the win of a pawn, and therefore Black must immediately determine his pawn structure on the queenside.' (Vasyukov)

Even so, this is a responsible decision: White presents his opponent with the advantage of the two bishops. 'An ordinary player, naturally, would first have played 14 axb5. What distinguishes a world champion is an ability to take non-routine decisions! A normal person would be simply horrified by the prospect of losing his "Spanish" bishop!' (Kholmov)

In the event of 14 axb5 axb5 nothing would be given by either 15 ♗f4, in view of 15...b4 16 ♘b5 (16 ♘c2 ♘a5) 16...♖xa1! (Geller and Lein's move 16...♗a6 is not so clear because of 17 e5) 17 ♕xa1 ♕d7, or 15 d5 (14 d5 really is better) 15...♘e5 16 ♖b1 ♕d7 or 16 ♖a2 c6. Therefore my trainers and I studied 15 ♖b1 ♘a5 16 ♘xb5 ♗a6 17 e5 or 15...♗a6 16 ♘c2 ♘a5 17 ♘b4 ♘xb3 18 ♕xb3 ♗b7 19 d5 with a minimal plus for White. But this was not used, since after the present game the variation with 13...♘b6 practically went out of use.

14...bxa4 (3)

The correct reply, of course: 14...b4?! drives the knight towards the centre – 15 ♘c2, and after 15...♘a5 16 ♘xb4 Black has no compensation for the pawn.

15 ♗xa4 ♘xa4

None of the experts commented on this natural and instant exchange, and only Vasyukov suggested 15...♘b4 16 ♗b3 a5 (½-½ Balogh-Naiditsch, Sibenik 2009), but

after 16 ♘c2! a5 17 ♗b5 White has an enduring advantage; I noticed that 15...a5 was also dubious because of 16 ♗b5!.

16 ♕xa4

In return for his 'Spanish' bishop White has a dynamic pawn pair in the centre and the possibility of pressure on the queenside. Black is forced to defend patiently, but for the moment he has a comparatively acceptable game.

16...a5 (1)

Also a seemingly logical move – creating a support pillar for the knight on b4. 16...♕d7? 17 ♘c4 (threatening ♘a5) 17...♖ad8 18 d5 favours White, but 16...♕e8 came into consideration: for example, 17 ♘c2 ♘d8! 18 ♕b3(b4) ♕b5, approaching equality, or 17 ♕c4 (occupying the place of the knight) 17...♕d7 with the idea of ...♘e7-g6, and Black's sufferings are only slight.

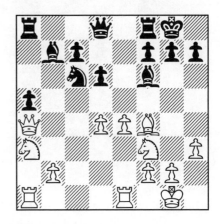

17 ♗d2! (5)

After 17 ♘c2 ♘b4 18 ♕b3 c5 or 18...♖e8 it is hard for White to achieve anything tangible.

17...♖e8 (1)

Again a sensible idea – pressure on the centre. In the event of 17...♖a6 18 d5 ♘b4 19 ♘c4! Black has more problems: 19...♘d3 20 ♖e3 ♘xb2 (20...♘c5 21 ♕c2) 21 ♘xb2 ♗xb2 22 ♖b1 ♖b6 23 ♖b3 ♗f6 24 ♗xa5 ♕a8! 25

♕a3! ♖xb3 26 ♖xb3 c5 27 ♗c7 ♗e7 28
♕xa8 ♗xa8 29 ♖b6, stealing up on the d6-
pawn. Polugayevsky recommended 17...♕e8
(with the threat of ...♘xd4) 18 ♕b5 ♖b8 or
18...♗a6, but 18 ♘b5! is stronger.

'17...♖b8 suggested itself, in order to answer 18 d5 with 18...♘b4. However, after 19
♗xb4 axb4 20 ♘c4! (20 ♕xb4? ♗xd5)
20...♗c8 21 ♖ac1 ♗d7 22 ♕b3 all the same
Black ends up as the defending side *[18 ♘c2!
is even better – G.K.]*. Therefore Karpov
prefers to give up a pawn immediately, in
order to open the position and gain counter-
chances, exploiting the power of his long-
range bishops.' (Kholmov)

18 d5 (5)

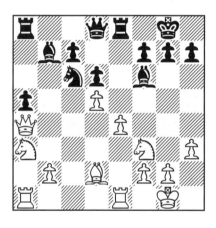

18...♘b4!? (1)

Following the scheme of play planned in
home preparation. In the event of 18...♘e5
19 ♘xe5 ♗xe5 20 ♘c4 Black would have
lost a pawn without sufficient compensation: 20...f5?! 21 exf5 ♗xd5 22 ♘xe5 ♖xe5
23 ♖xe5 dxe5 24 ♕g4! etc, or 20...♗d4 21
♗c3 ♗c5! (if 21...♗xc3 22 bxc3 f5, then 23
♕b3!) 22 ♕c2! ♕g5 23 ♖xa5 ♖xa5 24 ♗xa5
♗c8 25 ♕c3, repulsing the threats on the
kingside (true, in this position Black has
some counterplay in the spirit of the Ark-
hangelsk Variation of the Spanish).

19 ♗xb4 (7) **19...axb4** (1) **20 ♕xb4 ♖b8** (1)

Karpov very confidently and quickly reproduced the first 20 moves on the board,
spending just 16 minutes on them. But my
next move came as such a surprise to him
that he thought for a whole hour!

21 ♕c4! (9)

This paradoxical move (a counter-sacrifice
of the b2-pawn!) provoked a furore in the
press centre. Since 21 ♘b5 c5! (Vasyukov) is
dubious for White, everyone was analysing
the obvious 21 ♕d2!? c6! (pointed out by
Spassky in the match bulletin). After this
both Kholmov and Polugayevsky gave only
22 ♘c4 cxd5 23 exd5 ♖xe1+ 24 ♘xe1(?!),
after which 24...♖c8! is possible, with good
counterplay. But after 24 ♖xe1! it is more
difficult for Black to obtain full compensation for the pawn: now if 24...♖c8 there is
both 25 b3 and 25 ♕f4! (25...♗xd5? 26
♘xd6, winning), if 24...h6 or 24...♕c7, then
25 ♘e3 is strong, or if 24...♕d7 – 25 b4.

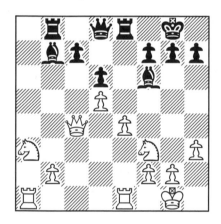

I think that the commentators rather
over-praised my queen move to c4 ('a deep
penetration into the secrets of the position',
'a brilliant way of transforming one form of
advantage – material, into another – positional', etc). It deserves a '!' mainly for its
surprise effect and for the fact that I managed to figure out a complicated problem at
the board. It somehow dawned on me that

Karpov and his helpers would almost certainly not have looked at 21 ♕c4. And I guessed right! The opponent's reaction exceeded my expectations...

21...♕c8? (63)

A serious mistake, made after an agonising think of record duration (only I thought for longer in our 1987 match). Its psychological origin is of interest. Why did Black not risk taking on b2 and fighting with equal material, but instead went in for a difficult and, above all, unpromising defence a pawn down?

Karpov was probably unsettled by the unanticipated move 21 ♕c4, and after 21...♗xb2 22 ♖a2 he imagined all sorts of horrors. And not only he! As Roshal reported from the scene of events, 'in the press centre at that moment they were unable to find an acceptable continuation for Black'. And indeed, 22...♕f6(?), hoping for 23 ♕xc7(?) ♖ec8 24 ♕d7 (Spassky, Vasyukov) 24...♗a6! does not work because of 23 ♖b1! ♗a8 24 ♘b5 ♗e5 25 ♖a7 and wins, while after 22...♗xa3?! 23 ♖xa3 followed by ♘d4 Black is in a vice (and also the c7-pawn is very weak).

In the opinion of Geller and Lein, 'Black's position is not eased in any way' by 22...♗f6(!) 23 ♘b5 ♕d7 24 ♘fd4! (24 ♘bd4 is inaccurate because of 24...♖a8!, as is 24 ♖a7, given by me in *Informator*, in view of 24...♗a6 or 24...c5 with equality). Spassky and Vasyukov also add 24...♗xd4(?) 25 ♘xd4, and this is indeed bad for Black: ♖a7 is threatened, and after 25...♖a8 26 ♖xa8 ♖xa8 27 ♖c1 he cannot breathe. 24...♖a8? also will not do in view of 25 ♖xa8 and ♕xc7.

However, 24...g6! was more or less acceptable, with the idea of 25 ♘xc7?! ♖ec8 26 ♘db5 ♗d8 27 ♖c1 ♗xd5 28 ♕xd5 ♖xb5, equalising. Although after 25 ♖a7 White retains appreciable pressure (say, 25...♖e7

26 ♘c3! ♕c8 27 ♖b1), there is still all to play for. But Karpov thought it more promising to try for counterplay against the backward b2-pawn – 21...♕c8 and ...♗a6.

22 ♘d4! (14) **22...♗a6 23 ♕c3**

The only move, but sufficient.

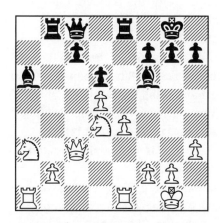

23...c5?! (3)

This attempt to enliven the play proves unsuccessful, since in the end it merely makes things easier for White. But what should be done instead? Geller and Lein recommended 23...♖b6 with the variation 24 ♘ac2 ♕b7 25 b3(?) ♗b5 26 ♕d3 c5 27 dxc6 ♗xc6, 'and it is not at all easy for White to convert his material advantage.' However, 25 b4! ♗b5 26 ♖a5 is obviously stronger. 'In the event of 24 b4 ♕b7 25 ♖ab1 Black also has nothing to hope for' (Kholmov): for example, 25...♖b8 26 ♕e3 ♗xd4 27 ♕xd4, and 27...♖xb4? fails to 28 ♖xb4 ♕xb4 29 ♖b1.

Apparently, Black should have preferred the waiting move 23...♕b7 24 ♘ac2 (Polugayevsky) 24...♗b5!? (24...♕b6 25 ♖a4! and ♖ea1), and although after 25 ♖a5 ♗d7 26 b3 Black's position is also unenviable, at least he is not losing by force. However, my opponent did not like to 'stand and wait' in permanently inferior positions.

24 dxc6 ♗xd4 25 ♕xd4 ♕xc6 26 b4! (8)

Getting rid of the weakness on b2. It would appear that, when he played 23...c5, Karpov underestimated this move and was only expecting the quiet continuation 26 ♖ac1 ♕b6(b7), when Black would retain chances of a draw, by aiming to exchange his d-pawn for the b-pawn and exploit the 'backwardness' of the knight on a3.

26...h6 (6)

After 26...♕b6? 27 ♕xb6 ♖xb6 28 b5! ♗xb5 (if 28...♗c8(b7), then 29 ♘c4!) 29 ♖eb1! and ♖xb5 the weakness of the eighth rank causes Black's downfall.

27 ♖e3 (1) **27...♖e6** (12) **28 f3!** (3)

The game is essentially decided: White has firmly supported his e4-pawn, and his extra passed b-pawn has been transformed from a weakness into a real strength.

28...♖c8 (5) **29 ♖b3** (3) **29...♗b5** (12)

If 29...♕a4 the best is 30 ♖c3 and ♘c2, quickly centralising the knight.

30 ♖b2! (3) **30...♕b7** (2) **31 ♘c2** (3) **31...♕e7** (3)

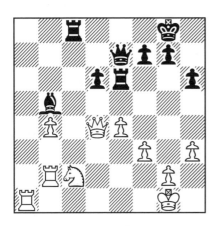

32 ♕f2?! (9)

Again, as had already occurred many times in this match, in anticipation of a quick win my aim lost its accuracy. 'It is not clear why the queen was withdrawn from its strong position.' (Geller and Lein)

I wanted to play ♘d4 as soon as possible,

in order to drive the bishop from b5 and begin advancing my b-pawn, but: '32 ♘e3 ♕g5 33 ♘f5! would have won quickly, for example: 33...♖c1+ (33...♖g6 34 f4!) 34 ♖xc1 ♕xc1+ 35 ♔h2 ♕f4+ (35...♖e5 36 ♖f2) 36 g3 ♕e5 37 f4! ♕f6 38 ♕xf6 ♖xf6 39 ♘d4' (Polugayevsky). Or 39 ♘e7+! and ♘d5. And after the more resilient 33...♔h7 or 33...♖c4 there is the strong reply 34 h4!.

32...♖g6 (2)

Trying to exploit the opponent's inaccuracy. The other attempt 32...d5 is hopeless in view of 33 ♘d4 ♖a6 34 ♖d1! ♗d7 35 exd5 or even 35 b5.

33 ♘e3 (11)

Now in the event of 33 ♘d4?! ♗d7 the h3-pawn is hanging, and after 34 ♔h1 (34 b5! ♗xh3 35 ♕e3 is stronger, but one does not want to give up an extra pawn!) 34...d5! 35 exd5 ♕e5 36 b5 ♕xd5 37 b6 ♖b8 Black retains saving chances.

33...♕e5 (2) **34 ♖bb1** (34 ♕d2!?) **34...♗d7** (3)

After 34...♖b8 (Polugayevsky), 35 ♖a7 followed by ♘d5 or ♘f5 is strong. Here I realised that with the help of inactive manoeuvres alone the game could not be won, and I forced myself to concentrate.

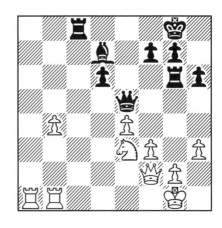

35 ♖a5! (3) **35...♕e7** (3)

In the opinion of Geller and Lein, 35...♕d4

36 ♖d5 ♕b6 was more resilient, but White would have defended against the threat of ...♗xh3 by 37 g4 or 37 h4!? and then continued proceeding towards his goal.

36 ♖a7 (3) **36...♕d8** (1) **37 ♘d5** (1) **37...♔h7** (of course, not 37...♗xh3? 38 ♘e7+) **38 ♔h2** (2)

In slight time-trouble I played as solidly as possible. 38 b5! would have been more quickly decisive, since 38...♗xh3 fails to 39 ♘f4.

38...♖b8 (1) **39 f4** (1)

'An inaccuracy' (Spassky), but in my opinion, although this move is not obligatory, it does not spoil anything.

39...♖e6 (39...f5?! 40 ♖c1! fxe4 41 ♖cc7 and wins) **40 ♕d4** (2) **40...♕e8!** (1)

The time control was reached, and here the game was adjourned.

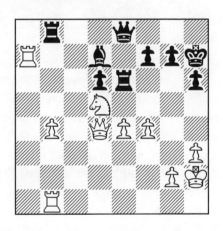

41 ♖e1! (3)

With this sealed, 'generally consolidating' move I avoided an amusing trap: 41 ♘c7? ♖xe4, when the artless 42 ♕xd6 ♕c8! 43 ♘a6 (43 ♖b3! is nevertheless better) leads after 43...♗xh3! 44 ♘xb8 ♕g4! 45 ♖a2 ♗xg2! 46 ♕d7 f5! 47 ♖xg2 ♕h4+ 48 ♔g1 ♖e1+ to perpetual check. True, White can play more subtly – 42 ♕d3, but here too after 42...♕e7! 43 ♘d5 ♗b5! 44 ♕xb5 ♕xa7 45 ♘f6+ gxf6 46 ♕f5+ ♔g7 47 ♕xe4 ♕a4

he loses nearly all his advantage. That is also the case after 41 e5(?) dxe5 42 fxe5 ♗c6! 43 ♘c7?! ♖g6! with equality (Spassky) or 43 ♕d3+ ♔h8 44 ♘c7 ♕e7 (Polugayevsky), and if 45 b5, then 45...♗xg2! 46 ♔xg2 ♖xe5.

Now, however, it was possible to find the best way of converting the extra pawn in calm analysis at home. The adjournment session, which took place the next day, did not last very long.

41...♗c6 (1) **42 ♕d3!** (1)

The fruits of our high-quality analysis are immediately seen: White makes a series of strong, energetic moves.

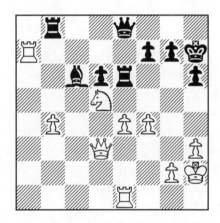

42...♕f8 (2)

A difficult choice (the fork ♘c7 was threatened).

43 ♖c1! (20) **43...♗xd5** (1) **44 exd5+!** ♖g6 (1) **45 ♕f5** (2) **45...♔g8** (2)

If 45...♕e8 46 ♖xf7 ♕e3 White decides matters with 47 ♖xg7+! ♔xg7 48 ♖c7+ followed by 48...♔h8 49 ♕xg6 ♕xf4+ 50 ♕g3 ♖xb4 51 ♖c6.

46 ♖ac7 ♖f6 (46...♖d8 47 b5) **47 ♕d7 ♖d8** (5) **48 ♕xd8!**

Transposing into a rook endgame with the black rook cut off is the simplest way to win.

48...♕xd8 49 ♖c8 (1) **49...♕f8** (1) **50 ♖1c4!** ♖f5 (2) **51 ♖xf8+** (1) **51...♔xf8 52 ♖d4**

One can only feel sympathy for the black rook, but there is no way of helping it.

52...h5 (1)

52...g5 53 g4! or 52...♔e7 53 g4 ♖f6 54 b5 ♔d7 55 ♖c4 h5 56 b6 was equally hopeless.

53 b5 (2) **53...♔e7** (1) **54 b6 ♔d7**

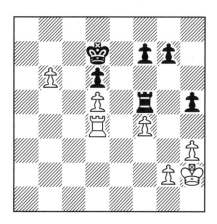

55 g4!

'It is all over – the rook is forced to abandon the 5th rank (where it was attacking the d5-pawn) and the passed pawn cannot be stopped. No, the Leningrad variation of 1986 did not apply. The spiral of history made a sharp turn.' (Vasyukov)

55...hxg4 (1) **56 hxg4 ♖f6 57 ♖c4**

Faced with an invasion of the 7th rank, Black resigned (**1-0**). Times: 2.56–2.34.

An important win, gained at a moment when the opponent had levelled the score in the match and was full of optimistic hopes. I again took the lead (9½-8½), but more importantly, I undermined Karpov's belief in the possibility of regaining the title, although, as was his custom, he continued fighting with all his might to the very end.

Before the next game the ex-champion took his second time-out. It was clear that he would try to recoup his losses (in this match we both won only with White), and so I gave up the ill-starred Grünfeld Defence and reverted to the King's Indian. This proved to be a happy choice.

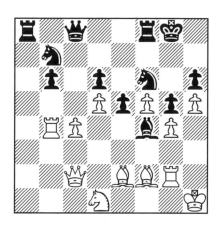

34...♘c5!

An unexpected pawn sacrifice. Karpov was probably expecting 34...♘xd5 35 ♖b5, when after both 35...♘f6 36 ♖xb6 (Azmaiparashvili and Giorgadze), and 35...♖a5 36 ♕b1 (Geller and Lein) or 36 ♕b3 (Averbakh) White has counterplay. Now, however, his task is far harder.

35 ♖xb6 (1) **35...♘ce4!** (1) **36 ♖c6!** (1)

'If 36 ♗e1, then 36...♘xd5' (Averbakh), but after 37 ♖b1 ♘df6 38 ♗f3 ♕c6 the position is equal. 36...♕c5! 37 ♖b3 ♖a1 is better, with a sizeable advantage for Black: 38 ♗f3 (this defence was suggested by Speelman) 38...♖c1 39 ♕d3 ♖xc4 40 ♖e2 ♘g3+!? or 38 ♕d3 ♕d4! 39 ♖b1 ♖fa8 etc.

The following lines were also insufficient: 36 ♗f3 ♘xf2+ 37 ♘xf2 ♕c5! 38 ♖b1 ♖a3 (Azmaiparashvili and Giorgadze), or 38 ♖b5 ♕d4! 39 ♖b1 ♖fc8 40 ♘e4 ♖xc4 41 ♘xf6+ ♔f7 etc.

36...♕b7 (4) **37 ♗e1?** (2)

In the opinion of Geller and Lein, this is a 'serious mistake' and 'better was 37 ♗d3 (or first 37 c5) 37...♘xf2+ 38 ♔xf2 ♖a1+ 39 ♖g1' etc. But here 38...♗e3! is stronger: for example, 39 ♖xd6 (...♖a1+ was threatened, and if 39 ♖g1, then 39... ♖a3) 39...♕b4! 40 ♖xf6 (forced, alas) 40...♗xf6 41 ♖g1 ♖fa6 or 41 ♕e2 ♕c5, and White does not have sufficient compensation for the exchange.

It was also not good to play 37 ♗f3?! ♘xf2+ (Averbakh) 38 ♔xf2 ♖a3! or 38 ♖xf2 ♖a1!. But 37 c5! would indeed have retained hopes of equalising: 37...♖a1 (37...♘xf2+ 38 ♖xf2!) 38 cxd6 ♖c1 39 ♕d3 ♘xf2+ 40 ♖xf2 ♖xc6 41 dxc6 ♕xc6+ 42 ♖f3 e4 43 ♕c4+ or 42...♔g7 43 ♕c4, and White should hold on.

Now, however, Black acquires real chances of winning.

37...♖a1 (3) **38 ♗f3** (1) **38...♘c5** (2)

The move that suggests itself, but 38...♖b8 was also interesting, although the best was 38...♕a7! 39 ♗xe4 ♕a3, when White is on the verge of defeat (40 ♗d3 e4!).

39 ♗c3 ♖c1 (6)

Black has a clear advantage, but here came an unexpected finish, which provoked a great commotion in the chess press.

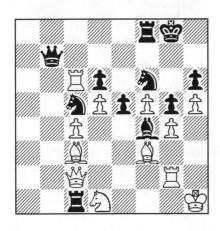

Draw agreed (½–½) – on Black's proposal!
Times: 2.25–2.19.

It is said that when the clocks were stopped and we shook hands, in the press centre they decided that Karpov must have resigned. It is indeed easy to believe this, looking at the final position. After the forced 40 ♕b2 (40 ♕a2? ♘fe4!) Black has two tempting possibilities:

1) 40...♕xb2, and if 41 ♖xb2, then not 41...♘a4 (Spassky) 42 ♖b3 with equality, but 41...♘d3! 42 ♖g2 (42 ♖b3 ♘f2+) 42...♖a8! with the terrible threat of ...e5-e4 (and if 43 ♔g1 or 43 ♖c7, then 43...♘e4!). 41 ♗xb2 is more resilient, for example:

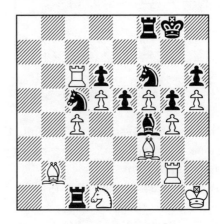

Analysis diagram

a) 41...♖xc4, and 'White faces a struggle for a draw' (Averbakh), but by 42 ♗e2 (42 ♖xd6 is also possible) 42...♖c2 43 ♗f1 ♖xg2 44 ♔xg2 ♘xg4 45 ♖xd6 he achieves his aim;

b) 41...♖b1! 42 ♖g1 (42 ♖xd6? e4!; also weak is 42 ♗a3 e4 43 ♗e2 ♘fd7 or 42 ♗c3 ♘a4! 43 ♖c2 ♘xc3 44 ♖xc3 ♖a8 45 ♖xd6 ♔g7) 42...♘ce4, and 'Black's chances are to be preferred, despite him being a pawn down' (Krogius). After 43 c5!? (43 ♔g2? ♖b8!, while if 43 ♖b6, then 43...♘g3+) 43...♘xc5 44 ♗a3 (44 ♗c3 ♘fe4!) 44...e4 45 ♗e2 ♘d3! 46 ♗xd6 ♗xd6 47 ♖xd6 ♘f4 48 ♗a6(c4) ♘xg4! or 47 ♗xd3 cxd3 48 ♖xd6 ♘xg4! White is probably unable to save himself;

2) 40...♕a7! (recommended by Azmaiparashvili and Giorgadze; 40...♕a8 allows 41 ♖xc5!) 41 ♕a2 (the only move: 41 ♖xd6? ♕a4! or 41 ♗d2? e4! and wins) 41...♕a4! 42 ♕xa4 ♘xa4.

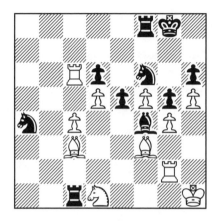

Analysis diagram

This ending is even worse for White than the one examined earlier, and no way of saving it is apparent:

a) 43 ♗a5 e4 44 ♗e2 ♖a8 45 ♗b4 ♘b2 and ...♘xd1;

b) 43 ♗b4 e4 44 ♗e2 ♖b1! 45 ♗xd6 (45 ♗e1 ♘b2) 45...♗xd6 46 ♖xd6 ♘c3 47 c5 ♘xe2 or 47 ♖b6 ♖c1 and ...♘xe2;

c) 43 ♗b2 ♖b1 44 ♖a6 (44 ♖c2 ♖b8!) 44...e4 45 ♗xf6 exf3 46 ♖g1 ♘c5 47 ♖a1 ♖xa1 48 ♗xa1 ♘e4 49 ♖e1 f2!.

But before the time control at move 40 I was so exhausted that I could no longer delve into the subtleties of the position, and I was desperate to relieve the burden of the intense pressure as soon as possible. The very thought of the forthcoming adjournment, an endless night of analysis and playing on the following day was unbearable for me. My brain was demanding a rest, and I offered a draw.

However, this story had not only regrettable, but also positive consequences for me:

in the next, 20th game Karpov with Black went in for open play, taking a risk. Well, that day he himself sowed the wind – and he reaped the whirlwind, allowing me to create the most brilliant game of the match.

> ## Game 74
> ## G.Kasparov-A.Karpov
> ## World Championship Match
> ## 20th Game, Lyons 15.12.1990
> ## *Ruy Lopez C92*

Razuvaev: 'In the early 1980s grandmaster Lev Psakhis and I were once discussing Kasparov's style of play. Lev found an interesting and, in my opinion, accurate description. "You see", he said, "when Tal attacks it is like a storm. Wave after wave, roller after roller. And each one needs to be endured. But with Kasparov it is a tsunami. The entire board is engulfed, and only a miracle can enable the opponent to emerge unscathed." Quite nicely said. And here is another curious observation: the first hurricane came in the 2nd game, and the second in the 20th. The world champion's liking for the magic of numbers is well known.'

1 e4 e5 (5)

As far as I remember, Karpov was not considering playing the Caro-Kann, but was simply slightly late.

2 ♘f3 ♘c6 3 ♗b5 a6 4 ♗a4 ♘f6 5 0-0 ♗e7 6 ♖e1 b5 7 ♗b3 d6 8 c3 0-0 9 h3 ♗b7

Again the Zaitsev Variation while 9...♘d7 (*Game No.73*) is sent off for repairs.

10 d4 ♖e8 11 ♘bd2 (1) **11...♗f8** (1) **12 a4 h6** (1) **13 ♗c2 exd4** (1) **14 cxd4 ♘b4 15 ♗b1** (2) **15...c5** (not 15...bxa4 – *Game No.69*) **16 d5 ♘d7 17 ♖a3** (2) **17...f5**

A repetition of the risky variation from the 4th game. Karpov had decided to engage in a large-scale battle!

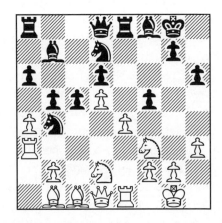

18 ♖ae3 (4)

An attempt to improve White's play compared with 18 exf5 (4th and 22nd games). This line, along with others, was one that I had analysed with Beliavsky (and he, I remember, disputed the immediate 18 ♘h2 with 18...♕e7!?).

18...♘f6 (4)

Quite a rapid reply, although in the earlier game Timman-Karpov (9th match game, Kuala Lumpur 1990) after 18...f4 19 ♖3e2(?!) ♘e5 (19...♕f6!?) 20 ♘f1?! (20 ♘xe5 dxe5 is equal) 20...♘xf3+ 21 gxf3 ♕h4 Black had no problems (21...♕g5+! 22 ♔h1 ♗c8 is even better, Bezgodov-Yakovenko, Tomsk 1998). However, the rook on e2 is badly placed, and I was planning 19 ♖a3!: for example, 19...♕f6 20 ♘b3 ♘e5 (20...♘b6?! 21 ♘a5, De Firmian-A.Ivanov, Chicago 1988) 21 ♘a5 ♗c8 22 ♗d2 ♗d7 23 ♕c1 or 19...♘e5 (Timoshchenko-Shapiro, USA 1990) 20 ♘xe5!? (20 ♘f1 ♕f6 21 ♗d2 was also studied) 20...dxe5 21 b3 and ♗b2, retaining a small plus.

19 ♘h2! (1)

An unexpected novelty (previously 19 ♖3e2 had occurred), after which for the first time Karpov sank deep into thought, on seeing that in the event of 19...fxe4?! 20 ♘xe4 the threat to the d5-pawn is ephemeral:

20...♘bxd5? 21 ♘xf6+ ♘xf6 22 ♖xe8 ♘xe8 23 ♕d3 ♘f6 24 ♘g4 or 20...♘fxd5? 21 ♖g3! (the point of my idea) 21...♖e6 (21...♔h8 22 ♗xh6!, and if 22...gxh6 then 23 ♕g4 ♘f6 24 ♘xf6 ♖xe1+ 25 ♘f1, mating) 22 ♘g4 ♔h8 23 ♘xh6! with crushing threats. 20...♘xe4 21 ♖xe4 ♖xe4 22 ♗xe4 ♕f6 23 ♕h5 ♗e7 24 ♖d1 also favours White.

How should Black respond, in order to restrain the opponent's attacking surge?

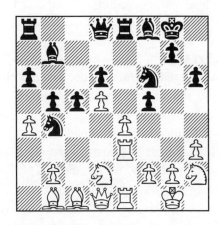

19...♔h8?! (23)

A questionable reply: Black wastes a tempo, without solving the problem of his king. Annotating this game in *Informator*, I recommended 19...♕d7!?, and six months later Karpov played this against me in Amsterdam (Game No.33 in *Kasparov vs. Karpov 1998-2009*).

True, the move 19...♔h8 also had its virtues: in our analysis we had not looked at it. We had mainly studied 19...fxe4 and briefly 19...♖e5 20 b3. Therefore here also, after a good think, I advanced my b2-pawn.

20 b3! (23)

'An important link in White's plan – the bishop is needed on the long diagonal.' (Krogius). I think that this decision was psychologically unpleasant for Karpov: the black king has only just taken shelter on h8, and suddenly the bishop takes aim from b2.

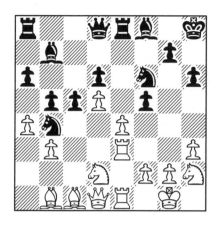

20...bxa4 (20)

'After again spending a good deal of time, Karpov did not find anything better.' (Polugayevsky). And, indeed, 20...fxe4?! 21 ♘xe4 was still dubious, for example:

1) 21...♘bxd5? 22 ♘xf6 ♖xe3 (22...♘xe3 loses immediately to 23 ♕d3) 23 ♖xe3! ♘xf6 24 ♘g4 d5 25 ♕c2 and wins;

2) 21...♗xd5? 22 ♘xf6 ♖xe3 23 ♖xe3 ♕xf6 24 ♘g4! (24 ♗d2, given by me in *Informator*, is inaccurate because of 24...♕f7) 24...♕d4 (now if 24...♕f7 there is the strong reply 25 axb5 axb5 26 ♗b2 ♕h5 27 ♖g3!) 25 ♗d2 bxa4 (25...♔g8 26 ♖g3) 26 ♘xh6! and wins;

3) 21...♘fxd5?! 22 ♖g3! (in *Informator* I gave 22 ♖f3 ♘f6 23 ♖xf6 gxf6 24 ♘g4, but this is unclear in view of 24...♗xe4 25 ♖xe4 ♖xe4 26 ♗xe4 d5) 22...♘f6 (not 22...♕c7? 23 ♘g4 ♖e6 24 ♘xh6!) 23 ♘xf6 ♕xf6 24 ♗d2! ♖xe1+ (24...d5? 25 ♘g4) 25 ♗xe1 ♕f7 (25...♕e6? 26 ♗xb4! cxb4 27 ♕d3 ♕g8 28 ♘g4 etc) 26 ♗c3 ♘d5 27 ♗a1 with a strong attack;

4) 21...♘xe4 22 ♖xe4 ♖xe4 23 ♗xe4, and the long-range white bishops cause Black a mass of problems (as is also the case after 19...fxe4?! 20 ♘xe4 ♘xe4 21 ♖xe4 ♖xe4 22 ♗xe4).

21 bxa4 (3) **21...c4?**

'Karpov's striving to sharpen the play on the queenside is readily understandable and explicable.' (Razuvaev). But this quickly-played move is apparently wrong, and 21...fxe4!? 22 ♘xe4 should finally have been preferred. Here it is again dangerous to play 22...♘fxd5?! 23 ♖g3! ♘f6 24 ♘xf6 ♕xf6 25 ♗d2! (Geller and Lein), but 22...♗xd5! 23 ♘xf6 ♖xe3 24 ♖xe3 ♕xf6 has become possible, since after 25 ♘g4? there is no time for ♘xh6 because of 25...♕a1! 26 ♗d2 ♗a2! – there is where the nuance lies!

And 'in the event of 25 ♗d2 ♗g8(?!) it is not easy for White to continue the attack' (Krogius). However, the bishop retreat (to say nothing of Geller and Lein's variation 25...♕d4? 26 ♘f3, winning) in fact makes things easier for him after 26 ♘g4. More interesting is 25...♕f7 26 ♘g4 or 25...♖b8 26 ♘g4 ♕f7 27 ♗c3, when White has excellent compensation for the pawn, but the play is still very unclear and double-edged.

22 ♗b2 (16)

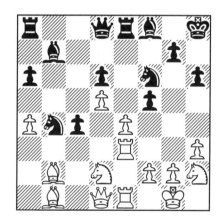

22...fxe4?! (34)

Exchanging at this particular moment loses the battle, but it is already hard to offer Black good advice. Thus he cannot be satisfied with 22...♘d3?! 23 ♗xd3 cxd3 24 exf5 (Razuvaev) 24...♖xe3 25 ♖xe3 and ♖xd3.

In the press centre grandmasters Spassky

and Polugayevsky examined 22...♖c8, and considered it to be the best defence. Geller and Lein were of the same opinion, since after 23 ♕f3! ♕d7 (again 23...fxe4? 24 ♘xe4 is weak) 24 ♗xf6 gxf6 'the c4-pawn becomes dangerous'. But the obvious 25 ♖c1, pointed out by me in *Informator*, would have left White with a stable advantage: 25...♘d3 26 ♗xd3 cxd3 27 ♖xc8 ♗xc8 28 ♖xd3 ♕xa4 29 exf5, and Black has a difficult position – 29...♖e5 30 ♖b3! or 29...♖e1+ 30 ♘hf1 ♕d1 31 g4 etc. Here one can probably talk only about practical saving chances.

23 ♘xe4 (9) **23...♘fxd5** (9)

The other capture 23...♘bxd5? did not work: 24 ♘xf6 ♖xe3 (24...♘xe3 25 ♕h5 and ♕g6) 25 ♖xe3 and ♕c2 (Polugayevsky).

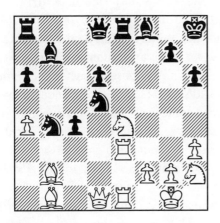

24 ♖g3 (14)

'The strongest and most accurate. 'Deep Thought', a debutant in the press centre, unexpectedly suggested here the sentimental 24 ♕h5(!?) ♘xe3(?) 25 ♕xh6+ ♔g8 26 ♘g5 and wins (or 26 ♘f6+! ♕xf6 27 ♕h7+, suggested by Polugayevsky – G.K.). But the cold human reply 24...c3! would have repulsed computer imagination.' (Razuvaev). However, after 25 ♖xc3! ♘f6 (25...♘xc3? 26 ♗xc3 ♘d5 27 ♕g6! ♘xc3 28 ♘f6! and wins) 26 ♕g6 ♖xe4 27 ♖xe4 ♗xe4 28 ♗xe4 ♘xe4 29 ♕xe4 d5 30 ♕g4 or 25...♖e5 26 ♕g6 ♕e8

27 ♖g3 White would retain winning chances.

The clever 24...♖e5 did also not bring any relief in view of 25 ♗xe5 dxe5 26 ♘g4 ♕e8 (26...♘xe3 27 ♘xe5 ♕b6 28 a5!) 27 ♕xe8 ♖xe8 28 ♖f3 ♔g8 29 ♘c3 etc.

24...♖e6! (14)

'An important defensive resource' (Geller and Lein). 'With White Karpov likes to play his rook to the 3rd rank, and with Black – to the 6th. I think that this move was found intuitively.' (Razuvaev)

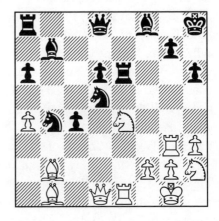

25 ♘g4? (19)

Building up the pressure. Alas, this is an imperceptible but significant error, after which Black could have equalised. 25 ♘f3!, suggested immediately afterwards by me and Polugayevsky, was correct. Now in the event of 25...♕d7? 26 ♘fg5! White gives mate: 26...hxg5 27 ♕h5+ ♔g8 28 ♘xg5 ♖xe1+ 29 ♔h2 or 26...♖e7 27 ♕h5 c3 28 ♗xc3 ♘xc3 29 ♕g6 etc. 25...♕e8? 26 ♘xd6! is also fatal, so Black has to choose between two knight jumps:

1) 25...♘f4 26 ♘d4! ♖e5 27 ♕g4 ♘bd3 (27...♘bd5 28 ♘e6!) 28 ♗xd3 ♘xd3 29 ♘e6!, and 29...♕e7 30 ♗xe5 dxe5, suggested by me in *Informator*, is bad because of 31 ♕g6! ♘f4 (31...♕e8? 32 ♕f5 ♘xe1 33 ♘f6!) 32 ♘xf8 ♖xf8 33 ♕d6!, and 29...♕f6

30 ♗xe5 ♕xe5 in view of 31 f4! ♕b2 32 ♕f5 ♘xe1 33 ♘xf8 ♕d4+ 34 ♘f2 or 32...♗xe4 33 ♕xe4 ♖e8 34 ♕c6, winning;

2) 25...♘d3 26 ♘eg5! (instead of the routine 26 ♗xd3 – an unpleasant surprise) 26...♖xe1+ 27 ♘xe1 hxg5 28 ♕h5+ ♔g8 29 ♘xd3, and there is no way to save the game.

Thus, to all appearances, 25 ♘f3 would have won, whereas 25 ♘g4 casts doubts (for just one half move!) on White's advantage.

I will explain why I nevertheless played to g4. Firstly, I was in a fighting mood (Karpov sensed this) and I did not calculate everything to the end, but simply threw my pieces into the vicinity of the enemy king. And secondly, White's attack looked very threatening: 25...♘f4? 26 ♘ef6! ♖xe1+ (26...♗c8 27 ♖xe6 and ♕f3!) 27 ♕xe1 ♘bd3 28 ♗xd3 cxd3 29 ♘xh6! or 25...♕h4? 26 ♘c5! ♖xe1+ 27 ♕xe1 dxc5 (27...♗c6 28 ♘e6) 28 ♕e4 ♘d3 29 ♖xd3! cxd3 30 ♗xd3 ♘f6 31 ♕xb7 ♖e8 32 ♗xf6 and wins, to say nothing about the line which occurred in the game.

Here Karpov stopped to think, and for me these were agonising minutes...

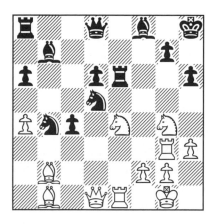

25...♕e8? (17)

A fatal mistake. All the commentators, and the first was Spassky in the match bulletin, recommended the saving move 25...♘d3! (after the game Karpov also said

that he saw this move, but to his misfortune he decided to take a risk – trying to exploit the pin on the e-file). Now nothing is given by 26 ♖xd3? cxd3 27 ♕xd3 ♕h4! etc.

White has to play 26 ♗xd3 cxd3, and here 27 ♘xh6? ♖xh6 28 ♘g5 is incorrect in view of 28...♕d7 29 ♖e6 ♘f6! 30 ♕xd3 ♖e8, winning. Also nothing is given by 27 ♖xd3?! ♕e7! (my *Informator* move 27...♕a5 is worse because of 28 ♖f3, as is Krogius's 27...♘b4 because of 28 ♖de3) 28 f3 ♘f4 with advantage to Black, or 27 ♕xd3 ♕e7! (but not Krogius's move 27...♕e8? in view of 28 ♘ef6! ♖xe1+ 29 ♔h2 and wins) 28 ♕b1 ♖e8 with approximate equality.

There remains the recommendation of Geller and Lein: 27 ♕d2 ♕e8(?!) 28 ♔h2 (28...♖xe4? 29 ♕xh6+ ♔g8 30 ♗xg7! ♖e1 31 ♘e5! or 30...♗xg7 31 ♘f6+!) or 27...♕e7(!) 28 ♔h2, and 'White still has a great advantage'. However, this is an illusion: in the second case 28...♖xe4 is now possible, when 29 ♕xh6+? ♔g8 30 ♗xg7? (30 ♕g6 ♖xg4!) does not work in view of the simple 30...♗xg7, while after 29 ♖xe4 ♕xe4 30 ♕xh6+ Black is saved by 30...♕h7. I should add that 28 ♘xh6 leads only to a draw: 28...♖xe4 29 ♖xe4 ♕xe4 30 ♘f7+ ♔g8 31 ♘h6+ ♔h7 32 ♘f7.

Schussler's recommendation 25...♕d7(?!) is less good. This move leaves Black with far more practical problems, and White with various combinative possibilities – there is 26 ♘ef6!? ♖xf6 27 ♗xf6 ♘xf6 28 ♘xf6 gxf6 29 ♕d4 ♗g7 30 ♕xc4 a5 31 ♗f5! ♕xf5 32 ♕f7 ♖g8 33 ♕xb7 and 26 ♕d4 ♖c8 27 ♘xh6!? ♖xh6 (27...c3!?) 28 ♘xd6 ♕xd6 29 ♖xg7 ♕f6 30 ♖xb7, as well as 26 ♕c1 ♘d3 (26...♖c8 27 ♘xh6) 27 ♗xd3 cxd3 28 ♘xh6!?. On the whole here White's chances are better.

But 25...♕e8, the move made by Karpov, is even worse, since it allows the capture on h6. 'It is easy to explain such a mistake with time-trouble approaching. When you are under a violent attack, you don't want to throw your pieces far forward. On the contrary, the desire to concentrate your forces in defence is quite natural.' (Razuvaev)

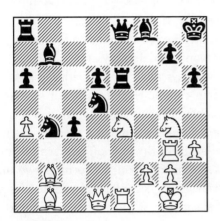

26 ♘xh6! (5)

From this moment on I carried out a sustained attack. Moreover, I played very quickly – for some reason I had not a shadow of doubt about the correctness of White's attacking construction.

26...c3 (4)

If 26...♖xh6 White would quickly conclude matters with 27 ♘xd6! ♛d7 (27...♖xe1+ 28 ♛xe1 ♖xd6 29 ♛e4!) 28 ♛g4! ♛xg4 29 ♘f7+ ♚g8 30 ♘xh6+ gxh6 31 ♖xg4+ ♚f7 32 ♗g6+ or 27...♛h5 28 ♖g5! ♛xd1 29 ♘f7+ ♚g8 30 ♘xh6+ ♚h8 31 ♖xd1 c3 32 ♘f7+ ♚g8 33 ♗g6! ♘e7 (33...cxb2? 34 ♖h5, and mate) 34 ♗xc3 ♘xg6 35 ♗xb4 ♚xf7 36 ♖d7+ ♚f6 37 ♖xg6+ and ♖xb7.

It would appear that Karpov was pinning great hopes on 26...c3, thinking that Black was seizing the initiative. But here came another powerful blow.

27 ♘f5! (2) **27...cxb2** (8) **28 ♛g4! ♗c8** (1)

It is too late the help the king – White has a colossal advantage in force. Black is not saved by 28...♘c3 29 ♘f6! ♖xe1+ 30 ♚h2, 28...g6 29 ♚h2! ♛d7 (29...♚g8 30 ♘exd6) 30 ♘h4!, 28...♖c8 29 ♚h2! ♛g6 30 ♘g5, or

28...♛d7 29 ♚h2! ♖h6 30 ♘xh6 ♛xg4 31 ♘f7+ ♚g8 32 ♖xg4 (and if 32...♚xf7 33 ♘g5+ with mate).

29 ♛h4+

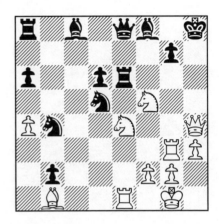

29...♖h6

In the event of 29...♚g8, again 30 ♚h2 (or 30 ♖e2) is decisive – Black is in a kind of zugzwang: for example, 30...♖a7 31 ♘exd6 ♗xd6 32 ♘xd6 and wins.

30 ♘xh6 gxh6 (1)

31 ♚h2! (13)

My patent prophylactic move in the Ruy Lopez. 'Specially for aesthetes: the king moves away from possible checks and the counterplay evaporates.' (Razuvaev) True, 31 ♖e2 would also have won.

31...♛e5

Mating motifs have appeared: 31...♗g7 32 ♘xd6 ♕xe1 33 ♕xh6+! ♗xh6 34 ♘f7 mate. **32 ♘g5** (another sacrifice) **32...♕f6** (2) **33 ♖e8** (1) **33...♗f5**

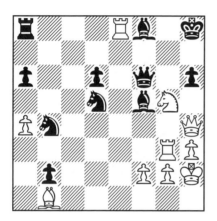

34 ♕xh6+! (1)

34 ♘f7+ ♕xf7 35 ♕xh6+ ♗h7 36 ♖xa8! would have led to a quick mate, but I chose a more elegant way with a queen sacrifice.

34...♕xh6 35 ♘f7+ ♔h7 36 ♗xf5+ ♕g6 37 ♗xg6+

Here I still regret that I didn't play 37 ♖xg6! ♘e7 38 ♖xe7! ♗xe7 39 ♖g4 mate! 'There were very many coincidences. In the time scramble in the 2nd game the world champion missed an immediately decisive stroke on g6, and now he captures on g6 with the wrong piece. However, even as it is, the battle does not last long.' (Razuvaev)

37...♔g7 38 ♖xa8 (1) **38...♗e7** (1) **39 ♖b8 a5 40 ♗e4+ ♔xf7 41 ♗xd5+**

The time trouble came to an end, and Black resigned (**1–0**). Times: 1.58–2.28.

For the first time I managed to crush Karpov with a direct mating attack, without any particular counter-chances for the opponent. The score became 11-9 in my favour, and to retain the title of world champion, I only needed to score one more point. But all the four remaining games were played – and in all of them, as at the finish of the 1985 match, there was a fierce battle. The reasons for this were Karpov's amazing fighting qualities and my slight relaxation, although, of course, I tried to master myself. On the evening of 31st December 'from a position of very great strength' I forced a draw in the 24th game and won the match 12½-11½.

Two days later, on 2nd January 1991, the closing ceremony of the match took place, and there I received my fourth world champion's laurel wreath and a special prize from the jewellery firm Korloff – an impressively heavy monogram in the form of two interwoven letters 'K', made of gold, bronze and 1018 black and white diamonds, mounted on a chess board. I soon sold it, and all the money – 300 thousand dollars, converted into 10 million roubles – went towards the fund which I set up to help refugees from Baku. This unusual prize was bought by the new millionaire Kirsan Ilyumzhinov, who at that time had only just appeared on the chess horizon, but five years later, with the blessing of the Kremlin and Campomanes, he unexpectedly became FIDE President.

Today, more than twenty years later, after soberly assessing the unprecedented complexity and drama of the situation prior to the match, I wonder by what miracle my team nevertheless managed to cope with the challenges of those turbulent times. Despite all the difficulties and extreme fatigue, I was sustained by confidence in my playing superiority over the opponent (as in the 1986 match, not once was he able to take the lead).

The fifth match of the 'two Ks' was destined to be my last classical match for the world championship under the aegis of FIDE and the last in my lengthy battle with Karpov for the chess crown, although at the start of 1991 this was far from obvious.

Chapter Three

Fall and Rise

Challenge to the Champions

International Tournament in Linares (22 February – 15 March 1991): 1. Ivanchuk – 9½ out of 13; 2. **Kasparov** – 9; 3. Beliavsky – 8; 4–5. Yusupov and Speelman – 7½; 6. Salov – 7; 7–8. Timman and Karpov – 6½; 9–11. Ljubojevic, Anand and M.Gurevich – 6; 12. Gelfand – 5½; 13. Ehlvest – 3½; 14. Kamsky – 2½.

As the chess experts had predicted, at the start of the 1990s a farewell was bid to the generation of the Fischer era and new stars joined the battle with the Karpov and Kasparov generations. They announced their presence in the summer of 1990 at the Interzonal Tournament in Manila (1–2. Gelfand and Ivanchuk – 9 out of 13; 3–4. Short and Anand – 8½, etc), in January 1991 they all won their Candidates matches (Ivanchuk's win over Yudasin was especially impressive – 4½-½!), and then they challenged the strongest players in the world at the ninth, traditional tournament in Linares.

It was this event that began the history of annual super-tournaments of fourteen leading grandmasters – events of the highest category, which the journalists aptly christened the 'chess Wimbledon'. As the press remarked, *'here, for the first time, the two inseparable "Ks" played together with both of their "predicted rivals" – Vassily Ivanchuk and Boris Gelfand, while among the other contestants were only Candidates of the present world championship cycle and finalists of the second World Cup. The only place "not by ranking" was allotted to the young Gata Kamsky, and he very much felt the heavy hand of his senior colleagues.'*

During the opening ceremony, apart from the usual drawing of lots, the pairings for the Candidates quarter-final matches were also made. As in the previous cycle, Karpov joined the proceedings at this stage. I remember how he literally beamed with delight when he 'drew' the 21-year-old Vishy Anand (the other pairings were Ivanchuk-Yusupov, Gelfand-Short and Timman-Korchnoi). For the first time Karpov had a match opponent who was young enough to be his son! It seemed improbable that the very talented and promising, but as yet too young and inexperienced Indian grandmaster would be able to put up a serious resistance against the great Anatoly Karpov. It would appear that the ex-champion did not imagine what a dangerous opponent fate had assigned him – but perhaps he began to gain an insight when he lost his game to Anand with White in the 2nd round.

In the first round I was paired with Black against Ivanchuk. He flew in late in the evening, was late for the opening ceremony, and the next day he played against me 1 e4 c5 2 ♘f3 d6 3 ♗b5+. I thought that it was probably in order to obtain a solid position. But I played uncertainly, whereas, by contrast, Vassily played very strongly – and his win was fully deserved. As it later transpired, this game decided the outcome of the battle for first place. For me it was a warning signal: for the first time in ten years of tournament play I lost not as a result of some oversight, but because I was outplayed by my opponent.

In the 2nd round I won a very complicated game against Gelfand, and also subsequently points were gained with great difficulty. Only by the 8th round, after beating Gurevich and Kamsky, and drawing with Timman, Speelman and Salov, did I reach a more or less respectable 'plus two'. And here I had Black against Karpov, who had also lost to Ivanchuk and was on just 'minus one': what told on his play was the enormous fatigue that had accumulated after our match and his January victory in the double-round tournament in Reggio Emilia. But I was happy with a draw, since without particular exertion I was able to solve my opening problems – a good sign, after a match that had been so difficult for Black (Game No.32 in *Kasparov vs. Karpov 1988-2009*).

That same evening Beliavsky won against Timman, and Ivanchuk against Anand, and the two leaders increased the gap between them and their pursuers: Beliavsky – 6½ out of 8 (!); Ivanchuk – 6; Kasparov – 5, etc.

In the 9th round I had White against the formidable Alexander Beliavsky, and to retain chances of first place in the tournament I had to win 'to order'. The game took place after a free day, so that each of us had time for preparation. A particular piquancy was added to the situation by our recent analytical collaboration before my match with Karpov.

Game 75
G.Kasparov-A.Beliavsky
Linares, 9th Round, 8.03.1991
English Opening A19

1 c4 e6 2 ♘c3 ♘f6 (for some reason my opponent rejected 2...d5 and his customary Queen's Gambit) **3 e4 c5 4 e5 ♘g8 5 ♘f3**

In the quiet variation 5 d4 cxd4 6 ♕xd4 ♘c6 7 ♕e4 d6 8 ♘f3 Beliavsky had achieved draws with Black against Seirawan (Lucerne 1989) and Azmaiparashvili (Amsterdam 1990).

5...♘c6 6 d4 cxd4 7 ♘xd4 ♘xe5 8 ♘db5 a6 9 ♘d6+ ♗xd6 10 ♕xd6 f6 11 ♗e3 ♘e7 12 ♗b6 ♘f5 13 ♕c5!? d6 14 ♕a5

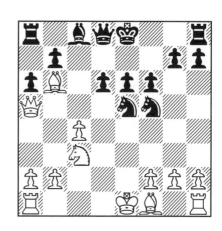

Up to here this was a repetition of my Belfort game with Andrey Sokolov, and I was pleased by Beliavsky's choice: White has good compensation for the pawn, and his active piece play gives him more winning chances than strict manoeuvring in the classical set-ups of the Queen's Gambit.

14...♕d7!? (but here is a new move instead of the previous 14...♕e7 – *Game No.40*) **15 f4!** (15 0-0-0 ♕c6!) **15...♘c6**

Of course, with gain of tempo. 15...♘g4?! 16 ♗e2! or 15...♘g6?! 16 ♗d3! with the threat of ♗xf5 is worse.

16 ♕a3

A critical moment.

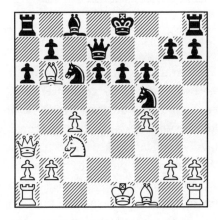

16...e5?

A mistake, leading to great difficulties on account of the weakness of the d5-point, whereas it is not possible to exploit the d4-point. Soon the correct defence was found – 16...♘ce7! 17 0-0-0 ♕c6 with sharp play. After 18 ♕b3 White retains pressure, and Black his extra pawn: 18...♗d7 19 ♖g1 d5 (19...h5!?) 20 ♔b1! (20 g4 ♘d6 21 cxd5 ♘xd5 is not so clear, Psakhis-A.Greenfeld, Israel 1991) or 18...0-0 19 ♖g1 d5 20 g4 ♘d6 21 c5 (21 ♕b4 ♖e8) 21...♘f7 22 ♗g2 (L'Ami-Wells, London 2008).

17 ♗d3!

It would appear that Beliavsky was hoping for 17 0-0-0?! exf4 18 ♘d5 0-0, which is quite acceptable for Black, and he underestimated my reply, which intends 0-0.

17...0-0

17...exf4 is no better: 18 0-0 g5 (my *Informator* suggestion 18...♘e5(?) is fatal on account of 19 ♗xf5 ♕xf5 20 ♘d5 ♔f7 21 ♖xf4 etc) 19 ♖ae1+ ♔f7 20 ♘d5 (more energetic than 20 ♗xf5 ♕xf5 21 ♘e4) 20...♘e5 21 ♗e4 or 21 g3!? with an escalating attack.

18 0-0 exf4

It is already not easy to find a satisfactory move: 18...♘fd4? 19 fxe5 dxe5 20 ♗xh7+!. In subsequent correspondence games 18...♕f7 19 fxe5! (my suggested 19 ♘d5 is weaker in view of 19...♘fe7! 20 ♕xd6 ♗f5) 19...fxe5 was tried, and here I would have preferred 20 ♖f2! and ♖af1 with an obvious plus.

19 ♖xf4 ♘fe7 20 ♖d1

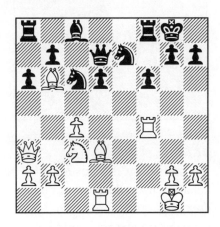

Now White concentrates his efforts on eliminating the d6-pawn. The pair of powerful bishops guarantees him an enduring initiative.

20...♘g6 21 ♖ff1 ♘ge5

21...♘ce5 22 ♗e4 ♕g4?! (22...♕f7 23 b3) 23 h3 ♕h4 24 ♗f2 ♕h5 25 ♕xd6 was even more dismal for Black.

22 ♗e4 ♕f7 23 b3 ♗e6 24 ♕xd6

With the threat of ♘d5. The centralisation of the queen is more appropriate than 24 ♖xd6, although the immediate 24 ♘d5!? also deserved consideration.

24...♔h8 25 ♕c7?!

The exchange of queens reduces White's domination, which would have been especially perceptible after 25 ♘d5! ♖ac8 26 h3 ♖fe8 27 ♖fe1, when Black runs out of useful moves: 27...f5 28 ♗c2 ♗d7 29 ♘f4 etc.

25...♕xc7

Little was changed by 25...♖fe8 26 ♘d5, but 25...♕e8!? 26 ♗f2! would have led to a more tense battle.

26 ♗xc7 ♖f7 27 ♗b6 (27 ♗d6!?) **27...♖e8 28 h3**

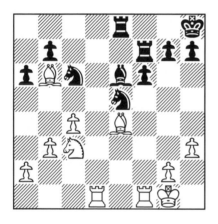

28...♖d7?!

Disheartened by the unsuccessful opening, Beliavsky had ended up in time-trouble and lost almost without a fight. Whether good or bad, 28...f5! was essential.

29 ♘d5 (threatening ♘c7) **29...♖c8**

The imprudent 29...♗f7? would have lost to 30 ♗f5! ♗e6 31 ♘c7, but the clumsy regrouping 29...♗g8!? 30 ♗f5 ♖f7 was a try.

30 g4 ♘g6?! (an unexpected blunder of a pawn; 30...♘e7 was more resilient) **31 ♔h2**

Continuing to intensify the pressure, although 31 ♗xg6!? hxg6 32 ♘f4 suggested itself.

31...♘ce5 (31...♘ge5!?) **32 a4 ♖d6 33 a5**

♘d7?

A final time-trouble error, although after 33...♖d7 34 ♖fe1 White has an imposing advantage (34...♗xd5 35 cxd5!).

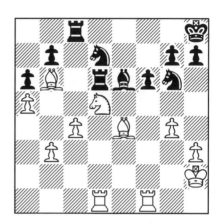

34 ♘c7! 1-0

Then, in a complicated and error-strewn game I won with Black against Ehlvest, and three rounds before the finish I finally caught up with my rivals, having scored, like Beliavsky and Ivanchuk, 7 out of 10.

The 11th round proved to be the turning-point in the tournament race. Beliavsky again ended up in desperate time-trouble and lost after blundering against Salov. All evening Ivanchuk put Gurevich's position under pressure, and he adjourned the game with an extra pawn and good winning chances. And I, in my first duel with the future world champion Vishy Anand, was ready to employ some lethal opening preparation.

Game 76
G.Kasparov-V.Anand
Linares, 11th Round, 11.03.1991
Petroff Defence C43

1 e4 e5 2 ♘f3 ♘f6 3 d4

Usually I played 3 ♘xe5 (Game Nos.50, 100 in *Garry Kasparov on Garry Kasparov Part I*), but I prepared this line with Timoshchenko before the Leningrad half of the third match (1986), although I employed it only in the 10th game of the fifth match (1990).

3...♘xe4

The most topical line. Karpov replied 3...exd4 4 e5 ♘e4 5 ♕xd4 d5 6 exd6 ♘xd6 7 ♘c3 (7 ♗d3!?) 7...♘c6 8 ♕f4 ♘f5!? 9 ♗b5 ♗d6 10 ♕e4+ ♕e7, but White could have retained some initiative by 11 ♗d2!? and 12 0-0-0 (cf. Game No.17 in *Kasparov vs. Karpov 1988-2009*).

4 ♗d3 d5 5 ♘xe5 ♗d6

This sharp plan, developed by Makarychev, Dvoretsky and his pupil Yusupov, was for a long time the main line, but from the spring of 1992 it almost disappeared from serious practice, giving way to the plans with 5...♘d7 (*Game No.95*).

6 0-0 0-0 7 c4 ♗xe5 8 dxe5 ♘c6 9 cxd5 ♕xd5 10 ♕c2 ♘b4 11 ♗xe4 ♘xc2 12 ♗xd5 ♗f5 13 g4 ♗xg4 14 ♗e4 ♘xa1

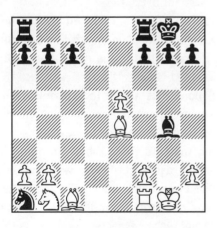

Black has won the exchange, but his knight is in danger, and he hopes to maintain the balance by returning his extra material at the right time.

15 ♗f4!

The weaker 15 ♘c3 allows Black to equal-

ise by 15...♗h3 16 ♖e1 f5 17 exf6 ♖ae8! intending ...♖xe4 and ...♘c2 (Tal-Karpov, Milan 1975), or immediately 15...f5 (Makarychev-Karpov, Oslo 1984).

15...f5

White is better after 15...f6 16 ♘c3 fxe5 17 ♗e3 (17 ♗g3!?) 17...♗f3 18 ♖xa1 ♗xe4 19 ♘xe4 (Kasparov-Timman, Paris (rapid) 1991).

16 ♗d5+! ♔h8 17 ♖c1 c6 (the attempt 17...♖ad8 18 ♘c3 b5? does not work because of 19 e6!) 18 ♗g2! (another accurate move) 18...♖fd8 19 ♘d2!

Not 19 f3 ♗h5 20 ♘a3 ♖d4 21 ♗e3 ♖b4 with a quick draw (Sax-Yusupov, Thessaloniki Olympiad 1988).

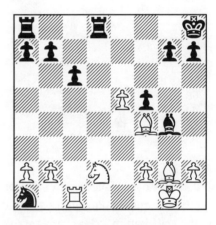

I studied the well-known variation 19...h6 20 h4 ♖d3 (Rozentalis-Gelfand, Vilnius 1988) before the 1990 match, and my assistant Sergey Dolmatov (also a pupil of Dvoretsky) found the good set-up with 21 ♗f1! followed by the sacrifice of the e5-pawn in order to occupy this square with the knight. The strength of this idea was demonstrated a year later in Timman-Yusupov (6th match game, Linares 1992): after 21...♖d4 22 ♗e3 ♖d5 23 ♖xa1! (Yusupov and Dvoretsky had only looked at 23 f4, 23 f3 or 23 e6) 23...♖xe5 24 ♘c4 White gained an enduring advantage and scored an important win.

I wanted to catch Anand with this novelty, but an unpleasant surprise awaited me.

19...♖xd2!?

Vishy chose a line mentioned by Rozentalis in his *Informator* notes to his game with Gelfand. Strangely enough, in our analysis we had not even considered this possibility.

20 ♗xd2 ♖d8 21 ♗c3!

Later it transpired that after 21 ♗e3 ♖d1+ 22 ♖xd1 ♗xd1 23 ♗xa7 ♘c2 the most probable outcome is a draw.

21...♖d1+ 22 ♖xd1 ♗xd1

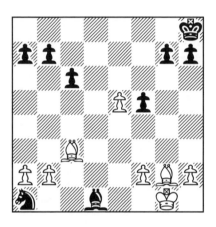

23 f4?

Alas, at the board I failed to find the correct 23 ♗f1! (the end of Rozentalis's variation with the evaluation 'clear advantage to White'), which was later studied in detail in correspondence tournaments. After 23...♔g8 24 ♗c4+ ♔f8 25 b4 ♘c2 26 ♗b3! Black would have faced a very difficult defence.

23...♘c2 24 ♔f2 ♔g8 25 a4 a5! 26 ♗xa5 ♘d4 27 ♗f1 ♗b3 ½-½

The competitive significance of this game was enormous: by not winning it, I also failed to win the tournament. In the 12th round Ivanchuk quickly beat Gelfand (Boris blundered a piece and resigned as early as the 18th move), Beliavsky defeated Kamsky, and, after being on the verge of defeat, I beat Ljubojevic. Then the adjournments took place, and just before the finish the leading trio looked like this: Ivanchuk – 9 out of 12; Kasparov – 8½; Beliavsky – 8.

In the last round Beliavsky lost to Karpov, I could do nothing against Yusupov and I saved the game only by a miracle in a time scramble, while Ivanchuk drew with Timman and retained sole first place. This was his finest hour! After such a triumph the 22-year-old Lvov player was now firmly recognised in the chess world as the main challenger for the crown.

For the first time in the nearly ten years that had passed since Tilburg 1981, I failed to take or at least share 1st place. It was not only a matter of the crisis that was natural after a world championship match, and not only due to my lack of a constant trainer or the growing pressure of the young wave (Ivanchuk and Gelfand had been joined by Anand). The slump in my play was also caused by my enormously chaotic Moscow existence, the lack of order in my life and my involvement in politics.

At that time I outlined my beliefs in an article 'Is it not too much for the champion...', published in the newspaper *Moscow News* (1991 No.2):

'I should like at last to explain myself. To those for whom my ideas away from the chess board seem like the extremism of a young man. To those who, shrugging their shoulders, ask in perplexity: why does he get involved in politics? In chess he is the leader, the world champion, and, as the satirist said ironically – a respected person. Perfectly successful and even independent in comparison with most of his contemporaries. And if he were to stick to playing, he would add to the achievements of Soviet sport. But instead of this – participation in democratic rallies, risky political forecasts in the press, and even the refusal to play under the USSR flag in the last match with Karpov... Is it not too much for a chess player, even if he is the champion?

'I think that the main role in my current views has been played by several factors. The first is the situation in which I have found myself. After all, the motto "Chess is above politics", widely propagated in our country for decades, was in fact a screen, behind which the essence was concealed. The idea of the country's ideologues was that, with their victories abroad and their titles, sports people should "once again" demonstrate the superiority of the socialist system, and its successes in promoting the complete development of a person. Chess players, in particular, were earmarked for demonstrating on the international arena the successes of our society as regards intellect.

'This political reality arose back in those distant years when Mikhail Botvinnik distinguished himself in chess. And when in the 1970s the Karpov-Korchnoi confrontation arose, the situation was politicised in the extreme. The matches for the title of world champion were played not by two outstanding grandmasters, but by a representative of the foremost ranks of Soviet youth, enjoying comprehensive state support, against a renegade and traitor, who had dared to express his dissatisfaction with the existing order in the country.

'Willy-nilly it turned out that, in entering the battle for the supreme title, a chess player became involved in high-level politics. He had to "conform" to the views of the ruling structure, and to be a "person of the system". Otherwise the system would not compromise its principles. And they, alas, were by no means to do with sport. And so it turns out that in our country the world chess champion is not a title, but a duty, and one that is rather politicised.

'It is said that for a serious politician I spend too much time on chess, and for a chess player – an unjustified amount on politics. But after all, an ability to assess your actions critically, analyse a situation and anticipate your opponent's moves is necessary in any matter. If, of course, you want to achieve something in it. In chess I have achieved. And it is largely thanks to this that politicians are already listening to my opinion about the developing situation in our country. It is a pity that for the moment this is only in the West.

'Chess is a black and white game, without compromises. At least, for anyone who wants to come first. In making this choice I was helped by my character and upbringing. And the battle for and around the title of world champion helped to determine my attitudes. I began with democratic changes in the chess world, I was the first to speak out for the democratisation of Soviet sport, and now I am doing what I can to further this process in society. The title of champion is not only for the satisfaction of personal ambition. It is to advance and proceed further. Everything is rapidly changing. In 1985 I criticised the directors of chess, and today I am publicly disagreeing with the president of the country...'

Incidentally, my autobiography *Unlimited Challenge*, published in 1989, concluded with these words: 'I regard 1987 as a turning-point in my life. The publication of my book *Child of Change* and the ensuing rift with the Soviet Sports Committee can really be said to have determined my relations with the system. Today I am free of illusion; in the words of Robert Jordan in Hemingway's *For Whom the Bell Tolls*: "There were fifty years of undeclared war against fascism ahead, and I had signed on for the duration".'

One-off Inspiration

Euwe Memorial Tournament (Amsterdam, 2–13 May 1991): 1–2. Salov and Short – 6 out of 9; 3–4. Karpov and **Kasparov** – 5½; 5. Korchnoi – 4½; 6–7. Hjartarson and Timman – 4; 8. M.Gurevich – 3½; 9–10. van der Wiel and Ljubojevic – 3.

Two months after Linares, Karpov and I met at the Euwe Memorial – a tournament of ten grandmasters in Amsterdam. Due to my participation in the turbulent social and political life of the country (I should remind you: this was the last year of the USSR's existence), I was unable to run into good form and on this occasion I performed terribly. Moreover, although on the whole Amsterdam was somewhat weaker than Linares, I found points even harder to come by.

Playing the Sicilian Najdorf against van der Wiel in round 1, after 6 ♗g5 e6 7 f4 I chose 7...♕c7 (instead of the critical 7...♕b6) 8 ♕f3 ♘bd7 (instead of 8...b5) which allowed a forced drawing variation, and in an attempt to devise something I almost lost. In a better position in the 2nd round I was unable to finish off Gurevich. In the 3rd round I had a very complicated game with Short – I gained an advantage, but lost it as time-trouble approached. Something similar occurred in the next game with Salov. Then I had excellent King's Indian play against Hjartarson, but Black's initiative, alas, was insufficient for a win.

In the 6th round I played Karpov, who by that time had managed to win one game and together with Salov and Korchnoi was half a point behind the leader, Short. A win over me by the ex-champion could have become the springboard for overall victory in the tournament, but I turned up for the game in a fighting mood, hoping finally to make full use of the white pieces (incidentally, in Horgen

1995, immediately after the match with Anand, I also began with five draws, and then lost in nightmarish style with White against Ivanchuk, who in the end became one of the tournament winners). Karpov as though sensed that there was a large-scale battle in prospect, and he again chose the very sharp line in the already complicated Zaitsev Variation of the Ruy Lopez, in which he had suffered a severe defeat in the 20th game of our recent match. He had prepared an improvement (cf. *Game No.74*, note to Black's 19th move) and then, exploiting my uncertain play, he seized the initiative and was very close to a win, but in desperate time-trouble he allowed me to save the game.

By the 7th round, in which I had to do battle with the uncompromising Viktor Korchnoi, for the first time I was seriously in contention for the title of 'drawing king'. I had never played worse, and there were only three more rounds before the finish. Korchnoi was in the mood for a grand battle, clearly realising that a better chance of beating me might not present itself. I was also not intending to back out – it was time I won! The choice of opening variation in our duel was pre-determined.

Game 77
V.Korchnoi-G.Kasparov
Amsterdam, 7th Round,
10.05.1991
King's Indian Defence E99

---

1 ♘f3 ♘f6 2 c4 g6 3 ♘c3 ♗g7 4 e4 d6 5 d4 0-0 6 ♗e2 e5 7 0-0 ♘c6 8 d5 ♘e7 9 ♘e1

The fanciful 9 a4 allows Black a comfortable game: 9...a5! 10 ♘e1 ♘d7 11 ♗e3 f5 12 f3 ♘c5 13 ♘d3 b6 14 b4 ♘xd3 15 ♕xd3 axb4 16 ♘b5 ♔h8! 17 ♕b3 ♘g8 (Korchnoi-Kasparov, Barcelona 1989).

9...♘d7

A year later as an experiment I employed against Shirov (Manila Olympiad 1992) and Korchnoi (Debrecen 1992) the risky variation 9...♘e8 10 ♗e3 f5 11 f3 f4 12 ♗f2 h5 13 c5 g5 (cf. Game No. 40 in *My Great Predecessors Part V*).

10 ♗e3

Korchnoi's favourite set-up, which earlier was considered rather slow and less good than 10 ♘d3 f5 11 ♗d2 (*Game No.64*), but which has now become very topical.

10...f5 11 f3 f4 12 ♗f2 g5

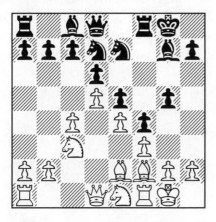

13 a4!?

Piket played 13 b4 against me (*Game No.58*). Korchnoi also tried 13 ♘b5 (Game No.39 in *My Great Predecessors Part V*), but from 1996 he switched to 13 ♖c1!? with the idea of 13...♘g6 14 c5! ♘xc5 15 b4 ♘a6 16 ♘d3 h5 17 ♘b5 ♗d7 18 a4 ♗h6 19 ♖c3 (Piket-Kasparov, Linares 1997; Korchnoi-Cvitan, Pula 1997).

13...♘g6

If 13...h5, then 14 a5! (Korchnoi-Forster, Switzerland 1994; Korchnoi-Xie Jun, Prague 1995). But consideration should be given to 13...a5!? 14 ♘d3 b6 15 b4 axb4 16 ♘xb4 ♘f6 17 ♖a3 ♗d7 with double-edged play (Yusupov-Kasparov, Yerevan Olympiad 1996).

14 ♘d3 (14 a5! is more energetic – in the 1990s Korchnoi won half a dozen games with this move) **14...♘f6**

There is no sense in keeping the knight on d7 any longer: the c4-c5 break is inevitable.

15 c5 h5

With the obvious threat of ...g5-g4. The alternative is 15...♖f7 or 15...♔h8 16 a5 ♖g8 (as played by Landa against Korchnoi), for the moment managing without ...h7-h5 and leaving the h5-square for the knight.

16 h3

A questionable novelty – a weakening in the place where White is being attacked: now the opening of lines on the kingside will be even more dangerous for him. 16 cxd6?! is also inaccurate: 16...cxd6 17 a5 g4 18 ♘b5 g3! with a counterattack (Larsen-Torre, Bauang 1973). However, 16 a5! g4 17 c6 (Korchnoi-Xie Jun, Amsterdam 2001) or 17 a6 bxa6 18 ♘b4 is sounder.

16...♖f7 17 c6

This was the idea of my highly-experienced opponent, but it all turned out rather differently than he had planned...

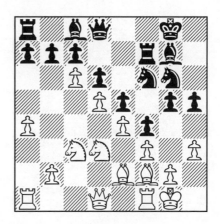

17...g4? is incorrect in view of 18 fxg4 hxg4 19 cxb7 ♗xb7 20 ♗xg4. After 17...♗f8 there is the unpleasant 18 ♘b4! (my *Informator* suggestion 18 ♘b5 is weaker because of 18...bxc6) 18...b6 (otherwise cxb7 and

♞c6) 19 a5! etc. And after 17...bxc6 18 dxc6 ♝e6 19 ♞b4 White seizes the d5-point and the initiative: 19...g4 20 hxg4 hxg4 21 fxg4 ♜b8 22 ♞bd5! ♜xb2 23 ♝xa7 ♛a8 24 ♝f2 ♛xc6 25 ♝f3 and a4-a5.

17...a5!

I was terribly proud of this unexpected move, impeding White's offensive. Black also plays on the opponent's territory (as though to counter-balance 16 h3), hoping later to make progress on the kingside while White is creating a passed pawn on the a-file.

18 cxb7

The immediate 18 b4 allows 18...b6 19 bxa5 bxa5!, when White's activity comes to a standstill, whereas Black calmly prepares an attack by ...♝h6, ...♜g7 and ...g5-g4.

18...♝xb7 19 b4

The attempt to play against the c7-pawn – 19 ♜c1 ♝c8 20 ♞b5 g4 21 ♛c2 runs into 21...g3! 22 ♝e1 ♝xh3! 23 gxh3 ♛c8, when White is forced to return the piece – 24 ♞f2 (24 ♝d1?! ♞h4!) 24...♞e8 (not rushing with 24...gxf2+? 25 ♜xf2!) and then ...♞h4 with a comfortable game for Black.

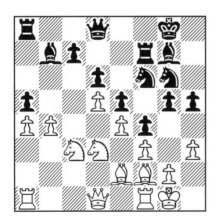

19...♝c8! (to support ...g5-g4) **20 bxa5 ♝h6!**

With the intention of breaking out after ...g5-g4 and ...♝g5-h4. Here the routine 20...♝f8?! has no point: the d6-pawn does not need defending.

21 ♞b4

After the game Korchnoi claimed he could have gained an advantage by 21 a6. After 21...♝xa6 22 ♞b4 White's position, thanks to his passed a-pawn, is indeed better.

But after 21...g4! 22 fxg4 hxg4 23 hxg4 ♝g5 he is forced to find almost the only moves to defend: for example, 24 a7 ♛f8! 25 ♜e1 ♛h6 26 ♜b1 ♜h7 27 ♔f1 ♛h1+ 28 ♝g1 ♞h4 29 ♝f3 ♞xg4! 30 ♜b8! ♞xf3 31 ♛xf3 ♞h2+ 32 ♔e2 ♞xf3 33 ♜xa8! (in *Informator* I expressed doubts about Black's attack because of 33 gxf3(?) ♛g2+ 34 ♔d1 ♛xf3+ 35 ♔c2, overlooking the winning 35...♜xa7! 36 ♜xc8+ ♔g7 37 ♝xa7 ♜h2+) 33...♛xg2+ 34 ♝f2 ♛h3! 35 ♜b8! ♞xe1 36 ♞xe1 ♛xc3 37 ♜xc8+ ♔g7 38 a8♛ f3+ 39 ♞xf3 ♛c4+ 40 ♔e1 ♛xe4+ 41 ♔f1 ♛xf3 42 ♜xc7+ ♔h6 43 ♜xh7+ ♔xh7, and the wild complications end in a draw.

21...g4 22 ♞c6 ♛f8

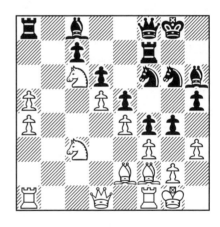

23 fxg4?

Equivalent to capitulation: in White's defences there are now yawning gaps, through which the black pieces now inexorably infiltrate his position.

Korchnoi was probably unnerved by the threatened capture on h3, which it would appear can be parried by 23 a6! (to decide on such a move on the threshold of time-trouble is not easy). If 23...gxh3?! 24 gxh3 ♗xh3 the exchange sacrifice 25 a7! is good: 25...♘e7 26 ♔h1! or 25...♕g7 26 ♔h2!. However, Black can sacrifice a piece on h3: 23...g3! 24 ♖e1 (24 ♗a7? ♗xh3! 25 gxh3 ♕c8! 26 ♖f2 ♖xa7!) 24...♗xh3! 25 gxh3 ♘h4, forcing White to give up a rook – 26 ♖f2 with very sharp, roughly equal play.

23...hxg4 24 hxg4 (after the obviously worse 24 ♗xg4? ♘xg4 25 hxg4 f3! Black wins) **24...♗g5**

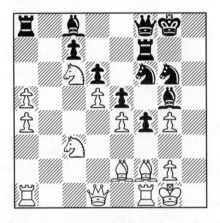

25 ♗f3

A vain attempt to plug the hole. However, even the slightly more resilient 25 ♖a3 did not help in view of 25...♕h6 26 ♘b5 f3! 27 ♗xf3 ♖h7 28 ♗g3 ♗e3+ 29 ♖xe3 ♕xe3+ 30 ♖f2 (30 ♗f2 ♕f4!) 30...♕h6! 31 ♖f1 ♗xg4 32 ♗xg4 ♘xe4 33 ♗h3 ♘xg3 and wins.

25...♕h6 26 ♖e1 ♘h4!

The right way! The stereotyped 26...♗h4? would have sharply reduced Black's attacking potential: 27 ♔f1 ♗xf2?! 28 ♔xf2 ♘xg4+ 29 ♔e2, and White is still afloat.

27 ♗xh4

Alas, White is forced to give up bishop for knight: things are altogether catastrophic after 27 ♔f1 ♘xf3 28 gxf3 ♘xg4! (my earlier 28...♗xg4 is less good because of 29 ♕d3) 29 fxg4 f3 or 29 ♗g1 ♘e3+ 30 ♗xe3 ♗g4! etc.

27...♗xh4!

In this game the King's Indian bishop has made a brilliant career for itself! 27...♕xh4? was incorrect: 28 ♔f1 ♘xg4 29 ♔e2. Now, however, the white king is unable to break out of the mating net.

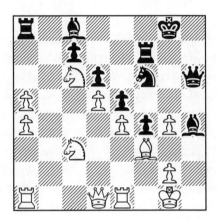

28 g5

A desperate pawn lunge. If 28 ♔f1 Black decides matters with both 28...♗xe1 29 ♔xe1 ♘xg4 30 ♔d2 ♘e3 31 ♕e2 ♖g7, and 28...♘xg4 with the threats of ...♘e3+, ...♗xe1 and ...♖g7: for example, 29 ♗xg4 ♗xe1 30 ♔xe1 f3! or 30 ♗xc8 ♕h1+ 31 ♔e2 f3+!.

28...♕xg5 29 ♖e2 ♘g4 (29...♗g3!) **30 ♖b1 ♗g3 31 ♕d3** (desperation) **31...♕h4**

The threat is ...♘e3 and ...♕h2 mate, so White resigned (**0-1**).

An impressive rout. This spectacular game was voted the best in the 51st volume of *Informator*. At that time this is what happened in my games with Korchnoi: even if I was performing indifferently in a tournament, against him I played with inspiration and usually I won.

Karpov also launched a belated pursuit of the leaders, by winning against Timman. But in the next, penultimate round, I failed to break down the Dutch grandmaster, who played without any serious mistakes. And although at the finish I beat Ljubojevic, I caught up only with Karpov, who was unable to beat Short with White. As a result Salov and Short finished half a point ahead of us.

Whereas Karpov performed significantly better than in Linares, I suffered an obvious slump: instead of 2nd place with a high score, I shared only 3rd-4th places, winning just two games. Alexander Roshal gave an interesting commentary on this situation:

'Gradually they have ceased "demanding" only first places of Karpov. With regard to Kasparov, as yet public opinion is not so compliant. During his first five years as champion, everyone became accustomed to applauding victory for him at the end of any tournament in which he played. Kasparov's slight hitch in Linares was put down to Ivanchuk's rapid rise, without which, it was said, nothing would have changed.

'The Amsterdam tournament has also concluded. Well, what is unusual about the success of Salov and Short, who are undoubtedly among the strongest grandmasters in the world? In any event, the discussion again involves Karpov and especially Kasparov. Like the tournament winners, both the ex-champion and the champion were undefeated. But there is also a significant difference: at no time was either of the favourites in the lead. Karpov was closer to success, as indicated by his game with his eternal opponent, and other unrealised possibilities. It follows that Kasparov's play is the most in need of explanation. Well known are the conflicts of political life in our country, and the vigour with which the world chess champion takes part in this life and tries to influence it. And all this is bound to have an adverse effect on Kasparov's tournament performances. He himself decides what is now more important, but we are obliged to draw attention to the certain lowering of his chess ambitions, as though he has lost his appetite for the game.

'Eye-witnesses have also noticed something altogether unexpected – Kasparov's customary superiority in the openings has disappeared somewhere. It is quite probable that, "being programmed for Karpov", he has not had time – he has been occupied with other things! – to readjust to other opponents. And, since now he hardly plays 1 e4, he avoids the forcing continuations which previously were such favourites.'

Fruits of Preparation

Double-round Super-tournament in Tilburg (16 October – 5 November 1991): 1. **Kasparov** – 10 out of 14; 2. Short – 8½; 3. Anand – 8; 4. Karpov – 7½; 5. Kamsky – 7; 6. Timman – 6½; 7. Korchnoi – 5½; 8. Bareev – 3.

To return to my former level, I needed again to concentrate on chess, and I began looking for a permanent trainer. From the summer of 1991 I began working with the well-known Moscow grandmaster Sergey Makarychev – in 1985-86 he had helped Karpov, he had successfully captained the Olympiad team, and our collaboration lasted about three years.

As a year earlier, I was forced to arrange a lengthy training session outside of the USSR – now on the west, oceanic coast of the USA, in California. This at least partially replaced my native Zagulba: without the sea I would have been unable to regain my strength before the new chess battles. We spent the whole of August and part of September there, enduring from afar the dramatic events in Moscow associated with the August putsch (appearing on the evening of 19th August on the Larry King program on CNN, I predicted that it would all be over within 48 hours). At the same time I began preparing the ground for a future world championship match in Los Angeles, where I found some potential sponsors.

Despite all the anxiety, disorder and intense stress of that time, Makarychev and I managed to carry out some high-quality analytical work (in particular, to refresh the already half-forgotten move 1 e4 with new ideas), and its results were soon seen at the October super-tournament in Tilburg.

Meanwhile, the Candidates quarter-final matches in August produced the following results: Karpov overcame Anand with enormous difficulty, Ivanchuk sensationally lost on the tie-break to Yusupov, Short beat Gelfand and Timman beat Korchnoi. On returning from my distant wanderings to Moscow, I commented on events at the chess summit in an interview for the *Sport-Express* newspaper:

'In all the Candidates matches the opposite results would have been logical. Anand completely outplayed Karpov, and for victory all that he lacked was maturity... Short beat Gelfand, but if Boris had won the 8th game – and it was completely won – everything would have turned out differently... Short has begun playing better, more calmly and more confidently. Taking account of his distinctive style, it can be stated: he can look to the future with great optimism. I think that in the forthcoming Karpov-Short semi-final match it is very important that Short should absolutely not be afraid of Karpov.

'The Yusupov-Ivanchuk pairing was the only one which really interested me from the standpoint of creating a great stir in the forthcoming world championship match. Ivanchuk is now playing stronger than the rest. But for all his obvious virtues, he is too unpredictable. As the person who persuaded the Americans to fork out for the world title match, I realise that for quite obvious reasons they would like my opponent to be Short. But for me as a chess player, my interest in the cycle was significantly reduced as soon as Ivanchuk was eliminated. Although Ivanchuk is the most dangerous opponent, it is he whom I would have liked to play. For me this would have been a stimulus to study chess seriously.'

In the meantime, the ex-world champion, having hardly rested after his match with Anand, was successful in the initial tournament of the second World Cup (Reykjavik 1991): 1. Ivanchuk and Karpov – 10½ out of 15, etc. Altogether five tournaments were planned, and each participant had the right to play in three of them. I was due to join the fight in the second tournament (July 1992), in the third (November 1992) I would face the direct rivalry of Ivanchuk, and in the concluding, fifth (May 1993) – of Karpov. Alas, at the end of 1991 financial and organisational problems forced the GMA to give up the further staging of the World Cup, and Bessel Kok resigned from his presidential post.

In the second half of October, Karpov and I met at a very strong double-round tournament of eight grandmasters in Tilburg: the champion was playing, as well as all the Candidates, apart from Yusupov. From the press: *'The average rating of the players reached the highest mark in the history of chess competitions – 2666! The magnificent eight competitors were well matched by the organisation of the tournament. Tilburg became a place of pilgrimage for chess fans from all corners of Holland, with most of the spectators hurrying not into the playing hall (they did not drop in there for long – to soak up the atmosphere of the tournament, and see the stars "in the flesh"), but to a special foyer with demonstration boards. Constantly present there were commentators, spontaneously describing the course of the play.'*

On this occasion I started in my usual style, scoring quite good wins over Timman, whom I struck with 19...♘xf2! in a King's Indian middlegame, and Korchnoi, who was unable to hold out in the Exchange Variation of the French Defence – 1 e4 e6 2 d4 d5 3 exd5 exd5 4 ♘f3 ♘f6 5 ♗d3 c5 6 0-0! c4 7 ♖e1+ ♗e7 8 ♗f1 etc. Korchnoi was terribly annoyed by this outcome, and in the game from the second cycle, wishing to teach me a lesson, he chose an exchange variation against the King's Indian.

Then came a difficult draw with another rising star – the 17-year-old 'new American' Gata Kamsky (in Tilburg 1990 he shared 1st-2nd places with Ivanchuk). And in the 4th round I met a player making his debut in the tournament, the 25-year-old Muscovite Evgeny Bareev, who by that time was a prize-winner in two USSR championships, had won Hastings 1990/91, taken second place in Biel 1991, and attained the solid rating of 2680. But the clash with the seven leaders of the world chess elite was a severe test for him.

> ### Game 78
> **E.Bareev-G.Kasparov**
> Tilburg, 4th Round, 21.10.1991
> *King's Indian Defence E92*

1 d4 ♘f6 2 c4 g6 3 ♘c3 ♗g7 4 e4 d6 5 ♗e2 0-0 6 ♘f3 e5 7 d5 a5 8 ♗e3

Although Gligoric and Petrosian played it, to me this move seems inferior to 8 ♗g5 (*Game No.47*). It is good only after 7...♘bd7 (Kramnik-Kasparov, Moscow (rapid) 1994; Kasparov-Vescovi, Rio de Janeiro (simul') 1996).

8...♘g4 9 ♗g5 f6 10 ♗h4 ♘a6! (now Black has a comfortable game) **11 ♘d2 h5!?**

More active than 11...♘h6 and ....♗d7 (Gligoric-Geller, Belgrade 1970, 2nd round).

The weakening of the kingside did not frighten me: I had studied similar positions a year earlier, before my match with Karpov.

12 a3 ♗d7

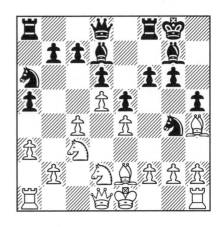

13 h3?!

White begins losing precious time. 13 0-0 ♕e8 (13...♘c5? 14 b4) 14 h3 ♘h6 15 b3 f5 is sounder, with approximate equality (Petrosian-Geller, Sochi 1977).

13...♘h6 14 ♖b1 (again a non-essential move) **14...♘c5!**

Of course: White was threatening b2-b4, cutting off the knight on a6.

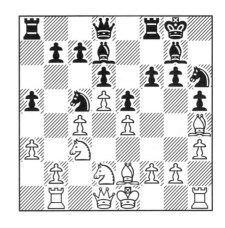

15 b4?!

If 15 0-0 the constricting 15...a4 is now possible, although 15...g5 16 ♗g3 h4 17 ♗h2 f5 is also not bad. In *ChessBase* Wahls and

Anand recommend 15 b3, although here too after 15...g5 16 ♗g3 h4 17 ♗h2 f5 the initiative is on Black's side.

15...axb4 16 axb4 ♘a4 (resolving the problem of the 'bad' knight) **17 ♕c2**

There is also little joy in 17 ♘xa4 ♗xa4 18 ♕c1 g5! (not my *Informator* suggestion 18...♗e8 19 f3!) 19 ♗g3 h4 20 ♗h2 (Morovic-Kamsky, Las Palmas 1994) 20...f5! 21 b5 (21 exf5 ♘xf5 and ...♘d4) 21...g4 etc.

17...♘xc3 18 ♕xc3 g5 19 ♗g3 h4! (19...♕e8 allows time for 20 f3!) **20 ♗h2 f5**

Rarely in the King's Indian Defence is Black 'allocated' such a promising position.

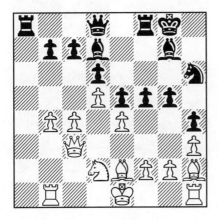

21 c5

As it later transpired, it was only here that we diverged from the well-trodden path. The alternatives are no better: 21 ♖a1 ♖xa1+ 22 ♕xa1 g4! (Rogers-Piket, Groningen 1990), or 21 f3 g4! 22 c5 ♕g5 23 hxg4 fxg4 24 c6 bxc6 25 dxc6 (Danner-Navrotescu, Budapest 2001) 25...♗e6!

21...g4 22 c6 ♗c8!?

Keeping the light-squared bishops on the board. In the event of 22...bxc6 23 dxc6 ♗e6 24 ♗c4 it would be easier for White to defend, although after 24...♗xc4 25 ♕xc4+ ♖f7 26 hxg4 ♘xg4 Black would retain some advantage.

23 hxg4 fxg4 24 cxb7 (also after 24 0-0 b6

followed by ...♘f7 and ...♕g5(f6) White would not have solved the problem of activating his bishop on h2) **24...♗xb7 25 0-0 ♕g5**

The critical moment of the battle.

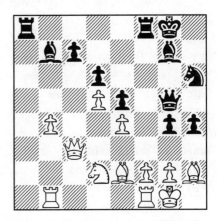

26 ♖a1?

A tactical error. The *Informator* suggestion 26 g3(?!) is unaesthetic in view of 26...h3, but White should have made a solid move, such as 26 ♘b3 with the intention of ♘a5.

26...♖xa1 (the immediate 26...♗xd5!? was also possible) **27 ♖xa1**

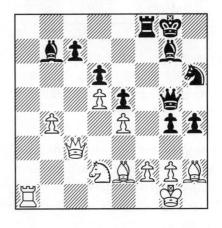

27...♗xd5!

My flamboyant suggestion 27...♘f5(?!) is, in fact, less effective: 28 exf5 e4 29 ♕xc7 g3 30 ♖d1! gxh2+ 31 ♔h1! h3 32 gxh3 ♗xd5 33

♕xd6 ♖xf5 34 ♘c4 e3+ 35 f3 ♔h7 36 h4!, and White has every chance of holding on. **28 ♖a7** (28 exd5? e4) **28...♗e6 29 ♖xc7 ♕f6 30 ♕e3 ♘f7 31 ♗c4 ♗h6 32 ♕e2 ♗xd2?!**

32...♘g5? was incorrect because of 33 b5, but 32...♖b8! was more accurate, with the inevitable win of the b-pawn.

33 ♗xe6

If 33 ♕xd2, then 33...♘g5 34 ♕e2 (34 ♗xe6+?! ♘xe6 35 ♕xd6? g3! and wins) 34...♖a8 or 34...♔h8 with an enduring advantage for Black, who is practically playing with an extra piece.

33...♕xe6 34 ♕xd2 ♕b3! (an unpleasant invasion for White) **35 ♔h1** (35 b5 ♖a8!) **35...♕b1+?!**

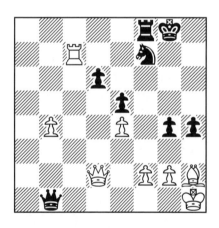

Winning the tasty e4-pawn. But 35...h3! was objectively stronger: 36 ♕c2(e2) hxg2+ 37 ♔g1 (37 ♔xg2? ♕h3+) 37...♕f3 with the threat of ...♘g5-h3 mate.

36 ♗g1 ♕xe4 37 ♕c2?

Hoping to save himself in a difficult endgame a pawn down, Bareev does not notice the paradoxical defensive resource 37 b5! h3 38 f3! gxf3 39 gxf3 ♕xf3+ 40 ♔h2, when the strong passed b-pawn almost compensates White for his material deficit: 40...♕g4 (threatening ...♘g5) 41 ♗e3! or 40...♔g7 41 ♕g5+ (41 b6 ♔f6!) 41...♔h7 42 ♕g3 with drawing chances.

37...♕xc2 38 ♖xc2 d5!

Consistent play aimed at restricting the white bishop and king – the threat is ...d5-d4. Now there is no way of saving the game.

39 b5

If 39 f3 d4! 40 fxg4?! there was the decisive 40...d3 and ...e5-e4. And the desperate 39 f4 would have been refuted not only by 39...exf4 40 ♖d2 ♖b8, but also by the pretty 39...g3! 40 ♖d2 ♘d6! 41 ♖xd5 ♘e4 or 41 fxe5 ♘e4 42 ♖d1 ♖f2!.

39...d4 40 f3 g3 (40...♖b8!?) **41 b6**

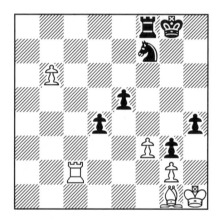

41...♖d8

I was proud of this 'subtle' move and I condemned the 'crude' 41...♖b8(!) because of 42 ♖c6, although after 42...♔g7 Black would also have won: 43 f4 d3! 44 ♗e3 ♖d8 45 ♖c1 e4 etc.

42 ♖c6

It would not have helped to play 42 b7 ♘d6 43 ♖b2 ♖b8 44 ♖b6 ♘xb7 45 ♖b3 (45 f4? d3) 45...♔f8!, or 42 ♖c5 ♖b8! 43 ♖b5 (43 ♖c6 ♔g7, as in the note to Black's 41st move) 43...♔g7 44 b6 ♔f6 45 f4 d3.

42...♘d6! 43 ♖c7

If 43 ♖c5 I saw a straightforward win after 43...♔f7 44 ♖xe5 ♘c4 and ...d4-d3, while Bareev pointed out 43...♘b7 44 ♖xe5 d3 45 ♖e1 d2 46 ♖d1 ♖d3! when White is paralysed.

43...♖b8 44 ♖c6 ♘f5 45 ♖e6 ♘e3!

With the threat of ...♘d1-f2+. White resigned (**0-1**) – if 46 ♖xe5 ♖xb6.

With a score of 3½ out of 4, I took the lead, but Vishy Anand was only half a point behind. And in the next round I arrived for the game with him with a great desire to win.

Game 79
G.Kasparov-V.Anand
Tilburg, 5th Round, 22.10.1991
Sicilian Defence B48

1 e4 c5

Not repeating the Linares choice 1...e5 (*Game No.76*) – already Anand had an extensive opening repertoire. I did not imagine that I would encounter the Paulsen Variation, but from the summer I had an interesting idea stored up in it.

2 ♘f3 ♘c6

After 2...e6 3 d4 cxd4 4 ♘xd4 a6 I was also planning 5 ♘c3 ♕c7 6 ♗d3 ♘c6 7 ♗e3, although later in a game with Movsesian (Prague 2001) I preferred 7 ♘xc6.

3 d4 cxd4 4 ♘xd4 ♕c7 5 ♘c3 e6 6 ♗e3

The alternative is 6 ♗e2 a6 7 0-0 ♘f6, and here I employed both 8 ♔h1 (against Kengis, Riga 1995), and also the main line 8 ♗e3 ♗b4 9 ♘a4 (including against Anand, Frankfurt (rapid) 1999; Linares 2002).

6...a6 7 ♗d3

Nowadays the variation 7 ♕d2 ♘f6 8 0-0-0 ♗b4 9 f3 is more topical (an example: Kasparov-Ye Jiangchuan, Bled Olympiad 2002).

7...♘f6 8 0-0 ♘e5

8...b5, 8...♗d6 and 8...♘xd4 9 ♗xd4 ♗c5 are also played, but the set-up with the knight on e5 is the most critical.

9 h3 ♗c5

White was judged to be better after 9...b5 10 f4 ♘c4 11 ♗xc4 ♕xc4 12 ♕d3! ♗b7 13 a4! ♕xd3 14 cxd3 b4 15 ♘ce2 or 12...d5 13 e5 ♘d7 14 ♕xc4 dxc4 15 f5! (Fischer-Petrosian, Santa Monica 1966).

10 ♔h1!?

This line, which used to be considered harmless, was one that I developed together with Makarychev. More prominent were 10 ♕e2 d6 11 f4 ♘ed7 12 ♘b3 (Spassky-Petrosian, 23rd match game, Moscow 1969), 10 ♘a4 ♗a7 11 c4 d6 12 ♖c1, as Tal played against Eingorn (Sochi 1986) and Panno (Buenos Aires 1991), and the sharp 10 f4 ♘c6 11 ♘f5 (Durao-Hartston, Praia da Rocha Zonal 1969).

10...d6 11 f4

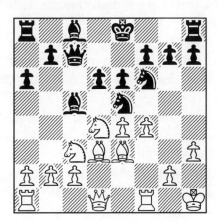

11...♘c6?

Anand made this move almost without thinking – in those years he used to play very quickly. Meanwhile, two other knight moves were much better:

1) 11...♘ed7 (11...♘xd3?! 12 cxd3 is unfavourable for Black) 12 a3 b5 (12...0-0 13 ♕e1!, Kasparov-Ivanchuk, Novgorod 1994) 13 ♗xb5!? (13 ♕e1!) 13...axb5 14 ♘dxb5 with a dangerous initiative (Kasparov-Lautier, Amsterdam 1995) or 12 ♕e1! (12 ♕f3!?, Tal-Najdorf, Belgrade 1970, 1st

round) 12...♕b6 (12...b5?! 13 b4!; 12...0-0 13 ♕g3!) 13 ♘a4 ♕b4 14 ♕xb4 ♗xb4 15 ♘b3 b5 16 ♘b6 with the better ending (Ivanchuk-Lautier, Horgen 1995);

2) 11...♘g6 12 ♕e1 (the sharp 12 f5!? or the quiet 12 ♕d2!? is more interesting) 12...0-0 13 f5 (a strategically risky move) 13...♘e5 14 ♕h4, and if 14...b5 I had prepared the questionable exchange sacrifice 15 ♖f3!? with the idea of developing an attack on the g-file. However, 14...♗d7 is sounder: 15 g4 (here also 15 ♖f3!? was analysed) 15...♕b6 16 g5 ♘h5 17 ♕xh5 ♗xd4 18 ♗xd4 ♕xd4 19 f6 ♗c6, maintaining the dynamic balance (Kasparov-Milos, Rio de Janeiro 1996).

12 e5!

This sudden breakthrough emphasises the lack of harmony in the placing of the black pieces (the c5-bishop would definitely be better on e7!).

12...♘xe5?

Already the decisive mistake. It was also obviously bad to play 12...dxe5? 13 ♘db5! axb5 14 ♗xc5 ♘d4 15 fxe5 (15 b4!?) 15...♕xc5 16 exf6 and ♘e4, or 12...♘d7? 13 ♘xe6! fxe6 14 ♕h5+ ♔d8 (14...♔f8? 15 f5!) 15 ♕h4+ ♘e7 16 ♘e4 with a winning attack. But there were three other possibilities:

1) 12...♗xd4?! 13 ♗xd4 dxe5 (13...♘xd4?! 14 exf6 gxf6 15 f5!) 14 fxe5!, when the following lines will not do: 14...♘d5? 15 ♘e4 0-0 (15...♘xd4 16 ♘d6+ or 15...♘xe5 16 ♕h5! is also weak) 16 ♘f6+!, or 14...♘d7? 15 ♘e4 ♘cxe5 (15...♘dxe5 16 ♗c5) 16 ♕h5! (Goloshchapov-Al.Kharitonov, Yekaterinburg 1999), or 14...♘xe5? 15 ♖xf6! gxf6 16 ♘e4 ♘d7 (16...f5 17 ♘f6+ ♔e7 18 ♕e1!) 17 ♕e1! b5 18 ♕b4 with a decisive attack, while after 14...♘xd4 15 exf6 g6 16 ♗e4 Black will have to suffer;

2) 12...♘xd4?! 13 exf6 g6 (if 13...gxf6? there is the decisive 14 ♘e4 f5 15 ♗xd4 or 14 ♗xd4 ♗xd4 15 ♗b5+ and ♕xd4 – Stohl)

14 ♗xd4 ♗xd4 15 ♗b5+ and ♕xd4, or 14 ♕e1!, threatening ♘d5 and ♖d1, with an obvious advantage;

3) 12...♘d5! (the most resilient defence) 13 ♘xd5 exd5 14 ♘xc6!? (14 ♕e1 or 14 c3 is also not bad), retaining an enduring initiative after all of 14...bxc6 15 exd6 ♗xd6 16 ♕h5, 14...♕xc6 15 ♗xc5 dxc5 16 f5!, and 14...♗xe3 15 ♘b4 ♕c5 16 ♕f3! ♕xb4 17 ♕xe3 0-0 18 f5!.

13 fxe5 dxe5

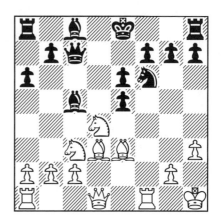

14 ♗b5+!

White would have won equally prettily by 14 ♘db5! axb5 15 ♗xb5+, and if 15...♔e7 16 ♗g5! ♗d7 (after 16...h6 my *Informator* move 17 ♗h4 is good, but 17 ♕h5! ♖h7 18 ♗xf6+ gxf6 19 ♖ad1 ♗d4 20 ♕h4 is more forceful) 17 ♕f3! ♔e8 18 ♖ad1. At the board I rejected this because of 15...♗d7 16 ♗xd7+ ♘xd7, overlooking the obvious 17 ♗xc5 ♕xc5 (17...♘xc5? 18 ♘b5) 18 ♖xf7! 0-0-0 19 ♕g4 or even 18 ♘e4! ♕d5 19 ♘d6+ ♔e7 20 ♕h5! with the threats of ♖xf7+ and ♖ad1.

14...axb5

If 14...♗d7 15 ♗xd7+ ♘xd7, then Stohl's 16 ♕f3 is not bad, but 16 ♘xe6! fxe6 17 ♗g5! is far more resounding: 17...g6 18 ♘e4 ♕c6 19 ♕d3 or 17...♗e7 18 ♗xe7 ♔xe7 19 ♕g4 ♖ag8 20 ♕b4+, and Black has no defence.

In the event of 14...♔f8!? I would have had to make another sacrifice – 15 ♖xf6!, also depriving Black of any saving hopes. Since 15...gxf6? 16 ♗h6+ ♔e7 17 ♘f5+! exf5 18 ♘d5+ is fatal for him, one of the captures on d4 is all that remains:

1) 15...♗xd4 16 ♗h6! (this move of Stohl's is far stronger than 16 ♖xf7+(?!)♖xf7 17 ♗xd4, which I gave in *Informator*) 16...gxh6 (16...♗xc3 17 ♖xf7+! ♔xf7 18 ♕h5+ ♔e7 19 ♖d1 or 16...♕e7 17 ♘e4 and ♕h5 is even worse) 17 ♕h5 ♖g8 (if 17...♗e3 18 ♖af1 ♗f4, then 19 ♖6xf4! exf4 20 ♕xh6+♔e7 21 ♕g5+ ♔f8 22 ♖d1!) 18 ♕xh6+ ♖g7 19 ♗e8! ♗e3 20 ♕xe3 ♔xe8 21 ♘e4, or 16...axb5 17 ♕h5 e4 18 ♘xb5 ♕e7 19 ♗xg7+ ♔xg7 20 ♕h6+ ♔g8 21 ♘xd4 ♕f8 22 ♕h5 and ♖af1, winning;

2) 15...exd4 16 ♗h6! (my *Informator* suggestion 16 ♗f4(?!) ♕e7 17 ♘e4 axb5 is weaker, even after the best move 18 ♗e5!) 16...dxc3 (16...axb5? or 16...gxh6? loses to 17 ♕h5!) 17 ♕f3! (now if 17 ♕h5? Black is saved by 17...♗d4!) 17...axb5 (earlier I recommended 17...♗d4, missing the winning 18 ♗xg7+! ♔xg7 19 ♖f1 ♖f8 20 ♗d3! – Stohl) 18 ♖f1 ♔e8 19 ♖xf7 ♕c6 20 ♕h5! ♕d5 (20...g6 21 ♕e5) 21 ♗g5! g6 22 ♕h6, or 19...♗d7 20 ♕xc3 e5 21 ♗xg7 ♖g8 22 ♕d3! and wins.

15 ♘dxb5 ♕c6 16 ♗xc5 ♕xc5 17 ♘d6+ ♔e7

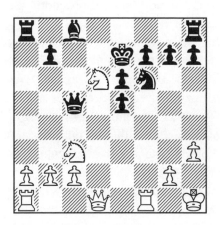

If 17...♔f8, then 18 ♘ce4 ♕d5 19 ♕f3 and ♖ad1, winning.

18 ♖xf6!

This is both stronger and prettier than the prosaic 18 ♘ce4 ♕d4 (18...♕d5 19 ♕e1) 19 ♕f3 ♘xe4 20 ♘xe4 (20 ♘b5!?) 20...f5 21 ♕g3! ♔f7 22 ♘g5+ and ♖ad1, which also wins.

18...gxf6 19 ♘ce4 ♕d4 (19...♕e3? 20 ♘f5+!, while if 19...♕c7(b6) there is the decisive 20 ♕h5 ♖f8 21 ♕h6!) **20 ♕h5 ♖f8 21 ♖d1! ♕e3** (21...♕xb2 22 ♕h6) **22 ♕h4 ♕f4 23 ♕e1! ♖a4**

There is nothing else: 23...f5? 24 ♘xc8+ and ♕b4+, mating.

24 ♕c3 ♖d4 25 ♖xd4 ♕f1+ (25...exd4 26 ♕c7+ ♗d7 27 ♘c8+!) **26 ♔h2 exd4**

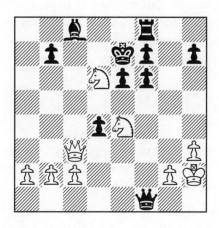

27 ♕c5! (the final touch) **27...♔d7** (or 27...♕f4+ 28 g3 ♕e5 29 ♘xc8+, also with mate) **28 ♘b5! ♕f4+ 29 g3**

And in view of mate after 29...♕xe4 30 ♕c7+ or 29...♕e5 30 ♘xf6+! Black resigned **(1-0)**. Such a crushing win against a dangerous rival gave me great creative satisfaction.

As is usual in double-round tournaments, so that no one should play three successive games with the same colour, the organisers switched some rounds – the 6th with the 7th, and also the 13th with the 14th. In the rearranged round I drew with Short, after missing a win in the second time scramble, and before my game with Karpov, which concluded the first cycle, I was confidently leading with 5 out of 6.

But what about my eternal opponent? From the press: *'Many assumed that the tournament would see a sharp duel between Kasparov and Karpov. This did not happen: the ex-world champion began in very poor form. What told was fatigue after the first stage of the World Cup, which concluded literally a couple of days before Tilburg, and the arduous flight from Reykjavik to Holland. The outcome of the first cycle was uncommonly poor for Karpov: in seven games he scored six draws and not a single win. After this, of course, he was unable to fight for first place. But the next brick in the fundamental edifice of duels between Kasparov and Karpov proved uncommonly attractive.'*

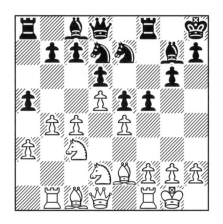

13 f3

Nothing is given by the gambit 13 c5 axb4 14 axb4 dxc5 etc. If 13 ♕c2 again 13...♘g8 is good (Salov-Short, Skelleftea 1989), although there is also the sharp 13...axb4 14 axb4 ♘f6 15 f3 g5!? 16 c5 ♘g6, abandoning everything for the sake of an attack on the king (Vaganian-Kasparov, Manila Olympiad 1992).

13...♘g8!?

Black manoeuvres with his knights, maintaining the pawn tension in the centre and retaining the choice between ...f5-f4 and ...fxe4. Makarychev: 'The world champion's strategic plan probably became the most important contribution by Black to the theory of the classical variation after the famous game Taimanov-Najdorf (Zürich Candidates Tournament 1953)'.

The old move was 13...f4: for example, 14 ♘b3?! axb4 15 axb4 g5 16 ♗d2?! ♘g6 17 ♖a1 ♖xa1 18 ♕xa1 ♘f6 19 ♕a7 (19 g4 fxg3!) 19...g4! 20 fxg4 (20 ♘a5 g3!) 20...♘xg4 21 h3 ♘h6 22 ♗e1 ♖g8 23 ♘d2 ♗f6! and ....♗h4 with excellent play for Black (Ljubojevic-Kasparov, Linares 1993).

After 13...♘g8 White must guard the e4-point and prepare c4-c5. But how?

14 ♕c2

This is the main line. In Skelleftea Karpov

Game 80
A.Karpov-G.Kasparov
Tilburg, 7th Round, 25.10.1991
King's Indian Defence E97

1 d4 ♘f6 2 c4 g6 3 ♘c3 ♗g7 4 e4 d6 5 ♘f3 0-0 6 ♗e2 e5 7 0-0 ♘c6 8 d5 ♘e7 9 ♘d2 (9 ♘e1 – *Game Nos.58, 64, 77*) **9...a5 10 a3**

Of course, not 10 b3?! c5 (Game No.44 in *Kasparov vs. Karpov 1986-87*).

10...♘d7 11 ♖b1 f5 12 b4 ♔h8!

A useful move, in contrast to 12...b6?! (*Game No.42*). Black's objective is to relieve the congestion in his position. He should not hurry with ...f5-f4, but play ...♘g8, and for the moment keep his other knight on d7, hindering White's c4-c5 (if 12...♘f6?!, then 13 c5!). The first time I employed this new plan, which became the most popular, was against Karpov in Skelleftea (1989).

responded inaccurately – 14 ♘b3?!. Now after c4-c5 White will no longer have the strong manoeuvre ♘d2-c4, and Black gains time to create counterplay: 14...axb4 15 axb4 ♘df6! – the knight begins operating on the kingside, at the same time making way for the bishop on c8 (Game No.7 in *Kasparov vs. Karpov 1988-2009*).

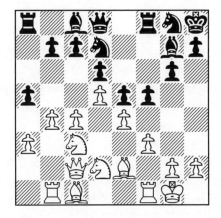

14...♘gf6

A month later I successfully played 14...axb4 15 axb4 ♘df6?! 16 c5 ♘h5 17 ♘c4! ♘f4 18 cxd6?! cxd6 19 ♘b5 ♖a6 20 ♖b3 fxe4 21 fxe4 ♗d7! 22 ♘c3?! ♖a1 23 ♗xf4 ♖xf1+ 24 ♗xf1 exf4 25 ♕f2 ♘h6 26 h3 ♘f7 27 ♘e2 ♘g5 28 ♘xf4? ♕f6... 0-1 (Khalifman-Kasparov, Paris (rapid) 1991), but 18 ♗e3! with the idea of b4-b5-b6 is stronger.

At that time 14...♗h6 was also fashionable – after 15 ♘b5 axb4 16 axb4 ♘df6 17 c5 ♘h5! (17...fxe4 18 ♘xe4 is advantageous to White, Ivanchuk-Gelfand, Linares 1992) 18 ♘c4 ♗d7! both sides have chances (Dokhoian-Velikhanli, Helsinki 1992), but 15 c5 or 15 ♘b3 and c4-c5 is more promising.

15 ♘b5

For the moment everything is following a familiar pattern. The exchange 15 exf5 gxf5 weakens White's foundations in the centre: 16 ♗d3 axb4 17 axb4 ♘b6 18 ♘b3 ♘h5 19 g3 c6! with counterplay. But soon a new,

problematic variation appeared: 15 ♗d3!? f4 (forced) 16 ♘b5 b6, and this quickly became the main one. Its author, Ivanchuk, in a game with me (Linares 1992) sacrificed a pawn – 17 c5!?, and after 17...dxc5 18 bxa5 ♖xa5 19 ♘c4 ♖a8 20 a4 ♘e8 I did not achieve full equality. 17...bxc5 (Khalifman-Kamsky, Biel Interzonal 1993) is perhaps safer. However, Gurevich's move 17 ♗b2! with the threat of c4-c5 became more popular (here I prepared 17...♘e8 followed by a counterattack on the kingside, but I did not in fact test it in practice).

15...axb4 16 axb4 ♘h5 17 g3 ♘df6

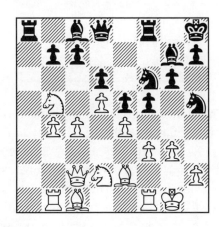

18 c5!

More energetic than 18 ♖b3 fxe4, when Black equalises (Lobron-Gelfand, Dortmund 1990).

18...♗d7

The alternative is 18...fxe4 19 fxe4 ♗h3 20 ♖f2 ♕d7 (if 20...♘g4, then 21 ♖xf8+ ♗xf8 22 ♘f3 h6 23 ♘h4!, Polugayevsky-J.Polgar, 2nd match game, Aruba 1991) 21 c6 bxc6 22 ♕xc6 ♗h6 23 ♘c4, and instead of 23...♗xc1 24 ♖xc1 ♘xe4 25 ♕xd7 ♗xd7 26 ♖xf8+ ♖xf8 27 ♘xc7 ♖b8, which after 28 ♗d3! and b4-b5 (Ftacnik) gives White an advantage, 23...♕g7!? 24 ♕xc7 ♘xe4 25 ♕xg7+ ♗xg7 26 ♖xf8+ ♗xf8 is better, with a complicated, roughly equal endgame.

19 ♖b3!

A strong, multi-purpose move: the rook not only aims for c3, but also defends the kingside. Before the 1990 match my trainers and I studied 19 c6?! here and concluded that after 19...bxc6 20 dxc6 ♗e6 Black has a perfectly acceptable position.

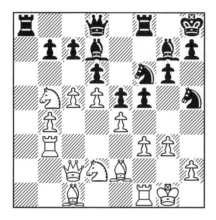

The culmination of the theoretical duel. After the quiet 19...♗h6 20 ♖c3 fxe4 21 fxe4 ♗h3 22 ♖e1 (Epishin-J.Polgar, Brno 1991 and Vienna 1991) White's chances are somewhat better, and 19...fxe4?! 20 fxe4 ♗h3 21 ♖e1 ♗h6 is inaccurate in view of 22 ♘f3!?, Gelfand-Kasparov, Paris (rapid) 1991.

The move 19 ♖b3, confidently made by my opponent, provoked in me a surge of emotion, and after some thought I decided to sharpen the play to the utmost with a daring knight sacrifice.

19...♘xg3?!

It is interesting that, the following year, after 19...♗h6 20 ♖c3 I launched an attack with successive sacrifices against Kamsky (Dortmund 1992): 20...♗f4?! 21 cxd6 (21 ♖f2 ♘xg3! 22 hxg3 ♗xg3 23 ♖g2 ♘h5 with two pawns for the piece, and an attack) 21...♘xg3? (now this is a blunder) 22 hxg3 ♘h5 23 gxf4 ♘xf4 (23...♕h4 also fails to save Black after 24 ♖f2 ♘xf4 25 ♗f1 ♗xb5 26 dxc7 ♕g3+ 27 ♖g2 ♘xg2 28 ♗xg2 ♕e1+

29 ♘f1) 24 ♗c4!, and White won.

Of course, the cool-headed 21...cxd6! was essential (threatening of ...♕b6+), when 22 ♘c7 ♖c8 23 ♘e6 ♗xe6 24 dxe6 ♗e3+! 25 ♔g2 ♖xc3 26 ♕xc3 f4 27 ♘b3 ♗xc1 28 ♖xc1 fxg3 29 hxg3 ♘xg3! 30 ♔xg3 ♘h5+ 31 ♔g2 ♕h4 could lead to perpetual check.

And even so, the attack with 20...♗f4 is dubious in view of 21 gxf4! ♘xf4 22 ♗c4: for example, 22...♘6xd5 23 exd5 ♕g5+ 24 ♔f2 ♗xb5 25 ♗xb5 ♕h4+ 26 ♔e3 ♘xd5+ 27 ♔e2 or 25...c6 26 dxc6 bxc6 27 ♔e1 cxb5 28 cxd6 – Black has insufficient compensation for the material deficit. Therefore he apparently has to reconcile himself to the approved 20...fxe4 21 fxe4 ♗h3.

20 hxg3 ♘h5 21 f4!

The best reply (White loses after 21 ♔g2? ♘xg3 22 ♔xg3 f4+, while if 21 ♖f2 ♘xg3 his extra piece is not felt), although it seemed to me that also after it Black should be okay. But the longer I thought over my 21st move, the more anxious I became...

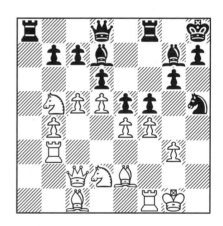

21...exf4?!

Alas, nearly half an hour's calculation did not help me to make the correct choice – 21...♗xb5! 22 ♗xb5 exf4, when 23 gxf4 ♘xf4! 24 ♘f3 fxe4 25 ♕xe4 ♖c8! (Khalifman-Kindermann, Munich (rapid) 1991) or 23 ♗b2 ♘xg3 (Beliavsky-Khalifman, Reggio

Emilia 1991/92) gives Black good play.

It is stronger to play 23 exf5! ♘xg3 (23...dxc5!? deserves consideration too) 24 ♖xf4 ♘xf5 25 ♘f3 dxc5, and here not 26 bxc5 ♕xd5 (Rublevsky-Pugachev, Russia 1992), but 26 ♕xc5!, and White's extra piece is nevertheless superior to the black pawns: 26...c6 (26...♖a1 27 ♗f1) 27 ♗d3 b6 (otherwise ♗xf5) 28 ♕c2 ♘d4 29 ♖xf8+ ♕xf8 30 ♘xd4 ♗xd4+ 31 ♔g2 cxd5 32 ♗b2 etc. True, with only one surviving pawn, it is hard for White to hope for success.

22 c6! (I underestimated this strong intermediate move) **22...bxc6 23 dxc6 ♘xg3?**

Now Black's position is close to being lost. However, even after the more resilient 23...♗e6 24 ♗xh5 gxh5!? (but not my *Informator* suggestion 24...♗xb3? 25 ♘xb3 gxh5 in view of 26 ♘3d4!) 25 ♗b2! fxe4 26 ♗xg7+ ♔xg7 27 ♕xe4 ♗xb3 28 ♘xb3 or 23...♗xc6 24 ♕xc6 ♘xg3 25 ♖xg3 fxg3 26 ♘f3! fxe4 (26...♕e7?! 27 ♗d3) 27 ♘g5 ♖xf1+ 28 ♗xf1 ♕f8 29 ♘xe4 I would have faced a depressing struggle for a draw.

24 ♖xg3 fxg3 25 cxd7 g2

Of course, not 25...♕h4? 26 ♘f3 ♕h3 27 ♗b2 g2 28 ♗xg7+ ♔xg7 29 ♖e1 and wins. From afar it had seemed to me that the resulting position was not so bad for Black, but this was an illusion.

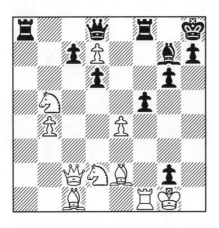

26 ♖f3?

White has three (!) minor pieces for the rook and pawns, and to be able to play for a win he needs to retain at least one of his pawns, or, at the worst, the queens, in order with the support of the minor pieces to attack the enemy king. Black's aims are directly the opposite. Thus in the event of 26 ♖f2 ♕xd7 27 ♗b2 fxe4 28 ♘xe4 ♖xf2 29 ♘xf2 c5! he would succeed in exchanging White's last pawn and half solve the difficult problem of achieving a draw. Therefore in *Informator* I recommended 27 exf5 – after 27...c5? 28 bxc5 dxc5 29 ♗b2 White has a fearfully strong attack, but with 27...c6! Black can still resist.

However, the strongest was 26 ♖d1! with a powerful activation of the pieces. Now the c1-bishop is defended, and therefore it is bad to play 26...♕xd7? 27 ♕xc7 ♕xc7 28 ♘xc7 – the fate of the game is decided by the passed b-pawn. There is also no point in 26...♕h4?! 27 ♘f3 ♕h1+ 28 ♔f2 fxe4 29 ♕xe4 and wins, while if 26...♖b8?! (with the idea of 27 ♕xc7? ♗d4+!) there follows the unexpected 27 e5!! ♕xd7 28 ♕xc7 or 27...♗xe5 28 ♘f3 ♗f6 29 ♕xc7 etc. That only leaves 26...fxe4 27 ♘xe4 ♕xd7 28 ♔xg2 (of course, not 28 ♕xc7? ♕h3!, forcing a draw – 29 ♕xg7+ ♔xg7 30 ♗b2+ ♔h6 31 ♗c1+) 28...♖ae8 29 ♕c4, but here White retains both the b4-pawn and the queens, and with them every chance of converting his enormous advantage.

26...♕xd7

In *Informator* I recommended 26...♕h4 27 ♔xg2 ♕g4+ 28 ♔f1 fxe4 29 ♕xe4 ♕xd7, but here the invasion of the knight is unpleasant for Black – 30 ♘d4! c5 31 ♘e6 ♖xf3+ (31...♖fe8 32 ♗c4! cxb4 33 ♖h3 with a winning attack) 32 ♕xf3 ♖a1 33 ♘b3 ♖xc1+ 34 ♘xc1 ♕xe6 35 b5 and wins.

27 ♗b2

My earlier recommendation 27 exf5 c6 28 ♗b2 (28 ♘a3 ♕e7!) does not stand up to criticism because of 28...cxb5 29 f6 (29 fxg6 ♖ac8) 29...♗xf6! 30 ♗xf6 (30 ♖xf6? ♕h3) 30...♗xf6 31 ♘e4 ♗e5, when Black is alright. And after 27 ♕xc7 ♕xc7 28 ♘xc7 ♖ac8 he would have regained one of the pieces and successfully coped with the passed b-pawn.

27...fxe4 28 ♖xf8+ ♗xf8

Another turning-point in the game.

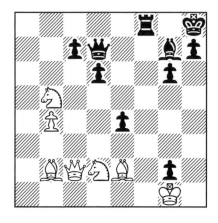

29 ♗xg7+?

Speelman was right in reproaching Karpov for this hasty exchange of bishops and in recommending 29 ♘xe4. And although after 29...c5?! (apparently the lesser evil was 29...♗e8) White's last pawn is exchanged, he could continue playing for a win, even despite the open position of his own king: 30 bxc5! dxc5 31 ♕xc5 ♖b8 32 ♗xg7+ ♕xg7 33 ♘bd6, and under the threat of a mating attack I would soon have also had to give up rook for bishop. White would have remained with two extra knights, but with the queens on (and even without the queens Black would be hindered by his own pawns).

29...♕xg7 30 ♕xe4 ♕f6!

30...c5 was also possible, but it is more important first to exchange the queens. Equality is already close, although there is an extremely rare and original balance of forces

on the board. It should be borne in mind that the fantastic endgame looming on the horizon – two knights and bishop against rook – is drawn in view of the possibility, when no pawns remain, of giving up the rook for the bishop or playing for stalemate. But Black must play very accurately!

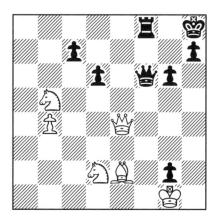

31 ♘f3 ♕f4 32 ♕e7 (avoiding 32 ♕xf4 ♖xf4 33 ♘xc7 ♖xb4 with a draw) **32...♖f7 33 ♕e6 ♖f6**

A draw would immediately have been forced by 33...g5!? 34 ♕e8+ (34 ♔xg2?! g4, winning the knight) 34...♔f8 35 ♕e7 g4 36 ♗d3 ♖f7 37 ♕e8+ ♖f8 38 ♕e7. But as it is, there is no longer anything that White can do.

34 ♕e8+ ♖f8 35 ♕e7 ♖f7 36 ♕e6 ♖f6

Again avoiding 36...g5!? – I was expecting that at any moment a draw offer would follow. But Karpov suddenly decided to continue the fight.

37 ♕b3!? g5

The seemingly tempting 37...c6?! with the idea of 38 ♘bd4 g5! (suggested by me after the game) would have been refuted by the typically computer move 38 ♘c7! followed by 38...d5 39 ♕c3! ♚g8 40 b5! ♖f7 41 b6 (that's progress for you!).

38 ♘xc7

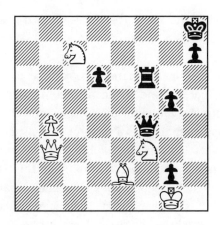

38...g4?!

A sign of time-trouble. 38...♕c1+ 39 ♚xg2 ♕xc7 40 ♕e3 ♕b7 or 40 ♕d5 g4 would have drawn more quickly and simply.

39 ♘d5 ♕c1+ 40 ♕d1 (if 40 ♚xg2 gxf3+ 41 ♗xf3 ♕d2+ 42 ♚f1 there is the good reply 42...♖f8! 43 b5 ♖c8) **40...♕xd1+ 41 ♗xd1 ♖f5 42 ♘e3 ♖f4 43 ♘e1 ♖xb4**

'So Black has succeeded in eliminating White's last pawn. But there is still tremendous potential for suffering in the position!' (Speelman). A valid observation: at this moment I did not definitely know whether I would be able to hold out with my rook against the armada of minor pieces.

44 ♗xg4 h5!

44...♖xg4? 45 ♘xg4 was premature – with pawns on the board, the white knights,

supported by the king, should sooner or later construct a mating net. Therefore I firmly decided to give up all my pawns – and what would be, would be.

45 ♗f3 d5 46 ♘3xg2 h4 47 ♘d3 ♖a4 48 ♘gf4 ♚g7 49 ♚g2 ♚f6 50 ♗xd5 ♖a5 51 ♗c6 ♖a6 52 ♗b7 ♖a3 53 ♗e4 ♖a4 54 ♗d5 ♖a5 55 ♗c6 ♖a6 56 ♗f3 ♚g5 57 ♗b7 ♖a1 58 ♗c8 ♖a4 59 ♚f3 ♖c4 60 ♗d7 ♚f6

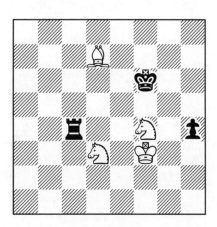

The second time control was reached, and the game was at last adjourned, with both players having used nearly all their time. On arriving at the hotel, I was not sure that this was a drawn ending, but I quickly found a reliable plan – to play my king to the dark corner (of the opposite colour to the bishop) and keep my rook at the other end of the board (to avoid knight forks), while threatening to sacrifice it. White has no way of breaching this fortress.

But upon the resumption Karpov battled on 'to the last bullet'.

61 ♚g4 ♖d4 62 ♗c6 ♖d8 63 ♚xh4

Today the mighty endgame program *Nalimov* has ascertained that two knights and a bishop cannot win against a rook, irrespective of which corner – dark or light – the king is driven to.

63...♖g8 64 ♗e4 ♖g1 65 ♘h5+ ♚e6 66 ♘g3 ♚f6 67 ♚g4 ♖a1 68 ♗d5 ♖a5 69 ♗f3

♖a1 70 ♔f4 ♚e6 71 ♘c5+ ♚d6 72 ♘ge4+ ♚e7 73 ♚e5 ♖f1 74 ♗g4 ♖g1 75 ♗e6 ♖e1 76 ♗c8 ♖c1 77 ♚d4 ♖d1+ 78 ♘d3 ♚f7 79 ♚e3 ♖a1 80 ♚f4 ♚e7 81 ♘b4 ♖c1 82 ♘d5+ ♚f7 83 ♗d7 ♖f1+ 84 ♚e5 ♖a1 85 ♘g5+ ♚g6 86 ♘f3 ♚g7 87 ♗g4 ♚g6 88 ♘f4+ ♚g7 89 ♘d4 ♖e1+ 90 ♚f5 ♖c1 91 ♗e2 ♖e1 92 ♗h5 ♖a1 93 ♘fe6+

Methodically confining the black king, although it is also quite comfortable on the edge of the board.

93...♚h6 94 ♗e8 ♖a8 95 ♗c6 ♖a1 96 ♚f6

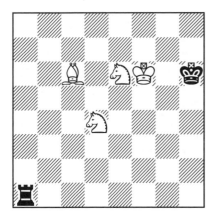

96...♚h7

96...♚h5 was also possible here, but not the alternative 96...♖f1+ 97 ♘f5+ ♚h5? 98 ♗g2! ♖f2 99 ♗h3! with the threat of ♘eg7 mate.

97 ♘g5+ ♚h8 98 ♘de6 ♖a6 99 ♗e8 ♖a8 100 ♗h5 ♖a1 101 ♗g6 ♖f1+ 102 ♚e7 ♖a1 103 ♘f7+ ♚g8 104 ♘h6+ ♚h8 105 ♘f5 ♖a7+ 106 ♚f6 ♖a1 107 ♘e3 ♖e1 108 ♘d5 ♖g1 109 ♗f5 ♖f1 110 ♘df4 ♖a1 111 ♘g6+ ♚g8 112 ♘e7+ ♚h8 113 ♘g5 ♖a6+ 114 ♚f7

After exhausting the 'fifty move' limit, White allows the long-awaited sacrifice.

114...♖f6+!

Draw agreed (½-½) in view of 115 ♚xf6 – stalemate! The longest game of the tournament and an unforgettable, study-like finish.

After the first cycle the leading trio was Kasparov – 5½ out of 7, Anand – 5, Short – 4½.

The entire tournament took place against the background of constant discussions about the venue for the future world championship match. As a counter to my suggestion of Los Angeles, a bid from Morocco suddenly appeared. I think that this was another of Campomanes's intrigues, a game aimed at raising the 'American stakes'. Fortunately, a conflict did not occur: Rabat soon withdrew its bid – there, apparently, they took account of the world champion's opinion. But I wonder how chess history would have turned out, if I had nevertheless agreed with the Morocco variation?

The November FIDE Congress in Berlin approved Los Angeles without any particular discussion, and in Moscow on 18th February 1992 Campomanes and the organisers signed a 'final' contract, in accordance with which about 20% of the prize fund was to be allocated to FIDE, the GMA and a special chess fund. The start of the match was set for 14th August 1993. Who could have known then, that in August 1992 serious financial and political causes would force the organisers to pull out of staging the match, FIDE would begin collecting new bids, and this would be the prelude to extremely dramatic events in the chess world...

During the second cycle in Tilburg I won against Timman and Bareev, and drew with Korchnoi and Kamsky. Three rounds before the finish it appeared that the question of the tournament winner was already decided: I was on 8½ out of 11, Anand had 6½ and a slightly better adjourned position against Kamsky, while Short and Karpov, who had made a spurt, were on 6½. However, in the 12th round I contrived to lose from an excellent position to Anand, completely wasting a valuable novelty with a queen sacrifice. For an instant it appeared that Vishy might catch me, but in the 13th round he lost to Karpov, and then, with a blunder on the 99th move, he also lost his adjourned game against Kamsky.

As for me, in the 13th round I drew with difficulty against Short. Thus before the concluding meeting of the two 'Ks', the destiny of first place was already decided: with 9 out of 13, I was one and a half points ahead of Karpov, Anand and Short. Nevertheless, our game was just as competitive as ever.

Game 81
G.Kasparov-A.Karpov
Tilburg, 14th Round, 4.11.1991
Scotch Game C45

1 e4 e5 2 ♘f3 ♘c6 3 d4!?

Let's see, after our last year's match, what the opponent has prepared against the Scotch!

3...exd4 4 ♘xd4 ♘f6 (4...♗c5 – *Game No.88*)
5 ♘xc6 bxc6 6 e5 ♕e7 7 ♕e2 ♘d5 8 c4 ♗a6
(8...♘b6 – *Game No.71*) **9 b3 g6**

To judge by Karpov's rapid reply, my choice did not come as a surprise to him. In contrast to 9...0-0-0 (*Game No.70*), 9...f6 or 9...♕h4?!, the 9...g6 variation was still little-explored.

Four years later Ubilava's aggressive move 9...g5!? also appeared (Kasparov-Anand, 8th match game, New York 1995). Now the e5-pawn is in danger (White does not have f2-f4 and in some cases ...♘f4-g6 is threatened). I replied 10 ♗a3, and after 10...d6 11 exd6 ♕xe2+ 12 ♗xe2 ♗g7! 13 cxd5 ♗xe2 14 ♔xe2 ♗xa1 15 ♖c1 0-0-0! I obtained sufficient compensation for the exchange, but not an advantage. 10 g3 (Kasparov-Nikolic, Linares 1997) or 10 h4!? (Palac-Giorgadze, Pula 1997) is more topical.

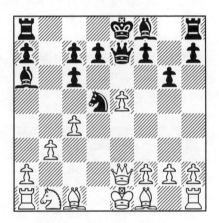

10 f4!?

A novelty. Analysing this variation before the start of the Lyons part of the 1990 match, my trainers and I concluded that this was the most energetic reply (in the hope of exploiting the insecurity of the black knight and the bishop on a6). Later I was also attracted by other continuations:

1) 10 ♗a3?! ♕g5 with unclear play (Kasparov-Ivanchuk, Amsterdam 1994), but soon it was established that 10...♕h4! is stronger, planning if 11 ♗xf8? the unexpected invasion 11...♕d4. And after 11 ♗b2 ♗b4+ 12 ♔d1 (12 ♘d2 ♘c3) 12...♘f4 Black has no difficulties;

2) 10 ♗b2 ♗g7 11 ♘d2 ♘b4!, and here 12 ♘f3 c5 13 g3 0-0 14 ♗g2 has occurred, followed by 14...d5! 15 0-0 (Sveshnikov-Kharitonov, Leningrad 1991) 15...♖ad8! (Svidler-Adams, Tilburg 1997), while in 1993, trying to find even a hint of an advantage for White, I spent a long time analysing 12 0-0-0 ♘xa2+ 13 ♔b1 ♘b4 14 ♘e4. But after 14...0-0 Black's defences are solid: 15 ♘f6+ ♗xf6 16 exf6 ♕xe2 17 ♗xe2 d6, or 15 ♕f3 ♖fe8 16 ♘f6+ (16 h4 d5 17 ♘f6+ ♗xf6 18 exf6 ♕e4+) 16...♗xf6 17 exf6 ♕c5 18 h4 d5 19 h5 g5 etc;

3) 10 g3 ♗g7 11 ♗b2 0-0 12 ♗g2 ♖fe8 (12...♖ae8!?) 13 0-0. Nowadays this is a fashionable set-up, where Black has played both 13...♗xe5 14 ♕xe5 ♕xe5 15 ♗xe5 ♖xe5 16 cxd5 ♗xf1 17 ♔xf1 cxd5 18 f4 with slightly the better chances for White, and 13...♘b6 14 ♖e1 d5 (Kasparov-I.Sokolov, Yerevan Olympiad 1996), or 14...f6!.

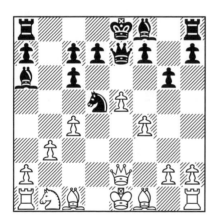

10...f6

By no means the only move. White has a small advantage after both 10...♗g7 11 ♕f2 (van der Wiel-Beliavsky, Groningen 1994), and 10...♕b4+ 11 ♗d2 ♕b6 12 ♘c3 ♗b4 13 ♕d3! (but not 13 ♕f3 ♘xc3 14 ♗xc3 ♗b7 15 0-0-0 c5 with equality, Gelfand-Karpov, Linares 1992), or 12 ♕f3! (slightly more accurate than 12 ♕e4 f5 13 ♕f3, Kasparov-

Bacrot, Sarajevo 2000).

But the most interesting and perhaps the most promising is the sharp 10...g5!? (attacking the base of the pawn chain as recommended by Nimzowitsch!): for example, 11 ♗a3?! (Motylev-Ivanchuk, Moscow (blitz) 2002) 11...♘b4! 12 f5 (12 ♗b2 gxf4 13 ♕f2 c5) 12...d5 13 ♗b2 dxc4 14 ♕e4 0-0-0, seizing the initiative, or 11 fxg5 (11 f5?! 0-0-0 12 ♗a3 d6 is worse) 11...♗g7 12 ♗b2 (Pavasovic-Balinov, Pula 2003) 12...♕xg5 13 ♘d2 0-0-0 with double-edged play.

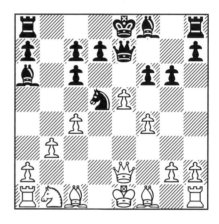

11 ♗a3!?

After 11 exf6 ♕xe2+ 12 ♗xe2 ♗b4+! 13 ♗d2 ♗xd2+ 14 ♘xd2 ♘xf4 15 ♖f1 Black equalises with 15...♘xe2! 16 ♔xe2 ♔f7 17 ♔d3 ♖ae8 (Radjabov-Kasparov, Linares 2004).

11...♕f7?!

An incorrect manoeuvre, in my view, although up to now it has been thought to lead to equality. In the event of 11...c5 12 g3! fxe5 13 ♗g2 c6 14 ♗b2 ♗g7 15 0-0 (15 fxe5 0-0 16 ♘d2 ♘c7!) 15...0-0 16 ♘d2 ♘b4 17 ♘f3 e4 18 ♗xg7 ♕xg7 19 ♕xe4 ♖ae8 20 ♕b1 ♕c3 21 ♕c1 ♘c2 22 ♖b1 ♖e2 23 ♖f2 ♖fe8 24 ♗f1! White's chances are also somewhat better.

11...♘b4! is correct: 12 ♗b2 ♗h6! (but not 12...c5 13 ♘c3 fxe5 14 a3!, as given by me in *Informator*, or 12...fxe5 13 a3 ♘d5 14 ♕xe5! ♘f6 15 ♗e2 ♗g7 16 ♘d2) 13 a3 (13 ♘c3 fxe5!) 13...♘d5 14 exf6 (14 g3 0-0 is equal) 14...♕xe2+ 15 ♗xe2 ♘xf4! 16 f7+ ♔xf7 17 ♗xh8 ♖xh8 18 0-0 ♔g7 with full compensation for the exchange (Sutovsky-Nielsen, Reykjavik (rapid) 2004).

12 ♕d2! (12 exf6+?! ♔d8 13 ♕d2 ♘xf6! favours Black) **12...♘b6**

12...♘e7 is hardly any better: 13 ♗d3! fxe5 14 0-0 with the initiative.

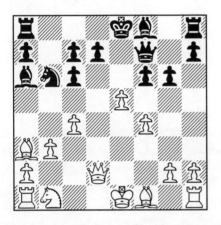

13 c5! (an unpleasant tactical stroke, which unsettles Black) **13...♗xf1 14 cxb6 axb6?!**

For some reason I sensed that this move might be made, although it is a step towards the precipice. Let us analyse two other possibilities:

1) 14...♗a6(?) 15 bxc7 fxe5 (15...♗xa3 16 ♘xa3 is no better) 16 ♕a5 ♕xf4 17 ♕xa6 ♕h4+ 18 ♔d1! (otherwise it is a draw: 18 g3 ♕e4+ or 18 ♔f1 ♗xa3! etc) 18...♕d4+ 19 ♔c2! ♕e4+ 20 ♕d3 ♕xg2+ 21 ♘d2 ♗xa3 22 ♖hf1! with the threat of ♕a6, and Black cannot save the game: 22...♔e7? 23 ♖ae1 d6 24 ♕a6 ♗b4 25 c8♘+! ♖axc8 26 ♕b7+ and ♕xb4, or 22...♕d5 23 ♕a6 ♗b4 24 ♖ad1 ♔e7 25 ♕e2! ♖hf8 (if 25...♗xd2? 26 ♖xd2 ♕a5 there is the spectacular ambush 27 ♕e1!! ♕xa2+ 28 ♔c3 ♕a5+ 29 ♔b2) 26 ♘c4 ♕e6 27 ♘xe5 ♗d6 28 ♖fe1 ♗xe5 29 ♕xe5

♖f2+ 30 ♔c3 ♕xe5+ 31 ♖xe5+ ♔f6 32 ♖de1, and the c7-pawn quickly decides the outcome;

2) 14...♗xa3! (the best reply) 15 b7! ♖b8 16 ♘xa3 ♗a6 17 0-0-0 ♗xb7 (17...♖xb7? 18 e6!) 18 ♖he1 0-0 19 ♕xd7 fxe5, and White's advantage in this position is comparatively slight.

15 e6!!

When, thinking about 13 c5, I saw this elegant stroke, I literally began to shake with excitement. I can imagine what a shock it must have been for Karpov, who thought that Black was quite alright. Indeed, after, say, 15 ♗xf8? ♗xg2! 16 ♕xg2 ♖xf8 17 0-0 fxe5 18 fxe5 ♕xf1+ 19 ♕xf1 ♖xf1+ 20 ♔xf1 ♖a5 he has a sufficient number of pawns for the knight.

15...dxe6

In the event of 15...♕xe6+?! 16 ♔xf1 ♗xa3 17 ♘xa3 0-0 (17...♖xa3? 18 ♖e1) 18 ♘c2 with two pawns for a piece Black can still play on for a long time, but – without hopes of success.

16 ♗xf8 ♖d8! (the only resource that offers any resistance) **17 ♕b2!**

An accurate reply: after 17 ♕f2? ♕xf8! 18 ♖xf1 ♕b4+! 19 ♘d2 ♕c3 20 ♖d1 ♖d3! Black's activity would fully compensate for his material deficit.

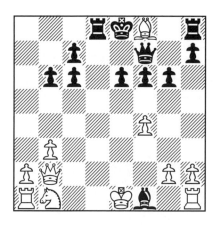

17...♗xg2?

After this capture the battle essentially concludes, and the phase of converting the extra piece ensues. Only the retreat of the bishop could have made White's task harder: 17...♗a6 (after this I was intending 18 ♗b4! followed by ♘d2 and 0-0-0), or 17...♗d3!? 18 ♗a3! g5!, and since 19 fxg5?! is weak because of 19...♕h5!, I would have had to make a difficult choice between 19 ♘c3 ♕h5 and 19 ♘d2 gxf4. In general, these positions are far more complicated than the one which arose in the game.

18 ♕xg2 ♔xf8 19 ♕xc6 ♖d6 20 ♕c3 (a solid move 'towards the centre', although the computer is also not afraid of 20 ♕b7!?) **20...♔g7 21 ♘d2 ♖hd8**

If 21...♖d5 (with the idea of 22 0-0-0? ♖c5) there is the good reply 22 0-0 ♖hd8 23 ♘e4 c5 24 ♖f3 or 24 ♖ae1.

22 0-0-0! ♕e8?!

An inexplicable oversight: why did Karpov suddenly give up a pawn? After the natural 22...♕d7 23 ♕c2 ♖d5 24 ♘e4 the conversion would have taken White longer.

23 ♕xc7+ ♖8d7 24 ♕c2 ♕b8 25 ♘c4! (clarifying the picture as being dismal for Black) **25...♖d5**

Perhaps the ex-champion had been counting on 25...♖xd1+ 26 ♖xd1 ♕xf4+, but

here he noticed the simple 27 ♖d2!, when both 27...♖xd2 28 ♕xd2 and 27...b5 28 ♘d6 are hopeless.

26 ♕f2 ♕c7 27 ♕xb6 ♕xf4+ 28 ♕e3

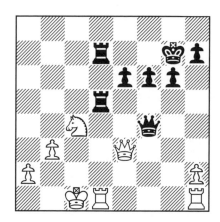

28...♕g4

Also in the event of 28...♖xd1+ 29 ♖xd1 ♖xd1+ 30 ♔xd1 ♕xh2 the outside passed pawn comes into play – 31 a4!. The rest is clear without any commentary.

29 ♖dg1 ♕h4 30 ♖g3 e5 31 ♖h3 ♕g4 32 ♖g1 ♖d1+ 33 ♖xd1 ♕xd1+ 34 ♔b2 h5 35 ♖g3 ♕h1 36 ♕f2 h4 37 ♕g2 ♕xg2+ 38 ♖xg2 g5 39 a4! ♔g6 40 a5 e4 41 b4 h3 42 ♖g3 ♖h7 43 a6 f5 44 ♖a3 1-0

This heavy defeat was the result of a typical opening disaster. As early as the 10th move Karpov had to follow an unfamiliar path and faced problems that were new for him. This was greatly to the credit of the Scotch Game. The resulting irrational positions, without any clear guidelines, with pieces scattered around various parts of the board, were to my liking, whereas, on the contrary, they were not to Karpov's taste. In subsequent 'black' games with me he replied to 1 e4 only with the Caro-Kann or the Petroff.

Although I won the tournament quite easily, by a large margin, I was nevertheless not fully satisfied with my play, because I was unable to land such a 'blow' as in Tilburg 1989. But it was still high-quality chess.

Under the Italian Sky

International Tournament in Reggio Emilia (27 December 1991 – 6 January 1992): 1. Anand – 6 out of 9; 2–3. Gelfand and **Kasparov** – 5½; 4. Karpov – 5; 5–7. Ivanchuk, Khalifman and Polugayevsky – 4½; 8–9. Salov and M.Gurevich – 4; 10. Beliavsky – 1½.

The year 1991 had been an uncommonly difficult one for me. It was a tense, crazy period, involving, apart from appearances in tournaments, my resettlement along with that of my relatives in Moscow, participation in the stormy political life of the country, endless discussions regarding the future match for the world championship, and the reorganisation of the USSR Chess Union, of which I was the head: on 15th December 1991 a meeting was held, at which in view of the break-up of the USSR it was transformed into an International Chess Union.

It was probably because of this that in events at the end of the year I again underperformed. First in the Immopar Cup in Paris – a rapid-play knock-out tournament, where I won against Khalifman (1½-½), Gelfand (2-0) and Bareev (2-0), but lost in the final to Timman (½-1½). And then I made a comparatively modest result at the Christmas super-tournament of ten grandmasters in Reggio Emilia.

In my entire career this was my only tournament in Italy. Not without reason it was called a 'meeting of the leaders of different chess eras': in an attempt to compete with Linares, the organisers had assembled a brilliant line-up. True, playing during the days of the new year celebrations proved a rather unusual experience.

In the 1st round I was paired with Black against Mikhail Gurevich, one of my helpers in two title matches (1986 and 1990), and Anand's second in the 1991 Candidates matches. Incidentally, Vishy's only loss in the tournament was in fact at the hands of Gurevich, which is not surprising: the latter played very strongly. In 1985 Mikhail became USSR champion, but the authorities did not allow him to play in the Interzonal Tournament – supposedly the documents were lost! He had already finished 1st in Reggio Emilia (1988/89) and was close to a triumph in the Interzonal Tournament in Manila (1990) – he was leading two rounds before the finish but he cracked under the pressure, losing to Anand and Short. Soon Gurevich moved his permanent place of residence to Belgium, and now he appears under the Turkish flag.

Game 82
M.Gurevich-G.Kasparov
Reggio Emilia, 1st Round,
28.12.1991
English Opening A21

---

1 c4 (in this tournament 1 e4 did not occur in any of my 'black' games) **1...g6 2 ♘c3 ♗g7 3 g3**

Avoiding d2-d4 and the King's Indian, my opponent chooses a quiet version of the English Opening, which did not come as a surprise to me.

3...e5 4 ♗g2 d6 5 d3

5 e3 f5 6 ♘ge2 ♘f6 7 0-0 0-0 8 b3 c6 9 ♗a3 a5 10 d4 e4 leads to complicated play (Biehler-Kasparov, Frankfurt (simul') 1986).

5...f5 6 e3

Also possible is 6 ♘f3 ♘f6 7 0-0 0-0 8 ♖b1 a5 or 6 e4 (this was played by Reshevsky and Smyslov) 6...♘f6 7 ♘ge2 0-0 followed by ...c7-c6 and ...♗e6 – in this way I defeated

Gruenberg (Hamburg (simul') 1987) and Ljubojevic (Linares 1992).

6...a5!?

In *Informator* I incorrectly gave a different move order – 6...♘f6 7 ♘ge2 a5. After 7...0-0 8 0-0 c6 Black has to reckon with 9 b4!? ♗e6 10 b5, as Hübner and Ljubojevic (Brussels (blitz) 1987) played against me. True, Mikhail preferred 9 f4 ♗e6 (9...a5!?) 10 b3 (Gurevich-Bukal, Bundesliga 2004).

7 ♘ge2 (7 d4!?) **7...♘f6 8 0-0 0-0 9 b3 c6**

I always liked the flexible set-up without ...♘b8-c6, in which Black retains the option of developing his queen's knight at a6 or d7.

10 ♗b2

White plays with exaggerated solidity, avoiding any weakening of his position (such as 10 e4?! ♘a6 11 h3? f4! 12 gxf4 ♘h5! with an attack, Poldauf-Lau, Bad Neuenahr 1991), and intending to suppress the opponent's activity on the kingside with f2-f4. But I had another plan.

10...♘a6 11 ♕d2 ♗d7!

Gurevich did not expect this: Black suddenly begins preparing to seize space on the opposite wing! 11...♗e6 or 11...♖e8 (Nakamura-Short, London 2011) are less energetic.

12 ♔h1?!

Not only the loss of a tempo, but also a tactical oversight. It is better to develop the

queen's rook – 12 ♖ae1 (Serper-Markovic, Arnhem 1989), 12 ♖ad1 (Kosten-D.Gurevich, Geneva 1993), 12 ♖ab1 (Csom-Agrest, Budapest 1997) or even 12 d4 (Bilek-Groszpeter, Hungary 1993). However, in any case Black has a comfortable game.

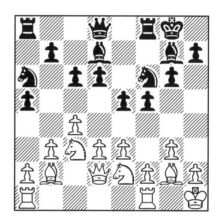

12...♖c8 (with the king on h1 there is no longer any need for the modest 12...♖b8) **13 ♖ae1**

The rook does not really do anything here. 13 ♖ad1 or 13 f4 is more appropriate.

13...b5 14 e4?!

On seeing that after 14 cxb5 cxb5 Black is okay – 15 ♘d5 (15 ♗b7?! ♖c7 16 ♗xa6? ♕a8+ and ...♕xa6) 15...♘xd5 16 ♗xd5+ ♔h8 17 ♗b7 ♖c7 (18 ♗xa6? ♕a8+ and ...♕xa6), Gurevich tries to justify the move ♖ae1. But from this point of view 14 f4 was more appropriate.

14...♘c5!

Seizing the initiative: the pawn tension in the centre is clearly to Black's advantage in view of the more harmonious placing of his pieces. It is hard for White to find an acceptable plan of further action.

15 cxb5

If 15 f3 there is the unpleasant 15...fxe4! 16 dxe4 (16 fxe4?! b4) 16...bxc4 (16...♕c7!?) 17 ♕xd6 (17 bxc4 ♗e6!) 17...♘d3 18 ♖b1 ♘e8 19 ♕a3 ♗e6. Apparently 15 exf5 ♗xf5

16 ♘c1 was the lesser evil, but Mikhail decided to place the other knight on e4 and open the c-file, along which exchanges are possible.

15...cxb5 16 exf5 ♗xf5 (of course, not 16...gxf5?! 17 d4! when White gets away with a slight fright) **17 ♘e4 b4**

Restricting the knight on e2. 17...♘d5!? was also not bad, with the idea of 18 ♘xc5 dxc5 19 ♘c3?! ♘b4!.

18 ♖c1 ♘fxe4! 19 dxe4 ♗d7!

Aiming for b5. Black is also better after 19...♗e6 20 ♖cd1 a4! (my *Informator* 20...♖c6(?!) 21 f4! ♛b6 22 f5 allows White counterplay) 21 ♛xb4 (21 bxa4 ♛b6!) 21...♖b8 22 ♛d2 axb3 23 axb3 ♘xb3 24 ♛e3 ♛b6! etc.

20 ♖cd1

The d6-pawn is poisoned: 20 ♛xd6? ♗b5 21 ♗xe5 (21 ♛xd8? ♖fxd8 22 ♖c2 ♗d3 and wins) 21...♗xe5! (not 21...♗xe2? 22 ♖xc5) 22 ♛xe5 ♖e8 23 ♛b2 ♘d3 24 ♖xc8 ♘xb2 25 ♖xd8 ♖xd8 26 ♗f3 ♖d2 27 ♖e1 ♘d3 28 ♖a1 ♘xf2+ 29 ♔g2 ♘d3 with a won endgame.

20...♗b5 21 ♛e3 a4 (it was also tempting to active the dark-squared bishop – 21...♖f7, then ...♛f8 and ...♗h6) **22 ♖fe1 ♛b6** (22...♖f7! and ...♛f8 with the threat of ...♗h6 was again strong) **23 ♘c1**

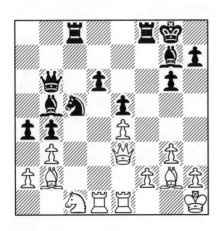

23...a3 (tightly fixing the a2-pawn) **24 ♗a1**

♗d7?!

This regrouping is too slow: now the white knight comes into play. 24...♖c6 or 24...h5!? was better.

25 ♘d3 ♗e6 26 f4! (White has revived!) **26...♖c6** (26...♛b5 27 ♘f2! is also unclear) **27 ♘f2**

Weaker was 27 fxe5?! ♘xd3 28 ♛xd3 dxe5 or 27 ♘xc5?! ♛xc5! 28 ♛xc5 dxc5 29 f5 ♗f7 and ...c5-c4. However, consideration should have been given to 27 f5!? ♘xd3 (27...♗f7 28 ♘f2!) 28 ♛xd3 ♗f7(c8), when Black's advantage is comparatively slight.

27...♘d7!

Following my *Informator* suggestion of 27...♛c7(?!) White maintains the balance by 28 ♛d2!, while Ribli's recommendation in *ChessBase* of 27...♔h8(?!) is parried by 28 ♗h3 or even 28 ♔g1. A piece sacrifice looked tempting – 27...♘xb3!? 28 axb3 ♛xe3 29 ♖xe3 exf4 30 gxf4 ♖fc8! with the threat of ...♖c1, but after 31 ♘d3 ♗xb3 32 ♖g1 ♖b6 33 e5! Black's advantage might not be sufficient for a win.

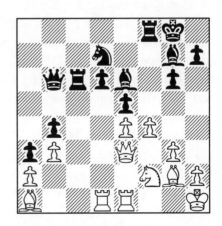

28 ♛d2!

The best chance. After 28 ♛xb6 ♖xb6 White has a difficult ending: ...exf4 is threatened, and if 29 ♘d3, then 29...♘c5! 30 fxe5 ♘xd3 31 ♖xd3 dxe5 etc.

28...♘c5?!

Black marks time – an imminent time scramble gradually begins to interfere. 28...罩fc8! was far more energetic – in *Informator* I condemned this move because of 29 ②d3(?!), but after 29...罩c2! 30 豐xb4 奧g4 31 豐xb6 ②xb6 32 罩c1 罩xa2 White cannot save the game. Things are also difficult for him after 29 罩e2 罩c2 30 豐d3 罩c1! or 30 豐e1 exf4 etc.

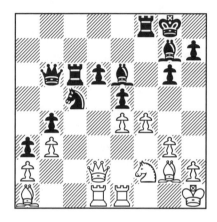

29 奧h3! 奧f7! (not allowing the opponent to achieve complete equality) **30 fxe5?!**

Instinctively aiming to simplify the play. But White should not have relieved Black of his weak d6-pawn and cleared the sixth rank for his manoeuvres. Again 30 f5!? came into consideration – in search of winning chances here I would have had to give up a piece: 30...gxf5 31 奧xf5 ②xb3!? 32 axb3 奧xb3 33 ②d3 奧xd1 34 奧e6+ 含h8 35 豐xd1 罩f6 36 豐a4 豐a6 37 豐b3, and here White is still afloat.

30...dxe5 31 ②g4 奧e6 32 ②h6+ 含h8 33 奧xe6 ②xe6?!

Time, time... 33...罩xe6! was far stronger: for example 34 含g2 豐c6 35 豐e3 罩d6 36 罩xd6 豐xd6 37 ②g4 ②d3 38 罩f1 罩c8 and Black remains with an enduring positional advantage.

34 ②g4 (34 罩f1!? 罩xf1+ 35 罩xf1 ②d4 would also have led to unclear play) **34...②d4!**

35 奧xd4?

This time-trouble exchange of the sleeping bishop for the powerful knight puts White on the verge of defeat. It was also bad to play 35 ②xe5? 奧xe5 36 奧xd4 豐xd4 37 豐xd4 奧xd4 38 罩xd4 罩c2, when the outcome is decided by the a3-pawn: 39 罩xb4 罩ff2 or 39 e5 罩ff2 40 e6 罩xh2+ 41 含g1 罩cg2+ 42 含f1 罩xa2 43 罩h4 罩hf2+! (instead of the *Informator* suggestion 43...罩af2+(?) 44 含g1 罩e2 45 罩e4! with a draw) 44 含g1 罩ae2 45 罩e4 罩xe1+ 46 罩xe1 罩f8 and wins.

Real saving chances were offered only by 35 罩f1! 罩xf1+ 36 罩xf1 豐c5 37 ②e3 奧h6 38 豐d3 奧xe3 39 豐xe3, when Black is restricted by the weakness of his own king.

35...exd4

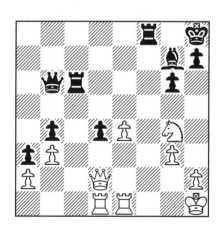

36 ♘f2?!

With the vain hope of placing the knight on the blockading square d3. 36 e5 was more resilient, although after 36...h5! 37 ♘f6 ♗xf6 38 exf6 ♖cxf6 or 37 ♘f2 ♖c3! 38 ♘e4 ♖e3 White has almost insuperable difficulties.

36...♖c3?!

Alas, in my haste I did not notice the winning 36...♗h6! 37 ♕xh6 (37 ♕e2 ♕c7!) 37...♖xf2 38 ♖d2 d3! 39 ♖xd3 ♖cc2 40 ♖ed1 ♖xh2 41 ♕xh2 ♖xh2+ 42 ♔xh2 ♕f2+ and ...♕xa2.

37 ♘h3?!

This panicky flight of the knight loses ig-nominiously. But even the 'planned' 37 ♘d3 was fatal for White, for the reason that his king is not on g2, but on h1: 37...♖f3! 38 ♘f4 (38 ♕e2 ♕f6!) 38...d3! 39 ♘d5 ♕e6! (39...♕f2 is also interesting, but not my earlier 39...♕d4(?) in view of 40 ♔g2!) 40 ♕g2 ♕g4 41 h3 ♕h5! 42 ♘f4 ♖xf4 43 gxf4 d2 44 ♖xd2 ♕h4! and wins.

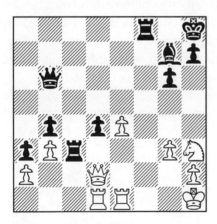

37...d3! 38 ♘f4 ♖c2 39 ♕xd3 ♖xa2 40 ♖f1 ♖f2

The last move before the time control. 40...♖b2, or 40...g5, or 40...♕f6! with the new threat of ...♕b2, was rather more forceful.

41 ♖xf2 ♕xf2 42 ♖d2

If 42 ♘e6 the best is 42...♖a8!, since my

Informator suggestion 43 ♕d5 will not do, mainly because of 43...♕f3+ 44 ♔g1 ♕xd1+ 45 ♕xd1 a2.

42...♕a7! 43 ♕e2 ♗c3 (43...♗h6!?) **44 ♖c2**

Or 44 ♖a2 ♕f7 (threatening ...♕xb3) 45 ♘d5 ♕f3+! 46 ♕xf3 ♖xf3 47 ♔g2 ♖d3 and wins.

44...♕f7 45 e5 (45 ♘d5 ♕f3+!) **45...♕b7+** (45...♕xb3!? 46 e6 ♖xf4! and wins) **46 ♕g2** (46 ♘g2 ♗b2 and ...a3-a2) **46...♕xg2+ 47 ♔xg2 ♗b2 48 ♖f2 a2** (48...♖c8(e8) and ...a3-a2 was cleaner) **49 ♘xg6+ hxg6 50 ♖xf8+ ♔g7 51 ♖f1 ♗xe5 52 ♔f3 a1♕ 53 ♖xa1 ♗xa1 54 ♔e4 ♔f6 0-1**

Such an opening win did not appear to herald any misfortunes. In my second round game with Anand I resolutely played 1 e4, but after 1...e6 2 d4 d5 I became anxious: I did not want to repeat the Exchange Variation, which had worked in my Tilburg game with Korchnoi, and Makarychev and I had not yet studied the complicated set-ups with 3 ♘c3 (*Game No.86*). And so I played 3 ♘d2, and after 3...c5 4 exd5 ♕xd5 I tried the rare 5 dxc5 ♗xc5 6 ♘gf3 ♘f6 7 ♗d3 0-0 8 ♕e2 followed by 0-0-0, but I did not gain the slightest advantage and in the end I lost.

The day after this saw the 160th (!) serious game in the history of my duels with Karpov. On this occasion the ex-champion chose the Sämisch Variation against the King's Indian Defence. In a very sharp, far from error-free battle I gained a decisive advantage, but in the time scramble I missed a win, and a draw was agreed on the 61st move (Game No.36 in *Kasparov vs. Karpov 1988-2009*). To some extent I settled accounts with Karpov for the 'present' which he made to me in the spring in Amsterdam.

To keep out of harm's way, my 4th round New Year's Eve duel with Vassily Ivanchuk had to be begun with 1 c4. From the press:

'In Reggio Emilia Kasparov was obviously not in his best form – he often got into time-trouble and did not display his customary easy play. But the world champion's class always remains high, and in several games he was successful. Garry's tastes against his own favourite weapon are demonstrated by the following important game.'

> ## Game 83
> **G.Kasparov-V.Ivanchuk**
> Reggio Emilia, 4th Round,
> 31.12.1991
> *King's Indian Defence E92*

1 c4 ♞f6 2 ♞f3

The little subtleties of top-class chess: by 1 c4 White avoids the opponent's Queen's Gambit Accepted, and by 2 ♞f3 he avoids the established variations with 2 ♞c3 e5 (*Game No.41*).

2...g6 3 ♞c3 ♝g7 (Vassily's choice surprised me: playing the King's Indian against a King's Indian player?) **4 e4 0-0 5 d4 d6 6 ♝e2 e5 7 ♝e3**

Karpov played this five times in our 1990 match, and I had had time to study the nuances of this variation.

7...c6 (the fashion nowadays is for 7...♞g4) **8 ♛d2**

8 d5 ♞g4 9 ♝g5 f6 10 ♝h4 is nevertheless more promising (Game No.26 in *Kasparov vs. Karpov 1988-2009*).

8...♞bd7

I myself preferred 8...exd4 (*Game No.87*), but Ivanchuk is aiming for complicated play with a closed pawn centre.

9 ♜d1?!

A strange move, which is unnecessary in the event of d4-d5. The usual 9 0-0 is better, with the possible continuation 9...♜e8 10 d5 or 9...♞g4 10 ♝g5 f6 11 ♝h4, while if 9...a6,

then 10 ♜fd1 ♜e8 11 dxe5 dxe5 12 b4 with the initiative on the queenside (Giorgadze-Kindermann, Bundesliga 1997).

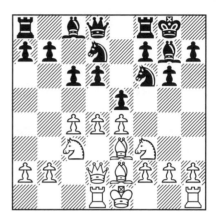

9...♜e8

A novelty! I was reckoning on 9...exd4?! 10 ♞xd4 ♜e8 11 f3 d5 12 cxd5 cxd5 13 ♞db5! with advantage to White (Speelman-Mestel, London 1986), or 9...♛e7 10 ♝g5!? (Giorgadze-Geenen, Manila Olympiad 1992). But now the threat of ...exd4 forces White to reveal his intentions in the centre.

10 d5 (strictly speaking, 10 dxe5 dxe5 11 0-0 is more logical, but in such positions the control of the open d-file usually proves illusory) **10...cxd5 11 cxd5 a6**

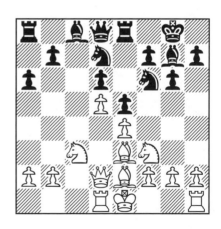

This is rather more solid than the typical manoeuvre 11...♞g4 12 ♝g5 f6 13 ♝h4 h5

(Giorgadze-Dolmatov, Krasnodar 1997).

12 0-0 b5 13 ♕c2 (White is forced to spend time regrouping) **13...♘b6**

Aiming to complete the development of the queenside as soon as possible, which looks sounder than 13...♘h5 14 ♖fe1 ♘f4 15 ♗f1 ♘f6 (15...♘b6 16 ♘d2!) 16 h3 ♗d7 17 a3 with a small advantage for White.

14 a4!

To avoid variations such as 14 ♖c1 ♗d7 or 14 ♘d2 ♘g4 15 ♗xg4 ♗xg4 16 ♖c1 ♗d7 (and ...f7-f5) White urgently opens the queenside – this is where a rook on a1 would have been useful!

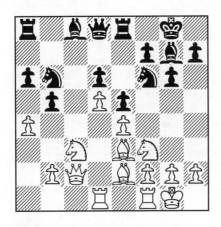

14...bxa4

14...b4?! was not good in view of the interposition of 15 a5!: for example, 15...♘bd7 16 ♘a4 ♕xa5 17 ♘b6! (17 ♘d2!?) 17...♘xb6 18 ♖a1 ♘a4 19 ♖xa4 ♕d8 20 ♖xb4, regaining the pawn with an obvious advantage. But 14...♘xa4 was probably more accurate, leaving White only 15 ♘xa4 bxa4 16 ♕xa4, transposing into a position from the game.

15 ♘xa4 (a temporary pawn sacrifice came into consideration – 15 ♖a1!? ♗d7 16 ♘d2 and ♖fc1) **15...♘xa4 16 ♕xa4**

Threatening both ♗b5-c6, and ♘d2-c4.

16...♖b8?!

Eliminating only the first of the threats. 16...♗d7 was much stronger: 17 ♕c2 (17

♕b4?! ♕b8!) 17...♖c8! (my *Informator* suggestion 17...♕b8(?!) 18 ♘d2 ♖c8 is worse because of 19 ♘c4) 18 ♕b1 a5 (19 ♘d2 ♘g4 with equality).

17 ♘d2! ♘g4

Vassily was very much counting on this move when he played 16...♖b8. If 17...♖xb2 I gave the modest 18 ♗xa6 (when it is too late for 18...♘g4? in view of 19 ♗xc8 ♘xe3 20 fxe3 ♕xc8 21 ♘c4 and wins), but 18 ♕a3!? ♖b8 19 ♖b1 or 18 ♖b1!? also comes into consideration.

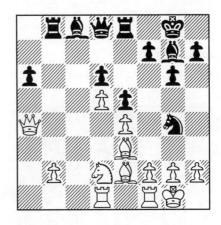

18 ♗a7!

An unexpected move, after which the position abounds in tactical nuances. The diverting 18 ♗g5 would have been elegantly refuted by 18...♗d7! 19 ♗xd8 ♗xa4 etc. With his two bishops Black also has no problems after 18 ♗xg4 ♗xg4 19 f3 ♗d7 or 19 ♖c1 ♗e2 and ...♗b5.

18...♖xb2

The alternatives are excessively passive: 18...♖a8?! 19 ♗b6 ♗d7 (19...♕e7 20 ♗b5!) 20 ♗xd8 (my *Informator* suggestion 20 ♕a5 is also not bad) 20...♗xa4 21 ♖a1 ♖exd8 22 ♖xa4 ♘f6 23 ♗d3 ♘d7 (otherwise ♘c4) 24 b4 with pressure on the queenside, or 18...♖b7?! 19 ♕xa6 ♕c7 20 ♖a1 ♖xb2 21 ♕d3 ♖b7 (but not 21...♕c2? 22 ♘c4! ♕xe2 23 ♘xb2 ♕xb2 24 ♖fb1) 22 ♕a3! etc.

19 ♗xa6?!

19 ♕a3! ♖b7 20 ♕xa6 ♕e7 21 ♗b6 ♖b8 22 ♕a5 is more accurate, when it transpires that the exchange of the queenside pawns does not yet guarantee Black a draw, since he is rather short of space and the d6-pawn is weak.

19...♖e7

Ivanchuk tries to exploit the vulnerable position of the bishop on a7. The status quo would have been more simply maintained by 19...♗xa6 20 ♕xa6 ♕c8! 21 ♕a4 ♖e7 22 h3 ♖bb7! or even 19...♕d7 20 ♕xd7 ♗xd7 21 ♘c4 ♖c2 22 ♘a3 (22 ♘xd6?! ♖a8! 23 ♗d3 ♖c3) 22...♖a2.

20 ♗xc8 ♕xc8 21 h3!

Of course, not 21 ♘c4? ♖xa7!

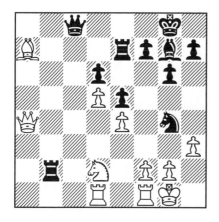

21...♕a8?!

The turning-point: Black does not sense the danger. The optimistic 21...♕c2? would have led to the loss of a pawn – 22 ♕a6! (my previous 22 ♕a3(?) is worse because of 22...♖d7) 22...♗f8 (22...♖d7? 23 ♖c1) 23 hxg4 ♖a2 24 ♕xd6 ♖axa7 25 g5 or 22...♖a2 23 ♕xd6 ♖exa7 24 ♕b8+ ♗f8 25 hxg4 etc. After 21...♗h6? 22 ♘c4 ♖xa7 23 ♕xa7 ♕xc4 24 hxg4 ♕xe4 25 ♕a3! (instead of 25 ♕d7(?) ♗e3!) 25...♖b4 26 ♕a8+ ♗f8 27 ♖c1 White is also close to a decisive material advantage.

However, 21...♖bb7! would have maintained the balance, since 22 ♕a6 (with the idea of 22...♕d7(?) 23 ♗c5!?), which seemed very strong to me, is refuted by 22...♕a8! 23 hxg4 and now 23...♘f8 24 ♕xd6 ♖e6! 25 ♕b8! ♖xb8 26 ♗xb8 ♖e8 27 ♗c7 ♖e7 with a probable draw, despite the power of the passed d-pawn, or 23...♖ed7! and ...♖xa7, when Black trusts in the impregnability of his fortress.

22 ♖a1!

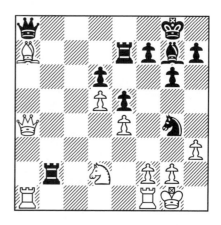

22...♘f6?

The decisive mistake! On seeing that his earlier planned 22...♖bb7? was bad because of 23 ♕c6! (this is much more forceful that my *Informator* move 23 ♗c5!?) 23...♕d8 (if 23...♖ec7? there is the insidious 24 ♗b6!) 24 hxg4 ♖xa7 25 ♘c4 ♗f8 26 ♕xd6, winning the d6-pawn and the game, Ivanchuk became rattled.

It was essential to play 22...♖xd2 23 hxg4 ♖b2! (23...♗h6? 24 ♖fb1!) 24 ♕a3 ♖eb7 25 ♗c5 ♕xa3 26 ♗xa3 ♖2b6, when after my *Informator* recommendation 24 ♕c6 ♕d8 25 ♗e3 Black is saved by 25...♖eb7! (25...♖b8?! 26 ♖a6!) 26 ♖fc1 ♗f8 (and if 27 ♕c8, then 27...♕xc8 28 ♖xc8 ♖b8). Although White has clearly more space, the front has become too narrow, and Black has every chance of holding out.

23 ♘c4! ♖bb7 24 ♗e3

By carrying out all his intentions, White has managed to gain an overwhelming advantage.

24...♛b8?

Desperation. 24...♛xa4 25 ♖xa4 ♖bd7 (Black loses after 25...♘xe4? 26 ♖a8+ or 25...♘e8? 26 ♖a8) was more resilient, but after 26 ♖a6 Black is not helped by any of 26...♘e8? 27 ♖a8, 26...♖e8?! 27 ♖xd6, or 26...♖d8 27 ♗g5! ♖ed7 28 ♘xe5!.

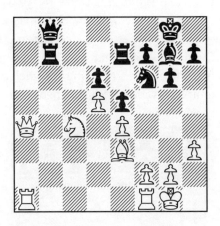

25 ♘a5! ♖b4 26 ♛d1 (or 26 ♛a3!? with the same threat of a triple knight fork – ♘c6!) 26...♖xe4 27 ♘c6 ♛f8 28 ♘xe7+ ♛xe7 29 ♖a8+ ♗f8 (29...♘e8 30 ♛c2 and ♛c6!) 30 ♛f3 (threatening ♗g5) 30...♖xe3 31 fxe3 ♘d7 32 ♖b1 1-0

After this important win I joined the leading group (Gelfand – 3 out of 4; Kasparov and Anand – 2½) and was hoping to achieve my usual form. But, alas, this did not happen.

True, after a fighting King's Indian draw with Gelfand (cf. *Game No.64*, note to Black's 12th move) I managed to win against Beliavsky, who was performing very badly: he found a way, literally in five moves, of ruining a promising position. After catching Gelfand and Anand, in the 7th and 8th rounds I satisfied myself with 'black' draws against Salov and Polugayevsky, but my rivals fared no better. Before the finish Anand, Gelfand and I all had 5 out of 8.

From the press: *'In the last round fortune smiled on Anand: despite every effort, Kasparov was unable to overcome Khalifman's resistance, and Gelfand gained only a draw in a protracted encounter with Karpov, but Vishy was greatly helped by the "eternally" uncompromising play with White by Beliavsky, who in the end overstepped the mark and lost.'*

That was how 1991, one of the most critical years in my chess career, concluded.

First Again!

International Tournament in Linares (22 February – 14 March 1992): 1. **Kasparov** – 10 out of 13; 2–3. Ivanchuk and Timman – 8; 4. Karpov – 7½; 5–7. Anand, Salov and Gelfand – 7; 8. Bareev – 6½; 9–10. Beliavsky and Yusupov – 6; 11. Illescas – 5½; 12. Ljubojevic – 4½; 13–14. Speelman and Short – 4.

Soon after Reggio Emilia, in January 1992, I continued my tradition of clock simultaneous displays against professional teams, and by defeating the German team (3-1) in Baden-Baden, I won what was by then my third car, this time a BMW. And on returning to Moscow I immediately set off with Makarychev to a training session on the outskirts of the city and began purposeful preparation for the next Linares tournament. We worked a great deal and, as it later transpired, very fruitfully. Incidentally, at that session I studied the Evans Gambit for the first time, but I decided to employ this romantic opening only three years later...

The line-up at Linares 1992 was uncommonly strong: the world champion, a quartet of Candidates – Karpov, Short, Yusupov and Timman (who were soon due to meet in the semi-final matches), young stars – Anand, Ivanchuk and Gelfand (participants in the quarter-final Candidates matches), and so on. This promised a gripping competitive intrigue. I remember that, in an interview after Reggio Emilia, Anand declared that Kasparov was now only the first among equals. However, I was burning with a desire to demonstrate that this was not so, and I arrived in Linares with a great store of ideas and strength.

From the press: '*This year the tournament was an obvious success! It had everything: a gripping competitive fight with dramatic episodes, important theoretical novelties, and a wealth of material for psychologists. A triumphant success was achieved by Garry Kasparov. His uncompromising character forces him always to aim for first place. A year ago Kasparov finished behind Ivanchuk, and now the champion was eager for revenge. He arrived for the start extremely composed and excellently prepared. And in the very first round he began "settling accounts", by repaying Jan Timman for his recent "King's Indian" defeat in the final of the Paris knock-out rapid-play tournament.*'

Game 84
J.Timman-G.Kasparov
Linares, 1st Round, 23.02.1992
King's Indian Defence E87

1 d4 ♘f6 2 c4 g6 3 ♘c3 ♗g7 4 e4 d6 5 f3 0-0 6 ♗e3 e5 (6...♘bd7 – *Game No.68*; 6...a6 – *Game No.91*) **7 d5** (7 ♘ge2 – *Game Nos.90, 98*) **7...♘h5**

Our November game (2nd match game, Paris (rapid) 1991) went 7...c6 8 ♗d3 (8 ♕d2 – *Game No.92*) 8...cxd5 (8...b5?! – *Game No.43*) 9 cxd5 ♘h5 10 ♘ge2 f5 11 exf5 gxf5

12 0-0 ♘d7 13 ♖c1 ♘c5 14 ♗c4!? a6 15 b4 ♘d7 16 a4 ♕e8 17 ♔h1 (17 a5!?) **17...♘df6 18 b5** with a small but enduring advantage for White. My improvement 16...♕h4!? (Game No.36 in *Kasparov vs. Karpov 1988-2009*) also does not completely equalise in view of 17 ♕b3.

It stands to reason that Timman wanted to continue the dispute in this branch, but I played differently, choosing one of the variations prepared for the 1990 match with Karpov. Here White must play 0-0-0, which for the opponent was more unpleasant: after all, Timman often played superficially, and with an open king it could lead to a swift catastrophe. And my psychological reckoning was completely justified!

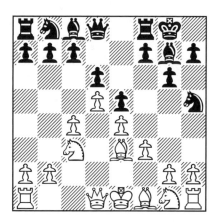

8 ♕d2 f5 9 0-0-0 ♘d7 (it is rather early for 9...a6?! – *Game No.28* in *Kasparov vs. Karpov 1988-2009*) **10 ♗d3 ♘c5**

If now 10...a6, then 11 exf5 gxf5 12 ♗xf5! ♖xf5 13 g4 is strong. And after the traditional 10...♘df6 11 exf5! gxf5 12 ♘ge2 White has too easy a game. But later my attention was drawn to the crazy gambit 10...♘f4?! (cf. *Game No.98*, note to White's 7th move).

11 ♗c2 a6

An old counterattacking idea of Beliavsky and Mikhalchishin's, which I decided to test in this game.

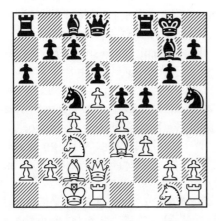

12 ♘ge2

Provoking the reply ...b7-b5. 12 ♔b1! was more accurate, but even so I would have given up a pawn – 12...b5 (12...fxe4?! 13 ♗xc5! and ♘xe4) 13 cxb5 axb5 14 ♘xb5 ♗a6! 15 ♘c3 ♕b8 16 ♘ge2 ♕b4 17 ♗xc5 dxc5 18 a3 ♕a5 with quite good compensation (Wang Yue-Cheparinov, Khanty-Mansiysk 2007).

12...b5 13 b4!?

A confidently-made move, although it is obviously weakening. Black is no longer frightened by 13 cxb5 axb5 14 ♘xb5 ♖xa2 15 ♔b1 ♖a6!, or 14 ♗xc5 dxc5 15 ♘xb5 ♖xa2 16 ♗b3 ♖a1+ 17 ♔c2 ♖xd1 18 d6+! ♔h8 19 ♖xd1 c6! 20 ♘bc3 ♘f6 21 ♘g3 ♕b6 etc.

13...♘d7 14 cxb5

My *Informator* suggestion 14 exf5(?!) gxf5 15 ♘g3 is weaker in view of 15...♘xg3 16 hxg3 ♘b6!. And my other recommendation 14 c5(?!) a5 15 a3 axb4 16 axb4 dxc5 17 bxc5 b4 18 ♘b5 is dubious on account of 18...♗a6 19 ♕xb4 ♘f4!.

14...axb5 15 ♘xb5

15 ♔b2?! (A.Petrosian-Beliavsky, Riga 1973) is dangerous in view of 15...fxe4! 16 fxe4 (16 ♘xe4 ♖b8 and ...♘b6) 16...♘b6 17 ♗xb6 cxb6 18 ♖hf1 (18 ♘xb5 ♖f2) 18...♗d7

19 ♗d3 ♕h4 etc. But the attempt, not mentioned by anyone, to relieve the tension by 15 ♗g5!? is far more interesting: for example, 15...♗f6 (15...♕e8?! 16 ♘xb5) 16 ♗xf6 ♕xf6 17 exf5 gxf5 18 ♔b1 ♘b6 19 ♘xb5.

At that time it appeared that 15 ♘xb5 promised White an advantage, but practice did not confirm this evaluation: Black has real counterplay, which should not be underestimated.

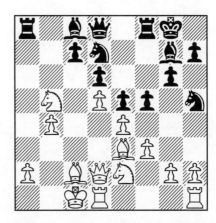

15...♖xa2 (15...fxe4!? is also good, with the ideas of 16 fxe4 ♖xa2 and 16 ♗xe4 ♘b6!) **16 ♘ec3 ♖a8** (16...♖a6!?) **17 ♔b2 ♘df6**

My *Informator* recommendation 17...fxe4! 18 fxe4 ♘df6 is more promising: for example, 19 h3? (Kasimdzhanov-Poldauf, Bundesliga 1999) 19...♗d7! or 19 ♖a1 ♖b8, and it is rather White who has problems.

18 ♘a7 (although it looks terribly dangerous to clear the path of the bishop on g7, 18 exf5!? gxf5 19 ♘a7! and ♘c6 came into consideration) **18...fxe4!** (now necessary) **19 ♘c6 ♕d7**

After 19...♕e8 the lunge 20 g4?! ♘f4 21 g5 is now dubious because of 21...♘6xd5! 22 ♘xd5 exf3, but 20 ♗xe4! is solid enough.

20 g4!?

A very optimistic move and perhaps not even a bad one. If Timman had foreseen all

its possible consequences, he would probably have played 20 ♗xe4! (20 fxe4 ♘g4)
20...♘xe4 21 fxe4 with a sound and slightly
more pleasant position for White. However,
he was obviously hoping for more!

20...♘f4 21 g5

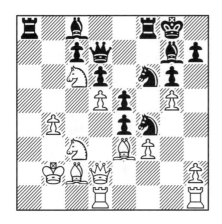

21...♘6xd5!

My opponent did not believe in the correctness of this sacrifice. On one occasion, in
Moscow 1981, in desperation I played
against him 17...♘d5?! – into an attack by
two pawns (cf. Game No.51 in *Garry Kasparov on Garry Kasparov Part I*, note to
White's 7th move). It would appear that here
Timman relaxed, confident that this was
another desperation sacrifice and that the
white king was in a safe position.

21...♘6h5 as not as bad as it appeared to
me at the board: for example, 22 ♗xe4 ♘h3
23 ♖a1 ♗b7 or 22 fxe4 ♗b7 23 ♘a5 (23 b5
♘h3) 23...♗a6 24 ♖a1 ♕h3. But I sensed
that more could be achieved here, and I
landed a blow which decided the game
within four moves!

22 ♘xd5 ♘d3+!

An abrupt change of scene. This sudden
check stunned my opponent. Other continuations would hardly have been so effective:

1) 22...♗b7 23 ♘ce7+ ♔h8 24 ♗xe4

♕e6!? (24...c6? 25 ♘b6) 25 ♕c3 c6 26 ♘xf4
♖xf4 27 ♘xc6 ♖a2+ 28 ♔b1 ♖xe4 29 fxe4
♗xc6 30 ♖d5! ♖a6 31 ♕c4 ♗xd5 32 ♕xd5
♕xd5 33 exd5 ♖a3 34 ♗d2 ♔g8 35 ♔c2,
and the tactical skirmish concludes in an
endgame favourable for White;

2) 22...exf3!? (the most obvious move) 23
♘xf4! ♖xf4! (23...exf4+?! is worse in view of
24 ♗d4, with the terrible threat of ♗b3+
and h2-h4-h5) 24 ♕d5+ ♔h8 25 ♗xf4 (25
b5?! ♕e8!) 25...exf4+ 26 ♔c1 f2! with excellent compensation for the rook: 27 ♘d4 ♖b8
28 ♗b3 ♕e8 29 ♘c2 ♗b7 30 ♕e6 ♗xh1 31
♕xe8+ ♖xe8 32 ♖xh1 ♗d4, and the endgame is this time favourable for Black.

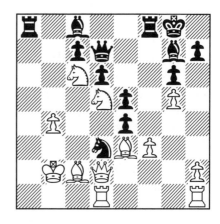

23 ♗xd3?!

In my old commentary I considered this
move to be the decisive mistake and I added:
'It was essential to play 23 ♔b1 ♖xf3 24
♖hf1 (24 ♕c3?! ♗b7!) with wild complications, which, as shown by analysis, should
lead to a draw after correct play by both
sides.' I had in mind the variations with
24...♖xf1 25 ♖xf1 ♗b7 26 ♘f6+! etc, although 25...♔h8!? sets White rather more
problems, and if 26 b5 or 26 ♕c3 – 26...♕h3.

In fact there is the simpler 23 ♔b3! ♕xc6!
– apparently it was this pretty move that
concerned Timman, but after 24 fxe4!
(instead of the suicidal 24 ♘e7+? ♔h8 25

♘xc6 ♗e6+ 26 ♔c3 ♖a3+ 27 ♔b3 ♖xb3+ 28 ♔c2 ♖b2+ 29 ♔c3 ♖xd2 30 ♔xd2 ♖xf3) Black's queen and knight are hanging, and nothing is given by 24...♘c5+ 25 ♗xc5!, so that he must force a draw: 24...♕a4+ 25 ♔c3 ♕c6+ 26 ♔b3 ♕a4+.

23...exd3

The culmination of the battle.

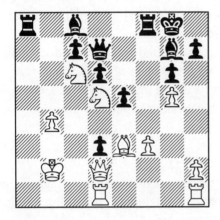

24 ♘ce7+?

White cracks under the pressure. The knight should not have been moved from c6: there it was somehow cementing the position together. Also bad was 24 b5? ♕f7! or 24 ♖c1? ♗b7! 25 ♕c3 (25 b5(?), given in *Informator*, is fatal because of 25...♗xc6! 26 bxc6 e4+ or 26 ♖xc6 ♕f7) 25...♖xf3 etc. The only saving chance was 24 ♕c3!, for example:

1) 24...♖xf3 25 ♕c4 ♔h8 26 ♖a1 ♖xa1 27 ♖xa1 ♕h3 28 ♖a8 ♖f8 29 b5 with sharp, roughly equal play;

2) 24...♗b7!? 25 b5 ♖xf3 26 ♕c4 ♔h8 27 ♖xd3 e4+ 28 ♖c3!, retaining dynamic equality, not without some difficulty;

3) 24...♕f7!? 25 ♖a1 ♗d7 26 ♗d2 ♕xf3 (26...♖ae8 27 ♘f6+!) 27 ♖hf1 ♖a2+ 28 ♖xa2 ♕xf1 29 ♘f6+! ♗xf6 30 gxf6 ♕xf6 31 ♖a7 ♗xc6 32 ♕xc6 ♕f2 33 ♕c4+ ♖f7 34 ♖a8+ ♔g7 35 ♕xd3 ♕xh2 36 ♕c3 and ♖c8(a7) with a probable draw.

24...♔h8 25 ♘xc8 (after the more resilient 25 ♕c3!? there was the decisive 25...c5! 26 bxc5 ♕b7+ 27 ♔c1 dxc5 28 ♕xd3 e4 or 28 ♗xc5 ♖xf3) **25...e4+**

And in view of 26 ♘c3 ♕a4 or 26 ♘f6 ♖xf6! 27 gxf6 ♗xf6+ White resigned (**0-1**). An amazing miniature!

My eternal opponent Anatoly Karpov also began the tournament with a win – against Ljubojevic. In the 2nd round came our next encounter, already the 161st.

Game 85
G.Kasparov-A.Karpov
Linares, 2nd Round, 24.02.1992
Caro-Kann Defence B17

1 e4 c6 2 d4 d5 3 ♘d2

Karpov had not played the Caro-Kann against me since Amsterdam 1988, and I was very pleased when he replied 1...c6. The point was that after his match with Anand, the ex-champion, accusing his opponent's assistant Mikhail Gurevich (my former second) of all kinds of offences, stated that against the Caro-Kann Vishy had used the variation with 3 e5, which I had apparently prepared for the 1990 match! However, after 3...♗f5 Anand went 4 ♘f3 e6 5 ♗e2, but I never played this and had not even looked at it. And now finally I had an opportunity to show what had in fact been prepared.

3...dxe4 4 ♘xe4 ♘d7 5 ♘g5 ♘gf6 6 ♗c4

In 1988 I tried 6 ♗d3, which was then only beginning to become popular (*Game No.34*), but now I chose a set-up which I had analysed in 1990 with Beliavsky.

6...e6 7 ♕e2 ♘b6 8 ♗b3 (more dynamic than 8 ♗d3) **8...h6**

In the 6th round Speelman played 8...a5 against me, which is a little early because of

9 c3! a4 10 ♗c2 a3 11 b3 ♘bd5 12 ♗d2 ♗d6 13 ♘1f3 (here Speelman recommended 13 g3, and I – 13 ♘e4 ♘xe4 14 ♕xe4) 13...♘f4, when by 14 ♗xf4!? ♗xf4 15 g3 ♗xg5 (15...♗c7 16 ♘e5) 16 ♘xg5 ♘d5 17 ♕d2 I could have retained a slight plus (17...♘xc3 18 ♘xf7). The bold a-pawn has rushed as far as a3, but what is it doing there?

9 ♘5f3 c5 (9...a5 – Game No.39 in *Kasparov vs. Karpov 1988-2009*) **10 ♗f4**

The bishop joins the battle for the key e5-square.

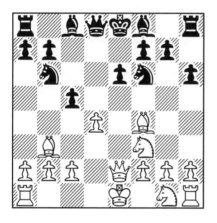

A well-known theoretical position. Before my first match with Karpov (1984/85), Andras Adorjan, who was then helping me, suggested playing the Caro-Kann with Black and sacrificing a pawn here with 10...♘fd5?! 11 ♗g3 c4 (Kupreichik-Speelman, Hastings 1981/82), but I was less than enthusiastic, about which I have no regrets.

The main continuation was 10...♘bd5 11 ♗e5 ♕a5+ 12 ♘d2 b5! (after 12...cxd4 13 ♘gf3 ♗e7 14 ♘xd4 0-0 15 0-0! ♗d7 16 c3 ♕b6 17 ♗c2 White's chances are better, Ivanchuk-Anand, Monte Carlo (rapid) 2000), and here Beliavsky and I analysed 13 dxc5 ♗xc5 14 c3!? ♕b6?! (not 14...0-0? 15 ♗xd5! ♘xd5 18 b4 winning a piece, Anand-Dlugy, Sharjah 1985) 15 a4! and now 15...♗xf2+ 16 ♕xf2 ♕xf2+ 17 ♔xf2 ♘g4+ 18 ♔g3 ♘xe5

19 ♖e1 with the better endgame, or 15...bxa4 16 ♗xa4+ ♗d7 17 ♘c4 also with advantage to White (Ivanchuk-Gulko, Riga 1995). However, we overlooked 14...♗b7! – the potential threat of ...♗xg2 forces 15 ♘gf3, and after 15...♕b6 (Anand-Ivanchuk, Wijk aan Zee 2001) the undermining move 16 a4 loses its strength in view of 16...a6.

But at the time, when studying the diagram position during preparations for the 1990 match, I came to the conclusion that the complicated play with 10...♘bd5 or 10...a6 was not at all in Karpov's style and that he would probably choose a rarer move – the quiet, simplifying 10...♗d6. And I succeeded in anticipating my opponent's choice!

10...♗d6 11 ♗g3

This reply seemed to come as a surprise to Karpov: he thought for nearly forty minutes. What to do next?

The exchange 11...♗xg3 12 hxg3 (Matanovic-Panov, Skopje 1970) merely opens the h-file for White, without giving anything in return. He also has a clear plus after 11...♘h5 12 dxc5 ♘xg3 13 hxg3 ♗xc5 14 ♘e5 (control of the centre!). The most natural continuations, which were also studied at home, were 11...0-0 12 0-0-0 and 11...♕c7, when 12 dxc5 ♕xc5 13 0-0-0 ♗xg3 14 hxg3

♗d7 is unclear (J.Polgar-Epishin, Geneva (rapid) 1996), but to me 12 ♘e5!? cxd4 13 0-0-0 seemed interesting.

Possibly on the basis of this, Karpov endeavoured to find a less obvious solution.

11...♕e7

A solid move, which has only one strategic drawback: Black concedes the e5-point without a fight. On the other hand, Beliavsky and I had not looked at this line.

12 dxc5 ♗xc5 13 ♘e5 (I responded in standard fashion to the opponent's unexpected reply) **13...♗d7**

Now the traditional manoeuvre 13...♘bd7 14 ♘gf3 ♘xe5 15 ♘xe5 ♘d7 would lead after 16 0-0-0 to an enduring advantage for White. 15...0-0 16 0-0-0 a5 is somewhat better, but here too after 17 ♗a4! Black does not have clear equality.

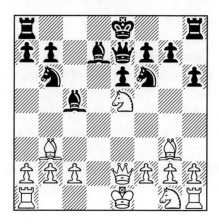

14 ♘gf3

14 0-0-0 was also quite possible, but after 14...a5! the position would have become sharper and Black would have gained real counterplay. On the other hand, 14 ♘gf3 allows him to exchange his knight for the strong bishop on g3 (after which, it is true, kingside castling becomes dangerous).

14...♘h5! 15 0-0-0

15 ♘xf7?! ♘xg3 16 fxg3 did not work, although not because of the line which I

gave immediately after the game – 16...♔xf7(?) 17 ♘e5+ ♔e8(?), since after 18 0-0-0! White has a powerful attack (and after 17...♔g8 18 ♘xd7 ♘xd7 19 ♗xe6+ ♔f8 20 0-0-0 ♘f6 21 ♖he1 – good compensation for the piece), but in view of 16...♕xf7! 17 ♘e5 ♕e7! (instead of 17...♕f5?? 18 ♖f1 ♕g5 19 ♘f7 and wins), when Black is better after both 18 ♘g6?! ♕f6 19 ♘xh8 ♕xb2 20 ♕h5+ g6! 21 ♕xg6+ ♔d8 22 ♘f7+ ♔e7, and 18 ♕h5+ ♔d8 19 ♘g6 ♕g5 20 ♕xg5+ hxg5 21 ♘xh8 ♔e7 22 ♘g6+ ♔f6.

15...♘xg3

The incautious 15...0-0-0?! could have led after 16 ♘xd7 ♘xd7 17 ♗e5! ♘xe5?! 18 ♘xe5 ♘f4 (18...♘f6? 19 ♘xf7!) 19 ♕c4 to serious problems for Black. 17...♘hf6 is better, although here too after 18 ♗f4! the two powerful bishops promise White the advantage (18...g5 19 ♗d2).

16 hxg3 0-0-0

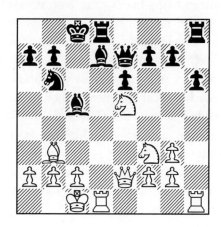

The first critical position in the game. At this moment my opponent looked very content. Indeed, it seems that Black has solved all his problems, and after 17 ♘xd7 or 17 ♖d3 and ♖hd1 with exchanges on the d-file, things will end in a quick draw. White has a strong knight on e5, but the bishop on b3, running up against the f7-e6 pawn pair, is in danger of becoming passive.

However, White does still have a little time, since for the moment Black has not overcome a certain lack of harmony in the placing of his pieces: his knight is obviously unhappy on b6, while the bishop on d7 will be forced, by retreating to e8, to disconnect the rooks.

17 ♖h5!

The white pieces behave as though they have just woken up; full of attacking energy they now turn to the creation of constant threats. Spassky once informed me of the amusing 'Bondarevsky rule': if for ten successive moves you attack the opponent's pieces, on the eleventh he will definitely leave something *en prise*. This 'rule' came in useful for me in my decisive game with Tukmakov at the finish of the 49th USSR Championship (Game No.67 in *Garry Kasparov on Garry Kasparov Part I*). It also operated in the present game.

After 17 ♖h5 the ex-champion stopped to think, and the contented expression on his face changed to one of anxiety. The threat is 18 ♘xf7 ♕xf7 19 ♖xc5, and 17...♗d6? is bad because of 18 ♖xd6!. Karpov was faced with a psychological problem: should he or shouldn't he weaken his position? And he decided to avoid moves which would create long-term weaknesses – in the hope that White's initiative would evaporate and then Black's two bishops and good pawn formation would begin to tell.

17...♗e8

Of course, 17...g6 gets rid of the pressure along the fifth rank, but after 18 ♖h4 White has a stable positional advantage, since the opponent's pawn structure on the kingside is hopelessly compromised: 18...g5 19 ♖hh1 ♗e8 (19...♗a4? 20 ♘xf7) 20 ♖xd8+ ♕xd8 21 a4!, and if 21...a5, then 22 ♕e1 ♗b4 23 ♕e3 ♘xa4 24 ♘xf7 ♗xf7 25 ♗xa4. There is also

not full equality after 17...♖hf8 18 c4!? ♗e8 (18...♗d6 19 ♘d3 or 19 ♔b1) 19 ♖xd8+ ♔xd8 20 ♘d3 ♘d7 21 ♘xc5 ♘xc5 22 ♗c2 f6 23 ♖h1 ♔c7 (23...e5?! 24 ♘h4) 24 ♘d4 ♗d7 25 b4 ♘a6 26 a3 etc.

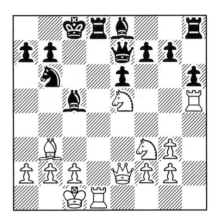

In playing 17...♗e8, Karpov apparently assumed that the problem of equalising had already been solved, and the subsequent constant 'little bites' proved very painful and unexpected for him.

18 ♖xd8+ ♔xd8 (18...♕xd8? 19 ♘xf7) **19 ♕d2+**

Nothing was given by 19 ♕d3+ (taking away this square from the knight on e5) 19...♔c7 20 ♕c3 f6, but a small plus would have been retained by 19 ♘d3!? ♗d6 20 ♖a5 ♘c8 21 ♕d2! or 20...a6 21 ♕e3(e4).

19...♗d6

It turns out that this is the only move: 19...♕d6? 20 ♘xf7+ (20 ♘d3 also wins) 20...♗xf7 21 ♖xc5, or 19...♔c8(c7)? 20 ♘d3 f5 (20...♗d6 21 ♕c3+ and ♕xg7) 21 ♖h1 ♗d6 22 ♖e1 and wins.

20 ♘d3 ♕c7

20...f6? 21 ♖a5!, 20...f5? 21 ♖h1 (followed by ♖e1), and 20...♔c8? 21 ♕c3+ followed by ♕xg7 were all suicidal, but 20...♗c7 was acceptable.

21 g4!

An important link in White's plan: the

opponent is avoiding pawn weaknesses, so some must be created for him. The threat of g4-g5 was a particularly unpleasant one for Karpov: just before he had absolutely no concerns about his pawn structure, but now suddenly it is about to be disrupted, and it is difficult to prevent this.

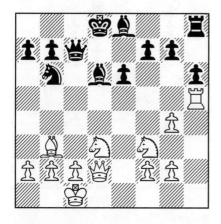

21...♔c8

In the end the king has to run away from the centre. 21...f6? 22 ♘c5! or 21...f5? 22 ♘g5! would have lost immediately. And if 21...♖g8 (preserving the unity of the pawn chain), then 22 ♕e3 ♗c6 23 ♘d4!? is good.

22 g5 ♗f8

A very solid move. The clever attempt 22...♗b5? 23 gxh6 ♗xd3 24 hxg7 ♖d8 (with the idea of 25 ♖h8? ♗h7!! 26 ♖xh7? ♗f4 or 26 ♘g5? ♗g8) would have been refuted by 25 g3! or 25 ♔b1! followed by ♖h8.

If 22...♔b8 23 gxh6 gxh6 I was intending to play 24 ♔b1 (24 ♖xh6? ♗f4!; also no advantage is promised by 24 ♘d4 e5 25 ♘f5 ♗f8 26 ♘e3 f6 27 ♖h4 ♗g6 28 a4 h5), and here Black would have had to see the move 24...e5! (24...♗c6 25 ♖xh6) with chances of equalising: for example, 25 ♘dxe5 f6 26 ♘f7 ♖h7 27 ♖xh6 (27 ♘xd6 ♗xh5) 27...♗f4 28 ♕e2 ♗xh6 29 ♕xe8+ ♕c8 30 ♕xc8+ ♘xc8 31 ♘xh6 ♖xh6 32 ♔c1, with no more than sufficient compensation for the ex-

change. However, after 25 ♘c1! e4 26 ♘d4 White would nevertheless have retained some initiative (if 26...♗f4, then 27 ♕e2).

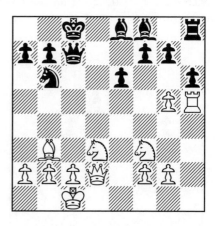

Thus, as before Karpov does not want to complicate the play and create defects in his position. Now if 23 gxh6 he replies 23...♖xh6, exchanging his passive rook and obtaining a draw.

23 ♖h4 (instead of the objectively better 23 g6!? fxg6 24 ♖e5, the rook switches to a different attacking position) **23...♔b8**

After 23...♗e7 24 ♖h1 h5 25 ♕e3 or 23...♗c6 24 ♘fe5 ♗xg2 25 g6! White would also have retained some pressure.

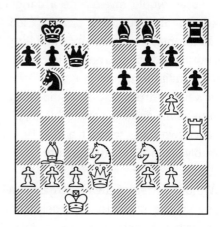

24 a4! (the 'bites' follow first from the right, then from the left) **24...♗e7**

Black would like to coordinate his pieces

by 24...♘c8 with the idea of ...♘e7-c6(g6), but after 25 g6! fxg6 26 ♘d4 or 26 ♖c4 White has an enduring advantage. However, 24...♗c6!? 25 a5 ♘d7 26 ♘d4 ♗e7 was a worthy alternative – Black is close to equality.

25 a5

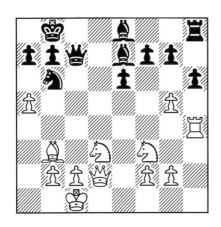

25...♘d5?!

The point of Karpov's previous move. Black chose the square for his knight without any particular calculation, largely on general grounds: on d5 the knight 'looks' better placed than at c8. And yet 25...♘c8 would in fact have been better – I thought that 26 a6 would give White a dangerous attack, but after 26...♗b5! 27 axb7 ♘d6 and ...♖d8 the play is very complicated, and the position, to all appearances, is one of dynamic equilibrium.

However, Karpov obviously did not want to retreat his knight: having his pieces on the back two ranks for such a long time was probably beginning to irritate him.

26 ♔b1!

Without frittering away his gains, White builds up the pressure. Strangely enough, after the prophylactic king move he acquires some real threats. In addition, with the black knight at d5, at an appropriate moment he can exchange his inactive bishop for it. It is

unlikely that the ex-champion was concerned about this exchange. Thus after the immediate 26 ♗xd5 exd5 27 ♘b4 ♗c6 28 ♘xd5?! (28 ♖h5 still retains some advantage) 28...♗xd5 29 ♕xd5 ♖d8 Black would get away with a slight fright.

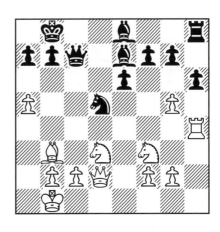

26...♗d8?

Short of time on the clock, Karpov makes another 'solid' move, after which Black's difficulties become insuperable. It was essential to move the rook off the h-file, creating the threat of ...hxg5. True, if 26...♖f8?! 27 ♗xd5 exd5 28 ♘b4 ♗c6? (28...hxg5 is also inadequate: 29 ♘xd5 ♕d8(d6) 30 ♖d4) White wins with the attractive 'draughts' combination 29 gxh6! ♗xh4 30 ♘a6+! bxa6 31 ♕b4+, ♕xf8+ and hxg7.

Practical saving chances were offered by 26...♖g8, although after 27 ♖c4! ♕d8! 28 gxh6 (29 g6!?) 28...gxh6 29 ♖d4! White would have retained an appreciable advantage.

27 a6! (breaking up the black king's pawn protection) **27...♕a5?**

Equivalent to capitulation. Karpov cracked under the strain – he simply lacked the strength to solve small, unpleasant problems for so long. Remember the 'Bondarevsky rule', which was mentioned in the note to White's 17th move? Since then the position has not particularly changed – White has merely advanced his g- and a-pawns. However, by all the time making little threats, within ten moves he has obtained a winning position.

27...b6? 28 ♗xd5 exd5 29 ♘b4 was also hopeless, but 27...bxa6 was far more resilient, for example:

1) 28 ♘b4 (28 c4?! ♘e7! is unclear) 28...♗d6! (not 28...♘xb4? 29 ♖xb4+ ♔a8? 30 ♖c4 or 29...♗b5 30 c4) 29 ♘xd5 exd5 30 ♗xd5 ♗b6 31 c4 ♗c6 32 ♗xc6 ♕xc6 33 ♘e5 ♕e6 34 ♖e4 ♔c8 35 gxh6 ♖xh6 36 ♖e1, and Black's defence is difficult;

2) 28 ♗xd5! (the most interesting continuation) 28...exd5 29 gxh6! with a powerful initiative, although considerable energy and resourcefulness are still demanded of White: 29...♖xh4?! 30 hxg7 ♖g8 31 ♘xh4 f6 (31...♖xg7 32 ♕b4+ and ♕f8) 32 ♘b4 ♕xg7 33 ♕xd5 or 29...♖xh6 30 ♖xh6 gxh6 31 ♕xh6 ♗b5 32 ♘b4 etc.

28 ♕e2

An infiltrating move with the threat of ♕e5+ and ♕xg7. 28 ♘b4! was also very strong.

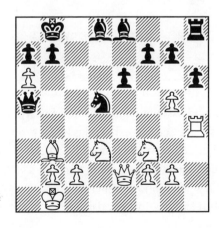

28...♘b6

It was also possible to play 28...♘c7 29 axb7 ♗xg5 30 ♘xg5 ♕xg5 31 g3 ♗b5! 32 c4 ♗c6 33 ♘e5 ♗b7 34 ♗e2, or 28...♘e7! (the

best chance) 29 axb7 ♘g6 30 ♖h3 (30 ♖h5 ♗e7) 30...♗xg5 31 ♘xg5 hxg5 32 ♖xh8 ♘xh8 33 ♕e3, and although White should win, there is still some fight in the position.

29 axb7

The obvious move, but 29 ♕e4! would have won more quickly, with the ideas of 29...♕xa6 30 ♕e5+ and ♕xg7, 29...bxa6 30 ♕d4, or 29...♗c6 30 ♕f4+ ♔a8 31 ♕xf7 ♗g5 32 axb7+ ♗xb7 33 ♕xg7 and wins.

29...♗xg5 (29...♗c6 30 ♘fe5 or 29...♔xb7 30 ♕e4+ ♗c6 31 ♕f4 ♕f5 32 ♕d6 also did not help) **30 ♘xg5 ♕xg5 31 ♖h5!**

After carrying out an enormous amount of 'off-screen' work, the rook again moves on to its favourite fifth rank, in order to strike a decisive blow on the queenside.

31...♕f6

An amusing variation could have occurred after 31...♕g2 32 ♘c5 (with the threat of ♕e5 mate) 32...♘d7 (32...f6 33 ♕d3) 33 ♕a6! (threatening ♕d6 mate) 33...♘xc5 34 ♖xc5 ♕xb7 35 ♕d6+ ♔a8 36 ♕d8+ ♕b8 37 ♖c8! (and here the rook has the last word!).

32 ♖a5! (the c5-square is intended for the knight) **32...♗c6 33 ♘c5 ♗xb7 34 ♘xb7 ♔xb7 35 ♕a6+ ♔c6 36 ♗a4+ ♔d6 37 ♕d3+ ♘d5**

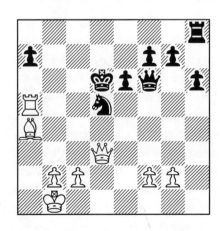

38 ♕g3+ (38 ♕a3+! was more forceful)

38...♕e5 (38...e5 39 ♕a3+! ♔e6 40 ♕h3+)
39 ♕a3+ ♔c7 40 ♕c5+ ♔d8 41 ♖xa7

The time scramble came to an end, and Black resigned (**1–0**). This memorable win was judged to be the best in the 54th volume of *Informator*.

The initial pairings proved quite difficult for me: immediately after Timman and Karpov I had to play in succession against Ivanchuk, Anand and Gelfand. In the first of these games, which was also very interesting, I, with difficulty, gained a draw. Against my King's Indian Ivanchuk employed a high-quality novelty and seized the initiative on the queenside (cf. *Game No.80*, note to White's 15th move), but I managed to defend, and in the time scramble there was even a chance of gaining an advantage.

In the 4th round I met Vishy Anand, and this was an especially critical encounter: I very much wanted to gain revenge for the recent defeats in Tilburg and Reggio Emilia.

Game 86
G.Kasparov-V.Anand
Linares, 4th Round, 27.02.1992
French Defence C18

1 e4 e6 (as expected) **2 d4 d5 3 ♘c3**

Having lost to Anand after 3 ♘d2, I got down to a serious analysis of the French. Makarychev and I even looked at 3 e5, but things did not get as far as employing this move in practice. By the time of the match with Short (1993) I was ready to play the most complicated variations with 3 ♘c3.

3...♗b4 4 e5 c5 5 a3 ♗xc3+ 6 bxc3 ♘e7

If 6...♕c7 there could have followed 7 ♕g4 f5 8 ♕g3 cxd4 (8...♘e7 – Game No.127 in *My Great Predecessors Part II*) 9 cxd4 ♘e7 10 ♗d2 0-0 11 ♗d3 b6 12 ♘e2 ♗a6 13 ♘f4

♕d7 14 h4! ♗xd3 15 ♕xd3 ♘bc6 (15...♖c8!? 16 ♖h3 ♖c4) 16 ♖h3! ♖ac8 17 ♖g3 with attacking prospects (Kasparov-Short, Novgorod 1997).

7 h4

The main move 7 ♕g4 would also soon appear in my arsenal, followed by 7...♔f8 8 h4 (Kasparov-Nikolic, Horgen 1994; Paris (rapid) 1994) or 7...0-0 8 ♗d3 (Kasparov-Short, Munich (blitz) 1994). But on this occasion I decided to test a comparatively rare – but also aggressive! – continuation.

7...♘bc6

The alternative is 7...♕c7 8 ♘f3 b6 or 8...♘bc6 9 h5 h6 (but not 9...f5? 10 h6!, Kasparov-Baude, Zurich (simul') 1988) 10 ♗d3 ♗d7 (Makarychev-Gruenberg, Sochi 1983).

8 h5 ♕a5 (8...h6!?) **9 ♗d2 cxd4** (later 9...♗d7 10 h6! became fashionable) **10 cxd4 ♕a4**

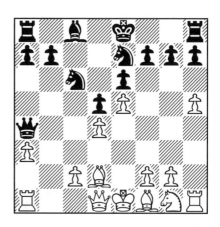

Anand was relying on well-known patterns – 11 ♗c3 (the harmless 11 c3 ♕xd1+ 12 ♖(♔)xd1 h6 allows equality) 11...b6! 12 h6 gxh6 (Short-Korchnoi, Wijk aan Zee 1987) or 12 ♘f3 ♗a6 (Short-Ivanchuk, Tilburg 1990), in both cases with a good game for Black.

11 ♘f3!?

'A novelty in true Kasparov style' (Stohl) – an unexpected pawn sacrifice. The other gambit attempt 11 h6 is parried by 11...♕xd4 12 ♘f3 ♕e4+ 13 ♗e2 ♘xe5! 14 ♗c3 f6

(Miton-Shabalov, Stratton Mountain 1999).

11...♘xd4 12 ♗d3 ♘ec6

After 12...♘xf3+ 13 ♕xf3 ♕d4 14 0-0 ♕xe5 15 ♖fe1 ♕f6 16 ♕g3 with the threat of ♗g5 White has excellent play on the dark squares, although correspondence games in the 1990s showed that by 16...h6 17 ♗c3! d4 18 ♗b5+ ♗d7 (18...♔f8 19 ♖ad1!) 19 ♗xd7+ ♔xd7 20 ♗xd4 ♘f5! Black nevertheless maintains the balance.

The safest and also most natural move is 12...h6!, nipping in the bud the threat of h5-h6 (recent examples: Nakamura-Shulman, Saint Louis 2010; Zherebukh-Robson, Moscow 2012). However, the move in the game is also not so bad.

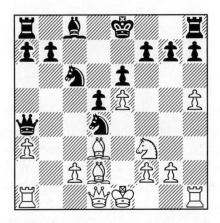

13 ♔f1!

Creating the threat of ♖h4. The rook emerges via the h-file – this was my idea: White voluntarily gives up the right to castle (if 13 0-0, then 13...♘xf3+ 14 ♕xf3 ♕h4! is good). 13 h6!? also comes into consideration (Fedorowicz-Yermolinsky, Durango 1992).

13...♘xf3

In the event of 13...b6? 14 ♖h4 ♗a6 15 ♘xd4 ♘xd4 16 ♗e3(c3) ♗xd3+ 17 ♕xd3 Black loses a piece. In *Informator* I recommended 13...♘f5!?, although here too White retains compensation for the pawn by playing 14 ♗xf5 exf5 15 h6, immediately 14

h6 or 14 ♔g1.

14 ♕xf3 b6?

14...h6? or 14...♘xe5? is also bad in view of 15 ♕g3!. The correct defence is 14...♕d4! 15 ♖e1 ♘xe5 16 ♕g3 ♘xd3 17 cxd3 (threatening ♖h4) 17...♖g8! (covering the g7-pawn – this move was not in our analysis!) 18 ♖h4 ♕b2 19 ♗b4 a5 20 ♗c5 ♕b5, and although White's dark-square initiative fully compensates for the material deficit, Black holds on (De Luca-Brizio, correspondence 1999). But in an unfamiliar position Vishy took me 'at my word' and quickly made a natural developing move.

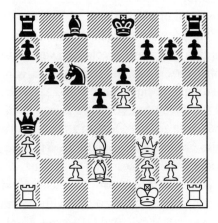

15 h6!

Apparently Black was reckoning on 15 ♕g3? ♗a6 16 ♕xg7 0-0-0, giving back the f7-pawn and obtaining a comfortable game. But now his kingside is crumbling and he is unable to complete his development quickly.

15...♗a6!

Comparatively the best try. The following alternatives were hopeless: 15...♘xe5? 16 hxg7 ♖g8 17 ♕h5 (with the threat of ♕xh7) 17...♘g4 18 ♖e1!, or 15...g6? 16 ♕f6 ♖f8 17 ♖h4 d4 18 ♗e4, as well as 15...♖g8 16 hxg7 ♖xg7? (16...♗a6!) 17 ♕f6 ♕g4 18 g3, when the threat of ♖h4 forces 18...♖g6 19 ♗xg6 ♕xg6 20 ♖h6 ♗a6+ 21 ♔g1 ♕xf6 22 exf6 and ♖xh7, winning.

16 hxg7 ♖g8

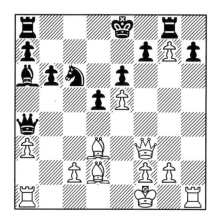

17 ♗xa6!

The fruit of a long think. 17 ♖xh7(?) ♘xe5 18 ♖h8(?) ♘xf3 19 ♖xg8+ ♔d7 20 ♖xa8 was tempting, but here a cold shower awaited White – 20...♕d4!, and instead of a win he would have to fight for a draw: 21 ♔e2 (21 ♖xa7+?! ♔c6!) 21...♕xg7 22 ♖xa7+ ♔c6 23 ♖xa6 ♘xd2 24 ♖d1 ♘e4(c4) 25 ♗xe4(c4) etc.

Also nothing was given by 18 ♕f6 ♗xd3+! 19 cxd3 ♕d4! 20 ♖e1 ♕xd3+ 21 ♔g1 ♕xh7 22 ♖xe5 ♖(♕)xg7 or 22 ♗b4 ♘xf3+ (22...♕h2+!?) 23 ♕xf3 0-0-0 with equality. However, 18 ♕e3! ♘xd3 19 cxd3 ♕e4! 20 ♕xe4 dxe4 21 ♖h8! ♔d7 22 ♗c3 would still have left White with chances of success.

As it later transpired, after 17 ♖xh7? the simplest is 17...♕xc2! 18 ♗xa6 ♕xh7 19 ♗b5 0-0-0! (I only looked at 19...♕h1+? 20 ♔e2 and wins) 20 ♕c3 ♕h1+ 21 ♔e2 ♕h5+ 22 ♔f1! ♕h1+ with perpetual check (Stohl). Queen moves were also blank shots – 17 ♕g3? ♘e7! or 17 ♕f6? ♗xd3+! (but not Stohl's move 17...♕d4(?) because of 18 ♖c1!) 18 cxd3 ♕c2 19 ♗g5 ♕xd3+ 20 ♔g1 ♕g6!.

17...♕xa6+ 18 ♔g1 ♖xg7

Hurrying to get rid of the dangerous pawn. 18...♘d4? was bad because of 19 ♕f6 ♘e2+ 20 ♔h2 with the winning threat of ♗g5. Black's position is also very difficult

after 18...♘xe5 19 ♕h5 ♘g6 (19...♘c4 20 ♗c3) 20 ♖e1 0-0-0 21 ♕f3! ♖d7 (21...♖xg7? 22 ♕c3+) 22 ♖xh7 ♔b7 23 ♕c3, or 18...♘c4(a4) 19 ♖xh7 ♘xe5 20 ♕f6! ♕d4 (20...♘g4 21 ♕g5!) 21 ♖e1 ♘c6 22 ♗g5(c3) ♕xf6 23 ♗xf6 and ♖h8, but objectively this was a more resilient defence.

19 ♕f6 ♖g8 20 ♖xh7 ♕b7

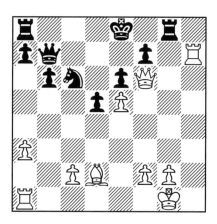

21 ♗g5?!

An annoying error. 21 c4! suggests itself – in order to target the black king, the centre must be opened. Black loses ignominiously after 21...dxc4 22 ♗g5 (threatening ♖d1) 22...♕e7 23 ♕f3! ♕c7 24 ♖d1 ♖c8 25 ♕h5 (with the threats of ♖h8 and ♖d6xe6), or 21...♖d8 22 ♗g5 ♕e7 23 ♖h8 ♔d7 (23...♖xh8 24 ♕xh8+ or 23...♕f8 24 ♗h6 is also bad) 24 ♖xg8! (more accurate than 24 cxd5, as I gave in *Informator*) 24...♖xg8 25 cxd5 exd5 26 ♕xc6+! (Stohl). And 21...d4 is little better: 22 ♗g5 ♖c8 23 ♖h8! ♖xh8 24 ♕xh8+ ♔d7 25 ♕g7, winning the f7-pawn and the game.

After the premature bishop sortie the situation could have become more complicated.

21...♘d4?!

Carried away by the idea of ...♘e2+ and ...♘c3-e4, Anand rejected the less clear 21...♕e7 22 ♕f4, and here not 22...♕c7? 23 ♖e1 ♖f8 24 c4! or 22...♕f8? 23 c4! d4 24

置d1, when White wins, but 22...置xg5! 23 置h8+ 含d7 24 置xa8 含c7! (my *Informator* suggestion 24...置f5(?) is weak because of 25 營a4!, winning) with some compensation for the exchange, although after 25 c4! (breaking up the opponent's defences) 25...d4 26 c5! White would retain chances of gradually converting his advantage.

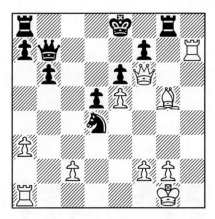

22 c4!?

At last! However, the prophylactic 22 含f1! was even stronger, and only after 22...置c8, 22...置f8 or 22...②c6 – the deadly 23 c4!, while if 22...②b5, then 23 置h3! 置g6 24 營f4 and once again c2-c4. But now Black begins jumping around with his knight.

22...②e2+! 23 含h2 ②c3 24 置h8 置xh8+ 25 營xh8+ 含d7 26 營h7?!

Another error, creating unnecessary problems for White. There was a forced win by 26 營f6! (or 26 營g7) 26...含c6 27 cxd5+! (alas, I only considered 27 營f3(?!) ②e4 28 cxd5+ exd5 29 置c1+ ②c5 and 27 置c1(?!) ②e4 28 cxd5+(?) 含b5!) 27...②xd5 28 置c1+ 含b5 29 營f3! (here with 26 營g7 played there is 29 營h7! 含a6 30 營d3+) 29...含a6 30 營d3+ b5 31 a4! 營b6 32 置b1 or 31...營d7 32 置c7!.

26...置f8 27 ②h6 置e8 28 營xf7+ 置e7

It is now Black who is a pawn down, but his pieces have taken up good positions, and for the moment the superiority of the bishop

over the knight is not perceptible. In addition, I was running into time-trouble, whereas Anand still had a mass of time: he used to play very quickly.

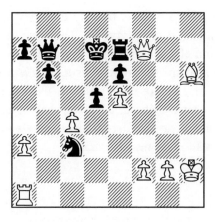

29 營g6

29 營g8!? also came into consideration, since if 29...營c7 there is the very strong 30 ②g5! (Stohl, who pointed out this move, parries my *Informator* suggestion 30 f4(?) with 30...置e8! 31 營f7+ 置e7 32 營g6 含c8) 30...營xe5+ 31 f4 營g7 32 營b8 置f7 33 置e1 ②e4 34 營xa7+ 含c6 35 營a8+ 置b7 36 營c8+ 含d6 37 cxd5 exd5 38 ②h4 with an extra pawn and an attack. 29...營c8 is better, but in the endgame after 30 營xc8+ 含xc8 31 cxd5 ②xd5 (31...置h7? 32 置c1) 32 ②d2!? 置h7+ 33 含g3 White also has every chance of converting his material advantage.

29...營b8! 30 cxd5 (30 f4?! 營e8! 31 f5 營h8! with equality – Stohl) **30...②xd5!**

Anand is again resourceful: 30...營xe5+? 31 f4! 營h8 (31...②xd5 32 ②g5) 32 dxe6+ 置xe6 33 營g7+! is worse for Black.

31 置d1?

A time-trouble blunder. 31 置e1?! 營h8! is inaccurate (Stohl). After 31 f4! I was also frightened by 31...營h8!? (31...營e8 32 f5!) 32 含g1? 置h7, when White is in trouble (33 ②g5? 置h1+), but 32 含g3! would have retained the extra pawn and good winning chances.

31...♕xe5+ 32 f4 ♕h8 33 f5 ♕e5+ 34 ♔h1

Also after 34 ♔h3, the simplest is 34...exf5 35 ♕g8 ♕e6. Draw agreed (½-½).

It was painful not to win such a won position, but what can you do... The initial result – 3 out of 4 against the 'heavyweights' and a share of the lead with Yusupov – was not bad, and before my 5th round 'black' game with Boris Gelfand, who was half a point behind, I tried to cast off any negative emotions and take myself in hand.

> ## Game 87
> ### B.Gelfand-G.Kasparov
> Linares, 5th Round, 28.02.1992
> *King's Indian Defence E92*

1 d4 ♘f6 2 c4 g6 3 ♘c3 ♗g7 4 e4 d6 5 ♗e2 0-0 6 ♘f3 e5 7 ♗e3 (Boris more often played 7 0-0 against me – *Game No.64*) **7...c6**

If immediately 7...exd4 8 ♘xd4 ♖e8 9 f3 c6, then 10 ♗f2! (instead of the 'logical' 10 ♕d2) 10...d5 11 exd5 cxd5 12 0-0 ♘c6 13 c5 ♘h5 14 g3 ♗e5 15 ♕d2 ♘g7 (15...♗h3?! 16 ♖fe1 ♘g7 17 ♖ad1! ♖c8?! 18 ♘db5, Kasparov-Carlsen, Reykjavik (rapid) 2004) 16 ♖fd1! with some advantage for White.

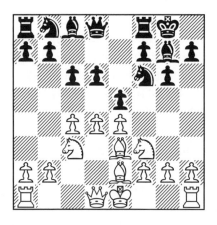

8 ♕d2

8 d5 is possibly more dangerous for Black (Game No.26 in *Kasparov vs. Karpov 1988-2009*), but Gelfand chose the move made by me in Reggio Emilia against Ivanchuk. The opponent was obviously trying to lure me into the very sharp position from the 11th game of my 1990 match with Karpov...

8...exd4 (8...♘bd7 – *Game No.83*) **9 ♘xd4 ♖e8 10 f3 d5 11 exd5 cxd5 12 0-0 ♘c6 13 c5 ♖xe3!?**

With this sudden sacrifice I literally stunned Karpov, but Boris was well prepared for it.

14 ♕xe3 ♕f8!

Black is threatening not only ...♕xc5, but above all ...♘g4.

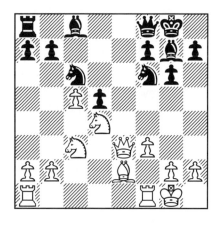

In the source game after 15 ♘xc6 bxc6 16 ♔h1?! (16 ♖ad1! was better) 16...♖b8 17 ♘a4 ♖b4 it all soon concluded in a spectacular perpetual check (Game No.18 in *Kasparov vs. Karpov 1988-2009*).

15 ♘cb5!?

And here is Gelfand's attempt to refute my variation. Of course, my trainers and I had also looked at this move, and, as it seemed to us, we had found clear equality. However, things are not so simple...

15...♕xc5 16 ♖ac1

After 16 ♘f5? d4! 17 ♘fxd4 a6 18 ♖ac1

♕b6 19 ♖xc6 (19 ♘d6 ♗h6!) 19...bxc6 20 ♘d6 ♗e6 White loses material. But Makarychev's recommendation 16 ♕f2!? is slightly more accurate (the source game: L.B.Hansen-Nielsen, Danish Championship 1992), when after 16...♗d7, apart from 17 ♖ac1, White has the resources 17 ♘b3 and 17 ♖fd1. However, here too Black has an excellent bishop with a pawn for the exchange and quite adequate counterplay.

16...♕b6 17 ♕f2 ♗d7

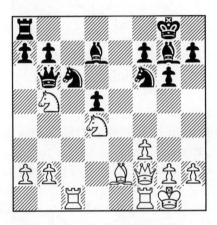

18 ♖fd1

Boris employs a novelty – and runs into our preparation! Earlier 18 ♘b3 ♘e8?! occurred (Fishbein-Rechel, Groningen 1990), after which 19 ♖cd1! is good, or 18...♗h6!? (Fishbein-Schandorff, Kerteminde 1991). The endgame after 18...♕xf2+ 19 ♖xf2 a6 20 ♘c3 ♗e6 (21 ♘a4 ♘d7) is also more or less acceptable for Black.

18...♖e8

This looks the most dynamic. The simplifying variation 18...♗h6 (it is a pity to move the bishop off the long diagonal) 19 ♖c3 ♘xd4 (19...♘b4!?) 20 ♕xd4 ♗xb5 21 ♕xb6 axb6 22 ♗xb5 ♖xa2 23 ♖b1 or 23 ♖c2 would have been a concession and would have given White a minimal advantage.

19 ♗f1 ♗h6

Now, when all the resources have been brought up, Black cannot delay the start of concrete action. However, first 19...♘b4! was more accurate, allowing White only 20 a3 or 20 b3!? ♗h6 21 ♖c3 (cf. the note to White's 21st move).

20 ♖c3 ♘b4!

The point of Black's idea. There was a battle for the d4-square, and suddenly he deviates from it with ...♗h6 and ...♘b4.

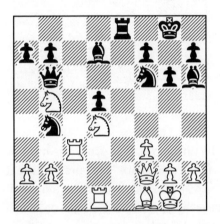

On encountering a surprise, for an instant Gelfand lost the thread of the play and offered to go into an ending, underestimating all the dangers associated with it.

21 ♘c2?

A serious error, sharply changing the evaluation of the position (back in 1990 we judged this move to be bad). First, it was possible to force a draw by 21 a3 ♘a2 22 ♖b3 ♘c1! (22...a6?! 23 ♘c3) 23 ♖c3 ♘a2. And second – to continue the fight for an advantage:

1) 21 b3!? ♘xa2 22 ♕xa2 ♗xb5 23 ♗xb5 ♖e1+! 24 ♖xe1 ♕xd4+ 25 ♔f1 ♕xc3 26 ♕xa7 ♕xb3 27 ♕xb7 ♗e3(d2), and White's poorly defended king denies him any hopes of success;

2) 21 ♖b3! (a risky but interesting idea) 21...a5! (21...♘xa2?! 22 ♘c2! is worse) 22 a4 ♗f8! (with the idea of ...♗c5) 23 ♖e3 ♖c8 24 ♘b3 ♗c6 with a complicated game in

which, in my view, White's chances are slightly better.

21...♕xf2+ 22 ♔xf2 ♘xc2 23 ♖xc2 ♗e3+

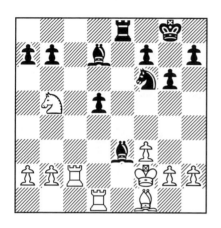

24 ♔e1

The only move. If 24 ♔g3? the most forceful is 24...h6! with the pretty threat of 25...♘h5+ 26 ♔h4 ♗g5 mate, and White is not saved by either 25 h4 ♗g1!, or 25 f4 ♗b6 26 h3(h4) ♗g1!.

24...♗f4+ (not rushing with 24...♗g1+!, Black gives two additional checks, in order later to avoid time-trouble) **25 ♔f2 ♗e3+ 26 ♔e1 ♗g1+! 27 ♔d2**

White's problem is that 27 ♖e2? fails to 27...♗xb5. Was it this that my opponent missed?

27...♗xh2

Thus, while keeping his rook on the board, Black has won a second pawn for the exchange. And although his material advantage is only slight, his playing advantage is obvious: he has two active bishops and numerous strengthening possibilities, thanks to the extremely weak squares in White's position.

28 ♖e1 (28 ♘d4!? ♗f4+ 29 ♔c3 a6 is less clear) **28...♗f4+ 29 ♔d1 ♖d8 30 ♘d4**

30 ♘xa7? did not work: 30...♖a8 (but not my earlier 30...d4(?) because of 31 ♗c4!) 31 ♘b5 ♖xa2 32 ♗d3 ♗g3 33 ♖h1 ♖a8! with

the threat of ...♘h5-f4.

30...a6 31 ♗d3

If 31 g4, then 31...h5 32 gxh5 ♘xh5 is possible, or the preparatory 31...♗g3.

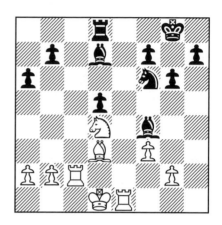

31...h5

Initiating a squeeze on the enemy kingside. It also made sense to conclusively weaken the dark squares by 31...♗a4!? 32 b3 ♗d7.

32 ♖c3 h4 (fixing the g2-pawn, which becomes a chronic weakness) **33 ♗c2 ♗g3 34 ♖e2**

34 ♖h1 ♘h5 35 ♘e2 d4! 36 ♖b3 ♗f2 37 ♖xb7?! d3! or 36 ♖d3 ♗b5 37 ♘xg3 ♘xg3 38 ♖xh4 ♘f5 39 ♖e4 ♗xd3 40 ♗xd3 ♘e3+ and ...♘xg2 was also not at all promising for White.

34...♔g7

After 34...♘h5!? in reply to 35 ♖b3 (35 ♖d2?! ♗f4 36 ♖e2 ♗d6!) there was 35...♘f4 36 ♖xb7 ♘xe2 37 ♘xe2 (37 ♔xe2 ♖e8+ 38 ♔d3 ♖e7!) 37...♗c8 with a sound extra pawn.

35 ♖b3 ♖b8

An unaesthetic move, but Black has no reason to hurry. I did not want to allow my opponent any hopes of counterplay in the variations with 35...b5 36 a4 bxa4 37 ♖b6 a5 38 ♖b7 or 35...♗c8 36 ♖e7 ♔f8 37 ♖bxb7! ♗xb7 38 ♖xb7.

36 ℤd2 (36 ℤb6 ♗c7) **36...b5!** (also seizing space on the queenside) **37 ℤa3 ℤb6**

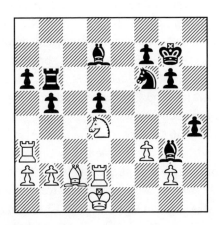

38 b4?!

A purely practical resource, creating fresh holes in White's position. 38 ♘e2 ♗d6 39 ℤad3 was more resilient.

38...♗d6 (38...♗f4!? should have been included, in order after 39 ℤe2 ♗d6 40 ℤb3 to play 40...♘h5 and then ...♘f4 with gain of tempo) **39 ℤb3 ♘h5 40 ♘e2 ♗e6 41 a3**

It is hard to offer White any good advice.

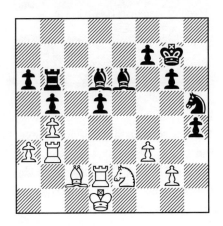

41...g5?!

All in the same unhurried manner, although 41...♘f4! was stronger: 42 ♘xf4 ♗xf4 43 ℤd4 ♗g5, threatening ...♗f6 and ...d5-d4, or 42 ♘d4 ♗e5 43 ♘xe6 ℤxe6 44 ℤe3 f6 with an overwhelming advantage.

42 ♘d4 (42 ♔e1!?) **42...♔f6** (42...♗f4!?) **43 ♘xe6!**

At least getting rid of one of the two bishops. The resulting opposite-coloured bishops increase White's hopes of a draw.

43...fxe6 44 ♗d3 (with the idea of ♗f1 – to defend the g2-pawn!) **44...♘f4?!**

Another error! White's defence would have been far more difficult after 44...♗e5! and ...♘f4.

45 ℤc3 d4?! (45...♗e5 46 ℤc8 is no longer so clear) **46 ℤc8 ♘d5**

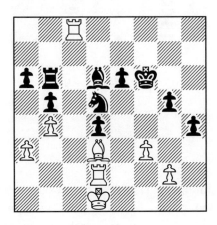

47 ♔e2?

Already again low on time, Gelfand ruins his game, missing a real saving chance – 47 ♗e4! (in *Informator* I gave only the cooperative 47 ℤe2(?) ♘c3+) 47...♘e3+ 48 ♔e2! ♘xg2 49 ℤxd4 ♘f4+! (49...♗f4 50 ℤd3!) 50 ♔f1! h3 51 ♔f2 h2 52 ℤh8 or 50...g4 51 ♗c6! ♗e5 52 ℤd7 ℤxc6! 53 ℤxc6 g3 54 ℤc8! h3 55 ℤf8+ ♔g5 56 ℤg8+ ♔h6 57 ℤg4!.

47...♗f4 48 ℤdc2 ♘e3 49 ♔f2?!

Desperate resistance: White returns the exchange – if only to avoid losing the g2-pawn. 49 ℤ2c6 was hopeless: 49...ℤxc6 50 ℤxc6 ♘xg2 51 ♔f2 (51 ℤxa6? h3 52 ♔f2 ♘e1!) 51...h3! (my earlier 51...♘e3 was also good) 52 ♗f1 ♘e3+ 53 ♔g3 ♘f4 54 ℤxa6 (54 ♔h2 d3!) 54...♔e5 55 ♗xb5 ♗g1! 56 ℤa7 d3 and wins.

49 ♖2c5 ♘xg2 50 ♖f8+ ♔g7 (50...♔e7?! 51 ♖h8!) 51 ♖cc8 ♗e3 52 ♔d1 ♘f4 53 ♗e4 was objectively more resilient, but here too after 53...♘d5 White would hardly have managed to hold out.

49...♗g3+! 50 ♔g1 ♘xc2 51 ♖xc2

Two pawns down, White is not even saved by the opposite-coloured bishops.

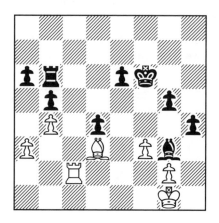

51...g4!?

Aiming to create a pair of connected passed pawns in the centre as soon as possible, in order to conclude the game without an adjournment and a resumption.

52 fxg4 ♔g5 53 ♔f1 e5 54 ♔e2

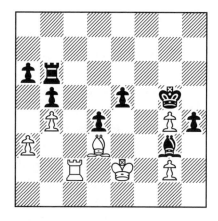

54...♔xg4

In the heat of the moment after the game I condemned this 'time-trouble error' and gave

a 'clear win' with an exchange sacrifice – 54...♖f6 55 ♗f5 ♖xf5 56 gxf5 e4! 57 ♖c5 ♗f4 58 ♖d5 d3+ 59 ♔e1 ♔f6 60 ♔d1 ♗g5 (the first zugzwang) 61 ♔e1 ♗c1 62 ♔d1 (62 ♔f2 ♗d2! 63 ♔f1 ♔g5 – the second, decisive zugzwang) 62...♗xa3 63 ♖d6+ (63 ♔d2 ♗xb4+ 64 ♔e3 ♗c3 65 ♔xe4 d2 etc) 63...♔xf5 64 ♖xa6 ♗b2! 65 ♔d2 (65 ♖b6 e3) 65...♗e5 and wins. Elegant – but not obligatory.

55 ♖c8 ♖f6 56 ♗e4

And here I condemned this 'time-trouble error in reply' and suggested 'resisting' by 56 ♖g8+ ♔f4 57 ♖e8. However, after 57...♖c6! 58 ♖f8+ ♔g5 59 ♖g8+ ♔h6 60 ♖h8+ ♔g7 61 ♖h7+ ♔g8 and ...♖c3 the game concludes.

56...♖f2+ 57 ♔d3 ♗f4 (57...♖b2!) **58 ♖g8+ ♔h5 59 ♗d5 ♗g5**

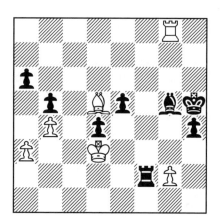

60 ♔e4

Little more resistance would have been offered by 60 ♖h8+ ♔g4 61 ♗e6+ ♔g3 62 ♖g8 ♖d2+ 63 ♔e4 ♖e2+ 64 ♔d3 ♖e3+ 65 ♔d2 ♔f4 or 64 ♔f5 d3 65 ♖xg5+ ♔f2 66 ♖g7 d2 67 ♗b3 e4 and wins.

60...♖xg2

Here the game was adjourned and Gelfand sealed **61 ♔xe5**, after which the simplest is 61...♗f6+! 62 ♔xf6 ♖xg8 63 ♗xg8 h3 64 ♔e5 h2 65 ♗d5 d3 or 62 ♔f4 ♖xg8 63 ♗xg8 d3, intending ...♗b2xa3. Without resuming the game, White resigned (**0-1**).

After this win I reached 4 out of 5 and finally assumed the sole lead. But then I slowed up, drawing with Speelman (cf. *Game No.85*, note to Black's 8th move) and Bareev – and I was caught by Beliavsky and by Karpov, who had won three games in a row. With 5 out of 7, we were a point ahead of our nearest pursuers – Ivanchuk and Timman. But here the ex-champion's strength deserted him. In the 8th round he lost to Timman, whereas I overcame Short, and our paths diverged...

In this tournament Nigel did not play very well: for him the main thing was the forthcoming semi-final Candidates match with Karpov in April. But our clashes were always of a crucial nature.

1 e4

Earlier against Short I almost exclusively played 1 d4 (*Game No.25*) or 1 c4 (*Game No.48*), but now I was ready once again, as in Tilburg 1991, to battle against his beloved French. But my opponent replied differently.

1...e5 2 ♘f3 ♘c6 3 d4 exd4 4 ♘xd4 ♗c5
(4...♘f6 is not in Short's style – *Game Nos.70, 71, 81*) **5 ♗e3**

The main variation from the old opening guides. Later I developed the line 5 ♘xc6 ♕f6 6 ♕d2 dxc6 7 ♘c3!? and now 7...♗e6 8 ♘a4! ♖d8 9 ♗d3 ♗d4 10 0-0, as in games of mine with Short (11th and 17th match games, London 1993) and Yusupov (Horgen 1994), or 7...♘e7 8 ♕f4, which was tested against Topalov (Las Palmas 1996) and Anand (Frankfurt (rapid) 1999). In the end Black began playing 7...♗d4!.

5...♕f6 6 c3 ♘ge7 7 ♗c4 (the 'newly fashionable' 7 g3 did not attract me) **7...0-0**

Short extremely rarely chose the main line – 7...♘e5 8 ♗e2 ♕g6 9 0-0, when after 9...d5?! 10 ♘h5! ♕xe4 for the 1990 match with Karpov I stored up the novelty 11 ♘d2! ♕d3 (11...♕h4?! 12 ♗xf7+!) 12 ♘4f3!, which appeared a year later (Sveshnikov-Varavin, Anapa 1991), but after 9...d6! White's searches for an advantage came to nothing.

8 0-0 ♗b6

At that time quite a popular line.

Against the usual 9 ♘a3 my opponent devised the interesting reply 9...♘xd4!? 10 cxd4 d5! 11 exd5 ♖d8 12 ♕h5 h6 and ...♗f5 with a comfortable game (Chandler-Short, 1st match game, London 1991). Even less good is 9 ♔h1?! ♖d8! 10 ♕h5 h6 11 ♘d2 d5! 12 exd5 ♘xd4, and already Black has a slight plus (Kasparov-Kamsky, Tilburg 1991).

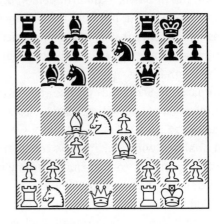

9 ♘c2!?

A novelty, prepared together with Makarychev. White prevents the freeing advance ...d7-d5 and hopes, after playing f2-f4, to gradually develop pressure in the centre and on the kingside. In this case the black queen will be uncomfortable on f6 – this is the place for the knight.

9...d6 10 ♗xb6

10 f4 ♗e6 11 ♗d3, which occurred later,

nevertheless allows 11...d5! 12 e5 (12 ♗xb6?! dxe4!) 12...♗xe3+ 13 ♘xe3 ♕h6 14 ♖f3 g6 with approximate equality.

10...axb6 11 f4

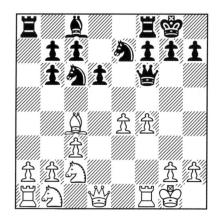

11...g5?!

Rather a wild move – with a pawn from in front of the king! Sometimes also in the Sicilian the f4-pawn is undermined, in order to win the e5-point, but here this advance is questionable and it may not give sufficient positional compensation for the weakening of the king's fortress.

Apparently Short did not like the natural continuation 11...♗e6! 12 ♗d3 ♖xa2 13 ♖xa2 ♗xa2 14 ♘d2 ♗e6 15 ♘e3, which I had analysed with Makarychev, considering White's position to be quite promising. Black's extra pawn, especially since it is doubled, is for the moment not felt, the opponent's forces are cramped, and White can calmly prepare an attack on the king. That said, after 15...♕h6 (Lastin-Grischuk, Moscow 1996) Black can hope for a successful defence.

12 f5

The drawbacks to Black's plan are more clearly emphasised by 12 ♘ba3!? ♗e6 13 ♗xe6 ♕xe6 14 ♘b5 or 12...gxf4 13 ♘b5 (the weakness of the c7-pawn is typical of the set-up with ...♕f6), when the counterattack

13...♖a5! 14 ♘xc7 ♖g5 is refuted by 15 ♕d2! ♘e5 16 ♗e2 ♗h3 17 ♘e1 ♖c8 18 ♘d5 ♘xd5 19 exd5 ♘g6 20 ♔h1 – an interesting combinative solution! But I was attracted by playing for a bind.

12...♘e5 13 ♗e2 ♗d7

13...d5?! is weak, not because of my *Informator* suggestion 14 ♘d2 (here 14...♕d6! is unclear), but in view of the simple 14 exd5! ♖d8 15 ♘e3 or 14...b5 15 ♘e3 ♖a4 16 b4.

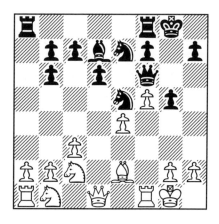

14 c4!

With the intention of ♘c3. 14 ♘e3 ♗c6 15 ♘d2 is more passive: 15...♖fd8 (but not the terrible *Informator* blunder 15...d5(?) in view of 16 exd5 ♘xd5 17 ♘e4 and wins) 16 ♗c4 b5 or 16 c4 h6.

14...g4?!

Too ambitious: Short aims for activity on the kingside, but this is not his sector of the board. In addition, now White acquires a transit point at f4. It was safer to play 14...♗a4!? 15 b3 (15 ♘c3!?) 15...♗c6 16 ♕d4! and ♘c3 with a small advantage for White.

15 ♘c3 h5

15...♔h8!? and ...♖g8 was somewhat better, not conclusively exposing the king: for example, 16 ♘e3 ♖g8 17 g3!? ♕g5 18 ♖f4 h5 19 a4! and b2-b4-b5.

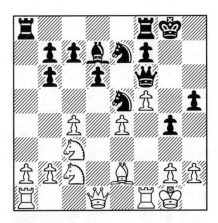

16 ♕d2 ♔h8 17 ♕f4 (here also 17 a4!? and b2-b4-b5 is interesting) **17...♗c6 18 ♘e3 ♘d7?**

A fatal weakening of the g4-pawn: Nigel obviously underestimated the bishop sacrifice, which gives White a decisive attack. 18...♖g8 was correct, although after 19 a4! ♘d7 20 b4 with the threat of b4-b5 Black has a difficult position, as a result of his reckless strategy.

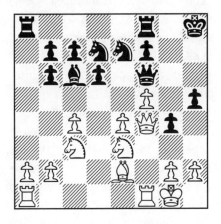

19 ♗xg4!

19 h3!? gxh3 20 ♖f3! ♖g8 (20...hxg2? 21 ♖h3 and wins) 21 ♖xh3 ♔g7 22 ♗xh5 is also clearly advantageous to White, but the piece sacrifice is stronger, and in addition it disheartened the opponent.

19...hxg4 (it is hard to call 19...h4 'more

resilient': White replies 20 ♘ed5 ♗xd5 21 exd5 with the threats of ♖f3 and ♘e4) **20 ♘xg4**

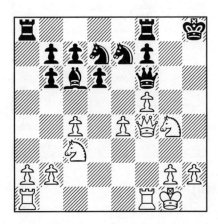

The positional play has concluded, and a mating attack begins.

20...♕h4 (20...♕d4+ 21 ♔h1 or 21 ♖f2 with the lethal threats of ♕h6+ and ♖d1) **21 ♖f3 ♘g6 22 ♖e3! ♕xg4**

I was already expecting capitulation, but Short suddenly began resisting fiercely. After the alternative 22...♔g7 White had four (!) 'roads to Rome': (a) 23 ♖g3 with the threat of fxg6; (b) 23 ♖af1 with the idea of 23...♕xg4 24 ♖g3 ♕h4(h5) 25 ♖h3; (c) 23 f6+ ♘xf6 24 ♘xf6 ♖h8 25 h3; and, finally (d) 23 fxg6 ♕xg4 (23...f6(xg6) 24 ♖h3!) 24 gxf7 ♕h5 25 ♖f5! ♕h4 26 ♖af1! ♖h8 27 ♖g5+ ♔f8 28 ♖g8+! ♔e7 29 ♘d5+ ♗xd5 30 exd5+ ♘e5 31 f8♕+ ♖xf8 32 ♖fxf8 ♕xh2+ 33 ♔f1 ♕h1+ 34 ♔e2.

23 ♕h6+ ♔g8 24 ♖h3

24 ♖g3!? was even better: 24...♕xg3 25 hxg3 ♘ge5 26 ♕g5+ ♔h7 27 ♔f2 ♘g6 28 ♖h1+ ♔g7 29 ♕h6+! (I underestimated this resource) 29...♔f6 30 fxg6 fxg6 31 ♖h4 and wins.

24...♕xh3 (after 24...♘f6, apart from 25 fxg6 fxg6 26 ♖g3, 25 ♖f1! is also strong) **25 gxh3 ♘ge5 26 f6** (26 ♔h1? f6) **26...♘xf6 27 ♕xf6 ♖ae8**

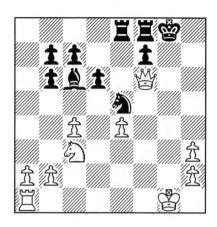

28 ♔h1!

Vacating a square for the rook and preventing 28...♖e6? in view of 29 ♖g1+ ♘g6 30 ♖xg6+. Black's hopes of setting up a fortress with rook and bishop for the queen are unfeasible.

28...♘g6 29 h4! ♖e6 30 ♕g5 ♖fe8 31 h5!? (the steady 31 ♖e1(f1) was also possible, but I took the direct course) **31...♖e5 32 ♕h6 ♖xe4!** (a desperate chance) **33 ♘xe4 ♖xe4 34 ♔g1**

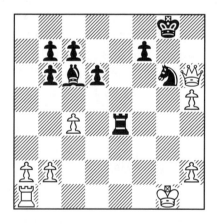

34...♘e5

34...♖g4+!? was rather more cunning: 35 ♔f1! (35 ♔f2 ♖g2+ 36 ♔e3! is also possible, but not 36 ♔f1? ♘e5 with the idea of 37 ♖e1? ♖f2+!) 35...♘f4 (35...♘e5 36 ♖c1) 36 a4! and ♖a3-g3, winning.

35 ♕g5+ ♔h7 36 ♕f5+ ♔h6 37 ♖f1 (37 ♖c1!?) **37...♖e2 38 ♕f6+** (38 ♖f4!?) **38...♔h7 39 ♕g5 ♗e4** (not 39...♖xb2 on account of 40 ♖xf7+! ♘xf7 41 ♕g6+, ♕f6+ and ♕xb2) **40 h6 ♗g6**

After the alternative 40...♖g2+ 41 ♕xg2 ♗xg2 42 ♔xg2 ♔xh6 43 b3 White would have converted his extra exchange without any problems.

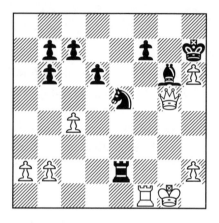

41 h4! (the second of the doubled h-pawns also comes in useful) **41...♖e4 42 h5** (42 ♖f4!?) **42...♖g4+ 43 ♕xg4 ♘xg4 44 hxg6+ fxg6 45 ♖f7+ ♔xh6 46 ♖xc7 ♘e5 47 ♖xb7 ♘xc4 48 b3 1-0**

An interesting opening and a tense middlegame battle!

That day Beliavsky drew and fell half a point behind. In our 'battle of the leaders' which took place in the 9th round he employed a novelty in the 'Seville Variation' of the Grünfeld Defence with 12 ♗xf7+!?, but I gained a draw (cf. *Game No.28*, note to White's 16th move).

It was time for a finishing spurt, and the 10th round decided the outcome of the event: Beliavsky lost with White to Yusupov (and 'in despair' he lost all his remaining games), whereas I was able to crush the 26-year-old 'home' player Miguel Illescas.

Game 89
G.Kasparov-M.Illescas
Linares, 10th Round, 9.3.1992
Sicilian Defence B45

1 e4 c5 2 ②f3 e6 3 d4 cxd4 4 ②xd4 ②c6 5 ②c3

The opponent was apparently expecting 5 ②b5 ②f6 6 ②1c3 d6, transposing into the Sveshnikov Variation, which was his main weapon.

5...②f6 6 ②xc6 bxc6 7 e5 ②d5 8 ②e4 ➌c7 9 f4 ➌b6 10 c4

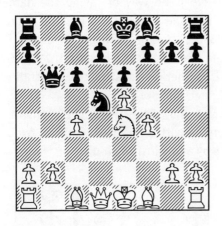

10...②e3

The character of the play in the main line with 10...②b4+ is not to everyone's taste: 11 ③e2 f5 12 exf6 (the old 12 ②f2 ②a6 13 ③f3 ②e7 14 ②e3 ②c5 15 ②xc5 ➌xc5 is also unclear) 12...②xf6 13 ②e3: for example, 13...➌d8 14 ②d6+ ②xd6 15 ➌xd6 ②b7 16 ③d1 (16 ③d1!?), and in search of counter-play Black has to sacrifice a pawn – 16...c5! 17 ➌xc5 ②e4 (Akopian-Radjabov, Heraklion 2007; Najer-Khairullin, Plovdiv 2008).

11 ➌d3 ②f5

A logical move: Black plans to occupy the d5-point, keeping ...②b4+ in reserve. After 11...②b4+ 12 ②d2 ②a6 13 ②xb4! ➌xb4+ 14 ③f2 ➌xb2+ (14...②d5? 15 ➌b3!, Chandler-

Nunn, British League 1999) 15 ②e2 the endgame favours White – 15...②f5 16 ②ab1 ➌d4+ 17 ➌xd4 ②xd4 18 ②d3, as does the sharp 15...②xc4 16 ②hd1! ➌b6+ 17 ➌d4 0-0 18 ②c5 (Macieja-Rogozenko, Bundesliga 2009).

12 g4

12 ②d2!? is probably stronger, since in the event of 12...➌xb2 13 ②b1 ➌d4 14 ➌xd4 ②xd4 15 c5 White has powerful pressure for the pawn (Ivanchuk-Radjabov, Bazna 2009).

12...②d4 13 ②g2! (13 b3 ②b7 14 ②e3(b2) allows Black time for 14...c5 15 ②g2 ②d8! and ...d7-d5) **13...h5!**

Gaining control of the f5-point. At that time the theory of this variation was only just developing, and the players were groping for the correct path. 13...②b7 was also played, after which it transpired that the sudden 14 b4!! a5 (14...②xb4+? 15 ③f1! and wins) 15 ②b2 c5 16 b5 is very strong.

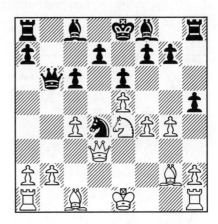

14 g5

A novelty, hastily devised before the game. If 14 h3, then 14...②b7 is now completely safe (15 b4?! hxg4!). 14 ③d1? hxg4 is clearly bad, when 15 ②e3? is not possible on account of the double attack 15...➌xb2. But 14 ③f1!? hxg4 15 ②e3 c5 16 b4! is interesting, initiating a tactical fight (Stellwagen-van der Wiel, Wijk aan Zee 2003).

14...♗b7?!

A routine reply. I examined two other possibilities: 14...h4 15 ♗d2!? (instead of the insipid 15 b3) 15...♕xb2 16 0-0 ♘f5 17 ♖ab1 (the *Informator* suggestion 17 ♗c3?! ♕b6+ 18 ♖f2 is less accurate) 17...♕d4+ 18 ♕xd4 ♘xd4 19 ♖fd1, and 14...♘f5!? (the most consistent) 15 ♗d2!? (15 ♘g3, given in *Informator*, is weaker because of 15...♗c5!) 15...♕xb2 16 ♖b1 ♕d4 (16...♕xa2?! 17 0-0 is dangerous) 17 ♕xd4 ♘xd4 18 ♔f2, in both cases with good compensation for the pawn and chances of an advantage.

15 ♗e3

Now the b2-pawn is poisoned (after 15...♕xb2? 16 0-0 c5 17 ♖ab1 the bishop on b7 is hanging). 15 ♗d2!? also came into consideration: 15...c5 16 ♗c3 ♘f5 17 0-0-0 0-0-0 18 ♕d2 ♕a6 19 b3 d5 20 exd6 ♗xd6 (Meier-Socko, Kallithea 2008) 21 ♕f2! with an enduring advantage for White. But the variation in the game seemed prettier to me.

15...♘c2+ 16 ♔f2 ♘xe3 17 ♕xe3

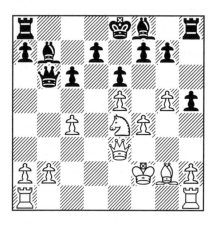

17...♕xb2+?

The decisive mistake: with the queens on Black is absolutely defenceless! Therefore 17...c5?! is also weak: 18 ♖hd1! ♖d8 (18...♕xb2+? 19 ♔g1 and wins) 19 ♖d2 or 18...0-0-0 19 ♖ab1 etc. 17...♕xe3+! 18 ♔xe3 c5 was essential, although after 19 g6! (but

not 19 ♖hd1?! d5! 20 exd6 0-0-0 with equality) 19...fxg6 20 ♖hg1 ♖b8 (20...0-0-0? 21 ♘g5!) 21 b3 ♗e7 22 ♖ad1 Black would have had to fight for a draw in an inferior ending.

18 ♔g3! (the king gets out of harm's way)
18...♗a6

An instructive variation goes 18...h4+ 19 ♔h3 ♗c8 20 ♖ab1 ♕c2 21 ♖hc1 ♕a4 22 ♘d6+ ♗xd6 23 exd6 ♕a5 24 ♗e4, and Black is on the verge of collapse.

19 ♖ab1 h4+ 20 ♔h3 ♕c2 (not 20...♕a3? 21 ♕xa3 ♗xa3 22 c5!, when the bishop is trapped: 22...♗d3 23 ♘d6+ ♔e7 24 ♖b3) **21 ♖hc1 ♕a4 22 ♕c3! ♗a3**

There is no way of saving the game: if 22...♗c8 the simplest is 23 ♘d6+ ♗xd6 24 exd6 0-0 25 ♖b3 with the threat of ♖a3, while after 22...♗e7, apart from 23 ♘d6+ or 23 ♖b3, there is the attractive 23 ♗f3!? with the new threat of ♗d1.

23 ♖c2 ♗e7 24 ♖b3 (for the moment not hurrying with 24 ♘d6+!? ♗xd6 25 exd6 0-0 26 ♖b3 and wins) **24...0-0**

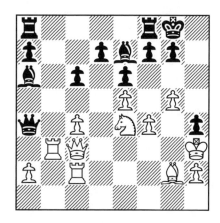

25 ♘f6+!

Of course, 25 ♘d6!? ♗xd6 26 exd6 would also have won, but after a long think I could not deny myself the pleasure of playing for mate.

25...gxf6 (25...♔h8 26 ♕e1! and ♕xh4+) **26 gxf6 ♗c5**

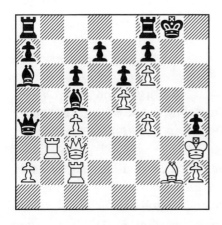

27 ♗e4!

There would also have been a spectacular finish after 27 ♔xh4!? ♖fb8 28 ♕g3+ ♔f8 29 ♗f3 ♖xb3 30 ♖g2! ♔e8 31 ♕g8+ ♗f8 32 ♕xf7+! ♔xf7 33 ♗h5 mate – an interesting mating construction.

27...♖fb8 28 ♔xh4 (28 ♕f3 or 28 ♖g2+ was more forceful) **28...♔f8 29 ♖g2 ♕xc4**

29...♔e8 30 ♖g8+ ♗f8 31 ♖xf8+! ♔xf8 32 ♕g3 would also have led to mate. The end could have been delayed by 29...♖xb3! 30 axb3 ♕a3 31 ♕g3 ♔e8 32 ♕g8+ ♗f8 33 ♖g7 ♔d8 34 ♗xc6! dxc6 (34...♖b8 35 ♕xf7) 35 ♖xf7, and if 35...♔e8, then 36 ♖h7, nevertheless mating.

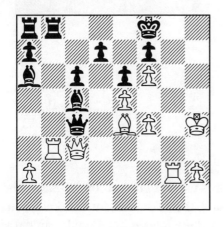

30 ♕xc4 (30 ♕g3 would have mated more quickly, but I was carried away by another

variation) **30...♗xc4 31 ♗h7 ♗f2+** (or 31...♔e8 32 ♖g8+ ♗f8 33 ♖xf8+! ♔xf8 34 ♖g3) **32 ♔h5**

After the 'spite' check 32...♗e2+ 33 ♔h6 mate is inevitable, and so Black resigned **(1-0)**.

The leading trio was now Kasparov – 7½ out of 10; Karpov and Timman – 6. In the 11th round I beat Yusupov in a King's Indian (cf. *Game No.66*, note to White's 8th move) and thereby won against all four Candidates!

In the 12th, penultimate round Salov chose against me the Sveshnikov Variation of the Sicilian, which Makarychev and I had analysed in 1991. I was ready for a dispute in the sharp line with 9 ♗xf6 gxf6 10 ♘d5 and from the opening I gained an enduring advantage. But when the opponent attacked my f4-pawn with his knight, instead of the obvious 21 fxe5 I suddenly replied 21 0-0-0?! (for other instances of late castling – cf. *Game Nos.12 and 62*). Ivanchuk, who was watching the game, froze in astonishment with his mouth agape. Standing up from the board, I asked him: 'What, is the move against the rules?' Vassily was embarrassed – and he rushed off. In the end I reached an endgame with an extra pawn, but in the second time scramble I missed excellent winning chances.

Then at the finish I beat Ljubojevic with Black (cf. *Game No.82*, note to White's 6th move), and for the first time in the history of Linares I won the tournament by a margin of two points. So much for any concept of 'first among equals'!

In April, on the same stage in Linares, the Candidates semi-final matches took place. With the identical score 6-4 Timman won against Yusupov, and Short – against the great Karpov! This sensational event provoked a genuine furore in the chess world. The ex-champion was let down by his nerves and incredible time-trouble. Already in Reggio Emilia and Linares it was apparent that he was in poor form. This also showed itself in the match with Short... At the time many thought that this was the end of the Karpov era. No one could have imagined how chess history would change direction just a year later...

Dortmund Fever

International Tournament in Dortmund (16–26 April 1992): 1–2. **Kasparov** and Ivanchuk – 6 out of 9; 3. Bareev – 5½; 4. Anand – 5; 5–6. Kamsky and Salov – 4½; 7. Hübner – 4; 8–9. Adams and Shirov – 3½; 10. Piket – 2½.

Although lacking the elite status of Lina-res, the short super-tournament of the ju-bilee 20th Dortmund festival gave an oppor-tunity for talented young players to show their worth. Three 'veterans' – the 43-year-old Hübner, the 29-year-old Kasparov and the almost 28-year-old Salov – were opposed by players whose average age barely ex-ceeded twenty. 'Young lions surround the leader of the herd' joked a reporter for the newspaper *Frankfurter Allgemeine*.

For the first time in a serious event I saw Shirov, Adams and the 16-year-old Kramnik (he became one of the winners of the open tournament). All three arrived in Dortmund from a strong junior open in the English town of Oakham, where Shirov brilliantly took first place and Kramnik shared second. A worthy performance by former pupils of the Botvinnik-Kasparov school!

In the initial game I was in fact paired with Black against the 19-year-old Riga grandmaster Alexey Shirov, who was already No.8 in the world rating list. A duel between two King's Indian players was in prospect,

and all the indications were that it would be an uncompromising battle.

Game 90
A.Shirov-G.Kasparov
Dortmund, 1st Round, 17.04.1992
King's Indian Defence E86

1 d4 ♘f6 2 c4 g6 3 ♘c3 ♗g7 4 e4 d6 5 f3 0-0 6 ♗e3 e5

Shirov himself has successfully played the gambit variation 6...c5!?. Apart from the move in the game I also tried 6...♘c6 (Game No.51 in *Garry Kasparov on Garry Kasparov Part I*), 6...a6 (cf. *Game No.91*), 6...c6 (Game No.8 in *Kasparov vs. Karpov 1988-2009*), and 6...♘bd7 (*Game No.68*).

7 ♘ge2 (7 d5 – *Game Nos.43, 84, 92*) **7...c6 8 ♕d2 ♘bd7 9 0-0-0** (the most aggressive plan if White rejects d4-d5; 9 ♖d1 – *Game No.98*) **9...a6**

One of the *tabiyas* of the Sämisch Varia-tion.

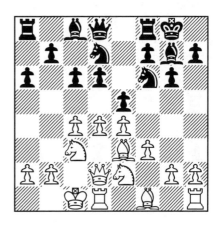

10 ♔b1

It is useful to defend the a2-pawn and to vacate the c1-square for the knight. If 10 dxe5 there follows 10...♘xe5! – an old idea of Geller's (a topical example is Ljubojevic-Timman, Linares 1992).

The frontal attack 10 h4 is more dangerous for Black: 10...b5 11 h5 ♕a5! 12 ♗h6 ♗xh6! 13 ♕xh6 b4 14 ♘b1 ♕xa2 15 ♘g3 (15 ♖d2 ♘b6!) 15...♘b6 16 c5! ♘c4 17 ♖d2 ♘xd2(?) 18 ♘xd2 ♕a1+ 19 ♔c2 ♘a1+ 20 ♔c1 ♘b3+ with perpetual check (Beliavsky-Kasparov, Linares 1993).

But Shirov chose a more popular, positional plan, which was also in Kramnik's armoury.

10...b5 11 ♘c1

Until the mid-1990s this was played automatically, but then, largely through the efforts of Graf, the sharp 11 c5!? came to the fore.

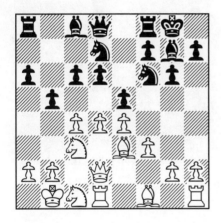

11...exd4!

The correct move: I sensed that Black had a good game, and that the centre had to be opened. The old 11...♖e8 can be met by either 12 d5 (as in the source game of the variation, Khasin-Boleslavsky, Gorky 1954), or 12 dxe5 (Barbero-Schandorff, Copenhagen 1991). And if 11...♗b7?!, then 12 dxe5 is even more unpleasant: 12...♘xe5 (12...dxe5?

13 g4!) 13 ♕xd6 ♖xd6?! (13...♘d5! is more resilient) 14 ♖xd6 (Kramnik-Remlinger, Gausdal 1992). 11...bxc4 12 ♗xc4 is also unattractive for Black (Kramnik-Akopian, Oakham 1992).

12 ♗xd4 ♖e8

Quite sound, but 12...b4! was more accurate: 13 ♘a4 c5 14 ♗xf6 (if 14 ♗e3, then 14...♘e8 15 h4 ♕c7 16 h5 ♗b7 17 hxg6 fxg6! or 17 b3 ♗c6 18 ♘b2 a5 – as Makarychev and I established, Black has good counterplay) 14...♗xf6 15 ♕xd6 ♗e7! 16 ♕g3 (16 ♕d5?! ♖a7) 16...♗h4! 17 ♕h3 ♗e7 18 ♕g3 ♗h4 19 ♕h3 ½-½ (Kramnik-Kasparov, Linares 1993). And although this quick draw greatly enraged Senor Rentero, after it the variation disappeared from serious tournament play.

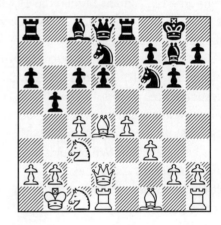

13 ♗xf6?!

Played after not much thought. To be honest, the exchange of the important dark-squared bishop for the knight was something that I did not consider at all – back in my youth, periodic chess contacts with Gufeld instilled in me the thought that such exchanges could not be good. But Shirov demonstrates a concrete approach to the solving of problems, typical of modern chess: he hopes that his extra pawn will outweigh Black's activity. Moreover, other attempts do not promise White any particular dividends:

1) 13 ♗f2 ♗f8 14 h4 (not 14 ♘b3?! b4 15 ♘a4 c5 16 ♗g3 ♖e6, Meshkov-Petrushin, Kazan 1980) 14...♘e5 15 c5 (Riazantsev-Sakaev, Linares Open 2001) 15...d5! or 14...♗b7!? (with the idea of ...b5-b4 and ...c6-c5) 15 a3 ♘e5, and Black is perfectly alright;

2) 13 ♘b3!? (a more energetic move, introduced by Sakaev in the same year, 1992) 13...♖b8 (not my *Informator* suggestion 13...♘b6 because of 14 c5! ♘c4 15 ♕c1 d5 16 g4) 14 ♗a7 ♖b7 15 ♗f2 (Jobava-Smirin, Beer Sheva 2005) 15...♗f8! 16 c5 b4 17 ♘a4 d5, or 13...♗f8! with the intention of ...b5-b4 and ...c6-c5, and if 14 c5, then 14...dxc5 15 ♗xc5 ♗xc5 16 ♘xc5 ♕b6 with equality.

13...♕xf6!

The right way! Strangely enough, with the queens on – 13...♗xf6 14 ♕xd6 ♕b6 15 ♘b3 it is more difficult for Black to develop his initiative: 15...bxc4 16 ♗xc4 ♗xc3 (16...♗e5!?) 17 bxc3 ♘e5 18 ♗e2 (18 ♕d4? c5!, but 18 ♖d4!?, a move of Slovakian correspondence players, is good) 18...♖b8 (my *Informator* 18...♗e6(?!) is worse because of 19 ♕c5! ♕b8 20 ♔a1! ♗xb3 21 ♖b1) 19 ♔a1 ♗e6 20 ♖b1, and White holds on.

14 ♕xd6 ♕xd6 15 ♖xd6 ♘e5

It is already not so easy for White to find the correct path.

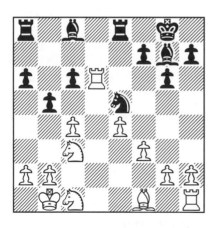

16 f4?!

A pseudo-active move, leading to unnecessary difficulties. 16 cxb5 axb5 17 a3 (to my *Informator* 17 ♘d3(?) there is the strong reply 17...b4! 18 ♘e2 ♗f8) 17...♗f8 18 ♖d1 (later this was played by some correspondence players) was steadier, although after 18...♗e6 Black has excellent compensation for the pawn.

16...♘g4!

An unexpected outflanking manoeuvre, with the threat of ...♘f2xe4 or ...♗xc3! and ...♖xe4. After 16...♘xc4 17 ♗xc4 bxc4 18 ♘1e2! (my earlier 18 e5 is worse in view of 18...♗f5+ 19 ♔a1 ♖ad8) White would have emerged unscathed.

17 e5 ♘f2! 18 ♖g1 ♗f5+ (or first 18...b4) 19 ♔a1 b4! 20 ♘a4

20 ♘3e2? ♗f8 or 20 ♘d1?! ♗f8 21 ♖d2 ♘e4 was weak.

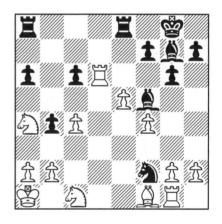

20...f6!

This undermining move (with the idea of 21 exf6? ♖e1!) was obviously underestimated by Shirov. After the opening of the position it is very difficult for White to coordinate his pieces.

21 e6?

Confusion: by returning the pawn, White reconciles himself to an inferior ending. It was essential to play 21 g4! ♘xg4! 22 ♗d3 fxe5! 23 ♗xf5 gxf5 24 h3 exf4! 25 hxg4 f3 26 gxf5 (but not 26 ♘d3? ♖ad8! or 26 g5?! f2 27 ♖f1 ♖e1 28 ♖d1 ♖xd1 29 ♖xd1 ♖e8 30 ♘d3 ♗d4 31 ♔b1 ♖e2! etc) 26...f2 27 ♖f1 ♖e1 28 ♖d1 ♖ae8 29 ♘d3 ♖xd1+ 30 ♖xd1 ♖e2, when the formidable passed f2-pawn together with the powerful bishop more than compensate Black for the piece deficit (also, for the moment the knight on a4 is out of play): 31 ♔b1?! ♖d2! 32 ♖f1 ♖xd3 33 ♗xf2 ♖d4 34 ♖g2 ♔f7 35 ♖h2 h6 etc. But White can gain a draw, by exchanging his f-pawn for the potentially dangerous h-pawn and giving up his knight for the f2-pawn: 31 ♖h1 ♗d4 32 ♔b1 ♔g7 33 c5 ♗f6 34 b3 ♗d4 35 ♘b6 ♗c3 36 f6+! ♔xf6 37 ♘xf2 ♖b2+ 38 ♔c1 ♖xf2 39 ♖xh7.

At the board both players saw the variations with 21 g4 ♘xg4, but to Alexey the passed f2-pawn seemed too dangerous (White is forced to find the only moves to save himself), and instead of this he tried at least to slightly block the position.

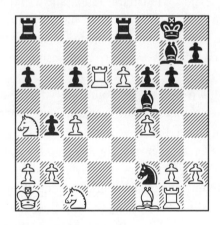

21...♖xe6

21...♗xe6!? (for the moment retaining both rooks) is also promising: 22 ♗e2 ♘e4 (22...♗f8!?) 23 ♖dd1 f5, or 22 ♘c5 (Stohl) 22...♗f8! 23 ♖xc6 ♖ac8 24 ♖xc8 ♗xc8 25 ♘5d3 ♗f5! 26 c5 ♘xd3 27 ♗xd3 ♗xc5 and ...♗c8! with an enduring initiative.

22 ♖xe6 (22 c5 ♖xd6 23 cxd6 ♖d8 and ...♖xd6 or 23...♗f8!? 24 d7 ♖d8 and ....♗xd7 was no better for White) **22...♗xe6 23 ♗e2 f5 24 ♘b3 ♗f7 25 ♘a5**

After my *Informator* suggestion 25 c5, there is the strong reply 25...♗d5!, and if 25 ♗d3 ♖d8 26 c5 (Stohl), then 26...♘e4!.

25...♖d8

Previously I attached an exclamation mark to this move, but 25...♖e8!? 26 ♗f3 ♘d3 27 ♖d1 ♘xf4 followed by ...g6-g5 also came into consideration, when all Black's pieces, including his two long-range bishops, are extremely active.

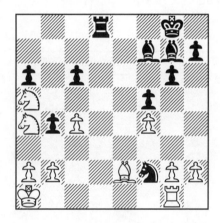

26 ♖f1?

In severe time-trouble Shirov makes a decisive mistake. While correctly pointing out in *Informator* that the variation 26 ♘xc6? ♖d2! was unsuitable – if 27 ♗f3 there is 27...♗e8! 28 ♗d5+ ♔f8 and ...♘d1(d3), I overlooked the most resilient defence – 26 ♔b1! (escaping from the corner) 26...♘e4! (26...♖d2 27 ♖e1 and ♘b3) 27 ♖d1 ♖xd1+ 28 ♗xd1 ♘d2+ 29 ♔c1 ♘xc4 30 ♘xc6, and although after 30...♘e3 31 ♗f3 ♗f8 32 b3 ♗d6 Black retains the advantage, White has far more chances of a draw.

26...♘g4! 27 ♖d1 (there is nothing else) **27...♖xd1+** (27...♖e8!?) **28 ♗xd1 ♘e3!** (28...♘xh2?! 29 ♘c5! and ♘xa6) **29 ♗f3**

♘xc4 30 ♘xc6

Things are hopeless for White after 30 ♘xc4?! ♗xc4 31 ♗xc6 ♗d4! (threatening ...♗b5) 32 ♔b1 ♗d3+ 33 ♔c2 ♗e3+ 34 ♔d1 ♗b5! 35 ♗d5+ ♔g7 36 b3 ♗xf4 37 h3 ♔f6 etc.

30...a5! 31 ♘d8

Alas, with his king stuck in the 'box' on a1 (31 ♔b1? ♘d2+ and ...♘xf3), White will never be in time: 31 ♗e2 ♘e3! (far more forceful than my earlier 31...♔f8) 32 ♗f3 ♘c2+ 33 ♔b1 ♘e1, or 31 g3 ♗e8! 32 ♗d5+ ♔h8 33 ♔b1 ♘e3! 34 ♗h1 ♘f1 35 ♘c5 ♗xc6 36 ♗xc6 ♘xh2 37 ♗g2 ♘g4 with the threats of ...♘e3 and ...♗d4-f2.

31...♘d2!

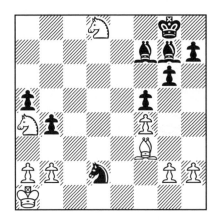

32 ♗c6

If 32 ♘xf7 I had two ways to my goal:

1) 32...♔xf7 33 ♗d5+ ♔e7 34 ♘b6 (not 34 ♗g8 ♗d4, cutting off the knight) 34...♔d6 35 ♗g8 ♔c5 36 ♘a4+ ♔b5 37 ♗f7 ♗d4 or 36 ♘d7+ ♔c6 37 ♘e5+ (37 ♘b8+ ♔d6!, and if 38 ♗xh7?, then 38...a4!, mating) 37...♗xe5 38 fxe5 h6 39 ♗h7 ♔d5 40 ♗xg6 ♔xe5, and with his king on a1 White has no saving chances;

2) 32...♘xf3 33 gxf3 (after Stohl's move 33 ♘d6 the simplest is 33...♘e1(h4) 34 g3 ♘f3! etc) 33...♔xf7 34 ♘c5 ♗d4! (much stronger than 34...♗f8 35 ♘d3 etc given in *Informa-*

tor) 35 ♘d3 ♔f6 36 h3 ♗e3 37 ♔b1 g5! 38 ♔c2 h5 (38...♗xf4 also wins) 39 ♔d1 g4 40 fxg4 fxg4 and wins.

32...♗h6 (32...♗d4!?) **33 g3 ♘f1** (beginning the mopping-up) **34 ♘b6**

Or 34 ♘c5 ♘xh2 35 ♘d3 ♗g7 36 ♗g2 (36 ♔b1? ♘f1 and ...♘xg3) 36...♘g4 and wins.

34...♘xh2 35 ♘d7 (also after 35 ♗g2 ♗f8 the evaluation of the position is obvious) **35...♗g7! 36 ♘e5 ♗xe5 37 fxe5 ♔f8 38 e6 ♗e8 39 ♗xe8** (at last exchanging bishops, but too late...) **39...♔xe8 40 ♘c6 ♘f1 0-1**

A good start to the tournament. More-over, in the 2nd round I won unexpectedly easily against Anand, who on the 16th move – a very rare occurrence! – left a knight *en prise* (cf. *Game No.97*, note to Black's 8th move). It would appear that Vishy faltered psychologically, unable to withstand the 'burden of leading': before this game he had a better score against me (+2−1=2), but after it he lost a further three serious games in succession – in Linares (1993 and 1994) and Riga (1995), and he scored his only remaining 'classical' win against me in the 9th game of our world championship match (1995).

But from the 3rd round, in which I met the youngest, but already experienced contestant, the 17-year-old Gata Kamsky, my play became extremely feverish. My games with this representative of an altogether different generation initially went badly for me: after winning against Gata in Linares 1991, I with difficulty gained two draws with him in Tilburg 1991. And in Dortmund, thinking only about winning, I clearly over-stepped the mark and lost (cf. *Game No.80*, note to Black's 19th move). However, soon I became familiar with Kamsky's style of play and, beginning with Manila (*Game No.92*), I defeated him three times in succession in 'classical' play.

The next day I won in a Scotch against Piket and took the lead together with Ivanchuk – 3 out of 4. In the 5th round we contested a fighting draw and retained the lead. But in the 6th round we both suffered a catastrophe: in a complicated King's Indian battle (cf. Game No.66, note to White's 13th move) I unexpectedly lost to Hübner, although before that I had a score of 6-0 against him with eight draws, while Ivanchuk tragically lost on time against Bareev, who overtook us on a sharp bend!

In the 7th round, not yet recovered from my previous failure, I achieved nothing against Bareev in his favourite French Defence and I even had to make a draw 'from a position of weakness'. Two rounds before the finish my chances of 1st place were miniscule: Bareev, Ivanchuk and Salov – 4½ out of 7; Anand and Kasparov – 4. In the 8th round Bareev and Anand were satisfied with draws, Ivanchuk beat Salov and became the sole leader, and I managed to win with Black against Adams and catch Bareev.

At the finish all the other games were drawn, but I overcame Salov's resistance and as a result caught Ivanchuk, sharing 1st-2nd places with him. But in general, in view of my nervy and uneven play (+5–2=2), I did not deserve this. The tournament showed very clearly that, to successfully oppose the new generation, I needed to be less diverted by extraneous matters and to work more on my chess.

An Acquaintance with Asia

30th World Chess Olympiad (Manila, 7–25 June 1992): 1. Russia – 39 out of 56; 2. Uzbekistan – 35; 3. Armenia – 34½; 4. USA – 34; 5–7. Latvia, Iceland and Croatia – 33½; 8–10. England, Georgia and Ukraine – 33, etc (altogether – 102 teams). The winning team comprised **Kasparov** (8½ out of 10), Khalifman (6 out of 10), Dolmatov (6 out of 9), Dreev (4 out of 9), reserves Kramnik (8½ out of 9) and Vyzhmanavin (6 out of 9).

Six weeks after Dortmund came the 1992 Olympiad in Manila, one of the most intriguing in the history of chess. The global political changes in the early 1990s had led to the break-up of the two leading chess powers – the Soviet Union and Yugoslavia, in place of which twenty new states had been created. The teams of these countries constituted a considerable force and threat to the traditional favourites – the ambitious English, Americans, Hungarians and so on.

The press wrote: '*When the line-up of participants in the present Olympiad was decided, with a dozen teams from the republics of the former USSR and three from the former Yugoslavia (although without Serbia!), the long-standing leader of the Filipino team Eugenio Torre said: "To finish 17th here will be the same as 7th in Thessaloniki" (that was the result of the Filipino team in 1988).*'

There were also problems for the young Russian team. Quite recently Karpov and I, who were playing a match for the title, with an easy conscience had missed the 1990 Olympiad in Yugoslav Novi Sad, where the USSR team (Ivanchuk, Gelfand, Beliavsky, Yusupov, reserves Yudasin and Bareev) confidently scored another win. But now the situation had radically changed: Ivanchuk and Beliavsky were heading the Ukrainian team, Gelfand – the Belarussian (he did not play in Manila), Vaganian – the Armenian, Ehlvest – the Estonian, and Shirov – the Latvian... For various reasons none of Karpov, Yusupov, Salov and Bareev appeared for the Russian team (and Yudasin had emigrated to Israel).

In this situation the Chess Federation

Praesidium had no doubts about the quartet of main players – Kasparov, Khalifman, Dolmatov and Dreev, but there were heated arguments about the candidates for the reserve places. I insisted on the inclusion in the team of the brilliantly performing Kramnik, but the worldly-wise trainers objected, referring to his youthful age (at the end of the Olympiad Vladimir would be just 17 years old). Fortunately, I was supported by the one of the most prestigious experts – the chairman of the trainers' council, Yuri Razuvaev, and Kramnik was taken to Manila. As it later transpired, this was a fateful decision.

Before the start, with five debutants in the team, Russia by no means looked the main favourites, and we anticipated a difficult battle. A first appearance in Asia was a new challenge for me: I set myself and my colleagues the objective of demonstrating that all the same we were the strongest! But first we had to reach the Philippines, which at that time was no simple matter: after the break-up of the USSR the former organisational links had been destroyed. Even so, the Armenians succeeded in organising a special flight from Moscow to Manila, on which many of the teams flew. On the way our valiant Ilyushin-86 made two stops – and the 12-hour flight proved to be a very tiring adventure.

But, paradoxically, despite all the problems and the unaccustomed atmosphere, this Olympiad became one of my most successful, in both the competitive and the creative respect.

In the first two 'limbering-up' rounds I was rested: as it was, Russia easily dealt with The Philippines 2nd team (4-0) and Switzerland (3½-½). In the 3rd round match with the Dutch I very much wanted to beat Timman with White, but I instead reached an inferior position, then repaired matters and in a sharp time scramble I offered a draw. But thanks to Kramnik's win – the third in succession! – we nevertheless won the match (2½-1½). And then by the identical score 3-1 we defeated Croatia and Latvia. I won against Cebalo comparatively easily, but in an ultra-tense King's Indian duel with Shirov (cf. Game No.77, note to Black's 9th move) there were mutual time-trouble errors, and the last mistake was made by my opponent.

This was how the surprises at the start were described by Sergey Makarychev (he and Razuvaev were our team's trainers). *'Tell me, who would you have put your money on in the Kyrgyzstan-France and Uzbekistan-Germany matches? To us the chances seemed roughly equal. But our western colleagues were unpleasantly startled to see some new Asian teams successfully competing with them. A few matches concluded sensationally: Latvia crushed Spain (3½-½) and Lithuania overcame the USA (2½-1½). In the 3rd round the English, who the day before had whitewashed the Finns, looked extremely insipid in their match with the Estonians (2-2). And in the 5th round, to judge by the nature of what happened, they underestimated the Uzbek team, who performed splendidly in Manila. Three of the Uzbeks – Serper, Nenashev* [he later adopted the name Graf – G.K.] *and Zagrebelny simultaneously succeeded in "achieving the impossible". In the match with the English only one of them won, but no one in the team lost.'*

It was the 5th round that first produced a single clear leader: Russia – 16 out of 20; Uzbekistan – 14½, etc. In the 6th round we crossed swords with our unexpected rivals. The situation vividly resembled a USSR Spartakiad. On top board I was opposed by a three-times Uzbek champion, the 36-year-old grandmaster Valery Loginov (after returning to Russia in 1995, he also became three-times champion of St. Petersburg!). Although an enormous rating difference separated us, at Olympiads this is not so important as in individual tournaments.

Game 91
G.Kasparov-V.Loginov
World Chess Olympiad
6th Round, Manila 13.06.1992
King's Indian Defence E84

1 d4 ♘f6 2 c4 g6 3 ♘c3 ♗g7 4 e4 d6 5 f3

We knew that Loginov played the King's Indian, and that against the Sämisch Variation he employed the line from my games with Timman (Bugojno 1982) and Spassky (Niksic 1983). And Kramnik advised me once again to go in for this variation.

5...0-0 6 ♗e3 a6 (6...e5 – *Game Nos.43, 84, 90, 92, 98*; 6...♘bd7 – *Game No.68*) **7 ♕d2**

Beliavsky once tried 7 ♗d3 against me and ran into 7...c5! (Game No.81 in *Garry Kasparov on Garry Kasparov Part I*).

7...♘c6 8 ♘ge2 ♖b8

Not wasting time on 8...♖e8?! – Game No.51 in *Garry Kasparov on Garry Kasparov Part I*.

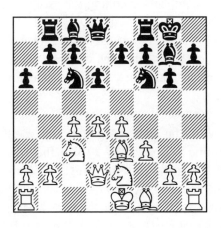

9 h4!?

Another fashionable line is 9 ♘c1 e5 10 d5 (the weaker 10 ♘b3 exd4 11 ♘xd4 ♘e5 12 ♖d1 c6 13 ♗e2 b5 allows equality, Beliavsky-Kasparov, Linares 1990; Beliavsky-Loginov, Azov 1991) 10...♘d4 11 ♘b3 (11 ♘1e2 c5 12 dxc6 ♘xc6!, Arbakov-Loginov, Katowice 1992) 11...♘xb3 12 axb3 c5! 13 g4 h5 14 h3 ♘h7 15 gxh5 ♕h4+ 16 ♕f2 ♕xh5 (16...♕xf2+ 17 ♔xf2 is slightly worse, Razuvaev-Loginov, St. Petersburg 1998) 17 ♗e2 f5 or 13 b4 cxb4 14 ♘a4 ♘h5 (14...b5!?) 15 ♕xb4 (15 ♗b6 ♕e7!) 15...f5 with counterplay on the kingside.

9...b5

9...h5 is more usual, but after 10 ♘c1 e5 11 d5 ♘d4 12 ♘b3 ♘xb3 13 axb3 c5 apart from the most popular move 14 ♗e2 (this was also recommended by Kramnik, with the idea of 14...♘h7?! 15 g4 or 15 b4!?), 14 b4!? (Portisch-Nunn, Szirak Interzonal 1987) 14...cxb4 15 ♘a4 is tempting, since in contrast to the line with 9 ♘c1 Black does not have the resource ...♘h5.

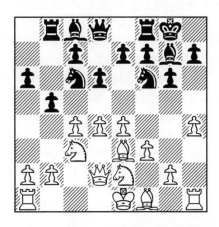

10 h5 e5

I also played this against Timman, whereas after 10...bxc4?! 11 g4! Spassky ran into difficulties (Game No.87 in *Garry Kasparov on Garry Kasparov Part I*). 10...♘xh5? 11 g4 ♘f6 12 ♗h6 is even more dangerous.

11 d5 (of course, not 11 dxe5?! ♘xe5!, Mi.Tseitlin-Loginov, Omsk 1985) **11...♘a5 12 ♘g3 bxc4**

12...♘xc4 13 ♗xc4 bxc4 14 0-0-0 (Tarjan-Nezhni, USA 1982) did not become established at grandmaster level.

13 0-0-0

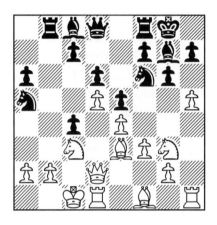

13...♖b4!

After confidently playing the opening, Loginov 'fires off' an interesting novelty. After my 13...♘d7?! Timman gained a big advantage with 14 hxg6 fxg6 15 ♘b1! ♖b5? (15...♘b7 16 hxg6 and ♘a3! or 15...c5 16 dxc6 ♘xc6 17 hxg6 hxg6 18 ♘c3 also fails to equalise) 16 b4!.

Now, however, Black has created a firm construction on the queenside (14 ♘b1 ♖a4!), and is intending ...♕e7, ...♗d7 and ...♖fb8. If White does not undertake anything, it will not be clear why he has given up a pawn. But his attack on the kingside involves the exchange of the dark-squared bishops, which is strategically also to Black's advantage! And nevertheless...

14 ♗h6 ♗xh6

After 14...♗d7 15 ♗e2 ♗xh6 (15...♕b8? is bad in view of 16 ♗xg7 ♔xg7 17 f4!, which occurred by transposition in Gheorghiu-Santana, New York 1988) 16 ♕xh6 ♔h8 17 hxg6 fxg6 18 ♖df1! (18 ♘f1 ♖g8 and ...♕f8!,

Psakhis-Djurhuus, Gausdal 1994) 18...♕e7 19 f4 White retains the initiative (Seydoux-Gorge, correspondence 2000), while if 15...♕e7!? (Stohl), then 16 ♖df1!? with the ideas of f3-f4 and ♘d1-e3 is equally interesting.

15 ♕xh6

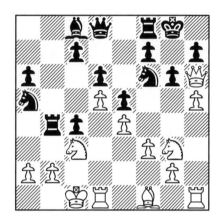

15...♕e7

My *Informator* recommendation of the move 15...♔h8(?!) is inadequate in view of 16 hxg6 fxg6 17 ♗e2 ♗d7 (17...♕e7? 18 ♕xg6 ♖g8 19 ♘f5! ♗xf5 20 ♕xf5) 18 ♖df1! and f3-f4, as in the previous note.

16 ♗e2 ♗d7

16...♘d7 (to enliven the play by ...♘c5) also came into consideration: 17 ♖df1! g5 (17...♘c5?! 18 f4) 18 ♘f5 ♕f6, transposing into a complicated ending, where after 19 g3 ♕xh6 20 ♘xh6+ ♔g7 (20...♔h8 21 f4!) 21 ♘f5+ ♔h8 (21...♔f6 22 f4!) 22 f4 exf4 23 gxf4 gxf4 24 ♖xf4 ♘e5 25 ♘d4 White has no more than good compensation for the pawn.

17 ♘f1!

With the idea of g2-g4 and ♘e3(g3). Nothing was given by 17 f4 ♖fb8 18 ♖df1 (18 ♖d2 exf4 19 ♕xf4 ♕e5!) 18...♖xb2 19 hxg6 fxg6 20 f5 ♗a4! 21 ♘xa4 ♖xa2 22 ♗d1 ♘b3+ 23 ♗xb3 ♖xb3 24 fxg6 ♖a1+ with perpetual check. If 17 ♖d2, then 17...c6?! is dubious in view of 18 ♘f1! ♔h8? (18...cxd5 19 ♘e3 ♗e6 is more resilient) 19 hxg6 fxg6 20 ♕xg6 cxd5 21 ♘e3! and wins (Lautier-Svidler, internet 2004), but 17...♖fb8 18 ♘f1 leads to a simple transposition of moves.

17...♖fb8 (not 17...♘xh5? 18 g4, when 18...♘f6 19 ♘g3 and g4-g5 is bad, as is the desperate 18...♖fb8 19 gxh5 ♖xb2 20 hxg6 fxg6 21 ♘e3!, winning) **18 ♖d2**

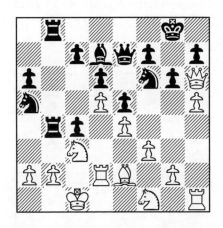

18...c5?

A serious positional error: by depriving his knight of the c5-square, Black sharply reduces his chances on the queenside. The consistent 18...♗e8! (18...♕f8 19 ♕g5! ♕e7 20 ♕h4, avoiding the exchange) 19 g4 ♘d7 20 hxg6 fxg6 21 ♘e3 (earlier I assessed this in favour of White) 21...♘c5! (Stohl) 22 g5 ♗d7 (threatening ...♘ab3+) 23 ♔b1 ♕g7 or 19 ♘e3 ♘d7 20 ♖h3 ♔h8 (20...♘c5? 21 ♘f5!) 21 hxg6 fxg6 22 g4 ♘c5 23 ♖d1 ♘a4! would have given him good play.

19 ♗d1!

Useful prophylaxis. My opponent was reckoning on the unclear 19 g4 ♗a4!, for example:

1) 20 g5?!, and now not 20...♘xh5? 21 ♘g3! or 20...♘e8?! 21 f4! exf4 22 hxg6 fxg6 23 ♖h4 (threatening both ♖xf4, and ♗g4-e6+), but 20...♘g4! 21 fxg4 ♕b7 22 hxg6 fxg6 with the counter-threat of ...♖xb2!;

2) 20 ♘e3 ♕b7?! 21 ♘f5 ♘e8 22 ♗f1! ♖xb2 23 ♘e7+! ♕xe7 24 ♖xb2 ♖xb2 25 ♔xb2 ♕b7+ 26 ♔c1 ♕b4 27 ♕e3(d2), and although Black has two pawns for the exchange, White can hope to maintain his advantage by activating his rook. However, it is possible to go totally on to the defensive – 20...♕f8 21 ♕g5 ♕g7.

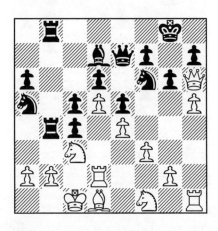

19...♘e8?!

A passive move, which accelerates Black's defeat. 19...♗e8 20 g4 ♕b7? was now pointless in view of 21 ♖hh2!, firmly reinforcing the b2-pawn and beginning a decisive storm on the kingside. But 20...♕f8 was more resilient, or immediately 19...♕f8 (Stohl), although here too after 20 ♕g5 the play is all one way: 20...♘e8 21 hxg6 fxg6 22 g3!, threatening ♖dh2 and f3-f4, or 20...♕g7 21 h6! (now there is little sense in 21 hxg6 fxg6) 21...♕h8 22 ♘e3 followed by ♖f2 and f3-f4.

20 hxg6 fxg6 21 g4! ♕g7 (21...♘f6 22 ♘g3 ♕g7 23 g5! would hardly have changed anything) **22 g5! ♕xh6 23 ♖xh6**

It unexpectedly transpires that the exchange of queens has not eased Black's situation: his pieces are just too badly placed.

23...♘g7

The attempt to switch the rook to f7 did not succeed – 23...♖4b7 24 ♖dh2 ♗c8

(24...♗b5 25 a4) 25 ♗a4! and wins. White is also clearly better after 23...♘b7 24 a3! ♖b6 25 ♖dh2 ♘d8 26 ♖xh7 ♘f7 27 ♘e3 ♖6b7 28 ♖7h4! with the idea of 28...♘xg5 29 ♖g2 or 28...♗b5 29 a4, and otherwise 29 ♘xc4 (Gallagher-Sutovsky, Biel 1996).

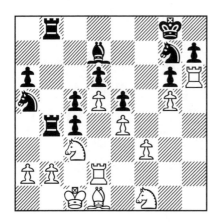

24 f4!

White could also have won by 24 ♖dh2!? (but not 24 ♘g3? ♘b7! and ...♘d8-f7) 24...♘h5 (24...♗e8 25 f4!) 25 ♘g3! (Stohl) 25...♘xg3 26 ♖xh7 ♘h5 27 ♖xd7 ♘b7 28 ♗e2 ♖d8 29 ♖c7, but I found the most effective continuation: the opening of the f-file decides the fate of the black king.

24...exf4

If 24...♖f8, then 25 f5! gxf5 (otherwise ♖dh2) 26 ♖xd6 fxe4 (26...♗c8 27 ♖h2) 27 ♖xd7 (or my *Informator* move 27 ♘e3) 27...♖xf1 28 ♘xe4 c3 29 ♘f6+! ♖xf6 30 bxc3 and wins.

25 ♖dh2 ♖e8

Things were also hopeless after the more resilient 25...♗e8 (25...♘h5? 26 ♗xh5 gxh5 27 ♖xd6) 26 ♖xh7 ♘h5 27 ♖h6 (Stohl) 27...♖4b6 28 ♗xh5 gxh5 29 ♖f2! ♖8b7 (the position of the knight on a5 is terrible, but if 29...♘b7, then 30 e5!) 30 ♖e6 ♗f7 (30...♗d7 31 ♖g6+ etc) 31 ♖f6 followed by ♖2xf4 and ♘e3(g3)-f5.

26 ♘d2!?

The obvious 26 ♖xh7 was no worse – say, 26...♖e5 27 ♖2h4 with the threat of ♖h8+ and ♖xf4+. However, with such an overwhelming superiority in the quality of his pieces, White has no reason to hurry.

26...♖eb8 (if 26...♖e5 there would have followed 27 ♖xh7 ♖xg5 28 ♖h8+ ♔f7 29 ♖a8! or 27...♔f7 28 ♘f3 ♖e8 29 ♖2h4 and ♖xf4+) **27 ♖xh7 ♖xb2 28 ♖2h4!** (the prelude to the execution of the king) **28...♖2b7 29 ♖h8+ ♔f7 30 ♖xf4+ ♔e7 31 ♖h7 ♖g8 32 ♖f6 ♗e8**

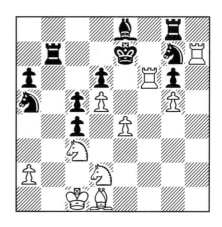

33 e5!

After this breakthrough in the centre Black quickly suffers enormous loss of material.

33...♖b6 (33...dxe5 34 ♖xa6) **34 ♘de4 ♘b7 35 exd6+ ♘xd6 36 ♖e6+ ♔d7**

And without waiting for 37 ♘xd6 ♖xd6 38 ♗a4+, Black resigned (**1-0**).

As a result we defeated Uzbekistan 3-1. And in the next round we also crushed our inveterate rivals – the USA team. This key match went very well for us from the very start.

On top board I had Black against the new leader of the American team, Gata Kamsky, and again, as in Dortmund, I employed my favourite King's Indian.

Game 92
G.Kamsky-G.Kasparov
World Chess Olympiad
7th Round, Manila 14.06.1992
King's Indian Defence E88

1 d4 ♘f6 2 c4 g6 3 ♘c3 ♗g7 4 e4 d6 5 f3

Gata chose 5 ♘f3 in Dortmund, but now he prefers the Sämisch – probably both under the influence of my game with Loginov, and taking into account the difficulties that I had encountered in this variation.

5...0-0 6 ♗e3 e5 (6...♘bd7 – *Game No.68*; 6...a6 – *Game No.91*) **7 d5** (7 ♘ge2 – *Game Nos.90, 98*) **7...c6**

After some thought I decided to avoid my recent variation with 7...♘h5 (*Game No.84*), for which Kamsky would have certainly prepared.

8 ♕d2 (8 ♗d3!? is more promising – *Game No.43*) **8...cxd5 9 cxd5 a6**

9...♘bd7 deserves consideration, with the ideas of 10 ♘b5 ♘c5 11 ♖c1 b6 (12 b4 ♘fxe4!) 10 ♗d3 ♘c5, 10 ♘h3 a6, as in the 3rd game of my match with Psakhis (cf. *Game No.68*, note to White's 7th move), and 10 ♘ge2 a6 (cf. below).

10 ♗d3

10 ♘ge2 ♘bd7 occurred six times in my games with a score of +3=3 in Black's favour – details in *Kasparov vs. Karpov 1988-2009* (cf. *Game No.36*, note to White's 8th move), and in the next volume of *Garry Kasparov on Garry Kasparov*.

10...♘h5

This is more active but also more risky than 10...♘bd7: Black immediately prepares ...f7-f5.

Usually White fights for an advantage by 11 ♘ge2 f5 12 exf5 gxf5 13 0-0, but Kamsky suddenly staggered me with a strange move.

11 g4?

This is how they played at the dawn of the King's Indian, when it was not yet understood that the knight should not be driven to f4, since its exchange on this square – even with the loss of a pawn – gives Black a powerful initiative after ...exf4, thanks to the activation of the bishop on g7. Such a move by the strong but still very young grandmaster can be explained only by his lack of King's Indian experience.

11...♘f4 12 ♗c2 (12 ♗xf4? exf4 13 ♕xf4 ♕b6 and ...♘d7-e5 is altogether bad for White, Szmukler-Wexler, Buenos Aires 1978) **12...b5 13 ♕f2 ♘d7 14 ♘ge2 b4!**

Not missing the opportunity to give the white knight a push.

15 ♘a4

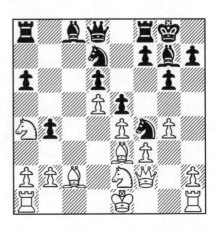

15...a5!

15...♕a5?! 16 0-0-0 was inaccurate, but now ....♗a6 is threatened. 'Sooner or later the f4-knight will have to be taken, after which the bishop on g7 will become fearfully strong. Of course, in taking this standard decision Kasparov did not think for long.' (Makarychev)

16 ♘xf4 exf4 17 ♗xf4 ♘e5

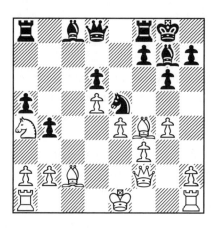

18 0-0-0?!

Sending his own king to the scaffold! White is unable to create any dangerous threats at all on the kingside, as long as the g7-bishop is alive. Therefore it was also fatal to play 18 ♗xe5?! (18 ♘b6? ♘xf3+) 18...♗xe5 19 0-0-0 ♖b8! and ...♗d7 with an escalating attack. He should have removed his king to the opposite wing – 18 0-0 (18 ♔f1?! f5!), although here too after 18...♗a6 19 ♖fc1 ♗b5 or 19 ♖fd1 ♖c8 20 ♖ac1 ♗b5 Black has an excellent game. In all variations the knight on a4 is a constant headache for White.

18...♘c4! 19 ♗e3

Gata can no longer find anything better than to give up his valuable dark-squared bishop for the knight. And, indeed, if 19 ♔b1?! there is the sacrifice 19...♘a3+! (20 bxa3?! ♕f6), while the attempt to block the terrible diagonal at the cost of the exchange

– 19 ♗b3 ♗d7 20 ♗xc4 ♗xa4 21 ♖d4 is unsuccessful because of 21...♕c7! (more accurate than my *Informator* suggestion 21...♕b6 22 ♗e3 ♕c7) 22 b3 ♗xb3! 23 axb3 a4 or 22 ♔d2 ♕c5 23 ♔d3 ♗b5! and wins. These spectacular variations merely illustrate the ruinous nature of White's plan.

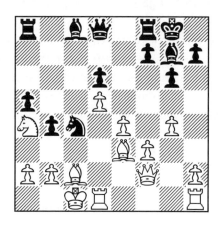

19...♘xe3 20 ♕xe3 ♖b8! (not allowing the knight to go to b6 – the threat is ...♗d7 and ...♕e8) **21 ♗b3**

It is hard to offer White any good advice. Thus he would have lost ignominiously after 21 ♔b1 ♗d7 22 ♖d2 ♗b5 23 ♖c1 ♕d7 24 b3 (24 ♘b6 ♕b7) 24...♗xa4 25 bxa4 b3!! or 23 b3 ♗xa4 24 bxc4 ♕e8! 25 e5 b3!! and ...♕xa4.

21...♗d7 22 ♔b1 ♕e8 23 ♘b6 ♗b5 24 ♖d2

24 ♖c1 ♖xb6! would have led to the loss of a piece, since if 25 ♕xb6? Black concludes prettily with 25...♗d3+ 26 ♔a1 ♗xb2+!, mating, or 26 ♖c2 ♕e5!.

24...a4?!

Black could have immediately won material and the game with the subtle 24...♕d8! 25 ♘a4 ♕d7 26 ♘b6 ♕a7! 27 ♘c4 ♕a6, with the threats of ...♗xc4 and ...a5-a4.

25 ♗d1?!

25 ♗c4!? ♖xb6 26 ♕xb6 ♗xc4 27 ♕xb4 was more resilient, although after 27...♗h6! 28 ♖g2 ♗d3+ 29 ♔a1 ♕a8 or 28 ♖d4 ♗e2

29 ♖e1 ♗xf3 30 ♕xd6 ♗xg4 White cannot withstand the onslaught of the rampant bishops.

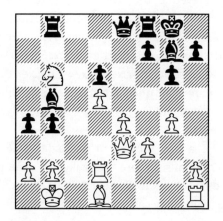

25...♖b7

While preparing ...b4-b3, Black vacates the b8-square for his queen, but he could also have decided matters with the immediate 25...b3! 26 axb3 (26 a3 ♕d8!, trapping the knight) 26...axb3 27 ♗xb3 ♖b7! (threatening ...♕b8; 27...♕d8!?) 28 ♘c4 ♗xc4 29 ♗xc4 ♕a4!.

26 e5 b3! 27 axb3 axb3

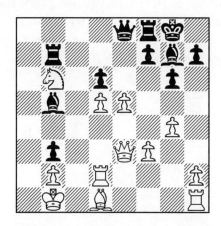

28 ♗xb3 (if 28 e6 both 28...♕b8 and 28...♕d8 29 ♘d7?! ♕a5! 30 ♗xb3 ♖a7 are good) **28...♕b8 29 ♘c4 ♗xc4 30 ♗xc4 ♗xe5**

White is still a pawn up, but this is of no

importance. If White's king were on g2 and his pawn on b3, Black would simply have excellent compensation for the pawn in the form of his dark-square domination. But, alas, the king is on b1, and its execution cannot be avoided.

31 ♕e2

White also fails to save the game with 31 b3 ♖c8 32 ♔c2 ♖xc4+ 33 bxc4 ♖b2+, or 31 ♕a3 ♖a7 32 ♕d3 (32 ♕b3 ♕a8) 32...♕b4 etc.

31...♕a7 32 ♖c1 ♖a8 33 b3 ♗f4 34 ♔c2 ♖e7 35 ♕d3 ♕c5 36 ♖b1 ♖e3 37 ♕d4 ♖a2+ 38 ♔d1

Or 38 ♖b2 ♖xb2+ 39 ♕xb2 ♗e5 40 ♕a2(c1) ♖c3+.

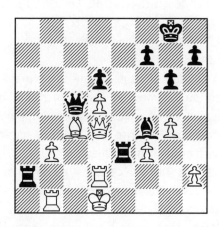

38...♖xf3

38...♖e8!? was more flamboyant: 39 ♖bb2 ♖a1+ 40 ♔c2 ♖c1+! or 39 ♖d3 ♕b4 40 ♕c3 (40 ♖c3 ♖ee2) 40...♕xc3 41 ♖xc3 ♖d2+ 42 ♔c1 ♖e1 mate!

39 ♕xf4 ♖xf4 40 ♖xa2 ♕g1+ 41 ♔c2 ♕xh2+ 0-1

As he usually did at that time, Kamsky fought on to the very end.

An important game. The team supported my success: Khalifman outplayed his former compatriot from Leningrad, Yermolinsky, and the young Kramnik succeeded in overcoming the distinguished Seirawan!

The outcome of the match exceeded all our expectations: 3½-½!

The lead over our pursuers increased, but in the next round we faced another important match with a very dangerous rival – the strong Ukrainian team, which was always among the favourites at the USSR Spartakiads. The central encounter that day was my game with Vassily Ivanchuk, who was then rated No.2 in the world.

Game 93
G.Kasparov-V.Ivanchuk
World Chess Olympiad
8th Round, Manila 16.06.1992
English Opening A35

---

1 ♘f3

A change of tune: in my three previous victorious games against Ivanchuk I had played 1 c4 or 1 d4. In reply my opponent decided to surprise me with a curious branch of the English Opening.

1...c5 2 c4 ♘c6 3 ♘c3 ♘f6 4 g3 d6 (in order if necessary to defend the c6-knight with ...♗d7) **5 ♗g2 g6 6 d4 cxd4 7 ♘xd4 ♗d7**

Here I stopped to think about my subsequent plan.

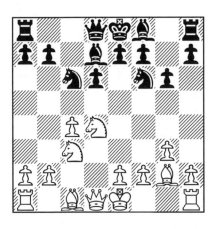

8 e4

A rare instance of a novelty as early as the 8th move – in a position where White usually played 8 0-0 (the most natural way, promising White a minimal advantage) 8...♗g7 9 b3 or 9 ♘c2, while later, without particular success, he tried 8 ♘xc6 bxc6 9 c5 d5 10 e4 dxe4 11 ♘xe4 ♘xe4 12 ♗xe4 ♗g7 (Kasparov-Kramnik, 7th match game (blitz), Moscow 1998).

8...♗g7

Not a bad move, but 8...♘xd4! 9 ♕xd4 ♗g7 equalises more forcefully: for example, 10 c5 0-0 11 cxd6 ♗c6! or 10 0-0 0-0 11 ♕d3 ♘g4. This may cast doubts on the idea of e2-e4: White has no positional compensation for the restriction of his g2-bishop.

9 ♘xc6 ♗xc6

And here 9...bxc6!? deserved consideration – in *Informator* I put my trust in 10 c5!? (10 0-0 ♕a5!?, Gelfand-Kramnik, Monte Carlo (blindfold) 2000) 10...dxc5 11 e5 (11 0-0 ♗e6!?, Lerner-Baklan, Ordzhonikidze Zonal 2000) 11...♘g4 12 f4 (12 e6? is weak: 12...♗xe6 13 ♗xc6+ ♔f8! 14 ♗xa8 ♕xa8 15 0-0?! h5! or 15 f3 ♗c4, with an attack and a pawn for the exchange), but after 12...0-0 there would have been a very double-edged game in prospect.

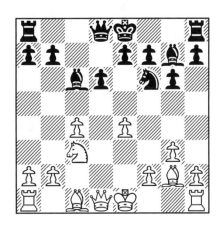

10 ♗e3!

10 0-0 is inaccurate in view of 10...♘d7!, when the threat of ...♗xc3 forces either the passive 11 ♗d2, or 11 ♘d5, but the knight cannot be maintained on its proud outpost: 11...0-0 (the immediate 11...e6 is also possible) 12 ♕e2 (Grischuk-Gashimov, Monte Carlo (rapid) 2011) 12...e6! 13 ♘b4 ♕b6 14 ♘xc6 bxc6 with equality.

But with the text, my plan is justified: by developing my c1-bishop at the right time, I have created a classical Maroczy set-up.

10...0-0

10...♘xe4?! 11 ♘xe4 f5 12 ♘xd6+ exd6 13 0-0 or 12...♕xd6 13 ♕xd6 exd6 14 ♗xc6+ bxc6 15 0-0-0 is obviously better for White. And the 10...♘d7 manoeuvre is no longer as strong as before in view of 11 ♖c1! (an important move), when the greedy 11...♘c5?! 12 0-0! ♗xc3?! 13 ♖xc3 ♗xe4? is punished by 14 ♗xc5! ♗xg2 15 ♗d4! ♗xf1 16 ♗xh8 ♗h3 17 g4 and wins.

11 0-0

Nowadays this is one of the popular lines.

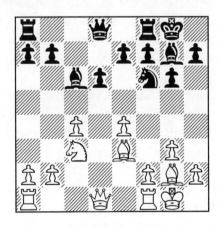

11...a5

Black has also tried 11...a6 (Kramnik-Kamsky, Monte Carlo (blindfold) 1995; Kasparov-Carlsen, Reykjavik (blitz) 2004), 11...♕a5 (Kramnik-Ivanchuk, Nice (rapid) 2008), and 11...♕d7 (Khalifman-Rasulov, St. Petersburg 2011). But the best resource

looks to be 11...♘d7 (nevertheless) 12 ♖c1 ♕a5!? (instead of the fashionable 12...a5) 13 a3 (my *Informator* recommendation) 13...♘b6!? 14 ♕e2 ♘a4 or 13 ♕d2 ♖fe8 14 b3 ♖ac8, with quite a flexible position and reasonable equalising chances.

12 ♖c1 a4

After devising the interesting plan with ...a7-a5-a4 and ...♕a5, Ivanchuk obviously decided that in this way Black obtains a very comfortable game. However, the position is full of tactical nuances, which I begin to exploit.

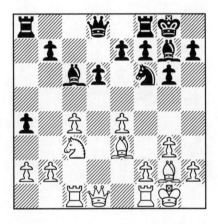

13 ♕e2

The premature 13 c5?! dxc5 14 e5 (14 ♗xc5 ♖e8 is no better) 14...♕xd1 15 ♖fxd1 ♘g4 16 ♗xc5 ♘xe5 17 ♗xe7 ♖fe8 allows equality. 'But White has no need to force events: there are still possibilities for improving the coordination of his pieces, while Black will soon experience all the burdens of his cramped position.' (Makarychev)

13...♕a5 14 ♖fd1 ♖fc8?!

In making this over-optimistic move, the opponent allows an unpleasant blow in the centre. One of the following continuations would have been far less of an evil:

1) 14...♘d7 15 ♘d5!, and here not 15...♗xd5?! because of 16 ♖xd5! with the threats of ♖b5 and c4-c5 (16 cxd5 ♖fc8 17

♖xc8+ ♖xc8 18 ♗h3 ♖c7 19 ♗xd7 ♖xd7 20 ♖c1 ♖c7 21 ♖xc7 ♕xc7 22 ♕b5, which I gave in *Informator*, leads only to a draw after 22...♕c8!), but 15...♖fe8!;

2) 14...♖fe8! 15 c5!? (it would appear that here too this is the best chance, but the rook is far better placed at e8 than at c8) 15...a3! 16 cxd6 (16 b3?! ♘d7! 17 ♘d5 dxc5) 16...axb2! (after 16...exd6 17 b3 ♘xe4 18 ♘xe4 ♗xe4 19 ♗xe4 ♖xe4 20 ♕f3 ♕e5 21 ♖c7 f5 22 ♖xb7 White has some advantage) 17 ♕xb2 exd6 18 ♗d4 ♕a3! with prospects of equalising.

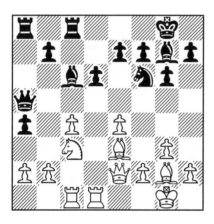

15 c5! ♘e8

Black already has a difficult choice. He could not be satisfied with 15...dxc5? 16 e5 ♘e8 17 ♘d5 ♗xd5 18 ♖xd5 with the threats of ♖dxc5 and ♖d7.

15...a3 would also have been worse than with the rook on e8 – after this in *Informator* I gave the flamboyant 16 cxd6 axb2 17 ♕xb2 ♘xe4(?) 18 ♗xe4 ♗xe4 19 d7! ♖xc3 20 ♖xc3 ♗xc3 21 ♕xc3 ♕xc3 22 d8♕+ ♖xd8 23 ♖xd8+ ♔g7 24 ♗d4+ ♕xd4 25 ♖xd4 with the exchange for a pawn and winning chances, but after 17...exd6 18 ♗d4 ♕a3! Black holds on. Therefore the correct reply is 16 b3!: for example, 16...dxc5 17 e5 ♗xg2 18 ♔xg2 ♘e8 19 ♘d5, retaining the pressure, or 16...♘d7 17 ♗d2! dxc5 (alas, 17...♘xc5?

runs into 18 b4! ♕xb4 19 ♘d5!) 18 ♘d5 ♕d8 19 ♗g5 f6 20 ♗e3 with an initiative which more than compensates for the pawn deficit.

16 cxd6 (the immediate 16 ♘d5!? was also good) **16...♘xd6 17 ♘d5 ♗xd5 18 ♖xd5 ♖xc1+** (after 18...♕b4?! 19 e5 the reply 19...♘c4? is not possible on account of 20 ♖d4!) **19 ♗xc1**

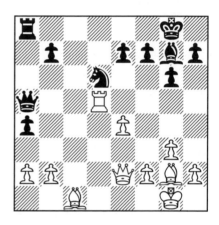

19...♕c7!

The best chance: if 19...♕a6, then 20 ♕d1! with the threat of e4-e5 is strong.

20 ♗f4 ♕c4! (this attack on the white pawns forces the exchange of queens) **21 ♕xc4 ♘xc4**

I think that Ivanchuk was hoping without particular anxiety to gain a draw in a somewhat inferior endgame. Therefore Black's problems, which suddenly began to snowball, shook him.

22 b3

After driving back the knight, White is pinning his hopes on the activity of his two bishops and his centralised rook.

22...axb3

Black's problems would not have been solved by either 22...e5?! 23 ♗g5, or the tempting 22...♘a5?! (with the threat of 23...♘xb3! 24 axb3 a3!) 23 bxa4! ♘c6 24 ♗f1!? (24 ♖d7 ♖xa4 25 e5 h5 26 ♖xb7 ♘xe5

27 ♗xe5 ♗xe5 28 ♖xe7 leads to the win of a pawn, but the opposite-coloured bishops may save Black) 24...♖xa4 25 ♗b5, and after 25...♖d4 26 ♗xc6 bxc6 27 ♖xd4 ♗xd4 28 ♔f1 White has an excellent bishop endgame with an outside passed pawn, while after 25...♖a8 26 a4 and ♖d7 he has an enduring advantage.

23 axb3

The critical moment of the game.

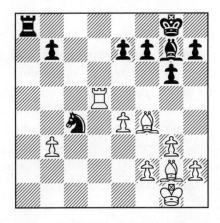

23...♘a5?

A by no means obvious mistake. 23...e5? 24 ♗g5 h6 25 ♗d8! was also weak, but real drawing chances were offered by 23...e6! with the idea of 24 ♖c5 ♘a5 25 ♖b5 ♗d4 26 b4 ♘c6 27 ♖xb7 ♖a2!, 24 ♖b5 e5! 25 ♗g5 ♘d6 26 ♖d5 ♖a1+ 27 ♗f1 ♗f8 28 f3 (28 ♖xe5 ♖b1! and ...♖xb3) 28...♔g7 etc, or 24 ♖d7 ♘e5! 25 ♖xb7 g5! (a sudden tactical trick) 26 ♗xe5 (26 ♗xg5? ♖a1+ and ...♘f3+, while after 26 ♗e3 ♖a1+ 27 ♗f1 h5 28 ♔g2 g4 White is paralysed by the threat of ...♘f3-e1+) 26...♗xe5 27 ♗f3 ♖b8, nevertheless reaching the drawing haven.

24 b4

24 ♖b5?! ♗d4! 25 b4 ♘c4 26 ♗f1 ♘d6 27 ♖d5 ♗c3 was unclear, with counterplay. But now Black's position deteriorates.

24...♘c6 25 b5 ♘d4 26 ♗f1

After advancing his pawn to d5 and se-

curely defending it with his bishop, White is threatening to invade with his rook on d7, and as yet the black king does not have an escape square.

26...h5?!

The spirited 26...g5?! 27 ♗e3 ♘f3+ 28 ♔g2 g4 no longer worked in view of 29 h3! (breaking up the trap) 29...♘e1+ 30 ♔h1 ♘c2 31 ♗c5. However, it was better either to confuse matters somewhat with 26...♘f3+!? 27 ♔g2 ♘e1+ 28 ♔h1(h3) h5, or to exchange rooks in the hope of saving the difficult minor piece endgame – 26...♘e6!? 27 ♗e3 ♖d8 28 ♖xd8+ ♘xd8 29 f4 ♗c3 etc.

27 ♔g2 ♘c2

In view of the weakening move ...h7-h5, the variation 27...♘e6!? 28 ♗e3 ♖d8 29 ♖xd8+ ♘xd8 30 f4 ♗c3 did not attract Black at all, but perhaps it would have enabled him to avoid the worst.

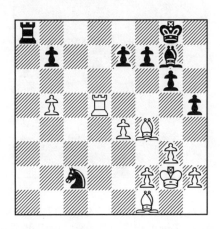

28 ♗d2! e6 (28...b6!? 29 ♖d7 e6 was more resilient, although here too after 30 ♖c7 or 30 ♗d3 things are most probably bad for Black) **29 ♖c5! ♘d4 30 ♗e3 b6 31 ♖c7** (threatening ♖d7 or ♖b7xb6) **31...♖a1?!**

This hastens the end, but also after 31...♖b8 (31...♗e5?! 32 ♖d7!) 32 ♗f4! (with the threat of ♖xf7) 32...e5 33 ♗e3 White completely dominates.

32 ♖c8+ ♔h7 33 ♖c7

Repeating moves to gain on the clock with time-trouble imminent. 'By the 20th move Kasparov was already rather short of time and he had less than a minute per move leading up to the first time control, whereas Ivanchuk had expended his time far more rationally.' (Makarychev)

33...♔g8 34 ♖c4! ♖d1 (34...e5?! 35 ♖c8+ ♔h7 36 ♖c7 and wins) **35 ♖c8+ ♔h7 36 ♖d8** (a deadly pin on the knight) **36...♗e5 37 h3?!**

There was a simpler win by 37 h4! ♔g7 38 ♗c4 ♗f6 (38...♔f6? 39 ♖d7!, as in the game) 39 ♖d7 ♔f8 40 ♗f4! ♔e8 41 ♖d6 and ♖xb6. **37...♔g7 38 ♗c4 ♔f6?**

Also a time-trouble error. 38...♗f6 39 ♖d7 ♔f8 was essential, although after 40 ♖d6 and ♖xb6 White has every chance of converting his extra passed pawn.

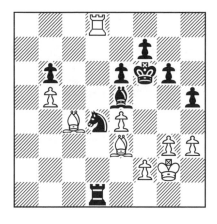

39 ♖d7! g5 (zugzwang: 39...♔g7 40 ♗xe6!) **40 ♗e2! ♘xe2 41 ♖xd1 ♘c3 42 ♖d8 ♘xe4 43 ♗xb6 ♘c3 44 ♖g8 ♘xb5 45 ♗d8+ 1-0**

A good positional win over a top-class grandmaster.

As a result we also defeated the Ukrainian team: 3-1. Makarychev: *'The match with the Ukrainians summed up the battle for Olympic gold, creating a kind of image of a Russian miracle. The results – 25½ out of 32 (!) and 6½ out of 8 against USA and Ukraine made a*

strong impression on "the entire Olympiad". After the 8th round the "adjournment session" for our team began. The next match, with Georgia, was won only because the opposing team was experiencing an even more difficult tournament period. However, the 10th round brought the Russians their only defeat in the tournament – against Armenia (1½-2½). The loss of the image of a team of super-heroes also had its positive aspects: now it could calmly proceed to the finish.'

In the 10th round I drew with Black in a sharp King's Indian clash with Vaganian, but in the 11th I defeated Hjartarson with White, which gave us victory over Iceland (2½-1½). After this the triumph of the Russian team was not in doubt. I was on 7 out of 8, and the next day I could have been rested. However, on encountering once again the problem of deciding on the line-up, I volunteered to play – seeing as our trainers had already 'worked out' the name of my next opponent and the colour of the pieces.

In the 12th round we faced the Bosnians, and I – their leader Predrag Nikolic, with not only the team's interests on my mind, but also the battle for the best result on board 1.

Game 94
G.Kasparov-P.Nikolic
World Chess Olympiad
12th Round, Manila 21.06.1992
Slav Defence D10

1 d4 d5 2 c4 c6 3 ♘c3 e5!?

At that time the ancient Winawer Counter-Gambit had come into fashion, not without the help of Nikolic, so that it was quite easy to predict his choice of opening. And I unearthed a variation in the hope of gaining an analytical advantage over my opponent in a position that appears harmless, but contains a mass of latent tactical possibilities.

4 dxe5

For a long time Black's audacious sortie was rejected because of 4 cxd5 cxd5 5 ♘f3 e4 6 ♘e5, but then it transpired that after 6...f6! (6...♗e7 is more modest, Nogueiras-Nikolic, Brussels 1988) 7 ♕a4+ ♘d7 8 ♘g4 ♔f7! (Wiedenkeller-Engqvist, Gothenburg 1990) or 8 ♘xd7 ♗xd7 9 ♕b3 ♗c6 (Lukacs-Janovsky, Budapest 1991) things are not so bad for him.

4...d4 5 ♘e4 ♕a5+

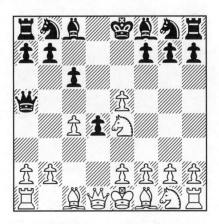

6 ♗d2!

It is staggering that this natural developing move was overshadowed and that everyone played 6 ♘d2: for example, 6...♘d7 7 ♘gf3 ♘xe5 8 ♘xd4 ♘xc4 9 e3 ♘xd2 10 ♗xd2 ♗b4 with equality (Seirawan-Nikolic, Reykjavik 1991) or 7 e6 fxe6 8 g3 ♘e5!? (instead of 8...e5 9 ♗g2 ♘gf6 10 ♘gf3, Karpov-Bareev, Linares 1992) 9 ♕c2 ♘f6 10 ♗g2 ♗e7 11 ♘h3?! (Timman-Nikolic, Manila Olympiad 1992), and here 11...♘eg4! with the idea of 12 0-0 ♕h5! gives excellent play.

6...♕xe5

It was thought that the complete relieving

of the central situation plus the absence of pawn weaknesses should ensure Black straightforward equality. In this game I was able to remind my opponent of a half-forgotten factor – a lead in development.

7 ♘g3 ♕d6

A quite rapid and correct reply (7...♘f6 8 ♘f3 ♕d6 comes to the same thing). After 7...c5 8 ♘f3 ♕c7 9 e3 White has more chances of retaining the initiative (Ionov-Tregubov, Orel 1992; Korchnoi-Schwartzman, Wijk aan Zee 1993).

8 ♘f3 ♘f6 9 ♕c2!

A novelty, which became the main continuation. In two earlier little-known games 9 a3 and 9 e4 were tried.

9...♗e7 (or 9...♗e6?! 10 0-0-0!) **10 0-0-0 0-0**

The first critical position.

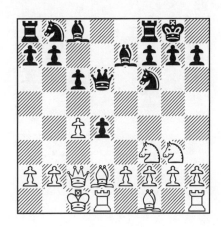

11 e3

11 ♗c3!? suggested itself, with the idea of developing activity in the event of 11...c5 (which was what Nikolic was intending) 12 e3 ♕a6 13 exd4 cxd4 14 ♘xd4 ♕xa2 15 ♘df5 (15 ♗d3!?) or 11...♕f4+ 12 e3! dxe3 13 fxe3 ♕xe3+ 14 ♔b1 etc. But 11...dxc3!? seemed unclear to me: 12 ♖xd6 cxb2+ 13 ♕xb2 ♗xd6 with decent compensation for the queen (although later this assessment was disputed by 14 e4 ♗f4+ 15 ♔b1 or 14 e3 etc). Therefore I chose a different, outwardly

paradoxical plan, the outlines of which had been worked out at home.

11...dxe3 12 fxe3

This way (or 12 ♗c3 ♕c7! 13 fxe3). Also interesting is 12 ♗xe3!? ♕c7 13 ♘f5 with a mini-plus, or 12 ♗a5!? (depriving the black queen of the c7-square) 12...♕e6! 13 ♘d4 (13 ♗d3!? g6 14 ♖he1) 13...♕e5 14 ♗c3 with sharp play (Nielsen-Hector, Denmark 2008).

12...♕c7 (the alternative is 12...♘a6 13 ♗c3 ♕c7!, but not 13...♕e6 14 ♘d4! ♕xe3+ 15 ♔b1 with a dangerous initiative for the pawn: 15...♘b4 16 ♕a4!) **13 ♗c3 ♗g4**

Natural development, but 13...c5!? and ...♘c6 is safer (Krasenkow-Morozevich, Pamplona 1998/99) or 13...♘a6!? 14 a3 ♗g4 15 ♖e1 g6! (Krasenkow-Nikolic, Bled Olympiad 2002).

14 ♗d3

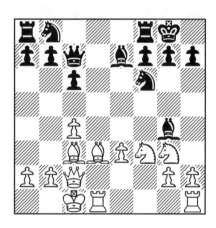

14...♘bd7?!

Now White can seize the initiative. 14...g6! with the idea of 15 ♗f5 ♘a6 (Stohl) would have set him far more problems.

15 ♗f5?!

15 ♘f5! was more accurate: for example, 15...♖fe8 16 ♘xg7! ♔xg7 17 ♗f5 or 15...♗xf5 16 ♗xf5 g6 17 ♗xd7 ♘xd7 18 h4! with chances of an attack.

15...♗xf5?

Nikolic fails to find the only defence. White

is also better after 15...♖ad8?! 16 ♗xg4 ♘xg4 17 ♘f5! (instead of the unclear *Informator* suggestion 17 ♗xg7 ♘xe3! etc) 17...♗f6 (17...♗c5? 18 ♘xg7! and wins) 18 h3 ♘ge5 19 ♖d6 and ♖hd1. But the accurate 15...♖fd8! 16 ♗xg4 ♘xg4 17 ♘f5 (here 17 ♗xg7? is now obviously weak in view of ...♘xe3 and ...♘xd1 – Stohl) 17...♗f8 would have led to double-edged play and dynamic equality.

16 ♘xf5 ♖fe8

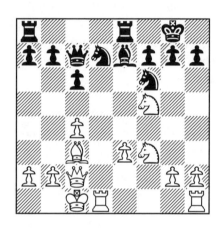

17 ♘xg7!

To demonstrate the correctness of this sacrifice it is not necessary to calculate too many variations, and I captured the g7-pawn without particular hesitation. On the other hand, the crux of the combination – the 'quiet' move 19 h4 – demanded an incomparably greater expenditure of intellect and energy.

17...♔xg7 18 ♕f5 ♘f8

Black would have lost quickly after 18...♔f8? 19 ♘g5! or 18...♔g8? 19 ♕g5+ and ♘h4!. It was also bad to play 18...♖ed8 19 ♘g5! (19 g4 ♔g8 20 ♕g5+ ♔f8! 21 ♖hf1 ♘e4 is not so clear) 19...♔g8 20 ♖hf1 ♘f8 (20...♕b6? 21 ♘xf7!) 21 ♖xd8 ♕xd8 22 ♘e4! or 18...♖ad8 19 g4! ♔g8 20 ♕g5+ ♔h8 (20...♔f8? 21 ♘h4!) 21 ♖hf1, when Black has no defence: 21...♖f8 22 ♕h4 or 21...♖g8 22 ♕f5 with the murderous threat of g4-g5.

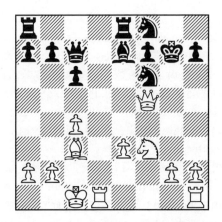

19 h4!?

One of the deepest and least obvious moves in my career, which surprised many spectators. It was possible to regain the piece immediately – 19 ♘g5 (19 g4?! ♚g8! is less good) 19...♚g8! (19...♛c8? 20 ♕f3 h6 21 ♖d6! and wins) 20 ♗xf6 ♗xf6 21 ♕xf6 ♕e7 22 ♖hf1 ♕xf6 23 ♖xf6, but in such an endgame it is not easy to convert the extra pawn. I thought that White could count on more than routine technical work in an ending, and I decided to retain both the queens, and the initiative. The following computer line was even stronger: 19 ♘e5! ♚g8 20 ♖hf1 ♖ed8 21 ♖de1!, threatening ♘g4: for example, 21...♕d6 22 ♘g4 ♘8d7 23 e4! or 22...♘g6 23 ♗xf6 ♗xf6 24 ♘xf6+ and ♕h5 with a decisive attack.

Although 19 h4 complicated the situation, it staggered my opponent, who was obviously expecting 19 g4. White simply advances his rook's pawn, not hurrying to regain the piece!

19...h6?!

I thought that this dubious move was the only defence, but I had failed to take something into account. Let us analyse the three other possibilities:

1) 19...♚g8 20 h5! h6 21 ♗xf6 ♗xf6 22 ♕xf6 ♖e6?! 23 ♕f5! (more accurate than my

Informator suggestion 23 ♕c3) 23...♕e7 (23...♖ae8 24 ♘d4!) 24 ♖h3 and wins, or 22...♕e7! 23 ♕xh6 ♕xe3+ 24 ♕xe3 ♖xe3 25 ♖he1 with the hope of nevertheless converting the extra pawn in the ending;

2) 19...♖ad8 20 ♖df1!, when it is bad to play 20...♕b6? 21 ♕g5+ ♘g6 22 ♘d4 or 20...♚g8? 21 ♕g5+ ♘g6 22 h5 ♘e4 23 hxg6! ♘xg5 (23...fxg6 24 ♕xg6+!, mating) 24 ♘xg5 f6 (24...fxg6 25 ♖xh7!) 25 gxh7+ ♚h8 26 ♖xf6! with a highly spectacular rout. There is also a strong attack after 20...♕g3 21 h5! ♚g8 22 ♗xf6 ♗xf6 23 ♕xf6 ♕g7 24 ♕f5! f6 25 ♖h4 or 24...♖d6 25 ♘d4. But after the best move 20...h6! 21 ♘g5! ♕d7! 22 ♗xf6+ ♚g8 23 ♘e4 ♕xf5 24 ♖xf5 ♘d7 25 ♗c3 ♗b4 26 ♗xb4 ♖xe4 27 ♖f4 White again has 'only' an endgame with an extra pawn and winning chances;

3) 19...♕b6 20 ♘d4! (even better than 20 ♖de1!?) 20...♚g8 (20...♕c5 21 ♕f3!) 21 ♖hf1 ♘e6 22 ♕f3 ♘g7 23 ♘c2, and in the event of 23...c5 – 24 g4!? or 24 ♖d5!? with an overwhelming advantage.

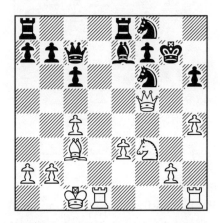

20 g4?!

An annoying error! Initially I had been planning the strongest move 20 ♕g4+!, for example:

1) 20...♘g6? 21 h5 ♕b6 (21...♕a5 22 ♕g3!) 22 hxg6 ♕xe3+ 23 ♚b1 fxg6 (23...♚f8

24 ♕h3!) 24 ♘h4 (24 ♕h4 is also decisive) 24...♕g5 25 ♕e6 and ♖d7 (Stohl) or 23...♖ad8 24 ♖de1! ♕d3+ 25 ♔a1 ♕xc3 26 gxf7+ ♘xg4 27 fxe8♘+! ♖xe8 28 bxc3 and wins. Alas, I did not immediately grasp the fact that the suddenly discovered defence 23...♕xc3!?, which concerned me, did not help in view of 24 ♕f4!;

2) 20...♔h7 (if 20...♔h8 White has both 21 ♕h5, and 21 ♘g5, forcing 21...♔g8, since 21....♗d8? 22 ♖xd8! or 21...♕a5? 22 ♕f4! etc. is bad for Black) 21 ♘g5+! ♔g8 22 ♗xf6 h5! 23 ♕f5(f3) ♗xf6 24 ♕xf6 ♕e7! 25 ♖hf1 ♕xf6 26 ♖xf6 ♖xe3 27 ♖xf7, and White, who with his h4-pawn has created a powerful outpost for his knight on g5, should be able to convert his extra pawn.

After rejecting 20 ♕g4+, I automatically played 'safely' and reconciled myself to the exchange of queens.

20...♕c8! (20...♔g8? 21 g5 and wins)

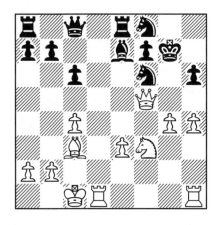

21 ♕xc8?!

White's position is so strong, that he could have permitted himself a temporary retreat – 21 ♕c2! ♔g8 22 g5, which promises a fearfully strong attack:

1) 22...♘h5? 23 gxh6 ♘g6 24 ♘g5 ♗xg5 25 h7+! ♔xh7 26 hxg5 ♕g4 – initially I called this defence 'comparatively best', not noticing the winning 27 ♖d4! ♕xg5 28 ♖dh4;

2) 22...♘g4 23 gxh6 with two branches:

a) 23...♗c5 (23...f5? 24 ♖hg1) 24 ♗d4! (24 ♖hg1!? – Stohl) 24...♖xe3 (24...♗xd4 does not help: 25 ♖xd4 ♖xe3 26 ♖g1 f5 27 ♖f4! and ♖xf5, or 25...f5 26 ♘g5! ♕e7 27 ♖g1) 25 h7+! ♘xh7 26 ♘g5! ♘xg5 27 hxg5 ♗xd4 28 ♖xd4 ♕e8! 29 ♕h7+ ♔f8 30 ♕h8+ ♔e7 31 ♕h4!, regaining the piece with an obvious advantage;

b) 23...♕e6 24 ♖hg1 ♗c5 25 ♔b1! ♗xe3 26 ♖de1 ♕e4! (the most resilient) 27 h7+! ♘xh7 28 ♖xe3 ♕xc2+ 29 ♔xc2 ♖xe3 30 ♖xg4+ ♔f8 31 ♗b4+ ♔e8 32 ♖g8+ ♔d7 33 ♖xa8 ♖xf3 34 ♖xa7 ♔c7 35 h5 ♖f2+ (35...♖h3 36 ♖a5 and ♖f5) 36 ♔d3! with winning chances (36...♖xc2?! is dangerous in view of 37 ♗d2!).

Moreover, 21 ♖hg1!? was also promising, with the pretty variation 21...♕xf5 22 gxf5+ ♔h7 (22...♔h8 23 ♖d6!) 23 ♘g5+! (a second piece sacrifice!) 23...hxg5 24 hxg5 ♖ad8 25 ♖df1 ♖d3 26 ♗e5 ♘h5 27 ♖h1 ♔g8 28 ♖xh5 f6 (the 'booty' has to be returned) 29 gxf6 ♗xf6 30 ♗xf6 ♖exe3 31 ♖f4, and Black is lost. 21...♔g8 22 ♗xf6 ♗xf6 23 ♕xf6 ♕e6! 24 ♕xe6 ♖xe6 (24...♘xe6 25 h5!) 25 ♘d4 ♖xe3 26 ♘f5 ♖e6 27 g5! h5! is more resilient, although here too after 28 ♖gf1 White has an obviously better ending.

21...♖axc8 22 g5 ♘8h7

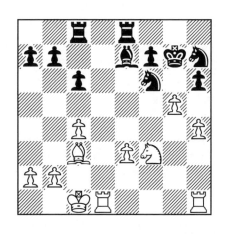

This endgame is by no means so clear.

23 e4!

White continues to pin his hopes on his initiative and c3-g7, 'the main diagonal of the game'. 23 gxf6+ ♗xf6 24 ♘d4 ♔f8 25 ♖hf1 was also not bad, but not the over-hasty 23 ♖d7? because of 23...hxg5 24 hxg5 ♘xg5! 25 ♘xg5 ♔g6!.

23...♖cd8?

Nikolic cracks under the pressure. How-ever, even after the best move 23...♔f8! 24 gxf6 ♘xf6 25 ♖hg1 Black would have faced a difficult and thankless defence: 25...♖cd8 26 ♗d2! or 25...♖ed8 26 ♖df1! (my *Informator* suggestion 26 ♗d2(?) h5 27 ♘e5 is weak on account of 27...♗d6, equalising) 26...♘xe4 27 ♗g7+ ♔e8 28 ♗xh6 etc.

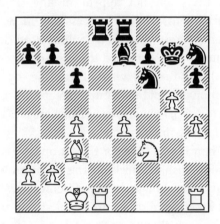

24 ♖df1

Again deferring the transition to technical lines – 24 gxf6+ ♘xf6 25 ♖df1 ♔f8 26 ♘e5 ♖d6 27 ♗d2 or 26 ♘d4 ♗c5 27 ♘xc6! bxc6 28 ♖xf6 ♗d4 29 ♗xd4 ♖xd4 30 b3 etc.

24...♔f8 25 gxf6 ♗xf6 (25...♘xf6 – cf. the previous note) **26 e5 ♗g7** (26...♗e7? 27 e6! and ♘e5!) **27 ♖hg1 c5**

Covering himself against ♗b4+. Without the queens and with material equal, Black continues to remain under attack.

28 ♔c2 ♖e6 29 ♖g4 (29 ♖g2!? or 29 b4! b6 30 bxc5 bxc5 31 ♖b1 was slightly more

accurate) **29...♗h8**

In the event of 29...h5 30 ♖f4 ♗h6? (30...b6 or 30...♖d7 was more resilient) White would have won prettily by 31 ♖xf7+! ♔xf7 32 ♘g5+ ♔e7 33 ♖f7+ ♔e8 34 ♘xe6.

30 b4! (by opening up the queenside, White creates new weaknesses in the enemy position) **30...b6 31 bxc5** (managing without the preparatory 31 a4 or 31 ♖b1) **31...bxc5 32 ♖b1 ♖a6**

If 32...♖ee8 there follows 33 a4! ♖b8 34 ♖b5! and wins.

33 ♖b2

Previously I attached an exclamation mark to this move, but there was a quicker win by 33 ♖b7! ♖xa2+ 34 ♗b2! (Stohl's move 34 ♔b3 is weak because of 34...♖f2!) 34...h5 35 ♖g1!, and it is time to give up the knight – 35...♘f6, since 35...♖e8 36 ♔b1 ♖a6 37 e6! is even worse.

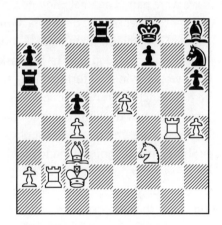

33...♗g7?

A final mistake in a difficult position. 33...♔e7? was bad in view of 34 ♖b7+ ♔e6 35 ♖f4 ♖f8 36 ♖c7 ♖xa2+ 37 ♔b3 and ♖xc5 (Stohl). Soon after the game I recommended 33...♖b6(?!) 34 ♖b5! ♖c8 (34...♖xb5?! 35 cxb5 and wins), but then 35 a4! is strong, with the threats of a4-a5, ♖g1-d1 and ♘e1-d3. Black also cannot hold out after 33...♖e8 34 ♖b5! ♖xa2+ 35 ♔b3 ♖e2(a6) 36 ♖xc5 or

33...h5 34 ♖g2! with the threat of 35 ♖b7(b5) ♖xa2+ 36 ♗b2.

34 ♖b7! (of course!) **34...♖xa2+ 35 ♔b3 ♖a6 36 e6!** (the decisive breakthrough) **36...♖xe6 37 ♖xg7 1-0**

Despite the errors made, this game was awarded the first brilliancy prize of 50,000 pesos.

As a result we defeated the Bosnians by our 'favourite' score 3-1, and in the 13th, penultimate round a 2-2 draw with Israel practically ensured us first place. After a short draw with Psakhis my score became 8½ out of 10 (85%). The fight for the best result on board 1 was a serious one: it is sufficient to say that a player by the name of Yang Xian from Hong Kong finished on 10 out of 12 (83.33%). And, to avoid spoiling the picture, I decided to miss the last round, in which we were paired against England.

My absence provoked the dissatisfaction of the leader of the English team, Nigel Short. A few days before this, journalists had asked me who would win the forthcoming final Candidates match – Timman or Short? – and how my next world championship match would end. To the first question I replied: 'It will be Short'. And, laughing, I made the same reply to the second question: 'It will be short.' On learning of this from the tournament bulletin, Short took offence – and on the day of the match with Russia he claimed that I was afraid of playing Black against him (six months later 'in revenge' I beat Nigel with Black in the European Team Championship).

Instead of me, Khalifman turned out against Short and he easily gained a draw, and the match itself concluded 2-2.

To the astonishment of the chess world, Russia performed no worse at the Olympiad than the USSR (Kramnik especially impressed – 8½ out of 9!), England and USA finished outside the prize-winners, and the silver and bronze medals were won by the hitherto unknown Uzbekistan and Armenia!

Also the Strongest in Europe

10th European Team Championship (Debrecen, 20–30 November 1992): 1. Russia – 25 out of 36; 2. Ukraine – 22½; 3. England – 21½; 4. Israel – 21; 5–8. Croatia, Sweden, Germany and Lithuania – 20½; 9. Georgia – 20, etc (altogether – 40 teams). The winning team comprised **Kasparov** (6 out of 8), Bareev (5 out of 8), Kramnik (6 out of 7), Dreev (3 out of 6) and reserve Vyzhmanavin (5 out of 7).

After the Manila Olympiad, for five months I did not appear in any serious tournaments, but I successfully flew to Buenos Aires, where in a double-round clock simultaneous I crushed the Argentine team (9-3), and to Paris, where I won the regular 'Immopar' rapid-play Cup, defeating Kramnik (1½-½), Polugayevsky (2-0), Kamsky (2-0) and, in the final, Anand (1-1; 2-0).

Then it was time for the European Team Championship, which on this occasion was held in the Hungarian city of Debrecen. With the emergence of a number of strong new teams, which had replaced the USSR and Yugoslavia, here, as at the Olympiad, the competition was expected to be much more intense. In addition, the number of boards had been reduced: at one time, in Skara 1980, it was eight (plus two reserves), in Haifa 1990 it was six (plus two reserves), and now it was only four (with one reserve).

The Russian team was again unable to field its strongest line-up: those who declined to play included Dolmatov and Khalifman, and the participants in the Alekhine Memorial in November – Karpov, Yusupov and Salov (it was in this year that the last two left

Russia: Artur – for Germany and Valery – for Spain). However, on board 2 there was now Bareev. Our new 'star striker' Kramnik moved up to board 3, and on the 4th and reserve boards, following the principle 'leave well alone' we took two more Olympiad players – Dreev and Vyzhmanavin (and if a second reserve had been needed, it would probably have been the young Tiviakov).

Usually in the 1st round of a 'Swiss' the opponents of the strongest teams are middle-ranking sides. Therefore I decided to miss the initial match, since from the 2nd round to the 7th such a possibility might no longer present itself. But that day it had to happen that the pairings came out the way they did: the opponents – the Swiss team, and the black pieces for Russia on the odd boards! The decision taken at the team meeting the previous evening had to be revised: after all, the name and chess reputation of the Swiss leader Korchnoi was incomparably higher than his current rating and especially than the strength of the team he was heading.

The entire morning was spent in a commotion, which had little to do with chess and especially little to do with preparations for the forthcoming game: the 'Yugoslav problem' was heatedly discussed. Under the pretext 'FIDE team', the FIDE president Campomanes unexpectedly tried to bring in a team from 'central' Yugoslavia, circumventing UN sanctions against this country, which was at war with its former republics (Yugoslav players had not been admitted to the Olympiad: the Philippines Ministry of Internal Affairs simply did not issue them entry visas). At a meeting of team captains, the overwhelming majority of participants presented a united front for the exclusion of the Yugoslavs. But the draw had already been made, no one intended to change the

pairings for the first round, and a decision regarding the fate of the 'FIDE team' was deferred for 24 hours.

While I was making my initial moves, rushing through my head was a fragmented mixture of the most varied chess and non-chess thoughts, preventing me from concentrating properly on the game. On that dramatic day my favourite King's Indian also misfired – Korchnoi gained an obvious plus (cf. Game No.40 in *My Great Predecessors Part V*, note to White's 16th move), and it was only at the cost of enormous efforts that I managed to confuse my opponent and gain a draw. By winning all the remaining games, we crushed the Swiss 3½-½.

And within a few hours the participation in the tournament of the 'FIDE team' (who beat Czechoslovakia 3-1 in the first round) also concluded. At a meeting of team representatives, 28 out of 29 of those present voted for its exclusion. Many were angered in particular by the hypocritical idea of including Yugoslavia not openly, but under some pseudonym (apparently money had been offered by the sponsor of the Yugoslav team, the notorious banker Jezdimir Vasiljevic, who not long before this had splashed out five million dollars on the Spassky-Fischer 'return match'). At any event, its inclusion would have had even more painful consequences: Bosnia and Croatia were ready to announce their withdrawal from the championship, and a further 17 teams agreed to take part, since they had already arrived – but only on condition that they did not play the 'FIDE team'!

Then we confidently overcame Lithuania and Bosnia (each 3-1), matches in which I beat Rozentalis and drew with Nikolic. The leading positions after three rounds were: Russia – 9½ out of 12; Ukraine and Holland – 8½; England – 8; Armenia – 7½.

In the 4th round one of the central matches of the championship took place: Russia-Ukraine. And once again I was paired with White against Vassily Ivanchuk.

> ### Game 95
> **G.Kasparov-V.Ivanchuk**
> European Team Championship
> 4th Round, Debrecen 24.11.1992
> *Petroff Defence C43*

1 e4

After trying 1 c4, 1 d4 and 1 ♘f3 against Ivanchuk, I switched to 'serving from the right'. In reply my opponent chose a very reliable defence.

1...e5 2 ♘f3 ♘f6 3 d4 ♘xe4 4 ♗d3 d5 5 ♘xe5 ♘d7

This variation (as well as 5...♗d6 – *Game No.76*) was one that I looked at a great deal with Makarychev – a leading Petroff expert.

6 ♘xd7

The line with 6 ♕e2 faded into the background after Karpov-Larsen (Tilburg 1980): 6...♘xe5! 7 ♗xe4 dxe4 8 ♕xe4 ♗e6! 9 ♕xe5 ♕d7 10 0-0 (or 10 ♘c3 0-0-0 11 ♗e3 ♗b4! and ...f7-f6) 10...0-0-0 11 ♗e3 ♗b4! (Game No.48 in *My Great Predecessors Part IV*).

6...♗xd7 7 0-0

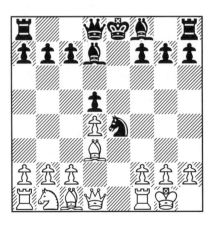

7...♕h4?!

A variation with castling on opposite sides which was fashionable at that time. Soon it was deemed dubious, and following the example of Yusupov 7...♗d6 became topical.

8 c4 0-0-0 9 c5! g5 10 ♗e3

10 ♘c3! is more forceful: 10...♗g7 11 g3 ♕h3 12 ♘xe4 dxe4 13 ♗xe4 ♗b5, and here White is better after both 14 ♗xg5 ♖xd4 15 ♗g2 ♕f5 16 ♕b3 c6 17 ♗e3 ♗xf1 18 ♖xf1 (Ivanchuk-Anand, Roquebrune (rapid) 1992), and 14 ♗g2 ♕f5 15 ♗e3! ♗xf1 16 ♗xf1 with excellent compensation for the exchange (Anand-Ivanchuk, Linares 1993). For many players, White's win in this game killed their desire to play 7...♕h4.

10...♖e8

At that time the main move. After the direct 10...f5 they replied 11 f3 f4 (we also analysed 11...♘f6 12 ♘d2!?) 12 fxe4 fxe3 13 g3 ♕h3 14 e5 with a small advantage for White. But it transpired that 10...♗g7! promises Black equality: 11 ♘d2?! f5! 12 ♘f3 ♕h6 (when 13 ♘e5? is weak in view of 13...f4! 14 ♘f7 ♕e6) or 11 f3 ♘f6 12 ♘c3 g4!.

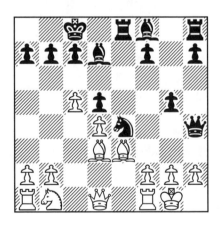

11 ♘d2!

A novelty that we had prepared. 11 f3 ♘f6 12 ♗f2 (or 12 ♕d2 ♖g8) 12...♕h6! 13 ♘c3 g4 leads to sharp play, which is what Black is aiming for in this variation (Makarychev-Ye

Rongguang, Belgrade 1988). Therefore White begins with prophylaxis – he changes course with his knight, avoiding f2-f3 and creating the threat of ♘f3.

11...♗g7

11...♘xd2 12 ♕xd2 does not altogether equalise, while if 11...f5 there follows 12 ♘f3! ♕h6 13 ♘e5 f4?! (13...♕e6 14 ♖c1 f4 15 ♗d2 is also unfavourable) 14 ♘xd7 fxe3 15 fxe3! ♔xd7 16 ♕a4+ ♔d8 17 ♕xa7 with a winning attack (this was what we had prepared).

12 ♘f3 ♕h5?!

Making things easier for me: now it is possible to transpose into a favourable endgame. 12...♕h6 deserved consideration, in order to answer 13 ♘e5 (13 h4 f5!) with 13...♖xe5! 14 dxe5 ♗xe5 15 g3 f5, with a pawn for the exchange and an unclear game.

13 ♘xg5 ♕xd1 14 ♖fxd1

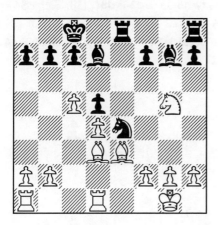

Certain additional resources were given by 14 ♖axd1!? ♘xg5 15 ♗xg5 ♗g4 (15...♗xd4?! 16 c6!) 16 ♖d2 ♗xd4 17 ♗b5!: for example, 17...♖e4 18 ♔h1! (apart from 18 h3) 18...♗e5 19 f3 ♖b4 20 fxg4 ♖xb5 21 ♖xd5 f6 (after 14 ♖fxd1 this would have refuted 18 ♔h1) 22 ♗xf6 ♗xf6 23 ♖xf6 ♖xb2 24 h4! ♖xa2 25 g5 or 17...♖eg8 18 ♖xd4 ♖xg5 19 f4!? (apart from 19 ♖e1) 19...♖g7 20 c6, in all cases with advantage to White.

14...♘xg5 15 ♗xg5 ♗g4

If 15...♗xd4 White would have retained the initiative by 16 c6! ♗e6 17 cxb7+ ♔b8 (17...♔xb7?! 18 ♗b5! ♖eg8 19 ♖xd4 ♖xg5 20 ♖c1 is worse for Black) 18 ♖d2 ♖eg8 19 ♗f4 ♔xb7 20 ♗e2 ♗f6 21 ♖c1 or 18...♗e5 19 ♗b5 ♖eg8 20 ♗e7 etc.

16 ♖d2 ♗xd4 17 c6?!

A tempting blow, but 17 ♗b5! was stronger: for example, 17...♖e4 18 h3! (18 ♖xd4?! ♖xd4 19 ♗f6 ♖b4 with equality) 18...♗f5 (not 18...♗xh3? 19 ♖xd4! 20 ♗f6 ♖g4 21 ♗xh8 ♖xg2+ 22 ♔h1 ♖xf2 23 ♖g1) 19 ♖ad1 ♖g8 (19...c6 20 ♗xc6!) 20 h4 h6 21 ♖xd4 winning a pawn, or 17...♖eg8 18 ♖xd4 ♖xg5 19 c6! (19 ♖e1 is also sensible, but not 19 f4?! ♖g7 20 c6 ♗f3 21 g3 h5!) 19...♗f3 20 g3, and White's chances are better.

17...♗e5! (17...♗b6? 18 ♗f6!) **18 ♗b5 b6!**

Again the best defence. My *Informator* suggestion 18...♖e6(?!) is weaker in view of 19 ♖xd5 (19 f4!?) 19...♖g8 20 h4 bxc6 21 ♗a6+ ♔b8 22 ♖a5(d3) etc.

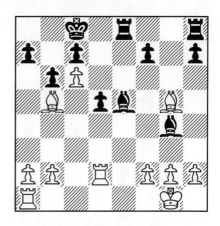

19 ♗h4! (in order to deal with the excessively active bishop on e5) **19...♖hg8**

Here Ivanchuk was already running into severe time-trouble. The 'active' 19...d4(?!) recommended by me would merely have increased Black's problems after 20 f3 ♗f5 21 ♔f1! followed by ♖ad1(e1).

20 &a6+

Dislodging the king. But the immediate 20 &g3!? was somewhat stronger, or even 20 ♖e1!? ♖e6 (not 20...&xh2+?! 21 ♔xh2 ♖xe1 22 f3!) 21 ♔f1 &d6 22 ♖xd5 ♖xe1+ 23 ♔xe1 &e6 24 ♖h5 &xa2 25 &d3! ♖xg2 26 &xh7 with slightly the better chances in an open battle (26...♔b8 27 &b1! ♖g1+ 28 ♔d2 &f4+ 29 ♔e2 &c4+ 30 ♔f3 a5 31 ♔xf4 ♖xb1 32 &f6 etc).

20...♔b8 21 &g3 &xg3

If 21...h5, then 22 a4 or 22 ♖e1 is possible, when 22...&xg3?! 23 ♖xe8+ ♖xe8 24 fxg3! is now to White's advantage.

22 hxg3 ♖d8 23 ♖d4 ♖d6 24 ♖c1 &c8

(24...h5!?) **25 &d3**

A critical choice: it is important to retain this strong bishop, but the main thing is that for the moment the black king remains penned in. Previously I criticised this move and recommended 25 &xc8 ♔xc8 26 b4 with the optimistic evaluation 'clear advantage to White', but after 26...h5! 27 b5 ♖g4 he has none: 28 ♖cd1 a6! 29 a4 ♖xd4 30 ♖xd4 axb5 31 axb5 ♔d8! or 29 ♖xd5 axb5 30 ♖xd6 cxd6 31 ♖xd6 ♔c7 and ...♖a4 with equality.

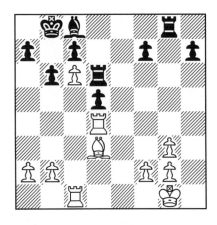

25...♖g4?!

After this move Vassily had literally just one minute left! 25...h5 26 &e2 ♖g5 was

safer, but even so the position is still within the drawing zone.

26○ ♖xg4 &xg4 27 f3

Also nothing was promised by 27 b4 d4 28 b5 &e6, but the straightforward 27 &xh7!? d4 28 &d3 &e6 29 b3 came into consideration.

27...&e6 28 b4?!

Succumbing to the temptation to play on the opponent's time-trouble, since no benefits are apparent from 28 g4 d4 29 b3 &d5 30 &b5 ♔c8 etc.

28...d4 29 a4 a5 (the immediate 29...&b3! 30 a5 bxa5 31 bxa5 &a4 was also good, with equality) **30 b5 &b3 31 ♖a1 ♔c8**

The equalising 31...h6 32 ♔f2 &e6 was more accurate. Now, thanks to such long-term trumps as the better pawn structure and the far-advanced c6-pawn, I am able to set Black some problems.

32 ♔f2 h6 33 ♔e2 ♔d8?! (33...♖e6+ 34 ♔d2 ♖e5 35 &c2 &c4 with the threat of ...♖e2+ was better) **34 ♔d2 ♔e7 35 &c2 &c4 36 ♖h1**

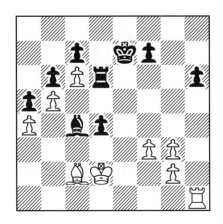

36...d3?!

A tempting and outwardly spectacular pawn advance with the flag about to fall, but now the bishop comes under attack along the fourth rank. Black should have marked time – 36...♖e6! 37 &d3 &b3 38

♖h4 ♖d6 39 ♗c2 ♗c4 40 ♖e4+ ♔f8 41 g4 ♖d8(d5), retaining a defensible position.

37 ♗d1 ♔f8 (37...f5!?) 38 ♖h4

Centralising the rook with gain of tempo. 38 g4!? also came into consideration, with the idea of f3-f4, ♖h5 and g4-g5.

38...♗a2 39 ♖e4 ♖g6 (39...h5?! 40 f4!) 40 g4

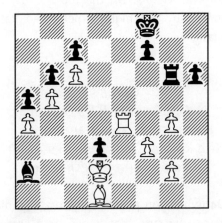

40...h5?!

Another step towards the precipice. My old recommendation 40...♖d6 was better – in the event of 41 ♖e5 f6 42 ♖e1 ♗g8 Black stands firm with the rooks on, while after 41 ♖e3 ♗e6 42 ♖xd3 ♖xd3+ 43 ♔xd3 ♔e7 he has every chance of saving the bishop endgame a pawn down (it is not clear how White can break through: his bishop is tied to the a4-pawn).

The time control was reached, and after calming down and having a proper think, I found a way of maintaining my initiative.

41 f4!

An unexpected rejoinder, which in his haste Ivanchuk had overlooked. 41 ♖d4 was weaker: 41...♗e6 42 gxh5 ♖xg2+ 43 ♔xd3 ♖h2 with counterplay.

41...hxg4 42 f5

To be followed by the capture on g4. White has sharply improved his position, by exchanging his doubled pawn and restricting the black bishop.

42...♖d6

In the variation 42...♖g5? 43 ♗xg4 ♗d5 44 ♖d4 ♗xg2 45 ♔xd3 f6 46 ♔e3 ♖g7 there is the decisive 47 ♗h5 ♖e7+ 48 ♔f4, but it is simpler to immediately transpose into a rook endgame by 47 ♔f2: for example, 47...♗h1 48 ♗h5! (not my *Informator* 48 ♔g1? ♗d5!) 48...♖e7 49 ♖d8+ ♔g7 50 ♗f3! ♗xf3 51 ♔xf3, or 47...♗d5 48 ♖xd5 ♖xg4 49 ♖d8+ ♔e7 50 ♖d7+ ♔e8 51 ♖xc7 ♖xa4 52 ♖c8+ ♔e7 53 ♖b8, and Black cannot hold out.

43 ♖xg4 ♗d5 44 ♖h4!

Reminding Black about the weakness of the c7-pawn. The win of the d3-pawn is far more harmless – 44 ♖d4?! ♔e7 45 g4 f6! 46 ♔xd3 ♗g8 47 ♖xd6 ♔xd6 with a drawn bishop ending.

44...♔g7 45 g3!

'Far from obvious prophylaxis.' (Makarychev). Again 45 ♖d4?! is harmless, this time in view of 45...♔f6! 46 g4 ♔e5 47 ♖xd3 ♗e4 with a draw, or 46 ♗b3 ♔e5 47 ♖xd5+ ♖xd5 48 ♗xd5 ♔xd5 49 ♔xd3 ♔e5 with a drawn pawn endgame (50 g4? ♔f4!).

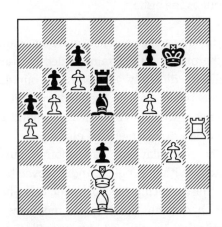

45...♔f6?

The decisive mistake! 45...f6? 46 ♖d4 and ♗b3! was also bad, but one of two bishop moves was far more resilient:

1) 45...♗a2 46 ♖g4+ ♔f8 47 ♖e4 ♗d5 (if

47...f6? 48 ♗h5 ♖d8 49 g4 ♗b3, then 50 g5! fxg5 51 f6 ♗f7 52 ♗d1! is strong) 48 ♖d4 ♔e7 49 ♖h4! ♖d8! 50 ♖h6 and g3-g4, retaining chances of success;

2) 45...♗g2! 46 ♔e3 d2 47 ♔f2 ♗d5 48 ♖d4 ♔f6 49 g4 ♔e5 50 ♖xd2, and here either 50...♗e4 51 ♖xd6 ♔xd6 52 ♗b3 ♔e5 53 ♔g3 ♔f6 (53...f6? 54 ♔h4 and wins) 54 ♔f4 ♗d3 55 g5 ♔e7, or 50...♗c4! 51 ♖xd6 ♔xd6 52 ♔g3 f6 53 ♔h4 ♗f7 54 g5 fxg5+ 55 ♔xg5 ♔e7 56 f6+ ♔f8 with a draw in view of the weakness of the a4-pawn.

46 ♖h8! (nevertheless breaking through to the c7-pawn) **46...♔e5**

The best practical chance was a piece sacrifice – 46...♔xf5 47 ♖c8 ♗xc6!? 48 bxc6 ♖xc6, although after 49 ♗b3 and ♔xd3 the conversion would not present any particular difficulty.

47 ♖c8 ♔d4 48 ♖xc7 (creating an ultra-powerful passed pawn) **48...♖h6 49 ♖d7! ♖h2+ 50 ♔c1 1-0**

Only not 50 ♔e1?? ♔e3 (Ivanchuk's desperate trap). An unusual technical endgame with pawns fixed on squares of the same colour as the bishop.

This was a key win: the three other games in the match with Ukraine ended in draws, and with difficulty we overcame our dangerous rivals: 2½-1½. The leading positions were now Russia – 12 out of 16; England and Armenia – 10½; Israel – 10, etc.

The next day we had another super-match – with the English, and it proved to be the most difficult. My opponent was Short, who had been thirsting to meet me in Manila, but I outplayed him with Black in a Sicilian, obtained a superior endgame and, despite inaccuracies, won on the 38th move. Nevertheless we only just saved the match: 2-2.

That same day Armenia defeated Holland

(3-1), and Israel crushed Moldova (3½-½), and now two teams were just half a point behind Russia!

In the 6th round came the match between the gold and bronze medal winners at the recent Olympiad, which was especially crucial for Russia, since we had lost to Armenia in Manila. On the top board I was opposed by the highly-experienced Rafael Vaganian.

Game 96
G.Kasparov-R.Vaganian
European Team Championship
6th Round, Debrecen 26.11.1992
Queen's Gambit Declined D37

---

1 d4 (when you play this against Vaganian, you can be sure that it will be a Queen's Gambit) **1...♘f6 2 c4 e6 3 ♘c3 d5 4 ♘f3**

A rare instance of my avoiding the 'Carlsbad' – 4 cxd5 exd5 5 ♗g5 (*Game Nos.37, 45, 51*). I very much wanted to test one of the sharpest lines of the 5 ♗f4 variation, which I had analysed a great deal and prepared for the fourth match with Karpov (1987).

4...♗e7 5 ♗f4 0-0 6 e3 c5

For many years this was the main line, but nowadays they often play 6...♘bd7, not fearing the bind with 7 c5.

7 dxc5 ♗xc5 8 ♕c2

More aggressive than 8 ♗e2 dxc4 (Smyslov-Kasparov, 4th match game, Vilnius 1984), 8 ♖c1 ♘c6 9 cxd5 exd5 10 ♗e2 d4!? (Game No.49 in *Kasparov vs. Karpov 1986-1987*), or 8 cxd5 ♘xd5! 9 ♘xd5 exd5 10 a3 ♘c6 11 ♗d3 ♗b6 12 0-0 ♗g4 13 h3 ♗h5 etc (van Wely-Kasparov, Wijk aan Zee 2001).

8...♘c6 9 a3 ♕a5 10 0-0-0

I had already played this against Khalifman in Reggio Emilia (1991/92). Since the times of the Korchnoi-Karpov matches it has been known that after 10 罝d1 奠e7 11 ♘d2 e5 12 奠g5 d4 13 ♘b3 ♛d8 14 奠e2 a5! Black has a good game (Alterman-Kasparov, Tel Aviv 1998).

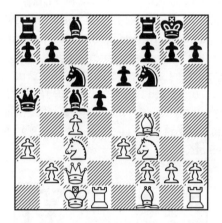

Black's main reply is 10...奠e7, after which the two most popular responses are:

1) 11 g4 dxc4! 12 奠xc4 e5 13 g5 exf4 14 gxf6 奠xf6 15 ♘d5 ♘e7 16 ♘xf6+ gxf6 17 罝hg1+ ♚h8, for example:

a) 18 ♛e4 ♘g6! 19 ♛d4 ♛b6! 20 ♛xb6 axb6 21 罝d6 fxe3?! 22 fxe3 罝a5 23 ♚d2 罝f5, and if I had played 24 奠d5!, Khalifman would have had to fight for a draw, but 21...奠h3! with equality is better (Gelfand-Yusupov, Linares 1993);

b) 18 e4 b5! 19 奠d5 ♘xd5 20 exd5 b4! 21 axb4 ♛a1+ 22 ♚d2 ♛a6! 23 ♛c6 罝d8 24 ♚c3 (24 ♛xa8? ♛c4!) 24...奠b7 25 ♛xa6 奠xa6 26 罝d4 罝ac8+ 27 ♚d2 (27 ♚b3 罝xd5!) 27...奠b7 with equality (van Wely-Short, Wijk aan Zee 1997; Anand-Kramnik, Leon 2002);

2) 11 h4!? dxc4?! (but here it is better to play 11...a6 or 11...罝d8, Kasparov-Ehlvest, Novgorod 1995) 12 奠xc4 b6? 13 ♘g5? (both players underestimated 13 奠b5! 奠b7 14 ♘d2 and ♘c4, trapping the queen) 13...奠a6 14 ♘ce4 g6 15 ♘xf6+ (15 ♘xf7!?) 15...奠xf6 16 ♘e4 奠e7 17 奠xa6 ♛xa6 18 ♚b1 ♛b7? (18...罝ac8 was more resilient) 19 h5! with a

powerful attack, which brought White victory as early as the 24th move (Kasparov-Vaganian, Novgorod 1995).

However, on this occasion Vaganian decided to test a fresh idea, to which the game Gelfand-Yusupov (Linares 1992) had drawn attention.

10...♘e4!?

My trainers and I analysed this move before my fifth match with Karpov (1990), and we came to the conclusion that in the event of 11 ♘xe4 dxe4 12 ♛xe4 奠xa3! 13 bxa3 ♛xa3+ 14 ♚d2 罝d8+ 15 ♚e2 ♛b2+ 16 罝d2 罝xd2+ 17 ♘xd2 e5 Black has excellent compensation for the piece. For example: 18 奠g5 (Timoshchenko-Mateus, Cappelle-la-Grande 1992) 18...h6! 19 奠h4 g5, when 20 奠g3? 奠g4+! and ...罝d8 is bad for White.

I remember Gia Giorgadze wondering what would happy after 11 ♘b5. I replied: 'What sort of ugly move is that? Somewhere off to the left...' But on examination we realised that Black's centre was beginning to creak, and also that an invasion on c7 was threatened.

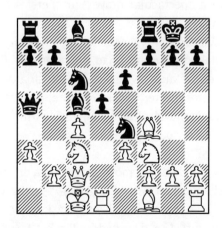

11 ♘b5!? a6

The reckless 11...e5? is weak not only because of 12 罝xd5 ♘f6 13 罝xe5! ♘xe5 14 奠xe5 奠e7 15 ♘c7, but also in view of 12 ♘xe5 ♘xe5 13 奠xe5 奠g4 14 f3 奠xe3+ 15

♔b1 ♘f2 16 fxg4 ♘xh1 17 ♗d3 or 12...♗f5 13 g4 ♘xe5 14 gxf5 ♘g4 15 b4.

12 ♘c7 e5

Hoping to achieve good play in the unclear complications.

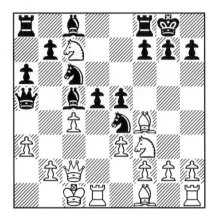

The aforementioned Gelfand-Yusupov game went 13 ♘xd5 ♘xf2! 14 ♘g5 (after 14 ♕xf2 exf4 15 ♗d3 fxe3 there only remains a colourful perpetual check: 16 ♗xh7+! ♔xh7 17 ♕h4+ ♔g8 18 ♘f6+! gxf6 19 ♕g3+) 14...♗f5! 15 ♕xf2 exf4 16 ♕xf4 ♘e7! 17 ♘xe7+ ♗xe7 18 ♖d5 ♕e1+ 19 ♖d1 ♕a5 with a spectacular draw. But there is also another idea...

13 ♖xd5!?

Makarychev and I had prepared this (we looked at and revised our 1990 analyses). The unexpected rook capture unsettled Vaganian, and after an agonising think he made a serious mistake.

13...f5?

A pseudo-active move, leading to a difficult position. 13...♗f5? 14 ♘xa8 ♘g3 15 e4! ♗xe4 16 ♗d2! or 13...♗e6? 14 ♖xe5! ♘xe5 15 ♗xe5 ♗f5 16 ♗d3 is bad for Black. 13...♘f6?! is also insufficient: 14 ♖xe5! ♘xe5 15 ♗xe5 ♖a7 16 ♗d3 with excellent attacking chances. And 13...♘xf2 is no longer so tempting: 14 ♕xf2 ♕xc7 15 ♘xe5 ♘xe5 16 ♗xe5 ♕b6 17 ♗d4 ♗xd4 18 ♖xd4 ♗e6 19 ♔b1 or

16...♕e7 17 ♗d4 b6 18 ♗d3, retaining an albeit weak but extra pawn.

However, 13...♕xc7 (or first 13...exf4) was correct: 14 ♕xe4 exf4! (but not 14...f5? 15 ♗xe5 fxe4 16 ♗xc7, Alonso-Diaz, Cuba 1993) 15 ♖xc5 fxe3, and although White wins a pawn, the weaknesses in his position give Black adequate counterplay: for example, 16 fxe3 g6 17 h4 ♖d8 18 h5 ♕b6 and ...♗f5, or 16 ♗d3 g6 17 ♕xe3 b6 18 ♖h5! (18 ♖g5 ♘a5!) 18...♗g4 19 ♖h4 ♗xf3! 20 ♕xf3 ♘e5 21 ♕g3 ♘xd3+ 22 ♕xd3 ♖ad8 23 ♕c2 ♖fe8 etc.

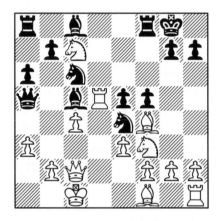

14 ♖xe5! ♘xe5 15 ♗xe5 ♖a7?

The decisive error! 15...♗d7? was also unsuitable: 16 ♘xa8 ♖xa8 17 ♗d3 ♗c6 (17...♗a4 18 ♕e2) 18 ♗d4 ♖d8 19 ♖g1! and wins.

The last chance was 15...♖b8!. In the event of 16 ♘xa6 bxa6 17 ♗xb8 White is now three pawns up, but 17...♗d7! 18 ♗e5 ♗a4 forces 19 ♗c3 ♘xc3 20 ♕xc3 ♕xc3+ 21 bxc3 with a sharp endgame, where Black can seek salvation by 21...♖xa3+ 22 ♔d2 ♖b8 23 ♘d4 ♖b2+ 24 ♔d3 ♗b3! with the idea of ...♗a2-b1+, or 21...f4!? 22 ♔d2 fxe3+ 23 fxe3 ♖b8. Therefore consideration should be given to the developing 16 ♗d3!? ♗d6 17 ♗xe4 ♗xe5 18 ♗d5+ ♔h8 19 ♘xe5 ♕xc7 20 f4 or 17...♕xc7 18 ♗d5+ ♔h8 19 ♗d4 ♕e7 20 c5 ♗c7 21 ♕c3

♗d7 22 h4 with two pawns for the exchange and powerful domination. Nevertheless, after 15...♖b8 some intrigue is still retained, whereas now the battle concludes.

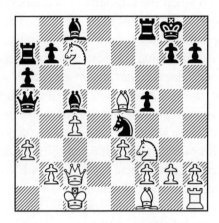

16 ♘d5! b6

If 16...♕d8 White decides matters with the unexpected 17 b4! ♗d6 18 ♗d4 ♖a8 19 c5 and ♗c4. All his pieces quickly join the battle, and Black cannot defend, his centralised knight remaining out of play.

17 ♗d3

It was also possible to win the bishop at once – 17 b4 ♕xa3+ 18 ♗b2 ♕a2 19 bxc5 bxc5 20 ♗d3, but I played more solidly.

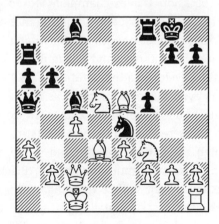

17...♗d7

Black would not have lost so submissively after 17...b5!? 18 b4! (18 cxb5 is also good)

18...♕xa3+ 19 ♗b2 ♕a2, when accuracy would still have been demanded of White: 20 ♘e5 ♗d6! 21 ♗xe4! fxe4 22 ♘c3 ♕xb2+ 23 ♔xb2 ♗xe5 24 ♔c1 etc.

18 b4 ♕xa3+ 19 ♗b2

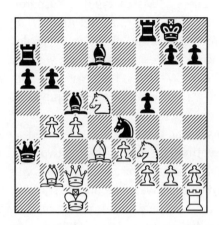

19...♕a4 (if 19...♕a2 apart from 20 bxc5 there is also 20 ♘c3 ♘xc3 21 ♕xc3 ♗e6(c6) 22 bxc5 bxc5 23 ♖d1 and wins) **20 bxc5 bxc5** (or 20...♘xc5 21 ♘e5) **21 ♘e5 ♕xc2+ 22 ♗xc2 ♗e6 23 ♘f4 1-0**

As a result we crushed Armenia 3½-½! The outcome of the tournament was decided. Makarychev: *'Between the 4th and 6th rounds three important wins were achieved, and very convincingly, by the world champion. Many even felt that if Kasparov turned out he would win his game without fail, irrespective of what colour he had, and that the opponents should only pin their hopes on the remaining boards.'*

In the last three matches – with Israel, Hungary and Georgia – we won by the identical score 2½-1½. In the 7th round I was rested, and in the 8th and 9th, realising that fatigue was setting in, I drew with Portisch and Giorgadze.

That was how my second European Championship concluded. Its three prize-winners – Russian, Ukraine and England –

were a real reflection of the order of chess strength on the continent.

Hurricane at the Finish

International Tournament in Linares (22 February – 15 March 1993): 1. **Kasparov** – 10 out of 13; 2–3. Karpov and Anand – 8½; 4. Shirov – 8; 5. Kramnik – 7½; 6–7. Salov and Ivanchuk – 6½; 8. Beliavsky – 6; 9–10. Bareev and Kamsky – 5½; 11–12. Yusupov and Timman – 5; 13. Gelfand – 4½; 14. Ljubojevic – 4.

As usual, Linares 1993 assembled almost the entire chess elite, including two new stars – Kramnik and Shirov. Only Short was not playing: three weeks before the start, on 31st January, he defeated Timman in the final Candidates match (6½-4½) and won the right to fight with me for the world title. Campomanes promptly announced that the last date for submitting bids to stage our match was 8th February, but then he granted an extension of two weeks. The first to submit a bid was Manchester (Short's native city), and Campo hastily declared Manchester to be the match venue, although FIDE had already received a bid from London with a larger prize fund than Manchester's 1.7 million dollars.

Of course, Short and I were unhappy about such lack of ceremony – the FIDE President had taken a decision about the venue and dates of the match, without even consulting the players. Just before the start of the tournament in Linares, Nigel phoned me and unexpectedly suggested playing the match outside the framework of FIDE, as in former times right up to 1948. Thinking that Short – at that time the last GMA President – would bring western grandmasters with him and that we would create a new, effective and professional organisation, I replied that I had been awaiting such a call for many years, and after some hesitation I agreed with my opponent's proposal. (Looking ahead, I should say that I overestimated Short, and the hopes of uniting the efforts of the GMA and PCA were not realised.)

And when the tournament was already in progress, on 26th February, Short and I made a sensational announcement, which was to have far-reaching consequences for the chess world: *'Since FIDE has shown disregard for its own rules and it cannot be trusted to organize the most important professional chess competition in the world, we have agreed to play our match outside the jurisdiction of FIDE, under the auspices of a new body – the Professional Chess Association. We have agreed to donate 10 per cent of the prize fund from this match to establish this body which is intended to represent chess professionals world-wide and work for the good of the game.'*

This statement, published in Linares, changed the psychological situation in the faction of leading grandmasters, arousing passions around the chess summit. It appeared to instil Karpov with new strength: he had lost hope of regaining the crown, and now suddenly, according to the new FIDE rules, there was a glimmer of a chance... On this occasion the ex-champion looked refreshed and he played in a fighting manner, seriously competing with me and Anand.

True, both Karpov and I caught very bad colds (I developed a temperature of 38.3 and I was even taken to hospital, as they were afraid I had pneumonia), and as an exception we were allowed to miss the 1st round. Joining the battle from the 2nd round, we both began the tournament with Black: I satisfied myself with a draw against Ivanchuk, after quickly equalising in a Scheveningen, while Karpov lost on time in a difficult game with Timman.

On the other hand, the adjournment day, when the postponed games took place, was a victorious one for us: Karpov overcame Salov with White, and I beat Ljubojevic with Black in my favourite King's Indian (cf. *Game No.80*, note to Black's 13th move).

But the effects of the illness were still being felt. I adjourned my 3rd round game with Yusupov in an endgame with the exchange for a pawn and good winning chances. Makarychev and I spent a long time analysing this endgame, but on the resumption – on the 102nd move! – I suddenly drove the enemy king out of the corner, and by a miracle Black saved himself (with the king in the corner White would have won easily thanks to zugzwang). In the 4th round came a draw with Kramnik – I employed an important novelty with Black (cf. *Game No.90*, note to Black's 12th move). In the 5th round I gained a very difficult win with White against Bareev in the rare Bishop's Opening (1 e4 e5 2 ♗c4). And in the 6th came a protracted draw with Salov in a Sicilian with 2 c3.

At that point there was four leaders on 4 out of 6: Karpov, Kasparov, Anand and Kamsky. Then Kamsky fell away, suffering a series of losses, and among the remaining three a fierce battle for victory in the tournament developed. In the 7th round I with difficulty converted an absolutely won position against Timman, and in the 8th I parried a dangerous attack by Beliavsky by gaining perpetual check (cf. *Game No.90*, note to White's 10th move).

Before the five concluding rounds the leading trio looked like this: Anand – 6 out of 8, Karpov and Kasparov – 5½. I was not in a very good mood, I was not playing well, and I faced a difficult finish – Anand, Karpov, Gelfand, Shirov and Kamsky! But I managed to summon my will-power and this stretch of the event became one of the best in my career. My genuine hunting fervour suddenly came to life – and everything began to work out.

It began with the 9th round game with Anand, which was very important in the competitive sense. By that time Vishy had already become the main favourite for the next world championship cycle. In the autumn of 1992 he had won the 'match of future champions' against Ivanchuk (5-3), and soon after Linares he qualified for both sets of Candidates matches – from the FIDE Interzonal Tournament in Biel, and from the PCA Qualifying Tournament in Groningen.

Game 97
G.Kasparov-V.Anand
Linares, 9th Round 8.03.1993
Slav Defence D18

1 d4 d5 2 c4 c6 (the expected choice: Anand played this against me in Dortmund 1992) **3 ♘f3 ♘f6 4 ♘c3 dxc4 5 a4 ♗f5 6 e3 e6 7 ♗xc4 ♗b4 8 0-0 ♘bd7**

That game, an ill-starred one for Vishy, went 8...0-0 9 ♕e2 ♘bd7 10 ♘e5 ♖e8 11 ♖d1 ♕c7 12 ♘xd7 ♕xd7 13 f3 ♘d5 14 ♘a2 ♗f8 15 e4 ♗g6 16 ♕e1!? f5?? 17 exd5, and in view of 17...exd5 18 ♗e2 Black resigned. **9 ♘h4**

9 ♕b3 – cf. *Game No.33*.

9...♗g6

Nowadays they more often reply 9...0-0, not fearing the exchange on f5: for example, 10 h3 (10 f3 – Game No.106 in *My Great Predecessors Part II*) 10...♖c8 11 ♕e2 ♘b6 12 ♗b3 ♘bd5 13 ♗d2 ♕e7 14 ♖fc1 ♖cd8 15 ♕f3 ♘e4 16 ♘xf5 exf5 17 ♘xe4 fxe4 18 ♗xb4 ♘xb4 ½-½ (Kasparov-Kramnik, Paris (rapid) 1994).

10 h3!?

An interesting waiting move. No real dividends are given by 10 g3 0-0 11 ♕b3 ♕b6 12 ♘xg6 hxg6 13 ♖d1 a5 (Kasparov-Beliavsky, Tilburg 1981).

10...0-0

A slightly second-rate reply. Vishy also tried 10...a5 (Karpov-Anand, Monte Carlo (blind 1993), and soon he tried 10...♗h5!? with the idea of 11 g4 ♘d5 12 ♘g2 ♗g6 (Topalov-Gelfand, Belgrade 1995) or 11 ♕b3 a5 12 f4 (if 12 g4 Black has both 12...♘xg4, and 12...♗g6 13 ♘g2 0-0 14 ♘f4 e5 with equality, Sakaev-Kasparov, Rethymnon 2003) 12...0-0! (Piket-Anand, Amsterdam 1993), and if 13 g4, then 13...♘xg4 14 hxg4 ♕xh4 with equality.

11 ♘xg6 hxg6 12 ♕c2! ♖c8

Now 12...e5? is not possible on account of 13 ♕xg6, but later they came to prefer 12...♕e7 13 ♖d1 (13 a5!?) 13...a5.

13 ♖d1

Also suppressing 13...c5? in view of 14 d5.

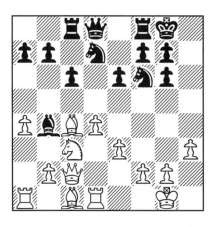

13...♕b6?!

A novelty, provoked by the inconvenience suffered after 13...♕a5 14 ♘a2 ♗d6 15 ♗d2 (Portisch-Hjartarson, Tilburg 1988) or 13...♕e7 14 a5!, depriving Black of his bulwark on b4 (Portisch-Kir.Georgiev, Reggio Emilia 1989/90). But Anand's move has its drawbacks.

14 e4

This resembles the position reached after the 22nd move in my game with Timman from Amsterdam 1988 (*Game No.33*): here White also has the two bishops and a strong pawn centre, while Black's freeing advances are hindered.

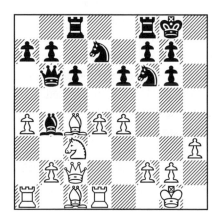

14...c5?!

A positional mistake. However, Black's position is also cheerless after 14...♕c7 15 ♗e3 or 14...♕a5 15 e5 ♘d5 16 ♘e4, while my *Informator* recommendation 14...e5 dangerously strengthens the position of the bishop on c4 – then 15 ♗e3 is good, and also 15 ♘e2 exd4 16 ♘xd4, as in a game between German correspondence players (2008), or 15 dxe5!? ♘xe5 16 ♗a2 with a small but enduring advantage for White.

15 d5 (of course!) **15...♘e5 16 ♗e2**

The simplest, although, as could have transpired three moves later, it was more accurate to play 16 ♗f1! exd5 17 ♘xd5

♘xd5 18 ♖xd5 ♘c6 19 ♗e3 (excluding the resource 19...♗a5 which was available in the game) 19...♘d4 20 ♕d1 ♖cd8 21 ♗c4 etc. However, 16 a5 ♗xa5 17 ♘a4 ♕c7 18 dxe6 ♘xc4 19 ♕xc4 a6 20 exf7+ ♖xf7 21 ♘c3 b5 22 ♕e2 c4 was far less clear.

16...exd5 (16...c4 17 ♗f4!) **17 ♘xd5 ♘xd5 18 ♖xd5 ♘c6 19 ♗c4**

After 19 ♗e3 ♘d4 20 ♗xd4 cxd4 21 ♕b3 a5 22 ♖d1 ♖fd8 23 ♗c4 ♖xd5 24 ♗xd5 ♖c7 25 e5 ♖e7 and ....♗c5 Black has merely a somewhat inferior position. Therefore White builds up the pressure, pinning his hopes on his two bishops, the passive position of the bishop on b4, and the fact that he effectively has an extra mobile pawn in the centre (since Black's queenside pawns are blockaded).

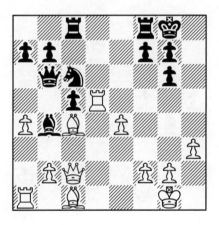

19...♘d4?!

If 19...♘a5?!, then 20 ♗g5 ♘xc4 21 ♕xc4 ♕e6 22 ♖ad1 is strong, as is 20 ♗a2 c4?! 21 ♖b5 ♕d6 22 ♗e3 or 20...♕e6 21 ♗g5(e3) and ♖ad1. However, 19...♗a5! (threatening ...♘b4) was more resilient: 20 ♕e2 ♘d4 21 ♕d3 (or 21 ♕d1 ♖fe8) 21...♘c6!? (again threatening ...♘b4) 22 ♕d1 ♖fe8, and White's advantage is reduced. True, after 20 ♖d1!? ♘d4 21 ♕d3 thanks to his strong light-squared bishop he still has quite good prospects.

20 ♕d3 ♖cd8 21 ♗e3 ♖xd5

There is little choice: if 21...♘e6, then 22 a5! is unpleasant: 22...♕c7 23 a6 or 22....♗xa5 23 ♕a3 ♗b4 24 ♕xa7 etc.

22 ♗xd5 ♖d8 23 ♕c4 ♖d7

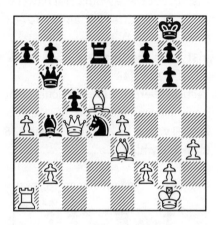

24 ♖c1

In the event of 24 ♗xd4?! cxd4 25 ♕c8+ ♖d8 26 ♕xb7 ♕xb7 27 ♗xb7 d3 Vishy would have been saved by the opposite-coloured bishops and the powerful passed d-pawn. 24 ♖d1!? was more purposeful – after 24...♕a6?! 25 ♕xa6 bxa6 26 h4! or 24...♘e6 25 g3 followed by ♔g2, h3-h4, b2-b3 and so on, Black has a strategically difficult position without any counterplay.

24...♕f6

The move ♖c1 would have been fully justified after 24...♗a5?! 25 b3 ♕b4 26 g3! ♕xc4+ 27 ♖xc4 (27...♘xb3? 28 ♖c2 and wins), but 24...♘e6!? should have been preferred.

25 ♖d1 ♘e6 26 ♕b3

After defending his b2-pawn, White intends gradually to increase the pressure (although at this moment I already had only 15 minutes left for 14 moves). The opponent's defence would have been eased by the exchange of the b-pawns after 26 ♕b5 ♖e7 27 ♗xb7 ♕xb2 28 ♗d5, but perhaps 26 b3!? was better, hindering the play with ...a7-a6 and ...b7-b5.

26...a5?!

By conclusively shutting in his bishop and devaluating his pawn majority on the queenside, Black deprives himself of his last counter-chances. 26...b6 27 g3 was also depressing, but there would still have been a glimmer of hope after 26...a6! 27 ♖d3 ♕d8 or 27...♖e7.

27 ♖d3! (with the threat of 28 ♗xe6 ♖xd3 29 ♗xf7+!) **27...♘f4?**

A tactical oversight in a difficult position. After any neutral move – say, 27...♕d8 or 27...♖e7 – I would have simply replied 28 g3, and Black is stymied.

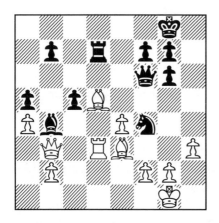

28 e5! ♕f5 (28...♕xe5? 29 ♗xf7+! would have been a tragic finish) **29 ♗xf4 ♕xf4 30 e6 ♖d8**

If 30...♖e7 White wins by 31 exf7+ ♔f8 32 ♗e6 ♕c1+ 33 ♖d1, and more elegantly with 31 ♕c4! ♕xc4 32 exf7+! ♔f8 33 ♗xc4.

31 e7! ♖e8

The fate of the game is decided: White has an irresistible attack on the king, with opposite-coloured bishops. However, Anand continues resisting with his customary resourcefulness, especially since in Linares he had twice escaped with a draw against me (*Game Nos.76, 86*).

32 ♖f3

It was simpler to play 32 g3! ♕f5 (32...♕f6

33 ♖f3) 33 g4 ♕f4 34 ♖f3 ♕c1+ 35 ♔g2 ♖xe7 36 ♗xf7+ ♔h7 37 ♗xg6+!, mating, or the computer line 33 ♖f3 ♕b1+ 34 ♔g2 ♖xe7 35 ♕c4! and ♗xf7+.

32...♕c1+ 33 ♔h2 ♖xe7 (after 33...c4 34 ♗xf7+ ♔h8 apart from anything else there is the elegant 35 ♕xb4!) **34 ♗xf7+ ♔h7 35 ♗xg6+!**

I made this sacrifice automatically, expecting immediate resignation. 35 ♕d3 or 35 ♖g3 would have led more quietly to the goal.

35...♔h6!

35...♔xg6 was hopeless in view of 36 ♕d3+ ♔h6 (36...♔h5? 37 ♕h7+) 37 ♕d6+ and ♕xe7. But now it suddenly seemed to me that the situation had become unclear, and I became slightly rattled.

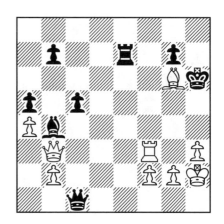

36 ♕d5

36 ♗c2!? would also have won without any problems: 36...♖e2 37 ♖f8! ♕xc2 38 ♕g3 or 36...♖e1 37 h4! c4 38 ♕xc4 ♗d6+ 39 ♔h3 ♖h1+ (39...g6 40 g3) 40 ♔g4 ♖xh4+ 41 ♔xh4 ♕h1+ 42 ♖h3 ♕xg2 43 ♕e6+ g6 44 ♕xg6+.

36...♕g5 37 ♗f5 (37 ♕c4(d8) was also good, but I instinctively withdrew my bishop) **37...g6 38 h4! ♕f6 39 ♗d3?!**

The alternative 39 ♗c2! was far stronger, since if then 39...♕e5+ 40 ♕xe5 ♖xe5 there is the immediately decisive 41 ♖f7! and g2-g4, weaving a mating net.

39...♛e5+ 40 ♛xe5 ♖xe5 41 ♖f6! (now if 41 ♖f7?! there is the diversion 41...c4!) **41...c4!** (the best practical chance) **42 ♗xc4?!**

Again delaying the win, which would have been achieved by 42 ♖xg6+ ♔h7 43 ♗b1, or, more simply, 42 f4! ♖d5 43 ♖xg6+ ♔h7 44 ♗e4 ♖d4 45 ♖e6+ etc.

42...♗e7!

Desperately struggling on in an endgame where he is two pawns down. I was expecting 42...♖e4? 43 ♖xg6+! and ♗d3 with an easy win.

43 ♖b6 (43 ♖f4! ♗d6(c5) 44 ♔h3 or 43...♖f5 44 ♖xf5 gxf5 45 ♗d3 etc would have been decisive) **43...♗c5!** (43...♖e4? 44 ♗d3!) **44 ♖f6**

Returning to the correct path. All chances would have been lost after 44 ♖xb7? ♗xf2 45 g3 ♖e3 46 ♔g2 ♗xg3 47 b4 axb4 48 a5 ♗d6 49 a6 ♖g3+ 50 ♔f2 ♖c3! or 50 ♔f1 ♖a3!.

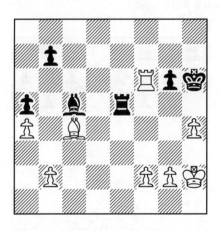

Here, after some thought, Anand realised that if 44...♗e7 there would now follow 45 ♖f4!, and he made a last attempt to confuse matters.

44...♖e4!?

There is an interesting winning method after the exchange of rooks – 44...♖f5 45

♖xf5 gxf5 46 f4!: for example, 46...♔g6 47 g3 ♔f6 48 ♔g2 b6 49 ♔f3 ♗d4 50 b3 ♗c5 51 h5! ♗f8 52 ♗d3 ♔e6 53 ♗xf5+! (the decisive sacrifice!) 53...♔xf5 54 g4+, and for the pawn avalanche Black will have to give up his bishop, but then White's queenside pawns will have their say.

45 ♗d3!

Now after 45 ♖xg6+? ♔xg6 46 ♗d3 ♗xf2 47 ♗xe4+ ♔f6 48 ♔h3 b6 Black succeeds in saving his b-pawn and, two pawns down, in constructing a fortress with the opposite-coloured bishops.

45...♖g4!

No problems would have been created by 45...♖xh4+ 46 ♔g3 ♖d4 47 ♖xg6+ ♔h5 48 ♗f5 ♖xa4 49 f4! or 47...♔h7 48 ♖d6+ ♔g7 49 ♖xd4 ♗xd4 50 b3 and wins.

46 ♔h3 ♗e7! 47 ♖e6! (47 ♔xg4 ♗xf6 48 b3 was also good enough to win, but why suffer any unnecessary difficulties?) **47...♖xh4+ 48 ♔g3 ♖d4 49 ♖xg6+ ♔h5 50 ♗f5**

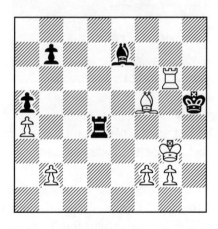

Or 50 ♗b1(c2). In any event, White has avoided all the pitfalls and is about to begin advancing his passed pawns.

50...♗d6+ 51 ♔f3 ♗c5 52 g4+ ♔h4 53 ♖h6+ ♔g5 54 ♖g6+ (54 ♖h5+!? ♔f6 55 ♗c2) **54...♔h4 55 ♗e4 ♖d6!? 56 ♖g7!**

Anand was hoping for 56 ♖xd6 ♗xd6 57 ♗xb7 ♔g5 with illusory drawing chances three (!) pawns down, although after 58 ♗c8 (threatening ♔e4) 58...♗c5 59 ♗f5 White would have won with the b2-b4 break-through. But with the rooks on it is all far simpler.

56...♖f6+ 57 ♗f5 ♖b6 58 ♖h7+ ♔g5 59 ♖h5+ ♔f6 60 ♗d3 (60 ♗c2!? ♗d4 61 b3) **60...♗d4 61 g5+ ♔g7**

After the alternative 61...♔e6 the rooks can be exchanged without fear: 62 ♖h6+ ♔e5 63 ♖xb6 ♗xb6, and after 64 ♔g3 the pawns advance.

62 ♖h7+ ♔f8 63 ♗c4 (63 ♗b5!?) **63...♖xb2?!** (63...♗xb2 was more resilient) **64 ♖f7+ ♔e8**

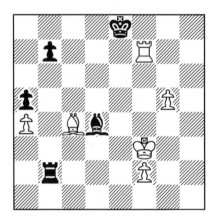

65 g6! 1-0

The last spectacular nuance: the g-pawn will cost a piece (65...♖xf2+ 66 ♔e4!).

And so I gained a half point lead over An-and! However, Karpov defeated Ljubojevic and also moved up to 'plus four'!

In the 10th round, which was played after a rest day, my 162nd encounter with Karpov took place – a genuine battle for the lead. My eternal opponent came on to the stage in a very determined mood, but that evening I was on form and something unforeseen occurred, astounding the participants, the spectators, and the entire chess world.

1 d4 ♘f6 2 c4 g6 3 ♘c3 ♗g7 4 e4 d6 5 f3 0-0 6 ♗e3 e5 (6...♘bd7 – *Game No.68*; 6...a6 – *Game No.91*) **7 ♘ge2**

Karpov made this move quickly – in the 8th round he had used it to defeat Kamsky, although before this for many years he played only 7 d5. Here I wanted to surprise my opponent with a sacrifice of two pawns: 7...♘h5 (7...c6 – *Game Nos.43, 92*) 8 ♕d2 f5 9 0-0-0 ♘d7 10 ♗d3 ♘f4?! (instead of the usual 10...♘c5 – *Game No.84*) 11 ♗xf4 exf4 12 exf5 ♘e5 13 fxg6 ♘xd3+ 14 ♕xd3 ♗f5 15 gxh7+ ♗xh7, and here we looked at 16 ♕d2 (16 ♘e4!?) 16...c5 17 ♘ge2 b5. In the computer age such play looks crazy, but from the human point of view it is very interesting and unusual.

7...c6 8 ♕d2 ♘bd7

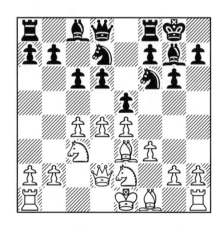

9 ♖d1

A rare and objectively second-rate move. 9 d5 or 9 0-0-0 (*Game No.90*) are more aggres-sive. Being well familiar with my style, in this important game Karpov wanted to exclude risk and sharpness, and therefore he chose a set-up that was quiet, but not without venom. However, there was something he failed to take into account.

9...a6 10 dxe5

Fundamentally not wanting to play 10 d5 (especially after ♖d1), after which there would have followed 10...c5 (with the threat of ...b7-b5: after the exchange on b5 the a2-pawn is hanging) 11 ♘g3 h5! (Evseev-Maslak, St. Petersburg 2000), or 11 g4 h5! with excellent play for Black (12 h3 ♘h7 13 ♗g2 h4 or 12 g5 ♘h7 13 h4 f6). But, strangely enough, the pawn exchange in the centre proves less good.

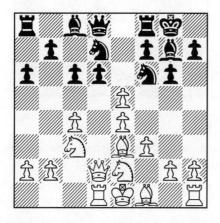

10...♘xe5!

A novelty! Karpov was counting on 10...dxe5?! 11 c5: for example, 11...♕e7 12 ♘a4 (Suetin-Uhlmann, Brno 1975), 11...♘e8 12 ♘c1 (Gavrikov-Barbero, Bern 1991), or 11...♕a5 12 a3, and White has a small but stable plus. But here there is the possibility of not shutting in the 'King's Indian' bishop: Black's lead in development and piece activity allow him to give up the d6-pawn.

11 b3

It doesn't look good to play 11 ♘c1 ♗e6 12 ♕xd6 ♕xd6 13 ♖xd6 ♗xc4 or 12 b3 ♘e8 (12...♘fd7 or 12...b5 13 ♕xd6 ♘fd7 is also interesting) 13 ♗e2 b5, developing play on the queenside.

11...b5

An interesting moment.

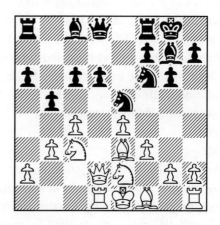

12 cxb5

'According to Anand, from this point Karpov does everything wrong. First, he incorrectly opens the a-file for the rook on a8. White could have subjected Kasparov's novelty to a critical test by 12 c5' (*Schach Magazin-64*). But this recommendation is dubious in view of 12...d5! with a dangerous initiative: 13 exd5 b4 14 ♘a4 ♘xd5 or 13 ♗g5 h6 14 ♗xf6 (14 ♗xh6 ♘xe4!) 14...♕xf6 15 exd5 (15 f4? ♕h4+) 15...♖e8 etc.

12 ♕xd6 ♕xd6 13 ♖xd6 bxc4 is also unfavourable for White. It was for this reason that Karpov exchanged on b5.

12...axb5 13 ♕xd6 ♘fd7!

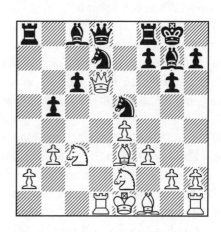

Unexpectedly Black has achieved excellent prospects. When before the game I devised the variation with a sacrifice of two pawns (mentioned in the note to 7 ♘ge2), my mood immediately lifted – and I wanted to fight for a win. In fact it proved sufficient to give up only one pawn, in order to obtain a position with colossal latent energy. On sensing this sudden change, Karpov became rattled.

14 f4?

A fatal mistake: White incautiously exposes his king, which is caught in the centre. Annotating the game in *Informator* and *New in Chess*, I also rejected 14 ♘d4? in view of 14...♖a6 with the threat of ...c6-c5 (14...♖e8 is perhaps even better). After the awkward 14 ♗g1?! I recommended an exchange sacrifice – 14...b4 15 ♘a4 ♖xa4 16 bxa4 ♕a5 17 ♗d4 c5 with full compensation, but the pressurising 14...♖e8! is even stronger.

However, White had several continuations which would have enabled him to retain approximate equality:

1) 14 ♕d2 b4 15 ♘a4 (if 15 ♘b1, then 15...♕a5 16 ♘c1 c5 17 ♗e2 ♘c6 and ...♘d4) 15...♖xa4 (a flamboyant sacrifice, but 15...♘c4!? is no worse) 16 bxa4 ♘c4 17 ♕c1 ♘xe3 18 ♕xe3 ♕a5 19 ♖d2, and although Black has obvious compensation for the exchange, White can defend;

2) 14 h4, and apart from the unclear 14...h5 Black can force a draw by 14...b4!? 15 ♘a4 (15 ♕xb4? c5! 16 ♗xc5 ♘xc5 17 ♕xc5 ♘d3+) 15...♖xa4 16 bxa4 ♘c4 17 ♕f4 (17 ♕d3 ♘b2) 17...♗e5 18 ♕h6 ♗g7 19 ♕g5 ♗f6;

3) 14 ♔f2 b4 (14...♖e8!?) 15 ♘a4 (15 ♘b1?! ♖xa2 or 15 ♕xb4?! c5 16 ♗xc5 ♘xc5 17 ♕xc5 ♘d3+ 18 ♖xd3 ♕xd3 is worse for White) 15...♘c4 16 bxc4 ♖xa4 17 ♖d2 or 17 ♘c1 with very sharp play;

4) 14 a4 bxa4 15 ♘xa4 ♖xa4 (15...♕a5+!?

16 ♔f2 f5) 16 bxa4 ♘c4 17 ♕d3 (there is also 17 ♕f4) 17...♘b2 (17...♕a5+!?) 18 ♕c2 ♘xd1 19 ♕xd1 ♕a5+ 20 ♔f2 ♘e5! 21 ♘f4 f5 22 exf5 ♗xf5 'with a very strong attack for only one pawn', I wrote in *New in Chess*, but after 23 ♕b3+ ♔h8 24 h4! it is hard for Black to find anything more convincing than 24...♖a8, intending ...♕xa4 with equality.

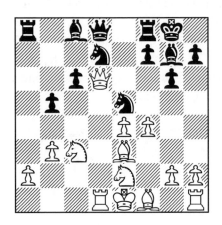

14...b4!

Unexpectedly it transpires that 15 ♕xb4? is bad because of 15...c5! 16 ♗xc5 ♘xc5! (a cunning stroke, which is easily overlooked from afar) 17 ♖xd8 ♘ed3+! or 17 ♕xc5 ♘d3+ 18 ♖xd3 ♕xd3 and wins. After quickly seeing this combination while considering the move 11...b5, I happily gave up my d6-pawn. And subsequently I played without especially delving into details and guided largely by intuition. This was one of those days when everything worked out for me.

15 ♘b1

A difficult choice. White is also poorly placed after other replies:

1) 15 ♘a4 ♖xa4! 16 bxa4 (16 fxe5 ♖xa2) 16...♘c4 17 ♕d3 ♘b2 18 ♕b3 ♘xd1 19 ♕xd1 ♕a5 20 e5 (there appears to be nothing else) 20...♖d8 21 ♕c1 ♕xa4 with an overwhelming advantage;

2) 15 fxe5 bxc3 16 ♘xc3! (16 e6? fxe6 17 ♕xe6+ ♔h8) 16...♖xe5! 17 ♕xc6 ♗xc3+ 18

♕xc3 ♕h4+ 19 ♔d2! – the best chance, but also insufficient in view of 19...♘f6! 20 ♔c1 ♗e6! (in previous analyses I only considered the unclear 20...♘xe4?! 21 ♕e5 ♗f5 22 g3!) with decisive threats: White is not helped by either 21 ♖d4 ♖xa2 or 21 ♗c4 ♗xc4 22 bxc4 ♖xa2, as well as the defence of the a2-pawn – 21 ♔b2 ♘xe4 22 ♕e5 ♖fe8 23 ♗d4 f6 24 ♕c7 ♘f2 25 ♗b5 ♖ec8, or 21 ♕c2 ♘xe4 22 ♗c4 (22 g3 ♕e7) 22...♖xc4 23 bxc4 ♖a3! etc.

15...♘g4

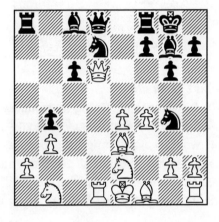

16 ♗d4

In the press centre during the game 16 ♗g1 ♖xa2 was discussed, but here White would also have lost: 17 h3 (17 ♕xb4 ♖e8 or 17 ♕xc6 ♕h4+ 18 g3 ♕e7 is worse for White) 17...♘gf6! (in *Informator* I analysed only the gambit line 17...♕h4+ 18 g3 ♖xe2+!? 19 ♔xe2 ♕xg3) 18 ♕xc6 ♖e8 19 e5 ♕e7, and the attempt 20 ♕d6 ♕xd6 21 ♖xd6 is parried by 21...♘e4 22 ♖d5 (22 ♖d4 ♘dc5) 22...♖a1 23 ♖d1 ♘xe5! 24 fxe5 ♗xe5, winning.

16...♗xd4 17 ♕xd4

It is hard to believe, but White can no longer save the game even after the 'developing' 17 ♘xd4, for example:

1) 17...♖xa2 18 ♘xc6 (18 ♖d2 ♖a1 19 ♗d3 ♕b6 is also hopeless) 18...♕h4+! 19 g3 ♘xh2!! 20 ♕d3 ♕f6 21 ♘xb4 ♘e5! with crushing threats;

2) 17...♘df6!? 18 ♕xd8 (18 ♘f5 ♕b6) 18...♖xd8 19 ♗e2 ♘e3 20 ♘xc6 ♖xd1+ 21 ♗xd1 ♖xa2 22 ♘xb4 ♘xg2+ 23 ♔f1 ♘e3+ 24 ♔e1 ♖b2 and wins.

17...♖xa2 18 h3

If 18 ♕xb4, then 18...♘e3 19 ♖d2 ♘c2+.

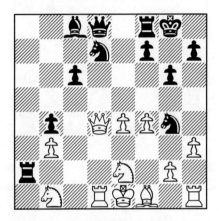

18...c5

A normal, human move, to which an exclamation mark was previously attached. But the computer finds another, pretty way to win, which is also the shortest – 18...♕h4+!? 19 g3 ♖xe2+ 20 ♔xe2 ♕xg3 21 hxg4 ♘c5!: for example, 22 ♕xc5 ♗xg4+ 23 ♔d2 ♖d8+ or 22 ♖d3 ♗a6 23 ♖h3 ♕xg4+ 24 ♔e1 ♘xd3+ 25 ♖xd3 ♗xd3 26 ♗xd3 ♕xf4 27 ♘d2 h5.

19 ♕g1

If 19 ♕d3 Black would win with the elegant 19...♗a6 20 ♕f3 (20 ♕xd7? ♕h4+ 21 g3 ♖xe2+ 22 ♗xe2 ♕xg3+) 20...♘de5! 21 fxe5 ♘xe5 22 ♕e3 ♘d3+ 23 ♖xd3, and now not 23...♕xd3(?) 24 ♕xd3 ♗xd3 25 ♘c1! ♗xb1 26 ♘xa2 ♗xa2 27 ♗c4 ♗b1 because of 28 ♔f2! (28 e5, given by me in 1993, is less good because of 28...♖e8! 29 ♔d2 ♗e4 30 ♖f1 ♖e7) 28...♗xe4 29 ♖e1 with drawing chances, but 23...♗xd3! 24 ♘c1 (24 ♘d2 c4! and wins) 24...♗xe4! 25 ♘xa2 ♖e8 26 ♕xc5 ♗xb1+ 27 ♗e2 ♗xa2, and White has no defence.

19...♘gf6 20 e5 (20 ♘d2 ♖xd2 21 ♖xd2 ♘xe4 and wins) **20...♘e4**

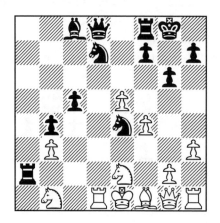

Karpov was already in severe time-trouble. Now the attempt to bring the queen back into play – 21 ♕e3 was too late because of 21...♗b7, for example:

1) 22 ♘d2 (22 ♘c1? ♕h4+) 22...♘xd2 23 ♖xd2 ♖xd2 24 ♕xd2 ♕h4+ 25 g3 ♕e7 26 ♖h2 (26 ♖g1 ♖d8!) 26...♖d8 27 ♕d6 ♕xd6 28 exd6 ♘f6 or 27 ♕b2 c4! 28 bxc4 ♘c5 29 ♘d4(c1) ♘e4 and wins;

2) 22 h4 ♕e7! (22...♖e8!?) 23 ♘d2 (23 h5 g5!) 23...♘xd2 24 ♖xd2 ♖xd2 25 ♕xd2 (25 ♔xd2 ♖d8) 25...c4! (again a typical breakthrough: the passed b-pawn will cost a piece) 26 bxc4 ♖d8, and 27 ♕d6 ♕xd6 28 exd6 does not save White in view of 28...♘c5 29 ♘c1 b3 30 ♘d3 ♗e4(xg2).

21 h4 c4! 22 ♘c1

A terrible disaster has befallen White: all of his seven pieces are entrenched on the back rank. But this could not have been successfully avoided: 22 ♕e3 c3! 23 ♕xe4 c2 or 22 bxc4 ♕a5 23 ♕e3 ♘dc5 and wins.

22...c3!?

A by no means essential, but spectacular rook sacrifice. 'Kasparov is accustomed to finishing with a flourish, but my modest contribution would be 22...♖b2.' (Anand). With the prosaic threat of ...♖xb1, and if 23

♕d4 Black has a whole raft of decisive continuations –23...♕b6, 23...c3 24 ♕xe4 c2, and 23...♘f2 24 ♕xb2 ♘xh1 25 g3 ♘xg3 etc.

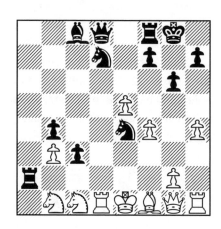

23 ♘xa2 c2 24 ♕d4

The last chance of stirring up trouble was 24 ♖c1, but the forceful 24...♘xe5! 25 ♖xc2 ♗g4! would have clarified the picture: 26 ♘d2 ♘d3+ (at the board 26...♕d3!? also appealed to me) 27 ♗xd3 ♕xd3, or 26 ♖d2 ♘xd2 27 fxe5 (27 ♘xd2 ♖e8) 27...♘e4 and wins.

24...cxd1♕+

Here, because of my carelessness and a mistake by the arbiter, an unpleasant incident occurred. After placing my pawn on d1, I automatically said: 'Queen!'. But there was no second queen to hand. If I had been more attentive, I would have said 'Rook!', and placed on d1 with check my rook which had just been captured on a2. However, as it was, I had to wait for a queen to be produced. But the arbiter, who apparently had something else on his mind, brought – a white queen! Here my patience snapped (all this was occurring at the expense of my own time on the clock) and, leaving my pawn on d1, I started my opponent's clock. At which point Karpov, in desperate time-trouble (one minute for 16 moves), instantly replied 25 ♕xe4!!?. 'You're in check', I exclaimed in surprise. 'From what? It might be a bishop on d1', retorted Karpov. The clocks were stopped and the ex-champion demanded that, in accordance with the rules, he should be given additional time: I had supposedly made an illegal move. Although in fact the illegal move had been made by Karpov himself! But, being one step away from victory, I did not bother to argue. The arbiter finally found a black queen, Karpov was given two additional minutes, and the game continued.

25 ♔xd1 (if 25 ♕xd1, both 25...♘g3 and 25...♕a5 are good) **25...♘dc5! 26 ♕xd8 ♖xd8+ 27 ♔c2** (27 ♔e1 ♗g4) **27...♘f2**

And in this hopeless position (28 ♖g1 ♗f5+, mating), White nevertheless lost on time (**0–1**).

This was probably the most crushing defeat in Karpov's career. Moreover, he did not blunder anything, but merely fell catastrophically behind in development (after the incautious 14 f4?). By losing on time 13(!) moves before the control, the ex-champion beat his own anti-record, established in the 8th game of our 1986 match, when his flag fell on the 31st move (*Game No.14*).

I was happy that at the decisive moment of the tournament race I had been able to create a minor masterpiece, and I said to the press representatives: 'This win over Karpov is noteworthy for me. Firstly, in that for the first time after the 24th game of our 1985 match (when I became champion) I have managed to win with Black. Secondly, the game proved so fascinating, that it as though served as an excellent present for Robert Fischer, who on that day, 9th March, reached the age of 50'. Yes, and White's position after the 22nd move was fully in the spirit of 'Fischer chess'! Need it be said which game was judged the best in the 57th vol-

ume of *Informator*?

Wins over both rivals enabled me to surge ahead: Kasparov – 7½ out of 10; Karpov and Anand – 6½. But the lead had to be consolidated, and for the next game with Boris Gelfand I arrived in an ultra-fighting mood. As was the case before the game with Karpov, that day I had the strange premonition that the battle would not last long...

Game 99
G.Kasparov-B.Gelfand
Linares, 11th Round 11.03.1993
Sicilian Defence B87

1 e4 c5 2 ♘f3 d6 3 d4 cxd4 4 ♘xd4 ♘f6 5 ♘c3 a6

Preparing for a 'white' game with Gelfand was simultaneously both easy and difficult: Boris had a very narrow, but finely honed opening repertoire. In the Sicilian Defence he, like myself, played the Najdorf Variation.

6 ♗c4

In those years this was my universal move. After 5...♘c6 Makarychev and I also prepared 6 ♗c4, but, alas, I was not able to employ the ideas developed in the Velimirovic Attack (6...e6 7 ♗e3 with the idea of ♕e2 and 0-0-0), since my opponents – Timman (Manila Olympiad 1992), Anand (Linares 1994) and Kramnik (Horgen 1995) – replied 6...♕b6.

6...e6 7 ♗b3 b5

The main line. Against Short, who terrorised me with 6 ♗c4 in our 1993 match and also later, apart from this I tried 7...♘bd7, 7...♘c6 and 7...♗e7 (details in the next volume).

8 0-0 ♗e7 9 ♕f3 ♕c7

In addition we studied 9...♕b6 10 ♗e3 ♕b7, which was also in my opponent's arsenal.

10 ♕g3 0-0 11 ♗h6 ♘e8 12 ♖ad1

In a previous Sicilian duel with Gelfand (Paris (rapid) 1991) I tried 12 ♖fe1?! ♗d7 13 a4 (instead of 13 ♖ad1 ♘c6 14 ♗g5 ♗xg5 15 ♕xg5 b4 with equality, Oll-Gelfand, Sverdlovsk 1987), but after 13...b4 14 ♘ce2 ♔h8 15 ♗g5 ♗xg5 16 ♕xg5 ♘f6 17 ♘g3 ♘c6 18 ♘xc6 ♗xc6 Black obtained comfortable play. 12 ♔h1 ♗d7 13 f4 ♘c6 14 ♘f3 b4 (Morozevich-Gelfand, Madrid 1996) is hardly any better.

12...♗d7

Boris has been playing this set-up all his life!

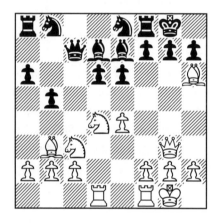

13 ♘f3!?

A novelty, involving the pretty idea of a piece attack on the king. Although at the time it created quite a stir, now I regard it sceptically: Black has a very solid position. He is also not frightened by 13 a3 ♘c6 14 ♘xc6 ♗xc6 15 ♗f4 ♕b7 (Short-Kasparov, 20th match game, London 1993), and 13 ♘ce2 ♔h8 (Lautier-Gelfand, Las Vegas 1999) or 13...♗f6 (J.Polgar-Karjakin, Benidorm (rapid) 2002).

But the logical 13 f4! ♘c6 is still the focus of attention – after this they have played 14 ♘xc6 ♗xc6 15 f5 ♔h8 16 ♗e3 (16 f6!?, Ivanchuk-Gelfand, Moscow (blitz) 2008) 16...b4 17 ♘a4 (17 ♘e2?! e5), and here not

17...♖b8? 18 fxe6 fxe6 19 ♖xf8+ ♗xf8 20 ♖f1 ♕e7 21 e5! with crushing threats (A.Sokolov-Gelfand, 56th USSR Championship, Odessa 1989), but 17...♘f6! with approximate equality. Later there emerged 14 ♗g5 ♗xg5 15 fxg5 ♘xd4 16 ♖xd4 ♕c5 (Morozevich-Gelfand, Istanbul Olympiad 2000), and 14 f5!? ♘xd4 15 ♖xd4 ♗f6 (Morozevich-Kasparov, Astana 2001), or 15...♔h8 (Mamedyarov-Gelfand, 3rd match game, Kazan 2011).

13...b4

The most natural reply, and apparently the most correct: Black immediately begins pursuing the bishop on b3. But after his defeat in this game they began seeking other ways: 13...a5 14 a4 b4 15 ♘e2 ♘c6 (Short-Kasparov, 18th match game, London 1993) or 13...♘c6 14 ♗f4 ♕b7!? 15 ♖fe1 b4 16 ♘e2 e5! 17 ♗g5! ♗e6 with sharp play (Kasparov-Gelfand, Moscow Olympiad 1994). **14 ♘e2 a5 15 ♘f4 ♔h8** (of course, not 15...a4? 16 ♗xg7! and wins) **16 ♗g5**

There is nothing else.

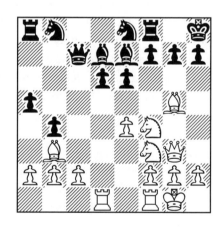

16...♘f6

16...♗xg5?! is dangerous: 17 ♘xg5 ♘c6 (17...h6? 18 ♗xe6!, Erashchenkov-Sjurgirov, Krasnodar 2004) 18 ♗xe6! ♗xe6 (18...fxe6? 19 ♘g6+! ♔g8 20 ♘xf8 ♔xf8 21 ♕f3+ ♘f6 22 ♘xh7+ is bad for Black) 19 ♘fxe6 fxe6 20

♘xe6 ♕e7 21 ♘xf8 ♕xf8 22 c3(c4), and the rook and two pawns are rather stronger than the knight.

But 16...♘c6!? comes into consideration. 17 e5?! ♗xg5 18 ♘xg5 ♘xe5 or 17 ♗xe7 ♘xe7 (Stupavski-Palac, Zadar 2007) is ineffective. 17 ♘d5 exd5 18 exd5 is more energetic, although here too Black has no real problems: 18...♘f6 19 dxc6 ♗xc6 or simply 18...♗xg5 19 dxc6 ♗xc6 20 ♘xg5 h6 21 ♘f3 ♖c8 22 ♕f4 ♘f6! 23 ♖xd6 ♘e4, forcing a draw by perpetual check – 24 ♖xh6+ etc. 16...♘f6 is more risky, but also not bad.

17 ♕h4!

Building up the pressure. My unusual attacking plan unsettled my opponent...

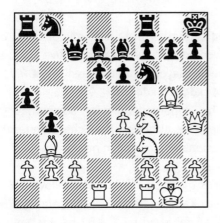

17...♗b5??

Black's only mistake, but a fatal one. 17...a4? would have been met by the stunning 18 ♘h5!, for example:

1) 18...axb3 19 ♘xf6! ♗xf6 (19...h6? 20 ♗xh6 ♗xf6 21 ♗g5+ ♔g8 22 ♗xf6 gxf6 23 ♘g5!, mating) 20 ♗xf6 gxf6 21 ♕xf6+ ♔g8 22 ♘g5! ♗b5 23 ♕h6 ♖e8 (23...f6 24 ♕xf8+! or 23...♖c8 24 e5! dxe5 25 ♘xh7 is no better) 24 ♕xh7+ ♔f8 25 ♖xd6! bxa2 26 ♖a1 ♖a6 27 e5 ♖c8 28 h4! with a victorious march towards the queening square;

2) 18...♖g8 19 ♘xf6 ♗xf6 20 ♗xf6 gxf6 21 ♕xf6+ ♖g7 22 ♘g5 ♔g8 23 ♖d3! axb3 24

♖g3! ♗b5 25 ♕xg7+! ♔xg7 26 ♘xe6++ ♔h6 27 ♘xc7 ♗xf1 28 cxb3! ♖a7 29 ♘e8 ♗e2 30 ♘xd6, and the black king is in trouble even without the queens;

3) 18...♕d8! (the most resilient) 19 ♗c4 (threatening ♖xd6!) 19...♘g8 20 ♗xe7 ♕xe7 21 ♕xe7 ♘xe7 22 ♖xd6 ♖c8 23 ♗d3 with an extra pawn in a complicated endgame.

It would appear that it was ♘h5 which concerned Boris, and he played 17...♗b5 in order to parry it with 18...♘bd7. But he did not notice the correct defence 17...♘c6!, which I pointed out in *Informator*. Now nothing is given by either 18 ♗a4 ♗d8! 19 ♖fe1 ♖c8 20 ♘h5 ♘xh5! 21 ♕xh5 ♘e5, or 18 ♘h5 ♘xh5! (safer than 18...♘g8, Rudak-Simantsev, Alushta 2002) 19 ♗xe7 ♘xe7 20 ♕xe7 ♖ac8! 21 ♖xd6 (21 e5?! ♘f4!; 21 a4?! bxa3!) 21...♘f6! 22 ♖d4 ♗b5 23 ♕xc7 ♖xc7, and White loses his bishop on b3, although he gains fair compensation for it: 24 ♖a1 a4 25 ♖xb4 axb3 26 axb3 ♖c5 27 ♘e1 etc.

Thus Gelfand's intuition did not let him down when he chose 13...b4: this active move kills the idea of 13 ♘f3, but only on condition that 16(17)...♘c6 is played.

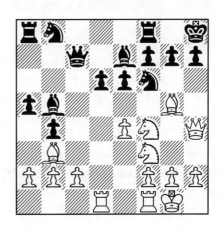

18 ♘d4!

A sudden regrouping of the fighting units: now Black suffers a classic Sicilian catastrophe on the e6-point (it was this that buried the variation for many years – such is the chess world!). Another argument against the panicky 17...♗b5?? is that even the modest 18 ♖fe1 ♘c6 (18...a4? 19 ♗xe6!) 19 ♖e3! and c2-c4 would have given White an advantage.

18...♗e8

After 18...♗xf1 there was the decisive 19 ♘dxe6 fxe6 20 ♗xe6 ♘h5 21 ♕xh5 ♖xf4 (otherwise mate) 22 ♗xf4 ♘d7 23 ♔xf1, and after 18...♗d7 – 19 ♖d3! (with the murderous threat of ♖h3) 19...e5 20 ♘h5! ♕d8 21 ♘f5 ♗xf5 22 exf5 ♘g8 (22...♘bd7 23 ♗a4!) 23 f6! ♗xf6 24 ♘xf6 ♘xf6 25 ♗d5! ♘bd7 26 ♗e4 and wins.

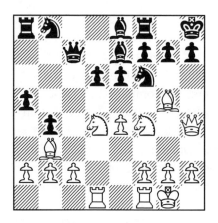

19 ♘dxe6!

There was also a spectacular win after 19 ♖d3 ♘bd7 20 ♖h3 ♕c5 21 ♘f5! exf5 22 ♘d5 or 20...♖g8 21 ♘f5! ♗d8 22 ♖d1, but there is no longer any need for all these subtleties.

19...fxe6 20 ♘xe6 ♕a7 21 e5! dxe5 22 ♘xf8 ♗xf8 23 ♗xf6 gxf6 24 ♖d8 ♘d7 25 ♕g4!

And in view of 25...♗g6 26 ♕e6 Black resigned (**1-0**).

In the next found I had a sharp King's Indian skirmish with Shirov (cf. *Game No.66*, note to White's 12th move), which at the

start of the second time control produced a level endgame and soon a draw.

Before the last round the leading positions were: Kasparov – 9 out of 12; Karpov and Anand – 8. At the finish both of my rivals had Black (and in the end they gained draws), while I had the white pieces against Gata Kamsky and in principle I could have satisfied myself with a draw, giving me sole first place, but all the same I decided to play for a win.

> *Game 100*
> **G.Kasparov-G.Kamsky**
> Linares, 13th Round 14.03.1993
> *Sicilian Defence B80*

1 e4 c5 (earlier Gata a couple of times employed against me his main move 1...e5, but here he played more aggressively) **2 ♘f3 e6 3 d4 cxd4 4 ♘xd4 ♘f6 5 ♘c3 d6**

The opponent's choice somewhat surprised me, although the Scheveningen had occasionally occurred in his games.

6 ♗e3

If 6 g4 there could have followed 6...h6 (Aseev-Kamsky, Barnaul 1988), and if 6 ♗c4 – 6...a6 followed by 7 ♗b3 b5 8 0-0 ♗e7 9 ♕f3 ♕b6 (9...♕c7 – *Game No.99*) 10 ♗e3 ♕b7 11 ♕g3 0-0 12 ♗h6 ♘e8 (A.Ivanov-Kamsky, 1st match game, Los Angeles 1991). After some thought I preferred the popular English Attack, which I had already encountered with Black.

6...a6 7 f3 ♘bd7

A far rarer move than 7...♗e7 (*Game No.39*) or 7...b5 (this line will be covered in more detail in the next volume). But the intriguing factor is that Gata is duplicating my play in my rapid match with Short (1987).

8 g4 h6 9 ♖g1!?

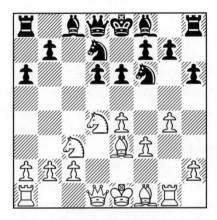

This interesting novelty is an attempt to get away from the standard 9 ♕d2 b5, and from 9 h4 ♘e5 10 ♖g1?! ♕b6! 11 ♕c1?! d5! with advantage to Black (Short-Kasparov, 6th match game (rapid), London 1987).

9...♕b6

Now 9...♘e5?! is weak on account of 10 f4!, since Black loses after 10...♘exg4? 11 ♖xg4 ♘xg4 (11...e5 12 ♖g3!) 12 ♕xg4 e5 13 ♘f5 g6 14 0-0-0! gxf5 15 exf5 etc. And the usual 9...b5 10 h4 leads to a position from the 2nd game of my rapid match with Short, which continued 10...g6 (10...♘b6!? 11 g5 ♘fd7 is more flexible, Anand-J.Polgar, Linares 1994) 11 g5 hxg5 12 hxg5 ♘h5 13 a4! b4, and here 14 ♘a2! would have retained the advantage.

9...g5!? with the idea of 10 h4 gxh4 also came into consideration. But Kamsky attacked the b2-pawn with his queen by analogy with my 10...♕b6 (cf. the note to White's 9th move). From the press: 'This idea belongs to Kasparov himself! On encountering his own invention, he had a serious think and found a very strong plan, casting doubts on his opponent's entire play.'

10 a3! (a typical idea: 10...♕xb2? 11 ♘a4)

10...♘e5 11 ♗f2!

Creating the threat of ♘xe6. 'This brilliant move was probably the most difficult deci-

sion in the game. The black pieces are thrown back from their active positions, and White's become excellently coordinated', wrote Sergey Janovsky in the magazine *Shakhmatny vestnik*.

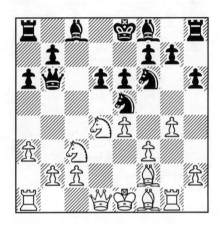

11...♕c7

A sensible reply. It would have been fatal to play 11...♗d7? 12 ♘xe6! ♕xb2 13 ♘c7+ ♔d8 14 ♗d4! or 11...♗e7? 12 ♘xe6! ♕xb2 13 ♘xg7+! (not now 13 ♘c7+ ♔f8!) 13...♔f8 14 ♗d4! ♘xf3+! 15 ♕xf3 ♕xa1+ 16 ♔d2 ♔xg7 17 ♕f4!!, winning a rook down (!): 17...♖g8 18 ♘b5! or 17...♔f8 18 ♗xf6 ♗e6 19 g5 ♗xf6 20 ♕xf6 ♖h7 21 gxh6 ♖c8 22 ♖g3! ♕xa3 23 ♕g5 with the decisive threat of ♕g8+ and ♕xh7. And the central blow 11...d5?! 12 exd5 ♗c5 (12...exd5? 13 ♕e2) would not have equalised in view of 13 ♖g3! exd5 14 ♕d2 and 0-0-0.

12 f4 ♘c4

In *Informator* I recommended 12...♘g6, but after 13 f5 ♘e5 14 ♕e2 followed by 0-0-0 and h2-h4 the initiative is also on White's side. 12...♘c6 (Makarychev) 13 ♕f3 e5 14 ♘f5 or 13...b5 14 ♘xc6 ♕xc6 15 0-0-0 etc is hardly any better.

13 ♗xc4 ♕xc4 14 ♕f3

With the obvious intention of 0-0-0. From the press: 'White's lead in development looks threatening, and Kasparov accurately converts it into a win.' Alas, not altogether accurately and not without the opponent's help...

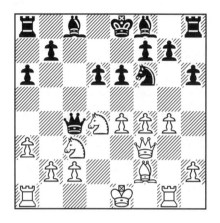

14...e5!?

Here the 'only' move 14...b5 was suggested, but after 15 0-0-0 ♗b7 (15...♘d7?! 16 e5! d5 17 f5!) 16 g5 hxg5 17 fxg5 ♘d7(h5) 18 g6 or immediately 15 g5 hxg5 16 fxg5 ♘d7(h5) 17 g6 White has an obvious advantage. It would appear that 14...e5, to which I attached a question mark, is in fact the best chance!

15 ♘f5

A critical moment, which was not re-marked on in earlier commentaries.

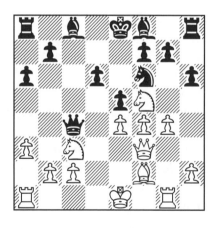

15...♗xf5?

A faulty exchange, which sharply increases White's positional superiority. 15...h5! 16 g5

♘g4 was far more resilient, for example:

1) 17 fxe5 ♗xf5! (now this forces simplification favourable for Black) 18 exf5 ♘xf2 (after 18...♕c6?! 19 ♕e2! ♘xf2 20 exd6+ ♔d7 21 ♕xf2 ♖e8+ 22 ♘e2 ♕xc2 23 ♖g3 ♕xb2 24 ♖d1 White has a dangerous attack) 19 ♕xb7 ♖d8 20 e6 fxe6 21 ♔xf2 (21 fxe6 ♗e7!) 21...d5 22 ♔g2 ♖d7 with drawing chances;

2) 17 ♘e3!? ♘xe3 18 ♕xe3 exf4 19 ♕xf4 ♗g4 20 ♖g3 ♕e6 21 ♘d5 ♖c8 22 c3 – White presses, but there is still all to play for.

16 gxf5 d5

This desperate freeing attempt is Gata's idea: otherwise there would simply have followed 17 0-0-0.

17 fxe5

Not bad, but there was a quicker win by 17 0-0-0! d4 18 fxe5 dxc3 19 exf6 cxb2+ 20 ♔b1! gxf6 21 ♗d4 ♖c8 22 ♖d2, when the black king is defenceless, or 17...♖c8 18 fxe5 ♘xe4 19 ♗d4 ♗xa3! 20 ♖d3! ♘xc3 21 ♗xc3 d4 22 ♔b1! etc.

17...♘xe4

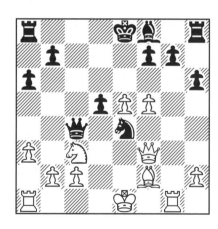

18 ♖g4! (the rook comes into play with considerable effect) **18...h5** (if 18...♖c8? there is the decisive 19 ♖d1!) **19 ♖h4**

It was probably simpler to play 19 ♖f4! ♕c6 (19...♖c8? 20 ♖d1!) 20 ♘xe4 dxe4 21 ♕xe4, winning a pawn and the game.

19...♗c5

If 19...♗e7 apart from the prosaic 20 ♘xe4, there is the lively 20 f6!? g5 21 ♖xe4! dxe4 22 ♘e4 ♗f8 23 0-0-0 ♖c8 24 c3 with an irresistible attack. And in the event of 19...♖c8 again 20 ♖d1! is strong – in *Informator* I condemned this because of 20...♗c5 21 ♗xc5 ♘g5!? (21...♕xc5 22 ♘xd5 ♕g1+ 23 ♕f1 is hopeless), underestimating the reply 22 ♕f4 ♕xf4 23 ♖xf4 ♖xc5 24 ♖xd5 ♖xd5 25 ♘xd5 0-0 26 ♘b4 and ♘d3 with excellent chances of converting the extra pawn.

In any event, White remains with a technically won position.

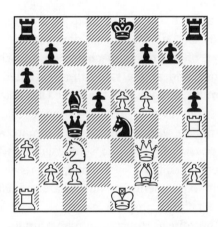

20 0-0-0! (there was no reason allow the harassment of the king after 20 ♘xe4?! dxe4 21 ♕xe4 ♗xf2+ 22 ♔xf2 ♕c5+ etc.) **20...♗xf2**

The symmetric flight of the king with 20...0-0-0!? was more resilient, although after 21 ♗xc5 ♕xc5 22 ♘xd5! ♖xd5 23 ♖xd5 ♕xd5 24 ♖xe4 ♖e8 25 ♕e3 the extra pawn in the heavy piece ending must bring White a win.

21 ♘xe4 dxe4 22 ♕xf2 ♖c8

22...0-0 23 ♖xh5 and ♖g1 was suicidal, but with his king in the centre Black is also condemned to a swift loss – say, after 22...♕a2 23 c3 or 22...♖d8 23 ♖xd8+ ♔xd8 24 ♖h3!. The

only way to prolong the resistance was by a tactical trick: 22...e3!? 23 ♕e1! ♕c5 24 ♕g3 ♖d8 (24...e2 25 ♖d2!) 25 ♖xd8+ ♔xd8 26 ♕xg7 ♖e8 27 e6! e2 28 ♖e4 and wins.

23 ♔b1 (essential prophylaxis before the start of the mating attack) **23...♖d8** (23...♖h6 24 ♕g2!) **24 ♖xd8+ ♔xd8 25 ♖h3! ♕d5 26 ♖c3 ♔d7**

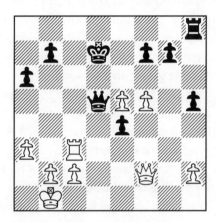

27 ♕b6

27 ♕g3 or 27 e6+! fxe6 28 ♕g3 was more forceful, but this no longer plays any role.
27...♖d8 (27...♖c8 28 e6+!) **28 ♖c5! ♕d1+ 29 ♔a2 ♔e8 30 ♕xb7 ♕g4** (30...♕d7 31 ♕xe4) **31 e6! fxe6 32 ♖e5 ♕g5 33 h4 ♕xh4 34 ♖xe6+** (34 ♕xg7!?) **34...♔f8 35 f6 1-0**

Vitaly Tseshkovsky: *'An important theoretical novelty, backed by energetic play, brought Kasparov another win. The world champion's unconditional success in this tournament gives a conclusive reply to the question who is who.'*

Yes, the tension over the withdrawal from FIDE did not prevent me from winning the 'chess Wimbledon' for the second successive year and with the same result +7=6. The finish of 4½ points out of 5 turned out to be my swan song in the capacity of FIDE world champion.

Immediately after the event, discussions

continued regarding the forthcoming title match. Campomanes went back on his word and urgently sought a reconciliation. Through the intermediary of FIDE, organisers from Manchester even arrived in Linares and expressed their readiness to improve the financial conditions. We had a chance to 'take a move back', but Short and Keene, who was lobbying for the match to held in London, were against any negotiations with FIDE, and I, in a state of euphoria after my Linares triumph, decided that I should also be able to win on a second front.

Three days later, 18th March 1993, speaking at a meeting of the Russian Chess Federation, I explained the reasons why Short and I had withdrawn from FIDE:

'I have spent two years trying to find money for the world title match. Many say that Kasparov was seeking money for himself. This is not true; I was seeking money for the creation of an effectively operating chess system. Chess must be dragged to a new level, carrying out a similar revolution to that which occurred at the turn of the 1960-1970s in tennis and golf. Tennis has an organisation similar to FIDE: it only sanctions the staging of events, without having any involvement with them and receiving 3-4% of the prize fund... But FIDE, while laying claim to more, does not fulfil its main objective, for the sake of which it obtained the world championship – I have in mind the efficient acquisition of money and (this affects all grandmasters) the creation of systems which in themselves produce money. Experience world-wide shows that this can be achieved only by "going out into the open sea". Which is what Short and I have done. Am I afraid of sanctions on the part of FIDE? No. Take boxing – there they have many world champions.'

At that time there was also a split in the Russian Chess Federation, linked to the political crisis in the country, and the upper hand was temporarily seized by the 'forces of revenge', supported by Karpov. Therefore, with the exit from FIDE, for me a completely new psychological situation arose: the official title of world champion had allowed me to feel invulnerable in my confrontation with FIDE, the State Sports Committee and the Soviet Federation, but now it turned out that with my own hands I had destroyed this defence, built up by many years of hard labour.

Sanctions were not long in coming. Already on 23rd March FIDE deprived me and Short of the rights of champion and challenger, and at the same time excluded us from its rating list. By the same FIDE decree, the right to play a match for the title of champion was granted to Timman and Karpov (as finalist and semi-finalist in the recent qualifying cycle) and, on receiving their agreement, it immediately invited tenders for staging the match.

The refusal to play the match under the aegis of FIDE was the worst blunder of my entire chess career. This decision led to an unexpected revival of Karpov and allowed FIDE to set up a protracted opposition with the PCA, by having its own 'world champion'. Of course, I should have agreed to play in Manchester – and only then, after defending the title of FIDE champion, thought about setting up a Professional Chess Association. I would have saved myself a mass of nervous energy, and the chess world would have retained a single champion.

Index of Openings

Index of Games